CRITICAL ETHNIC STUDIES

CRITICAL ETHNIC STUDIES

A READER

Critical Ethnic Studies Editorial Collective

NADA ELIA, DAVID M. HERNÁNDEZ, JODI KIM, SHANA L. REDMOND, DYLAN RODRÍGUEZ, AND SARITA ECHAVEZ SEE

Duke University Press · Durham and London · 2016

Printed in the United States of America on acid-free paper ∞
Designed by Courtney Leigh Baker
Typeset in Arno Pro and Trade Gothic by Westchester

Library of Congress Cataloging-in-Publication Data
Names: Elia, Nada, author, editor. | Kim, Jodi, [date] author, editor. |Redmond, Shana L., author, editor. | Rodriguez, Dylan, author, editor.See, Sarita Echavez, author, editor. | Hernández, David, [date] author, editor. | Critical Ethnic Studies Editorial Collective, author, editor.
Title: Critical ethnic studies : a reader / Critical Ethnic Studies Editorial Collective, Nada Elia, David Hernández, Jodi Kim, Shana Redmond, Dylan Rodríguez, and Sarita Echavez See.
Description: Durham : Duke University Press, 2016. | Includes bibliographical references and index.
Identifiers: LCCN 2015044104
ISBN 9780822361084 (hardcover : alk. paper)
ISBN 9780822361275 (pbk. : alk. paper)
ISBN 9780822374367 (e-book)
Subjects: LCSH: Ethnology—Research. | Race relations—Research.
Ethnicity—Research. | Minorities—Research.
Classification: LCC GN316 .C758 2016 | DDC305.80072—dc23
LC record available at http://lccn.loc.gov/2015044104

Cover art: Sofia Maldonado, *Decolonized*, 2013. Image courtesy of Sofia Maldonado and Magnan Metz Gallery. Photo by Zach Callahan.

CHAPTER 5, "Hateful Travels: Queering Ethnic Studies in a Context of Criminalization, Pathologization and Globalization" was previously published as Haritaworn, Jin, "Beyond 'Hate': Queer Metonymies of Crime, Pathology, and Anti-Violence," in *Jindal Global Law Review*, Vol. 4, Issue 2, November 2013, reproduced with permission of Jindal Global Law Review.

CHAPTER 12, "Becoming Disabled / Becoming Black: Crippin' Critical Ethnic Studies from the Periphery," was previously published as "Disability as 'Becoming': Notes on the Political Economy of the Flesh," in Erevelles, Nirmala, *Disability and Difference in Global Context* (Palgrave Macmillan 2011), reproduced with permission of Palgrave Macmillan.

CHAPTER 19, "Up in the Air and On the Skin: Drone Warfare and the Queer Calculus of Pain," was previously published as Kapadia, Ronak, "Up in the Air and On the Skin: Wafaa Bilal, Drone Warfare, and the Human Terrain," in *Shifting Borders: America and the Middle East/North Africa*, ed. Alex Lubin (American University of Beirut Press, 2014), republished with permission of the American University of Beirut Press.

CHAPTER 20 was previously published as Feldman, Keith, "Empire's Verticality: The Af/Pak Frontier, Visual Culture, and Racialization from Above," *Comparative American Studies*, Vol. 9 no. 4, online available at http://www.maneyonline.com/loi/cas, republished with permission of Maney Publishing.

CHAPTER 23 was previously published as Maldonado-Torres, Nelson, "Césaire's Gift and the Decolonial Turn," *Radical Philosophy Review* Vol. 9, no. 2, 2006, republished with permission of Philosophy Documentation Center.

CONTENTS

V. Fugitive Socialities and Alternative Futures

PREFACE

Critical Ethnic Studies Editorial Collective:

NADA ELIA, DAVID M. HERNÁNDEZ, JODI KIM, SHANA L. REDMOND, DYLAN RODRÍGUEZ, AND SARITA ECHAVEZ SEE

The canvas is dripping with blood. The abstraction suggests a decolonization without guarantees, meaning its goals, strategies, and imaginings of alternative futurities in multiple sites and scales are unpredictable, contingent, and stubbornly difficult. The corporeality of blood, on the other hand, makes concrete decolonization a project that is urgent, agonistic, and structured by violence. This dialectic of decolonization is also evoked by what is rendered in black—billowing featheriness versus piercing bolts of lightning.

Critical ethnic studies is a project saturated with the pasts of our making and the expectations for our futures yet to come. Our efforts to render that project here is, like the painting *Decolonized* by the Puerto Rican–born artist Sophia Maldonado, a narrative that is not singular but part of a larger oeuvre of thought that is instructive but not exhaustive. This anthology might be read as emblematic of a time, a place, and a group, but we encourage readers to consider it a meditation rather than a symbol. As such we begin with our meditations on this collection—filtered through Maldonado's art—which urges us not merely to write and think about but also to see, smell, and feel

FIGURE FM.1. Sophia Maldonado, *Decolonized*, 2013. Acrylic and urethane on canvas. 84 × 108 inches. Image courtesy of Sofia Maldonado and Magnan Metz Gallery.

the violence, beauty, dissonance, and desire that undergird the formation of material and political landscapes.

THE SHARDS, EXPLOSIONS, and layers that make up Maldonado's painting make it easier for me to articulate how we have been attempting to challenge the emphasis on the identitarian while creating a flexible yet politicized space of assembly within academia that in turn challenges the incarcerated nature of academic institutions and cultures.

Trusted and hallowed institutions, often the very ones that were articulated in founding iterations of ethnic studies and inculcated with presumptions of goodness—cities, conceptions of nature, blue skies in Maldonado's art, and identitarian politics, rights discourses, the law in the anthology—must be sites of decolonization.

Maldonado presents multiple struggles pasted elaborately across blue skies, covering nearly everything. These struggles are simultaneous, seemingly coordinated, and different in scale.

The blue skies gesture to a horizon beyond colonial violence, and the longing for such a horizon is tethered to a nonlinear and nondevelopmentalist rendering of decolonization.

. . . and then it seemed that something had happened—at first, akin to absolute disorder, total dysfunction, as if things were coming apart from the inside out, and we were part of an implosion, or perhaps a collapsing. For some it brought deep sadness, but not of the tragic kind. It was as if we were all being convinced—slowly, insidiously, but so, so effectively—that there were those with a future and those without. And the sadness was about being part of an aspiration to see the tomorrow that many knew was not theirs. That the ambition to enter that time and place meant that some were to be left for dead, forever gone to history, having been forced off the temporal coil itself. And now it seemed that the idea of freedom, the other side of the thing called decolonization that we had perhaps been invoking too easily—really, too freely—carried with it the gravity of someone's obsolescence. We knew it would not be all of us who disappeared, and we were beginning to accept that as simple fact, something to be spoken but not talked about. They had started looking for ways to eliminate those without future, and now we realized, in this happening, that they were extending an invitation to us. I wondered if it was too late to RSVP *my regrets.*

Moments of calm and eruption keep the eye moving between colors and depths made possible through various layers and tones. Her brush strokes in black are open, which allow for the exposure of other surfaces, even as they are filtered through that blackness. The running paint signals the organized and anticipated messiness of her project—our project—and adds a wily movement, announcing that the work is unfinished.

THE ORGANIZED AND ANTICIPATED messiness of Maldonado's project provided us, the editors, with a powerful point of departure, and we in turn invoke her work as an entrance into this anthology. Like our efforts in responding to *Decolonized*, we invite you to imagine through this image and our words your own spaces of possibility and contribute your ideas and energies to this critical experiment.

INTRODUCTION: A SIGHTLINE

Critical Ethnic Studies Editorial Collective:

NADA ELIA, DAVID HERNÁNDEZ, JODI KIM, SHANA L. REDMOND, DYLAN RODRÍGUEZ, AND SARITA ECHAVEZ SEE

It is a generally well-known (and often mythified) fact that the Third World Liberation Front (TWLF) model of solidarity- and alliance-based rebellion and revolutionary struggle structured the opening stanzas of ethnic studies as a political and cultural intervention into the white supremacist university during the late 1960s and early 1970s. A peculiar pedagogical narrative has sprung forth from this period of antiracist and anti-imperialist social movements. This narrative both draws from and selectively neutralizes the principled forms of *intellectual* self-determination that constituted the TWLF as a political and cultural practice. That is, the coherence of ethnic studies as such has relied on a changing, often vexed set of rationalizations, arguments, and stories regarding the necessity and propriety of convening different epistemic-institutional formations within a political-intellectual housing (whether an academic department, high school curriculum, or community-formed project). These critical and radical intellectual projects, each with its own autonomous genealogy, have become legible as black studies, African American studies, Native American studies, indigenous studies, Chicano/a studies, Puerto Rican studies, Asian American studies, Latino/a studies, Arab American studies, women of color feminisms, queer of color critique, and so forth. Ethnic studies, as a pedagogical and narrative rubric, attempts to convene these autonomous intellectual traditions within a shared institutional space, inciting both transformative possibilities and severe internal contradictions. The significance of the TWLF model is thus not only its historical contribution to the disruption and rearticulation of the white university but also its crystallization of an *insurgent narrative structure* that facilitates the adjoining of vastly disparate human oppressions and rebellions into an ostensible totality of shared, radical agency against empire, conquest, criminalization, and enslavement. TWLF is the recurring dream form of a colored, colonized, enslaved revolt against an oppressive white world, in which a *totality* of degraded and disfranchised peoples convene in struggle against a *totality* of humiliations, injustices, dispossessions, and dominations. How has such a political-cultural imagination enabled robust collective movements against oppressive hegemonies while also (necessarily) failing to fulfill the aspirations of a radical totality, which the TWLF often references as "unity," "the people," and so forth?

Perhaps the central, animating force of this narrative or dream form is its tendency to generate schematic, (implicitly) comparative, and sometimes hierarchical descriptions of epochal human (and dehumanizing) violences—from colonial displacement to chattel enslavement, racial labor exploitation to massive incarceration. This tendency simultaneously infers the irreducibility and uniqueness of such historical encounters while cohering them as a *generalized whole,* coexisting in a relative symbiosis with the irreparable brutalities of modernity and nation-building. The truth-effect of this narrative is a compartmentalization of human suffering into relatively discrete historical episodes and geographies: colonization, land displacement, chattel enslavement, wars of conquest, apartheid and segregation, physical genocide, forced labor migration, and more. In this iteration ethnic studies attempts to compose the epistemological foundations for critical activist labors that strive to make sense of a mind-numbingly oppressive global-historical totality.

What if this alleged totality of epochal violence cannot be so easily generalized into coherence nor *schematically and coterminously* apprehended? While we are not suggesting the dismissal or abolition of ethnic studies and related institutionalizations, we are not convinced that such narratives are sufficient to the ongoing task of catalyzing or sustaining insurrection against a global social order that is so clearly apocalyptic for select, targeted subjects, populations, and bodies. When the narrative schematic fails, the consequences are far graver than we are usually willing to admit.

On the one hand ethnic studies has been enfolded into the neoliberal institutional mandates of the university through a particular proliferation as commodified and domesticated "difference" that performs the ideological and material labor of buttressing late-capitalist mantras such as "diversity and excellence" and "global citizens." On the other hand various ethnic studies and related interdisciplinary units and programs have been rendered vulnerable and periodically threatened with eradication within a university structure that is surrendering to the twin pressures of increased corporatization and economic duress. It would seem, then, that ethnic studies is at once a necessary component of a "global" and globally competitive twenty-first-century university *and* an anachronistic holdover from 1968. What does it mean that ethnic studies has come to be so vulnerable and available to such a Janus-faced positioning and appropriation? In what manner was the TWLF's framing of "solidarity" co-opted into a liberal politics of multiculturalism? Are there alternative intellectual and political frameworks for articulating the solidarities of ethnic studies that can speak against these liberal multiculturalist appropriations? The emerging critical ethnic studies project is a collective attempt to build on the possibilities enlivened by the historical work of ethnic studies, while also inaugurating a radical response to the appropriations of liberal multiculturalism.

The Critical Ethnic Studies Project as Neither Even nor Owned

In the spirit of the 2011 inaugural conference of the Critical Ethnic Studies Association (CESA) held at the University of California, Riverside, this editorial collective seeks to prioritize the goals of invitation, provocation, and exhortation rather than foundation. In the purposeful absence of a static or prescriptive scholarly agenda that poses as a *definitive* redefinition of ethnic studies, the still-forming project of critical ethnic studies is in some ways better understood as a principled gesture toward a radical intellectual openness. The purpose of this scholarly activist critique is multilayered, and every iteration of such a praxis—from dense theorization to grassroots political education—can and must affect the manner in which people apprehend and engage in the historical relations of power and violence that permeate their particular everyday.

It is within this openness that the thinkers anthologized in this volume collectively signify an intellectual and political urgency that responds to disparate though coexisting and relationally linked historical moments and conjunctures. Perhaps, in this sense, the emergent work of critical ethnic studies (CES) can also be conceptualized as an attempt to convene these differently located, disparately conditioned scholarly labors into something resembling a field of political-intellectual struggle with dynamic, multiple, and radically divergent focal points. To take such a spatial conceptualization of the CES project seriously, this is to argue that the ostensible field of critical ethnic studies practices and struggles is neither *even* nor *owned*. There is not one thing, institution, or site called critical ethnic studies. Rather it is an impulse emerging from divergent conversations and sites desiring to build on previous work in ethnic studies while simultaneously respecting the political and intellectual movements that gave birth to it inside and outside of the academy.

Critical Ethnic Studies: A Reader convenes these multiple and at times divergent genealogies of ethnic studies and calls attention to the urgency of articulating a critical ethnic studies in and for the twenty-first century. In this sense the *critical* in critical ethnic studies is less a critique of ethnic studies projects as we have come to know them and more a gesturing to the dual meaning of the word as both vital and precarious. If the essays in this volume articulate vital or urgent critiques of their respective objects of analysis, the kind of intellectual risk-taking required to engage in such a critique undergoes a certain precariousness and vulnerability vis-à-vis disciplinary protocols, institutional mandates, and neoliberal instrumentalizations of knowledge. There is moreover another valence of precarity suggested by the institutional precarity of this kind of intellectual labor: actual lives rendered precarious. Advancing an acute refutation of racial capitalist, colonial, and settler modernity's installation of land as property (as well as of particular peoples as dehumanized epiphenomena of conquered landscapes and racial chattel alienated from land), the scholars engaged in these inaugural iterations of critical ethnic studies exhibit varying intimacy with the spatial and historical disequilibria produced by regimes of racial and racializing, epochal and ad hoc violence.

The attempt to convene such political-intellectual workers in the context of this book is thus not sufficiently characterized as a conventional effort to bridge academic divides, construct or revivify coalitions, or build new paradigms for ethnic studies research and scholarship. Contrary to the notion of an intellectual vanguard, the contributors to this volume convey a more generous understanding of the critical ethnic studies project. Reflecting the capacious spirit of the first CESA conference, held in March 2011, these authors suggest a notion of critical ethnic studies that is premised on a convivial sense of urgent participation, intellectual vulnerability, and scholarly audacity. Each of them articulates an intellectual excitement that is inseparable from the social-historical violences that have produced and necessitated such study.

Many readers of this volume will be familiar with recent works in one or more scholarly areas that have contributed to, challenged, or decisively departed from the broad intellectual contours of ethnic studies and related fields. Much of the critically incisive scholarship we understand to be centrally situated in black studies, queer studies, Native American studies, cultural studies, and gender studies, for example, has either rearticulated, radically disrupted, or transformed the generally (and often presumptively) coalition- and alliance-based intellectual infrastructures of ethnic studies. Along these lines the contributors to this anthology construct a dynamic, nonforeclosed working frame through which to bring focal attention to an ongoing problem that marks ethnic studies, including some of its critical ethnic studies iterations: that is, the changing apparatus of epistemological tensions, ontological discontinuities, and historical-experiential incommensurabilities that define the genealogies of the insurgent scholarly fields that ostensibly compose the intellectual and institutional moorings of ethnic studies. While there is no way to adequately schematize these tensions, discontinuities, and incommensurabilities here, it is nonetheless worth emphasizing that the intellectual lineages and lived historical materialities of black studies, Native American studies, indigenous studies, Chicano/a studies, Puerto Rican studies, Asian American studies, Latino/a studies, and other (presumably constituent) fields of ethnic studies simply cannot be encapsulated into a unifying institutional regime or discrete scholarly rubric. This generative impossibility echoes throughout the emerging field of critical ethnic studies and may come to animate rather than undermine it.

Of course critical ethnic studies is not contained within CESA or its conferences. In fact the cofounders of CESA structured the organization with the intent of being nonproprietary about its name, welcoming myriad configurations to self-organize as critical ethnic studies projects. Thus, in keeping with the divergent histories of critical ethnic studies, this volume does not purport to tell *the* story of critical ethnic studies. Rather it puts into conversation some of these multiple strands as a provocation to further this impulse. Similarly this introduction is not an exhaustive account of the problematic with which critical ethnic studies concerns itself but an invitation to a perpetual and always unfolding critical inquiry into the objects, methods, presuppositions, and analytics of ethnic studies.

This anthology is part of a project to imagine a collectivity and recognition beyond institutionally mediated hierarchies of difference, beyond disappearance for those of us whose bodies, thoughts, and cultures have been deemed disposable. Our method was collaborative, working across Ethnic Studies fields and subfields to achieve a conversation between pieces, scenes, and communities that are too often separated by discipline and geography. While interested in building a constellation of response, our efforts signal the ways in which difference must be respected and understood as a unique front for contestation and refusal against systems of imperialism, surveillance, and structural harm. The necessity of movement—personal, intellectual, collective, political—is stressed in the pages to come and, we hope, will carry over in abundance in our shared spaces of collective thought and struggle.

Section Descriptions

THE MULTICULTURAL NATION AND THE VIOLENCE OF LIBERAL RIGHTS

As a liberal corrective to long-standing histories of exclusion, the contemporary regime of hegemonic multiculturalism nominally includes previously marginalized and exploited peoples in selective institutional sites of civil societies. This pluralist dispensation of rights has fabricated a universal, liberated (multicultural) subject from material histories of domination, displacement, and unfreedom. Critical ethnic studies attempts to interrogate the grand telos emplotted by the narrative of liberal multicultural inclusion, recognition, and equality. The radical intellectual labors encompassed in this volume turn the multiculturalist institutional imperatives—of diversity, tolerance, civility, and the postracial, to name a few—against themselves in order to reveal how the formal dispensation of liberal rights at once conditions and covers over a dispersion of continued violence.

It has been precisely during the period of liberal multiculturalism's emergence as a hegemonic national cultural structure—an emergence that has included various liberal appropriations and rearticulations of ethnic studies—that the proliferation of gendered racial *state violence* has reached new heights. The rise of the U.S. and global prison industrial complex and carceral-criminalization regime, for example, offers a stark historical-empirical rebuttal to the ideological overtures of liberal multiculturalism. While liberal rhetorics of diversity valorize the possibilities of vindicated, multicultural citizenship, the cultural and material institutionalization of racist state violence has displaced or socially liquidated entire geographies and demographies of people through the technologies of policing and incarceration. In fact this example indicates how the very structuring of liberal citizenship is symbiotic with or constitutively dependent on forms of institutionalized violence.

Shana L. Redmond addresses how the politics of identity has contributed uncritically to a politics of identification. Guided by the genealogies and provocations presented by James Baldwin, Redmond's discussion of contemporary political mobilizations seeks to trouble the postracial move to identification as a means of liberal political advance. Troy Davis and Trayvon Martin are the subjects whose movement resurrection highlights the fiction of the "I am . . ." narratives that are used as a tactical shorthand within the imagined solidarity of redress. Redmond argues that the "method used as critique subscribes to and relies upon long-standing violences against the African-descended in the United States that further dismiss the particularities of black existence and thereby devalue black life."

In his treatment of black and brown alliances and fissures, John Márquez offers a critique of the structural maintenance and mobilization of the black-white binary by liberal actors in government, law enforcement, social movements, and academic institutions. His chapter, "Juan Crow," takes aim at the way a decolonial political future is crippled by liberal multiculturalism in schools and public discourse, becoming a way of "disremembering" histories of activism, from immigration and labor to officially sanctioned civil rights. By placing into conversation narrative strategies from across the United States, as well as the counterhegemonic articulations of postwar activists and intellectuals, Márquez diagnoses the fallacies and failures of postracial democracy and invites alternative practices of political, community, and discursive accountability and camaraderie.

João H. Costa Vargas asks, "Why is it that, when black suffering and death are momentarily centered, they are almost always displaced by conversations that recenter the experiences of nonblacks?" Vargas invites the reader to engage in freedom dreams that require exercising a political sensibility whose energy derives from at least two sources: first, an immanent critique of the employment of and belief in tropes related to modern, liberal-democratic citizenship principles, and second, the recognition that what is needed to break down regimes of objectifying subjection is to imagine the unimaginable, embody the abject, and venture into the terrifying. More specifically, when, and if, ever so reluctantly, non-, near-, or antiblack people become, in some measure, and even if temporarily, of all things, black themselves, an interesting opportunity to engage with freedom dreams presents itself.

Given the complicity of the state in its apparatuses of violence, Lindsey Schneider calls on critical ethnic studies to denaturalize the form of the nation-state. Building on the work of Native studies scholars who have critiqued the "politics of recognition," Schneider looks at how contemporary discourse around gay marriage and treaty rights positions these struggles in relation to the nation-state. Framing state-sanctioned rights as the ultimate goal—be they tribal members' rights to fish off the reservation or the tribal government's rights to regulate the institution of marriage—reinforces the legitimacy of the settler state. Linking these struggles, however, creates a space to rethink the meaning of sovereignty in terms of decolonization rather than a politics of recognition by the nation-state. In doing so Schneider calls for a critical ethnic studies that denaturalizes the nation-state.

At the same time, Jin Haritaworn interrogates social movements' complicity in white supremacy through their adoption of "hate crimes" organizing as the model by which to address racial violence. Haritaworn terms this model the "hate/crime paradigm," which sticks criminality and pathology to bodies and populations that are always already seen as hateful. Thus a critical ethnic studies analytic cannot be satisfied by allying with social movements without a robust interrogation of the contradictions within the movements themselves.

In a far-ranging conversation moderated by Sarita See, Glen Coulthard and Dylan Rodríguez confront a central political contradiction: How do we make sense of the fact that racist and colonial structures of human fatality have persisted, and at times seem to have grown in reach and sophistication, in the aftermath of the past half century's major movements for progressive social transformation as well as liberal shifts in racial and colonial social texts, including the emergence of multiculturalism and state-ordained national antiracism? In a conversation that ranges from George Zimmerman to the Occupy Movement, Idle No More, and the Pelican Bay hunger strike, Coulthard and Rodríguez reflect on the profound obligations and limits that confront the scholar of differential decolonizing movements, Native and non-Native.

CRITICAL ETHNIC STUDIES PROJECTS MEET THE NEOLIBERAL UNIVERSITY

While we do not further rehearse the narrations of the foundational moments of ethnic studies here, it is worth emphasizing that ethnic studies is in fact born of *multiple* conditions of possibility, which both encompass and exceed the vibrant, militant student- and community-based movements that have exerted demands for socially relevant and socially transformative educational infrastructures. In other words, the precedents of intellectual labor and historical experience that have constituted the material contexts for various institutional iterations of ethnic studies must now be seen to fundamentally exceed the TWLF moment, and the origin story of the field thus necessarily opens to new narratives and multiple intellectual genealogies.

The essays in this section grapple with how the white supremacist university is also now a neoliberal university. Against this institutional logic and rendering, these essays gesture to the ways critical ethnic studies projects have the potential to articulate profound challenges and alternatives to the neoliberal university.

Long T. Bui calls on ethnic studies scholars to question how the public university remains intact as an unproblematized social model of advancement by interrogating the necropolitics of the public university—the collateral damage that the academic industrial complex incurs in securing advantages for some. Bui reads Asian American studies and its scholars against neoliberal claims by the University of California to provide a "better life," in so doing challenging the precarious privilege of Asian Americans and constructions of the "model minority."

Nada Elia focuses on the international academic solidarity movement with Palestinian liberation. Engaging the current Boycott, Divestment and Sanctions (BDS) Campaign that targets the complicity of Israeli academic institutions in the occupation of Palestine and its apartheid practices throughout Israel, Elia calls on academics and others to mobilize support within the academy for the BDS Campaign and demonstrates that such action can refresh and enliven radical inquiry and scholarship in the United States.

As Tania Das Gupta argues, the academic industrial complex is not monolithic. While university restructuring, consolidation, and abuse of power are rampant, Das Gupta uses the case of the Atkinson College reorganization at York University as a way to highlight the fact that the university also harbors sites of resistance and possibilities for constructing alternative educational methodologies. From this specific location Das Gupta details the struggles of a program to build such alternatives within the confines of the neoliberal university.

David Lloyd provides an extended analysis of the neoliberal university. Through a discussion of critical ethnic studies and its multiply situated theorists, Lloyd analyzes how the temptation for ethnic studies to remain at the level of critique actually serves to solidify rather than challenge the academic industrial complex. Scales of institutional value—of persons, labor, and scholarship—are cited as that which the CES project must dismantle such that inquiry and the social movements aligned with it are fostered as contests to the academic industrial complex.

Similarly Dan Berger calls for a renewed project of camaraderie between ethnic studies projects and the sociopolitical movements from which they arise (and continue to study and announce). Using Foucault as a founding theorist of knowledge, Berger names an investment in new processes of its production by highlighting the work of scholar-activists beyond the academy, namely J. Sakai, Butch Lee, and Red Rover, who form part of a Chicago-based revolutionary intellectual circle. In noting their absence within contemporary works of academic scholarship, Berger begins to generate a new archive of documents and practices that will productively shape a twenty-first-century project of critical ethnic studies.

THE BODY AND THE DISPENSATIONS OF RACIAL CAPITAL

Racial capital's dispensations—as distribution, management, and disposal—operate nimbly on multiple scales, from the planetary to the corporeal. Just as continents, regions, colonies, territories, and nations have been and continue to be racial capital's sites of violent abstraction, extraction, and exploitation, the gendered racial and sexualized body is the intimate terrain that is simultaneously produced by such violent dispensations but also exceeds them. These precarious, vulnerable, and disposable bodies exist in intimate proximity to racial capital's thriving necropolitical regimes; racial capital depends upon their continued vitality as a site of exploitation, yet their very disposability is also a source of surplus value.

The essays in this section offer analyses that focus on the intimate violence wrought by racial capital at the scale of the body. They reveal how the body registers a capacity to bear such violence but also to thwart it. Whether laboring, performing, disabled, transgender, or queer, the body refuses to become the fresh body count of racial capital's skeletal remains even as it carries the living memories of the previous body counts produced by the epochal violence of racial capitalist modernity's symbiosis with a variety of colonialisms.

Nirmala Erevelles builds on the work of Hortense Spillers to question the assumption that the acquisition of a disabled identity always occurs outside historical context. In the specific historical context of slavery, the attribution of disability to the female captive body, for instance, enabled this body to become a site where the flesh was the prime commodity of exchange in the violent conflation of both profit and pleasure. Erevelles situates disability not as the condition of being but of becoming; this becoming is a historical event, and further, it is its material context that is critical in the theorizing of disabled bodies and subjectivities.

Bo Luengsuraswat also focuses on the nonnormative body, in particular the relationships between racial and gender identity. He argues that Bobby Cheung's art practice resignifies the cultural signifiers of femininity and womanhood into an articulation of Asian American transgender maleness. Luengsuraswat's essay engages in broader lines of inquiry concerning the limits of trans- and homonormativity, the contours of Asian American *gendered* racialization, the problematics of the art world, and the labors of global capital.

Andrew Uzendoski's essay addresses global capital, in particular the relationship between capitalism and violence through the work of Indra Sinha, whose novel *Animal's People* makes visible neoliberal capitalism's economic ferocity as a kind of "slow violence" that produces a gradually materializing genocide. Uzendoski argues that Sinha's novel provides an "alternative historiography" that challenges the temporality of neoliberal capitalism and its uneven allocation of risk.

Stephanie Nohelani Teves centers indigenous performance artists as a site for rearticulating indigeneity. Teves complicates the (non)performances of indigeneity by the Kanaka Maoli drag artist Cocoa Chandelier, whose performance at the Miss Gay USA drag pageant in Hawai'i is the scene of investigation and grounds Teves's theorization of Hawaiian cultural performativity, which serves as an act of revision within prevailing, iconic performances of indigeneity, such as the hula girl. Using performance and postcolonial theorists, Teves argues that Chandelier complicates visual exchange and rebuts long-standing colonial and capitalist practices of consumption, thereby contesting and expanding the space available to indigenous performance artists.

MILITARISM, EMPIRE, AND WAR: THE SECURITY STATE AND STATES OF INSECURITY

The national security state—most muscularly embodied by the United States but globally projected—generates and wages multiple wars on multiple fronts. Whether declared or undeclared, domestic or foreign, cold or hot, legal or extralegal, territorial or extraterritorial, wars proliferate and metastasize. U.S. militarism and empire are at once produced by and are themselves the products of a warfare state. The wars of settler colonialism conditioned and continue to condition the very formation and cohesion of the United States. Imperial adventures and nation-building projects abroad secure resources in the name of security and democracy.

What and whose security is named in the national security state's waging of permanent war? If such war becomes synonymous with genocidal and biopolitical violence, the targeting of variously gendered racial populations, corporate profiteering, and the extension of U.S. imperial hegemony, then what constitutes security? For whom is security guaranteed, and who becomes collateral damage in producing security? Indeed U.S. national security has ushered in radical states of insecurity and penury for a global majority. These states of insecurity—across political, economic, and ecological terrains—render lives and ways of life vulnerable to attack and apocalyptic transmogrifications. The essays in this section point to the urgent intellectual, political, and ethical task of imagining and creating alternative states of security in the double sense of carrying out insurrections against the state such that warfare is not its primary raison d'être and creating states or conditions of security that sustain ways in which communities can live the life they want to live.

David M. Hernández addresses the relationship between militarism, security, and immigrant incarceration. Immigrant detention in the United States is an obscured and flexible enforcement power executed historically by proxy entities and institutions, including a web of domestic and international carceral sites and partners. Ultimately institutional obscurity, Hernández suggests, makes detention a robust and flexible enforcement power, lending itself to other government agendas, from fighting crime, drugs, and terrorism to managing labor and producing political currency. Hernández problematizes the prevailing logics both guiding and seeking to reform the detention regime, unmasking and intervening in the obscured discursive and institutional formations of immigrant detention in the United States.

Jason Luna Gavilan's chapter addresses Filipino sailors' shifting racial locations in the military hierarchy of the U.S. Navy during World War II. Using archival documents Gavilan explores Filipinos' hierarchical location among a complex system of U.S. military racial segregation and explores varying "preferences" for Filipino messmen in relation to other racially subordinated military personnel as well as the civilian complaints about racial segregation in a time of war. Gavilan considers these civilian pressures and geopolitical relationship between the United States and the Philippines, which led to the U.S. military's reluctant and cosmetic makeover of its racist enlistment system before the ultimate integration of the U.S. military after World War II.

Gilberto Rosas explores contemporary complex racial dynamics resulting from the ongoing securitization of the U.S.-Mexico border. In particular Rosas explores the concept of a "thickening" border, expanding both north and south through interrelated social forces: global efforts at immigration and drug enforcement, cultural and racial mixing or *mestizaje*, and emerging forms of undocumented youth activism and identity formation. He suggests that borders, mestizaje, and "illegal" identities have been dramatically reworked and resignified on the ground.

Ronak K. Kapadia identifies art as an alternative site to deconstruct the logics of U.S. global warfare through an examination of the critical and social potential of the contemporary aesthetic works of Wafaa Bilal, an Iraqi artist based in New York City. In this reading Kapadia proposes the concept of a "queer calculus" as an alternative mode of understanding the proliferation of drone warfare and the dominant militarized vision of U.S. imperialism that lies at its core. Queer calculus is a theoretical strategy that generates an account of both persistent systems and structures undergirding U.S. global counterinsurgency warfare and alternative logics, affects, and affiliations produced by racialized subjects in response.

Keith P. Feldman excavates the historically dynamic technologies of war making and racialization within the visual field. By using the iconic scene of the Situation Room at the moment of Osama bin Laden's murder, Feldman articulates a theory of "racialization from above" that is made possible by the persistent flexibility of the U.S. border and frontier and its weapons of extermination, namely the aerial drones employed with alarming regularity by U.S. operatives in theaters of combat abroad as well as along the borders of the nation-state. Feldman links the logics of this extralegal and extraterritorial expansion to histories and presents of settler colonialism in the United States and Israel and in so doing places the "war on terror" within a genealogy of recognizable scopic regimes and imperial expansion.

FUGITIVE SOCIALITIES AND ALTERNATIVE FUTURES

The sheer variety of colonial and neocolonial formations has necessitated fugitive socialities, or ways of living, being, and relating that have taken flight from the dominant and can only be glimpsed in fleeting moments. How can CES contribute to long-standing and complex debates about the meanings and differentiations among decolonization, decolonial struggle, and anticolonialism? The essays in this section gesture to the alternative futures that various moments and projects of anticolonialism and decolonization have attempted to chart and might still realize. Between the regret of an imperfect past and the anticipation of a utopic future there lies an interregnum whose time can be seized for instants of critical reflection. The urgency of identifying the fatal unfreedom that the monumental yet banal violence of colonialism continues to produce nurtures political subjectivities that are compelled to imagine decolonial futures.

Neferti M. Tadiar's essay argues that decolonization entails a rethinking of existing social analytics and genealogies of empire. Tadiar offers such a rethinking by conceptualizing "remaindered life" as an alternative form of social reproduction consisting of "generative associations and acts, social capacities and aspirations, agencies of imagination and practice." This form of social reproduction corrodes dominant social relations and instead produces fugitive socialities, which may be made available to obstruct the spread of empire.

Robert Stam and Ella Shohat argue that critical ethnic studies and identity politics must be seen against the backdrop of the "seismic shift" created by the decolonization of world culture. Central twentieth-century events—World War II, the Jewish Holocaust, Third Worldist anticolonialism, the civil rights struggle, and minority liberation movements—all simultaneously delegitimized the West as the axiomatic center of reference and affirmed the rights of non-European peoples emerging from the yoke of colonialism and racism. Within this context Shohat and Stam critically interrogate the convergence of anti-identity politics in left- and right-wing discourse. They call for a recuperation of a nonessentialist identity politics that is capable of addressing identity-based oppression.

Nelson Maldonado-Torres elucidates the significance of decolonization and elaborates the significance of what he calls the "decolonial turn," a recognition of the ethical, political, and epistemological significance of decolonization as a project in the twentieth century. In particular he reads Aimé Césaire's *Discourse on Colonialism* as a discourse on decolonial methodology and the response of a black colonized subject to the Cartesian project. In doing so he reveals how Césaire critically dislocates the basis of the European civilization project.

Laura Pulido examines the debate over Mexican and Mexican American racial identity, in particular the debates over racial choices and prescriptions among national Latina/o organizations in the mid-twentieth century. Pulido provides an analysis of the Asociación Nacional México-Americana (ANMA), a radical political and civil rights organization in the Southwest linked to the Communist Party and the International Union of Mine, Mill, and Smelter Workers. Although short-lived, ANMA broke from peer Latina/o organizations that asserted a white identity as a strategy for achieving rights and self-protection from racial discrimination.

Alexander G. Weheliye interrogates the conceptual carte blanche granted to white European thinkers. Focusing on Foucault's notion of "biopolitics" and Agamben's idea of "bare life," Weheliye demonstrates that they place racial difference in a field prior to and at a distance from conceptual contemplation. In doing so he reveals just how comprehensively the coloniality of Man suffuses the disciplinary and conceptual formations of knowledge we labor under, and how far we have yet to go in decolonizing these structures.

I. THE MULTICULTURAL NATION AND THE VIOLENCE OF LIBERAL RIGHTS

ONE

"As Though It Were Our Own": Against a Politics of Identification

SHANA L. REDMOND

Only a handful of the millions of people in this vast place are aware that the fate intended for you . . . is a fate which is about to engulf them, too.
—JAMES BALDWIN, "An Open Letter to My Sister, [Miss] Angela Davis"

There is a disturbing tendency within liberal intellectual and political circles to un(der)critically identify with the targets of racism and violence or the subjects who become the vehicles of its scholastic critique. Proxy narratives with those afflicted populations take liberties with the histories and present of power and manifest themselves not as solidarities but as violent displacements, as the narrator becomes the subject under examination who in turn shields from view those who are most vulnerable. While this practice may be enacted or witnessed as a protective measure, its employment has recently developed as an end in and of itself. In their attempts to mobilize sympathy, justice-redress actors who devise slogans of identification like "I am Troy Davis"—a meme developed in the months leading to Davis's 2012 execution—are unwittingly contributing to the tidy demise of their subjects.[1] Identification rhetoric signals a relation to endangered women and men that takes for granted the structures that allow for and welcome its articulation. By adopting the status of imperiled life, liberal actors disappear particular negotiations and struggles, thereby allowing the processes that contain and legitimize that death making to remain untrammeled.

Although not wholly new, this practice was redefined and rejuvenated in the past decade. Identification *as* rather than *with* the subject of violence is made imminently passible in the present by the myth birthed of a failed capitalism: postracialism. In a desperate bid to stem the tide of the dispossessed masses, the state distracts us with charming fictions to convince us that our experiences and fates are the same—that there is no difference produced from capital's expansion or regression and no histories or future of its exception. From this reorientation developed a political ethos that ostensibly critiqued both capitalism and the "declining significance of race" theory even as it employed those rhetorics and logics for alternative visions of social change.[2] The election of the nation's first black president, Barack Obama, in 2008 inaugurated a more mature language and visual practice of intense identification in response to acts of state violence and white vigilantism. There are embedded privileges within this practice that were enabled by his presidency—privileges that rely on and reinforce the very structures of difference that his election was announced to resolve and that movement actors attempt to dismiss through claims to sameness with those who are too often deceased.[3] Black (and Other) death and its proximity is the precondition for a politics that has, notably since Obama, used identification to evidence the continued ruptures of race, class, nationality, and, to a lesser extent, gender, within U.S. society. While these deep and enduring cleavages require public displays and performances as acts of evaluation and refusal, I argue that the method used as critique subscribes to and relies upon long-standing violences against the African-descended in the United States that further dismiss the particularities of black existence and thereby devalue black life.

I highlight here two instances that epitomize this burden of identification as a means of liberal political advance. It is worth noting that what I articulate as liberal is, to the minds of the actors, often considered radical or even revolutionary. I seek to demonstrate the practices that dismantle this promise and disarticulate it from previous strategies of defense. The execution of a Georgia death row inmate, Troy Davis, and the murder of a Florida teenager, Trayvon Martin, were the catalytic events that highlight this troubled political method and throw its premise into crisis. By adopting their dead bodies, a liberal populace was able to both exorcise and exercise their racial and/or gender privilege in order to draw attention to the repeated violence that otherwise signals the healthy function of a white supremacist order. Their mobilizations of sympathy, however, did not disrupt this national vitality; they instead condoned it by isolating these events as spectacular and extraordinary when they are in fact quotidian, always already existing as the everyday possibility of life and death for black communities.[4] Traditions of black response to incarceration and death largely remain evacuated from contemporary national discourses on punishment. My work here relies on one activist-thinker who, under great threat, theorized the conditions of one of the century's icons alongside the nation that held her captive. James Baldwin's "An Open Letter to My Sister, [Miss] Angela Davis" provides a frame for understanding the necessity of alliance and the impossibility of identification.[5] His provocations and warnings offer correctives that may well salvage the impulses that do not yet but could lead to actionable outcomes and effective structural change.

Published in November 1970, "An Open Letter" was a deeply historical and impassioned announcement of solidarity with the political activist Angela Davis and those like her who remained unnamed, unknown, and unclaimed. At the moment of the essay's publication, Davis was none of those things; she was a cause célèbre after going underground in flight of charges for aggravated kidnapping and first-degree murder. The official record reasoned that she be charged for her purchase of guns that were later used in a shootout with California police. Although she was not present at the event, the state of California argued that Davis was as responsible as those who pulled the trigger, leading J. Edgar Hoover of the Federal Bureau of Investigation to add her name to the nation's "Ten Most Wanted" list. Facing the possibility of death after her capture in October, Davis continued to publicly expose the racist violences of the state by writing and offering interviews from jail. As I discuss later, her work on both sides of the prison wall accelerated not only her own defense but also that of the imprisoned black women with whom she communed. Baldwin brought his own exposure to the case, employing the hunt for Davis as a moment of intervention into (inter)national conversations on race and punishment, gender and war making, epistemology and ontology. His efforts in "An Open Letter" connect the variety of regimes and structures that I briefly investigate as the pieces constitutive of the problematic of identification within contemporary political mobilizations.

They appear to glory in their chains; now, more than ever, they appear to measure their safety in chains and corpses.—JAMES BALDWIN, "An Open Letter to My Sister, [Miss] Angela Davis"

Black and brown death as a precondition for white life was put on full display on May 2, 2011, with the murder of Osama bin Laden. The Navy SEAL invasion of his compound, in excess of numerous international laws, was the spectacle through which the United States again announced itself as exceptional, powerful, and vengeful. Although bin Laden's murder was tied to and justified by a discursive and proto-juridical matrix labeled "national security," the domestic murders of Troy Davis (September 7, 2011) and Trayvon Martin (February 26, 2012) were suspended within a national common sense of crime and punishment when they are better situated inside of the logics that made bin Laden's murder possible: the expansion of the security state, which, in addition to growing U.S. military presence throughout the world, enacts domestic warfare by building prisons with unprecedented rapidity and promoting the gated community as an oasis of safety and exclusivity. The death of black women and men through state violence, legal and extralegal, is represented in the mass caging of human beings and the eradication of the commons, no less than through the international expansion of the war complex. It is precisely the acceleration and proliferation of an armed U.S. citizenry—whether through the nation's military, community paramilitary organizations like the Minutemen Project, or individual citizens—that condones and normalizes death as an appropriate punishment and response to difference.

Crime is the mobilizing language that encodes the two scenarios that I discuss here. The word is made impenetrable as a way to forestall criticism of state violence even though it is dialogic—in conversation with a wider field of constructions. As Nils Christie has detailed, "Crime does not exist. Crime is created. First there are the acts. Then follows a long process of giving meaning to these acts."[6] Ruth Wilson Gilmore argues against a common sense that links "crime" with the "prison" because "what counts as crime in fact changes, and what happens to people convicted of crimes does not, in all times and places, result in prison sentences. Defined in the simple terms of the secular state, crime means a violation of the law. Laws change, depending on what, in a social order, counts as stability, and who, in a social order, needs to be controlled."[7] This domestic warfare may well be considered the laboratory for international war making, such that it is in the logics and procedures of settler colonialism and chattel slavery that one finds, for example, the design of enforced enclosures that redline poor and of color communities from goods and services, or the extralegal and long-term captivity of subsidiary citizens or noncitizens at Pelican Bay State Prison or Guantánamo Bay Detention Camp.

These long and interdependent histories are both more available and tenuous within the discursive lexicon of the university, which employs a number of activist-scholars of the prison but is often an uneasy space that brings with it concerns and realities that exacerbate the injustices that these scholars have laid bare.[8] From university hedge fund investment in private prisons to the pervasive, university-funded patrolling of the black, brown, and poorer neighborhoods contiguous with their campuses, the experience and reality of violence is never too far from the work of the places to which we are sent to learn.[9] Knowledge production in some ways works as a foil for these experiences of difference. As Roderick Ferguson argues, the university has been not only the product of the brutalities of the state and capital but is a unique site of experimentation for its goals of minority body and discourse integration. Ethnic studies and women's studies have become part of the "archival economy" of power, thereby "producing formulas for the incorporation rather than the absolute repudiation of difference, all the while refining and perfecting its practices of exclusion and regulation."[10] Just as the United States in 1964 labored to legislatively fold an unruly blackness into itself, so too have universities sought to recuperate and reprogram the energies of a rebellious student body who demanded the intellectual venues to study and validate their experiences and knowledge. This move to incorporation offers a structural precedent and training ground for the political practice of identification that I examine here. The black bodies on display in my scenarios are not popularly positioned as agents in the same way as the striking undergraduate students of the 1960s; they are rather the collateral damage of this explosive moment in the institutionalization of Other knowledge formations. The failures of the incorporative agendas of the state, capital, and the university are on full display in the violent deaths of Davis and Martin, and the institutional representation of black communities in U.S. colleges and universities over the past fifty years has done little to stem the tide of disfranchisement that makes black death widely permissible. The evidence of an assimilable black body in the university, government, and law enforcement has further distinguished those good from bad in the rhetoric and legislation of the state that has reconfigured the landscapes and sightlines of its exclusions, in the process growing the numbers of cages and caskets.

The haphazard availability of knowledges based in communities of color, free from rigorous institutional investment or community cooperation, facilitates a false familiarity as all parties within increasingly uniform higher education institutions are somehow made universally recognizable and heard.[11] Students often are encouraged to understand black life through their own experiences of loss or frustration; only rarely do they engage it as the result of a distinct logic of abuse and exclusion. My experiences of this phenomenon in the classroom include students whose limited recognition of policing oppressions is filtered solely through their liberal investments in the legalization of marijuana or those students who, in response to discussions of the 1994 Rwandan genocide, cannot muster a response but through the history and language of the Jewish Holocaust. While we all approach the world through unique lenses and investments, this is too often where the students and their elders begin and end their discussions; the experiences of the African-descended are not considered distinct from their own, in the process abandoning the histories that position black people in discrete ways.[12] Black representation then stands in for substance, and inclusion masquerades as equality. The university constructs and applauds these moves as it announces its diverse future through a shared imaginary. "Part of the signature achievements of these affirmative modes of power," according to Ferguson, "was to make the pursuit of recognition and legitimacy into formidable horizons of pleasure, insinuating themselves into radical politics, trying to convince insurgents that 'your dreams are also mine.'"[13] These working-class, black, brown, gendered, and queer dreams then are evacuated in the process of an artless identification. Instead of true parity, transference occurs where whiteness is validated for its dimensionality and sympathetic embrace of a hollowed-out minority life. These beliefs and practices invaded the ranks of progressive political mobilizations, where they became the method of response to the violences of the state and its excess vigilantism, thereby producing a modality of political "radicalism" coalesced not by robust engagements with antiblack racism but instead by facile identifications with vulnerable peoples.

The relationship between knowledge production, politics, and identity is evidenced in the sociopolitical fights within and over contemporary Arizona. The 2010 Support Our Law Enforcement and Safe Neighborhoods Act, or Arizona Senate Bill 1070 (SB 1070), expanded police power in the streets and allowed for immigrant profiling in order to check women and men for documentation of U.S. citizenship. Within six months of SB 1070, Arizona's attorney general Tom Horne declared Tucson's Mexican American studies program illegal.[14] The proximity of these two policies exhibits their interrelatedness, which in combination stunts the minds and patrols the bodies of the nation's Others. Unions and community groups around the nation called necessary attention to the state and its escalation of terror against Latinas/os. The Todos Somos Arizona (We are all Arizona) campaigning that occurred in the wake of SB 1070 worked to make a national coalition of similarly positioned people, despite the fact that it was a particular condition of (non) being legislated for Latinas/os. SB 1070 sought to legally codify the distinct and concentrated difference of brown bodies, yet the sloganeering used to respond to those experiences attempted to make universal a specifically situated set of containments and abuses. As I will soon discuss, this movement was compromised by their efforts to gain legitimacy from black disidentification, thereby demonstrating not solidarity but rather the widely held and politically resonant structures of difference.

The intention behind the Todos Somos Arizona campaign is duly noted. Its project is to involve the entire nation in the public life of Arizona's residents, to implicate everyone in the fascist practices of the state, to rally all sympathies and empathies. There are, however, problems with this formulation. As I mentioned, the impact of SB 1070 was unevenly experienced. The spectrum was literally one of life and death, and those who marched against the bill included a sizable number on the safe end of the spectrum—those with the inalienable right to life. The mobilization of those whose rights and bodies are respected is a savvy tactic when highlighting the threat of violence, yet the right to safety that is accessible to some and not others remains underdeveloped in the rhetoric and public strategizing of many contemporary social movement formations. The Occupy Wall Street movement (OWS) is one example of a political collection consistently reported to have limited participation by black and brown members; its inability or unwillingness to address this absence and the differences of access and circumstance that make it possible will continue to threaten its effectiveness in response to our similar—not identical—experiences of abuse under capitalism and empire.[15] What groups like OWS have not entirely contended with is the fact that sidestepping the question of difference—experiential and structural—will continue to impede their goals and limit their ability to see and act beyond a parochial universalism that fails to disrupt, let alone resolve, the political and emotional currency of whiteness.

As long as white Americans take refuge in their whiteness . . . they will never . . . feel themselves sufficiently human, *sufficiently worthwhile*, to become responsible for themselves, their leaders, their country, their children, or their fate.—JAMES BALDWIN, "An Open Letter to My Sister, [Miss] Angela Davis"

The black body or its specter regularly plays boogey man to the conditions of critique within contemporary political mobilizations, providing an exemplar of compromise and failure. Instead of working in concert with and full appreciation of the gains of myriad black freedom struggles in the long twentieth century, current mobilizations too often portray themselves as the fully incorporative, antiessentialist torchbearers of a flawed emancipation project. The proof of those claims, however, has proven elusive. Universalism exposed its limits in the Todos Somos Arizona campaign as movement media machines encoded their message with black criminality and used it as the foundation from which to launch the innocence of their targeted subjects. "No Soy Criminal" was employed as a language of assimilability in distinction from anti-Arab and -Muslim discourses of terrorism but was regularly paired with an abstention from public assistance, such as food stamps and subsidized housing, two services regularly cited as examples of black depravity and laziness. In this political scenario black bodies were not inhabited like the rhetorical body snatchers of "I am Troy Davis" but were excised from the public "we" that was necessary for the broad Arizona coalition to retain political and narrative power. The relatively diverse collective established in response to SB 1070 exhibited its defeat when it defined itself against the glorified straw man of condemned and retrograde blackness.

As this scenario demonstrates, white people are not the only empowered players within the politics of identification. Nonblack(-identifying) people of color also mobilize their relative currency. Multiracialism, which theorist Jared Sexton argues is grown from entire industries of thought and performance around mixed-raceness, "not only proves complicit with white supremacy and antiblackness but goes on in that respect to announce itself as avant-garde." It is "less a classic *divide-and-conquer* strategy" than "a rationalizing discourse for the continued and increasing social, political and economic *isolation* of blacks."[16] Indeed this isolation has been structurally codified within our cities; as João Costa Vargas and Joy James argue, "The imagination, mechanics, and reproduction of the ordinary polis rely on the exclusion of ordinary blacks and their availability for violent aggression and/or premature death or disappearance (historically through lynching and the convict prison lease system, today through 'benign neglect' and mass incarceration). The ordinary black person can therefore never be integrated."[17] As such, multiracial politics, whose rudimentary identity collapse envisaged the postracial, relies on both neoliberal and conservative formations of redress and sociopolitical engineering in order to build its vision of inclusivity.

The promiscuity of political ideology across the issue spectrum has led to a movement schizophrenia that produces a rank and file who, in moments of confusion or jeopardy, illegibility or negotiation, compromise the collective by retreating into entitlement. Sociologists Debra Friedman and Doug McAdam explain, "To partake of a collective identity is to reconstitute the individual self around a new and valued identity."[18] This reconstitution is not automatic; it is a process that is regularly imperiled in antiracist social justice movements by what Baldwin argued was the "refuge" of whiteness—that separate and special place that allows white people to find safety in their power and possessions. Whiteness might be deployed as a helpful socioeconomic and political tool, but it comes with an escape hatch—a path of return for those who dare to play on the dark side. This out is a luxury unavailable to the majority of the black and brown people on whose behalf they claim to labor. It is precisely this always available escape or retreat into the comforts and rights of whiteness, wealth or privilege (including ability, heterosexuality, national citizenship, etc.) that distills the crises that grow from mainstream political mobilizations and become the affects and effects that limit people of color, queer, poor, and undocumented people's participation and safety within them. These too are the mechanisms of relativity that allow liberal movement actors of color to mobilize black vulnerability in service of their political identifications and movements. What I signal here is not the irredeemability of white or nonblack movement actors but rather the fact that whiteness and antiblackness as strategies of progressive political advance are impassable. The reliance on and mobilization of differential advantage and access inherently undercut the potential for thick camaraderie, relying instead on cheap exclusions and the thin bonds of sympathy.

If sympathy is a limited emotion, it is exponentially narrower as a mobilizing device, especially when race is an organizing element of the imagined political community. As Robert Solomon argues, "Insofar as sympathy involves actually sharing feelings, it is clear that the suffering one shares with the sufferer is, for the most part, pretty limp stuff and not nearly adequate to motivate ethical behavior."[19] History has revealed this fact. The grievances of black people have long been narrated by sympathetic white orators situated across the political spectrum. From white abolitionists who assumed the role of politico-intellectual executor, to the white benefactors of the Harlem Renaissance and the "superman" white teachers of impoverished urban and rural schools, white citizens have used sympathy as a narrative device in their managerial positions over black bodies and speech. Even those political projects that manifested positive result for the African-descended—including the abolitionist movement—regularly debated the level of humanity and movement role of black subjects.[20] Nineteenth-century sympathy was a "common construct across a wide spectrum of antislavery rhetoric" and, according to the historian Elizabeth B. Clark, was a "complex process in which the observer's willed attentiveness to another's suffering gave rise to an intuitive empathetic identification with the other's experiences." She exposes, however, that the will to empathy was not freely given in response to the suffering of the enslaved, even in the "enlightened" northern states of the union.

The tragic flaw of abolitionist universalism's application was that "the demand for equal treatment presupposed that all sufferers are similarly situated and deserving of sympathetic relief."[21] This too is a tragic flaw of contemporary political movements; in absenting the "historical richness, intellectual intensity, cultural expansiveness, and political complexity of black experience" described by Sexton, abolitionists and those who subscribe to a similar logic of sympathy fail to announce and account for the systems that make people's suffering different.[22] Identification unfolds as the collective mobilization of a responsive sympathy in political scenes of racialized violation. The rhetoric of the postracial has condoned and facilitated the move to identification by enforcing the invisibility of interracial difference and whiteness as power.

Postracialism in the United States is narrated primarily via the ventriloquism of white and elite communities who highlight the achievement of individual people of color in order to exorcize the guilt and anxiety of their possessions. A host of African-descended characters participate in this staging, falling along the spectrum between real and imagined. The science of postracialism is promoted within the realm of the popular, where it is the number of representations and superstars, not their quality or impact, that provides the evidence of its existence. For example, Kathryn Stockett's voice as Aibileen Clark's channeled through Viola Davis in the wildly successful film *The Help* (2011) is the chain of ventriloquism and habitation by which a white woman communes and identifies with the ghosts of black domestics past in a world of parity and reconciliation. Supreme relativity is the "racial calculus," to borrow from Saidiya Hartman, of postracialism;[23] either we're all oppressed or we're all fine. There are no distinctions and no hierarchies, at least none that warrant notice, let alone resolution.

The postracial oracle sent to manifest these truths is President Barack Obama, whose life constitutes both the contradictory facts and the unbearable fancy of the term. An algorithm that combines Obama's nonenslaved African ancestry with his Ivy League education provides the definitive solution to blackness, in spite of the fact that his narrative is not arranged or presented as a factorial—it is not a cumulative expression inclusive of all integers, all information.[24] There is missing evidence, those discarded factors that would disrupt a final outcome that has somehow equated individual black successes with the dismantlement of white supremacy. This is the platform from which Obama launched two successful bids to the presidency: he argued that his plight and its cure were identical to those faced and imagined by the rest of the nation, in the process relieving all involved of the histories and presents of race and racism.[25]

Baldwin refused to extinguish those formations from his thinking and public intellectualism. In "An Open Letter" he mapped an early genealogy for the postracial through his discussion of the national project to foment self-hatred in generations of black people. He wrote, "The American triumph—in which the American tragedy has always been implicit—was to make Black people despise themselves. When I was little I despised myself; I did not know any better. And this meant, albeit unconsciously, or against my will, or in great pain, that I also despised my father. *And* my mother. *And* my brothers. *And* my sisters. Black people were killing each other every Saturday night out on Lenox Avenue, when I was growing up; and no one explained to them, or to me, that it was *intended* that they should." This violence demonstrated the "triumph" and healthy function of the state; the death of black people was the inspired and expected result of centuries of enforced miseducation through which black men and women learned to hate themselves and each other. The postracial is a natural extension of this public education; it argues that "black people," as a heterogeneous yet distinctly situated and differently politicized coalition of individuals do not exist and, as Baldwin theorized, have never existed.[26] The enforced excision of blackness from the kaleidoscope of U.S. difference sought to remove the nation's most steadfast bulwark to the successful acceptance of developing myths like the postracial.

The dismissal of an unproblematic universal in tandem with a refusal of individualism are the acts that facilitate the robust and effective "claim to political, and delimited, claims" called for by Vijay Prashad, which call structure into question and advance its alternatives.[27] Anything short of these efforts will result only in receipt of the lowest-hanging fruits of American democracy as individual advancement charades as progress, leading the beneficiary to believe that the game has changed. What they and the believers in the postracial fail to recognize is that race is not soluble within this democracy; the bodies of difference always remain solid, and they eventually rise from the depths with names like Oscar and Aiyana and Sean.[28] The instances of postracial failure represented by these names are the material evidence of the dually structural and quotidian brutalities that the postracial and its politics of identification attempt to deny.

If we know, then we must fight for your life as though it were our own—which it is—and render impassable with our bodies the corridor to the gas chamber.—JAMES BALDWIN, "An Open Letter to My Sister, [Miss] Angela Davis"

As I've demonstrated, it is not only conservative or otherwise hegemonic groups and institutions that have used the postracial technique of identification for political gain. Liberal and progressive social mobilizations and demonstrations have been particularly adept at capitalizing on black death, in the process modeling the political circumstance that I question here. Recent deaths of black men enlivened feelings of identification across race that then were played out on a national stage. The execution of Troy Davis, an inmate on Georgia's death row, mobilized a number of communities and organizations. In 1989 Davis was charged and later convicted of the murder of a Savannah police officer. Over the years a campaign developed that mobilized the language of "too much doubt," as a number of witnesses recanted or changed their stories of Davis's guilt and a lack of physical evidence propelled a rigorous defensive strategy. Civil rights and liberties organizations took notice and sought to increase the coverage and scrutiny of the case in various media venues, including social networking sites. Identification developed as the point of access for the case and sent the phrase "I am Troy Davis" into the mainstream. Sponsored by groups like the National Association for the Advancement of Colored People (NAACP), this viral identification increased the exposure of his case but also obfuscated the stakes involved. While the death penalty received the bulk of the critical energies, the criminal justice system was regularly let off the hook either through silence or through highlighting the exceptional ignorance or abuses of key players within the Davis case. By focusing on the ineptness of a few, the "system" of the criminal justice system was contained and preserved. This selectivity showcases and buttresses the individualism of the postracial moment; the prison regime is largely pardoned as singular state actors take the fall for what is a structural result intended to happen again and again.

The logic of the "I am Troy Davis" campaign was like that of Todos Somos Arizona; in gathering an international body of sympathetic witnesses, the Davis family, the NAACP, and others hoped to play to the moral center of the system that could stay Davis's execution.[29] The appeal to morality, however, was one of the critiques that befell the campaign internationally. The conservative British journalist Toby Harnden argued, "If anything, the moral superiority of so many pontificating about Davis and the presumption of Europeans telling Americans how to run their justice system makes it more rather than less likely that executions will remain part of the American way."[30] The strategies of identification employed in this movement are what allow this critique to resonate; their exclusive focus placed Davis in a vacuum, even as others around the country and throughout the world aligned their identity with his.

Within six months of the Davis execution another black body was stilled and later revived as an international icon. Trayvon Martin was a seventeen-year-old high school student who, after a trip to the convenience store, was murdered by a neighborhood watch volunteer in the gated Florida enclave in which his father lived. In the wake of his death numerous individuals, in particular white women, found political voice through the claim "Trayvon is my son." President Obama similarly positioned himself with the comment "If I had a son, he'd look like Trayvon."[31] These claims reflect a deep reliance on the notion of the family within U.S. political discourse and revive a long-used method of engagement with black mobilizations.[32] What is lost in these filial attachments are the complexities and dangers of black life that made Martin vulnerable to death at age seventeen. The surveillance and unchecked violence that attended his life's last moments were exceptional only to *some*. The truth of that claim is masked by the demand for universal access to his body, his history, and the futures that are marked by his death. The identification claims outlined here argue the humanity of the plundered by narrating not interlocking but identical subjectivities: "I am you." The radical and unequal scales of disadvantage and vulnerability that structurally ground blackness as depravity and difference are evacuated by the forced relationships of movement activity. The cloak of progressive politics does not fundamentally change the unevenness of encounter with the state that the Davis and Martin scenarios elucidate. Black people's limited access to the rights and securities of citizenship cannot be excused by their adoption by a white and recognized minority whose comforts remain unquestioned.

The spectacularity of these events sparks conversation and contest while also feeding the systems that allow for their production. As Hartman argues in her theorization of enslaved subjectivity, the spectacles of violence attached to the black body "immure us to pain by the virtue of their familiarity."[33] The constant abuse faced by the African-descended is the visual that incites response, but its repetition is embedded within the expected functions of the state, thereby obscuring the scale at which they function and the structure that they bring to *everyone's* daily life. The experience of citizenship in the United States is built on the violence enacted against indigenous and black peoples; this is the metanarrative that must ground and rally progressive political communities. In order to expose the state's mobilization of black death, social movements have to first recognize it as such and, second, "illuminate the terror of the mundane and quotidian rather than exploit the shocking spectacle."[34] With that effort the deaths of Davis and Martin are recognized

FIGURE 1.1. Sticker from a July 14, 2013, Los Angeles rally in response to the murder of Trayvon Martin.

not as exceptional instances deserving of attention but as the very nature of our state's security apparatus that therefore requires dismantlement.

There is precedent for building a complicated and dimensional campaign of aligned movements in response to black abuse; the political narratives expressed in the lead-up to and during the murder trial of Joan (pronounced Jo-ann) Little model a more complex solidarity. In 1974 Little was the only woman incarcerated in a county jail in North Carolina while serving time for a breaking-and-entering conviction. On the night of August 24 a white male guard, with nothing but socks on from the waist down, was found stabbed to death in her cell; she had disappeared. After a weeklong national manhunt, Little turned herself in to authorities and was charged with first-degree murder, which, upon conviction, was automatically punishable in North Carolina by death. Her story gained national attention when she and her defense team argued that the murder was self-defense from sexual assault. In response black civil rights organizations, feminists, and anti–death penalty activists gathered together, forming a tenuous coalition that manifested not just sympathy but an urgent recognition of her fate as representative of a nation in rapid decline. Groups including the National Black Feminist Organization, Women's Legal Defense Fund, Southern Christian Leadership Conference, Feminist Alliance against Rape, Southern Poverty Law Center, National Organization of Women, and the North Carolina Commission on Sentencing, Criminal Punishment, and Rehabilitation joined the chorus to advance exposure of the case and put pressure on local, state, and national juridicopolitical systems.

This constellation of activists highlighted Little's intersectional identity; James Reston Jr. wrote in his coverage of the case for the *New York Times*, "Poor, Southern, undereducated and typical of the prisoner population, Joan Little is an ideal subject for reformist groups seeking to dramatize these issues for the public."[35] Indeed Little and the movement that developed around her epitomized the reality forwarded by the warrior-poet-theorist Audre Lorde, who argued, "There is no such thing as a single-issue struggle because we do not live single-issue lives."[36] The related and sometimes competing agendas of the various groups involved created a dynamic exchange of movement intellectualisms and strategies, leading to a diversity of voices that were able to critique and challenge each other in service of expanding the political terrain of their moment. Feminist organizations were able to maintain tension around the threat of a race-exclusive analysis, while the black civil rights groups demanded that race be centered within the policy recommendations of the prison activists whose labors were often directed at reform rather than abolition. They in turn put a spotlight on the prison as a factory of abuse and challenged the silence of a juridically oriented second-wave white feminism. Of course some of the organizations involved, including the National Black Feminist Organization, cut across these agendas and provided crucial leadership in thinking through intersectionality as a strategy of mobilization, yet there were always negotiations in play. As Genna Rae McNeil outlines, "As women's organizations interacted with one another within the context of the Free Joan Little (FJL) Movement, group leaders had to reexamine the concept of 'sisterhood' in light of *State v. Joan Little*. As a result, self-conscious recognition of *difference* created varying degrees of solidarity among women of diverse racial, socioeconomic, and personal backgrounds."[37] While this polyphonic debate posed real challenges for movement unity, it was ultimately productive and necessary in that the group's diversity also provided a mechanism of accountability and rigor: the identities and politics of those supporting

Little were put on display and made to be read against one another, unlike the current postracial identity collapse that demonstrates limited accountability with anyone other than those dead and gone. Through the FJL movement's internal structure of checks and balances a more representative and radical democracy was realized, in the process developing a cross-issue alliance that was Little's saving grace and her power.

Angela Davis assisted in bringing an intersectional approach to the public discussions of the case. Only a few years after her own incarceration and acquittal, Davis was a prominent ally for Little throughout her defense and spoke widely about the case, using her position to galvanize new supporters, activists, and strategies. In her 1975 *Ms. Magazine* article, "Joan Little: The Dialectics of Rape," Davis centers the accused within histories of white supremacy, patriarchy, and juridical violence; she tells of black women's violation as chattel property under slavery, the judicial system of North Carolina, which was responsible for the largest death-row population in the country, and the relationship between women's labor and their vulnerability to rape. "The reality of Joan Little's life as a prisoner, even before the rape, may have been one of sexual exploitation; a fate she consistently resisted," Davis argued. "The price of her resistance was a new threat of death, this time issuing from the government of North Carolina. And so she is being tried by the same state whose Supreme Court decided, in the 19th century, that no white man could be convicted of fornication with a slave woman." Davis's dense articulation of historical precedent was necessarily paired with the call to diversity displayed by the FJL movement. Her parting words framed the need for accountability in difference:

> Joan Little may not only have been the victim of a rape attempt by a white racist jailer; she has truly been raped and wronged many times over by the exploitative and discriminatory institutions of this society. All people who see themselves as members of the existing community of [the] struggle for justice, equality, and progress have a responsibility to fulfill toward Joan Little. Those of us—women and men—who are black or people of color must understand the connection between racism and sexism that is so strikingly manifested in her case. Those of us who are white and women must grasp the issue of male supremacy in relationship to the racism and class bias which complicate and exacerbate it.[38]

The efforts in support of Little by Davis and many other well-healed justice activists, including Rosa Parks, herself a longtime antirape activist, helped to make possible a scenario in which black women's complex identities could not be reduced to abstraction or caricature.[39] The mobilizations catalyzed by Little's detention capitalized not on an oversimplification of her identity but rather on her multiple oppressions, conjoining them in order to hold the nation accountable for the dimensionality of its violence.

The name recognition brought to the case by Davis, Parks, and others was a powerful element in the Little campaign, but its dynamism stemmed from its diverse methods, which were drawn from many decades of struggle among the groups involved. In addition to public protest actions in which bodies lined streets, there was a musical mobilization that forestalled any easy association between the protestors and their muse. In 1976 the African American women's a cappella ensemble Sweet Honey in the Rock released "Joanne [*sic*] Little," a 3:22 track born from Sweet Honey founder and former Student Nonviolent Coordinating Committee activist Bernice Johnson Reagan's recognition that Little epitomized "*any woman any where* who is violated."[40] The song was used as an anthem for Little's defense in large part because questions of identity, identification, and representation were central to its efforts; Sweet Honey contextualized and troubled the distortions used to contain and dismiss Little's body and experiences. Variously described as a prostitute, a sexual aggressor, and a predator, Little was mercilessly caricatured by a public that employed those ready tropes of black women's sexuality in its efforts to gain support for her death. According to McNeil, "Any authentic awareness of Little's complexity and humanity was likely to develop only among her supporters, the defense team, and select members of the jury."[41] Alongside the street-level activism, Sweet Honey in the Rock amplified an alternative public and counternarrative through which Little and those like her might speak.

The use of this song by those chanting "Free Joan Little" highlights the participants' recognition of, if not investment in, the differences among them. The song "Joanne Little" starts with a single voice that asks the haunting question "Who is this girl and what is she to you?" From the very beginning the song troubles our relation to this woman, forbidding any easy association between our bodies and the body being discussed. Sweet Honey begins the verse by situating themselves in relation to the uplift socialities that have so long governed minority communities. They sing of being told as young girls to "leave them 'no good' women alone" because "you're gonna be judged by the company you keep." These respectability politics condition us to see and preserve difference, to know that we are not the same and have no ties to those most reviled among us. Even in the face of this training Sweet Honey develops a rich rejoinder as they detail the Little case, which they understand as predicated on *structural* inequalities:

Now I ain't talkin' 'bout the roaring West.
This was 1975 at its most oppressive best.
North Carolina stayed the pride of this land,
made her an outlaw,[42] hunted on every hand.
Tell me, what did she do to deserve this name?
Killed a man who thought that she was fair game.

This passage provides the facts of the case against her and exposes the systems of inequality that made it possible. Sweet Honey's critique of progress narratives ("Now I ain't talkin' 'bout the roaring West. / This was 1975") and the continued sexual violence enacted against black women rightly pushed back against the civil rights paradigms of victory celebrated by mainstream race and women's organizations in the years prior to the trial. It also unsettled the artificiality of codified movements by arguing that there was unfinished business and that these histories of violence continued to have a present.

Joan Little was the figure that mobilized all of these concerns, making race, gender, class, location, education, and criminal status inseparable categories within hierarchies of power. In the context of movement mobilization, the question "Who is this girl and what is she to you?" is of utmost importance and insists on a rigorous response that considers two separate subjectivities: Little's and that of the person being questioned. The members of Sweet Honey were organizers who asked the tough questions and proceeded to offer answers as they sang:

Joanne Little,
she's my sister.
Joanne Little,
she's our mama.
Joanne Little,
she's your lover.
Joanne's the woman who's gonna carry your child.

These lyrics disrupt the easy assumptions made in the press about Little's sexuality; instead of running away from the lewd caricatures that have so long haunted black women's representation, Sweet Honey reorients their production, following in a line of black women popular artists who, according to Hazel Carby, "constructed themselves as sexual objects through song" in order to mount a different challenge to dominant frames of black sexuality.[43]

Sweet Honey positions Little as family, provider, and confidant whose sexual and emotional labor delivers the future.

In the absence of accompaniment, it is the percussive element within "Joanne Little" that brings another layer of meaning to these powerful lyrics. Patterned hand clapping is its organizing meter; the rhythmic emphasis on the up beat or "and" count (one *and* two *and* three *and* four, etc.) demands that you hear the lesser privileged pulses that organize Little's rebellion and recognize the "and" that structures her identity as "poor, [*and*] Southern *and* undereducated" *and* black *and* woman *and* incarcerated *and* victim of sexual assault. This sonic intersectionality frames the strategy already employed in the streets, which picked up on the language of this anthem, arguing alongside Sweet Honey that

> Joanne is you.
> Joanne is me.
> Our prison is the whole society.
> 'Cause we live in a land that brings all pressure to bear
> on the head of a woman whose position we share.[44]

The collectivity described by Sweet Honey provides an alternative model of identification that does not sacrifice difference for the sake of rhetorical or political clarity or consumption. It is not sympathy that makes the "we" of Sweet Honey's description; it is structure—"society"—that conditions us all to participate in, if not directly experience, racism and sexism and patriarchy and poverty. The cry released by Sweet Honey, in combination with the momentum and dynamism of a social movement invested in sustaining the three-dimensional *life* of a black woman who faced death, produced Little's unprecedented acquittal and made it possible for a tenuous though nonetheless powerful *we* to develop in response to the systems fed by difference and division.

> We live in an age in which silence is not only criminal but suicidal. . . . For, if they take you in the morning, they will be coming for us that night.—JAMES BALDWIN, "An Open Letter to My Sister, [Miss] Angela Davis"

The absence of a robust critique of racism and its relationship to national dogmas of security, family, and justice has led to limited political speech and mobilization. Identification has become the politics of the postracial, in turn discursively (not materially) minimizing the divisions that scaffold the apparatuses motivated by and dependent upon black death. Instead of "benevolent correctives and declarations" that too often "intensif[y] the brutal exercise of power upon the captive body," the real task of these movements is to make the connections and challenge the conventions that the state denies exist.[45] This language, and its effective mobilization, will not happen without intramovement contests and experiments that grapple with the nature of the individual within a collective. The language of Baldwin's imperative is important here; he was not forwarding a one-to-one relation between himself and Davis: he was in fact articulating how he, along with everyone else, was responsible for her caging and was prepared for this present of capture and disappearance to endure into the future. In order to work against this inevitability, he argued, solidarity and camaraderie could be achieved only through an understanding of the particularities of blackness and a refusal of individual possessions. His efforts did not eradicate the possibility of identification but necessarily complicated it by using the histories and experiences of the African-descended in the United States as the evidence of entrenched difference. In light of that he situates the scene of violence in the hypothetical ("*as though* it were our own") and cautiously proceeds ("which it is") to clarify the stakes of his prediction that those not yet taken will be next.

Identification must be troubled if not completely abandoned as a movement strategy because its genuine practice is beyond the pale of contemporary, large-scale political practice. To argue that I am you requires more than an intense sympathy or even empathy; it must include a suspension of singular rights and privileges, a refusal of self, a series of conscientious and sustained acts that condemn individualism in service of complicating, developing, articulating, and protecting a radical whole. This is where the sloganeering of contemporary political mobilizations breaks down. The instances of black death represented by Davis and Martin appear to be flashes in the pan because they erupt as spectacle and quickly die as such. Their lifespan tends to last only as long as narrow victories are achieved or the news cycle will cover them. This is a function of the nation's limited attention span, but it is also a failure of movement methods. The sound bites used to represent black dispossession and violence only nibble at the edges of democratic critique, never fully attacking or digesting the structures of abuse that continue to make these scenarios not only possible but inevitable. Ultimately the goal of effective movement participation is not to recognize that you "are" Troy Davis or that Trayvon Martin "is" your son but instead that you "could be" Troy Davis or Trayvon Martin "could be" your son, because, though unevenly experienced, we are all vulnerable to attack by the systems that perpetuate punishable difference. When we recognize this, we will begin to build powerful and enduring solidarities, not shortcuts. This appreciation for difference is better fitted to account for the structures of white supremacy, capitalism, and settler colonialism that hold us all in (unequal) bondage.

NOTES

1. I use this language of "social redress actors" to distinguish their efforts from what may otherwise be considered by witnesses or pundits as a social movement.

2. This theory was argued by the sociologist Wilson in *The Declining Significance of Race*. These types of political logics are witnessed on the contemporary left in those moments that applaud and adopt narratives of a white supremacist American Dream, which has led to integration rather than transformation. Bids to inclusion within existent and exclusive systems, rather than their meticulous deconstruction and reenvisioning, ultimately affirm those rights as privileged rather than universal.

3. Rodríguez discusses how Obama's election mobilized a "multiculturalist white supremacy" that is a "refurbishing, not an interruption or abolition, of the normalized violence of the American national project." See Rodríguez, "Inaugurating Multiculturalist White Supremacy."

4. Since I wrote this essay this tragic truth has been borne out on black flesh in locations including but not limited to Milwaukee, Madison, Ferguson, Baltimore, Atlanta, Los Angeles, New York City, Cleveland, Charleston, Chicago, and Detroit.

5. The letter originally appeared as an editorial in the *New York Review* on November 19, 1970.

6. Christie, *Crime Control as Industry*, 22.

7. Gilmore, *Golden Gulag*, 12.

8. I want to highlight those scholars and thinkers whose labor and vision have been particularly important to my own understanding of the prison, its appendages, and responses: João Costa Vargas, Angela Y. Davis, Sarah Haley, Craig Gilmore, Joy James, Mariame Kaba, Khalil Gibran Muhammad, Yusef Omowale, Jessie L. Redmond Sr., Dylan Rodríguez, Damien Sojoyner, David Stein, and Ruth Wilson Gilmore.

9. Examples of these practices include the 2006 campaign launched by the Graduate Employees and Students Organization at Yale University, which called for university divestment from Corrections Corporation of America, the nation's largest private prison company. In 2012 the surveillance and policing structures of the University of Southern California grew exponentially in collusion with the Los Angeles Police Department after two graduate students were killed off campus. Since that event the jurisdiction and arrest powers of USC security officers were extended into surrounding communities, their collaborations with the Los Angeles Police Department are more extensive, and additional private security staff stand watch at campus checkpoints and neighborhood corners throughout the day and evening.

10. Ferguson, *The Reorder of Things*, 12.

11. In addition to rollbacks on affirmative action decisions, the increasing debt burden faced by students—especially working-class students and students of color—has undercut

efforts to diversify higher education. See "Diversity in Academe, 2013," *Chronicle of Higher Education*, 2013, accessed March 14, 2014, http://chronicle.com/section/Diversity-in-Academe-2013/163/.

12. This is not to say that commonality is inappropriate or erroneous, but it has limits that its practitioners do not appreciate enough. The differences among conditions are as important a consideration as their similarities.

13. Ferguson, *The Reorder of Things*, 13.

14. In this case the fear of an otherwise tamed ethnopolitical history was still palpable and dangerous. Peter Rothberg, "Challenging Arizona's Ban on Ethnic Studies," *Nation*, February 1, 2012, accessed December 21, 2012, http://www.thenation.com/blog/165989/challenging-arizonas-ban-ethnic-studies#.

15. For commentaries on the OWS divisions, see Rinku Sen, "Race and Occupy Wall Street," *Nation* online, October 26, 2011, accessed December 30, 2012, http://www.thenation.com/article/164212/race-and-occupy-wall-street#; Bridget Todd, "Racial Fractures and the Occupy Movement," Racialicious blog, November 16, 2011, accessed December 30, 2012, http://www.racialicious.com/2011/11/16/racial-fractures-and-the-occupy-movement/. There is historical precedent for critiquing and debating racial difference within social movement mobilizations. When black activists of the Student Nonviolent Coordinating Committee ousted the white organizers, they argued that the services of their white comrades were best used to educate and mobilize their segregated communities.

16. Sexton, *Amalgamation Schemes*, 31, 15, 35, 6.

17. Vargas and James, "Refusing Blackness-as-Victimization," 194.

18. Friedman and McAdam, "Collective Identity and Activism," 157.

19. Solomon, "Sympathy and Vengeance," 301.

20. If we are to believe Tony Kushner and Steven Spielberg, black people played no role in their emancipation other than limited military service in the U.S. Civil War. See the film *Lincoln* (Touchstone, 2012).

21. Clark, "'The Sacred Rights of the Weak,'" 476, 475.

22. Sexton, *Amalgamation Schemes*, 15.

23. Hartman, *Lose Your Mother*, 6.

24. "There is an under-theorized, though not unnoticed, aspect of the Obama ascendency that constitutes a necessary dimension of his cross-racial attractiveness as a national symbol. His racial persona is significantly defined by the fact that he is not a descendant of slaves" (Rodríguez, "The Black Presidential Non-Slave," 25).

25. President Obama additionally is used to dismiss the black insurrections that continue to unfold over incarceration and police power, urban poverty, agricultural readjustment, and reparations, to name but a few. Simply by virtue of his *presence*, a diverse liberal public argues that black people have overcome, thereby forfeiting claims to injustice or racism.

26. Of course Baldwin was attuned to the ways black people were constructed in service of the labors of capitalism and empire. In that way there was subjectivity, albeit negative and wholly uncontrolled by the subjects themselves.

27. Instead of multiculturalism Prashad advances the idea of "polyculturalism," a category "that not only encourages the inherent complexity of cultures, but that also

stakes its claim to political, and delimited, claims rather than the pretense of universal, and nonembodied, values" (*The Karma of Brown Folk*, 40).

28. Oscar Grant, a twenty-two-year-old black man, was murdered while unarmed on the platform of the Bay Area Rapid Transit system by metro police in Oakland on January 1, 2009. A member of the Detroit SWAT team murdered Aiyana Jones, a seven-year-old black girl, in her home on May 16, 2010, during a raid of the home that she shared with her family. Sean Bell, a twenty-three-year-old black man, was murdered while unarmed in a hail of fifty bullets from the New York Police Department on November 26, 2006.

29. The stay was the intended result. Far from advancing demands of prison abolition, the Davis coalition publicly announced reform and individual amends as their vision of victory and justice.

30. Toby Harnden, "American Way: The Shallow Anti-Americanism of the 'I Am Troy Davis' Crowd," *Telegraph* (U.K.), September 24, 2011, accessed January 8, 2013, http://blogs.telegraph.co.uk/news/tobyharnden/100106968/american-way-the-shallow-anti-americanism-of-the-%E2%80%9Ci-am-troy-davis%E2%80%9D-crowd/.

31. Sam Stein, "Obama on Trayvon Martin Case: 'If I Had a Son, He'd Look Like Trayvon,'" *Huffington Post* online, March 23, 2012, accessed December 28, 2012, http://www.huffingtonpost.com/2012/03/23/obama-trayvon-martin_n_1375083.html.

32. The black cultural theorists Wahneema Lubiano and Paul Gilroy have deconstructed a reliance on the family as a normative site of sociality and stability. See Wahneema Lubiano, "Black Nationalism and Black Common Sense: Policing Ourselves and Others," in *The House That Race Built: Original Essays by Toni Morrison, Angela Y. Davis, Cornel West and Others on Black Americans and Politics in American Today*, ed. Wahneema Lubiano (New York: Vintage, 1998); Paul Gilroy, "It's a Family Affair: Black Culture and the Trope of Kinship," in *Small Acts: Thoughts on the Politics of Black Cultures* (New York: Serpent's Tail, 1993).

33. Hartman, *Scenes of Subjection*, 3.

34. Hartman, *Scenes of Subjection*, 4.

35. James Reston Jr., "The Joan Little Case," *New York Times*, April 6, 1975, ProQuest Historical Newspapers, "The New York Times (1851–2007)," http://www.jrobsessions.com/uploads/9/1/4/8/9148611/the_joan_little_case.pdf.

36. Lorde, *Sister Outsider*, 138.

37. McNeil, "Joanne Is You and Joanne Is Me," 267.

38. Angela Davis, "Joan Little: The Dialectics of Rape," *Ms. Magazine* 12.2 (1975), accessed July 15, 2013, http://www.msmagazine.com/spring2002/davis.asp.

39. For more on the three-dimensionality of Parks's activism and her role in the Joan Little defense, see Danielle L. McGuire, *At the Dark End of the Street: Black Women, Rape and Resistance—A New History of the Civil Rights Movement from Rosa Parks to the Rise of Black Power* (New York: Knopf, 2010).

40. Quoted in McNeil, "Joanne Is You and Joanne Is Me," 266.

41. McNeil, "Joanne Is You and Joanne Is Me," 262.

42. The language and charge of "outlaw" is more than simply a reference to characters of the fictive Wild West; in response to Little's evasion of arrest, North Carolina mobilized its outlaw statute of 1866, which permitted citizens' arrests and detentions

of wanted men and women accused of crimes. Death was a justified response to flight, making Little's fugitivity after the event all the more dangerous.

43. Carby, "It Jus Be's Dat Way Sometime," 10.

44. Sweet Honey in the Rock, "Joanne Little," track 5 of *Sweet Honey in the Rock.*

45. Hartman, *Scenes of Subjection*, 5.

TWO

Juan Crow: Progressive Mutations of the Black-White Binary

JOHN D. MÁRQUEZ

Oscar Vélez was a nineteen-year-old resident of Tijuana, Mexico, who was shot to death by a U.S. Border Patrol agent in September 1998. He was an amateur boxer who routinely crossed into neighboring San Diego to purchase needed sports supplies, school clothes for his younger siblings, and other staples. Oscar's death was but one incident in an epic increase in shooting deaths at the border that year, an uptick in police brutality that activists on both sides of the border attributed to border militarization, a byproduct of neoliberal free trade agreements such as the North American Free Trade Agreement and the Dominican Republic–Central America Free Trade Agreement and a corollary system to render displaced workers more vulnerable to exploitation under late global and racial capitalism. No charges were filed against the officer who killed Oscar, despite numerous eyewitness accounts of the officer's unwarranted aggression. The Vélez case represents one of numerous cases where police brutality has transpired with relative impunity at the border since the early 1990s (to say the least). Oscar's mother, Leticia, became an activist against border militarization after losing her son and being denied justice by U.S. courts of law, helping to form an organization of mothers whose sons had been killed by U.S. Border Patrol agents in a similar fashion. In the fall of 1999 she accepted an invitation to speak at a rally held near the spot where Oscar died that was organized by anti–border militarization organizations from the United States and Mexico. There she exclaimed, "The injustice at the border against immigrants is the same as the brutality against Blacks and other people in the U.S."[1]

Four years later, in 2002, African American and Chicano/a residents of Baytown, Texas, a blue-collar suburb of Houston, joined forces as activists to protest the death of a Mexican immigrant named Luis Torres who was beaten and choked to death by four police officers upon being falsely profiled for a crime.[2] Torres's beating, which was videotaped, was brutal and without rationale. Weeks later a Harris County medical examiner's report ruled that Torres's cause of death was homicide, countering claims by local officials that he likely died of a preexisting medical condition. Despite the video and autopsy evidence, no charges were filed against the officers who killed Torres, thus drawing comparisons to the Rodney King case in Los Angeles a decade earlier. Those activists who rose to Torres's defense popularized the slogan "Rodney King en Español" on posters and other paraphernalia, raising critical awareness about police brutality and the more pervasive legacy of state-sanctioned racial violence in which they situated it, a legacy of violence that once targeted African Americans nearly exclusively in the Gulf South and that has increasingly targeted Latinos/as as they have grown in number in that region.

In the Torres and Vélez cases, African American history was appropriated to justify and publicize resistance on behalf of Latino/a victims of police brutality. This maneuver, I believe, derives from a haunting presupposition that the death of persons like Torres and Vélez will not spur much alarm from the body politic, that the names of those Latino/a victims will never be recognizable as are names such as Rodney King and Trayvon Martin within debates on race and racism in the United States, and that the mass-scale police brutality mandated by border militarization and other harsh measures to police and punish immigrants will not receive much attention in the "lives matter" campaigns that have proliferated as of late. The activism elicited by these cases implies that this invisibility is due, in part, to the black-white binary, a discursive condition through which "relations" between whites and African Americans are positioned as the epicenter of "race relations" writ large, and in part to the extent that the histories and struggles of groups like Latinos/as, American Indians, Asian Americans, and Arab Americans are routinely overlooked or marginalized in political discourse.

Critiquing the black-white binary is both difficult and useful. On the one hand, it does not seem to have provided much socioeconomic benefit to the general African American population, nor has it made African Americans any more immune to the kinds of conditions that befell Torres and Vélez. Names like Trayvon Martin, Oscar Grant, Michael Brown, Eric Garner, Rekia Boyd, and Freddie Gray are indeed morbid reminders of the pervasive nature of a violent and often state-sanctioned antiblack racism, the latest names to be associated with historical figures such as Emmett Till and the lynching campaigns that preceded him and them, all reminders that policing as we know it in the United States has always been informed by fears of black fugitiveness, the sovereign state's essential commitment to the quarantine and control of black bodies as a pillar of its racial or colonial architecture and structuring of the civil domain as we know it. On the other hand, the black-white binary does seem to obstruct a more comprehensive and critical understanding of the conditions that ended the life of victims with a Hispanic surname.

Young people of all racial or ethnic groups rally at their schools, in their communities, and on Facebook for kids like Martin and Brown and never know, much less mention, the large number of Mexican and Central American bodies that have been destroyed as a result of border militarization and a growing anti-Latino/a hysteria, many of them nameless corpses that mark the landscape of the U.S.-Mexico borderlands and beyond. The stories of Oscar Vélez, Luis Torres, Anastasio Rojas, Andy Lopez, Antonio Zambrano-Montes, and Marcelo Lucero, an Ecuadorian immigrant killed as the result of white teenagers playing a sport they call "beaner hopping" in Long Island, do not register with much alarm, almost as if their death is a plausible outcome of the nation-state's natural right to defend its borders or sovereignty against foreign invasion.[3] The significance of the black-white binary is deepened by the fact that African American success stories are often and strategically positioned as central to postracial discourse, to the state's post–civil rights reconciliatory gestures. Those stories and images are often displayed within the reformist vision and rhetorics of neoliberal multiculturalism, a maneuver intended to subdue a more critical dissent by conveying that this nation-state has grappled with and reconciled one of its grandest contradictions, namely the origin of so much of its capitalist infrastructure in slavery. That reconciliation has never transpired. The illusion of black inclusion is, I believe, designed to distract our attention from slavery's afterlife, the everyday erasure of black lives and quotidian experiences with expendability that characterizes twenty-first-century urban life.[4]

The significance of the black-white binary is deepened even further by demographic shifts and other time and space compressions (symbolic and structural) wrought by neoliberalism or globalization. Economic and war refugees from across the Global South (Africa and Latin America) have increasingly migrated to the Global North since the late 1970s as a consequence of being displaced by neoliberal free trade policies and the military hegemony that makes them possible. The arrival of these refugees in cities across the United States has had a tremendous impact on demography and social climates. For example, African Americans constitute a steadily declining percentage of the national population, whereas the Latino/a and Asian American populations are growing at an incredible rate, with Latinos/as surpassing African Americans as the nation's largest racial or ethnic minority group at the turn of the century and projected to make up more than 40 percent of the total national population by 2044. The 9/11 tragedy, moreover, has exacerbated the vulnerability of Global South immigrants, particularly those from the Middle East, South Asia, and North Africa (in addition to the effect of Islamophobia), to racial profiling and the state-sanctioned vigilante and police violence that often accompanies it.[5] David Slater has referred to such conditions across the Global North as components of a "post-colonial geopolitics," that is, as conditions exacerbated by the intensified migrations associated with late global and racial capitalism that have resulted in intensely militarized geopolitical boundaries and large increases in xenophobic nationalisms. These crises, he argues, invite a "re-thinking [of] north-south relations" and of the popular assumption that nations are becoming symbolically unbound. Neoliberalism and postcolonial geopolitics, in sum, provide a conjuncture, a unique moment and impetus for scrutinizing how domestic relations of power, local histories, and postcolonial discourses structure and are structured by the sustained racial and colonial architecture of European modernity as it has been manifest within late global racial capitalism.[6]

This essay furthers an ongoing conversation regarding local-global interfaces with a particular commitment to helping craft a more diverse and complex antiracist agenda, one within which Latino/a lives are not so easily ignored and that makes us more wary of other and similar blind spots. Building on Slater's provocation, this essay scrutinizes the salience of the black-white binary as a domestic condition that is strained by postcolonial geopolitics. I focus primarily on the relationship between the black-white binary and Latino/a politics and, more specifically, on debates regarding border militarization and other measures that have helped to routinely destroy Latino/a lives. I advance three interrelated arguments. The first is that the black-white binary, as a focal point of narratives on post–civil rights liberal reform, has contributed to some extent to a growing black-white and statist alliance in support of militarized borders and other anti-immigrant measures, conditions that are widely held as compromising or diluting the relative gains for African Americans that resulted from the civil rights movement of the 1950s and 1960s. For clarity I refer to this as a *regressive mutation,* a condition that attempts to isolate antiblack racism from a more extensive conversation regarding white supremacy and a hemispheric context of racial and colonial violence.

My second and pivotal argument is that the black-white binary also has a prismatic political effect, a *progressive mutation,* that is used to link the genealogy of domestic antiblack racism to the ill effects and affects of neoliberal globalization as it applies to Mexican and Central American immigrants in particular. The black-white binary is, in sum, an "imaginative fixity" that can be and has been manipulated so as to enable a more dynamic wariness regarding the aforementioned conditions as a fulcrum for the advent of solidarity.[7] Calls to abolish the black-white binary that proliferate in academic fields like Latino/a studies tend not only to be poorly theorized but also often are not constructive within real life and community-based organizing campaigns that function beyond the academic industrial complex, struggles for survival that require a dynamism and complexity, a blurring of borders between black and brown, that academics are too often not wary of or are restricted from due to their unwillingness to think about social phenomena beyond the protocols of traditional disciplinary methods and the identitarian-framed units that they occupy and are rewarded by within the academy and its post–civil rights maneuvering or neoliberal adjustment. In the Torres and Vélez cases, activists attempted to raise greater awareness of the lack of rights and expendability of Latinos/as and to encourage resistance against such conditions by imaginatively linking the bodies of those victims to narratives and images of violent antiblack racism that the body politic was more familiar with. In 2002, for example, activists literally summoned memories of the videotaped beating of Rodney King in order to get people to pay more critical attention to the videotaped beating of Luis Torres.

African Americans were an essential part of that coalition as leaders and visionaries of collective resistance linking the global to the local, thus shedding light on how they too operationalize progressive mutations, linking epistemologies of the U.S. South to the Global South and reclaiming some of the transnational vision and global vision of racial power movements that proliferated prior to the neoliberal turn and the appropriation of a black (and Latino/a) professional class as emblems of change and progress. Beyond the Torres case and across the U.S. South, a region where the black-white binary is particularly hegemonic (and for astute reasons), African Americans have often spearheaded organizing campaigns on behalf of Latino/a victims of racial profiling, police brutality, and brutal labor exploitation. They have done so by imaginatively linking those phenomena to collective memories of chattel slavery, Jim Crow, the civil rights movement of the mid-twentieth century, and what Cedric Robinson has famously described as a "Black radical tradition" of resistance to racial capitalism.[8] The title of this essay is derived from one such example of this imaginative solidarity or linkage. This maneuver does not imply that antiblack racism is a historical artifact being replaced or displaced by other kinds of struggle mandated by a postcolonial geopolitics. Instead it represents a vision for a more relational and dynamic form of black politics that is attuned to the growing complexities of the current moment.[9]

My third and last argument, therefore, is that *progressive mutations* reflect the kinds of dynamic political collectives or hybrid cultures that Stuart Hall, Gloria Anzaldúa, Paul Gilroy, Néstor García Canclini, and Walter Mignolo have theorized as emerging from unique ruptures and conjunctures associated with the combined wreckages left by racialized modernity and capitalism, collisions between global processes and local histories that enable a shared wariness of expendability and exploitability, a wariness that is often manifest within new forms of collective consciousness that retain a unique political potential, the kinds of coalition that once thrived and defined maroon colonies across the Americas and that are now visible in the urban spaces where groups like African Americans and Latinos/as are bound to one another in their shared experience of expendability. In this imaginative rather than embodied or corporeal example of race mixture, hybridity or hybrid political cultures are thus a central component of decolonial ethics, an alternative form of relation to the world, to one another, to our increasingly diverse and rapidly changing home spaces. Hybridity, in my appropriation and use of this concept, refers to a model and praxis of solidarity that unsettles and destabilizes the identitarian silos and colonial politics of recognition that are necessitated by neoliberal multiculturalism.[10]

Regressive Mutations

The largest civil rights demonstrations in U.S. history took place in the early twenty-first century and during the May 1 marches for immigrant rights in Los Angeles, Chicago, Washington, D.C., and New York. These events have been commonly described as components of a Latino/a political awakening and the advent of a new civil rights movement. African Americans have often resisted such comparisons, worried that they dilute their history of racial uplift and compromise their position within neoliberally reformed institutions. As he watched a May 1 march in Washington in 2007, for example, a liberal African American sociologist and academic named Brendan Laster commented to journalists, "I do think their struggle is, in fundamental ways, very different from ours. We didn't choose to come here; we came here as slaves. And we were denied, even though we were legal citizens, our basic rights. . . . There are still a lot of unresolved issues from the civil rights era. Perhaps we're going to be pushed to the back burner." Linda Branch Carter, the president of the Des Moines, Iowa, chapter of the NAACP, offered a similar opinion, explaining that if the Latino/a population and its activism continue to grow, "[African Americans] will have no power, no clout."[11] Laster's and Carter's critiques seem to suggest that postcolonial geopolitics necessitate a politics of ethnic entrenchment for some African Americans—that they sense a growing need to defend institutional turf by distinguishing their history as isolated from and never interwoven in the broader racial and colonial assemblage of the Americas, a kind of narrow vision that can marginalize groups like Latinos/as and that also contributes to the more general erasure of indigenous peoples and the settler colonial architecture of the United States, a foundational violence that Jodi Byrd has described as the underpinning for U.S. imperialism the world over.[12]

This partitioning of antiblack racism away from a more diverse conversation regarding white supremacy represents, to some extent, a politically conservative ethic that is cloaked by a progressive and antiracist veneer, a kind of post–civil rights and liberal bipolarism that is encouraged by the protocols of neoliberal multiculturalism and the persistent pressure for groups to accentuate all that is unique about their plight and to secure spaces and resources belatedly granted them by lamenting or sympathetic whites. There are, however, critical elements to that position that deserve to be analyzed. Laster's and Carter's entrenchment can be read as a reflection on the particularity of antiblack racism. To be sure, African Americans have experienced racism in unique and uniquely profound ways and largely as the result of chattel slavery, Jim Crow, and the advent of the prison industrial complex. In addition antiblack racism is not exclusive to white subjectivities and is evident across Latino/a, Asian American, Arab American and Native American communities.

The comprehensive nature of this antiblackness represents a particular life devaluation that has elicited Jared Sexton's critique of unifying terms such as *people of color* and that inspires a critical debate about our ability to express solidarity between indigenous and Afro-descended peoples in particular.[13]

Sexton explains blackness as produced as or within an ontological or existential void of the unsovereign, a provocative viewpoint that forces us to pause and reconsider the depth and foundational nature of antiblackness in modern social formations like the United States. While useful for how it complicates discourses regarding comparativity or solidarity, this theorization also retains the potential for refortifying the black-white binary. It can be (and has been, as I've witnessed among students and activists) perceived as a rationale for not building more vibrant and necessary coalitions, and it conflicts with the dynamic and everyday struggles of mixed black-brown urban barrios to survive and resist the pressures of death or quarantine.

Placing that political and pedagogical dilemma aside for the moment, it seems as if Laster's and Carter's resistance to comparisons is the result of a generally implicit and comprehensive rather than explicitly intended misunderstanding of Latino/a histories. Their position moreover reflects what I describe as a force-choice binary, a sociological underpinning of the black-white binary and a discursive trope through which groups like Latinos/as (and Asian Americans) are essentialized as immigrant newcomers who willfully submit themselves to racial denigration in hopes of assimilation into the U.S. middle class.[14] Those groups are, in sum, commonly perceived as political parasites, globally transient persons who have not paid their activist dues in the United States, and who aim to prosper, as Toni Morrison once described of southern and eastern European immigrants, on the "backs of blacks."[15]

As already suggested, this perspective overlooks the overlapping significance of conquest, genocide, imperialism, and slavery within the racial ordering of the Americas, mutually constitutive forces that have contributed to the racialization of Latinidad, Latinos/as, and Latin America.[16] The force-choice binary also causes African Americans, as with other people of color and whites, to overlook the significant resistance to those conditions that proliferated across the Western Hemisphere beginning in the late fifteenth century. More recently, and as evident in Laster's and Carter's opinions, the force-choice binary causes African Americans to overlook the significant sacrifices and contributions of Latinos/as to antiracist struggles in the United States and also to the vibrant coalition-building enterprises that African Americans participated in and often helped to lead. Black-brown coalitions have been central to antiracist struggles for more than a century.[17]

Last, the force-choice binary influences African Americans to overlook the complexity of their own population and history—the interplay of force and choice, the significant political (race, ethnicity, and nationality) divisions within the African American population, the roles that African Americans played in the military conquest of the U.S. western frontier and the subjugation of American Indians, the roles that African American scholars or elected officials play within neoliberally reformed institutions, and the significant intranational and transnational migrations that Ira Berlin has described as foundational to the making of African America.[18] The force-choice binary, then, ascribes Latinos/as (like Arab Americans and Asian Americans) to a racial purgatory, a neoliberal political waiting room for those who are not quite ready for significance within civil rights movement discourse. American Indians, by comparison, are made primative, commonly considered either extinct or too small in number for their lives to matter within contemporary political mobilizations against racial or colonial violence.

Latinos/as have not made coalition building any easier. They are likely more xenophobic and statist than African Americans, often despite their own immigrant origins.[19] This seems especially true among Mexicanos/as and Centro-Americanos/as. The antiblack racism of Latinos/as is also a serious obstruction to solidarity. It is well known that Latinos/as have routinely attempted to benefit from their legal definition as "white" by distancing themselves from African Americans and ignoring their own African and indigenous origins, verifying much of Sexton's concerns with antiblackness. These dedicated, troubling, and sustained attempts by Latinos/as at whitening and assimilation have never really, as aforementioned, resulted in much of a general socio-economic benefit for them, similar to how the black-white binary does not offer much real benefit or immunity from violence or exploitation for African Americans. In fact Latinidad as an ethnoracial signifier of both deficiency and menace has been produced and reproduced in stark opposition to discourses regarding U.S. citizenship, a form of "racialization" that is exacerbated by the U.S.-Mexico border to an insidiously fatal extent and that perpetuates the uninterrupted imperilment of Latino/a life.[20] This condition of racialized expendability represents an area that deserves more attention from the critical ethnic studies project, which thus far, I believe, has insufficiently addressed the histories and plight of Latino/a (and especially Chicano/a) peoples within conversations regarding genocide and settler colonialism and can do a better job at engaging the significance of the U.S.-Mexico border, of the U.S. relationship to Latin America, and of Latino/a and Chicano/a scholars and activists.

Myths regarding U.S. racial and ethnic uniformity (white and Anglo-American) were profoundly shaped in direct opposition to Mexicanos/as during the imperialist conflicts of the mid-nineteenth century that resulted in our current geopolitical border. At that time Mexicanos/as were popularly described as a "mongrel race" derived from sexual encounters between American Indians and African Americans and as inheriting the worst traits of both sides of their ancestry. Consequentially such mongrels were popularly demonized as the primary obstacle to the nation's manifest destiny, justifying an assortment of horrific measures that the U.S. state deployed to displace, quarantine, or obliterate them, as evident in the Texas War for Independence and the U.S.-Mexico War that followed.[21]

During the era that immediately followed those conquests, Latinos/as were legally defined as "white" and granted U.S. citizenship. Such whiteness, however, did not grant immunity from white supremacist violence, much of which the state either participated in or turned a blind eye to. During the late nineteenth and early twentieth centuries Latinos/as (namely Mexicanos/as) were being lynched in places like south and central Texas at a higher rate than were African Americans in southern states like Mississippi. Since then the U.S.-Mexico border has been a space where U.S. nationalism is violently regenerated against the indigenous populations of that region (Mexicano/a and Native American).

The recent militarization of that border is but the latest episode. Postcolonial geopolitics has exacerbated the significance of the border, further imperiling the Latino/a population via what Leo R. Chavez has described as a "Latino threat narrative"—post-1980s discourses regarding Latino/a invasion that have resulted in a sharp increase in anti-Latino/a violence, much of which has transpired with relative legal impunity and that has never raised much alarm among the U.S. polity.[22] Anti-Latino/a hate crimes have risen by more than 40 percent over the past decade and have quite often been inflicted in the name of patriotism.[23] Latinos/as account for the group most commonly victimized by police brutality in the United States if one considers the combined effects of urban policing and the policing of immigration associated with border militarization. The over 170 years that Latinos/as have been linked to whiteness, or as closer to white than African Americans, thus do not seem to have resulted in much if any white refuge or privilege for Latinos/as, ironically despite how dedicated Latinos/as often are to whitening themselves and their histories.

The force-choice distinction has been taken to other extremes. In southern California a Black Minutemen chapter has aided white vigilantes who patrol the U.S.-Mexico border for "illegal aliens" with relative legal impunity. Organizations like Choose Black America and the Crispus Attucks Brigade have claimed that African Americans are being victimized by a

Latino/a invasion. Their spokesperson, Ted Hayes, explained, "We're being overrun. . . . The compañeros have taken all the housing. If you don't speak Spanish they turn you down for jobs. Our children are jumped upon in the schools. They are trying to drive us out. . . . Illegal immigrants are claiming rights that had nothing to do with them, nor did they fight for, nor do they understand, yet they enter the United States over the heads of American Black citizens who did fight for those rights."[24]

These are, to be sure, extreme examples that more than likely do not represent the attitudes or opinions of the African American community writ large. They are worth some consideration, however, within a broader conversation regarding black-brown solidarity. Recent poll data, for example, show that many African Americans have serious anxieties about Latino/a population growth and about the security of the U.S.-Mexico border (anxieties that many Latinos/as share). Most significant is that white conservatives, as per usual, have been eager to capitalize on this, a maneuver intended to obstruct black-brown coalitions, isolating the epistemologies of each group from one another and making them compete over victim status.[25] In May 2006 U.S. Congressman Lamar Smith, a white man from Texas and the highest ranking Republican on the House Judiciary Committee at the time, encouraged the heads of four major African American civil rights groups to join him in opposing any amnesty for undocumented immigrants, the vast majority of whom are from Latin America. He explained to them, "The simple law of supply and demand dictates that flooding the job market with cheap foreign labor will undermine any initiatives that help the African-American population." Amnesty, Smith continued, would "devastate job opportunities for millions of African-Americans."[26] T. Willard Fair, head of Miami's chapter of the Urban League, accepted an invitation from Smith to testify before Congress that "illegal" immigration "is the largest single reason . . . for the unemployment of Black men."[27]

Similar tensions have been aired in the U.S. South. Latinos/as have been increasingly targeted in that region for legislation that would authorize racial profiling as an element of de jure enforcement of immigration law, further blurring the lines between military and law enforcement apparatuses. These measures would essentially roll back some gains made by the civil rights movement and reauthorize legal forms of segregation and policing that African American activists fought so hard against.

Many African Americans, however, are reluctant to make this connection, their justifications often reflective of the force-choice binary. An African American board member of the Dustin Inman Society, an anti-immigration organization in Georgia, argued that to compare recent Latino/a activism to African American history is "an insult": "To compare it to a civil rights issue—in my mind, it is ludicrous to do that. . . . How can you do it? They aren't citizens." An African American woman shared a similar view, commenting, "I scratch my head at many of our so-called black civil rights leaders that are so quick to accept that these people have come here illegally and to treat them as if they are entitled to the same measure of protection that we fight for every day in this country."[28] White conservatives were in full agreement, using the opportunity to stir black-brown tensions. Upon being critiqued for reinstating Jim Crow segregation in the state of Alabama against Latino/as, Alabama's white governor Robert J. Bentley states, "To equate this to the Civil Rights movement is an insult to the Civil Rights movement. It's an insult to the men and women who had their homes bombed, the children who were killed in Birmingham up at the 16th Street Baptist Church . . . so it's an insult to them."[29]

Similar sentiments have lately been aired in Arizona in debates about the Tucson Unified School District's decision to outlaw Latino/a studies programs and curricula in public schools for being anti-American and for stirring racial tensions.[30] Arizona's attorney general John Horne has led much of this anti–Latino/a studies campaign, causing critics to compare him to antiblack segregationists in the South during the 1950s. In response Horne has claimed that Latino/a studies students are "the [new] 'Bull Connors.' They are the ones re-segregating." Latino/a youth are thus being depicted as undoing the triumphant civil rights activism of African Americans and dishonoring the sacrifices they made to make us more democratic. Horne added that it would be impossible to consider him a segregationist because, as a teen, he participated in the historic March on Washington, where he was inspired by Dr. King's message of color blindness. Horne's purported allegiance to African Americans as a teenager is thus being invoked to grant him racial immunity, a position enabled by the sociologics inherent in the black-white binary and its relationship to broader narratives regarding liberal reform and the advent of the postracial.

Progressive Mutations

After T. Willard Fair's congressional testimony, Marc Morial, CEO of the Urban League, retorted, "Mr. Fair does not speak for the National Urban League . . . or the Urban League movement."[31] At the May 1 march in Washington in 2006 the civil rights movement veteran Jesse Jackson linked recent Latino/a causes to older African American causes: "We too were denied citizenship. We too were undocumented workers working without wages, without benefits, without the vote. . . . We should feel honored that other people are using tactics and strategies from our struggle. We shouldn't say they're stealing from us. They're learning from us."[32] U.S. Congresswoman Sheila Jackson-Lee, an African American from Houston, similarly said, "Those Blacks who forcefully oppose mass immigration are simply naive and are being 'baited' into such negative positions"[33]

African American civil rights veterans in the South have demonstrated strong opposition to growing anti-Latino/a sentiments in their home states. The Black Legislative Caucus of Mississippi thwarted bipartisan support for an anti-immigrant bill authorizing the racial profiling of Latinos/as and mass deportation of undocumented immigrants, a bill that one member described as "more venom and more hatred" in a state renowned for its history of racial strife toward African Americans.[34] Congressman John Lewis, an African American and veteran civil rights activist from Atlanta, spoke at a large immigrants rights rally outside of the state capitol to protest two state bills in Georgia that would similarly criminalize undocumented workers and encourage racial profiling. Lewis drew upon memories of his work with Dr. Martin Luther King Jr. and declared his willingness to engage in civil disobedience alongside Latinos/as, explaining, "We are all brothers and sisters. It doesn't matter whether we are black, white, Latino/a, Asian-American, Native American. We are one people. We are one family. . . . We all live in the same house. If any one of us is illegal, then we all are illegal." Georgia State Senator Emanuel Jones, an African American, also fought against those bills by citing memories of Jim Crow: "It wasn't that long ago when vigilante groups, militia groups . . . routinely rounded up citizens just to exact their own form of vigilante justice." Georgia's NAACP and the Coalition for the People's Agenda, led by Rev. Joseph Lowery, an African American, have also been quite vocal in their opposition to those bills. Rev. Timothy McDonald III, an African American and veteran civil rights activist, described the current Latino/a cause as "the civil rights issue of the 21st century." He explained, "Ultimately, it is about discrimination. They are targeting a particular group as African-Americans were targeted."[35]

This solidarity has also been evident in Alabama, a place where the growing presence of Latinos/as has galvanized new debates about the meaning and significance of the civil rights activism of African Americans, their lifelong dedication to not only challenging antiblack racism but also the more complex phenomenon of white supremacy. Conservative lawmakers have routinely scapegoated Latinos/as as a drain on local economies and a threat to the safety and security of Alabama citizens. African Americans, most of them veterans of local civil rights struggles, have not stood silently as new legislation has been introduced to authorize racial profiling as a method to police immigration. Emanuel Ford, an African American school board member in Birmingham, commented on recent anti-immigrant bills targeting Latinos/as, "If this isn't racism, if this isn't Jim Crow, this is a disgrace before God. I can't believe that in 2011, we would do something so blatant." Rev. Robert Graetz, a white pastor of a Lutheran church in Montgomery, veteran civil rights activist, and former ally of Rosa Parks and Dr. King, joined a new Latino/a organization called Vamos Together, describing it as "one more phase of the civil rights movement." Graetz said, "To single out Hispanic people for unequal treatment violates the teachings of the Bible and is similar to the treatment of Black people."[36] Lekan Oguntoyinbo, a journalist, argues that Alabama's new anti-immigrant bill rebirths the state's Fugitive Slave Act by criminalizing those citizens who grant refuge to undocumented immigrants, similar to how those who granted refuge to runaway slaves in the nineteenth century were once criminalized.[37]

There have been comparable responses from African American artists such as Talib Kweli, Chuck D, Rhymefest, Jasiri X, and Tom Morello. Each reinforces the significance of expressive cultures within black politics and stretches the meaning of such politics beyond the black-white binary.[38] They each also reflect a more dynamic critique, riffs on the black radical tradition, that have been advanced by black and Latino/a youth activists across the United States, a dynamism that transcends the silo effect of neoliberal multiculturalism and that reflects real-life survival strategies in really imperiled and diverse communities. After the state of Arizona passed Senate Bill 1070 into law, Kweli released a song describing the bill as "Jim Crow en Español," which railed against this measure as a form of resegregation that further justifies the significance of black-brown coalitions. Chuck D, of Public Enemy fame, followed suit by recording and releasing the tune "Tear Down That Wall," a song that builds upon and samples Public Enemy's previous critique of Arizona, a critique that began a decade prior to SB 1070 with their song "By the Time I Get to Arizona." That earlier song was the result of Arizona's refusal to acknowledge the Dr. Martin Luther King Jr. Holiday.[39] "Tear Down That Wall" samples parts of "By the Time I Get to Arizona," building a sonic and imaginative bridge between African American and Latino/a struggles. In the newer tune Chuck D identifies the irony of Ronald Reagan's advocacy of "tearing down" the Berlin Wall in the 1980s while a wall dividing the United

States and Mexico was being built and militarized just a few years afterward. He attributes this phenomenon to lingering racial prejudices underlying cold war tensions, in addition to the conjuncture of neoliberal global/racial capitalism. Neoliberalism, according to Chuck D, has created a "modern day slavery" that targets and victimizes Latinos/as in particular: "While these situations [the MLK Day fight and the immigration fights] are different, the politics of both things stay around like a stain. Once again, Arizona has put itself into this mix. I don't know what the hell was on Gov. Jan Brewer's mind or what contingent is behind her, but to make a decision like this, and to be told to ignore the people who have been in this area on this earth the longest period of time—it just kind of resonates with me as being crazy." "Tear Down That Wall" is thus not only an explicit critique of "modern-day slavery"; it is also an implicit critique of a symbolic wall between African Americans and Latinos/as, obstructing solidarity.

New activist organizations have followed suit. Gerald Lenoir, an African American and veteran civil rights and anti-apartheid activist from Louisiana, joined forces with other veteran African American activists to form the Black Alliance for Just Immigration (BAJI) in 2006 in Oakland, California. Lenoir feels that African Americans are often politically crippled by their "ethnic chauvinism," what he describes as a post–civil rights condition resulting from belated, albeit differential inclusion and the roles that African Americans have been asked to perform in the theater of neoliberal reform and its emphasis on the bourgeois politics of respectability. This, he contends, causes many African Americans to believe that their own struggles and sacrifices against racism grant them immunity from being more conscious or critical about racism toward other groups, either domestically or globally, and especially within the context of the current neoliberal conjuncture. One of four BAJI founding principles states, "African Americans, with our history of being economically exploited, marginalized and discriminated against, have much in common with people of color who migrate to the United States, documented and undocumented. . . . BAJI provides the African American community with a progressive analysis and framework on immigration that links the interests of African Americans with those of immigrants of color. BAJI's analysis emphasizes the impact of racism and economic globalization on African American and immigrant communities as a basis for forging alliances across these communities."[40]

In addition to ethnic chauvinism, Lenoir and BAJI also cite a "divide and conquer logic of economic globalization" as a condition that impedes African Americans from understanding the true sources of their economic anxieties within a global and neoliberal capitalist economy, causing them to uncritically join whites in scapegoating immigrants of color (namely, mestizo or indigenous Mexicanos/as and Centro-Americanos/as but also black immigrants from Latin America, the Caribbean, and Africa) as the source of their currently high levels of unemployment, incarceration, and other detrimental conditions, turning their attention away from the more insidious logics of this postindustrial political economy and its relationship to prisons and imprisonment.

Putting words into action, Lenoir and other African American BAJI members traveled to Amite, Louisiana, in 2006 to organize a protest on behalf of Mexican immigrants working, according to BAJI, under "slave like" conditions for a small agricultural corporation. In defense of those workers, Lenoir claimed, "As African Americans we recognize what you're describing, and we are with you." Such statements allow for African American histories to be mobilized in defense of Latinos/as, considering how their current plight is reflective of the kinds of life devaluation or expendability inherent in slavery and Jim Crow. BAJI members also organized a citizens' arrest of the corporation's owners, forcing them to comply with demands for more equitable treatment.[41] Lastly, BAJI's Braving Borders, Building Bridges: A Journey for Human Rights, is a bus tour that takes African Americans to the U.S.-Mexico border to witness firsthand the effects of border militarization in addition to the depraved or what BAJI members often refer to as "Third World" living conditions of American Indians and Chicanos/as along the borderlands. Doing so, BAJI members explain, is an eye-opening experience for them and has been highly effective at creating a rationale for solidarity that they otherwise were likely to miss.[42]

The Limits of Belated Inclusion

In a statement regarding his frustration with the ethnic chauvinism of African Americans, BAJI's Lenoir asked, "What happened to the internationalist tradition and spirit of solidarity of the post-war and 1960s years? Back then, it seemed like African Americans were more in touch with all liberation struggles. . . . We understood the binding links between the Chicano struggle, the American Indian Movement, apartheid in South Africa, and the anti-imperialist/anti-colonial struggles in Latin America and Asia. But now, we are tainting our own histories and helping to ruin our own future through senseless isolation."[43]

Activist struggles of the past are certainly and often romanticized, but there were significant intergroup tensions in the past, just as there are significant coalitions in the present. Lenoir's lament, however, is instructive for those of us who are dedicated to practicing solidarity in the current moment. Something has changed, resulting in what he describes as an increase in "senseless isolation" among not only African Americans but also all groups of color. Latinos/as are also guilty of this, especially in their seemingly unending quest to access whiteness. In the least there was a vibrant intergroup and international solidarity evident within the civil rights and racial power movements of old, reflective of Chairman Fred Hampton of the Chicago Black Panther Party and the original Rainbow Coalition's famous quote:

> We got to face some facts. That the masses are poor, that the masses belong to what you call the lower class, and when I talk about the masses, I'm talking about the white masses, I'm talking about the black masses, and the brown masses, and the yellow masses, too. We've got to face the fact that some people say you fight fire best with fire, but we say you put fire out best with water. We say you don't fight racism with racism. We're gonna fight racism with solidarity. We say you don't fight capitalism with no black capitalism; you fight capitalism with socialism.[44]

Lenoir's lament is more than a critique of historical amnesia. It refers to a structural order and system of incentives that encourages and rewards such outcomes, our forgetfulness, dis-remembering, and decisions to not fight oppression with solidarity but rather through ethnically compartmentalized struggles. What, precisely, has changed since the cold war era? Much of the resistance that Lenoir laments as dis-remembered in the United States targeted historically undiverse institutions of privilege. Those institutions often responded to activist pressures with belated inclusion, meaning they allocated space and resources for the recuperation and integration of subaltern histories, subjectivities, and representation.[45] Belatedness, a term that I borrow from Dipesh Chakrabarty, has offered some benefit, this very publication a product of space and resources afforded to scholars of color like myself within the academy.

There are significant repercussions, however. One is that there is now a significant class division between communities of color and the academics, social welfare administrators, and elected officials that are now (and often rather handsomely) rewarded to speak for them, generally before white and liberal audiences who are eager to express their sympathies for the oppressed and lament the oppression that continues to take place, maneuvers geared toward their desire to be viewed as postracial and neoliberal subjects, not like their parents' generation, good-hearted and thus likeable, employable, and financially rewardable people within this increasingly globalized political economy.

Another repercussion is neoliberal multiculturalism: the management model, language, or protocol of belated inclusion that I've been referring to. Neoliberal multiculturalism imposes a value system for gauging the significance of "difference" within reformed liberal institutions. That reform has transpired via mere addition of subaltern representation to create a mirage of reconciliation or progress. The power-knowledge interfaces that are inherent in reformed and neoliberal institutions, that is, their ethical architectures, have been merely obscured. They thus retain the capacity to both produce and police subalternity and indigeneity, to decide when, where, and how the subaltern or indigenous subject shall be acknowledged, a strategy to subdue a more critical dissent.

The black-white binary bears a unique influence on these protocols. Symbols of African American suffering and triumph generally carry what is arguably the heaviest moral weight within the politics of liberal reform in the United States. This makes African American history a unique ground of and for racial contestation in the current moment. Activists like Gerald Lenoir and artists like Chuck D understand that. They understand that a trench or a silo is a static and easy target, that we are never more equipped to battle oppression by knowing less about it, and that black politics carries far more potential when it is less pro-black than it is anti–white supremacy. They engage in a thinking and a politics beyond their ascribed group and thus exemplify a shift away from uncritical representations of who a race is and toward a more critical theorization and dialogue about what race does, meaning an increased attention to the kinds of expendability and exploitability that it produces.

NOTES

1. Leticia Vélez, press statement, November 12, 1999. Attained by author at a demonstration held at Cd. Tijuana–San Ysidro border.
2. Márquez, "The Browning of Black Politics."
3. Cara Buckley, "Teenagers Violent 'Sport' Led to Killing on Long Island," *New York Times*, November 20, 2008.
4. Hartman, *Lose Your Mother*.
5. Rana, "The Story of Islamophobia."
6. Slater, *Geopolitics and the Post-Colonial*.
7. Bhabha, *The Location of Culture*, 66.
8. Robinson, *Black Marxism: The Making of the Black Radical Tradition*.

9. This argument regarding *progressive mutation* marks an extension beyond Kim's racial triangulation model in *Bitter Fruit*. It refers not only to how Latinas/os are "racialized" in relation to white and African Americans but also to the effects of such triangulation on contemporary forms of antiracist resistance, ones that unsettle the sociologics and segregating effects of liberal multiculturalism.

10. Hall, "New Ethnicities"; Anzaldúa, *La Frontera/Borderlands*; Gilroy, "British Cultural Studies and the Pitfalls of Identity," 34; Bhabha, *The Location of Culture*; Canclini, *Hybrid Cultures*; Mignolo, *Local Histories / Global Designs*.

11. Rachel Swarns, "Growing Unease for Some Blacks on Immigration," *New York Times*, May 4, 2006, accessed September 26, 2015, http://www.nytimes.com/2006/05/04/us/04immig.html?pagewanted=all&_moc.semityn.www&_r=0.

12. Byrd, *The Transit of Empire: Indigenous Critiques of Colonialism*.

13. Sexton, "People-of-Color-Blindness"; Sexton, "The Veil of Slavery."

14. Márquez, "The Browning of Black Politics."

15. Toni Morrison, "On the Backs of Blacks," *Time*, December 2, 1993.

16. Smith, "Indigeneity, Settler Colonialism, White Supremacy."

17. See Márquez, *Black-Brown Solidarity: Racial Politics in the New Gulf South*.

18. Berlin, *The Making of African America*.

19. Gutierrez, *Walls and Mirrors*; Vila, *Crossing Borders, Reinforcing Borders*.

20. Mbembe, "Necropolitics."

21. De Leon, *They Called Them Greasers*; Horsman, *Race and Manifest Destiny*.

22. Chavez, *The Latino Threat Narrative*.

23. Márquez, "Latino/as as 'Living Dead.'"

24. Crispus Attucks Brigade, "The Mission of the Crispus Attucks Brigade."

25. Doherty, "Attitudes towards Immigration."

26. De Wayne Wickham, "Immigrants a Scapegoat for Blacks' Unemployment," *USA Today*, August 7, 2007.

27. U.S. House of Representatives, Hearing before the Subcommittee on Immigration, Citizenship, Refugees, Border Security, and International Law of the Committee on the Judiciary, House of Representatives, 110th Congress, First Session, U.S. Economy, "U.S. Workers, and Immigration Reform," May 9, 2007, Serial No. 110–35.

28. Jeremy Redmon, "Civil Rights Leaders Join Fight against Immigration Bills," *Atlanta Journal Constitution*, April 9, 2011, accessed September 10, 2012, http://www.ajc.com/news/news/local-govt-politics/civil-rights-activists-join-fight-against-immigrat/nQsP8/.

29. Farley, "Alabama Immigration Law and a Modern-Day Civil Rights Movement"; "On the Rise in Alabama," editorial, *New York Times*, November 13, 2011, accessed September 18, 2012, http://www.nytimes.com/2011/11/14/opinion/on-the-rise-in-alabama.html.

30. *Precious Knowledge*, Dos Vatos Films, 2011.

31. Wickham, "Immigrants a Scapegoat for Blacks' Unemployment."

32. Swarns, "Growing Unease for Some Blacks on Immigration."

33. Stevan Malanga, "The Rainbow Coalition Evaporates," *City Journal* 18.1 (2008), accessed June 19, 2015, http://www.city-journal.org/2008/18_1_blacks_and_immigration.html.

34. Marcello Balve, "Black Legislators on Front Line against AZ Style Immigration Bills," New American Media, April 20, 2011, accessed September 25, 2012, http://

newamericamedia.org/2011/04/black-legislators-on-the-frontline-of-battle-against-az-style-immigration-bills.php.

35. Redmon, "Civil Rights Leaders Join Fight against Immigration Bills."

36. Marie Leech, "Birmingham Board of Education Will Condemn Alabama's Immigration Law Officially, Members Say," *Birmingham News*, November 8, 2012.

37. Lekan Oguntoyimbo, "Alabama's New Immigration Law Evokes 'Fugitive Slave Act,'" *Birmingham News*, June 19, 2011, accessed, July 1, 2015, http://blog.al.com/birmingham-news-commentary/2011/06/my_view_alabamas_new_immigrati.html.

38. Iton, *In Search of the Black Fantastic.*

39. Public Enemy, "By the Time I Get to Arizona," *Apocalypse '91. . . . The Enemy Strikes Back*, Def Jam, 1991; Mistachuck, "Tear Down That Wall."

40. Black Alliance for Just Immigration, Informational Pamphlet, "Who We Are." Attained by the author at a BAJI event in 2008.

41. Quant, "Slavery in the Fields." See also The Black Alliance for Just Immigration, press release, 2008; "Gerald Lenoir: Black Alliance for Just Immigration," Hub, May 28, 2008, September 26, 2015, http://hub.witness.org/en/USHRN/08/GeraldLenoir.

42. Black Alliance for Just Immigration, Media Release, "Black Leaders to Investigate Human Rights Violations at the U.S.-Mexcio Border," April 19, 2007. Attained by author from BAJI representatives.

43. Lenoir, lecture delivered at Northwestern University.

44. Fred Hampton, "Power Anywhere There's People," Chicago, ca. 1970, Black Panther Party, Political Pamphlets, P201234, Special Collections, Northwestern University, Evanston, Illinois.

45. Chakrabarty, "Belatedness as Possibility."

THREE

Can the Line Move? Antiblackness and a Diasporic Logic of Forced Social Epidermalization

JOÃO H. COSTA VARGAS

Why doesn't black suffering and death appeal and effectively mobilize beyond seemingly unique catastrophic moments? Why is it that, when black suffering and death are momentarily centered, they are almost always displaced by conversations that recenter the experiences of nonblacks? Although this essay draws on social events in the United States and Brazil, I am more concerned with the realm of possibilities rather than fully actualized, embodied practices. Improbable possibilities. Like many I remain dismayed, although not surprised, at the ultimate irrelevance of or refusal to fully engage with black suffering and death. Heeding the analytical efforts expressed mainly in works of self-defined Afro-pessimists and Afro-optimists, not only do I feel compelled to center black suffering;[1] I take some of its contemporary experiences, manifestations, and reverberations as mostly unrealized yet potentially transformative political visions. To engage my initial questions, then, is to somehow listen to echoes of a future, maybe already present, whose dystopia holds possibilities beyond the antiblack structure of antagonism. Elusive as it may seem, freedom as an ethical imperative animates this exercise. Although I am not prepared to fully do away with the strategic employment of the protocols and concepts of formal justice, the focus on freedom, even as an unrealized, perhaps unrealizable condition, forces us to move beyond, if not against, the very grammars, practices, and traditional claims of justice.[2] Recognizing and moving beyond the traps of integration, citizenship, and nationhood, the freedom dreams that I invite the reader to listen to with me require exercising a political sensibility whose energy derives from at least two sources.[3] First, an immanent critique of the employment of and belief in tropes related to modern, liberal-democratic citizenship principles, if only because the critique's protagonists are themselves victimized, killed by, notions and practices routinized as precisely the embodiment of such principles. Here I am talking about social death, but not only.[4] The deaths are of the flesh as they are of the person, as a liberal, rights-bearing individual, and spirit.[5] Second, the recognition that what is needed to break down regimes of objectifying subjection is to imagine the unimaginable, embody the abject, and venture into the terrifying.[6] More specifically, when, and if, ever so reluctantly, non-, near-, or antiblack people become in some measure and even if temporarily, of all things, black themselves, an interesting opportunity to engage with freedom dreams presents itself.[7]

This is an interesting opportunity because the dystopia of black suffering—whose myriad manifestations suggest a genocidal field—as it spills over nonblack populations, may bring about the almost unthinkable possibility of nonblacks' insight into the black condition.[8] Insight here does not mean empathy—although insight does not completely negate empathy.[9] Insight means a fleeting awareness resulting from one's involuntary participation in morbid rituals. Although you are new to the process and are apparently different from those who numerically and by way of their structural positionality dominate the scenes, you recognize and become acquainted with the dynamics in such a way that they resonate both personally and genealogically—you become of the scene; you become, or almost become, one of them; you are, or almost are, one of them; they almost become you. So these nonblack groups, by force of their vulnerability, become soon-to-be, almost, or symbolically black. Across space and a few generations this process forcibly socializes experiences until then exclusive to or disproportionately concentrated among the Afro-descended. It is this *becoming black* with which I want to linger.

Inspiration for this exercise can be captured in Angela Davis's writing: "If the prison continues to dominate the landscape of punishment throughout this century into the next, what might await coming generations of impoverished African-Americans, Latinos, Native Americans, and Asian Americans? Given the parallels between the prison and slavery, a productive exercise might consist in speculating about what the present might look like if slavery or its successor, the convict lease system, had not been abolished."[10] In this essay I speculate about regimes of confinement, which include carceral dystopia and militarized surveillance at the local, urban, everyday levels, not as rupture but as drawing many of its foundational dynamics and concepts from the regime of slavery.[11] The blackness of slavery, including the middle passage and its schemes of containment,[12] blackness as slavery, becomes—or is parallel to—the blackness of the prison system, the blackness of urban spaces and its attending institutions of enforcement. In black diasporic perspectives, these phenomena generate conditions of possibility for their own expansion and in the process of their expansion impact and blacken blacks and nonblacks.

Although I don't want to completely negate the potential of relative empathy that this very queer, blackening process generates, at this time the question I'm most concerned with is: Can this involuntary proximity to and imposed incarnation of paradigmatically black experiences, produce new sensitivities, awareness, social critique, and support for black freedom dreams? In these regimes of transgenerational (thus genealogical) confinement, what does one's forced closeness to black experiences, even the temporary wearing of black skin, suggest as imaginative and thus transformative potentials? The dystopian scenario is a compelled dance of death with blacks—the unmentionable dance that nonblacks refuse and cannot fully grasp and that blacks often avoid yet cannot escape.[13] Defying normative coherence, this coerced dance of death reconfigures (yet reenacts, at a distinct scale and composition) the very structural antagonism that excludes and constitutes blacks as nonhuman, not of this social world. These expanded scenes of carceral subjection result from morbid subpoenas. Less to do with empathy and more to do with uneasy, enforced symmetry, becoming black becomes becoming dead, or—if blackness is, after all, irremediably without analogue as an ontology and as a manifestation in space and time—becoming intimate with rituals of social, psychic, corporeal, spiritual, and living death. This intimacy is of a quality distinct from that of the intimacy obtained via the gaze; this intimacy is that of the reluctant participant, the reluctant being whose existence, henceforth nonexistence, is superimposed, or at least permeated, by blackness. Which of course, if we are to engage with the very black ontological imperative of resistance, which means resistance to the imposed ontological irrelevance, the question becomes that of raising the dead or of objection to subjection.[14]

THE QUESTIONS, AND THE conditions from which they emanate, are almost unimaginable because it is the intimacy between blackness and death that both formulates blackness and renders it practically impermeable to nonblacks.[15] To put it in another way, it is the various degrees of intimacy between nonblackness and life, rights, and citizenship that constitute the modalities of being nonblack.[16] To imagine the unimaginable allows for sensing beyond the dystopia of black genocide. It allows for instrumentalizing, and therefore moving beyond and negating, a scenario whose logic opposes continuity, movement, resurrection. There and then the imperatives of black survival, improvisation, and performance of freedom, specific to black conditions, become less foreign to nonblacks, to the next blacks.

This is certainly a stretch, a contortion of the imagination—one that embraces the dystopia of black death as producing, because of its physics of void and excess, the very possibilities that would make viable, at least as a prospect, a specter, a degree of compelling and sustainable recognition of black people, spaces, and condition. No more distant, foreign, unimaginable because so graspable, impregnated, blackness is resignified, reconfigured, as dreaded but almost inevitable layers of experiences, self-understanding, and interpellation. If Frantz Fanon focuses on epidermalization as internalization to analyze black ontology,[17] the scenes this essay focuses on include the unwilling conscientization of an imposed, structural, and therefore experiential black epidermis. Such imposed epidermalization, a necessary product of the technologies of containment, produces reluctant black cyborgs, not so much endowed with superpowers but generated by overwhelming forces—the forces of warfare in the U.S. and Brazilian homelands.[18]

Still, lest we become enamored in or of such landscapes, it must be underlined that the mechanics of what I'm trying to imagine, even though it may generate the possibility of pro-black, oppositional forms of consciousness and action, is intrinsically antiblack, in many ways organized against some of the perceived threats and gains of insurgent black radical traditions, in Brazil and the United States.[19] This essay is about antiblackness reaching a saturation point and the identification possibilities that emerge out of such dystopian setting. Increasingly over the past few generations and across contemporary social networks, the bodies targeted and rendered socially dead are those that, until recently, were not affected so intensely or so broadly by various forms of antiblack violence. The antiblack mechanics are not unprecedented. It is their range, intensity, and the times in and spaces on which they are applied that make them morbidly promising. An interesting, because potentially transformative, collateral consequence of antiblack genocidal processes may be a forced or accepted embodiment of blackness by those who until now, quite understandably, have resisted it as a mode of self-definition.

Because contemporary antiblack technologies are required to continuously expand, they inevitably interpellate nonblack (but potentially soon to be) black bodies;[20] at their limit these technologies dilute difference into a mass that, because of its imprinted familiarity with death—social death, spiritual death, physical death—becomes a black mass. This essay is attentive to this dilution process and what happens when until then nonblack bodies become interpellated as black—perhaps not directly but as a consequence of various repressive technologies.

The two sets of scenes that follow provide a sense of the excesses that antiblack mechanisms of domination produce. Applied to defined residential areas, aimed at specific racialized bodies (bodies whose genders and ages index variations of perceived danger, hardly ever the absence of danger), these mechanisms, however, are not able to precisely delimit their target. The antiblack wars—intense, technologically cutting-edge, charged with the imperatives of control, separation, ownership, purity, and life—produce collateral consequences that render black, or blacken, the unintended targets. Such is the case in Rio de Janeiro, Brazil, and Austin, Texas. The seemingly disparate geographical locations and the social actors whose proximity with blacks blackens them (Latinas/os in Austin; white, almost white, and not yet black people in Rio) reveal these technologies' diasporic nature, as well as the means by which blackness becomes, by force of repressive forces of containment—police operations and prisons—highly contagious. The language of contagion is meant to suggest the communication of social stigma resulting from a situational imperative: that of occupying zones paradigmatically associated with and defining blackness. That such zones are realms of life in social death renders the dystopian phenomenon one of great and terrible transformative potentials.

THE FIRST PART of the essay, focusing on recent joint police and army operations in Rio de Janeiro, explores the ways in which the targets of such operations—people inhabiting historical black neighborhoods[21]—although defined in the dominant imaginary, could not be precisely delimited in time and space. Indeed while the televised and written news media coverage expressed predictable antiblack dispositions, it also revealed some of the dynamics by which blackness expands, saturates, and thus demands constant reformulations of both the zones of death and the zones of life. Live television reporting of such military occupation operations provides interesting moments when professional commentators, forced to improvise their script, suggest socially shared representations about those deemed dangerous and in need of containment. Preemptively applying to the dangerous bodies and spaces the violence that allegedly they,[22] the dangerous bodies, would direct at the virtuous citizenry and spaces if left unchecked, the joint military operations did more than retake control of embattled zones. They also made obvious the porous and not always controllable boundaries of belonging, of nonblackness and thus of blackness.

The second part of the essay shifts to Austin, and more precisely to a juvenile detention facility where, between 2008 and 2012, together with two collaborators, I facilitated a writing workshop for incarcerated youth. Drawing on three years of interaction with the incarcerated youth and the staff, I propose an analysis of dystopian, transgenerational, and spatially wide-reaching institutional practices that result in extreme time and space dispossession. That such practices forcefully blacken the youth is both a symptom of a logic of social death and an opportunity when blackness is reconstituted, perhaps as an insurgent, albeit reluctant, consciousness.

Rio de Janeiro

In 2007 nineteen people were killed in a single police operation at the Complexo do Alemão, a working-class, mostly black, residential area known as a favela. Photographs of the operation, taken by the press and residents, propose an unmistakable link between race, segregation, and death: the fatal victims were black persons, while the agents of the state, although at times embodied by black individuals, carried out a policy of social and spatial control whose drive and results were in essence antiblack.[23] The state of Rio de Janeiro's branch of the Ordem dos Advogados do Brasil, the Brazilian equivalent of the U.S. Lawyers Guild, filed a dossier showing evidence of execution in the bodies of at least thirteen of the people killed in the operation.

I bring up this relatively recent fact in the annals of Rio's employment of deadly force against favela residents to remember a morbid connection between police operations and sport mega events. This particular massacre occurred a few weeks before the XV Pan American Games opening, on July 13, 2007. The Pan-American Sports Association had awarded Rio the hosting over San Antonio, Texas. During and after the deliberations urban violence and security for athletes and audience were major concerns. The police operation in the Alemão neighborhood catered to such concerns and forcefully demonstrated that the military police were in charge. By occupying a well-defined urban area and isolating it from the rest of the city, to the point where schools were shut down and residents had to show their identification document at checkpoints around the neighborhood—the siege lasted as long as the sporting event, which was considered successful mostly because no violent incidents were reported.[24]

Following the October 2, 2009, announcement that Rio was to host the 2016 Olympic Games, the security concerns voiced during the long host-city selection process carried over to the preparation phase. Rio state's governor, Sérgio Cabral, signaled his resolve to assure social control by hiring Rudolph Giuliani, New York City's former mayor, as the Games' security advisor. While Giuliani drew much of his municipal and national approval from his zero-tolerance stance on crime, among his city's black population few administrators have surpassed his level of disapproval.[25] The brutality the New York Police Department employed on members of disadvantaged communities, especially the black, were notoriously exemplified in Amadou Diallo's murder: in 1999 in the Bronx he was shot at forty-one times by four plainclothes officers. Earlier, in 1997, Abner Louima was brutalized and forcibly sodomized with the broken handle of a plunger by police officers in Brooklyn.[26] These constitute additional chapters in a foretold story of antiblack violence that is at once diasporic and local.

WHAT PRECEDED AND what followed the 2007 Alemão massacre suggest a permanent state of war. In Rio de Janeiro between January and August 2003 the police killed nine hundred people, almost 75 percent of them in favelas, which are predominantly black communities. For the entire year of 2003 police executions were projected at 1,500 in Rio state alone—a figure comparable to Baghdad's 1,700 civilian fatalities in the same period. In a month Rio police kill over 2.5 times more people than the New York Police Department kills in a whole year.[27]

On November 25, 2010, the conflict reached an apex when a joint police, marines, and air force operation was launched to take control over two highly contested areas, Vila Cruzeiro and Complexo do Alemão, a region where over 400,000 people live and a growing number of drug dealers found refuge as they were pushed out of their original communities. By the next day twenty-five people were dead, most of them young black men supposedly associated with drug dealing.

Whereas the 2007 massacre was presented as evidence that the city could host the Pan American Games, what has happened since must be seen in the context of the 2014 soccer World Cup and the 2016 Olympic Games. The one-day massacres exemplify trends whose numbers even out as evidence of the Brazilian state's impetus—if not by design, then certainly by its effects. Black death marks Rio's dystopian scenes of subjection and resistance.[28]

Let me focus specifically on the Vila Cruzeiro operation, the first and most significant of this particular police-military campaign. It was preceded by intense confrontations between police forces and armed gang members. Since Sunday, November, 21, 2010, twenty-three people had died, forty-seven had been incarcerated, and 112 had been detained for investigation. Two police officers were shot, and fourteen civilians had been injured in the crossfire. A list of the materials the police apprehended during the confrontations provides a sense of the urban battles' nature and intensity: twenty-nine handguns and pistols, ten rifles, two shotguns, a machine gun, five grenades, and two homemade bombs. In the possession of arrested suspects were a Molotov cocktail, two explosive artifacts, and nine liters of gasoline, among other items.[29]

Reacting against the state repression, as well as expressing their willingness to engage broader public attention, the alleged bandits set on fire thirty-seven vehicles. Unlike in relatively common events of previous years, when mostly buses were set ablaze as protest against police intervention in territory the drug gangs deemed their own, this time the arsons were not only seemingly coordinated; they included passenger cars and trucks and were widespread throughout greater Rio.[30]

On Tuesday, November 24, all military police officers, including those working behind desks, in hospitals, as mechanics and cooks, were ordered to join the street patrols. According to the Fecha Quartel (Close the Barracks) order, all administrative activities were suspended.[31] Rio state's security secretary, José Mariano Beltrame, affirmed that the police were going to get tougher on criminals. To emphasize his resolve and to stress the need for the concerted police efforts, he suggested that the city's two main factions, the Comando Vermelho and Terceiro Comando, were joining forces. Still, even with the reinforcements, the attacks on civilians and police continued: burned cars, buses, and shooting were widely reported in the newspapers and on television.[32]

Early on Wednesday, November 25, the military police general commander, Mário Sérgio Duarte, ordered that all officers remain on duty, while those troops at home were told to go back to their posts. That same afternoon, when Special Operations officers (Batalhão de Operações Especiais, BOPE), the equivalent of SWAT teams in the United States, entered Vila Cruzeiro, they were immediately fired upon. The many small stores along the Nossa Senhora da Penha Avenue immediately shut down, as did all the other commercial venues nearby. Perhaps sensing that the police and military buildup was threatening their territories in unprecedented ways, the local gangs did not measure efforts in their attempts to repeal the state operation. Even the *caveirão* (the big coffin), the black-painted military modified armored vehicle BOPE had been using in the past few years, became a target. The object of both fear and scorn—both well expressed in a number of popular rap songs—the caveirão was attacked as two homemade bombs were thrown under it. In an apparent victory for the local rebels, the armored assault vehicle had to retreat, turn around, and drive down the avenue so that the fire that quickly began to consume it could be extinguished. It finally stopped in front of the landmark Nossa Senhora da Penha Church, at a safe distance from the intense gunfire. Yet this temporary setback would not deter the larger, and final, massive operation that materialized a few hours later, when a number of military vehicles and personnel engaged the conflict and effectively put an end to it.[33]

THE LIVE TELEVISION reporting of these events was central to how the police and their adversaries were portrayed. As it became more apparent in the succeeding days of conflict, the television reporting provided an extra set of data—much of it in real time—that could potentially favor the operations against the bandits. Providing an important link in this news media and police symbiosis, at key points in the police operations former officers turned reporters suggested that the live images TV Globo produced be immediately forwarded to the commanding officers. Lauded as a "watershed moment in the city's public security," the Vila Cruzeiro invasion relied heavily on the powerful collaboration between real-time reporting and employment of military technologies in densely populated urban areas.[34]

The local newscast on RJ TV, one of TV Globo's most watched programs, hosted by Ana Paula Araújo, opened its Wednesday edition with a recapitulation of the past days' events. In quick succession clips of burning buses, gun battles between the police and alleged drug dealers, and footage of officers handling a number of assault rifles, guns, drugs, grenades, and money, allegedly confiscated from the criminals, were shown as Araújo's grave voice and facial expression described the events.[35]

As had become expected during Globo's coverage of these military operations, Araújo followed her introduction with a live call to the Globocóptero, the TV station's helicopter. Hovering over Vila Cruzeiro, the reporter Tatiana Nascimento provided a quick account of real-time, on-the-ground developments.

The camera showed several two-passenger motorcycles making their way to and stopping at a high point in the neighborhood and hurriedly dropping off what Nascimento described as members of the drug trade: "We made some impressive footage. A lot of armed bandits arriving at this place; some of them fired. . . . A truly scary scene [uma imagem verdadeiramente assustadora]. We just received the information that an 81-year-old man has been shot here in Vila Cruzeiro." She recited the litany of deaths, burnings, and arrests that had occurred in the preceding hours. While her voice was firmer and calmer than that of her colleague in the studio, her facial expression was in synchronicity with Araújo's, suggesting concern and traces of fear.[36]

THE GLOBOCÓPTERO—AS A provider of information as well as a vessel that enables the capture and dissemination of images without having to establish physical closeness to those on whom it focuses—is a powerful technology and symbol of the city's fractured geographies of privilege, race, and violence. Most Rio favelas are characterized by their hilly topography, the highest points of which, where the streets become steep and quite narrow, are difficult to access by car or any larger ground vehicle. Motorcycles are the quickest means of transportation in neighborhoods such as Vila Cruzeiro, where they are often utilized as taxis and freight vehicles, as well as for everyday commuting. It is common to see 125s and 250s, mostly Hondas and Yamahas, circulating through Rio favelas, many of them used as efficient (and often a little frightening, if you are not used to them) *moto-táxis*.

Back in the studio Araújo mentioned that Rodrigo Pimentel, "special commentator on security, a former officer in the special operations BOPE," noticed that the alleged gang members were using very powerful weapons. Pimentel described a scene in which, while most suspected bandits were leaving the spot where they had been seen concentrated, a man armed with an assault rifle apparently took a position, waiting for the police officers and army troops. The bandits, Pimentel explained in a concerned, hurried, almost stumbling voice, were showing evidence of a plan of resistance against the police operation. Pimentel's militarily trained eye quickly interpreted the movement along the narrow street he saw broadcast via Globo's helicopter camera: "This suspect [*elemento*] is helping with containing the police's advance. . . . This gang member is waiting for the police's entry [into the neighborhood]." Now on screen, Pimentel delivered a short statement that reveals much of TV Globo's—and, we can surmise, the broader public—expectations about the so-called suspect elements: "Even with all this police apparatus, you see the will to resist." Araújo quickly repeated the statement verbatim, for emphasis.[37]

Resistance, in Pimentel's explanation, is not only a blatantly unlawful act; it is also a challenge to the foundational imperative of favela control. The reporters' primordial response to the gang members' actions reveal a socially shared recognition that such acts of resistance ultimately threaten the very basic elements structuring privilege and belonging: insurgent agency, symbolized forcefully in the heavy weaponry utilized by the young men determined to resist the police operation, openly challenged spatial separation, control, and predictability, all based on the necessary monopoly of violence. To employ both the local police and the army suggested the magnitude of the threat as well as the urgency with which the bases of Rio's apartheid sociability had to be reestablished.[38]

The gang members' audacity notwithstanding, Pimentel's expert commentaries reassured the viewers that military supremacy at Vila Cruzeiro was inevitable: "The bandits have nowhere to go." A few days earlier the Jacarezinho favela, the second largest in the metropolitan region, where the same gang faction, Comando Vermelho, dominated the drug trade, had been once again forcefully occupied by the police. In the process gang members were either incarcerated, killed, or seen fleeing. As Pimentel presciently noted, for the ever challenged members of Comando Vermelho, in Vila Cruzeiro as in other key areas in the greater Rio, the neighborhoods of the Complexo do Alemão were the only remaining options for escape and refuge.[39]

Jornal Hoje, a TV Globo afternoon news program, provided continuity to the day's reporting on the developments in Vila Cruzeiro. As the Globocóptero scanned the neighborhood in search of evidence of the bandits' movement and the police-military operation's progress, Pimentel was asked to comment on the technicalities involved in the operation. Answering a question about what the people who lived in the neighborhood should do in case of gunfire, he stated that, because "a brick wall cannot take a high-powered bullet's impact," persons in those areas should seek protection behind a second wall, preferably in a corridor. Pimentel concluded by saying that the dweller (*morador*) should lie on the ground.[40]

At this moment Pimentel, as if improvising, went on to say, "Unfortunately, the favela dweller in Rio already does that [lies on the ground almost automatically at the sign of gunfire]." His side note led him to an apparently logical sequence: "Who does not live in such areas may not know any of this.

[The fact is that] one of those high-powered bullets can strike any of the nine neighborhoods around the Vila da Penha region . . . where 240,000 people live."[41]

THIS BRIEF BUT VERY significant statement contains what I've been trying to grasp and reflect on: the military responses against drug dealers in Rio inevitably affect people not involved in drug commerce, and drug dealers' reactions against police intervention affect persons not involved in the disputes. Drug dealers are usually a fraction of those who live in the neighborhoods undergoing intense police and military operations.[42] As important, the weapons used in these operations can potentially—and indeed frequently do—reach areas geographically quite removed from the immediate conflict zones. What was at first a focused military intervention—one that was as much about black bodies (black and nonblack bodies rendered black by their time and space coordinates) as it was about reclaiming black land—spills over unintended people and neighborhoods. The spillover is enhanced by the seemingly concerted operations that target the state, its agents, and the city's nonblack areas. The scenes that develop are such that the embattled semantic and geographic fields blacken susceptible subjects caught up in the crossfire. Of course not all subjects in the crossfire are rendered black; the process is just as effective in redefining whiteness and belonging. The subjects that are blackened already inhabit allegedly suspect liminal racial, spatial, age, and legality parameters.[43]

THE BEYOND-BLACK EXCESS of suffering and death is a fact, an opportunity, if tragic, that presents innovative, if not surprising, political possibilities. This excess recomposes a black body out of violent and lethal dystopias: as a result of technologies of domination, of carefully orchestrated tactics whose dominant public eye/I gains expression in and through Globo's airborne vantage point, the black body, dangerous and defiant, is also mutant. At times it is clearly indexed in the young men who refuse to give up control of their territory and their trade, the same young men who both attract and repel the white gaze. At other times the black body morphs and recomposes itself as greater than the sum of the visible threats, as the maps, movements, and plans that accompany technologies of domination; those times are marked by the unexpected outreach of such desires of domination, when bodies until then not necessarily marked as black become blackened due to their location, their victimization, and even their willing attempt to resist their subjugation.

Whereas in the Rio context there is certainly a high dosage of interpellation in the production, death, and reconstitution of the black body, there are agency moments, gestures of empowerment, and even interruptions in the dominant flows of desire for control that also contribute to the recomposition of the scrutinized, hunted, abject black body. What's different, what's promising, what's almost unthinkable is that both blacks and nonblacks are reconfigured as black insofar as both are caught up in and engage a web of the foundational, excessive, antiblack proclivities of the state and society. Antiblackness produces involuntary relationalities between nonblacks and blacks; the emerging politics of inhabitation, although not a given, is nevertheless a compellingly transformative possibility.[44]

Austin

Between 2008 and 2012, together with members of a local organization, we used poetry and music as means of debate, awareness, and critique in a writing workshop in a youth detention facility in Austin. The workshop consisted of two weekly visits at the facility, where youths of both genders, between the ages of thirteen and seventeen, served sentences ranging from a few weeks to many months.

Based on 2008 data, while Anglo youth in Texas made up 40 percent of the state's juvenile population, they accounted for 26 percent of referrals to juvenile probation departments. Latinas/os were the most populous group in the state, 44 percent, and accounted for 48 percent of referrals. Black youth accounted for 13 percent of the population and 25 percent of referrals. By far the larger racial group in the juvenile prison population, Latina/o youth are becoming familiarized with transgenerational rituals of incarceration that define blackness. If we consider the historical condition of blackness, in particular that of being familiar with death, as incommensurable to the experiences of whites and Latinos, and if we take seriously the proposition that social death is what animates and is enabled by the carceral logic, then when exploring the identification possibilities in the midst of the Texas dystopian landscapes we may begin to sense an opening.[45] The opening is that, by virtue of their forced, transgenerational, and intimate familiarity with the radical dispossessions brought about by incarceration, Latinas/os gain insights based on experience into what constitutes one of the defining—structuring and structural—traits of the black experience.

Why is death the most palpable aspect of this juvenile facility? Death is as present as the blackening dystopia that this bureaucracy embodies. To grasp this dystopia, to come to terms with the scenes of subjection it creates and reproduces, is to explore the terrain of an expanding black death and black resurrection in mutant, syncretic configurations—a dystopia buried in and actualized by geographies of criminalization in such a way that to excavate it is to engage the very possibilities of a reconfigured, expanded blackness.

Such a dystopia is apparently disavowed by the legal discourse and everyday practices within the detention facility. Legally the institutionalized youth are still children—and are treated as such in the juridical guidelines that inform the juvenile courts, probation, and detention facilities. Title 3 of the Texas Family Code structures the state juvenile justice system. Emphasis is placed on the rehabilitation of the youth through accountability, guidance, counseling, diversion, and treatment.[46] In the bylaws and in many of the actions and statements of the staff in this particular facility, the youth still possess that which defines their condition: their theoretically extended and plastic, malleable futures. They can be educated, guided, rendered responsible; they can be rehabilitated, reinserted in society as productive, law-abiding subjects. A better future, a yet to be positive reality is theirs to be grasped. It is quite telling that, in almost three years of work at the facility, only once did I hear a staff person explicitly demonstrate frustration about a youth who was allegedly beyond rehabilitation—a youth who therefore was devoid of potential to bring about a worthy future for himself, impermeable to good sense as he seemed to be. In the staff's words, the young black man was "a criminal and not a child."

Still this exceptional moment of unselfconscious frustration was the exception that brought home the norm. Insofar as the staff's orientation and the codes by which it is supposedly governed stress potentialities yet to be actualized, it would not be an exaggeration to call it a discourse of redemption, care, and hope—quite the opposite of the death-laced dystopias with which the orientation cohabits. That a repressive institution employs concepts that negate the fundamental nature of, or at the very least render compassionate, its confinement practices seems hardly surprising. The naturalization of imprisonment, and in particular that of young people, depends on this and other, similar processes by which the time and spatial experiences in confinement are represented as ultimately beneficial to both the incarcerated and to those who are not incarcerated.

I want to linger on the elementary forms of dystopian institutional practice as they become naturalized and acceptable. This exercise can provide two sets of related information.

The first is about the actual everyday mechanics of juvenile institutions. That is, by focusing on the ways seemingly edifying narratives are incorporated into and effectively become the expression of essentially life-negating practices, we can get a better sense of how and why such practices manage to present themselves as their precise opposite—as life-affirming, transformative—and why they become effective and accepted without continuous explicit coercion. The use of imperative commands, shackles, handcuffs, time-outs, and solitary confinement is carefully calibrated by educational programs, camaraderie, even affection between staff and inmates. Rubbing against the grain of the hegemonic, normalized everyday dynamic of confinement, the apparent absence of continuous institutional coercion should make us attentive to moments of infrapolitical insurgency—moments when the youth, and even staff members, while following the institutional orientation, find imaginative ways to appropriate, negate, and ultimately reveal not so obvious and benevolent facets of the carceral narratives.

The second set of information that an analysis of the dystopian environment provides is about potentially transformative sensibilities and processes. I would like to reflect on whether and how we can locate insurgent potentials in times and spaces of overwhelming, albeit often veiled, dehumanization, of which juvenile confinement is a particularly sad example. The continued and recurrent incarceration of young black and brown women and men makes all of this urgent. The window of time between their current incarceration and the next is brief, as is the turning point at which they legally become adults and are criminalized as such. Not to mention the limited options that define the occupied, highly segregated territories from which they come.

TO BEGIN THE PROCESS of locating and probing the dystopian tropes that can be easily confounded with tropes of rehabilitation and care, let me focus on the basic fact of incarceration. Youth incarceration marks symbolically and in practice processes that reinforce its own perverse logic, one that negates at every turn an existential condition of childhood, that of becoming—more specifically becoming as a process that is not already predetermined and reinforced by technologies of confinement. It is perverse because, at any given moment, over half of all the youth in a juvenile facility have previously been institutionalized. This means that for the majority of young people locked up, their condition is a sequel of and probable prelude to imprisonment. Data from 2008, the latest made available, illustrate the point. In that year

53 percent of all 99,276 referrals were of juveniles with previous referrals; of those, 32 percent had four or more previous referrals, and 35 percent had one prior referral. Among the juveniles with a prior referral, 46 percent had a felony as the most severe offense (including probation violation), and 9 percent had Conduct Indicating a Need of Supervision, a noncriminal offense.[47]

The groups we worked with exemplify the trends. During a writing session on October 25, 2010, in a girls unit that housed seven fifteen-, sixteen-, and seventeen-year-olds doing time for drug offenses, all the young women told us that they been incarcerated before. One girl was black, one was white, five were Latina. The strange familiarity the youth encounter when inside the juvenile facility is one of a foretold legal and experiential ritual. This familiarity is the result of two interrelated processes: the first process happens via social networks—kin, friends, and acquaintances; the second is that of becoming incarcerated. For the brown and especially the black youth caught up in the system, the incarceration experience provides a window into a considerable likelihood of future incarceration. Although rates vary by region, for black men there is an overall 32 percent lifetime chance that they will be incarcerated; for Latinos the probability is 17 percent, while for all men in the United States it is 11 percent.[48] That two out of three young black men are expected to be either on parole, on probation, or incarcerated by 2020 (if trends recorded in the 1980s and early 1990s persist) renders the specter of recurring incarceration an almost consolidated presence. Women's incarceration rates compound and reflect the specter: in 2011 black females were incarcerated at between two and three times the rate of white females, and Latinas experienced incarceration at a rate between one and three times the rate of white females.[49]

SUCH PREDICTABLE, CIRCULAR EXPERIENCES of incarceration extrapolate discrete units of time, space, and social distance; they constitute persistent, intergenerational, and far-reaching events. Incarceration affects social networks in scope as it reaches a considerable number of people connected by kinship or otherwise. This process in turn suggests an expanded territorial area onto which the social networks are mapped. Even though the youth that become the objects of incarceration are from residential areas segregated by race, such areas are not continuous: the young people hail from similar but distinct, not always contiguous residential areas. To grasp the expanded time horizon incarceration depends on and further dilates, consider that, within a given family, the experience of being behind bars is common to individuals belonging to one's own generation as well as to distinct generations. With a mixture of pride and sorrow young people mention that they have brothers, sisters, and cousins behind bars; they also speak of incarcerated parents, uncles, aunts, and grandparents.

The time distention that the carceral logic actualizes also expands control over racialized spaces: spaces of residence, spaces of confinement. As the time-space expansive carceral logic intensifies its control over black and brown bodies, it operates a corresponding dispossession of time and space among those it supervises. The confined youth, as with any prisoner, will say she has no control over her time, that being at the facility is a waste of time, that time does not belong to her, that she's just doing time. Without irony—evidence that they believe in and work for the redemptive qualities of incarceration—the staff will tell the young people that now, locked up, they have time to think about their lives, time to gain new skills, time to plan for when they are released, time to dream. Staff frequently utter the words *transformation* and *hope* by way of encouragement. Some of the youth try to embrace these suggestions and make the most out of what are presented as opportunities: so-called life-management skills as well as school curriculum content. For example, young women who are pregnant or who already have a child are trained in mothering skills and carry dolls during the day under the close scrutiny of staff.

THE OPPORTUNITY TO LOOK forward to something, anything, is eagerly embraced, at least temporarily. Able to glimpse an attractive, yet to be realized time, the youth gain time, their own unbounded time, as they do time, supervised time, legally imposed time. As a dividend paid to conformity, a sense of unbounded futurity is made graspable, if only during the few moments the facility's optimism seems credible.

Time becomes both the medium (experienced while doing time) and the product (time subtracted from one's sentence, time credit gained) of supervised effort.[50] This powerful, contradictory synthesis of institutional consent and apparent virtual, yet to be realized freedom, must account for the power that seemingly enabling, caring narratives have among the youth. Yet some, if not most, of the youth sense the contradictions of a bureaucracy that on the one hand imprisons them and on the other offers what seem like attractive possibilities that exceed the death zones of ghettos and barrios. Added to the loneliness and isolation felt in the facility, young men and women often express in writing the institutional ambiguities as well as their internal conflicts. The moments of frustration as well as the ambiguities the youth experience were well captured by a young black woman's writing:

> It's kind of weird: I'm afraid to go to bed.
> I'm tired of being tired, I'm fed up
> And I wish it was over 'cause
>
> I'm tired of going through what
> I'm going through
>
> I'm Phase 2 and I don't do what
> I'm supposed to do. People are here
> To help me, not hurt me,
> So I'm tired and confused.
> I'm sick of being
> This person that is trapped inside
> That I don't know how to get out.[51]

Being "trapped inside" suggests helplessness; it also indicates a psychological correspondence to being physically incarcerated. The young woman's despair arises as she is in possession neither of her body, her time, nor her mind.

Almost all the youths' activities—exercising, studying, eating, sleeping—are controlled for them, in spite of them. The activities are carefully matched to specific times and spaces within the facility. Time dispossession—doing time, paying back in time—is compounded by the lack of control over one's immediate spatial surroundings. In a similar way space dispossession is compounded by lack of control over one's time.

When focusing more closely on this peculiar time and space dispossession, we are able to grasp moments and places in which the seemingly redemptive tropes of rehabilitation can't resist the evidence of things seen and unseen. This peculiar time and space dispossession suggests a dystopia—one in which, rather than movement, autonomy, and becoming, the youth are forced into a cycle of almost unavoidable, permanent, life-negating state of confinement. In significant moments of their reflections rendered evident to the youth are both the ever-present narratives of their current confinement and their hardly unavoidable future confinement. Young men and women go back and forth between affirming that they don't want to ever return to the juvenile facility and recognizing the high likelihood of a repeated incarceration.

An irony that does not escape the youth's attention is that, in such a state of dispossession, they are reduced to bearers of time—the currency with which they pay their initial juridical debt and the currency with which they pay for transgressions while locked up. Time, whose management is taken away from the young men and women as they are forced to abdicate control of their body movements in the meticulously monitored space, is the substance of which they find themselves having an abundance. Attempting to balance the dispossession of their own time and body while having to produce time in the form and quantity demanded by the facility's staff is quite a daunting task. Tiredness and confusion are not surprising—what should be the cause of scandal is that anyone, let alone young people, is subjected to such anguished rituals.

It is this cycle of time and space dispossession that imposes a logic of death on the youth. We could speak of the young incarcerated subjects as genealogical isolates insofar as they have no direct access to and are not free to utilize the social heritage of their previous generations, the alive and the deceased.[52] While the facility's programming and staff allow family and group narratives that link the youth to their families—narratives of slavery, migration, standard ethnic pride, civil rights, and so on—the very fact of incarceration forcefully interrupts these narratives' logic of forward motion, of redemption and integration. As well the facility's rules of conduct, which include restrictions on vocabulary and the emphatic prohibition against "glorifying" drugs, gangs, and violence, often mean that, given the youth's symbolic universe, marked precisely by social structures that produce that which seems glorified, the young women and men often encounter barriers to integrating the experience of their elders into their lives, their memories, and as templates from which to make sense of their predicament and possibilities. Still the carceral logic is deceiving; it floats over, scrambles, and thus operates regardless of chronology; it reaches forward in genealogical time as much as it reaches back. The past, present, and future become one. Dispossessed of their ascendants' social heritage, incarcerated subjects will likely have no access to the social realizations of their progeny. Multigenerational and spatially all-encompassing, the carceral logic will probably reach the daughters and sons of those presently incarcerated. When we take into account that many of the incarcerated youth have children of their own, the transgenerational reach and scrambling of time of the carceral logic become quite graspable, reaffirming the mechanics by which genealogical isolates are produced.[53]

What makes the carceral logic deceiving is that, while it brings about the social and spiritual death of successive generations, it provides a sense of continuity across communities separated by time and space. By mentioning, being aware of, and communicating with relatives and friends behind bars, the youth bring these people closer to themselves, at least spiritually. Yet it is the very carceral system that mediates that sense of belonging—the same institution that has so thoroughly uprooted the youth from their communities and dispossessed them of their most basic control over their body, time, and space. If the carceral logic is a logic of death, and if the carceral logic connects generations, then generations become connected through a logic of death.

Although the sense of inter- and intragenerational communion depends on and is therefore about death, it nevertheless provides virtual comfort, melancholic as it may be. Being among the socially dead while supposedly alive is the source of reassurance; this morbid familiarity could be what best captures the condition of juvenile incarceration. Dystopian imagined communities, while providing some very palpable, even necessary solace to young people finding themselves radically dispossessed, also contribute, even if by very tortuous ways, to the naturalization of incarceration. It is this naturalization that produces and reflects the morbid sense of belonging that the carceral system provides. One thing is to belong to a community of resistance; another thing, related but that should be quite apart, is to belong to a seemingly inevitable, perpetual state of incarceration. While resistance is about life, incarceration is about death.

The Line Has Moved. Has the Line Moved?

The prison system in Texas, like its counterparts in other U.S. geographies, has plantation slavery as its main ideological and historical matrix. While Latinas/os in Texas have been violently and widely forced into the bowels of the state's prison system and subjected to the attendant, race-based, broader Jim Crow laws, such experiences suggest a level of contingency that link them to political arrangements that, according to some specialists, were plastic enough to allow for Latinas/os' relative incorporation into Texas social landscapes.[54] Such perspective lends credence to the view that civil society, and indeed the "wholeness of the social body, was made possible by the banishment and abjection of blacks, the isolation of dangerous elements from the rest of the population, and the containment of [racial] contagion."[55] The forced passage into fundamentally antiblack institutional mechanics, and the experiences that such passage involves, may bring about a potentially expanded or even unprecedented sensibility about that which is essential to the complexities of racial rule and the nature of the racial state and therefore about antiblackness. Diasporic in its effects (if not nature), antiblack racial states enact policies of control that are not able to prevent collateral damage. The Rio scenes of forced contagion show an expanding will of power spilling over unintended human targets and geographies. What these scenes announce as political possibilities—the coerced acquaintance and indeed embodiment of blackness, even if temporary—is quite a transcendental, if improbable and certainly disquieting dystopia in their expandable dimensions. New bodies and spaces of reconstituted blackness, while indeed imprinted with (and defined by) death, are nevertheless transformative as they engage and thus contest the ways by which antiblack structures of antagonism operate, incorporate, and kill.

It is within this black dystopia, spreading over nonblack racialized groups, that I hear, I hope for a shift, a syncope, that will allow for blackness to resuscitate in an expanded, even if utterly contradictory, embattled set of experiences and worldviews. This resurrected and expanded blackness, rendering previously nonblacks reluctant blacks, can expand the horizon of political possibilities. When many unwillingly become black, a generative crisis ensues. Civil society becomes a state of war; the empire-state becomes a naked genocidal machine;[56] reform will sink in as fascism. So here is the opening, the syncope, the momentary death that can lead to imagining extended sensibilities, altered scales of humanity, freedom.

In the guise of an unstable conclusion, let us listen again to a voice engaged in reflections on antiblackness: "Why do Humans take such pride in self-adjustment, in diminishing, rather than intensifying, the project of liberation (how did we get from 1968 to the present)? Because, I contend, in allowing the notion of freedom to attain the ethical purity of its ontological status, one would have to loose one's Human coordinates and become Black. Which is to say, one would have to die."[57]

The meanings and possibilities I am trying to grasp, not without a dose of quixotic optimism in the midst of otherwise overwhelming antiblack genocidal processes, suggest an angle from which to reflect projects of liberation. As nonblacks seemingly become more vulnerable to forms of social death brought by antiblack forces, it is the very notion of freedom, in its most urgent and irreducible forms, that becomes engaged. On the other hand, if such an expanded dance of death seems unlikely, impossible even, then this essay's negation would constitute the reaffirmation of the ultimately incommensurable black condition. Even the temporary forced wearing of black skin would not produce a corresponding nonbeing, rendering the black nonbeing without analogue and thus without effective allies.

NOTES

Many thanks to Dylan Rodríguez, who closely engaged, challenged, and greatly improved this text. A number of his suggestions and insights appear verbatim in the notes.

1. Wilderson defines the Afro-pessimists this way: "Though they do not form anything as ostentatious as a school of thought, and though their attitudes toward and acknowledgement of Fanon vary, the moniker *Afro-pessimists* neither infringes on their individual differences nor exaggerates their fidelity to a shared set of assumptions. It should be noted that of the Afro-pessimists—Hortense Spillers, Ronald Judy, David Marriott, Saidiya Hartman, Achille Mbembe, Frantz Fanon, Kara Keeling, Jared Sexton, Joy James, Lewis Gordon, George Yancey, and Orlando Patterson—only James and Patterson are social scientists. . . . The Afro-Pessimists are theorists of Black positionality who share Fanon's insistence that, though Blacks are indeed sentient beings, the structure of the entire world's semantic field—regardless of cultural and national discrepancies—'leaving' as Fanon would say, 'existence by the wayside'—is sutured by anti-Black solidarity. Unlike the solution-oriented, interest-based, or hybridity-dependent scholarship so fashionable today, Afro-pessimism explores the meanings of Blackness not—in the first instance—as variously and unconsciously interpellated identity or as a conscious social actor, but as a structural position of noncommunicability in the face of all other positions; this meaning of noncommunicable because, again, as a position, Blackness is predicated on modalities of accumulation and fungibility, not exploitation and alienation" (*Red, White, and Black,* 58, 59). Earlier Moten suggested a reading of Fanon, which "might misrepresent itself as a kind of refusal of Fanon," that is able to conjure a measure of optimism: "My reading is enabled by the way Fanon's texts continually demand that we read them—again, or deeper still, not or against again, but for the first time. I wish to engage a kind of preop(tical) optimism in Fanon that is tied to the commerce between the lived experience of the Black and the fact of Blackness and between the thing and the object—an optimism recoverable, one might say, only by way of mistranslation, that bridged but unbridgeable gap that Heidegger explores as both distance and nearness in his discourse on 'The Thing'" ("The Case of Blackness," 182). Moten suggests a problematic incorporation of tropes derived from assumptions of black pathology into Afro-pessimists' analyses, including those of Fanon. As well it is suggested that the discourse on Afro-pessimism, articulating a notion of blackness related to death, reveals itself as invested not only in the tragic but also in the neurotic. Sexton lingers on Moten's essay and locates in it—not surprisingly, given his attention to the antiblack semantic field that overdetermines even the most astute critiques—traces of the same tendency Moten hears in the Afro-pessimists perspectives: "What I find most intriguing about the timbre of the argument of the 'Case of Blackness,' and the Black optimism it articulates against a certain construal of afro-pessimism, is the

way that it works away from a discourse of Black pathology only to swerve right back into it as ascription to those found to be taking up and holding themselves in 'the stance of the pathologist' in relation to Black folks" ("The Social Life of Social Death," 20). Sexton concludes by way of an unstable, perhaps impossible synthesis that on the one hand criticizes the black optimist project for its insistence on agency and resistance as ontological irreducible priorities that are not always able to engage their reduced conditions of possibility. On the other hand Sexton proposes an alternative formulation of Afro-pessimism: "In this perverse sense [putting the emphasis on antiblackness as structuring the ontological position of blackness], Black social death is Black social life. The object of Black studies is the aim of Black studies. The most radical negation of the anti-Black world is the most radical affirmation of a Blackened world. Afro-pessimism is 'not but nothing other than' Black optimism" (32). I attempt to engage this polemic by stressing the field of possibilities in antiblack, dystopian scenes. As such I draw from both the Afro-pessimists' insistence on blackness as structural position and Moten's emphasis on the unscripted, unknowable, unpredictable outcomes and imperatives of blackness that are both its ontological requirements and worldly manifestations. Where this essay is attempting to go, however, is the place where and when blackness itself explodes its structural and performative confines, spilling over, as it were, to nonblack subjects. Whether this is a purely unrealizable and unconceivable possibility would indicate which perspectives, in the range of ontological challenges and opportunities contained in the Afro-pessimist–black optimism continuum, are meaningful. And of course such conversation begs interrogating to whom and why such perspectives would become meaningful at all.

2. Such a critical stance regarding traditional arenas of justice is well exemplified in Assata Shakur, Safia Bukhari, and Kuwasi Balagoon's refusal to recognize the legitimacy of courts. See, for example, Shakur, *Assata*; Bukhari, *The War Before*; Wilderson, "The Vengeance of Vertigo." On dominant and alternative notion of justice, see Young, *Justice and the Politics of Difference*. A focus on black suffering, however, demands that the very discussion of justice be suspended, as justice, in its various dimensions, is a constitutive part of a social architecture whose foundational logic is antiblack. Whether distributive or attentive to "issues of decision making, division of labor, and culture," as Young proposes, leaves intact the fact that blacks' exclusion is the condition of possibility of the very notion and practice of justice (*Justice and the Politics of Difference*, 33).

3. Kelley, *Freedom Dreams*. See also Bell's unflinching analysis of the ultimate impossibility of blacks' belonging in U.S. society as full citizens: "In spite of dramatic civil rights movements and periodic victories in the legislatures, Black Americans by no means are equal to whites. Racial equality is, in fact, not a realistic goal. By constantly aiming for a status that is unobtainable in a perilously racist America, Black Americans face frustration and despair. . . . While implementing Racial Realism we must simultaneously acknowledge that our actions are not likely to lead to transcendent change and, despite our best efforts, may be of more help to the system we despise than to the victims of that system we are trying to help" ("Racial Realism," 302, 308).

4. "Institutionalized marginality, the liminal state of social death, was the ultimate cultural outcome of the loss of natality as well as honor and power. It was in this too

that the master's authority rested. For it was he who in a godlike manner mediated between the socially dead and the socially alive" (Patterson, *Slavery and Social Death*, 46).

5. For a critique of liberalism and the racial state, see Mills, "Liberalism and the Racial State": "Far from being in principled opposition to racism, as a blatant infringement on individual rights and freedoms, liberalism has too often been complicit with it. The origins of both in modernity have tended to be manifested more in symbiosis than contradiction, the liberal individual being so conceptualized that whiteness is a prerequisite for individuality. And the liberal state, correspondingly, has historically functioned as a racial state, the Lockean sovereign denying self-ownership rights to people of color and the Kantian state treating nonwhites as subpersons incapable of self-rule" (28). Afro-pessimists will specify the categories whiteness, the racial state, and people of color by stressing their antiblack characteristics.

6. Holland, *Raising the Dead.*

7. Moving among essays by Moten, Sexton, Wilderson, Hartman, Spillers, Fanon, and Patterson, I suggest a syncretic analytic framework that recognizes both the ontological impossibilities of the black condition and the freedom drive as ontological necessity.

8. For an analysis of antiblack genocide in diasporic dimensions, see Vargas, *Never Meant to Survive*. On the impossibility of insight, see Fanon, *Black Skin, White Masks*: "Ontology—once it is finally admitted as leaving existence by the wayside—does not permit us to understand the being of the black man. For not only must the black man be black; he must be black in relation to the white man. Some critics will take it on themselves to remind us that this proposition has a converse. I say that it is false. The black man has no ontological resistance in the eye of the white man" (110).

9. This of course draws from, although not exactly following, Hartman's analysis of whites' selective and self-serving recognition of black humanity under slavery, which ultimately constitutes "an exercise in violence" (*Scenes of Subjection*, 35).

10. Davis, *Are Prisons Obsolete?*, 37.

11. Rodríguez's formulation helps to frame this proposition: "The status of the enslaved-imprisoned Black subject forms the template through which white Americana constructs a communion of historical interest, mobilizations of political force, and, more specifically, the production and proliferation of a regime of mass-based human immobilization. Thus, my theoretical centering of Black unfreedom here is not intended to minimize or understate the empirical presence of 'non-Black' Third World, indigenous, or even white bodies in these current sites of state captivity but, rather, to argue that the technology of the prison regime—and the varieties of violence it wages against those it holds captive—is premised on a particular white-supremacist module or prototype that is in fact rooted in the history of slavery and the social and racial crisis it has forwarded into the present" ("Forced Passages," 41). It is precisely the presence of nonblack bodies in contemporary sites of black death—that include but are not restricted to imprisonment, as my discussion of Rio de Janeiro illustrates—that this essay lingers on.

12. Spillers's account of the parallels between the spatial arrangements in the slave ships and the transformation of the black body as a gender- and genealogical-less entity is indicative of this paradigmatic moment. See Spillers, "Mama's Baby, Papa's Maybe": "Those African persons in the 'Middle Passage' were literally suspended in the oceanic, if we think of the latter in its Freudian orientation as an analogy on undifferentiated

identity: removed from the indigenous land and culture, and not-yet 'American' either, these captives, without names that their captors would recognize, were in movement across the Atlantic, but they were also *nowhere* at all. . . . Under these conditions, one is neither female, nor male, as both subjects are taken into account as *quantities*" (214–15).

13. Commenting on the "dance with death," Wilderson elaborates on the political and imaginative challenges that a focus on antiblackness generates: "If a social movement is to be neither social-democratic nor Marxist in terms of structure of political desire, then it should grasp the invitation to assume the positionality of subjects of social death. If we are to be honest with ourselves, we must admit that the 'Negro' has been inviting whites, as well as civil society's junior partners [the nonblack worker, the immigrant, the nonblack woman], to the dance of social death for hundreds of years, but few have wanted to learn the steps. They have been, and remain today—even in the most antiracist movements, such as the prison abolition movement—invested elsewhere. This is not to say that all oppositional political desire today is pro-white, but it is usually antiblack, meaning that it will not dance with death" (Wilderson, "The Prison Slave as Hegemony's [Silent] Scandal," 32). The scenes that I engage with provide insights into this forced contact and familiarity with the positionality of subjects of social death. Besides including a discussion of political horizons and possibilities, there is a question about the role of black studies in particular, and theoretical efforts in general, even progressive ones, that seem deeply implicated in antiblack perspectives—antiblack because unwilling and unable to engage with the full consequences of that which constitutes the quintessential black experience: that of nonbeing, of social and living death.

14. I draw this ontological imperative from Moten's *In the Break*: "This is to say that this book is an attempt to describe the material reproductivity of black performance and to claim for this reproductivity the status of an ontological condition. This is the story of how apparent nonvalue functions as a creator of value; it is also the story of how value animates what appears as nonvalue. This functioning and this animation are material. This ani*materi*ality—impassioned response to passionate utterance—is painfully disclosed always and everywhere in the tracks of black performance and black discourse on black performance. It is both for and before Marx in ways delineated by Cedric Robinson's historical analysis of the 'making of the black radical tradition'" (18). See Fanon's sentence on the black body producing no ontological resistance to the white gaze (see note 10). See also Holland, *Raising the Dead*. Contending that "the transmutation from enslaved to free subject never quite occurred at the level of imagination," Holland continues: "If Black subjects are held in such isolation—first by a system of slavery and second by its imaginative replacement—then is not their relationship to the dead, those lodged in terms like *ancestor* or *heritage*, more intimate than historians and critics have heretofore articulated? . . . In existential terms, knowledge of our own death determines not only the shape of our lives but also the culture we live in" (15). Moten's *In the Break* is the source of "objection to subjection."

15. On social death, see Patterson, *Slavery and Social Death*; Wilderson, *Red, White, and Black*.

16. See note 13, where Davis and Rodríguez explain the black matrix informing imprisonment. In relation to nonblacks, Wilderson proposes the following: "Whereas the positionality of the worker (whether a factory worker demanding a monetary wage, an

immigrant, or a white woman demanding a social wage) gestures toward the reconfiguration of civil society, the positionality of the black subject (whether a prison slave or a prison-slave-in-waiting) gestures toward the disconfiguration of civil society. From the coherence of civil society, the black subject beckons with the incoherence of civil war, a war that reclaims blackness not as positive value but as a politically enabling site, to quote Fanon, of 'absolute dereliction.' It is a 'scandal' that rends civil society asunder. Civil war, then, becomes the unthought, but never forgotten understudy of hegemony. It is a black specter waiting in the wings, and endless antagonism that cannot be satisfied (via reform or reparation) but that must, nonetheless, be pursued to the death" ("The Prison Slave as Hegemony's [Silent] Scandal," 33).

17. Fanon, *Black Skin, White Masks*, 11.

18. James, *Warfare in the American Homeland*. James has articulated the idea of the black cyborg in many public and private occasions in the past few years. See Vargas and James, "Refusing Blackness-as-Victimization." Inspiration for my thoughts on forced black epidermalization also comes from Butler's *Mind of My Mind*, where a timeless spirit, Doro, attempts to create a new type of being, endowed with psychic powers. There is an interesting tension between Doro's original black body and the successive bodies that he takes, not always black, after killing their spirits, apparently without ethical concerns. Mary, one of his creations, with whom he ultimately struggles, is a light-skinned black woman. Although endowed with unusual psychic powers, unlike Doro she is not able to inhabit other bodies; when her body dies, she dies. Her ethical boundaries—she will not consume, and thus kill, the subjects over whom she has control—seem to be related to her body, her epidermis.

19. There is a case to be made about the intensification of repressive and punitive law-and-order approaches, culminating in the current mass incarceration and the unprecedented public visibility and local effectiveness that black and nonwhite organized groups achieved in the mid-1960s until the early 1970s. The FBI-Cointelpro operations mark a paradigm shift in policing writ large, targeting specifically black and nonwhite groups and individuals. See Churchill and Vander Wall, *Agents of Repression*.

20. Here I have Foucault's reflection on penal justice: "The ideal point of penalty today would be an indefinite discipline: an interrogation without end, an investigation that would be extended without limit to a meticulous and ever more analytical observation, a judgment that would at the same time be the constitution of a file that was never closed, the calculated leniency of a penalty that would be interlaced with the ruthless curiosity of an examination, a procedure that would be at the same time the permanent measure of a gap in relation to an inaccessible norm and the asymptotic movement that strives to meet in infinity" (*Discipline and Punish*, 227).

21. Oliveira, "O Caso do Estado e as Questões Raciais."

22. I purposefully emphasize the black diasporic resonances of such preemptive, violent acts. See Butler, "Endangered/Endangering."

23. Salles, "A Chacina do Complexo do Alemão."

24. Candido, "O Haiti é Aqui, no Complexo do Alemão."

25. Michael Powell, "In a Volatile City, a Stern Line on Race and Politics," *New York Times*, July 22, 2007, accessed February 15, 2012, http//www.nytimes.com/2007/07/22/us/politics/22giuliani.html.

26. That Diallo was a Guinean immigrant and Louima is originally from Haiti suggest deep and broad diasporic resonances, which ask for an analysis of the necessary place that the Brazilian nation-state occupies in these webs of gendered inflections of race, impacting and impacted by struggles over rights to the city and ultimately landownership. On black land struggles in Brazil, see a growing literature on the topic. While providing analysis of the strategies organized groups utilized to appeal to the state and civil society actors (lawyers, anthropologists, clergy), this literature tends to assume Brazil's unique race-relations matrix. Here, however, based on historical and social similarities and the actual collaboration between blacks of the United States and Brazil on similar problems, I use a diasporic framework that emphasizes continuities rather than difference. See, for example, Vargas, "The Inner City and the Favela." Paixão et al., *Relatorio Anual das Desigualdades Raciais no Brasil* use census data and national sample research to show that Blacks are consistently disproportionately impacted by violence, poverty, and hunger.

27. Human Rights Watch/Americas, *Police Brutality in Urban Brazil.*

28. In 2007, in twenty-six of twenty-seven Brazilian states, the rates of mortality by homicide for black men (that include the categories *preto* and *pardo*, "black" and "mixed") were greater than the rates for white men, and the asymmetry acquired exponential magnitude; in the state of Paraíba, for example, it was 1,181.4 percent higher; 806.9 percent in Pernambuco. It was 130.0 percent in the state of Rio (Paixão et al., *Relatório Anual*, 255, 256). More telling, perhaps, is what is called "homicide by legal intervention," that is, homicides committed by individuals working for the state, especially the police. Notwithstanding the documented underreporting patterns regarding such homicides, between 2001 and 2007 blacks responded for 61.7 percent of their total, 64.5 percent for 2007 (Paixão et al., *Relatório Anual*, 259).

29. Ana Claudia Soares, "Operações da Polícia em Favelas têm Mortos, Presos e Armas Apreendias," *O Globo*, November 24, 2010, accessed November 29, 2010, http://oglobo.globo.com.

30. Soares, "Operações da Polícia em Favelas."

31. As reported by the daily newspaper *O Dia*, November 24, 2010.

32. Ronaldo Braga and Tais Mendes, "Novo Balanço da PM: 192 Presos e 25 Mortos até Agora," *O Globo*, November 26, 2010, accessed November 29, 2010, http://oglobo.globo.com.

33. "Rio Police Claim Victory Against Gangs," *Boston.Com*, November 29, 2010, accessed September 16, 2015, http://www.boston.com/news/world/latinamerica/articles/2010/11/29/rio_police_claim_victory_against_gangs/.

34. As reported in the midday televised news broadcast, *Jornal Hoje*, November 25, 2010.

35. RJ TV news, November 25, 2010.

36. RJ TV news, November 25, 2010.

37. "Mesmo com todo esse aparato policial, Ana Paula, você verifica a disposição da resistência. . . . Eles estão ali para atirar nos policiais" (RJ TV news, November 25, 2010).

38. Elsewhere I develop the notion of Brazilian apartheid, not as an attempt to juxtapose a specific South African political formation to another context but rather as a framework that emphasizes continuities in the ways in which urban space, economic

and social opportunities, and indeed life and death become overdetermined by antiblack everyday and institutional arrangements that have little relation—and indeed often negate—the formal juridical architecture supposedly sustaining Brazilian color blindness, democracy, and universal citizenship. See Vargas, "Apartheid Brasileiro."

39. RJ TV news, November 25, 2010.

40. *Jornal Hoje*, November 25, 2010.

41. *Jornal Hoje*, November 25, 2010.

42. Such was the case in the city's second largest favela, Jacarezinho. See Vargas, "The Inner City and the Favela."

43. Yet while initially focused on the supposed drug dealers, these othering narratives are also about the nonothers, "we." Pimentel, as well as the news reporters more generally, mobilize always already known tropes (of danger, vulnerability, crime) that, if they make descriptive claims about Vila Cruzeiro, as important, although not obviously so, they also establish bases on which the nonfavela, nonblack, respectable, stable society stands. As much as Vila Cruzeiro seems dangerous and distant, the imagined, preferred, and graspable "other side of the city" functions as a symbolic reservoir that is constantly replenished. Providing elementary moral, political, and racial guidelines, the nonfavela zones define Rio's social geography according to boundaries of belonging. When Araújo, following Pimentel, assured her viewers that "Zona Sul, Barra da Tijuca, Ipanema, Copacabana, Campo Grande, the Zona Oeste—all remain normal," she drew a map of Rio's metropolitan region that was marked on the one hand by successful "pacification" campaigns against recalcitrant drug factions strongly associated with their territories, and on the other hand, by the remaining ten neighborhoods, in the Penha region, that resisted what seemed like the unavoidable reclaiming of the land by the combined forces of the state.

44. I thank Dylan Rodríguez for suggesting this and other synthetic statements emerging out of his close engagement with the text. On the night of April 4, 2013, a light-skinned twenty-four-year old worker was shot by the occupying police unit in Jacarezinho, a historical black area in Rio. Residents protested against and confronted the police. The images of the events suggest just what I've been trying to point to, namely, the multiracial effects of fundamentally antiblack violence. Regardless of color and race, Jacarezinho felt threatened by and therefore opposed the brutal police. See Favela em Foco, "Assassinato na Favela do Jacarezinho."

45. On black incommensurability, see Wilderson, *Red, White, and Black*. "In the states of the Deep South, 30 percent of all black men are barred from voting because of felony convictions, but all of them are counted to determine Congressional representation and Electoral college votes. If one wants to wonder why the South is so solidly white, Republican and arch-conservative, one need look no further" (Ira Glasser, "Drug Busts=Jim Crow," *Nation*, July 10, 2006, 26).

46. "Texas Juvenile Probation Commission."

47. "Texas Juvenile Probation Commission," 23. Conduct Indicating a Need of Supervision includes public intoxication, truancy, running away from home, inhalant abuse, and expulsion for violating a school disciplinary code.

48. Bonczar, "Prevalence of Imprisonment in the U.S. Population, 1974–2001."

49. Carson and Sabol, "Prisoners in 2011," 8.

50. On this, Rodríguez suggests in a personal communication, "This is where we can see, collapsed, the logic of commodification (time leveraged as 'credit' on one's carceral duration) and the banality of a protogenocidal institutionalization (time as slow-killing, civil death, actually experienced social liquidation/neutralization)."

51. Quoted in Valdez and Thelen, *I Come from a Teardrop*, 41.

52. Patterson, *Slavery and Social Death*; see note 6.

53. On February 18, 2012, in a writing workshop session at the juvenile facility, a young black woman, sixteen years old, broke down in tears of desperation as she read her poem about her child. The child had been taken away from her by a state agency. Upset, the young woman got up from the table around which nine other young women were participating in the workshop and went to her room. "They didn't have to do that," she repeated a few times. In this group two other young women have children, whom they mentioned in the poems they wrote that day. The following week, on February 25, another young mother became upset when one of the staff persons, a white woman, asked to look at the poem she was writing. The white woman told her that the poem was not appropriate: it glorified gangs by mentioning a specific zip code number as well as graphically described drug transactions. The young woman claimed that there was nothing wrong in what she was writing and repeatedly refused to heed the staff's order not to read the poem aloud. Sensing that she had no way to argue her point that the staff was in fact picking on her, the young woman said, "You can call this a code blue or green or whatever." At that point the staff in charge ordered everyone to their room—"Everyone fall out"—and radioed other staff for a "code blue." We the facilitators were also asked to wait in another room. The young woman was restrained and confined to the time-out solitary room. The young mothers in both episodes were black.

54. One such specialist, David Montejano, suggests the following on integration: "This industrial period [following the demise of segregation and the rise of an urban-industrial order], unfolding roughly from World War II to the present, encapsulated the emergence of urban mercantile and consumer interests as a social and political force in Texas. Accompanying this emergence was a weakening of race segregation, reflecting a shift from a dominant class order of growers and farm laborers to one where merchants and urban consumers were prominent. The collapse of Jim Crow was accelerated by the Mexican American political activism of the 1960s and 1970s. Contemporary Mexican-Anglo relations, I suggest, represent a form of political integration, meaning that Texas Mexicans have been accepted as legitimate political actors and accorded a measure of influence" (*Anglos and Mexicans in the Making of Texas*, 9).

55. Hartman, *Scenes of Subjection*, 199.

56. On the United States as an empire-state rather than a nation-state, see Jung, "Constituting the U.S. Empire-State and White Supremacy."

57. Wilderson, *Red, White, and Black*, 23.

FOUR

(Re)producing the Nation: Treaty Rights, Gay Marriage, and the Settler State

LINDSEY SCHNEIDER

As part of its quest to theorize and interrogate racist state violence, critical ethnic studies necessarily requires not just a critique of the nation-state's complicity in historical patterns of genocide, chattel slavery, and conquest but a critical analysis of the ways those processes structure the present and how a presumption of the state's ongoing existence can work to constrain the possibilities for decolonization. The conversation between critical ethnic studies and indigenous studies is an important and productive one because the sustained contestation Native peoples have made against the encroachment of the state on their life and lands can help to break down the false sense of permanency and inevitability that surround the settler nation-state. This chapter contributes to that conversation by exposing the connections between the seemingly disparate issues of treaty fishing rights and tribal authority over gay marriage in order to reveal the depth of the state's investment in structuring the ongoing genocidal terms of existence of Native peoples.

Since shortly after they signed treaties with the United States in the first part of the nineteenth century, tribes in the Northeast have had to wage battles over the legal definition and modern interpretation of fishing rights on ceded lands. The conflict reached a high point in the "fish wars" of the 1960s through the 1980s, although it is by no means over. In more recent years a number of tribal governments have ruled on the issue of gay marriage. The Cherokee, Chickasaw, Muscogee Creek, and the Navajo Nation have passed acts prohibiting gay marriage, while the Colville, Coquille, Suquamish, and a handful of other tribes have voted to allow it. Although treaty fishing rights and gay marriage might not seem to have much in common at first glance, a closer look reveals that the origins of both contemporary issues lie in federal policies, such as the Allotment Act, which worked to assimilate Native people into a capitalist system as nuclear family units, thereby shaping Indian subjectivity. By examining how treaty rights to traditional food sources and tribal authority over gay marriage have both been used as testing grounds in the struggle for Native sovereignty through the operation of state licensure, this chapter seeks to uncover the ways in which they are actually cohering projects, linked by the capitalist heteropatriarchy of the nation-state. The legal and public discourse that has shaped the historical trajectory of fishing and marriage licenses reveals the schism between the representation of "licensed" capitalist (re)production of food and family through heteronuclear units as legitimate, and of unlicensed, "undisciplined" production of food and reproduction of family through traditional kinship structures as perverse.

Allotment: A Shift in Subjectivity

While the U.S. government's never-ending quest for access to Indian land and resources has remained a constant, allotment-era policy represented a major shift in the methodology of its acquisition project. Whereas the reservation system sought to constrain the extent of Indian land claims (under a genocidal presumption of the inevitable extinction of all Indian people), allotment policy worked to fundamentally reshape the nature of landownership for Native people, based on the (still genocidal) assumption of eventual assimilation. The Allotment Act, also known as the Dawes Act, was passed in 1887. It divided collectively held reservation lands into individual units or allotments. While the act certainly furthered the settler colonial project of acquiring Indian land, in that it drastically reduced the area of land seen as Indian property in the eyes of U.S. law, the means by which the act redistributed Indian lands and the language describing its purpose also reveal a number of other important functions with far-reaching consequences for conceptions of space, property, and production.

Heads of households were "awarded" a quarter of a section (160 acres); single adults and orphan children received half of that. The act made it clear that once divided, the land was to be used for agricultural or grazing purposes, and the acreage that wasn't "needed" for individual allotments or that was allotted to an Indian deemed unable to "personally and with benefit to himself occupy or improve his allotment or any part thereof" was to be leased out to non-Indians for farming, mining, or grazing.

By awarding twice as much land to heads of households, and defining households exclusively as heteronuclear families, the act worked not just to dismantle or eradicate traditional kinship structures but to replace them with a particular state-sanctioned model of family through which resource production and distribution would be organized. While the act did not require a state-licensed marriage for the inheritance of land, it did describe domestic cohabitation in explicitly heteronuclear terms.[1] Mark Rifkin has argued that the Allotment Act worked to transform Indian subjectivity and affect by "detribalizing" Native peoples: once land was allotted to individual Indian people, it would cease to be under tribal control.[2]

Rifkin points out that allotment policy was "characterized as an effort to shift the objects of native feeling—from clans and communities to nucleated families, from collective territory to private property, from the tribe to the nation-state—so as to create proper, individuated citizens out of primitive masses." By privatizing Indian land, the policy sought to reduce the power of "collective geographies" that had been maintained through traditional kinship structures.[3] In essence the Allotment Act set the stage for twentieth-century legislation that would further define modes of food and family (re) production deemed appropriate by the settler state.

The act was also implicated in the creation of "proper" citizens through the imposition of settler-style sedentary farming. Many tribes had practiced a variety of forms of agricultural production for thousands of years, based on an intimate understanding of localized ecosystems and natural cycles. I use the term *production* specifically because taking hunting and gathering out of the discursive realm of production devalues and erases the actual work that goes into those types of food production. It makes it seem as if prior to their "salvation" through settler farming methods, Native people just wandered the forest looking for food until they stumbled upon it rather than *working* for food by engaging in a complex set of intentional practices aimed at maximizing and maintaining those food sources over time. Additionally, framing hunting and gathering as historically anterior to the inception of "real" food production subjects Indian people to the same regimes of development discourse that María Josefina Saldaña-Portillo identifies in her work on revolution and development, putting Indian people on a universalized linear trajectory out of the darkness of "ethnic particularity" and into the rational light of the capitalist day.[4] The narrow definition of farming that was attached to civilization at the time, however, was predicated on what Rifkin calls "bourgeois nuclearity," individual land tenure, and European food crops. Rifkin describes "bourgeois nuclearity" as a kind of normative family unit, fundamentally linked to whiteness and the (re)production of the nation-state.[5] This link between the Allotment Act and production is critical to understanding how the act set the stage for modern-day battles over fishing rights and gay marriage.

Landscapes of Production and Consumption

The Allotment Act was not the only legislation of its day that worked to codify a capitalist model of organizing production in space and time. Where the Allotment Act sought to impose particular methods of production on land previously considered unproductive, the act that created Yellowstone Park in 1872 worked to "save" land seen as pristine from the encroachment of capitalist development. The legislation that created the park and others like it was part of an "unprecedented outburst of legislation" that used territorialization to delineate appropriate usage of space.[6] Many political ecologists have argued that the idea of wilderness—the conceptual impetus for the creation of the national park system—is a cultural construction. Both Gina Crandell and Bruce Braun discuss the European development of the ideology that gave rise to the conservation movement, which played a major role in the creation of the early national parks in America.[7] Where Crandell emphasizes the "pictorialization" of nature or the process by which Western assessments of the beauty of nature rely on the degree to which it conforms to pastoral European landscape paintings, Braun focuses on the artistic movement of "sublime nature," or nature "constructed around awe-inspiring vastness and grandeur."[8] According to Roderick Neumann, both pastoral and sublime nature played a role in American wilderness romanticism and the process of territorialization: "'Framing' nature in painting, whether pastoral or sublime, transformed it into picturesque scenery, where the observer is placed safely outside the landscape. Likewise, surveying, bounding, and legally designating a 'wild' space makes it accessible for the pleasure and appreciation of world-weary urbanites." Neumann goes on to argue that the changes to Western social and economic structures brought about by the industrial revolution in the nineteenth century have fundamentally shaped modern ideas about wilderness and nature. Pastoral scenes previously considered "natural" were transformed into spaces of production when agriculture became a part of industrial capitalism. The human labor imposed on the landscape made it unnatural. At the same time, as the working classes migrated to the cities, an idealized version of nature, untouched by human labor and its attendant effects of change and progress, began to be seen as diametrically opposed to crowded urban spaces. Neumann notes, "Parallel to their spatial separation, production and consumption began to occupy distinct temporal spheres of work time (production) and leisure time (consumption). . . . Leisure became a mass phenomenon . . . dependent on the existence of picturesque landscapes."[9] Thus the organization of (legitimate) capitalist production was organized in both space and time by the settler state.

Understanding how nature came to signify a landscape of leisure and agriculture simultaneously shifted from signifying the picturesque and pastoral to a landscape of production is crucial because it allows us to see how discourse around Indian land has created a double shift in ideologies of "appropriate" methods of productivity: as Indians assimilated into the settler capitalist system, Indian food production *should* happen in the developed space of private property and *should not* happen in the undeveloped "pristine" space that had become "nature" or wilderness. The legislative act of parceling out land with the intent of putting it to agricultural use reveals a discursive shift from Indian land as the "untamed frontier" to Indian land as a landscape of production—or, more accurately, what *should* be a landscape of efficient capitalist production. It is significant that any land that allottees were not able to occupy and improve or that was occupied but not needed for agricultural production became available for outside development—landscapes of production necessitated maximum efficiency. Furthermore by territorializing land intended for productivity as separate from wilderness, allotment policy essentially disavowed nonagricultural (noncapitalist) methods of food production such as gathering, hunting, and fishing. The historian Karl Jacoby traces the link between the territorialization of wilderness through the national parks system and the criminalization of acts of production in the nineteenth century: hunting became poaching and gathering became theft because subsistence and nature were fundamentally incompatible in the capitalist imaginary.[10] The idea of Indian fishing as criminal and, I suggest, "perverse" became further entrenched in the late twentieth-century "fish wars" over treaty fishing rights.

These major objectives of the Allotment Act—individual land tenure, heteronuclearity, and settler-style sedentary farming—have become so interwoven and entrenched in the settler colonial subconscious that parsing out their individual implications is nearly impossible. The imposition of capitalist agricultural production did not just dictate the *where* and *what* of Indian food production but also the *how*. In other words, it was imperative that Indians should start growing wheat like white settlers and also that they plant, grow, gather, and eat it *as heteronuclear family units*. It was not only the type of food that was being regulated; it was also how it was produced and by whom. From beginning to end the entire process of food production was to be governed by the organizational system of the heteronuclear family. This shift in social organization has been analyzed in terms of its role in assimilation and cultural genocide, but less has been said about what the imposition of heteronuclear families meant for Native peoples' ceremonial and practical relationships with the land. Prior to the act traditional kinship structures were intimately involved in how, where, and what kind of food was produced.[11] The gendered system of land tenure embedded in allotment policy reorganized labor and also worked to erase the significance of women's work. Shifting from the kinship system to bourgeois nuclearity as an organizing principle initiated the discursive split between the public and private spheres, so that only men's labor in the public sphere was acknowledged as legitimate production. Thus the act fundamentally shaped the relationship between food and family and ultimately changed what each of those concepts meant for Indian people and restructured their societies in the process.

The Nature of the Great Lakes Conflict

In recent years the meanings of *food* and *family* have been revisited in legal battles over treaty fishing rights and tribal ordinances on the legal definition of marriage; each has served as a testing ground of sorts for the limits of Native sovereignty. Fishing rights issues have often been linked to allotment-era policies, but I suggest that the nature of responses to demands for treaty fishing rights by the general public reveals that the conflict actually runs deeper than just the number of fish Indians catch or even the legitimacy of claims on ceded land. Rhetoric used by anti-Indian groups and even public officials in the Great Lakes area in the 1980s demonstrates that the most common objection is not to the validity of the treaties themselves but to the fishing methods the Indians used. The crux of the issue was the act of production in space that had come to represent wilderness and the "perverse" nature of non-heteronuclear, noncapitalist use of resources.

Non-Native settlers were most upset because Indians were going out in groups and spearing large numbers of fish at a time, supposedly violating state fish and game regulations that non-Indians were obligated to follow. In interviews with the *New York Times* in 1988 and 1991, Dean Crist, the leader of Stop Treaty Abuse–Wisconsin, one of the biggest and most violent anti-Indian groups, said, "I can't fish out of season—I can't go out and take thousands of walleye at one time," and "The Indians are raping the resources. . . . It's a blatant attempt at economic terrorism. They're going out of their way to fish off the reservation."[12] In another interview in 1991 he said, "There's no sport to spearfishing. It's like shoveling up potatoes."[13] The town chairman of Boulder Junction, Wisconsin, told the *New York Times*, "We see the walleye as a resource to attract tourists. The Indians see it as a commodity, something to be taken for food," essentially collapsing the distinction between commodity and subsistence production.[14]

Clearly more is at stake than the legal interpretation of treaty rights on ceded land or the economic value of walleye in the Great Lakes. Crist's remarks about the "sportsmanship" of Indian fishing reveal more than just a personal bias: at the heart of this issue is the question of "legitimate" methods of food production and resource distribution. Indians did not appear to pay for their right to fish (unlike non-Indian fishers, who had to purchase a state license), nor did they appear to work for their fish (because spearing fish is supposedly easy); even beyond that, Indians fished in large groups, defying the normative scheme of capitalist production and revealing affiliations and attachments outside settler heteronuclearity. For Crist and others, Indian spearfishing was a problem because it appeared to be unregulated by the state and did not conform to a bourgeois model of food production and passive consumption of nature organized through the heteronuclear family. Crist's comment about Native people "raping the resources" pointedly attacks Indian fishing as a form of undisciplined consumption, without regard for wise use of a resource to sustain it over time. Furthermore the designation of spearfishing (and other forms of Indian food production, for Crist's comment is by no means the only one of its kind) as "rape" demonstrates the discursive representation of noncapitalist Indian production as perverse and obscene—a violation of the sanctity of capitalism. This designation also alludes to the connection between legitimate methods of (food) production and (family) reproduction in the settler state.

The characterization of Indian fishing as "economic terrorism" indicates the shift in ideologies of land tenure. To Crist and others like him, Indian fishing is economic terrorism partly because it is the intrusion of commodity production into space designated as wilderness and partly because it is seen as a threat to the tourism and leisure industries of places like northern Wisconsin. An act that was once indicative of the "primitive" nature of Indian food production is thus seen as quite the opposite. Aside from being racist nonsense, Crist's comment is also problematic in that it belies the *actual terrorism*, especially in the form of sexual violence, visited on Native people by settlers throughout U.S. history. Sadly it is no surprise that threats of sexual violence, such as signs, slogans, and verbal taunts that declared "Save two walleye, spear a pregnant squaw" and "We won't kill your women if you don't kill our walleye," figured prominently in the anti-Indian protests.[15]

The Boulder Junction chairman's comment about seeing the walleye as a food commodity rather than a draw for tourists reveals another dimension of the conflict: the colonial roots of class privilege. Neumann and Jacoby both trace the historical linkages between the emergence of class divisions and "the hunt" as a leisure or sports activity.[16] As land was divided into spaces of supposedly undeveloped wilderness and developed spaces of capitalist production, activities such as hunting and fishing for sport became the purview of the dominant elite as a leisure activity, while subsistence hunting by Indians and working-class settlers became criminalized as poaching. Indian fishing, especially when it is a form of commodity production and not just subsistence, is fundamentally threatening to the settler state because it destabilizes the boundaries between work and play upon which the logic of capitalism rests.

Another often-cited objection to Indian fishing, particularly in the Great Lakes, was the use of "nontraditional" methods to catch fish, such as the use of electric lamps to stun fish, making them easier to spear. Although the 1983 *Voigt* decision in Wisconsin had upheld off-reservation treaty rights and specifically protected the use of modern and traditional methods, many non-Indians objected on the grounds that treaties guaranteed only culturally specific rights—when Indian people assimilated into the dominant culture, they no longer needed treaty rights, and thus treaties should have been abrogated.[17] This type of logic creates a discursive trap for Indian people: either reject economic development as a whole and remain in a "primitive" state of ethnic particularity, or transcend out of it into a fully modern, developed, assimilated, capitalist individual.[18] Scott Richard Lyons problematizes this fundamentalist notion of traditional, arguing instead that the Ojibwe culture of the spearfishers should be understood not as "stable content or rules but rather as pragmatic processes geared towards the production of more life."[19] Lyons's reformulation of culture and tradition disrupts the trajectory of capitalist development and speaks to the ways Indian (re)production—cultural and otherwise—threatens the logic of the settler state.

While tribal laws passed by the Cherokee and Diné that ban gay marriage may seem only distantly, if at all, related to treaty fishing rights, I suggest that articulations of marriage are not just about who can marry whom but also about legitimate and appropriate ways of organizing the distribution of resources and (re)producing the nation. Many arguments have been made both for and against the existence or "traditionality" of third, fourth, or even simply non-Western genders and same-sex partnerships in traditional kinship systems and Indian societal frameworks. Lyons's argument against treating tradition as static or "pure" and the need he has articulated to destabilize and de-essentialize the concept of tradition are relevant here as well. It is easy to misconstrue the tribal gay marriage issue as a contest over who is right about tradition, as if tradition were a literal text that requires interpretation (similar to another heavily contested text that always seems to come up in gay marriage debates). But, as Lyons points out, what we often mean when we discuss tradition is actually *culture*, and when we use tradition as a "rallying cry" for problems like gay marriage legislation (appealing as that might be), we are "asking culture to solve problems that are not always cultural in nature."[20] Thus I am less interested in the question of whether or not gay marriage is traditional and more interested in the link between legislating marriage and circumscribing Indian sovereignty within the confines of a politics of recognition by the settler nation-state. That is to say, I'm concerned with how we deploy tradition to justify political stances on state-licensed marriages and the ways in which doing so subsumes tradition within a consolidation of state power as the primary regulatory authority over food and family for Native people.

Jennifer Denetdale has argued that the "rhetoric of tradition" has specifically been used "in different ways and with the aim of legitimizing and validating contemporary attitudes and practices," such as militarism and heteropatriarchy and specifically the banning of gay marriage within the Diné nation.[21] Calling for a gendered analysis that would expose "how women are simultaneously invoked as cultural symbols . . . and denied access to scarce resources," Denetdale describes the passage of the Diné Marriage Act as a wartime response that reinscribed Western values and thus privileged masculinity.[22] In other words, in outlawing gay marriage, the Diné and other tribal governments did not take an uncomplicated stand for Indian sovereignty but further entrenched themselves in the logic of the settler state. Rifkin has identified how the "bribe of straightness" encourages Native peoples to disidentify with the elements of tradition the settler culture deems "perverse."[23] At the level of legal discourse we can see this happening with tribal nations that have banned gay marriage. Their right to ban gay marriage, whether or not it is traditional, is defended with claims of sovereignty. This type of sovereignty, however, is the type that Taiaiake Alfred has identified as limiting because of its "accommodation of indigenous peoples within a 'legitimate' framework of settler state governance."[24] In other words, Native nations are trading the disavowal of gay marriage for recognition by the nation-state.

The connection between treaty fishing rights and gay marriage can be confusing because in the case of fishing rights the exercise of sovereignty means the *defense* of something traditional, and with gay marriage the exercise of sovereignty results in the *banning* of something traditional. Of course traditionalism can be argued both ways in each instance (spearing fish might be traditional, but using electric headlights to stun them is perhaps less so, or perhaps one could say that Indians have "traditionally" used the best technology available at the time), but the justification for each from the perspective of the tribes involved is always about protecting something that is supposedly traditional.

Ultimately what connects the two issues is that they are about *seeking government approval through state licensure*, whether it is a fishing license to feed one's family or a marriage license to create a family. Both issues position the state as the appropriate body to mete out those rights and therefore to order schemes of production and organize the distribution of resources through the heteronuclear family structure. Thus the sovereignty native peoples seek in each instance is not really self-determination or autonomy; it is approval by the state through a politics of recognition. Glen Coulthard explains, "The politics of recognition in its contemporary form promises to reproduce the very configurations of colonial power that Indigenous peoples' demand for recognition [has] historically sought to transcend."[25] Although he is referring specifically to a Canadian context, his insights are useful here. Treaty fishing rights seek to transcend a colonially imposed scarcity of resources and property law configuration, but they do so through the settler state's power. Under a politics of recognition, a successful battle for treaty rights does not mean Indian people have full authority over the lakes and rivers out of which they have been fishing for millennia; it means the state approves of a certain percentage of the yearly catch being delegated to Indian fishers.[26] Likewise, if the tribal laws prohibiting gay marriage stand, it doesn't mean Native people are free to determine for themselves what constitutes a family, how kinship should be structured, or how procreation should be organized. What it means is that those tribal governments have implemented and enforced a narrow definition of what is fundamentally a settler institution, and the nation-state has sanctioned their right to do so. In both cases the definition of sovereignty is limited to what can exist within the reach of the state and looks to state-sanctioned rights as the ultimate goal and the state as the ultimate source of validation.[27]

Defined this way sovereignty actually legitimizes the settler nation-state and reifies the state's role as the appropriate distributor of resources. With marriage and fishing rights this happens on a direct level, as the state approves and issues licenses, and on an indirect level, because of the ways resource distribution is and has been organized through the heteronuclear family, such as taxes, commodity food distribution, and land allotments. The redistribution of resources through the bourgeois family serves to entrench and validate the racialized and gendered colonial logic of capitalist production, thereby legitimizing the existence and power of the settler state.

As Alfred has noted, this state-sanctioned version of sovereignty limits our sense of what options are open to us. Instead of looking for new and alternative means of resource distribution through Lyons's "production of more life" or Coulthard's "on the ground practices of freedom," the struggle for licensed treaty rights and marriage simply seek to either acquire more resources from the state in the public sphere or consolidate and reinforce the state's version of how resources should be distributed in the private sphere.[28]

This line of argument has serious implications in terms of how sovereignty is defined as well as how we organize around it. Gay marriage and treaty rights have both been sites of coalition between Indian and non-Indian activists, when settlers themselves realize that their heteropatriarchal capitalist system is not working for them. Unfortunately the potential for work in coalition tends to go hand in hand with the potential for co-optation. We can see how this has played out in terms of the environmental movement: white people working with Indian people on fishing rights see treaty rights not as a step toward political autonomy for Indian people but as a tool for protecting the environment. Native identities are romanticized and idealized as being part of, or at least in harmony with, nature rather than being engaged in long-term projects of *production* of food and other commodities by maintaining and extracting resources. This essentialized version of Indian identity then becomes available for appropriation by non-Indians who imagine themselves as having some sort of intuitive or primordial connection to nature.

Over the past several decades this has happened in the environmental movement with the "ecological Indian" and Sierra Club types who use this idea to promote their campaigns without actually engaging with Indian people on real terms. There is a very real danger that the "two-spirit Indian" in queer communities will go the way of the "ecological Indian" in the environmental movement.[29] When they are used as a cultural trope by non-Native settlers to deal with problems (heteropatriarchy and environmental destruction) caused by their own settler culture, the ecological Indian and the two-spirit Indian erase the reality of actual Indian people, two-spirited and otherwise. The ways their lives are affected by environmental racism and the infiltration of heteropatriarchy into tribal governments are obscured. Scott Lauria Morgensen notes that this process of identification with Indian histories by non-Indian queers can elide the connections that non-Indian queers have to settler colonialism and the "terrors of sexual colonization visited on Indian peoples." He argues, "At its extreme, non-Native queer longing for Native histories of sexuality or gender can seem to invite alliance when it performs a racial or national 'passing' that appropriates Native culture in order to indigenize non-Native queers."[30] I argue that non-Indian sport fishers see themselves as the rightful heirs to former Indian territories now designated as wilderness, and the violent backlash to treaty fishing rights is at least in part a reaction to the disruption of that settler imaginary.

Decolonizing Sovereignty

In the end framing state-sanctioned rights as the ultimate goal of sovereignty movements—be they tribal members' right to fish off the reservation or the tribal government's right to regulate the institution of marriage—reinforces the legitimacy of the settler state. Furthermore allowing treaty rights and two-spirit justice to exist as separate issues elides the state's role in imposing settler notions such as marriage and fishing licenses while leaving the underlying authority of the nation-state intact. Linking these struggles in terms of their shared basis in federal Indian policy creates a space to rethink the meaning of sovereignty. A state that imposes settler heteronuclearity on Native peoples as a primary method of resource distribution is not a state we want setting the terms of what sovereignty can mean for us. We have to conceive of sovereignty in terms of decolonization and "self-recognition" rather than a politics of recognition by the nation-state.[31]

Despite its inception in activist movements that sought to transform educational institutions, ethnic studies has sometimes failed to fully grasp the extent to which settler colonialism is a condition of possibility for those institutions to exist in the first place. A critical engagement with (rather than an umbrella-like inclusion of) indigenous studies is necessary for both fields to develop a nuanced analysis of the nation-state's role in enforcing hegemonic norms that does not presume the state's existence. Theorizing and actively working toward indigenous sovereignty provides the space to move beyond the false dualism of reformist work within the state's parameters and a rejection of the state's authority that ignores the extent of the state's power to infiltrate everyday life. Instead it can help us toward the kind of decolonial future where dismantling the state and its genocidal raison d'être go hand in hand.

NOTES

1. An Act to Provide for the Allotment of Lands in Severalty to Indians on the Various Reservations (General Allotment Act or Dawes Act), 1887, sec. 388–91.

2. Rifkin, *When Did Indians Become Straight?*, 152, 181–82.

3. Rifkin, *When Did Indians Become Straight?*, 181–82.

4. Saldaña-Portillo, *The Revolutionary Imagination in the Americas*, 6, 28, 31.

5. Rifkin, *When Did Indians Become Straight?*, 33.

6. Jacoby, *Crimes against Nature*, 1.

7. Crandell, *Nature Pictorialized*; Braun, *The Intemperate Rainforest.*

8. Neumann, *Imposing Wilderness*, 16.

9. Neumann, *Imposing Wilderness*, 15–17, 21–22.

10. Jacoby, *Crimes against Nature.*

11. Berman, *Circle of Goods*, 35.

12. Dirk Johnson, "Indian Fishing Dispute Upsets North Woods' Quiet," *New York Times*, April 24, 1988, accessed November 17, 2010, http://www.nytimes.com/1988/04/24/us/indian-fishing-dispute-upsets-north-woods-quiet.html?scp=23&sq=walleye+indian&st=nyt; William E. Schmidt, "Wisconsin Spring: New Fishing Season, Old Strife," *New York Times*, May 21, 1991, accessed November 17, 2010, http://www.nytimes.com/1990/04/08/us/wisconsin-spring-new-fishing-season-old-strife.html?src=pm.

13. Don Terry, "Indian Treaty Accord in Wisconsin," *New York Times*, May 21, 1991, accessed November 17, 2010, http://www.nytimes.com/1991/05/21/us/indian-treaty-accord-in-wisconsin.html?pagewanted=2&src=pm.

14. Schmidt, "Wisconsin Spring."

15. Nesper, *The Walleye War*, 215; O'Brien, *Exxon and the Crandon Mine Controversy*, 74; Treuer, *Ojibwe in Minnesota*, 50.

16. Jacoby, *Crimes against Nature*, 58–60; Neumann, *Imposing Wilderness*, 34–37.

17. Whaley and Bresette, *Walleye Warriors*, 13–33.

18. Saldaña-Portillo, *The Revolutionary Imagination in the Americas*, 7, 65–66; Lyons, *x-Marks*, 9.

19. Lyons, *x-Marks*, 93.

20. Lyons, *x-Marks*, 58.

21. Denetdale, "Securing Navajo National Boundaries," 144.

22. Denetdale, "Securing Navajo National Boundaries," 136, 142.

23. Rifkin, *When Did Indians Become Straight?*, 149.

24. Alfred, "Sovereignty," 34–35.

25. Coulthard, "Subjects of Empire," 439.

26. Even if, by some miracle, Indians were given full control over waterways, the logic of that control would still rest on a Western theory of property rights and the settler logic of territorialization—it would not mean that all the inhabitants of the land were living in a right relationship to it or to the people who were given the original instruction for that land.

27. This analysis could be expanded with the addition of Jeff Corntassel's work on the "federal era" of U.S. policy toward Indians, *Forced Federalism* (Norman: University of Oklahoma Press, 2008).

28. Lyons, *x-Marks*, 93; Coulthard, "Subjects of Empire," 456.

29. Braun describes this phenomenon as it occurred in British Columbia in the 1990s in great detail in *The Intemperate Rainforest*.

30. Morgensen, "Settler Homonationalism," 121–22.

31. Coulthard, "Subjects of Empire," 456.

FIVE

Hateful Travels: Queering Ethnic Studies in a Context of Criminalization, Pathologization, and Globalization

JIN HARITAWORN

In her lecture "Death and Rebirth of a Movement: Queering Critical Ethnic Studies," Cathy Cohen tentatively opens up the possibility that from the ashes of the white conservative LGBT movement another queer politics and theory might arise. This movement would be accountable to young people of color who, in a neoliberal context of neglect, militarization, and institutional and interpersonal violence, are prepared for premature death,[1] regardless of their sexual and gender identity. In calling for such a "politics that springs from the lives of folks of color," Cohen once again challenges both the identitarian assumptions of an institutionalized and professionalized movement that requires lives worthy of survival to look queer, and the postidentity claims of a queer canon whose default stance toward racialized subjects is one of indifference or competition.[2]

Given this lack of accountability, it may be unsurprising that the setting for Cohen's intervention is a critical ethnic studies conference rather than a queer or gender studies setting. This reminds me of the stakes involved in doing radical queer of color scholarship in variously disciplined spaces.[3] While gender studies is expanding in ways that often repeat rather than interrupt the harnessing of dominant women's and LGBT movements to the projects of nation and empire, ethnic studies is facing a brutal backlash, despite some of its gatekeepers' attempts to perform themselves as respectable multicultural citizens. As critical ethnic studies is reinvented as an insurgent knowledge formation that resists rather than diversifies capitalism, colonialism, and imperial war, it enters into possibility as a tentative site for antiracist queer and trans scholarship.[4]

One of the dominant political methods that Cohen singles out, besides marriage and gays in the military, is hate crime activism. She thus echoes Yasmin Nair's humorous characterization of gay equality campaigns as the "usual Holy Trinity of Hate Crimes Legislation, Marriage, and Don't Ask Don't Tell."[5] Both join a steadily swelling chorus of voices that critique the hate crime paradigm, now one of the top issues for LGBT movements globally, for strengthening a criminal "justice" system that disproportionately targets people who are poor, black, or unable or unwilling to conform to norms and standards around gender, sexuality, health, and consumption. These critical voices have so far been limited to the United States, currently the leading exporter of punitive methods and technologies.[6] The experience there suggests that those categorized as needing protection from violence often end up criminalized themselves for supposed hate crimes against whites, heterosexuals, and other structurally more powerful people.[7] As trans and queer of color organizations like the Audre Lorde Project, FIERCE, Gender Just, and the Sylvia Rivera Law Project have shown, this is compounded for sexually and gender-nonconforming people who are poor and of color.[8] For many this was amply demonstrated by the fate of CeCe McDonald, an African American transgender woman who was violently attacked and then sentenced to prison after her attacker died in the ensuing fight. Similar criminal *in*justice was done to the New Jersey 7, a group of black lesbians and gender non-conforming people who likewise defended themselves and were subsequently, all but one, sentenced to prison.[9]

Nevertheless what I call the hate/crime paradigm—the "sticking," in Sara Ahmed's terms, of criminality and pathology to bodies and populations that are always already seen as hateful, where *hate* functions as a racialized psy discourse—must be further analyzed. The German context, where terms like *Hasskriminalität* (hate crime) and *Hassgewalt* (hate violence) arrived very recently and are far from naturalized, may be instructive here. Until the late 2000s violent homophobia was not primarily understood as the deed of hateful individuals or as necessarily a cause for incarceration. Foregrounding a transnational race, gender, and disability studies lens and placing it in critical dialogue with affect studies and scholarship on biopolitics and necropolitics, I argue that the hate/crime paradigm travels in a context where capital, identity molds, and carceral and biomedical methods cross borders instantly, while critiques and alternatives often do not.

This chapter examines how the hateful homophobe, who, in a northwestern European context of war on terror and crime is immediately recognized as Muslim, arrived in close proximity with another figure of hate, the *Intensivtäter*—the multiple, chronic, or "intensive" offender—that is in turn forged in close hybridity with, and in a longer *duree* of, antiblack methodologies that target poor, racialized communities in the United States and elsewhere. In the late 1990s, *he*[10] became the latest folk devil whose basic incapacity for empathy and integration (often figured as mental and physical deficiency) has produced consent not only for faster, harsher prison sentences for young people but also for the cultural exiling of barely nationalized populations from the realm of human intelligibility and entitlement.

By starting with the proximities and overlaps between sexual and criminal justice, carceral and biomedical discourses on hate, violence, and crime, and between racialized, perverse, and mad figurations, we may approach the ascendancy of queer, multicultural, and disabled subjects in a different way, one that abolishes rather than diversifies systems of murderous inclusion and frees us to perceive, formulate, and strengthen radical alternatives.

Hate as a Psy Discourse

Many are now aware that the label *criminal*, including in its *hateful* variation, is more likely to stick to racially and sexually oppressed people than to racists, homophobes, and transphobes. Few, on the other hand, have asked how the label *hate* may function in a similar way. This may be due to the sense that "people have fought for this," as a senior colleague from the United States stated to a group of queers of color and allies in Berlin, who asked what the recent arrival of the "homophobic hate crime" discourse in Berlin might mean for racialized people. Even those who reject hate crime as a model of organizing often partly remain within its logics. Thus while the *crime* part of *hate crime* is sometimes debunked, its *hate* counterpart is rarely interrogated. While learning immensely from the compelling antiviolence methodologies formulated in radical women of color and queer and trans of color activisms in North America, including community accountability, prison abolition, and transformative justice, I am struck by how *hate* (now as *hate violence* rather than *hate crime*) has survived as a rationale for much of this work.

My intention is not to dismiss these important responses that have taught me so much about community building against multiple forms of violence, including those carried out by the state as the most powerful bully of poor, racialized, and gender-nonconforming people. Rather I wish to propose that we further expand our abolitionist imagination by asking how hate is ascribed in tandem with not only crime but also pathology in ways that defend and expand the prison as well as psychiatry and other institutions of care and reform. In particular I argue that hate always already emanates from racialized bodies and minds in ways that call for their assimilation and segregation in the form of treatment, education, policing, confinement, and deportation.

In taking this further step and interrogating hate alongside crime and pathology as twin pedagogies that educate us about the need for murderous systems of inclusion, we may draw on affect studies as a useful methodology to examine how meaning is ascribed to racialized bodies and populations. Particularly helpful to me is Ahmed's argument that affect sticks to bodies differentially, producing affect aliens such as the "melancholic migrant," who, in his or her backward orientation toward lost belongings and bad experiences, stands in the way of multicultural happiness.[11] In considering the hateful Other as an affect alien who threatens a nostalgic vision of a violence-free community, I am further struck by the call for action that this figure provokes from its onlookers. It appeals to authoritative intervention and thus demands a distinctly institutional critique. In particular it is noteworthy that figures like the melancholic migrant, the black rioter, and the hateful homophobe invoke psychiatric authority—the diagnosing, profiling, and treatment of "depressed," "schizophrenic," or otherwise "maladjusted" populations unable to control their impulses or function in a civilized society. Following insights by antiracist disability and mad studies scholars, we can trace how the trope of the mental and physical inferiority of racialized and colonized populations has informed successive projects of colonialism, slavery and genocide and continues to underwrite carceral, biomedical, military, border and other regimes of control and reform.[12]

In paying closer attention to the sites where bodies are sorted into populations according to evaluations of their "stock," I am inspired by current engagements in critical race and ethnic studies, which interrogate how subjects and populations are carved out for life and death, often along older lines of degeneracy that must be understood within ongoing histories of racism, eugenics, colonialism, and genocide, and the spatial practices of segregation, confinement, and deportation that have arisen from them. Some of these engage with biopolitics and necropolitics in asking how racialized bodies become recognizable as those against whom, in Foucault's words, "society must be defended."[13]

If this is more apparent with regard to death-making processes, it has equal purchase on the question of how subjects become viable for life, public visibility, and citizenship. In our introduction to *Queer Necropolitics*, Adi Kuntsman, Silvia Posocco, and I note that the vitalization of (white) queer subjects often stays close to the sites where queer and trans people were (and often continue to be, post-homophobic and -transphobic claims to the contrary) sentenced to social or actual death. Gay assimilation requires an ascent from madness and criminality that is best performed as expertise over those who properly belong with the segregated. What might an abolitionist project look like that attends to caring alongside more obviously punishing institutions and examines processes of exclusion alongside processes of "murderous inclusion"?

Narratives of hate are instructive here. In the crime reports, activist writings, and media texts on violent crime and homophobic hate crime that I review here, the two regularly appear alongside each other as related labels invoked to profile working-class, racialized youth. They work at each other's service, making those marked as hateful—who fail at emotional management—appear destined to become violent, criminal, and in need of punishment or reform. The hateful personality resembles the "dangerous individual" described by Foucault. In his reflection on the growing presence of psychiatric experts in court, Foucault noted a shift from the crime to the criminal, where what is punished is no longer something that has already happened but something that might happen in the future, a potential for harm that can be forecast by dissecting its carrier's inner workings. As Nikolas Rose and Dorothy Roberts have each observed, this is currently rehearsed with the rise of biopsychiatry and biocriminology and the renewed attempt to identify future criminals by their genes or forebrains.[14] But while Roberts, from her black feminist perspective, highlights the survival of scientific racism in discourses on crime in experiments on black inner-city schoolchildren in the United States, Rose, commenting on the same material but from a purely Foucauldian perspective that misses race, comes to a different, somewhat optimistic conclusion. Unlike the older criminological figure of the born criminal, he argues, the new scholarship, about whose uses and abuses he remains partly open, is distinctly posteugenics in that it only assumes a *potential* for violence which must first be triggered.[15]

I propose that this binary view of biology versus social construction, natural versus social science, nature versus nurture misses the point of how publics are seduced into viewing some as less than human and come to consent to their banishment from this category and its benefits. In fact the personality profiles that I review next are all designed to appear postrace and posteugenics and distance themselves from purely biological explanations. In media case studies as in statistical reports, perpetrators are described as young men of color who have suffered family violence, school exclusion, failed social mobility, and discrimination. Moreover marking the end of eugenics as the beginning of social constructionism becomes problematic when we revisit accounts by early twentieth-century eugenicists that already fused social and biological explanations and were less purely biologistic than we imagine today.[16] A more useful approach might therefore be to examine how seemingly opposite frameworks of nature versus nurture, punishment versus care (and we might add gays versus Muslims) combine to script racialized bodies as degenerate in ways that usher into consent highly diverse constituencies, including those that position themselves on the right side of power. Narratives of hate, which, as I will illustrate, is often described as an emotion that is both caused by harm and harm*ful*, are productive in this. Hate is similar to anger, whose oppressive ascriptions have been more widely explored and contested, including in antiracist and feminist discussions of oppression and resistance to pathologization.[17] Both are often described as responses to bad experiences and belittled as excessive, irrational, and misplaced. Yet, unlike hate, anger has also been described as a righteous reaction against oppression, as in this frequently cited statement from Malcolm X: "Usually when people are sad, they don't do anything. They just cry over their condition. But when they get angry, they bring about a change."[18] A prime gender studies example is the figure of the angry black feminist, whose anger is celebrated and glorified even as those who are interpellated this way are also regularly demonized and pathologized. Hate, in contrast, lacks positive connotations and reclamations. Though constantly explained in proliferating etiologies, it characterizes the humanly inexplicable, thereby rendering its subject seemingly irredeemable.

I will explore how case studies of violent perpetrators nevertheless often take the generic form of empathy narratives, honing in on evidence of child abuse, poverty, discrimination, and other "bad experiences" that at first sight look like understandable reasons to feel bad. Nevertheless if the causes of hate are understandable, the hateful reaction and subsequent action are not, rendering them immediately atrocious. This serves to rewrite the old chain of race, class, and crime as one of present or absent empathy with suffering. To hate is to reveal one's impulsiveness and irrationality as well as one's failure to perform oneself as a civilized subject who has the capacity to master destructive impulses, empathize with others' pain, and prove one's potential for change.

In the personality profiles that follow, the hateful perpetrator appears as the constitutive outside to the neoliberal citizen, who manages and is able to talk about hir feelings and expresses and takes responsibility for hirself, thus constantly striving toward emotional intelligence, communication, and self-actualization.[19] If this is a strategy of classification through which, as Beverley Skeggs argues, the white middle class distinguishes itself from the reformable white working class, the racialized perpetrator remains uncultivable.[20] Hir hate is a failure to love and forgive, to perform hirself according to the Christian values of an avowedly secular community and as a peaceful subject in times of war. Indeed in the personality profiles and unassailable statistical regression analyses that I examine, one's propensity to crime rises with one's degree of religiosity for Muslims but not for Christians, as the love of one's neighbor renders the latter more peaceful and tolerant.

Is it a coincidence that hate has become a Muslim property, that it is gaining currency as the bulk of the racialized in northwestern Europe are recast as Muslim, as one globally interchangeable population?[21] What bodies appear as hateful in different times and places? In the German texts that I examine, English-speaking studies of crime that have been formulated in the antiblack context of the United States are effortlessly assimilated into an anti-Muslim framework that is itself highly transnational.[22] How do the hateful criminal and the hateful homophobe each bring home globalized specters of Muslim terror and Muslim rage, re-posing the seemingly unanswerable question "Why do they hate us so much?" for diverse constituencies and at various scales? As I shall explore, the figure of the hateful Other has also been key to the dual emergence of a respectable queer subject who is innocent and worthy of inclusion and recognition and of a gay-friendly community that is willing to protect it. It is to this "drama of queer lovers and hateful Others" that I turn next.[23]

Queer Lovers and Hateful Others

In 2012 and 2013, I interviewed fifteen trans and queer people of color at various Berlin kitchen tables about the state of queer politics in the city.[24] The following statement is by Charlie Abdullah Haddad, a trans of color activist living in Berlin:

> I was at a friend's living room, all white people, there was a guy I had known for a while, he had just finished taking hormones: he is a cismale now who was trans in the past. He had some spare medication at home which he didn't need any more. I said I'm having trouble finding a doctor who would give me health insurance. I'll buy them off you. And very kindly he gave them to me for free later on. The other white people in the room asked him to share some of his experiences as a white trans person in Berlin, he was living in Kreuzberg. So within maybe 4, 5 minutes he started talking about how the Turks in Kreuzberg and Neukölln were looking at him when he was walking on the street, make derogatory comments and so on. And I said "Turks, what do you mean by Turks?" And then he said "Oh yeah, and also the Arabs." I went silent. There were three other people in the room. . . . They all looked at me because they knew that what he said was disgusting, and they knew that I would have a problem with him. And I mean I'm not stupid, I saw their eyes, and they were saying "Let it go," that his pain is more valuable, needs to be more visible than mine. So I let it go, but it built. So a week later I said to the other three, "Do you know how fucked up that was? When he was narrating that transphobic experience in the street, how does that construct my own experience as a trans Arab? It means I'm transphobic. And if you're giving out medals, he has a right to talk about transphobic experiences in the street, then honey give me some medal." . . . So they were talking about white injury at the expense of perpetrating another injury in the same room, and rendering that completely unspeakable.

Charlie Haddad's words help me make sense of the processes that have enabled some queer narratives to find a public while others get trapped in queer living rooms (or under queer tongues). The experiences that are described here do not give us unmediated access to violence against trans people, queers of color or other newly desirable subject positions that have become recognizable under conditions of gay imperialism and homonationalism. Rather Charlie's retelling of different scenes of violence—the street, the queer living room—invites us to question the very economies and relations of production, circulation, and exchange through which truths about violence are manufactured and attachments to scenes and states of injury occur. This retelling enables us to understand violence narratives as generating and distributing biovalue, by which I mean the embodied ability of individuals to perform themselves as valuable and "properly alive."[25] Formerly degenerate subjects find speakability, visibility, publicity, and vitality in front of publics and counterpublics that are able to come together for the first time on a racialized terrain that is populated by violent, criminal, and *criminally homophobic* populations, whose degenerate properties are much harder to contest. "Gay-friendly Berlin" takes shape in affective landscapes and biopolitical narratives of "Kreuzberg and Neukölln" as the "dangerous" inner city that belongs to "Turks . . . Oh yeah, and also Arabs." Yet the circulation of queer bodies and intimacies is uneven. While some bodies become visible in this criminal setting, others disappear from view. And while some stories roll off the tongue easily, others are best let go. The ones that body forth are current and become currency.[26] They are rewarded, gain "medals," as Charlie puts it. They generate biovalue by converting the suffering queer body into a resource whose energies and injuries can be extracted to accumulate capital for others, who in the process become more firmly rooted in the realm of the properly alive.

Nevertheless, if the promise of inclusion is made to many, the returns from these "intimate investments," as Anna Agathangelou, Morgan Bassichis, and Tamara Spira put it, are not the same from all queer starting points. Charlie's statement brings to the fore how the transgender body, whose ascendancy from the prison and the asylum is painfully recent and incomplete, becomes interesting within a changing landscape that is shaped by gentrification, the war on terror, and moral panic over crime and integration. Long excessive to "LGB-fake-T" politics, its spectacular proximity to death (as the always already injured or dying target of hate) makes it the ideal victim subject.[27] This complicates earlier theorizations of wounded attachments and traumatized citizenship. Wendy Brown's argument that claims to recognition are often made in the cadence of the wound is helpful, especially in understanding the global purchase of hate crime activism as the latest single issue politic.[28] Yet wounded performances do different work for different bodies. In the place of a universally injured subject, it may be more helpful to examine the conditions under which some injuries become spectacular while others appear self-inflicted or insignificant. This is well illustrated by the changing landscape of transgender recognition, which, as Charlie demonstrates, does not open equally to all trans people. While it invites some as experts, consultants, and coalition partners, often those who happen to be less vulnerable to violence as a result of their race and class privileges and professional qualifications, those trans people who are most vulnerable to violence become if anything less capable of telling stories that reach the status of the political and are capacitated mainly in their (social or actual) deaths. According to Charlie, a trans Arab who refuses to authenticate a racist etiology of violence has no value in this exchange system. In the absence of a queer community that is willing to consider trans (especially trans feminine) of color lives as vulnerable and trans women of color as coalition partners, to participate in violence talk in the queer living room would only mean risking losing fragile ground. In the space that is available to Charlie, violence and antiviolence talk follow a racialized binary of perpetrators (non-trans people of color) versus victims (white trans people). In the logic of this binary to be a trans Arab means to be transphobic.[29] Indeed, as mentioned earlier, the case of the United States, where hate crime laws already exist, shows that gender-nonconforming people of color who experience violence rarely receive protection from the criminal justice system but are more likely to be criminalized themselves.[30] The policing of nonsingular tellings of violence extends to the queer living room. Sharing one's experiences not only fails to elicit empathy but makes one sound mean, incoherent, and undeserving of community. For queer and trans people of color, antiracist antiviolence talk can land us in a corner where we are forced to watch the space around us contract at multiple scales: from the gender-nonconforming body to the queer living room to the gentrifying neighborhood. In this economy of violence and antiviolence, value and pathology are not distributed randomly but follow the powerful lines where populations are carved out, resources (from hormones to housing) distributed, and chances of life and death extended or withheld.[31]

Let us take a closer look at the queer intimacies that have appeared as worthy of protection in this economy. In German publics, queer kisses have mushroomed. One example is the photographed kiss between two white men that adorned an article in a big daily newspaper on a psychological study commissioned by the country's biggest gay organization. The study compared "migrant" schoolchildren's attitudes to homosexuals to the attitudes of their "German" counterparts, thus intimately marking the former as an alien, unhyphenatable population.[32] Other examples are the state-sponsored kissing posters and annual kiss-ins that were repeatedly deployed in Berlin's "problem areas," teaching their inhabitants (in German, Turkish, and Arabic) that "love deserves respect!"[33] The reform of the uneducable Other finds its material reflection in the regeneration of the inner city. With the fall of the Wall the former *Ausländerghetto* moved to the heart of the city, beginning its rebirth as the "multicultural inner city" where the rich and upwardly mobile now like to live, eat, and work. As Charlie's account documents, queers with race and class privileges have been among the gentrifiers and have left their marks on these areas by declaring them dangerous. In what I call the drama of queer lovers and hateful Others, some become a lovely sight and emerge as

17. Mai 2010, 21:16 Uhr   Migrantenkinder gegen Schwule

Homophobes Berlin

Sie finden es "anstößig", wenn sich Männer auf der Straße küssen. In Berlin stößt Homosexualität vor allem bei Migrantenkindern auf starke Ablehnung, das hat eine Studie nun ans Licht gebracht.

Von Philip Grassmann

Eigentlich könnte man meinen, dass in einer Stadt, in der ein schwuler Politiker bereits zwei Mal zum Regierenden Bürgermeister gewählt worden ist, eine gewisse Toleranz gegenüber Homosexuellen herrschen sollte. Vor allem, wenn man bedenkt, dass Klaus Wowereit in Umfragen bei den Sympathiewerten seit Monaten unangefochten an der Spitze liegt, während der heterosexuelle CDU-Oppositionsführer Friedbert Pflüger regelmäßig ganz hinten landet.

Für viele Migrantenkinder anstößig: Küssendes Schwulenpärchen. (Foto: Foto: dpa)

FIGURE 5.1. Screenshot of an article entitled "Migrant Kids against Gays: Homophobic Berlin."

innocent and worthy of protection and survival, while others are reinscribed as degenerate pathogens that must be displaced from the areas to which they were once confined so that these may "recover."[34]

The queer lover, who has barely escaped from the closet, the prison, and the asylum, moves into the daylight through inscription into neoliberal, national, and *transnational* values, including whiteness and gender conformity; privacy, respectability, and beauty; freedom and free choice; integration, security and protection; and diversity and vitality. Lisa Duggan's formulation of homonormativity as a "new neoliberal sexual politics . . . that does not contest dominant heteronormative assumptions and institutions but upholds and sustains them while promising the possibility of a demobilized gay constituency and privatized gay culture anchored in" domesticity, consumption, and privacy is instructive here.[35] If the innocence and worthiness of the queer lover in these images is encoded in the terms of neoliberalism—through hir recognizability as "like us" (mediated through hir whiteness, masculinity, and gender conformity and in the aesthetics of global consumer culture)—hir sudden ascent into loveliness nevertheless occurs in landscapes that are shaped by ongoing histories of racism that predate neoliberalism and are irreducible to it.

This becomes clearer when we attend to the hateful Other as the figure without whom, I argue, this ascendancy would not be possible. We have at our disposal a range of analytics to make sense of the queer lover and hir new desirability to the newly gay-friendly publics that rally around hir. Besides homonormativity, affect studies—in particular critiques of romantic love—help us understand why institutions like marriage that were historically used to demonize queers not only become objects of desire for queers but enable homonormatively figured queers to become desirable as well.[36] Yet unlike love, hate has so far been insulated from critique. How might we denaturalize its hold on anti-oppressive imaginations?

A transnational analysis is insightful here. In contrast to the United States, where the hate crime discourse is associated with the legacy of the civil rights movement, its arrival in Germany is more recent and reflective of the asymmetric travel of political methodologies in globalizing social movements. Until the late 2000s terms like *Hasskriminalität* (hate crime) and *Hassgewalt* (hate violence) were not widely used or even intelligible in antiviolence activism in Germany. Attempts by antiracist activists to scandalize the pogrom-like outbreak that accompanied the integration of the reunified Germany as *hate crimes* did not stick. This contrasts with the LGBT hate crime discourse that hit the headlines in 2008, arriving on fertile ground plowed in over a decade of moral panicking over "Muslim homophobia." I have described the landmarks of this moral panic elsewhere, but I will briefly repeat some of them now.[37] Its earliest incarnations can be found in press releases of the biggest gay organizations in Berlin in the late 1990s, which presented the phantom of migrant homophobia to an initially insubstantial public.[38] By the mid-2000s this public had expanded as these organizations managed to strategically chain the newly born "homophobic migrant" to bigger figures of "honor killers," "terrorists," and "integration refusers." The homophobic migrant appeared prominently on the horizon of the German nation with the debate around the "Muslim Test," the proposed citizenship exam that claimed to test the democratic, women- and gay-friendly propensities of a clearly denominated population against a brand-new set of what, following Hobsbawm, I suggest to be *invented* traditions.[39] By 2008 the Simon study of Berlin schoolchildren, commissioned by Germany's biggest gay organization and carried out by a white gay psychologist at Kiel University, "scientifically" proved what by then everyone knew: that "the migrants" are more homophobic than "the Germans," and that the twain shall never meet.[40] Designed in what I call the "plastic activism" of the homo-assimilationist NGOs—something that claims to be a mass movement but is really the work of a handful of paid functionaries and their graphic designer—the moral panic over hateful homophobic migrants did not stop there. It found its first bodies in 2008 in the radical queer alternative scene, when a group of drag kings, trans people, and queer women were beaten up during the internationally publicized Drag Festival.[41] The ensuing debate, which immediately (and many argue falsely) attributed the incident to "homophobic Turks," first let the word *Hasskriminalität* roll off German tongues. What made the term *hate crime* assimilable in the late 2000s as opposed to the early 1990s was not a sudden outbreak of homophobia or even transphobia that dwarfed the arson attacks on asylum-seeker homes and migrant-owned shops in the newly unified Federal Republic. On the contrary, the small handful of cases (that once the new discourse was consolidated largely disappeared from public debate) were highly contested.[42] I argue that the criminally hateful homophobe became intelligible through *his* family resemblance to other criminal figures. If the queer lover has become recognizable through hir familiality with national or transnational neoliberal ideals of respectability and privacy, the hateful Other entered into the German landscape by joining a rich archive peopled by dysfunctional families from deficient communities in the degenerate "ghetto."

The Hateful Homophobe and the Intensive Offender

I sometimes show my students two YouTube videos next to each other in the same projection.[43] One is from the year 2007 and is a TV news clip based on closed-circuit camera shots. It is on the Serkan A. and Spyridon L. case, which, true to its status as a case, served to familiarize German TV audiences with a new figure of moral panic: the *Intensivtäter* (intensive or repeat offender), a thus far administrative category whose punitive application and criminalizing impact on young people of color has been compared to the "three strikes" policy in the United States.[44] As Lauren Berlant notes in "On the Case," the case is pedagogical and exemplary in that it offers "an account of the event and of the world" and is the primary communicative action through which biopower, in the name of experts, sorts individuals into populations.[45] The case is also crucial to moral panics over crime, which, according to Chinyere Oparah, need offending bodies primarily in order to demonstrate the need for tough action regardless of actual crime numbers.[46] This is also the case with Serkan A. and Spyridon L., who beat up an old white man on the Munich subway just before Christmas. The media describe the victim as a frail pensioner who told the judge, 'I have been a teacher my whole life and then . . ."[47] For months the act was replayed on TV with an intensity and brutality that had its own performative force.[48] It was central in manufacturing consent for faster, harsher sentences for young people and led to debates about whether "criminal children" who bring us to the "end of our patience" (in the words of Judge Kirsten Heisig, whom the moral panic made a media star) should be put in closed homes or education camps. This was the second famous *Intensivtäter* case after the "Mehmet case," which, in November 2001, produced consent for the deportation of children born and raised in Germany who, until then, had secure status. Both are spectacular cases in Ruthie Gilmore's sense: their dramatic mediatization creates consent for new instruments of criminalization even as crime statistics are falling.[49] But while fewer youth offend, the criminal energy of these "terrible few" is so intense that "we" have to act quickly. Both hate and intensity produce an affective urgency that justifies quick and ruthless intervention.

The other video is called "CCTV" ("Überwachungskamera"). It also shows a terrible attack by young people marked as poor and racialized, this time against two white men who are kissing in a parking lot at night. Unlike the first video, "CCTV" is no documentary but an advertising film for a local gay antiviolence NGO called Maneo (also author of some of the posters and kiss-ins discussed earlier). It was shown at the Berlinale, on public television, and in the advertising program at Berlin cinemas. It precedes the "case of Serkan A. und Spyridon L." by a year, yet its plot, visualities, and technologies bear uncanny resemblances to this case. The hateful Other exists even before the figure finds its bodies and materializes into the very action it has been cast and forecast to perpetrate.

In both videos the homophobic migrant and the intensive offender look identical. They are recognized through the same forensic media and the same affective scripts. The frail pensioner and the bashed gay men slide into one sentimentalized, white, victim subject. Their interchangeability is confirmed by a growing army of experts who loyally repeat each other. For example, the report *Violence Phenomena among Male, Muslim Youth with Migration Background* cites the Simon study that is in turn commissioned by the biggest gay organization, LSVD (the Lesbian and Gay Association Germany), that designed and distributed the kissing posters.[50] And when Judge Heisig, long the most prominent expert on the Intensivtäter, dies (first, we hear, by suicide, then at the hands of Arab family clans), both the LSVD and Maneo publish obituaries of a "valuable partner and supporter."[51]

In the Simon study, the LSVD press releases, the articles and special issues on the Drag Festival, and the many reports on violent Muslim youth, the profile is nearly identical. To stylistically retrace the formulaic manner in which the hate or intensive offender is profiled: he is *badly integrated* and *religious* but only where he can be construed as Muslim. The most influential of the violence reports, the Pfeiffer study, whose findings are disseminated through headlines such as "Young, Muslim, Brutal," goes to particular lengths to highlight, in typical post-Christian secular and divide-and-rule manner, the positive effects of a Christian socialization (including for Christians who are not white Germans) in *reducing* rather than *increasing* delinquent behavior.[52] Moreover, and synonymously, the hate or intensive offender *is non-German.* According to Pfeiffer and colleagues, schoolchildren who "do not themselves have German nationality or were not born in Germany, or to whose biological parents the same applies," cannot call themselves German.[53] But when they answer "no" to the question of whether they perceive themselves as German, they are classified as badly integrated. These studies are thus performative: they remind both participants and readers that Germanness equals whiteness. In a citizenship context that has only just let go of its blood principle and is, for the first time, softening the biological borders of its nationality law, this is crucial. The figure of the criminal (and the criminally homophobic) migrant is a central technique by which the border is forcefully redrawn.

The border runs not only through blood but also through space. The hateful or intensive offender is described as coming from a "rural-patriarchal family."[54] He is not from here, no matter how many generations have been here before him.[55] He is described as investing in honor and thus placed in fertile kinship with "honor killers." He is from "problem neighborhoods" or "places of self-segregation," where "immigrants form big proportions of the population."[56] These are the same areas that urban planners now praise for their "good social mix."[57] To live there means something different to the immobile, racialized subject than to the mobile, white—including white queer—subject, whose arrival and displacement of dangerous bodies and intimacies is a symptom of the area's recovery and regeneration.

The hate or intensive offender is further characterized by his pathological attachments. He has few German (or, in Simon, homosexual) friends, and his whole "gang" is delinquent, which is correlated with the fact that their language of communication is Turkish or Arabic.[58] If bilingualism was briefly celebrated as intercultural competence, it has now lapsed back into its older, deficient status. It signifies backwardness: it is a "bad orientation" (in Ahmed's terms) to bad objects, bodies, communities and places.[59]

Another feature of the hate or intensive offender is his adherence to "violence-legitimizing masculinity norms" (*Gewalt-legitimierende Männlichkeitsnormen*, GLMN), a freshly coined criminological concept which in the qualitative studies is generically scripted as the signifying chain of Oriental despotism: violent dad, submissive mom, no communication skills, no impulse control.[60] How does this clunky new label, mystifyingly abbreviated as GLMN, serve to reformulate larger debates about the correlation between masculinity and violence? We might compare this account to feminist accounts of the family as a site where violence is normalized and gender difference is enforced and reproduced. While criminologists have long assumed a higher tendency to violence in boys (that is, male-assigned children), this is rarely accompanied by a critique of male socialization. On the contrary, formulae such as GLMN work to insulate violence in "chronically delinquent" boys who can be profiled and segregated from "regular" boys.[61] This distinction is not stable or secure, as shown by the ongoing attempt to find objective criteria to distinguish boys whose violence must be acted upon from those who are merely acting out and for whom violence is a "normal" step on their "normal" path to masculinity.[62] GLMN also offers new solutions to the old eugenicist problem of how to identify families that pass on violence. In particular it is a variation on the old classist theme of the "bad child from the bad family."[63] But while, in the generalized trope, delinquent children spring from excessive gender *symmetry* (working mother and weak or missing father in the white or black working-class family), in its Orientalized variant the intensive offender results from excessive gender *difference* (weak mother, authoritarian father).[64] As black feminists and queer of color critics have argued with regard to the "cultures of poverty" thesis, which blamed black and Latino families for producing dysfunctional children, racialized families are treated as sexually and gender nonconforming regardless of their apparent heterosexuality.[65] And as antiracist disability theorists have shown, this view racializes bodies and communities as deficient, inferior, and as reproducing problematically, in a way that resembles disablism but importantly does not allow its objects recognition as disabled.[66] The conceptualization of violence as GLMN thus serves both to repeat white middle-class, heteronormative, able-bodied reproduction as the uncontested norm and to normalize the everyday, banal violence through which categories of race, age, gender, disability, and class are upheld.

Racism is also normalized and Orientalized in other ways. While both the hateful homophobe and the Intensivtäter are often discussed in terms of underprivileged, underachieving, and failed masculinities, the *Intensivtäter,* as the older and better-researched figure, reflects this in greater detail. He lacks "structural integration," also measured as "educational aspirations." The high rate of children racialized as Muslim who leave school before graduating is not the responsibility of one of the world's most class-differentiated educational systems but of deficient, uneducated parents who fail to "integrate" their children.[67]

These failures are measured ever more imaginatively. Besides the tried and tested pathologization of bilingualism, experts bemoan the fact that racialized parents doom their children to limited horizons, limited verbal and emotional skills, and limited social capital by failing to play parlor games with them or to send them to *Schützenvereine* and *Trachtenvereine* (rifle and traditional costumes clubs).[68] Integration here becomes the nostalgic performance of a petit bourgeois Germanness that exists mainly as a *Heimatfilm* fantasy.[69] If this parochial landscape seems an odd site for the reproduction of the globalized affects of neoliberal citizenship (imagine learning conflict resolution skills at the local rifle club!), this is in part enabled by the *Intensivtäter*'s spectacular performance as an affect alien who is unable to talk about his feelings and to express himself other than through violence. He is the constitutive outside of a neoliberal citizen whose autonomy, self-responsibility, and emotional intelligence are evidenced by his capacity to constantly work on himself.[70] This narrative is at least as much about the integration of the national into the transnational as about the integration of the migrant into the nation. The dis-integrating migrant, who is redundant to both the national and the global, becomes the container into which these national and transnational anxieties are displaced, enabling the nation to globalize without losing its identity.

Besides his bad attachments to bad places and intimacies, the hate or intensive offender suffers from "perceptions of discrimination."[71] This trait again brings home the workings of bio- and necropower in the invention of this population. Violence is always already in those thus labeled, as well as in anyone who could be caught in this extensive profile. It cannot happen to you; to mention or even perceive it in its most toned-down version (as "discrimination" rather than racism) increases your risk of being criminalized as well as pathologized as paranoid. We can contextualize this with the punishable status of antiracist discourse more generally. In Germany use of the term *racism* is largely confined to the 1933–45 era.[72] *Ausländerfeindlichkeit* (hostility against foreigners) has been a common euphemism that psychologizes and depoliticizes racism as a somewhat natural reaction to "foreign" bodies that are, by definition, outside of and antithetical to Germanness. Even this limited frame is turned on its head in the figure of the *Intensivtäter* and the wider debates about migration and integration that it has mediated. In these debates the real problem, from which the politically correct obsession with hostility against foreigners has apparently distracted us, is revealed to be "hostility against Germans" (*Deutschenfeindlichkeit*).[73] Set in the schoolyards of Kreuzberg and Neukölln, this drama lets the taboo word *racism* finally enter the German language, but only to turn the victims into perpetrators and anti-oppression discourse into both completely unspeakable and punishable language. We must understand this drama in its institutional logics, whose murderous orientation Angela Davis aptly sums up as the "school-to-prison pipeline."[74] In Germany too schools prepare many children for social death rather than enhancing their life chances and thus participate in the trans-institutionalization of surplus populations between institutions of care, punishment, and reform.[75] This again intersects with the pathologization of the political as Deutschenfeindlichkeit or homophobia, a term that queer scholars have often contested and yet continually repeat.[76]

In the Simon study of migrant versus German schoolchildren, homophobia finally *becomes* a phobia, "a psychological tendency to react to homosexuals with a negative evaluation," which includes "negative affects or feelings, negative cognition and negative behavioral tendencies."[77] The conversion of sexual oppression into a psychological problem of dysfunctional youth radically disappears the everyday and institutional stuff that makes the world, in so many ways, hard to survive for sexually and gender nonconforming people. Instead it turns it into a property of deficient bodies that are precluded from life chances on the basis of their mental and physical traits. The metonymy between the German and the homosexual victim is highly productive in sexually expanding and racially contracting a German identity that no longer needs to feel guilty for the Holocaust but itself becomes its victim. For gays too were persecuted, and the hatred of homosexuals carries the same names as the hatred of Germans: "German pig," "German whore," "gay pig," "pig eater."[78]

The ghosts of a past that, as black German theorists and mad activists in particular maintain, began long before national socialism and reaches far into the present haunt both the hate crime and the wider violence discourse.[79] The first conjures them loudly. I lack the space to discuss the coincidence of hate crime and remembrance activisms in the same organizational and temporal setting. Nevertheless some brief thoughts on the activism surrounding the Memorial for the Homosexuals Persecuted under National Socialism, erected in 2008, will illustrate my point. In many LGBT commemorations, the homosexual victim of national socialism is put in competition with the Jewish victim, an (anti-intersectional) metonymy that serves to inscribe the homosexual subject into the foundational myth of a free democratic, postracist Federal Republic. This happens through mimicry: the Homo-Memorial, as it is often called endearingly, perfectly imitates the older Memorial for the Murdered Jews in Europe, completed in 2004.

It is from the same material and of the same color and shape. Yet instead of the 2,711 gray slabs, "we" have to make do with one, which is bent (not straight).[80] The Homo-Memorial hosts several of the kisses and kiss-ins I have already mentioned: one is continually projected inside, in a film of gay kissers that is an inbuilt part of the sculpture. Others are performed outside, in remembrance ceremonies and kiss-in actions that commemorate the dead and place them in continuity with today's injured lovers.[81] Today's victims (of homophobic migrants) seamlessly join a teleology of the *Never Again!* The irony—that the memory of a past of incarceration and deportation should orient us to a future of more of the same so that the Holocaust will not repeat itself, is lost.

In contrast to the hate crime debate, which loudly claims its historic heritage, the noisy hauntings of the wider violence debate remain unspeakable to the point of punishment. The intensive offender appears as a new phenomenon that requires new methodologies. The spatial and cultural typology of the patriarchal family in the ghetto is joined by a multitude of statistics that correlate an "integration index," "religiosity scale," and other "factors of influence" (such as "violence in the family," "family in proximity to poverty," and "life in disadvantaged housing areas") in countless regression analyses.[82] The numbers thus produced must be understood in a historical context that simultaneously birthed racism, eugenics, and statistics as kindred "white logic[s] and white methods." As Zuberi and Bonilla-Silva's collection of the same name demonstrates, these indeed have the same fathers in scientists such as Francis Galton.

The memory of this history enables us to understand violence narratives and their numerologies in their racist, classist, and eugenicist echoes, as well as in their transnational travels. This is why seemingly disparate and parochial debates such as the (currently revived) "culture of poverty" thesis in the United States and the crime and integration panics in northwestern Europe produce easily transposable explanations that nevertheless appear intrinsically local and authentic.[83] How might we turn around the gaze and begin to travel too, borrowing analytics that help us come to grips with these highly mobile racist scripts of bodies, minds, and spaces? For example, Sherene Razack's analysis of race, space, and Canadian settler colonialism has purchase for the European inner city. In Razack's analysis, the racialized inner city and the reservation are cast as degenerate spaces producing degenerate bodies: the indigenous and racialized people who live there are always already cause and origin of violence (both in the figure of the racialized perpetrator and in that of the non-rapeable woman of color).[84] Race, class, gender, and colonial violence thus disappear and become utterly unremarkable, self-inflicted phenomena that naturally inhabit racialized bodies and their surroundings.

Profiling the *Intensivtäter*

The search for the *Intensivtäter* does not stop at constructionist explanations. Besides being a focus of criminological, sociological, and pedagogical expertise, he is also the subject of psychologists and psychiatrists.[85] In the descriptions of the psy experts, he becomes a type, a personality profile, a genus. No longer at stake is the punishment of deeds that have already been done. In risk profiles "at-risk" children age five or younger are prepared for "early detection." This is Foucault's "shift from the crime to the criminal." In the collection *Jugendliche Intensivtäter* (English: intensive adolescent offenders), a youth psychiatrist complains that the *Diagnostic and Statistical Manual* of the American Psychiatric Association (DSM, which long included homosexuality and Gender Identity Disorder, and still lists many queer and trans practices and identities as mental disorders) has no diagnosis specifically for intensive offenders.[86] At the same time, the existing *DSM*, whose menu of diagnoses has grown exponentially since its first edition (from sixty to soon over four hundred), is invoked continually. Among the existing labels, Attention-Deficit Hyperactivity Disorder (ADHD) and Antisocial Personality Disorder (ASPD) are cited repeatedly.

While a genealogy of these diagnoses is beyond the scope of this chapter, both resound heavily with eugenicist specters of degeneracy and are deeply raced and classed in their application. Rachel Gorman describes hyperactivity as the successor of "moral imbecility," which was frequently diagnosed in children of color considered "turbulent, vicious, rebellious to all discipline; they lack sequence of ideas and probably power of attention."[87] More harmlessly, it seems, the *Intensivtäter* debate invokes ADHD as a prognostic tool to spot future chronic delinquents as "difficult babies."[88] In North America the widespread diagnosing of ADHD and commonplace medicating of children has been linked to the aggressive marketing of pharmaceutical companies.[89] The expansion of this diagnosis into unsaturated European markets must be observed against the background of a medical industrial complex that capacitates bodies anew.[90] We must ask how the medical industrial complex, as many working on the intersection of race and disability have shown, treats bodies differentially.[91] We must further interrogate how it renders surplus populations productive beyond their labor power. In the context of neoliberal racism, bodies labeled chronically delinquent are—not incidentally—those affected disproportionately by the exodus of manufacturing and the resulting mass unemployment.[92]

This is also apparent in the second diagnosis cited in the *Intensivtäter* debate: Antisocial (or Asocial or Dissocial) Personality Disorder. On the checklist of this diagnosis are traits such as "failure to conform to social norms," "lack of the capacity for empathy," "irresponsibility and disregard for social norms," "impulsiveness," "low threshold for discharge of aggression, including violence," and "incapacity to experience guilt."[93] Here the carceral and the biomedical are intertwined in a manner that recalls older eugenicist notions of the innate criminal—and personality disorders are generally considered incurable. In the words of two psychologists in the same collection who support the view that chronically delinquent youth represent their own "type" (the "LCP" or "life course persistent" type), it can "hardly be assumed that individuals of the LCP type will learn pro-social behaviors as adults."[94] Both chapters in *Jugendliche Intensivtäter* cite the increasingly popular brain and gene theories that treat violence as hereditary. This may occur either biologically or socially—aggressiveness can also be caused by violent damage to the head!

Recalling the debate over born versus socialized criminals, this logic fuses not only nature and nurture but also science and Christian morality: the frontal brain is the seat of both impulse control and conscience. It also brings to mind the scandals over proposals to experiment on children in black and Latino neighborhoods in the United States in the name of preventing violence and rioting, and the recurrent calls for brain scans and gene tests to "screen and intervene."[95] In the United Kingdom researchers have begun to assemble risk profiles that include biomarkers alongside social factors such as alcoholism, poverty, experiences of violence, and ethnicity; these may soon become available to judges, teachers, and doctors for diverse purposes.[96]

Again a transnational perspective is important here. While the German experts rely heavily on the English-language literature on ASPD, which interchangeably describes an "antisocial," "dissocial," or "asocial" type, I have not so far spotted the term *asozial* in the German literature, possibly because this was the exact term that the Nazis used to mark poor people, sexual deviants, and Rroma and Sinti for sterilization or internment. Nevertheless we can take Razack's thoughts on the degeneracy of racialized bodies and spaces—which are only ever perceptible as origins and never as targets of violence—further by attending to the return of explicit eugenics to Germany: from the racist theory of the German politician Thilo Sarrazin that people of Turkish origin have lower and Jewish people higher IQs, which hit the headlines around the same time as the *Intensivtäter* panic and is cited in the debate on the panic over the "cultural practice" of cousin marriage to violence reports that open with demographic prognoses about the disproportionate growth of migrant populations.[97]

These are narratives of decline that locate the social and biological downfall of the nation in the reproduction of racialized populations. Following queer of color theorists such as Rod Ferguson and Cathy Cohen, we may juxtapose these improper heterosexualities with queer investments in reproduction and regeneration through figures such as gay marriage, rainbow families, and the queer lover who comes to life in the shadow of the degenerate bodies and the regenerating buildings of the gentrifying ghetto. The vitalization of the queer subject is necropolitical in that it occurs in or close to the very death worlds from which Others are ghosted.[98]

The queer subject's new vitality contrasts with the inescapably asocial heritage of the *Intensivtäter*. So far this appears to occur in a random rather than a systematic manner. A study by Ohder and Huck, a criminologist and a psychologist who reviewed files on youth with this label at the prosecution service in Berlin, highlights constructionist explanations but also lists the physical, mental, and social "conspicuities" of the surveyed individuals. These include "impairment speaking (stammering, mute)," "motoric conspicuity (hyperactivity, coordination problems)," "chronic visible physical conspicuity (stunted growth, limping)," "brain organic conspicuity (early-childhood brain damage, Down syndrome, epilepsy)," "conspicuities with harm of others ('extraversion') [or] of self ('introversion')," "(delusional) distortion of perception," "running away from home," "prostitution," and "suicide attempts."[99]

While the figure of the *Intensivtäter* has disability, class, and race written all over it, his innate deficiency—physical and mental inferiority; poverty; social and sexual deviance; a criminal, mad, or alcoholic genealogy—distinguishes him from the recognizably disabled subject, the homonormative subject, the reformable working-class subject, and the good multicultural subject. The hate or intensive offender remains ungrievable in this landscape of commemoration and the futures that open up from it. While his prognosis seems bleak he is at first sight also an object of care and reform. In media representations of hate or violence, offenders' own experiences of abuse are described with apparently sensitive detail. In the aftermath of the Drag Festival debate Ahmet Toprak, thus far cited as an expert of the *Intensivtäter*, was invited to apply his tried and tested diagnostics to hateful homophobes, who indeed stem from the identical suspect group. In an interview in the Berlin queer magazine *Siegessäule* he states, "Similarities consist in offenders' difficulties in talking about their emotions. They never learned to talk about their inside and to resolve conflicts, since this isn't considered masculine." [100]

Serkan A. and Spyridon L., the well-mediatized *Intensivtäter* case, have likewise suffered. Serkan A.'s father is violent, his mother mentally ill. He was in a children's home, Spyridon L. in a youth psychiatric institution. Yet our empathy contrasts with their emotional coldness, as in the following profile of Serkan A. in *Stern* magazine: "The Munich crime policemen were speechless faced with such coldness. Psychologists speak of a shallowing of affect. [A violence researcher is cited:] 'These youth have difficulty talking about their feelings. We don't know if it's a deficit in language or a deficit in experience.'"[101] This empathy narrative nevertheless orients us away from Serkan A. Our empathy with him contrasts with his lack of empathy, his utter lack of emotion, which is firmly rooted in him. His dismissal from the realm of humanity and the humanly intelligible nevertheless occurs in the name of reform. The pedagogues and masculinity researchers in particular occupy themselves with the question of how we may teach the intensive offender, in spite of everything, to manage his anger and his hatred and develop empathy for his victims.[102] Our speechlessness nevertheless already points toward the futility of such attempts.[103] As we are left to connect the dots, the question that comes to the fore is whether well-meaning efforts may not be completely wasted on young minds so deeply steeped in hate.

Toward an Abolitionist Imagination

What lessons are there in thinking through the queer metonymies of sexual and criminal justice, carceral and biomedical knowledges, and racialized, perverse, and mad figurations that I have traced? Beginning with a queer of color critique of queer whiteness, I have ended up with an institutional critique that is inspired by an abolitionist imagination of (in Davis's words) "a world without prisons—or at least a social landscape that is no longer dominated by the prison."[104] This abolitionist imagination must extend to psychiatric and other institutions of care in ways that resist nostalgic longings for a welfare state that, for racialized people, was always ambivalent.[105] In the place of any wishful thinking that young people labeled violently hateful are simply in the wrong institution, we should attend to the symbiotic relationship between punitive, biomedical, and other "helping" apparatuses, each of which serves to administer surplus populations that, profiled by one, become recognizable to the other. This is especially relevant for racialized and colonized populations, whose conformity to white norms (especially of gender and sexuality) and identities has always been the remit of experts of punishment as well as of psychiatrists and other experts of care.[106]

Besides understanding the close relationship between criminalization and pathologization across multiple formal and institutional sites,[107] an abolitionist imagination might also involve attending to the way punitive and pathologizing logics undergird informal sites, including those that identify as alternative, radical, or progressive. I have suggested antiviolence organizing against *hate* as one such site, which, given the global spread of hate crime activism and the twin carceral and biomedical paradigms that undergird it, demands a transnational critique.

I propose that hate is a problematic sign to organize under for several reasons. First, describing violence as hatefully motivated partly misses the point. What of the many acts of violence accompanied by glee, indifference, or solidarity with others rather than by hate and lack of empathy? The most powerful face of violence may indeed not be hateful at all but indifferent and neglectful toward those who must have inflicted it upon themselves or appear unworthy in a meritocratic system that will give you equal opportunities if only you try hard enough. Hate thus has the same individualizing, depoliticizing tendencies as neoliberal discourse overall. Most worryingly its usefulness as an antiviolence method is limited by its tendency to stick to racialized bodies that are unable to perform a global multicultural citizenship fit for neoliberal subjectivity, to borrow from Jodi Melamed.[108] It serves as the latest descriptor of disposable populations marked as monocultural, irrational, backward, criminal, patriarchal, and *homophobic*, a marking that we must further identify as disablist. Besides producing consent for ever more dehumanizing measures and representations, the figure of the hateful Other also becomes the ground against which all racialized people must perform conformity to our oppression. I have described it here as a psy discourse that disciplines, but it is also a productive ingredient of governmentality in that it incites us to become docile subjects who labor hard to not appear hateful when confronted with this dehumanization.

While critiquing the victim subjectivity as a political paradigm, my analysis complicates an account of injury as universally experienced and mobilized. For example, Brown's discussion of the "wounded attachments" of dominant identity politics is helpful in explaining the global purchase of hate crime.[109] Nevertheless the drama of queer lovers and hateful Others brings to the fore the differential status and effects of these figures of violence and antiviolence. How do narratives of injury perform different work depending on their authors? Why do trauma narratives attached to homonormative victims and subjects circulate at such volume and speed while experiences of racism, poverty, or police violence remain unspeakable and unremarkable? To return to Charlie Haddad's sobering analysis, how do white transgender injuries become grounds for citizenship claims while trans of color injuries must be managed in private, buried under the tongue, because to voice them would be to lose one's small claim to queer community and the meager resources that come with it? The personality profiles I have examined bring home the immense pressures on the survivors of race and class oppression to present themselves as unscathed by it and to bear it as its containers and recipients.

In formulations of queer necropolitics that go beyond a happy inclusion framework of sexual citizenship, the paradox of who must die so that "we" can live (or rather who must live so that "they" can be killed with impunity) is clearly brought to the fore. While focusing on the forces that are death making, we must simultaneously ask what a queer and trans politics would look like that genuinely fosters survival, a task that may well begin with race and class oppression rather than with hetero- or even homonormativity. Such a politics would create spaces where safety is not won by bolstering regimes of exploitation and neglect and where the violence of the most powerful becomes a bigger scandal than the acts of those subjugated, who need not be innocent in order to deserve solidarity and for whom healing and transformation would take much more than the diversification of the unbearable status quo.

NOTES

1. See Gilmore, *Golden Gulag*.

2. Cohen, "Death and Rebirth of a Movement," 131.

3. While this describes disciplinary and interdisciplinary formations in the United States, we also need accounts of other parts of the world, including outside the Global North. In Germany, where most social movements have remained very white, gender studies has had some success in finding institutional homes; see Haritaworn and Weheliye, "Ethnic Studies in Deutschland?"

4. See the CESA calls for papers, https://www.criticalethnicstudies.org/content/conference-information. Theorists and activists on these intersections have made interventions where they could, but it is interesting that while gender and sexuality studies have in some ways become more reluctant homes for women's, queer, and trans of color scholarship, critical ethnic, race, and legal studies, while undoubtedly cis-heteropatriarchal, are tentatively promising to become more open. This might reflect their lesser investment in narratives of progress, rights, and protections and their longer history of questioning how the criminal legal system, even in its nicer faces, acts against oppressed people in a way that is neither accidental nor aberrant. It remains to be seen whether critical ethnic studies will expand to include queer and trans of color scholarship in particular, whose unique contribution to wider race and ethnic studies lies precisely in its potential for dismantling the white gender and sexuality norms that are at the heart of coloniality.

5. Nair, Yasmin, "Why I Won't Come Out on National Coming Out Day" (9 October). Available at http://www.bilerico.com/2009/10/why_i_wont_come_out_on_national_coming_out_day.php, accessed June 1, 2013.

6. For example, Conrad, *Against Equality*; Spade, *Normal Life*; Spade and Willse, "Confronting the Limits of Gay Hate Crimes Activism."

7. Bassichis and Spade, "Queer Politics and Antiblackness"; Smith, "Unmasking the State"; Smith, "Against the Law."

8. For example, Reina, "SRLP Announces Non-support of the Gender Employment Non-Discrimination Act."

9. See Incite! Women of Color against Violence, "Critical Lessons from the New Jersey 7"; Support Cece McDonald.

10. While female-assigned and transgender subjects are significantly targeted and criminalized in the wake of these moral panics, representations of multiple and severe offenders generally figure these as male.

11. Ahmed, *The Cultural Politics of Emotion* and *The Promise of Happiness*.

12. Gorman, "Mad Nation?"; Kanani, "Race and Madness"; Tam, "Governing through Competency."

13. Foucault, "About the Concept of the "Dangerous Individual," 1.

14. Roberts, "Crime, Race, and Reproduction"; Rose, "Screen and Intervene." See also Breggin, "Campaigns against Racist Federal Programs by the Center for the Study of Psychiatry and Psychology."

15. See also Singh and Rose, "Biomarkers in Psychiatry."

16. See Halmi, "Kontinuitäten der Zwangspsychiatrie."

17. For example, hooks, *Killing Rage*.

18. See Breitman, *Malcolm X Speaks*. Interestingly, googling this quote first pointed me to this self-help website: Change Management Coach, http://www.change-management-coach.com/change-quotes.html. My point is that antiracist states labeled as depression are often pathologized even in antiracist communities.

19. See Rose, *Governing the Soul*.

20. Skeggs, "The Value of Relationships."

21. See Yıldız, "Turkish Girls, Allah's Daughters."

22. Given the pervasiveness of antiblackness in Germany, criminalizing measures that find consent through anti-Muslim racism nevertheless regularly have antiblack effects.

23. Haritaworn, *Queer Lovers and Hateful Others*.

24. See also SUSPECT, "Where Now?"; Khalass!!! We're vex!, *We Are Here*. My interviews with queer and trans of color activists in London and Berlin suggest that queer of color positionalities that critique the racialization of LGBT politics and cultures continue to be suppressed even as the topic of German homonationalism, following the Pride racism scandal in 2010 that became better known as "Butler's refusal," has gained much international interest. I am also interested in making sense of the simultaneous desire for queer of color and transgender bodies (largely figured anti-intersectionally) and the failure to make sense of the foundational role of racism in vitalizing much queer and trans organizing in northwestern Europe at this moment. Against this my chapter foregrounds whiteness, whose critique in my view must precede the demand to render queer and trans of color lives transparent.

25. My concept of biovalue draws on Rose and Novas' definition of the term, coined in the context of genetic research, to describe how "bodies and vitality of individual and collective subjects have long had a value that is as much economic as political—or rather, that is both economic and political." I depart from the authors' proposal that ideologies of stock have ceased to be salient, and extend the concept beyond the realm of health. Rose and Novas, "Biological Citizenship," in Ong and Collier, eds., *Global Assemblages*, 439–63.

26. In Adi Kuntsman's terms in *Figurations of Violence and Belonging*.

27. On the victim/subject, see Kapur, *Erotic Justice*. On the LGB-fake-T, see Spade, "Fighting to Win." For a more detailed discussion of the place of injured trans of color bodies in transgender ascendancies, see Haritaworn and Snorth, "Trans Necropolitics."

28. Wendy Brown, "Wounded Attachments." For an earlier critique, see Coulthard's keynote speech at the Critical Ethnic Studies conference in 2012. Future critiques could focus on how the figure as a wound reifies illness and disability as undesirable and reduces them to a metaphor.

29. Of course trans Arabs too have been discovered as victim subjects that authenticate racist and imperialist discourses, in a way that enables white trans people to enter into sovereignty as their rescuers and representatives. This renders an antiracist trans Arab positionality even more inauthentic and impossible.

30. For example, Stanley and Smith, *Captive Genders.*

31. See Gilmore, *Golden Gulag;* Spade, *Normal Life.*

32. The term *migrant* was once forged in multigenerational and multidiasporic struggles against the racist construction of racialized people as "foreigners" but has since become its euphemistic substitute. For a critique of the "eternal migrant" as a figure that keeps Germanness white, see El-Tayeb, *European Others.*

33. The posters, which were funded by the local government in response to the Drag Festival, were long available on the organization's website but later taken down (at http://zeig-respekt.lsvd.de/index.php?option=com_content&view=frontpage&Itemid=133, accessed October 28, 2012). For a more detailed discussion, see Haritaworn, "Kiss-Ins, Demos, Drag" and *Queer Lovers and Hateful Others.*

34. See also Petzen, "Gender Politics in the New Europe"; Decolonize Queer, "From Gay Pride to White Pride?"; Hanhardt, "Butterflies, Whistles, and Fists."

35. Duggan, *The Twilight of Equality,* 50.

36. For example, Love, "Compulsory Happiness and Queer Existence."

37. See Haritaworn and Petzen, "Invented Traditions, New Intimate Publics."

38. See El-Tayeb, "Begrenzte Horizonte."

39. Hobsbawm, "Introduction: Inventing Traditions," 193.

40. By "scientific," I describe how a nonacademic discourse gains value by being converted into academic knowledge. As Zuberi and Bonilla-Silva and their contributors detail in *White Logic, White Methods,* racism, eugenics, and scientific methods have a shared genealogy.

41. See Haritaworn, "Colorful Bodies in the *Multikulti* Metropolis."

42. See Yılmaz-Günay, *Karriere eines konstruierten Gegensatzes.*

43. "Brutale Münchner U-Bahn-Schläger gefasst," accessed June 1, 2013, https://www.youtube.com/watch?v=EzxzNuj6DFA&oref=https%3A%2F%2Fwww.youtube.com%2Fwatch%3Fv%3DEzxzNuj6DFA&has_verified=1; Christoph Heller, "Überwachungskamera Security Camera Social Spot Berlinale," May 29, 2008, accessed June 1, 2013, http://www.youtube.com/watch?v=yvxR-OAGB-I.

44. So far the *Intensivtäter* is mainly an administrative category applied to youth who have been convicted of a given number of crimes (in Berlin, ten per year)—*or who are on their way to becoming Intensivtäter.* Its main purpose, besides marking a young person for harsher, faster sentences in court, seems to be surveillance; thus every Intensivtäter is assigned a personal police officer to watch over him *and his surroundings* (that is, his friends, his family, his neighborhood). In addition to youth penal law, people labeled Intensivtäter are governed through a (proliferating) arsenal of pedagogical, social and youth work and psychiatric instruments, including forensic and youth psychiatry, secure children's homes and boot camps, antiviolence training, and *Sicherungsverwahrung* (safe custody), a mixed penal and psychiatric form of confinement that has repeatedly been found in violation of human rights by the European Court for Human Rights. I thank Nadija Samour for explaining these legal facts to me.

45. Berlant, "On the Case," 665.

46. Cited in Oparah (fka Sudbury), "Celling Black Bodies."

47. Malte Arnsperger, "U-Bahn-Schläger-Prozess: Die schlagen mich tot," *Stern*, June 24, 2008, accessed August 1, 2014, http://mobil.stern.de/panorama/u-bahn-schlaeger-prozess-die-schlagen-mich-tot-624986.html.

48. See Ahmed, *The Cultural Politics of Emotion*.

49. Gilmore, "Globalisation and U.S. Prison Growth." The experts on intensive offenders admit to this. See Ohder and Huck, *Intensivtäter in Berlin*.

50. Toprak and Nowacki, *Gewaltphänomene bei männlichen, muslimischen Jugendlichen mit Migrationshintergrund und Präventionsstrategien*; Simon, "Einstellungen zur Homosexualität."

51. Maneo, "Zum Tod von Kirsten Heisig."

52. *Spiegel Online*. "Kriminologische Studies: Jung, muslimisch, brutal" (June, 2010). Available at http://www.spiegel.de/panorama/justiz/kriminologische-studie-jung-muslimisch-brutal-a-698948.html, accessed August 1, 2014; Baier et al., *Kinder und Jugendliche in Deutschland*.

53. Baier et al., *Kinder und Jugendliche in Deutschland*, 12.

54. LSVD, "Schluss mit Diskriminierung und Gewalt."

55. See El-Tayeb, *European Others*.

56. Haug, *Jugendliche Migranten—Muslimische Jugendliche*; Ohder and Huck, *Intensivtäter in Berlin*, 60.

57. TOPOS, "Sozialstruktur und Mietentwicklung im Erhaltungsgebiet Luisenstadt." For a critique, see Lees, "Gentrification and Social Mixing."

58. Baier et al., 64; Haug, *Jugendliche Migranten—Muslimische Jugendliche*, 69.

59. Ahmed, *Queer Phenomenology*. The category of the gang, which is often determined in highly arbitrary ways, is another globalizing instrument that allows lawmakers and enforcers to criminalize young people of color through their proximity to other low-income youth of color. See Critical Resistance Oakland, *Annual Report*.

60. Baier et al., 64; Toprak and Nowacki, *Gewaltphänomene bei männlichen, muslimischen Jugendlichen mit Migrationshintergrund und Präventionsstrategien*, 61.

61. Roth and Seiffge-Krenke, "Frühe Delinquenz und familiäre Belastungen in der Kindheit."

62. I thank Nina Mackert for our conversations about this.

63. Rose, *Governing the Soul*.

64. Toprak and Nowacki, *Gewaltphänomene bei männlichen, muslimischen Jugendlichen mit Migrationshintergrund und Präventionsstrategien*, 61.

65. For example, Cohen, "Punks, Bulldaggers, and Welfare Queens."

66. See Gorman, "Mad Nation?"

67. For a typically muddled response to Germany's bad results in international comparisons of educational achievement such as the PISA study, see A. Himmelrath, "10 Years of PISA Testing: Taking Stock," trans. C. Cave trans. Goethe Institute, available at http://www.goethe.de/wis/fut/sul/en8729860.htm, accessed October 24, 2012.

68. Baier et al., *Kinder und Jugendliche in Deutschland*, 64; Toprak and Nowacki, *Gewaltphänomene bei männlichen, muslimischen Jugendlichen mit Migrationshintergrund und Präventionsstrategien*, 61.

69. This genre became popular after the Second World War and typically depicts a sentimental world set in the mountains, where white gender-conforming boy romances girl, that is nostalgic for an innocent Germany unspoiled by racial or sexual Others.

70. See Rose, *Governing the Soul*; Skeggs, "The Value of Relationships"; Toprak and Nowacki, *Gewaltphänomene bei männlichen, muslimischen Jugendlichen mit Migrationshintergrund und Präventionsstrategien*.

71. Haug, *Jugendliche Migranten—Muslimische Jugendliche*, 19.

72. See Barskanmaz, "Rasse"; Melter and Mecheril, *Rassismustheorie und -forschung in Deutschland*.

73. Shooman, "Der Topos 'Deutschenfeindlichkeit' in rechtspopulistischen Diskursen." Pfeiffer and colleagues also mention *Deutscheinfeindlichkeit* as a common trait among their subjects (Baier et al., *Kinder und Jugendliche in Deutschland*, 64). The theme of reverse racism (as a criminal trait) is a globalizing phenomenon, as the prosecution of the antiracist activist Houria Bouteldja for "antiwhite racism" in France also illustrates.

74. Davis, *Are Prisons Obsolete?*

75. Ben-Moshe, "Resistance to Incarceration."

76. See Bryant and Vidal-Ortiz, "Introduction to Retheorizing Homophobias."

77. "Unter einer homosexuellenfeindlichen Einstellung ist die psychologische Tendenz, auf Homosexuelle mit einer negativen Bewertung zu reagieren, gemeint. Diese Bewertung beinhaltet negative Affekte oder Gefühle, negative Kognition und negative Verhaltenstendenz" (Simon, "Einstellung zur Homosexualität," n.p.).

78. M. Heyl et al., "Mein Vater hat mich geprügelt: U-Bahn-Schläger spricht im Knast," *Bild*, January 3, 2008, accessed August 1, 2014, http://www.bild.de/news/vermischtes/vater/schlaeger-3399928.bild.html; Schütz, "Kriminelle Ausländer"; Waltraud Schwab, "Homophobie-Expertin der Berliner Polizei: 'Gewalt fängt nicht erst an, wenn es blutet,'" *Tageszeitung*, June 22, 2009, accessed August 1, 2014, http://www.taz.dè/!5161044/.

79. For example, El-Tayeb, "Begrenzte Horizonte"; Halmi, "Kontinuitäten der Zwangspsychiatrie."

80. See also Haakenson, "Queers in Space."

81. The 2009 commemoration speech organized by the LSVD asked us to remember a long-term middle-class relationship that ended in a "love death" during national socialism. The same speech also cited the litany of racialized hate crime cases that was circulating at the time and warned us to not let the past repeat itself. Another example of how the hate crime discourse has been invoked to wed the "terror of the present" with the "terror of the past" (and white gay men as victims of both) is the annual kiss-in of the antiviolence organization Maneo that was performed in front of the memorial that year, after targeting "problem neighborhoods" in previous years.

82. These are the "factors" cited by the Pfeiffer study (Baier et al., *Kinder und Jugendliche in Deutschland*). For other reports, both quantitative and qualitative, that have repeated similar themes of integration, religiosity, inner-city background, and inherited violence and poverty, see Haug, *Jugendliche Migranten—Muslimische Jugendliche*; Toprak and Nowacki, *Gewaltphänomene bei männlichen, muslimischen Jugendlichen mit Migrationshintergrund und Präventionsstrategien*.

83. The culture of poverty theory was popularized in the 1960s and attributed poverty among black and Latino people to the dysfunctional structure of their communities and families. See Moynihan, *The Negro Family*. For critiques, see Roberts, "Crime, Race, and Reproduction"; Cohen, "Punks, Bulldaggers and Welfare Queens."

84. See Razack, "When Place Becomes Race."

85. On the dispersal of psy discourse to other disciplinary and professional formations and throughout neoliberal therapeutic culture, see Rose, "Screen and Intervene."

86. Huck, "Intensivtäter aus jugendpsychiatrischer Sicht."

87. Gorman, "Mad Nation?," 275. Gorman also highlights the bifurcation of ADHD into "'hyperactive' children of colour [who] are segregated in special education, while 'attention deficit' middle class youth are provided with specialised computers and tutors," 275.

88. Roth and Seiffge-Krenke, "Frühe Delinquenz und familiäre Belastungen in der Kindheit," 256.

89. Breggin, "Campaigns against Racist Federal Programs by the Center for the Study of Psychiatry and Psychology."

90. See also Puar, "The Cost of Getting Better."

91. Hutson, "Unverschämt"; Roberts, "Crime, Race, and Reproduction," 97.

92. There is anecdotal evidence in activist communities that children labeled difficult or disruptive, often those racialized and gendered as Turkish or Arab boys, are now given this diagnosis at school (Racism and Mental Health workshop at the Decolonize the City conference in Berlin, September 23, 2012). I am grateful to Cengiz Barskanmaz and Meral El for sharing preliminary findings from research done in Berlin schools that confirms this trend (summer 2012).

93. See the following list assembled from the *DSM* and from the checklist of the World Health Organization, "Antisocial Personality Disorder," Wikipedia, accessed August 1, 2014: http://en.wikipedia.org/wiki/Antisocial_personality_disorder.

94. Roth and Seiffge-Krenke, "Frühe Delinquenz und familiäre Belastungen in der Kindheit," 255–56.

95. Rose, "Screen and Intervene." For a genealogy of biopsychiatric attempts to reinscribe the link between race and violence, see Breggin, "Campaigns against Racist Federal Programs by the Center for the Study of Psychiatry and Psychology."

96. For a somewhat uncritical account, see Singh and Rose, "Biomarkers in Psychiatry."

97. Haug, *Jugendliche Migranten—Muslimische Jugendliche*; Sarrazin, *Deutschland schafft sich ab*).

98. Haritaworn et al., *Queer Necropolitics*; Haritaworn et al., "Introduction: Murderous Inclusions"; Mbembe, "Necropolitics."

99. Ohder and Huck, *Intensivtäter in Berlin*, 60. Many of these terms, such as *Auffälligkeit* (conspicuity), sound odd in German. I argue that the choice of a more random, less medically precise vocabulary serves to obfuscate the eugenicist hauntings of this list.

100. Toprak, "Machtausübung," 15.

101. Rupp Doinet et al., "Der Fall Serkan A.: Eine klassische Karriere," *Der Stern*, January 13, 2008, accessed January 5, 2010, http://www.stern.de/panorama/:Der-Fall-Serkan-A.-Eine-Karriere/607151.html.

102. See Ohder and Huck, *Intensivtäter in Berlin.*

103. Besides analyzing how the disposability of youth of color is euphemized through emotional narratives like these, we must attend to the institutional practices that govern the intensive offender. While the intensive offender is amply studied, no research has been done on what actually becomes of young people with this label (see Ohder and Huck, *Intensivtäter in Berlin*, 23).

104. Davis and Rodriguez, "The Challenge of Prison Abolition," 218.

105. Efforts to resist prison abuse by highlighting the high incidence of mentally ill prisoners who should *really* be in a mental institution, often heard in the United States, where many psychiatric institutions were closed as a result of neoliberal austerity measures, reify sanist notions of mental illness and ignore how psychiatric institutions too are sites of confinement. Psychiatric system survivors have long argued that similar circumstances can lead to spending longer in psychiatric care than in prison and that, instead of a clearly defined sentence, the psychiatric patient is dependent on the whim of doctors, who have full discretion to confine him or her until they declare him or her "cured" (e.g., Dissidentenfunk, "Massregelvollzug/Forensische Psychiatrie").

106. See Chan et al., *Women, Madness and the Law*; Vergès, *Monsters and Revolutionaries.*

107. On the overlaps between U.S. prisons and the military, see Gordon, "Methodologies of Imprisonment." On the transformation of the big psychiatric institution into mental health services in the community, see Voronka, "Rooting Out the Weeds."

108. Melamed, "Reading Tehran in Lolita."

109. See also Coulthard's keynote speech, where he argues, contra Wendy Brown, that for indigenous people in Canada it is too early to let go of resentment. He concludes, "Let's wallow in it."

SIX

Critical Contradictions: A Conversation among Glen Coulthard, Dylan Rodríguez, and Sarita Echavez See

In July 2013 Dylan Rodríguez, Glen Coulthard, and Sarita Echavez See sat together for a conversation organized by two questions posed by Rodríguez:

1 How do we make sense of the fact that racist and colonial structures of human fatality have persisted, and at times seem to have grown in reach and sophistication, in the aftermath of the past half century's major movements for progressive social transformation, including the abolition of U.S. and South African apartheid, as well as liberal shifts in racial and colonial social texts, including the emergence of multiculturalism and state-ordained national antiracism?

2 What useful articulations can take shape between current forms of radical intellectual work (such as that emerging from the critical ethnic studies project) and other forms of rebellion, collective mobilization, and social insurgency?

What follows is a transcript of that exchange, presented with limited editorial voice.

SEE: Dylan, can I ask you about that first question and its central political contradiction? While we were organizing the first critical ethnic studies conference, we had several critical conversations about the repercussions of the turn to feminism for the Left. What kind of indictment has not been achieved at all? What might it mean to really assess the impact of feminism writ large? Not just as in "pure" feminism, white feminism. Might this be connected to the central political contradiction of your first question?

RODRÍGUEZ: I wasn't thinking about it that way. I wouldn't lay the contradiction at the feet of the political spectrum or legal continuums that get disrupted all the time within different feminist practices. I wasn't thinking about it in that sense. I was thinking about it in the sense of a modality of both activist praxis and critical theorization that I think continues to reproduce a kind of epistemic binary. In other words, the difference I'm trying to point out is more than one of theoretical focus or conceptual distinction. It's a binary—it's close to a generalized opposition between the forms of massive systemic human violence that are clearly grounded in a racial-colonial genealogy that reaches back several centuries and, on the other hand, modalities of practice and theorization that are addressing developments of the past half century or so.

What surfaces is a certain kind of contradiction that I am not sure how to engage at this point because we have the field of critique and expository analysis that addresses this thing we call neoliberalism—which is actually multiple things. I think we need to put that on the table. We need to understand that neoliberalism is not one thing. It's multiple things that work at multiple registers. More specifically once we consider that we're at the moment of its initial implosion as an economic apparatus, we have to come to grips with the fact that this doesn't mean that it's going anywhere as a cultural and political apparatus. So there's that field of critique and analysis that focuses on the complex we call neoliberalism, and, alongside that field, there's the work that I see Glen and others doing in which they are really, perhaps more fundamentally concerned with a colonial relation. A settler colonial relation. Which is not to say that it's not centrally structured in neoliberalism in its different iterations, but it's to say that there's an analytic that Glen's work generates that pushes at the theoretical and historical limits of a lot of the prevailing modes of critical theorization around the neoliberal political crisis now.

That's part of where I was trying to think with that first question. I want to engage the problem of how to engage the persistent logics of violence that seem to have grown in their elaboration, in their institutionality, but which continue to both translate and amplify the genocidal and proto-genocidal power of the racial-colonial and racial chattel. These forms of power have multiplied in the phenotype through which they're exercised—and by this I mean the rise of hegemonic, liberal, and even some progressive multiculturalisms in which so-called peoples of color, even formerly colonized people, genealogical survivors of genocide, are actually administering and at times in intellectual leadership of contemporary oppressive systems that reflect the very same logics of violence they have survived. This is what I mean by phenotype. I also mean phenotype in terms of institutional phenotypes: different organizational and bureaucratic apparatuses—including within social movements—that in my view tend to at least condone, if not proctor, those older logics of violence as they operate in the normative social dynamics of the present order. So to say they are "older" does not mean anything other than that they are still entirely present. I think about this most recently in the context of dominant strains of the Occupy movement, or even in the stuff that just unfolded this past weekend with the "not guilty" verdict for George Zimmerman. I'm observing the responses and the ways in which people participate in these critical movements, and I think these things help to illuminate the contradiction I'm struggling to articulate with that first question. And it's hard to get at.

COULTHARD: What I got out of the question was that you are clearly identifying a certain transition in modalities of rule in the wake of transformative social movements of a whole series of types, whether it's women's lib, queer, indigenous, black, and so on. What I find interesting about this question is that, especially in light of contemporary movements like Occupy, there's an emergent concern with older social movements insofar as they appear predominantly negative in their articulation. As such we are told that they risk reifying the very binaries that we ought to be seeking to transcend. Within this framework "resistance" itself gets kind of shit on because it's an oppositional stance that doesn't come up with an affirmative gesture.

RODRÍGUEZ: Yes.

COULTHARD: I think that these types of criticisms need to be tempered, especially in contexts like Canada. Since the late 1960s colonial power has sought to solidify its gains by rendering indigenous subjects complacent and conciliatory by offering promises of inclusion and recognition. In such a context the development of a purely oppositional stance or politics is a necessary precondition for creating or even thinking of alternatives. In the context of a co-optative multicultural politics, resistance is important as such, regardless of whether it is articulated along with alternatives.

In other words, I think that there has to be a reaffirmation of oppositional politics, drawing lines in the sand and maintaining that binary, because when it's not maintained the risk of co-optation is heightened. We are at a stage where we have to affirm even a reactive revolutionary politics in the way that Fanon spoke of it: a politics that recognizes that saying "no"—resisting—is a condition of possibility for the construction of alternatives.

RODRÍGUEZ: I'll just add that one of the things I find especially bothersome in the paradigms through which people analyze their thought and action is how there is a tendency toward easy disavowal of the kinds of binaries that Glen is talking about—the persistent binaries of oppositional power, along the lines of race and gender, of colonialism and coloniality, sexuality, and so forth. The way those binaries are disavowed as part of a set of critical analytics and practices has allowed the very same circuits of power that those binaries fuse to sneak back in through the back door and constitute liberal and progressive politics and subjectivities in their very modes of disavowal.

By way of example, there has been this proliferating liberal progressive outrage over the not guilty verdict for George Zimmerman this past weekend. I think it's fresh in everybody's mind. And what's interesting and disturbing about the nature of much of that expression of outrage—especially among nonblack people and nonblack people of color in particular—are three things: One is the identification with the fatality, with the death, of Trayvon Martin as a kind of universal signifier through which people can inhabit a position of collective or universalized resistance. I mean that's as old as the "black-white binary" itself. This is something that creates a certain type of political joy for people such that they have trouble seeing and critically analyzing it. Second, there are the cries for justice and the righteous roars over this alleged injustice that radically misrecognize the nature of jurisprudence and the nature of criminal law in particular. And third, and for me most important, there is the disavowal of how it is that "we," the very people who voice outrage over this verdict and the conditions it acutely reflects, are constituted by the very thing that George Zimmerman is lambasted for—that this "we" has also produced George Zimmerman. We want to turn him away, we want to disavow him, we want to say that he is this kind of social pathologue, this avowed racist—all of which he is—but there's a way in which by doing all of this, we aren't willing to fully engage with the kinds of binaries that Glen is talking about. It makes it harder to understand how the persistence of these power binaries has allowed us—in our very disavowal of those binaries—to actually condone somebody like George Zimmerman up until the moment in which he assassinates Trayvon Martin. That's the thing. No one would have a problem with George Zimmerman if he hadn't pulled the trigger—and now we need to deal with the complex ways we are accomplices to the fact that there are many, many more George Zimmermans out there poised to do exactly the same thing.

What I think is profound about the response to the moment of the Zimmerman acquittal is the failure to take ownership of how we both produce and in a sense continue to condone the George Zimmermans of the world. That he represents a position. He is not an individual. And that's the analytical step that I think is much scarier to make because then you are forced to come to terms with how it is that you might be positioned within binaries that we want to call obsolete but that are clearly not. And this is a discussion in which we need to talk about the fundamental genocidal or proto-genocidal violence of antiblack racism. That is a binary as far as I'm concerned. There's no in between there. It's not to say it's not complex and layered and sophisticated—because it is—but in terms of a constituting structure of power, it's entirely dichotomizing. To just identify with the black position is too easy. It doesn't work like that, especially in the age of this so-called postracial moment in neoliberalism and the different iterations of multiculturalism and so forth.

COULTHARD: What I've been doing in the Canadian context is marking a transition in the modality of colonial rule beginning in the late 1960s. The form of rule that emerged at this point claims to accommodate rather than eliminate indigenous difference within the framework of settler-colonial sovereignty and the capitalist mode of production. So I get what your original question hints at here: What are we to make of this transition? When thinking of this transition, I think that we ought to be careful that our work does not assume that violence has stopped playing a vital role in the reproduction of colonialism and its effects, being entirely replaced by softer techniques of multicultural accommodation. Instead we have to understand that hard and soft power always simultaneously exist alongside each other. Even following the shift to a more accommodating discourse of recognition and Aboriginal rights, state violence always looms in the background, always ready to be deployed when the management of indigenous difference and dissent through the accommodation of our rights fails to produce the conditions required for the accumulation of capital on indigenous lands.

Idle No More

RODRÍGUEZ: Glen, maybe you can talk for a minute about what Idle No More is and why it's significant.

COULTHARD: Idle No More is a lot of things, but it emerged in the fall of last year [2012] as an educational campaign established by four women from the prairies. It was in response to a particularly repugnant piece of Canadian legislation proposed by our very neoliberal and social conservative government under the leadership of Prime Minister Stephen Harper. The legislation in question, Bill C-45, was a budget implementation bill that essentially makes it easier for the state to approve various economic development projects with less environmental scrutiny, which indigenous people obviously saw as a threat to their way of life and treaty relationships. Idle No More emerged to challenge the imposition of these changes.

The Idle No More original aim was to provide information to Canadians about the impending impacts of Bill C-45 on Aboriginal rights and environmental protections prior to the legislation being passed by the Canadian Senate. Then, on December 4, Chief Theresa Spence of the Attawapiskat Cree First Nation announced that she would commence with a hunger strike beginning December 11 [2012] to bring attention to the deplorable housing conditions on her reserve in northern Ontario, to raise awareness about the impacts of Bill C-45, and to demonstrate her support for the emerging Idle No More movement. During her hunger strike Chief Spence consumed only liquids—a combination of lemon water, medicinal teas, and fish broth—which she claimed she would continue to do until she secured a meeting with Prime Minister Stephen Harper and Governor General David Johnston to discuss treaty rights. By the second week in December the movement had exploded on social media under the hashtag #IdleNoMore, with the first national "day of action" called for December 10. Protests erupted in cities across the country. At this point the tactics favored by #IdleNoMore participants involved a combination of "flash mob" round-dancing and drumming in public spaces like shopping malls, street intersections, and legislature grounds, coupled with an ongoing public education campaign organized through community-led conferences, teach-ins, and public panels. On December 21 an #IdleNoMore protest involving thousands of indigenous people and their supporters was organized on Parliament Hill in Ottawa. During roughly the same time #IdleNoMore tactics began to diversify to include the use of blockades and temporary train and traffic stoppages.

For many of us, by late December it was clear that something truly significant was under way. Indeed Canada had not seen such a sustained, united, and coordinated nationwide mobilization of indigenous nations against a legislative assault on our rights since the proposed White Paper of 1969. What had begun in the fall of 2012 as an education campaign designed to inform Canadians about a particularly repugnant and undemocratic piece of legislation had erupted by mid-January 2013 into a full-blown defense of indigenous land and sovereignty. I would suggest that the oppositional stance defended in Idle No More marks a turning point from which we cannot return. The soft power of indigenous accommodation was no longer serving its purpose of co-optation, and indigenous folks were starting to recognize this false promise.

RODRÍGUEZ: So, Glen, would you say that the importance of Idle No More is its strategic privileging, and necessary privileging, of what you were just calling the modalities of "hard power," that is, its centering of the structural and systemic—as well as epistemic—relations of violent domination over the sophisticated, bureaucratized, proliferated forms of "soft power"? Is that what's important about it?

COULTHARD: Yeah, I think we were seeing a breakdown in the kind of internalized forms of subjection that render the violence of colonial rule natural and inevitable. We are seeing a failure in these state-sanctioned gestures of recognition and reconciliation to produce docile subjects. And this emerged in quite public and widespread splits within communities as to whether or not we should be supporting mainstream political Aboriginal or Native political organizations like the Assembly of First Nations, which was starting to be identified just as it is—as a colonial appendage of the settler state.

These critical conversations, which have always occurred, were becoming very pronounced and actually quite common to a certain extent, especially over the spring. These were becoming common debates, not just among radicals and nationalists. They were emerging at the fore of many conversations in people's houses and communities. It was truly remarkable to watch this unfold. We also saw many hard conversations happening among the non-Native population—conversations about the nature and extent of authentic solidarity. On this front there is still much work to be done. Most nonindigenous folks in support of Idle No More expressed their solidarity on instrumental grounds. In other words, they were in solidarity with the movement not because of some commitment to support indigenous sovereignty but because they had, say, environmental commitments that happened to be shared by many First Nations. As soon as we saw the first roadblocks go up, however—the first acts of more disruptive direct actions—we saw the solidarity originally expressed begin to wane, to dissipate. All this suggests a need for a far more substantive politics of solidarity, one that reaches beyond the instrumental approach by mainstream Canadians.

RODRÍGUEZ: Isn't this always where it falls apart, Glen? Especially within those already uneasy and contingent coalitions alleging solidarity between progressive subsectors of hegemonic groups? Let's use the example of a certain kind of liberal environmentalism, which gets articulated as a colonial and white supremacist practice while invoking vague notions of solidarity with Native people and worldviews. That's what Earth Day is. Earth Day to me is a fucking white supremacist ceremony. This is what goes on in the context of some of these solidarities, right?

COULTHARD: Exactly. This has always been the case, but what I think was interesting in paying attention to the past six months is that there was a new, albeit subaltern, discourse starting to emerge that was taking the indigenous lead on this quite seriously. And that substantive subaltern alternative is based on an understanding of relationships that have always been articulated both in words and deeds from indigenous peoples, especially those geared around treaties premised on reciprocity, mutual nondomination and nonexploitation. These relationships are at the founding of non-Native peoples' legitimacy on these territories, and as such they must be upheld and honored. It's not about one's interests as a non-Native simply coinciding with the particular interests of First Nations; it's about respecting the relationship, which is about respecting the right of First Nations to land and freedom. This solidarity is founded on indigenous articulations of what a noncolonial situation might look like and grounded on very tangible recommendations on how we might achieve that—namely the reaffirmation of the historical relations that allowed people to live on this territory.

Coercion and the Politics of Generosity

RODRÍGUEZ: This brings up another concern that I thought might be relevant to our conversation. It seems to me that the developments that you are talking about are absolutely contingent on a profound and peculiar sense of generosity and invitation that structures Native politics. And so part of what I wanted to get at was—or is—whether and how you understand that sense of political generosity, given the kind of historical text in which Native people, colonized people, enslaved people, and so forth, in their political generosity seem to always, almost inevitably get burned by precisely the people who are alleging solidarity with them, who are accepting the invitation, so to speak. It seems to me that there is a way this kind of political generosity is historically coerced, in the sense that there is a whole condition that actively coerces the generosity. It's not voluntary generosity, it's not generous the way white people are "generous." But what's interesting about it is that part of the politics of the solidarity, for it to be substantial, requires a certain level of recognition from the others that they are in fact being invited into something. An acknowledgment that I think is missing from many examples of so-called solidarity politics. Often within the forms of solidarity and coalition politics we're talking about, there's no acknowledgment of being involved in an invitation to anything. Instead there is a sense of entitlement, as if one is rendering a favor by offering one's solidarity rather than being offered the opportunity to be part of a political genealogy that belongs to someone else. Is this something that you see being dealt with in the politics of non-Native engagement with movements like Idle No More, or is it something that is so constitutive that folks don't really talk about it?

COULTHARD: I just don't think it's understood because it has different ontological foundations. The generosity expressed by indigenous peoples is rooted in the relations of reciprocity that embody what is understood by many of us as "land." It is this relationship that still forms the core of many indigenous articulations of nationhood and community identity. The generosity expressed through treaty relations is a relationship that exists between humans and nonhumans as well as between different nations and communities. In my work I refer to the foundation of this profound generosity as "grounded normativity," by which I mean the place-based practices and associated forms of knowledge that inform indigenous peoples' normative understandings of proper relations—relations between peoples, communities, and the land. At its best this place-based ethical framework is antithetical to the imperatives of capitalist accumulation. It is a relationship founded on the principle of mutual self-determination of all elements of creation. This grounded normativity compels indigenous people to seek an equitable relationship with the settler society even though the actions of this society have proven it untrustworthy. When indigenous peoples demand justice in terms of land rights, it is this conception of land that is often being articulated—that is, land as a relation, not as something to be hoarded, exploited, and amassed as wealth or capital.

Transitions and Change

SEE: I wanted to just remark here that we've begun some of the conversation around the challenge of how to mark transitions and dramatic historical changes with a kind of coming up and insistence on a different sense of what is older and yet also present and continuous. Because what I'm seeing here in this conversation is also a struggle for how to come up with a critical historical sense of how to observe these transitions. I guess what I mean is this: Is there a way to think of Idle No More as dialectically critiquing the Occupy movement? It's a way to consider how the exhaustion of the planet is actually compelling, right? These forms of alliance and forms of violence that we are participating in and observing, condoning, as well as resisting. So I'm seeing two threads of the conversation around "What are ontological genuine differences?" as well as "What kind of sense of the historical do we need in order to mark both those long continuities as well as major changes?" This is what I see in both of your bodies of work with the phrase "suspended apocalypse," for example, in Dylan's work, which continues to be incredibly productively controversial and very difficult for Filipinos to even look at, let alone engage with.

COULTHARD: To my mind the differences between movements like Occupy and the best of Idle No More relate to questions of land in the sense that I have just described it. Occupy was premised on a reclamation of the commons, a demand to take back that which the 1 percent has gradually appropriated for their own interests over others. The problem, however, is that such ahistorical notions of the commons can inadvertently serve the same erasure of indigenous peoples' presence that the original Lockean enclosure did, this time espoused with socialist principles in mind. Idle No More poses a fundamental challenge to this colonial blind spot. It does so, however, not by making an exclusionary claim to land or resources—a form of enclosure now undertaken by the colonized—but rather it is a demand to establish relations of reciprocity and sharing based on an entirely different ontological understanding of land and relations to it. The problem we face as indigenous peoples is that we're not even included in these conversations, and as a result I think our radical imaginary has been compromised and colonial relations are being allowed to prevail.

RODRÍGUEZ: I could not agree with Glen more about this. At times it seems there are irreconcilable antagonisms that emerge when you recognize that you have enemies on the Left. Those people and positions are in some ways much more dangerous than the easily recognized enemies in the liberal-to-conservative mainstream. This is precisely the way the Left does damage in its "good intentions." And you know, I'm kind of tired of acknowledging that. I'm kind of sick of always having to concede that people on the Left have good intentions. It's an acknowledgment that becomes less and less meaningful to me the more I take seriously what I'm arguing about the existence of enemies on the Left. And when I say this, by the way, I mean this as a contingent political naming. Some of those enemies can come over real quick. But for this to happen I think that there is a strategic way that we need to identify how it is, for example, that there are ways that large elements of the Left are focused on very selective forms of hard power, say drones and Guantánamo Bay, and in this selective focus their positions have the potential to silently endorse or condone other forms of hard power that are still culturally and politically normalized and that are inarguably far more devastatingly violent and proto-genocidal than either drones or Guantánamo Bay.

So I actually don't think that good intentions have anything to do with it, and I also think that part of what we're getting at here is how we come to understand the relationship between violent power and mediated power—or hard power and soft power—with soft power being represented by things like the rise of hegemonic multiculturalism, the rise of what Glen has called a politics of indigenous recognition by hegemonic states, the rise of things like state-ordained and state-articulated feminisms and so forth. The point is that these forms of soft power are not just supplemented by colonialist, misogynist, racist state violence as a last resort, but rather that all these things are generally symbiotic with soft power. These forms of mediated, sophisticated, so-called soft power have as their very condition the constant exercise of a violent power that exceeds any notion of the Foucauldian disciplinary society. This is what I think sits within much critical discourse as an impasse. I think there's a way that this field of critical discourse has trouble apprehending the complexity of so-called binary relations of power. There's a certain dismissal of those forms of power and dominance that addresses them as if they are simplistic, or just exhausted, that is, as if they have already been critically exhausted. That to go back to those things—those binaries—is to revisit old paradigms in a way that is intellectually reactionary. So I think we need to constantly point out how those hard forms of dominance surface as the underside of the soft, mediated forms of domination that we still need to subject to constant analysis.

I think here about another insurgency or rebellion that has been revived in the past couple of weeks, which is the California prisoners hunger strike. I think about how this initially emerged in 2011, primarily fueled by the people locked up in the Pelican Bay Security Housing Unit, and how this rebellion or insurgency was and is a direct challenge to racist state violence. And then I think about how the direct challenge mounted by the people who are in prison then proliferated outward by way of their extended family members and loved ones, the overwhelming majority of whom were ordinary women, by which I mean women who did not previously identify themselves as activists or intellectuals or social movement architects but who instead saw themselves as having been coerced into the position of being activists, intellectuals, and social movement architects. What this movement of people names, in its own complicated way, in its own geographically distended way, is both the continued presence of hard forms of violent power and also the sophistication of those hard forms of violent power. That's the impasse that I think is sometimes lurking in the middle of the critical discourse. And the tools we have to analyze these persistent forms of violent dominance—gendered racial colonial dominance—might not come from critical academic circles, at least not initially. It might be that we have to rely on the generosity of people like the people rebelling in the California prison system and the extended families, the activist women and women in leadership positions in the so-called free world; that we may have to rely on their sense of invitation and generosity to enrich our version of critical work and our critical thinking, as well as our praxis around these forms of dominance and state power, and state violence in particular.

COULTHARD: I would probably gesture to strengthen that and say that it's not "it might come from them." Instead "it will overwhelmingly come from them."

RODRÍGUEZ: I was trying to be subtle, Glen!

Fanon, Revolutionary Emotion, and Irredeemability

SEE: Can I ask Glen to talk a little bit about your turn to Fanon in your talk on rage at the CES conference? I'm bringing that up because of my own interest in the psychic dimensions of the way people are fully capable of contradictorily identifying with the torturer and the tortured simultaneously. David Lloyd's work on political prisoners and what he is arguing, along with others, about the earlier colonial models for what we now call the era of torture suggests that it is actually literary as well as media figures like the detective who have trained us to be able to identify with both the police as well as the civilian, and with the torturer as well as the tortured. That forms our ethic, our fundamental ethical way of being. So, if you could Glen, perhaps return to that.

COULTHARD: What I find interesting about Fanon these days is his work on the role played by negative emotions—hate, envy, resentment, et cetera—and their role in consciousness raising and revolution building. In *The Wretched of the Earth* he is essentially exploring that moment when you no longer can identify with the torturer and what to do with that as a colonized subject. When you do identify with the torturer, with the colonist, or whatever, that's a very deep kind of alienation—that's when colonialism is, in his language, "interiorized" or "internalized," thus rendering its power invisible. Internalized colonialism structures your life in such a personal, subjective sense that it renders its constitutive hierarchies nonproblematic from the perspectives of the subjects of those hierarchies themselves.

Emotions like anger and resentment represent a break in this deep-seated form of subjection for Fanon. I think they represent the *externalization* of that which was previously *internalized*—a kind of purging of the so-called inferiority complex of the colonized subject. In the context of internalized colonialism, the material conditions of poverty and violence that condition the colonial situation appear muted to the colonized because they are understood to be the product of our own cultural deficiencies. In such situations the formation of a colonial "enemy" signifies a collapse of this internalized psychological structure. For Fanon, only once this collapse has occurred can the colonized then cast their politicized hatred and rage in the direction of the colonial social structure itself. This is some great stuff when you look at the recent rise of reconciliation politics in places like Canada and even the United States. Political apologies, demands for reconciliation, truth commissions, et cetera, all view negative emotions like anger and resentment as problems, and in doing so they fail to see the source of our oppression: the ongoing acts of colonial dispossession that these negative emotions critically call into question.

SEE: Although you do already map that out—I'm just looking at your contemporary political theory article on subjects of empire and the critique of the politics of recognition and the way in which you conclude that article through Fanon and a reconceptualization of what self- recognition, self-affirmation might be. So I see your CES talk on resentment as related to the critique of the politics of recognition.

COULTHARD: When I wrote that essay, though, I didn't see it. Even though it does play its way into that. I had to go back and look at Nietzsche rather than through Hegel, as I did in the recognition piece. In some respects the resentment stuff, and what I talked about at the critical ethnic studies conference in particular, was a personal exploration of why people react so poorly to my own anger and resentment. (laughs)

SEE: (laughs)

COULTHARD: And I was pretty damn sure that I had fucking something to be resentful of. I of course understand how these emotions can manifest themselves in disempowering ways, but regardless of that it nonetheless has a source and a legitimacy to it. Indeed they could manifest themselves in the worst way possible, for instance total self-destruction. But don't go blaming the emotion. Blame its structural referent, its source. Like destroying lives. Like the fact that that's the norm. The problem with blaming the emotion is that it's the effect, not the source.

RODRÍGUEZ: If I can add to the kind of thinking that Glen's reflections provoke on this: one of the reasons why I think Glen's dialogue with Fanon is so pedagogically useful is because it invites a revisiting of how Fanon also maps out the moment in which the colonized being begins to disidentify with the ways they are constituted by the colonizer. So it is not just a disidentification from the colonial order without—or a disidentification from the colonizer, the torturer, who is external—but arguably more important, it's the externalization of a constitutive identification. This is the disruption. In a sense, the killing, the suicide, the anti- and decolonial revolutionary suicide in which the colonized subject becomes something other, by way of first recognizing—and in a deep sense appreciating—and then disrupting, disembodying, destroying, or attempting to destroy, in a constant sense, the very things that constitute them. And that's a process that I think Fanon names that is so dense that I always am troubled by the easy ways in which different kinds of people use the terms *decolonize* or *decolonizing,* or even *decolonial.* Some people talk about it in a teleological sense, all the time, in different circles—in the classroom, in organizing and activist circles, and sometimes in academic work too. And I think that the importance of what Fanon maps out here is that when you are dealing with a system that's constitutive of your being as an oppressed subject, then that moment in which you disidentify is a perpetual moment. It never stops. I mean, this is the whole point of his critique in *Wretched of the Earth.* He is constantly pointing out all the different ways in which the constitutive logic of colonization and colonialism—the constitutive subjectivity of the colonizer—is resurfacing, especially at the moment when you think you've decolonized, especially at the moment when you think you've found a modality of self-determination.

And so that's the moment, that's the mapping that I find so pedagogically useful, especially in the context of the United States, where what remains among many of my colleagues who identify as being on the Left is the persistence of a belief in the recoverability of the American political order. I constantly come back to Fanon on this. This belief is so clearly evident in the ways America is constitutive of our subjectivity in ways that we have difficulty confronting. I somewhat wallow in my frustration over it. In a sense I think this is what animates a lot of what I think and do nowadays—to try to name and attack that very belief in the recoverability of America, especially because there is so much evidence to the contrary. That's the thing that I feel is so cumbersome because there is all this evidence to the contrary. That the American political order, American jurisprudence, that's what I am talking about—the American racial cultural economic order—all those things are so structurally conditioned by the historical text in ways that cannot escape that same historical text. So what blows my mind are the folks who identify as radical, as being on the Left—it's not even that they can't come to terms with that. It's that they won't approach it.

COULTHARD: Do you think that in that specific context, then, something like the Zimmerman case has an opportunity attached to it? Like some of the analysis has been "This isn't the question of the state or the legal apparatus veering off from its otherwise just foundations. It is the foundation of the white supremacist settler colonial apparatus itself. This is what we ought to have expected from a system that is structurally geared toward this end in this case. It is operating precisely how it should."

RODRÍGUEZ: Yeah, yeah. . . .

COULTHARD: That's funny, because with this you go back a little bit further and look at the Left response to the war on terror. It was very much like with the invasion of Iraq, and Andy [Andrea] Smith writes a little bit about this in her article "Against the Law." She finds surprising certain legal analyses emerging from otherwise quite radical and astute critics who argue that what's wrong with Guantánamo Bay, what's wrong with the war on Iraq, is that it is in violation of what is otherwise the United States' own just foundations, its constitutional core. So what has happened here is that we have veered off this path and it is resulting in war and terror and all these other unjust things. And Andy makes the simple point that the foundation they represent is ultimately just one of genocide, dispossession, and slavery. So this call to realign oneself with one's just constitutional order is really a problematic perspective that is ill-equipped to solve questions of injustice by means of law. The Zimmerman case brought similar analyses to light, analyses from Robin Kelley and others. They argued that we ought not fool ourselves here. This is the system operating precisely in the interests that it represents. So I would hope that even such a profound injustice and moment of sadness can also serve as an awakening, a gain, and a break with identifying with those interests who are a more clear kind of understanding of what we're up against.

Genocides

RODRÍGUEZ: I think on the one hand those forms of analysis, those voices are what constitute different radical traditions, and without them we wouldn't be here. You know, I think I probably would have gone crazy by now were it not for those voices, in moments like this, who name the system as operating exactly as it was intended to operate, from both its recent reiterations and its historical foundations. So I appreciate that you bring that up, because that's vital to appreciating our collective existence as the kind of political and intellectual beings that we strive to be. So I think we have to honor that as a certain kind of complex position that sustains us. So yes, that's there. It's always an opportunity, right? It's no different from other moments of racial national crisis that present radical opportunity.

The thing that I think is challenging about how these moments of opportunity emerge is to track how it is that the radical opportunity is so quickly foreclosed, or so quickly compartmentalized, into practical responses. So one response that you are going to get—one that overlaps in some significant ways with the radical critique of the system—has to do with all the folks who would want to go back and fix the law. What you're seeing now is an increasing national consciousness around the different versions of Stand Your Ground laws—how these things may or may not be linked to the history of slavery and the plantation and the chattel racial order and Jim Crow, but nonetheless that the thing to do is to go and fix it. Attorney General Eric Holder just said this today—Holder just endorsed this position, and I'm willing to bet my life that there will be various elements of a Left and radical spectrum that will in some way endorse Holder's position—that one of the primary agenda items now is to go and deal with this contingent problem in the American juridical order, which is to actually admit that the system works exactly as it is supposed to work in the moment that Zimmerman is acquitted. So this does not necessarily provoke a radical position that says that the system needs to be completely reconsidered or that the work to be undertaken is to undo the entire apparatus of the system, however we desperately try to do that. I'm not sure where it is we go from that point of radical analysis.

On the other hand the thing that most provokes me into different forms of political urgency is—I want to find a proper way to phrase this—that at the same time that you can have the articulation of radical critiques of the system (juridical, economic, etc.) as being inherently dehumanizing for particular people, there is also another sense in which folks seem to absorb the critique, acknowledge it intellectually, and move forward. I'm not saying that they are simply condoning what the critique is naming—I'm saying that I think what may be underdeveloped is the capacity to politicize misery and suffering in a way that doesn't *merely* name it. This is something that I think the colonialist and racist state structures accomplish: that they actually eviscerate the capacity of people to politicize their misery and suffering in multiple ways. The larger gendered racial national culture does that same work of undermining the capacity to politicize misery and suffering. So then you have moments like this, in which folks may or may not acknowledge that living in a genocidal social text means that you can have the circulation of a very clear critique of the system as one that endorses extermination, or at least the evisceration of particular people, and, in sophisticated contradictory ways, other people inhabiting that same social text who absorb that critique without revolt, without revolution, without a sense of the system being irreconcilable to the point of political emergency. That, to me, is the signature political logic of a genocidal social text that can operate without being forced to exercise the large-scale elimination of people in the physical sense. Because what is being constructed is a condition in which people can be *socially* liquidated, socially neutralized. That, to me, is what Trayvon Martin's state-endorsed, or state-condoned, assassination represents. It's that now, what we've done is, we've accomplished this fact. We've taken a leap beyond Rodney King and the LAPD now. We've taken a leap forward from fifteen years ago and the LAPD's Rampart Division scandal. What we're saying now is that civilians—not just cops—can do this shit.

And what I come back to is that one of the things that forestalls that sense of urgency is the generalized failure to recognize how many of us carry a piece of Zimmerman with us all the time. Our easy disavowals of him as being this exonerated criminal, this exonerated racist, are a denial of that self-recognition in a certain way. We created Zimmerman. We enabled him. We're the ones who signed off on Neighborhood Watch. We are the ones who wanted to move into gated communities. And so on and so forth. So that's what I think is the problem with the moments of opportunity that you are naming, Glen. There is this additional step that needs to happen in which the radical analysis has to be accompanied, has to be symbiotic with the politicization of suffering in ways that I don't know if we have a sufficient political vernacular to accomplish.

COULTHARD: I would say so, but I would also say, and this gets to your second question, and this gets to the relevancy of the radical analysis of intellectual practitioners in relationship to movements on the ground: we also have to be attentive that some of these changes are nonetheless necessary. I would hate to be that critic who hurls insults from my office about certain reforms not being radical enough when some of the changes that are being advocated for and pushed are not perfect but nonetheless necessary. Some of the most profound struggles of importance in the Canadian context are indigenous women's struggles against the kind of heteropatriarchal logic of colonial rule that has rendered their bodies and lives dispensable. To throw critiques at these groups for seeking justice through the law—that is, for seeking reforms—seems misplaced to me. They are doing what is needed to curb the violence. Their strategies seem to coalesce with longer term struggles to uproot the colonial system itself, in my mind at least.

RODRÍGUEZ: Right.

COULTHARD: But nonetheless we need to really be attentive to the fact that these are real lives and they need change no matter how they can get it.

RODRÍGUEZ: I'm on board with that, and I think part of the activist labor that radical intellectuals need to embrace is that this kind of practice, in which we understand that the immediacy of particular kinds of policy changes—or what we want to call reforms—can also serve as a modality to actively, must also concretely theorize conditions of gendered racial colonial proto-genocide and genocide. One of the most provocative and important recent examples I have for this is the California prison hunger strikers' sets of demands, which on their face are entirely reformist—one could argue that they are in fact barely reformist. Many of these demands are asking the system to simply do what it says it will do—which is not even a reform, right? These demands read as if they are calling for a basic measure of state accountability. But nonetheless, if you read the demands more closely, and if you can apprehend the condition from which the demands are being issued, which is without a doubt at least a proto-genocidal condition, then what you can read into the text of the demands—if you read line for line, word for word how the demands are articulated—is that what the strikers are theorizing is a method through which they might be able to temporarily survive proto-genocidal conditions. One of the demands that they make is to be allowed another photograph in their cell. They actually list this. They want to be allowed to possess one photo per year. That is one of their demands. And on the face of it, it seems like that is not even a reform. It seems fucking pathetic. What you are left asking is: Why are these guys not asking for fucking freedom? Right? That's what you *want* them to demand, from the outside looking in. But then you take these demands as a theorized text, as something that is materially conditioned by a certain geography, a certain space, a certain political moment. And you realize that what that particular subdemand—to be allowed a fucking photograph—is actually saying is that we, the people being held captive, are living in such a condition where that particular demand is in fact substantively radical. And what that communicates to those of us who are not locked up in Pelican Bay SHU is the severity of a condition that we otherwise might not have remotely understood or recognized.

So I think that to amplify what Glen is getting at here, one of the most urgent intellectual and political labors for—loosely speaking—people like us, people reading this volume and people who see themselves engaged in these conversations, is to rearticulate or re-elaborate or own that kind of theoretical position and to translate it into as many different pedagogical venues as possible so that we begin to understand that what seems to be reformist practices may, at another level, present an opportunity to name the genocidal logics of an existing condition. So I'm with you on that.

COULTHARD: (laughs) I'm gonna have to check out here. . . .

SEE: Yep.

RODRÍGUEZ: Oh come on, Glen!

SEE: I was gonna say!

RODRÍGUEZ: Always ruining the party.

SEE: This is . . . we've got a lot to work with here, I think. So with all this technology double recording—hopefully all that—we've got a transcript, and so what I'm going to do now is call it a day for now.

RODRÍGUEZ: I was just getting started, man.

SEE: I know you were.

II. CRITICAL ETHNIC STUDIES PROJECTS MEET THE NEOLIBERAL UNIVERSITY

SEVEN

A Better Life? Asian Americans and the Necropolitics of Higher Education

LONG T. BUI

This essay considers the vexed position of Asian Americans within higher education, focusing on questions of institutional representation, complicity, and privilege. Such issues stood out to me during my early induction into student activism at the University of California, Irvine, a campus that has the distinction of having the largest percentage of Asian-identified students in any U.S. university.[1] As a freshman I participated in my first public rallies and marches for Wen Ho Lee. Wrapped in the aura of a "man of science," Lee was the Taiwanese American nuclear scientist arrested in 1999 as a suspected spy for communist China and detained for a year in solitary confinement in a federal detention facility by the U.S. government. The case spotlighted the persisting view of Asians in this country as "perpetual foreigners" and "alien outsiders." A wellspring of support came from Asian American national advocacy groups and community organizations that came together to confront this prominent instance of racial profiling. As a young person coming into my own political consciousness, I joined thousands of students shouting the slogan "Free Wen Ho Lee," exposing yet another example of discrimination against Asian Americans due to constant suspicion about their national loyalties and cultural foreignness. However, throughout this time a nagging question burned in the back of my mind: What exactly does this man do for a living, and why does it matter?

As it turns out, Lee constructed computer models to make nuclear missiles and warheads to abet the United States in continuing its dominance as the world's preeminent military superpower. In the grassroots fight against state racism in the Lee case (protests by college students were instrumental in helping to publicize the case), the sensitive nature of this man's job was never critically examined or brought up in activists' desire to liberate him from prison (and us from our imagined prisons of communal oppression). Many supporters cast Lee in the innocent role of a proud citizen and American patriot unfairly subjected to anti-Asian bigotry.[2] Today the Wen Ho Lee case is taught around the country in ethnic studies classes as a textbook example of how, "no matter how smart you are, no matter how hard you work," as Lee writes in his autobiography *My Country versus Me,* Asian people "will never be accepted [since] we always will be foreigners."[3] The racialized charges leveled against this hard-working scientist and the racialized labor that many scientists like Lee perform as what Ling-chi Wang calls "high-tech coolies" obfuscate the more serious question of how Asian American professionals enable government operations and military agendas.[4]

The fallout from the Lee case led to a chilling effect on the number of Asians applying to work at the Los Alamos National Laboratory, even as the number of Asian scientists and professionals grew nationally.[5] After the state ban on affirmative action in 1997 under California's Proposition 209, the University of California was devastated by the plummeting enrollments of historically underrepresented minorities, while the proportion of Asian students stayed pretty much the same (though many predicted the numbers would soar after the policy's end since Asians would somehow benefit from color-blind standards). Meanwhile the Los Alamos National Laboratory, where Lee was employed, remained an affirmative action employer (EEO/AA). Such preferential targeting of minorities twisted a domestic policy used to rectify past racial discrimination against aggrieved groups by turning it into a political tool to recruit foreign scientists and talent for the U.S. security state. I believe the state racism found in Lee's case and the "color-blind" post–affirmative action state university form the critical nexus for grasping tricky issues about differential institutional treatment that should inform our identity politics but often get ignored or swept under the rug in the general fight against anti-Asian racism. Without addressing these underlying tensions, we end up deifying what the feminist scholar Grace Hong describes as "the hero of a privileged historical narrative, the telos and resolution of which is the eventual and complete attainment of the rights and privileges of citizenship."[6]

By adopting the concept of necropolitics from the postcolonial theorist Achille Mbembe, I bring into discussion militarism and empire, which are rarely broached in education studies. Mbembe argues that the traditional investment of modern societies in developing educated healthy populations (what Foucault describes as biopolitics or biopower) works as necropolitics in Third World contexts in which violence is profligate and members of nonwhite populations are frequently killed indiscriminately. While he speaks about colonies, war zones, and slave plantations, we can extend his theorization of necropolitics as the prioritizing of death over life to privileged First World civilian spaces deemed peaceful but where nonwhite bodies can also be found targeted for death in large numbers. Such an application of necropolitics can illustrate "the classification of people according to different categories; resource extraction [that constitutes] a large reservoir of cultural imaginaries [that give] meaning to the enactment of differential rights to differing categories of people for different purposes within the same space." Inasmuch as necropolitics is not simply about wanton murder and human destruction but the manufacturing of "enclave economies," the cycles of crisis and risk management in the corporatizing public university continue to push all of us to (dis)articulate an educational discourse that already employs the rhetoric of life and death.[7]

In this essay I sketch out some thoughts on the fraught place of Asians and Asian Americans within the University of California, considered the most prestigious public educational system in the world, discussing how the life-affirming and value-added privileges of getting a college education loop back into the political economy of death. In general much of the popular discourse on Asians within American higher education tends to focus on their accomplishments and numbers, crystallized within debates on the affirmative action policies in which Asian American students represent examples of how a "postracial" society works to help minorities improve their own lives without government support or intrusion. Such views hold up Asian Americans as a "model minority" ideologically fueling the modern university's desire to retreat from remedying its history of racism and the state's wish to escape blame for social inequality.[8] Countless academic experts have spent considerable energy debunking this model minority myth and how Asian Americans cannot be easily classified or lumped together as a model minority, but such criticisms lack a more critical edge. At best there is an expectation that academic institutions need to become more sensitive toward the diversity and specific needs of Asian Americans, but the university itself remains intact as an unproblematized model of the better life we all supposedly deserve. Beyond the necessary project of advancing minority representation and voices there needs to be further elaboration as well as scrutiny in terms of what I am describing as the necropolitics of higher education, defined as the conflict between life-and-death forces found within the modern university, a contradictory place of social enlightenment and uplift as well as death making.

The Military-Academic-Industrial Complex

If the task of critical ethnic studies scholars is to think about the genocidal contexts and conditions that undergird our precarious lives, it is imperative to consider the public university as more than an educational system and as a productive site for the war machine. Indeed the first computer networks, which helped give birth to the Internet, were linked together at UCLA, a project funded by the U.S. Defense Department, giving heft to the University of California as a powerhouse and node of technological innovators, whose products of creative innovation feed directly into the warfare state.[9] For six decades the University of California held primary responsibility for managing the nation's two major research centers under the Department of Energy: Livermore and the Los Alamos National Laboratory. Based in remote, clandestine locales, these laboratories employ an army of researchers conducting classified research and manufacturing, among other things, military arsenals under the protective cloak and aegis of national security. UC faculty helped establish these laboratories, embedding them in the university's high-research culture.[10] For decades the university played an illustrious role as the primary institution of education running those top-secret sites, developing the first nuclear weapons and atomic bombs under the Manhattan Project. While UC formally ended its ties to the laboratories in 2006, it succeeded in the contractual rebid to lead the autonomous corporate entity created in the wake of this split, called Lawrence Livermore National Security, a shrewd move that enables the hiring of UC scientists in coveted government jobs.[11]

These shadow research campuses broker institutional links between the corporate, military, and governmental networks and the university. While the University of California is no longer in charge of the production or storage of nuclear weapons, it is still a central player in overseeing the maintenance of U.S. nuclear technology. At the same time as a student movement has emerged to bring visibility to the plight of undocumented students, Janet Napolitano, the former head of the Department of Homeland Security in charge of monitoring terrorist activities and border patrol, assumed the presidency of the UC system in 2013—an "unusual choice," according to the *Los Angeles Times*, that "brings a national-level politician to a position usually held by an academic." For UC officials Napolitano was a wise choice because her background could enable her to fluently administer the nuclear energy and weapons labs already run by the university.[12] Before Napolitano other UC presidents were entangled in U.S. imperial projects; for example, as superintendent of tribal education in the Philippines, David Barrows was responsible for forcibly assimilating and reforming America's largest colony at the turn of the twentieth century. The study of necropower in higher education necessitates not just a demilitarizing plan of action but what Sarita See calls a "decolonized eye" open to seeing and unwinding the imperial structures that bind us.[13]

The fight for life over the machinery of death continues to make waves. Inspired by the principles of nonviolence, the Coalition to Demilitarize, composed of community leaders and students, since 2002 has been throwing light on the crisis situation bubbling under the veneer of intellectual work and academic enterprise. The nuclear abolitionists find it is their responsibility to "do whatever they can to prevent the UC Regents from facilitating nuclear militarism."[14] This prompted a "No More Nukes in Our Name!" hunger strike at UC Berkeley in 2007 during a meeting where the regents were discussing cutbacks in employee pensions and when the United States was planning to upgrade its nuclear weaponry to possibly fight North Korea and terrorism around the world.[15] The current U.S. nuclear weapons program, called the Reliable Replacement Warhead, hinges on UC's for-profit business partnership model with the Bechtel Corporation and other industrial development companies to facilitate the proposed construction of hydrogen bomb and plutonium bomb pits (not manufactured since 1949).

It is no coincidence that the reinvigorated militarization of the country and necropoliticalization of higher education occurred at a time when the number of foreign-born scientists working in the United States had doubled and college students from militarizing countries like China, Japan, India, and South Korea soared. (International students account for 40 percent of all doctoral degrees in science and engineering granted in the country.)[16] Almost 70 percent of Asian PhDs in the United States earn their degrees in the life sciences, physical sciences, and engineering, an upward trend as the hard sciences receive heavier promotion and funding to bolster the number of potential workers able to directly enhance America's global standing as the most powerful nation. In the so-called post-American Asian Century, when scientific know-how gives industrializing Asian nations a comparative advantage in their bidding for world power against the United States, skilled Asian workers are valuable players in leveraging a new world order. In light of all this, it behooves scholars to move away from discussing the Asian model minority myth as a false stereotype or fixating on the "bamboo ceiling" faced by Asian professionals in their lucrative careers and begin initiating tough conversations about the lethal costs of their labor productivity.

The Rise of the Model Majority: Asians as a New (Post)Racial Preference

During the late 1960s and 1970s student-led antiwar movements exposed the collusion of state-funded universities and the U.S. military state.[17] The radicalism of the Yellow Power movement built around what Yen Le Espiritu calls panethnic "reactive solidarity" to societal racism has been greatly anaesthetized,[18] co-opted by the university in its quest to reduce racial turmoil on campus. The Asian American scholar Glen Omatsu maintains that there has been a steady decline in progressive Asian American politics, which were initially not "centered on the aura of racial identity but embraced fundamental questions of oppression and power . . . not of seeking legitimacy and representation within American society." For Omatsu there has been an enlarging of the Asian American presence in American society and colleges but not "a corresponding growth in consciousness—of what it means to be Asian American." This absence of radical thinking is due to an ideological-political vacuum as the community now finds itself stuck between the goals of "empowerment solely in terms of individual advancement for a few, or as the collective liberation for all peoples."[19]

The historical push for more public accountability from the university has failed to disrupt positivist ideas of public education and illuminate its origins as an engine of war. The fast evolution of the University of California into an Asian-serving institution (seven of its ten campuses are majority Asian) owes much to the history of U.S. colonialism and military wars in Asia that set the precedence for the government's preference for skilled Asian labor in the post-1965 period and liberal immigration policies that favored the kinds of professional college-educated immigrant families from which many Asian American students originate.

The meteoric rise of the University of California to become an internationally renowned brand owes much to the establishment of new labor, migration, and consumer markets, technological transfers, and global trade between the

United States and Asian nations. After World War II the federal government awarded millions of dollars to support research for military weapons manufacturing, recruiting high-tech workers from Asia but also poor Asian and Latino workers to form a segmented labor force, buttressing the alliance between the military establishment and universities like UC Berkeley to build an invincible war industry.[20] Geopolitical realignments and economic restructuring allowed the American research university to establish close ties with state entities in Japan, Singapore, China, and South Korea to create a professionalized global economy built not on political neutrality, as the sociologist Manuel Castells finds, but on a field of networks.[21] Under the U.S. pivot toward Asia, research universities will continue to grow exponentially, just as they did during the cold war to expand the academic-military-industrial complex. The dream of higher education and the American Dream pursued by so many Asian youths today reflects what Jodi Kim calls the "protracted afterlife" of U.S. imperialism in Asia, a fact of historical reality that prompts an Asian American politics that does not solely look toward a better future but also looks back at how things came to be.[22] As Mbembe tells us, when subjects are found "laboring under the sign of death, the future is collapsed into the present."[23] The hopes for a better life are circumscribed by the martial laws under which we operate.

While more young people are attending college than ever before and the U.S. military is focused on finessing an all-volunteer fighting force since the ending of the draft after the Vietnam War, it would seem there is a dissociation between military servicemen and college-going youth. However, this faulty divide fails to grasp the blurred boundaries between civilian workers and military employees as well as the porous traffic between the ivory tower and the armed services. Colleges are still a major source for direct military recruitment, as David Pellow observes: "In higher education systems, military recruiters tempt students with the chance to join the armed forces and be frontline participants in the killing machine that stands in for U.S. diplomacy."[24]

This recruitment of students for war efforts is not always obvious. In 2005 *Time* magazine published an article titled "China's Big Export," in which FBI officials revealed their anxieties about U.S. universities as "soft spots" for penetration by foreign spies. The officials pointed to the more than 150,000 Chinese students studying in the United States as possible informants and agents of the PRC, which pilfers information from its vast overseas network of tourists, students, and workers.[25] After the Wen Ho Lee incident, several cases emerged involving Asian American researchers at UC Davis and UC San

Diego charged with selling sensitive information to foreign countries.[26] Secretly infiltrating and probing campuses, the FBI relies on embedded informants "to help sort the few who go to America to spy from the thousands who go there for a better life."[27] Seven out of ten of the top student-exporting countries to the United States are in Asia, and the University of California is the top choice for most Asian international students matriculating in the United States. Given the wars raging on college campuses, it becomes imperative I believe to not accept higher education as a good thing that should always grow exponentially and be open to everyone, unless there is an added awareness of the growing dangers and threats to our world-class education.

Compromising the Socially Dead for the Living Few

The University of California is slowly moving away from its historic legacy as an all-white institution (though the faculty remains overwhelmingly white and male); now Asian students are not simply model minorities but institutional model majorities, paragons of academic excellence and the upstanding good life offered by higher learning. The fact remains that many Asian American students are the children of war. When I asked students in my ethnic studies class about their family background, many of them told of their parents overcoming war and conflict to come to the states. Yet while many claimed ancestry in the former war zones of Taiwan, Cambodia, or the Philippines, they disassociated their violent Asian past from their improved American lives. One female student put it simply, "My parents left the civil war in China so I could come here to have a better life, and that means getting a good education."

This premise of public education as offering a better life has been challenged by critical race legal scholars such as Cheryl Harris and Devon Carbado, who suggest that the desire to make college more accessible to all citizens deploys the language of progress, neutrality, and merit to mask our public educational system's massive failure to boost social mobility and diversity in general.[28] In the aftermath of Proposition 209 there remains a "new racial preference" for certain minority groups (e.g., Asian Americans) able to capitalize on the university's demands for a diverse pool of talent targeted not because of their race but because of their skills. In this manner Asian Americans, as a desirable or worthy minority group, are rewarded with education.[29] This new preference ironically favors upwardly mobile Asian global elites, a phenomenon that ends up negatively impacting native-born Asian Americans who need the University of California as a less expensive alternative to private schools. According to the scholar-activist Don Nakanishi, "the University of California has been the major vehicle for social mobility for the Asian-American community," which values an affordable, high-quality public education.[30] The complex relationship between Asians and Asian Americans, which for decades has gone unnoticed due to the lumping of all Asians into one group, has now reached a turning point. While the number of U.S.-born Asian students in the UC system has reached critical mass and plateaued after decades of explosive growth, the number of foreign students from Asia has skyrocketed, particularly in the 2000s, due to increased allotment of spaces for them over in-state residents as a means of getting more outside sources of revenue. In 2009 the administrators at the San Diego campus reduced its number of in-state freshmen by five hundred and filled those spots with out-of-state and international students. As a result close to two hundred freshmen from China enrolled in the school, a twelvefold increase from just barely sixteen individuals the year before, while the number of Asian American California freshmen fell by almost 30 percent.[31] Asian American students must now fight against rising tuition prices and systematic efforts to push them out from the very place they helped build into prominence.[32]

That the university is a conduit for life-restricting forces and projects can be seen in a range of issues, such as the institution's ongoing diminishment of organized labor union rights, the erosion of indigenous tribal sovereignty and land rights, the restriction of student dissent and free speech protest on campuses, and the administration's resistance to calls for divestment of university capital funds in corporations operating in countries with a history of human rights abuses.[33] The battle over life-and-death matters can be discerned in the balancing act between state funding for prisons and schools. California's governor Arnold Schwarzenegger made this obvious when he publicly stated his interest in outsourcing the care and housing of inmates in California's overcrowded prisons to Mexico to pay for the state's insolvent college system. He hoped to restore the University of California to its former rightful place as the number-one public school system in the world lest it slip into obsolescence and face its own demise.[34] Such overtures to institutional martyrdom, sacrifice, and survival gesture to what Mbembe calls the "state of siege" characteristic of our everyday realities in late capitalist society.

Recognizing the necropolitical logics inherent in such neoliberal rationales serves to explain necropolitics at a broader level, which disavows certain undesirable populations to save the most productive and privileged groups in society. As state investment in public schools decreases every year, the ballooning funding deficit in California's prison system siphons precious monies and resources away from poorer schools, which in term further reduce the chances of marginalized youth and poor communities to get a basic education. (In 2010 state funding for education was 7.5 percent of California's total budget, with prisons receiving 11 percent, but ten years earlier universities received close to 10 percent and only 3 percent went to the penitentiary system.)[35] The interrelationship between state prisons and public schools is a moral crisis not addressed by many educational advocates, who focus only on the bureaucratic problems of schooling. That the steadily gaining numbers of Asian-identified students who make up more than 40 percent of the total UC undergraduate population might also speak to the growing incarceration of black, brown and indigenous youth (as well as Pacific Islanders and Southeast Asians) who make up the supermajority of the state's jails and prisons is a teachable moment that needs to be deconstructed. Left alone, we become blind to what Dylan Rodríguez describes as the "genocidal logics" buttressing the push toward a multicultural liberal society.[36] Schwarzenegger's wish to "terminate" California's responsibilities to its prisoners for the sake of assisting the college-bound pits those already consigned to "social death" against those with better life opportunities, enabling certain educated subjects prejudged as having the right to life, liberty, and happiness to receive more state entitlements and protection than criminalized people of color deemed undeserving in their "rightlessness" as nonwhite racialized subjects.[37]

Racialization of Asians is concealed, even though their overrepresentation at the University of California makes them powerful cultural liaisons (or potential disruptive spies) between the American university and Asian nations at a crucial time, when cash-strapped public universities with dwindling state financial support seek to magnify their outreach and partnerships in the East (e.g., UCLA-National University of Singapore). Coincident with the greater demand for more math and science education to bolster national security, there is increasing stress at the University of California on STEM fields (science, technology, engineering, mathematics), where students of Asian descent can be found in disproportionate numbers.[38] Asian minds and bodies, perceived as easily assimilated into neoliberal and neocolonial ideas of educational competitiveness, embody the type of modular (post) racial subjects able to fill the globalizing necropolitical economies of a multitiered U.S. college system skewed to match the competitive talents of graduates from Asia. This is not to suggest a direct causal relationship between the corporatization, militarization, and globalization of the university and the enlarging of the Asian presence in college, but there exists a connection between what the research university represents as the "best and brightest" and what particular racial *groups* appear to fit its high standards of excellence. The boundary between Asians' reliance on the life force of education and their inadvertent contribution to the military-academic industry is a testy relationship; as the activist Helen Zia notes, Asian Americans are "part of the problem [as] collaborators in our own oppressions."[39] Asians are not simply another minority easily lumped together with other nonwhite groups, since their de facto status as an institutional model majority essentially deminoritizes them in a state apparatus that wants to exploit them as racialized human capital but does not consider them racially marked in some way.[40] Within the blurred lines of academic life and death, one finds that higher education can be the pathway to our salvation or to our destruction.

Toward a Critical Pedagogy of Life and Death

If we view college education only as an exalted public domain for improving quality of life, this limited perspective misses out on a larger critique that implicates us all profoundly. According to the Chicana scholar Rosaura Sanchez, "The discourse of ethnic power, opportunity, and pluralism led to an unrealistic assessment of the extent of struggle possible at the institutional level and masked our incapacity to avoid serving privilege and class domination within academia."[41] Sanchez says the pressure to address educational social justice through ethnic empowerment is unsustainable once administrative concessions are made toward students, staff, and faculty. Identifying the institutional absorption of Asians and Asian Americans within the academic-industrial complex helps undercut the myth of educational meritocracy but makes noticeable the necropolitical forces through which the university derives its broad powers. Critical attention must be paid here to the defunding of the arts and humanities (fields often critical of institutional power schemes)—a revamping of the traditional liberal arts curriculum that relates to Asian Americans because their stunning success in vaunted niche science industries has augmented the university's desire to extract more foreign capital and value from Asian labor while diminishing the cultural capital of ethnic studies and Asian American studies in their longtime advocacy for the oppressed. Perhaps owing to the field's emphasis on professionalization, many ethnic studies scholars have argued that Asian Americans are *not* model minorities, for although many have been successful, many still face racism and some, such as Southeast Asians, have not found success. There is a flaw to this pedagogical-political strategy since it fails to critique the institution beyond not doing a good job for its clients, as students are called these days by school administrators. Acknowledging the crucial role that Asians and Asian Americans play in the necropolitics of higher education serves to redefine the vague parameters of ethnic studies to forge new philosophies, ethics, and forms of consciousness raising.

This chapter touched upon the ambiguous and thorny place of Asians and Asian Americans in higher education. It demonstrates how our sense of moral crisis regarding the public university as an endangered public good might relate to the specter of death that lurks within the dark corridors of learning. If Asians are the new preferential subjects within the neoliberal "postracial" university, how do ethnic studies scholars, students, and activists promote antiracist politics and educational policies beyond prima facie concerns with minority discrimination and representation? How might we better teach critical ethnic studies by drawing attention to the shifting demographic composition and reconfiguration of our classes produced as a historical byproduct of the American war machine and U.S. geopolitical relations in Asia? How do we advocate for improving education without dealing with the uncomfortable fact that our educational system participates in lethal practices and processes? To even attempt to answer these hard questions there needs to be a reeducation in the meaning of ethnic studies to launch a radical critique enabling new lessons in matters of both life *and* death.

NOTES

1. Asian Americans are the largest non-white minority racial group in the University of California (approximately 30 percent), even though Asian Americans as a whole make up only 12 percent of the state and 5 percent of the national total population, California Postsecondary Education Commission, accessed September 16, 2015, http://www.cpec.ca.gov/StudentData.

2. Lee was eventually indicted for one count of mishandling sensitive government documents of the original fifty-nine indictment charges made against him. He received a financial settlement from the government and major media outlets that made a scapegoat out of him.

3. Lee and Zia, *My Country versus Me*, 252.

4. Wang, "Model Minority, High-Tech Coolies, and Foreign Spies."

5. Normally four or five of the top finalists for a job at Los Alamos would be Chinese, yet lab director John Browne said that in the round of applications after the Lee case, there wasn't a single Chinese name. "I looked further down the list, and there weren't any Chinese names down there, either," he said. See Stober, "Lee Case Discourages Asian American Scientists."

6. Hong, "Past Legacies, Future Projects," 123.

7. Mbembe, "Necropolitics," 26, 33.

8. The University of California has been the target of numerous famous legal battles over race-based admissions policies in the past two decades, such as the landmark Supreme Court case *Regents of the University of California v. Bakke* (1978), which found unconstitutional race-based admissions for black students in law schools like those at UC Davis. Proposition 209 helped end affirmative action in California; the campaign was led by a former University of California regent, Ward Connerly. See Takagi, *The Retreat from Race.*

9. Castells and Hall, *Technopoles of the World.*

10. The Lawrence Berkeley National Laboratory (LBNL) represents the most direct collaboration with UC as a research campus; it lies next to the Berkeley campus. Over two hundred LBNL researchers are Berkeley faculty members, and four hundred graduate and undergraduate Cal students conduct their research at the laboratory. Sited proximally to Asian-dominated enclaves in Silicon Valley and nearby UC campuses, Lawrence Livermore has extensive UC connections. While more physically isolated, Los Alamos in New Mexico draws UC faculty and students through the National Security Education Center, composed of institutes with partner universities in UC Santa Cruz, UC Davis, UC Santa Barbara, and UC San Diego. The university sets aside federal grant money it receives for managing the laboratories to fund research collaborations among national laboratory scientists with researchers and students across the UC system. See President's Executive Office, "University of California Briefing Binder," 122.

11. The UC regents retain primary responsibility for appointing three positions to the board of governors, a group of academic, national security, and business leaders that jointly own and control Lawrence Livermore National Security. The University of California also gets to appoint three governors to the executive committee out of a total of six, including the chair, who has tie-breaking authority over most decisions of the executive committee.

12. Larry Gordon, "Janet Napolitano, Homeland Security Chief, to Head UC," *Los Angeles Times*. July 12, 2013.

13. See, *The Decolonized Eye*, 173

14. University of California Santa Barbara against War, "Students Arrested for Blocking UC Nuclear Labs," Los Angeles Indymedia, November 18, 2006, accessed January 9, 2013, http://la.indymedia.org/news/2006/11/188301_comment.php.

15. BB, "Statement put out by Coalition to Demilitarize," LA Indymedia, November 18, 2006, accessed December 13, 2013, http://la.indymedia.org/news/2006/11/188301_comment.php.

16. Kent, "More U.S. Scientists and Engineers Are Foreign-Born."

17. This collusion included the pervasive influence of police and military personnel on college campuses, the heavy recruitment of youth for military service, and the expansion and contracting of government-funded disciplines like area studies to contribute to U.S. intelligence operations.

18. Espiritu, *Asian American Panethnicity*, 198.

19. Omatsu, "The 'Four Prisons' and the Movements of Liberation," 165, 184, 194.

20. Pellow and Park, *The Silicon Valley of Dreams.*

21. Castells, "The University System."

22. Kim, *Ends of Empire.*

23. Mbembe, "Necropolitics," 37.

24. Pellow, "Activist-Scholar Alliances for Social Change," 107.

25. Brian Bennett, "China's Big Export," *New York Times*, February 13, 2005.

26. Chen, "The Spy Who Shanghaied Me," 3.

27. Bennett, "China's Big Export."

28. Carbado and Harris, "The New Racial Preferences."

29. A wave of new Asian professionals immigrating to the United States in the 1970s and 1980s helped to rejuvenate the civil rights discourse of the model minority. The U.S. media's fixation on Asian "whiz kids" turned the designation of this racial minority group from a historically underrepresented racial minority to merely a numerical minority. The focus on high-achieving Asian students at elite schools masks the fact that most Asian Americans are enrolled in state and community colleges, not elite four-year universities, and that many study business, human sciences, or social sciences rather than STEM fields.

30. Quoted in Oliver Staley, "Lure of Chinese Tuition Pushes Out Asian-Americans," *Bloomberg News*, December 28, 2011, accessed June 19, 2015, http://www.bloomberg.com.

31. Staley, "Lure of Chinese Tuition Pushes Out Asian-Americans."

32. New changes include raising college tuition despite income stagnation, outsourcing work and classes to independent contractors, firing or forcing into early retirement many staff members (many of whom are racial minorities or women), and entrenching forms of hierarchy that divide tenured full-time faculty and the large corps of temporary adjunct lecturers who teach a large bulk of undergraduate courses.

33. At UC San Diego and other campuses there has been a long drawn-out fight for reparation of Native remains, which have been "discovered" and kept for scientific study at the university upon their exhumation on campus grounds. Similar to the student-led divestment movement against South African apartheid during the late1980s, UC student activists are trying to force financial divestment in companies promoting violence by providing technology to warring countries around the world, such as Israel. For more on these issues and more at a national level, see Chatterjee and Maira, *The Imperial University*.

34. Nicole Allan, "Arnold: Send Convicts to Mexico," *AtlanticWire*, January 27, 2010.

35. Jimmy Carter, "Call Off the Global Drug War," *New York Times*, June 16, 2011.

36. Rodríguez, *Suspended Apocalypse*, 193.

37. Patterson, *Slavery and Social Death*. For more on rightlessness as a product and a legally unprotected status of being racialized, see Cacho, *Social Death*.

38. While there is an overrepresentation of Asian faculty members in the hard sciences, there is a serious underrepresentation of Asian faculty in the humanities, arts, and social sciences. Asian Americans students are overwhelmingly enrolled in the hard sciences, but this phenomenon is gendered since mostly men are found in these technical fields, attesting to a subtle gender bias in scientific training and recruitment. See Simpson, "Segregated by Subject."

39. Zia, "Oh, Say, Can You See?," 9.

40. Lee, "The De-Minoritization of Asian Americans."

41. See Sanchez, "Ethnicity, Ideology and Academia," 301.

EIGHT

Notes from a Member of the Demographic Threat: This Is What "We Are All Palestinians" Really Means

NADA ELIA

Behind every terrorist stand dozens of men and women, without whom he could not engage in terrorism. They are all enemy combatants, and their blood shall be on all their heads. Now this also includes the mothers of the martyrs, who send them to hell with flowers and kisses. They should follow their sons, nothing would be more just. They should go, as should the physical homes in which they raised the snakes. Otherwise, more little snakes will be raised there.—AYELET SHAKED, Israeli Knesset member

Human rights are not a prescription for national suicide.—JUSTICE ASHER GRUNIS, summarizing the majority opinion in a 2012 Israeli Supreme Court ruling

Movements that seek to redress wrongs in a partial manner, prioritizing some over others, are bound to ultimately fail, as they cement the priorities they had conveniently selected during the struggle. Lifting the siege on Gaza is beyond urgent, as the situation there has correctly been described as slow genocide, even without the recurrent Israeli incursions, assassinations, and large-scale military assaults, such as Operation Cast Lead in 2008–9, Operation Pillar of Cloud in 2012, and Operation Protective Edge in 2014. Ending the forty-seven-year occupation of the West Bank is also of paramount importance, as the psychological, environmental, educational, economic, and overall social damage of living with no dignity or sovereignty grows more detrimental with each passing day. Stopping the ethnic cleansing and home demolitions in East Jerusalem is critical, as the living circumstances for Palestinian residents of the city are now barely better than those in Gaza. And while Palestinians as a whole hold the unenviable title of being a refugee people for the longest period in modern history (sixty-seven years at the time of this writing), one thing we have learned from other struggles is that our liberation must not, cannot be "partial," a liberation of the few. Hence Palestinians today, in Israel, in the West Bank, in Gaza, in Lebanon, in the United States, and everywhere we happen to be organizing, are organizing for complete liberation, for equal political rights for all Palestinians: those who never left the ancestral homeland and the refugees, be they internally displaced or in Gaza, in the West Bank, in the United States—anywhere our diaspora has taken us. Today an estimated 12 percent of the Palestinian people live inside Israel, and 50 percent live outside of historic Palestine. Palestinians in the West Bank and Gaza include refugees from towns and villages within Israel as well as internally displaced people from land confiscated by Israel inside the West Bank to create military outposts, Jewish-only roads, and Jewish-only settlements. The fact that some of us in the diaspora are now unrecognized as Palestinians, as a result of our forced exile and dispossession, must not eclipse the reality that we are all Palestinians and that our assertion of this identity goes beyond the cliché of solidarity. Indeed as we enact the homeland in our everyday life, some of us do not identify with Palestine as a nation-state but rather as a state of identity. Denying us this identity plays into Israel's agenda of erasing us so as not to address our violated rights.

And as we are all Palestinians, so educators everywhere who support Palestinian rights must act in solidarity with the entire Palestinian people, wherever we may be living today, rather than with "the Gazans" or "Palestinians in the West Bank." Particularly scholars of ethnic studies and gender studies and faculty working in programs grounded in praxis, in the lived experience and understanding that the personal is collective and political must take the lead in modeling engaged scholarship, scholarship that does not theorize about liberation and anticolonial struggle but participates in bringing it about. The opportunities abound, and the path is clearly delineated.

In 2005, in a momentous historical development taking into account the entirety of the Palestinian people, a majority of Palestinian civil society organizations, representing the three pillars of the Palestinian people (within Israel, in Gaza and the West Bank, and in exile in the global diaspora), issued a call for global solidarity in the form of a Boycott, Divestment and Sanctions (BDS) Campaign against Israel until it complies with international law by ending its occupation of Arab lands, dismantling the apartheid wall, recognizing the rights of Palestinians in Israel to full equality, and respecting the Palestinian refugees' right of return. Modeled on the call for Boycott, Divestment, and Sanctions against Apartheid South Africa of the previous century, the Palestinian call specifically states:

> We, representatives of Palestinian civil society, call upon international civil society organizations and people of conscience all over the world to impose broad boycotts and implement divestment initiatives against Israel similar to those applied to South Africa in the apartheid years. . . . These non-violent punitive measures should be maintained until Israel meets its obligation to recognize the Palestinian people's inalienable right to self-determination and fully complies with the precepts of international law by:
>
> 1. Ending its occupation and colonization of all Arab lands and dismantling the Wall;
> 2. Recognizing the fundamental rights of the Arab-Palestinian citizens of Israel to full equality; and
> 3. Respecting, protecting and promoting the rights of Palestinian refugees to return to their homes and properties as stipulated in UN Resolution 194.[1]

Within a few years of its issue the campaign has grown to the point where it is considered an existential threat to the Jewish state, and organizers and activists are achieving small and large successes on an almost daily basis. Nevertheless a sobering number of scholars and cultural workers feel entitled to criticize the comprehensive nature of the call and conveniently select for denunciation only the siege on Gaza or only the occupation of the West Bank, or they boycott only Israeli products from the settlements—as if the settlements were not encouraged, funded, and protected by the Israeli government and military—rather than engage in the kind of blanket boycott that allowed this strategy to help defeat South African apartheid in the 1980s and 1990s.

Particularly U.S. academics feel that the call to sever links with complicit Israeli universities violates the much-cherished ideal of academic freedom. Thus these academics willingly blind themselves to the reality that, as most Palestinians do not enjoy the most basic human rights, the academic freedom that they would be protecting by violating the boycott and collaborating with Israeli institutions is not so much freedom as it is the oppressor's privilege.

Claiming, as the poet and musician Joy Harjo did in December 2012 as she took up a writer-in-residence position at Tel Aviv University, that heeding the BDS call would have prevented her from traveling to Palestine/Israel and witnessing the injustice for herself is an act of bad faith.[2] Harjo was contacted by her own personal friends and numerous allies who patiently explained the boycott guidelines to her and presented her with alternatives that would have cemented rather than violated solidarity with the oppressed Palestinian people. She was given the example of Naomi Klein, who visited Israel in 2009 without violating the call for boycott. In addition Harjo was sent an open letter by the Palestinian Campaign for the Academic and Cultural Boycott of Israel, urging her not to perform at Tel Aviv University, an institution that, as the letter explains, is notorious for its deep and well-documented collaboration with the Israeli military and intelligence establishment, its racially exclusivist university policy toward Palestinian citizens of Israel, and its refusal to acknowledge its past and to commemorate the destroyed Palestinian village on whose grounds it was built.[3] As is the standard practice with most campaigns that ask an artist to cancel a scheduled performance, the appeals were made through social media, and in Harjo's case there was ample discussion of the boycott guidelines on her own Facebook page, which she clearly administers herself, as she was responding to and, to the dismay of BDS activists trying to educate her, deleting our posts. Harjo ultimately ignored our pleas and went ahead with her scheduled collaboration with Tel Aviv University. Less than two years later the myth of academic freedom was shattered in the United States, when Professor Steven Salaita was "un-hired" from his tenured associate professor position at the University of Illinois at Champaign-Urbana over tweets he made about Israel's summer 2014 assault on Gaza. *L'affaire Salaita* is still unfolding at the time of this writing but has exposed to all the climate of censorship, intimidation, and recrimination stifling scholarship and activism surrounding Palestinian rights in American universities.

In stark contrast to the acts of bad faith exhibited by Harjo, and prior to her, in 2010, when Amitav Ghosh and Margaret Atwood jointly accepted the Dan David Prize, an Israeli literary prize worth $1 million, in early 2012 a delegation of U.S. scholars who visited Palestine succinctly described what they found: "Palestinian scholars and students do not enjoy academic freedom under occupation. Israel has routinely closed Palestinian universities under security pretext, denied visas to international and Palestinian scholars living abroad who have faculty appointments in the occupied West Bank, blocked imports of equipment needed to teach basic science and engineering, and prevented Gaza students from attending West Bank universities. . . . And yet, most Israeli (as well as U.S.) academic institutions have been either silent or complicit in the face of Palestinian scientific and educational suffocation."[4]

Fred Moten, a radical black studies professor, spoke about the solidarity of U.S. academics with the Palestinian people. Criticism of Israel, "however necessary and justified," Moten explained, "is not the equivalent of solidarity with Palestine which, in the United States, can only ever augment and be augmented by our recognition of and resistance to the ongoing counter-insurgency in which we live." He elaborated on how enacting solidarity through boycott "refreshes" American and Israeli radical thought: "Such refreshment takes the form of an anti-national (and anti-institutional) internationalism—the renewal of insurgent thought, insurgent planning and insurgent feeling as a radical insolvent exchanged between those who refuse to be held by the counter-insurgent forces of an already extant two-state (U.S./Israel) solution. Standing with the Palestinians gives us something to stand upon precisely so that we can stand against the horrifically interinanimate remains of state sovereignty and exceptionalism in its biopolitical, 'democratic' form."[5] Thus heeding the call for a boycott of Israeli institutional academic institutions is seen as serving two functions: that for which it was initially called for, namely contributing to ending Israel's violations of the Palestinian people's rights, as well as a secondary, unintended but significant function of invigorating critical scholarship and insurgent thought in the United States.

One People, beyond Fragmentation and Invented "Nation-States"

Interestingly there are many excellent and extremely important studies of Palestine and its indigenous Palestinian people. Some focus on Palestine before the Nakba and play an important role in disrupting the Zionist discourse on the nonexistence of a Palestinian people in historic Palestine. *Al-Nakba*, Arabic for "the Catastrophe," is how we Palestinians refer to our expulsion in 1948, the large-scale ethnic cleansing of 80 percent of the indigenous people from an estimated 550 towns and villages, to allow for the establishment of the settler-colonial state of Israel. Some of these studies include Walid Khalidi's *Before Their Diaspora: A Photographic History of the Palestinians, 1867–1948* and *All That Remains: The Palestinian Villages Occupied and Depopulated by Israel in 1948*, as well as the diaries of most Zionist leaders, many of whom became Israeli government officials upon the creation of the state. Indeed the writings of the early Zionist leaders alone provide ample evidence of their full awareness of the violence of the colonial enterprise they were engaged in. This awareness is summed up by Vladimir Jabotinsky's statement as early as 1923: "Zionist colonization, even the most restricted, must either be terminated or carried out in defiance of the will of the native population."[6] More recently the former deputy mayor of Jerusalem Meron Benvenisti also asserted the basic Zionist understanding that Israel is a settler colonial state dispossessing the indigenous population: "The basic story here is not one of two national movements that are confronting each other; the basic story is that of natives and settlers. It's the story of the natives who feel that people who came from across the sea infiltrated their natural habitat and dispossessed them."[7] Despite the wishfully delusional claims of certain American politicians who would have their constituents believe the Palestinian people are "an invented nation," these studies, as well as the prolific writings of proto-Zionists and early Zionists, all show that we not only existed, tended the land, and lived in hamlets, villages, and major cities, but that we also identified and were known as a distinct people, with specific cultural norms and traditions unique to us that distinguish us to this day from our closest neighbors in Lebanon, Syria, Jordan, and Egypt.

In addition to historical studies that look at pre-1948 Palestine, many of the more recent studies focus on the current circumstances of the Palestinian people as refugees in the Occupied West Bank. One particularly poignant book is Muna Hamzeh's *Refugees in Our Own Land: Chronicles from a Palestinian Refugee Camp in Bethlehem*. Other books look at the living conditions of Palestinians within Israel, the "'48 Palestinians," those who never left. Among these are Rhoda Kanaaneh and Isis Nuseir's edited volume *Displaced at Home: Ethnicity and Gender among Palestinians in Israel* and Ben White's *Palestinians in Israel: Segregation, Discrimination, and Democracy*.

Clearly there is no lack of documentation of Israel's nature as a colonial state that ethnically cleansed the indigenous people of the land it (un)settled. Nevertheless when our existence as the indigenous people of the land is recognized by the dominant discourse, it is generally dismissed as quasi illegitimate because Palestine did not exist as a nation-state prior to 1948. This is all the more offensive because the very concept of the nation-state is an eighteenth-century European idea, which should not be the determining criterion for whether or not a society—especially one that is not European—is grounded in its homeland. By this logic all indigenous peoples everywhere are "invented" because their existence as societies in their ancestral land predates European colonialism and the European concept of the nation-state. But more important, as M. J. Rosenberg points out, if the Palestinians are an "invented" people, then surely so are the Israelis, who were

Arab, European, and African Jews prior to 1948 and only started identifying as Israeli in 1948, when Israel as a nation-state was created, "invented," so to speak, by the United Nations.[8]

I cite all of these studies of the Palestinian people because they provide an important counterpart to the discourse coming out of and sanctioned by Israeli universities, where sociology books omit the Palestinian narrative, historical accounts and textbooks erase our Nakba, geography books erase the names of our towns and villages, and archaeology departments discard Palestinian artifacts, selecting only ancient Jewish finds as worthy of identification. This erasure of the indigenous people, which illustrates the complicity of the Israeli academy, is to be expected, considering the nature of Israel as a settler-colonial state seeking legitimacy as rightful owners of the land who would then dismiss the "transitory" nature of the people who inhabited it uninterruptedly for millennia. This denial of the indigeneity of the Palestinian people it has displaced is corroborated by Israel's official insistence that the Palestinians were a nomadic people who roamed the region from southern Lebanon to Egypt and Transjordan rather than a settled people who identified with cities such as Haifa, Yaffa, Jerusalem, and Gaza. Surely Golda Meir's flippant response to a British journalist in 1969, in which she describes the Palestinians as "southern Syrians" before claiming we "never existed," epitomizes this distancing of the Palestinians from our homeland. Answering a reporter's question regarding her feelings about having displaced a people to create the Jewish state, Meir said, "When was there an independent Palestinian people with a Palestinian state? It was either southern Syria before the First World War, and then it was a Palestine including Jordan. It was not as though there was a Palestinian people in Palestine considering itself as a Palestinian people and we came and threw them out and took their country away from them. They did not exist."[9]

The erasure of the Palestinian people takes an even more serious turn in allied circles who claim solidarity with the Palestinian people yet seem willing to jettison the rights of the exiled 70 percent majority who are now in the *shatat* (Arabic for "exile," "diaspora"). A notable exception is Gabriel Piterberg's aptly titled essay "Erasures," which documents the Zionist consensus around the denial of the Palestinian right of return. Piterberg concludes, "The easy use of the term [*final solution*, in reference to the refugee problem in Israel] is striking. Here lie the historical roots of the obsessive refusal to concede to the Palestinians the right of return, which—more than the unity of Jerusalem—is the widest consensual basis of Israeli politics today. It is this which explains the genuine—preposterous—belief that withdrawal from the territories occupied in 1967 and dismantling of the settlements would be a painful compromise."[10] Indeed no solution could be complete, final, or just that does not address the entirety of the Palestinian people.

Gender and the Demographic Threat

My contention throughout this essay (as well as throughout my activism) is that partial solutions and the "liberation of the few" (say, in the West Bank and Gaza Strip) are inadequate and can compound rather than solve a problem. As such my emphasis is always on the larger Palestinian people in the Diaspora, not because we are the majority but simply because we are Palestinians and as such wish to regain the human rights denied us both at home and in the Diaspora. Nevertheless so long as there is a normative discourse that views some Palestinians as a demographic threat and not others, the circumstances of those "threatening" Palestinians must be discussed separately. This normative discourse was foregrounded most recently in a January 1, 2013, report announcing that "Palestinians will outnumber Israeli Jews in 2020" and explaining that, while Palestinians in Israel, the West Bank, and Gaza currently number 5.8 million, compared to the 6 million Israeli Jews, with the Palestinian birth rate being slightly higher than that of Israeli Jews the two populations will be equal in 2016, and the balance will tip in favor of Palestinians in 2020, who will then number 7.2 million to Israeli Jews at 6.9 million.[11]

The gendered aspect of the racist discourse, which views a certain population as presenting a "demographic" threat, is multilayered in Israel. There is the universal racism that celebrates declining birth rates among the "undesirable" population—in this case Palestinian households—while seeking ways to increase the rate among the "chosen people," Jewish households. This racism is compounded by the unfounded accusation that Palestinian parents "hate Jews more than they love their children" and as such continue to engage in and provoke the "retaliatory" violence that leads to Palestinian deaths. Racist population control also relies specifically on violence against women. So it is not surprising that Mordechai Kedar, an Israeli military intelligence officer turned academic, matter-of-factly suggested that "raping the wives and mothers of Palestinian combatants" would deter attacks by Hamas militants. While Kedar later explained that he was not actually advocating rape as a national strategy, because, in his view, "Israel would never commit or condone immoral and illegal acts," his words nevertheless expressed the banality of concerted sexual violence in situations of war.[12]

Similarly an Israeli Knesset member, Ayelet Shaked, cited in the epigraph, who was later appointed Israel's justice minister, openly called for the murder of Palestinian women because they give birth to "little snakes."[13]

As a "modern" settler-colonial state, however, Israel has adopted a particular discourse on the gender dynamics of the "uncivilized natives" it must deal with, one that differs in outward manifestation, if not at its critical core, from Gayatri Spivak's famous observation that colonial powers justify their occupations by projecting themselves as "saving brown women from brown men."[14] Indeed while Israel frequently avails itself of the standard colonial trope of comparing its own "advanced" treatment of women with that of the (imputed regressive) colonized, it has focused on what constitutes the twenty-first-century colonial discourse on gendered modernity, namely homonormativity, the "advanced, civilized" country's treatment of its (select) gay citizens. Thus Israel has been very active in polishing its image as a gay-friendly country, waging a global pinkwashing campaign that would distract from its violations of human rights.

Pinkwashing, the attempt to project Israel as a gay-friendly country in a barbaric homophobic region, is then the twenty-first-century manifestation of the Zionist colonialist narrative of bringing civilization to an otherwise backward land—a narrative that sanitizes the violence of occupation while erasing indigenous experience, struggle, and resistance. And just as the Zionist myth of "making the desert bloom" completely distorted the reality of the ethnic cleansing of Palestine by failing to mention, for example, that native olive trees were uprooted so that imported pine trees could be planted, so pinkwashing distorts the reality of Israel's violence against all Palestinians, regardless of sexuality. Scholars of gender studies need to be cautious. After all, as the queer Palestinian activist Sami Shamali puts it, "there is no magic pink door in the Apartheid wall."[15]

Palestinian women and queers have long organized to counter sexism, homophobia, and colonialism and have been extremely eloquent in our response to this exploitation of our challenging circumstances by Israel. All Palestinian women know that their greater oppressor, who denies them freedom of movement, freedom of education, freedom to travel in and out of their country, freedom to elect the politicians who represent them and legislate their lives, and, in the case of Gaza, even the freedom to access adequate nutrition—basically the oppressor who violates their human rights—is not Palestinian heteropatriarchy but the Israeli occupation and apartheid policies. As the group Palestinian Queers for Boycott, Divestment, and Sanctions recently wrote in another affirmation that a selective approach and a partial solution are nonstarters for radical Palestinians, "Israeli policies and occupation do not distinguish between queer and straight. All Palestinians—queer and straight—must deal with the effects of the apartheid wall, checkpoints, and illegal settlements, and settlers' violence, not to mention living under Israeli military law that strips them of their rights as civilians. All Gazans, including queers, live under an illegal siege in the de-facto open-air prison that is the Gaza strip. And like all Palestinian citizens of Israel, queers are subject to institutionalized discrimination in laws, education, and throughout their public and private lives."[16]

The Global Demographic Threat

Beyond the birth rate of Palestinians in historic Palestine, the greater demographic threat to Israel is the one Israel does not acknowledge: the refugees scattered around the globe, beyond the borders of historic Palestine. Our circumstances are extremely diverse. Tens of thousands were born and have died in the squalor of Lebanon's refugee camps, set up as temporary tent shelters in the aftermath of the Nakba and scenes of large-scale massacres decades later, as they grew into concrete slums on the margins of the larger cities; Sabra and Shatila, on the outskirts of Beirut, and Nahr el-Bared, outside of Tripoli, are but the most prominent of these. With the U.S. war on Iraq we heard of the plight of the Palestinians who had been living in Iraq and had become displaced yet again, sheltered in temporary camps on the border with Syria. Yarmouk camp in Syria bears ghastly witness to the seemingly endless misery of displacement and homelessness. Other Palestinian refugees live in Jordan, many of whom have no option but to trade their national identity for the benefits they derive from Jordanian citizenship. Millions are scattered in the non-Arab diaspora, from Austria and Australia to Canada and the United States. And wherever we are, we are organizing to be recognized as one people, unwilling to give up on our UN-recognized inalienable human right, the right to return to our homeland. "The old will die, and the young will forget," Israel's first prime minister, David Ben Gurion, is reported to have told his general staff in the flush of euphoria that followed the creation of the state of Israel.[17] But from all corners of the globe, in a multiplicity of languages, the Palestinians are looking to Palestine and clamoring "We will return." Thus, more than any political ideology, we are the "demographic threat" confronting Israel as it seeks to erase our very existence. It does not matter whether we left out of fear for our lives or out of naïveté, in the belief that we would be back within two weeks. It would not even matter if the Zionist version were true, that we left because the neighboring Arab leaders told us they would fight our fight and regain our country for us and have thus utterly failed us. The circumstances of our having become refugees are irrelevant; our right of return is enshrined in the Universal Declaration of Human Rights and in United Nations Security Council Resolution 194. Whatever one may think of the human rights framework, as it is the United Nations that created Israel as a nation-state, Israel should comply with UN resolutions.

The real existential threat to Israel is the millions of Palestinians in the shatat, whose inalienable human right, the right of return, Israel continues to violate. We are the millions whom Israel refuses to even consider in negotiations, because if we were allowed to return or to vote for our representatives, the myth of "Jewish democracy" would be shattered beyond the illusion of repair. The "threat" that we represent was expressed in the bluntest terms by Justice Asher Grunis, representing the majority opinion of the Israeli Supreme Court when they decided against granting Israeli citizenship to the spouses of Israeli Arabs (the 1948 Palestinians) who marry Palestinian refugees from the West Bank, Gaza, or anywhere in the global Diaspora. "Human rights are not a prescription for national suicide," Grunis stated, thus agreeing that the preservation of the nation of Israel (as a Jewish state) necessitates the violation of the human rights of some of its citizens.[18]

It is within this context that the BDS Campaign, the Palestinian-led call for solidarity, appears as the only strategy for a solution to the circumstances of the entire Palestinian people. That solution, in turn, allows for a redefinition of sovereignty beyond the treacherous confines of nation-states and official ID cards so that all can live equally in their homeland, "from the river to the sea," while those of us who are culturally and ethnically Palestinian can not only claim this identity but have it recognized, so that we are reinscribed where we have been erased.

Academic Responsibility

If the implementation of a basic human right poses an existential threat to any system, then surely that system is seriously flawed and must be overcome, abolished. Merely writing an essay about Israel as a settler-colonial state and an apartheid regime will not change that sorry reality. Teaching about the injustice in Palestine is not enough. Education that does not translate into action is nearly worthless. As academics we must realize that writing and teaching are not all that we can do. If we want to act in solidarity with the Palestinian people, then we must comply with the call issued by Palestinian civil society.

The BDS movement has grown in leaps and bounds since the call was issued and gained more supporters globally after Israel's war on Gaza in 2008–9. In the aftermath of that war American scholars founded the U.S. Campaign for the Academic and Cultural Boycott of Israel, which now has over one thousand academic endorsers. These endorsers can play an extremely important role in bringing attention to Israel's violations of international law, yet there are tens of thousands of academics who shy away from even signing a statement in support of Palestinian rights. Lashing out against academic complacency in 1994, a full decade before the call for academic and cultural boycott was issued, Edward Said had written, "Nothing in my mind is more reprehensible than those habits of mind in the intellectual that induce avoidance, that characteristic turning away from a difficult and principled position which you know to be the right one, but which you decide not to take. . . . Personally I have encountered them in one of the toughest of all contemporary issues, Palestine, where fear of speaking out about one of the greatest injustices in modern history has hobbled, blinkered, muzzled, many who know the truth and are in a position to serve it."[19]

Today more scholars are speaking out. Over the past few years numerous scholars and cultural workers have visited Palestine to see for themselves the extremes of violent dispossession and discrimination the indigenous people of the land suffer on a daily basis. Most have issued strongly worded statements denouncing the twenty-first-century manifestation of apartheid that poisons every aspect of the lives of the Palestinians in Israel and the West Bank. Their statements reveal courage, integrity, and the impulse to stop these violations. More important, these delegates grasp the fact that a comprehensive boycott, which includes an academic boycott, is crucial for the success of the BDS Campaign, which in turn will bring about the solution to the problems facing the millions of Palestinians around the world. One recent example is the collective statement issued by five professors upon their return from a January 2012 visit to the West Bank. Explaining that boycott is "a tool of solidarity," these scholars write, "Neither periodic pressure from diplomats and non-governmental organizations, nor international legal judgments condemning Israel's wall in the West Bank, the settlements, or the siege on Gaza, nor the ongoing, and now visibly fraudulent 'peace process' itself, have pierced the veil of Israeli impunity. In response to a call from within Palestinian civil society, we therefore declare our support for the US Campaign for the Academic and Cultural Boycott of Israel."[20]

As engaged academics we must acknowledge the complicity of the Israeli academy in facilitating and maintaining the occupation and dispossession of the Palestinian people, along with the denial of their basic human rights. Writing about South Africa's struggle with apartheid and the strategy that put an end to that brutal system of institutionalized discrimination, the South African academic Jacklyn Cock explains, "I think opposition to academic boycotts tends to privilege the university as an ivory tower that is divorced from its social context, and in the South African case, the notion of isolating the regime was a very significant nonviolent action."[21] The intimate complicity of the Israeli academy in Israel's dispossession and violation of the human rights of the Palestinians has been amply documented, and as academics we are in a unique position to contribute to the solution by boycotting Israeli universities, thus exerting upon them the kind of pressure that brought about the end of apartheid in South Africa.[22]

It is simply not enough to write about the issue. As the Palestinian spoken word artist Remi Kanazi put it, "We don't need another book explaining the situation, we need a lesson plan to stop the next bomb from dropping."[23] For engaged scholars the success of an article or book must not be determined by whether it was published in a prestigious scholarly journal or university press. Instead it must be judged by the impact it has on the situation it is analyzing. All scholarship is political. Scholars of ethnic studies, critical race theory, postcolonial studies, and women's and gender studies must embrace the subversive politics and praxis that birthed their disciplines and must do more than write about settler-colonialism and racial and gender apartheid. They must, and can, contribute to ending these institutionalized systems of racial oppression by acting in solidarity with the oppressed against the oppressors. As Rima Merriman put it in her critique of artists and scholars who continue to work with Israeli institutions:

> Being in solidarity entails being able to take direction from those one claims to be in solidarity with. Learning how to take direction, as to what is it that those we are in solidarity with wish us to do, is a huge aspect of shifting the relationships of power between the oppressed and the oppressor. It is also a way to really come face to face with our own true commitment and power issues. To do as we wish, is not being in solidarity. It is practicing supremacist charity. I say supremacist, because even when people claim to be in solidarity, they refuse to relinquish their own power and privilege as individuals. They refuse to surrender their own interests. They refuse to recognize that the collective must always

> be greater than the individual, or we are not in solidarity at all. We are then independent actors who cannot accept taking direction for whatever reason.[24]

Fortunately there is a detailed road map, the Boycott, Divestment, and Sanctions movement, with its history of success in redressing institutional wrongs. Heeding that call is the only way critical activist scholars can claim to be genuinely in solidarity with the entirety of the Palestinian people, so that liberation, when it finally happens, is genuinely that, rather than a privileging of the few. Because wherever we may have ended up as a result of our shatat, we are all Palestinians.

NOTES

1. BDS Movement, "Palestinian Civil Society Call for BDS," July 9, 2005, accessed October 1, 2015, http://www.bdsmovement.net/call.

2. Harjo wrote on her public Facebook page, "Signing the petition would have denied me this right to travel and see for myself." See her entry on December 13, 2012, at https://www.facebook.com/joyharjopoetsax?ref=ts&fref=ts. Here I need to disclose that I am one of the many activists who reached out to Harjo, only to find my explanatory notes deleted from her public Facebook page. Refusing to hear from those most impacted, while claiming that she is trying to educate herself, is what I consider an act of bad faith.

3. Palestinian Campaign for the Academic and Cultural Boycott of Israel, "Open Letter to Joy Harjo: Heed the Call of Conscience and Cancel Your Tel Aviv Show!," December 8, 2012, accessed October 1, 2015, http://www.pacbi.org/etemplate.php?id=2072.

4. Kauanui et al., "Educators Can't Stay Silent about Israeli Apartheid."

5. Moten, "The New International of Insurgent Feeling."

6. Jabotinsky, "The Iron Wall."

7. Cited in Shavit, "Cry the Beloved Two-State Solution."

8. M. J. Rosenberg, "One Invented Nation or Two?," *Jewish Journal*, December 23, 2011, accessed December 30, 2014, http://www.jewishjournal.com/opinion/article/one_invented_nation_or_two_20111223/.

9. Golda Meir, interview in *Sunday Times*, June 15, 1969, reprinted in *Washington Post*, June 16, 1969.

10. Piterberg, "Erasures," 46.

11. "Palestinians Will Outnumber Israeli Jews by 2020," *Yahoo News*, January 1, 2013, accessed June 19, 2015, http://news.yahoo.com/palestinians-outnumber-israeli-jews-2020-173656342.html;_ylt=AoLEVzaDQ8JVwX8AGDhXNyoA;_ylu=X3oDMTEyMWRpcWo2BGNvbG8DYmYxBHBvcwMxBHZoaWQDQjAzNDFfMQRzZWMDc3I-.

12. Mordechai Kedar, "On Rape, the Culture of Shame—and Radio Interviews," Middle East Insights, July 24, 2014, accessed October 1, 2015, http://mordechaikedar.com/rape-culture-shame-radio-interviews/.

13. "Mothers of All Palestinians Must Be Killed: Israeli MP," Press TV, July 16, 2014, accessed October 1, 2015, http://www.presstv.ir/detail/2014/07/16/371556/israel-must-kill-all-palestinian-mothers/.

14. Spivak, "Can the Subaltern Speak?" (1994), 93.

15. Cited in Segar, "Palestinian Queer Activists Challenge the Pinkwashing of the Israeli Occupation."

16. "World Social Forum: Free Palestine Call for Papers: Queer Visions, BDS, and Pinkwashing," Palestinian Queers for Boycott, Divestment and Sanctions, June 18, 2012, accessed October 1, 2015, http://www.pqbds.com.

17. Quoted in Ben-Zohar, *Ben-Gurion*, 157.

18. https://electronicintifada.net/blogs/ben-white/israels-high-court-upholds-racist-citizenship-law-avoid-national-suicide, accessed October 1, 2015.

19. Said, *Representations of the Intellectual*, 11.

20. Kehaulani et al., "Educators Can't Stay Silent about Israeli Apartheid."

21. Jacklyn Cock, personal communication, 2006.

22. I have written about Israeli academic complicity in another essay, "The Brain of the Monster." My own research as a Diaspora Palestinian not allowed into my homeland was facilitated by the publications of the Alternative Information Center, based in Israel, and notably their extremely well-documented sixty-four-page booklet, "Academic Boycott of Israel and the Complicity of Israel Academic Institutions in Occupation of Palestinian Territories," October 2009, available online at http://www.bdsmovement.net/files/2011/02/E0023–24-Web.pdf, and the more recent, 383-page *Targeting Israeli Apartheid: A Boycott, Divestment and Sanctions Handbook*, available at http://corporateoccupation.files.wordpress.com/2012/01/targeting-israeli-apartheid-jan-2012.pdf.

23. http://mondoweiss.net/2011/11/remi-kanazi-this-poem-will-not-end-apartheid, accessed October 1, 2015.

24. Rima Merriman, "Stanley Jordan: You Don't Get to Peace without Real Solidarity," *Palestine Chronicle*, January 4, 2013, accessed December 30, 2014, http://www.palestinechronicle.com/stanley-jordan-you-dont-get-to-peace-without-real-solidarity/#.

NINE

Restructuring, Resistance, and Knowledge Production on Campus: The Story of the Department of Equity Studies at York University

TANIA DAS GUPTA

The University as a Terrain of Struggle

Despite the fact that the educational system at all levels basically reproduces class, race, gender, and other relations of inequality and oppression, it is not a monolithic and deterministic structure. There are relatively autonomous spaces where individuals—teachers, researchers, administrators, and students—can and do exercise their sense of agency to resist hegemonic relations and ideas and aspire for alternatives. Many authors have described the university as a space where there is struggle in terms of what kind of knowledge is produced, how it is produced, and for whose benefit it is produced.[1] Indeed knowledge is cultural capital, as Bourdieu has argued,[2] and there are contested social relations of ownership and control over it, particularly in educational sites. Richard Johnson points out that progressive educators who are committed to "working with ethnic minority, working-class or mature students" face a tension between "what is really useful to students and to the subordinated collectives with which they identify and the institutional requirements of the academy."[3] In the 1960s and 1970s, when social conditions on and off campus in North America and beyond created the environment for furthering human rights and social justice, certain departments developed their work and their identity around working with historically marginalized students, focusing on providing access to them, creating support structures for their retention, and developing courses and programs addressing their experiences of oppression and their aspirations for social justice. Students from marginalized communities, or "nontraditional" students, as they are often referred to, continue today to negotiate and maneuver their existence in the proverbial ivory tower, seeking out supportive mentors, carefully choosing courses that are of interest to them, sifting through their readings, taking back skills and theories that they deem to be useful in their own lives and their community lives.[4] Although they may be marginalized in the process and many are unable to withstand the exclusions they encounter, they exercise their agency to steer through the corridors of higher learning, hoping to take back something of value to themselves and their communities. The School of Social Sciences at York University, which later transformed into the Department of Equity Studies, can be seen as exemplifying such processes.

A shift began to occur as we entered the 2000s, when inclusion of students from marginalized communities became more and more challenging and sustaining alternative pedagogies, innovative programs, and administrative structures seemed like an uphill battle as neoliberal values took hold on campuses. Such practices as the commodification of knowledge, the consumerism of the teaching and learning process, and the control of academic labor through increasing documentation transformed our work. This shift often became dramatically evident during restructuring exercises, where certain units and faculties historically associated with nonmainstream knowledge seemed to be targeted for retrenchment and rationalization. Of course these exercises continue to be couched in the discourse of benefiting students, transparency, knowledge for social relevance, and accountability, although market-oriented language also seep in, such as marketability, viability, feasibility, competition, and knowledge mobilization.

Focus of This Essay

On July 1, 2010, a two-year restructuring process closed down the Atkinson Faculty of Liberal and Professional Studies (formerly known as Atkinson College, both henceforth referred to as Atkinson) at York University, which had focused on adult education for working students for five decades. The School of Social Sciences (SSS), which was located in this faculty, had developed cutting-edge programs in such areas as antiracism, indigenous studies, human rights, ethnicity, and diaspora studies. It had built up a diverse faculty, arguably one of the most racially diverse on campus. With the closing of the faculty, the critical and innovative work of this unit was threatened with fragmentation and demise. Each of the programs of the SSS would be allocated to existing disciplinary and interdisciplinary units, and faculty teaching in those programs would be dispersed also. Within this context professors within SSS took a bold step and proposed the formation of a new department, called Equity Studies, in an effort to resist fragmentation and instead retain a space in which their work could continue in the new administrative structure. So the Department of Equity Studies (DES) came into being as the old faculty was terminated.

The story of the elimination of Atkinson and units like the School of Social Sciences and the formation of DES demonstrates that the university is an industrial complex, nonetheless providing a terrain of struggle and creating conditions for new challenges at every step. This essay is a case study of DES based on an autoethnographic account by the author, who was the chair of the SSS and the founding chair of the DES during the entire period of the second restructuring process, between 2004 and 2009. This first-person account is substantiated with related primary documentary and secondary literature. The essay illustrates two important realities. First, it shows that recent restructuring of postsecondary programs in a neoliberal capitalist context threatens the fragile gains of earlier decades in establishing social justice–oriented courses and programs, including those in critical ethnicity, indigenous, diaspora, and antiracism studies. Second, it suggests that the development of administrative units such as DES and other, similar units across Canada and the United States can not only resist fragmentation of earlier progress but can build them to a new height where a stand-alone unit is able to more effectively profile a vision based on alternative epistemologies, methodologies, and pedagogies, much like women's studies units did in the realm of feminism. Additionally such interdisciplinary units enable cross-fertilization across programs related to social justice to give rise to new and innovative programs, such as the ones produced by DES, including the Human Rights and Equity Studies Program and the Race, Ethnicity and Indigeneity Program, later renamed the Multicultural and Indigenous Studies Program. Such programs indicate the rise of new knowledge bases in individual silos and also a new politics of social justice, human rights, and equity based on a critique of status quo epistemologies mindful of how differently marginalized peoples are positioned in relation to each other.

Atkinson College

In 1991 I was hired into Atkinson College, in the Department of Sociology. At the demise of Atkinson Faculty in 2009, a celebratory volume was published to capture its unique history and vision.[5] Joan Gibson, a senior professor, wrote that "among its biggest beneficiaries were those generally debarred from continuing their education: early school leavers, those in full-time employment, the economically or socially disadvantaged, women and immigrants."[6] In later years more and more racialized immigrants (reflecting Canada's immigration trends following the Second World War) were entering the faculty in an effort to recuperate educational credentials that had been lost due to the devaluation of their pre-immigration educational qualifications and work experiences, a persistent problem for Canadian immigrants identified in many academic and government reports. An example of our student body was my mother (originally from India), who became a student in this college in her thirties. She completed a BA in sociology after ten years of part-time education while she worked full-time in the secretarial-clerical field and simultaneously raised two children and helped establish her newly immigrated family in Toronto. Her BA in India had been assessed as a grade 13–level education in Canada, which limited her economic and educational opportunities. She had not been able to access other postsecondary education due to systemic barriers against students with prior education outside Canada. Eventually she earned an MA, changed her career path, and became an adult educator, first as a teacher of adult English as Second Language and math classes and later as an administrator of such classes.

Given its mandate, most faculty members at Atkinson had a social justice orientation and had devoted years to developing unique, innovative, and flexible pedagogies, community outreach and activism, research trajectories, curricula, and educational approaches that were very different from other colleges and faculties within York University, which catered predominantly to traditional students who were younger and directly from high schools eager to pursue full-time education. Atkinson College, and the Sociology Department in particular, went beyond simply providing courses, instead creating cutting-edge programs that were unique in the university and indeed in the whole country. Atkinson's uniqueness was in providing full-time faculty and staff in creating the structures, services, and programs to serve nontraditional students rather than as an afterthought by those teaching full-time students. A former president of the university, H. Ian Macdonald, commented that

Atkinson took the vision of the university into the community through its students, many of whom were public school teachers.[7]

Reflecting back, I believe that the nature of the marginalized student population that Atkinson attracted also had an impact on the curriculum that was created in response to their social experience. Ironically I was hired into an innovative program, located in the same department that my mother had graduated from, several years after she graduated. Progressive faculty members with a history of teaching, research, and activism in anticolonialism and antiracism had developed a Certificate in Anti-Racist Research and Practice (CARRP) in 1989–90, then known as a Race Relations Certificate program, catalyzed by incidents of racism on and off campus and the antiracism movement in the city of Toronto.[8] This program was very innovative in that it conceptualized students as engaging in antiracist research and practice with communities outside the campus in addition to their in-class academic work. Evidently my antiracism activism in the city was viewed by Atkinson Sociology as an asset for this program. I share my experience with you just to provide an example of the kinds of students who attended Atkinson, the kinds of programs it created, and the kinds of academics it hired over the years. Brenda Spotton Visano and Kristin Taylor's volume contains more such stories.[9]

One of the things I perceived upon starting at Atkinson was that colleagues in the full-time programs of the university considered the college an inferior sibling. It was reported that "Atkinson was once referred to [by a colleague outside Atkinson] as a place for part-time students, part-time minds." We were constructed as deficient, while the rest of the university was perceived as the "main" university. We were in the margins of the university, often considered its "continuing studies" branch, as Rhonda Lenton, former dean, currently provost, mentions. And yet in terms of real work, our courses and research were equal to if not more innovative than what other faculties produced. A case in point is the Certificate in Anti-Racist Research and Practice, unique of its kind in the whole country. Atkinson always had more than its share of awards for teaching and research on campus. As one professor and former dean, Livy Visano, says, "Atkinson, that 'other' Faculty, contributed to York University by committing itself to enabling the 'othered' students, the 'othered' discipline."[10] It became evident that a "we/they" dynamic prevailed between Atkinson and our counterparts who taught full-time students. We were subjected to contradictory demands, on the one hand being required to harmonize with our full-time programs, and on the other being interrogated as to how we were unique. Atkinson also had a professional studies side, including a school of social work, several small health units, and a very large administrative studies unit. There was always a suggestion that liberal studies programs for part-time students offered in the evenings should not exist separately from the daytime degree programs, although during periodic reviews mandated by the provincial government, external reviewers invariably concluded against "amalgamation of units."[11] Perhaps as a result of such contradictory suggestions, Atkinson had developed a separate and strong identity of its own based on two features: its provision of adult education to part-time students and expertise in providing good quality evening and summer degree programs in a variety of formats. However, the talk of reorganization and restructuring was ever present as an invisible possibility ever since I had been at Atkinson.

Restructuring and Resistance

There were two rounds of restructuring in my time at Atkinson, once in 2000 and another in 2009, the latter of which is the focus of this essay. In the first round, as mentioned before, the college became known as the Faculty of Liberal and Professional Studies, thus adding a third distinctiveness to our collective existence, that of imbricating liberal arts with professional studies. With this development several independent liberal arts units (sociology, social science, political science, and geography) were merged to create the School of Social Sciences through a lengthy process of consultation with chairs and directors, the dean, and other administrators.[12] The amalgamation of these units was difficult as each department had its own disciplinary culture and history, not to mention personalities, and there was considerable resistance to the prospect of becoming interdisciplinary. We were mostly invested in our disciplinary identities and found it difficult to leave them. However, we were assured that each disciplinary degree program would be preserved (although in hindsight the demise of geography was a precursor to what was to come later) while strengthening and further exploring the development of new interdisciplinary degrees.[13]

I became a part of this unit, the School of Social Sciences, within Atkinson. After hard work on the part of its first two chairs, executive members (of which I was one), and administrative staff, the unit emerged as a much larger and more dynamic space in which many interdisciplinary, social justice–oriented programs, courses, research, and other activities developed. The inaugural chair emphasized the unique antiracism focus in the unit, and CARRP, originally developed within the Department of Sociology, was a flagship in this new unit. Affirmative action hiring was a strong focus, and we hired a number of exceptional faculty members, including two female indigenous scholars and an antiracism, feminist scholar. Despite the initial resistance, faculty members were able to find common cause in their commitment to equity and social justice. There was a sense of excitement, creativity, and collaboration that was palpable. We felt that we had overcome the constant need to justify our existence.

Reassured by the dean that there would be no further restructuring, I became chair of the SSS in July 2004. A sense of camaraderie developed in our unit, and new programs were collaboratively conceived, thus moving interdisciplinarity to a higher level. From our political science program colleagues conceptualized new interdisciplinary programs in public policy and administration and public administration and justice studies. Eventually these new programs were moved out to establish a new unit of public policy and administration, diverting some of our meager resources (people and courses). The Program in Race, Ethnicity and Indigeneity and the Certificate in Indigenous Studies grew, the latter jointly developed with another unit in the main university. These remained solidly in SSS and were faced with great obstacles in the approval process. The proposals for each of these new programs had to be taken forward through a process of what seemed like endless collegial consultations, approval in several committees and councils, and final approval by the senate and board of the university. These proved to be strenuous exercises often marked by opposition from a number of key departments.

No sooner had the new faculty and the units in it consolidated than talk of restructuring erupted once again. Within four months of my becoming chair of SSS, a letter was received from higher administration proposing a restructuring of liberal studies on our campus. It had been announced earlier that a new Faculty of Health would be established at the university to which all the health-related units from Atkinson would migrate. It was felt that this would affect the preexisting faculties, including Atkinson, in a fundamental way. Moreover it was felt that the restructuring of Atkinson would address the fact that it no longer held a monopoly over serving part-time students, who were apparently taking courses from all faculties (not just Atkinson), at all times of the day and evening. There was a suggestion that prospective students were confused by the provision of courses in these different faculties and that there was a need for "greater coherence, consistency and simplicity in its offerings."[14] To what extent students had been consulted about the prospect of restructuring and amalgamating degrees remained a question for some.

Restructuring was slow and protracted at first, and then drastic. Within months of becoming chair, I and program coordinators were called by administration to be a part of a committee along with other chairs, directors, deans, and administrators in relevant units to discuss restructuring. Colorful pages of statistics and PowerPoint presentations were made to demonstrate that our student body had changed to the extent that there was no rationale for the continuation of two faculties (arts, for full-time, day students; and Atkinson, for part-time, night students) and the stated duplication of our degrees and programs. The bottom line was that these programs would be amalgamated. My unit unanimously voted to oppose restructuring. Senior colleagues in my unit advised that the threat of restructuring was nothing new and that it would eventually dissipate. I represented my unit's strong opposition to restructuring in the chairs' and directors' meetings, arguing that Atkinson was a unique place and that our degrees in social sciences were very distinctive from the degrees of our full-time counterparts. We formed an ad hoc committee within my unit and developed a document to substantiate our point, but to no avail. I heard from a supportive colleague in another unit in Atkinson that there was no point being an ostrich and refusing to see what was inevitable. It was suggested to me that my unit and I should accept this situation and move on.

Retreat and Re-create

Once it became clear that restructuring was inevitable, we started looking at alternatives that would keep the unique interdisciplinary parts of our programs intact, such as in the Race, Ethnicity, and Indigeneity Program, the Indigenous Studies Certificate, the Certificate in Anti-Racist Research and Practice, and the Social Science Degree Program. We explored amalgamating with other units with shared social justice and equity goals; however, this did not seem to go anywhere. At an open community forum organized by administration during the consultation phase of restructuring, I asked whether a unit named Sociology and Equity Studies could coexist with the preexisting sociology unit. I pointed out that a similar model existed at the University of Toronto, which has a Sociology and Equity Studies Department coexisting with the Sociology Department. Administration seemed intrigued by the idea and did not respond with total negativity. They stated that we would have to demonstrate its uniqueness in order for such a unit to exist. Colleagues in my unit and I took that as a signal to proceed with that idea.

The idea was presented in our SSS meeting. Members felt that we should take the unprecedented step of declaring ourselves a Department of Equity Studies immediately. A unanimous vote solidified this proposal, and this new development was communicated to higher administration. A special meeting was requested with them, and a delegation from the SSS met with them to further discuss the specific requirements for the idea to become reality. Administration made it clear that in order to exist as a stand-alone unit, we would have to offer at least another degree program apart from the Race, Ethnicity and Indigeneity Program, which had just been approved and had no majors yet. After much deliberation among ourselves, we felt that a degree in human rights and equity would be logical given our decades of work in these areas and the fact that we had done some preliminary work in developing such a degree program a few years earlier, which for various reasons had not gone forward at the time. It was planned that a proposal for this new degree and a proposal for the new unit would go forward at the same time as the closure of Atkinson and the SSS. A senior professor in our unit with outstanding proposal-writing skills who had earlier penned the CARRP program was approached to start developing the proposal for such a degree program. The proposal with all its support documents was about the size of a telephone book and had to be taken around for consultation in related units for input and final approval. This was a huge task, requiring hundreds of hours of research, study, and writing. A lot of midnight oil was consumed in doing this. Consultations also required many hours of telephone conversations, meetings, receiving feedback, responding to feedback, including dealing with negative feedback, making new drafts of the proposal based on this feedback, delivering these back to those who had earlier objections, meeting again for further concerns, and final approvals at the end. Despite our best efforts at incorporating everyone's concerns, not everyone approved our proposal.

Opposition to New Programs

Although we received overwhelmingly positive and supportive feedback on our new program proposals, there were a few negative ones. Anyone who has engaged in program proposals knows that even one negative letter can jeopardize the entire project. For both our new programs—the Human Rights and Equity Studies Program and the Race, Ethnicity and Indigeneity Program—we had a small number of negative letters to deal with.

In a nutshell, a handful of departments stated from their viewpoint the redundancy of the proposed new programs because they were already doing what the new program proposed. The letters thus indirectly implied that we were "competing," "duplicating" what already existed, and were academically lacking. The discourse in these letters was polite and collegial but nonetheless appeared dismissive. From my vantage point, the situation was racialized as most of us were faculty of color defending our proposal in what seemed to us a sea of whiteness.

Names and titles of the new program proposals became a source of great concern, and we had to carefully avoid making use of words that had already been used by other units. It was reiterated that students could become confused with similar-sounding words in the titles of different degree programs. It seemed that knowledge was territorialized, and course titles and program names drew boundaries between different departments. Critical interdisciplinary programs such as the Human Rights and Equity Studies Program and the Race, Ethnicity and Indigeneity Program are based on the construction of new knowledge, challenging older boundaries and assumptions with resource implications.

Universities are bastions of ruling, hegemonic cultures with carefully designated canons, theoretical frameworks, methodologies, practices, and gatekeepers guarding the boundaries of mainstream knowledge. By and large the lives, experiences, and concerns of those who are marginalized in society are rarely included. When they are included, they are often articulated and represented by received "experts." Academics who are members of communities of color or indigenous peoples are rarely allowed to represent themselves. They are utilized as research assistants, native informants, and guest speakers, but they are often not full-time scholars and faculty members (although this is slowly changing at our university). Moreover the question of who speaks for whom is never a concern for the mainstream. There is rarely recognition of why and how a course on indigeneity taught by an indigenous person might be different from one taught by a nonindigenous person. There is denial of how research on immigration issues conducted by a first-generation immigrant woman academic of color could be different from research conducted by a nonimmigrant woman or man. And there is a general assumption that people of color and indigenous peoples are not experts: we have the experience, but not the scientific know-how or theoretical acumen that is required for academia. Such assumptions are reproduced by media, funding agencies, relevant unions, and other key institutions that work in conjunction with academia. In saying this, I am not saying that only people of color, immigrants, and indigenous scholars should be teaching antiracism and anticolonial courses or undertaking research in these fields, nor am I saying that only we are capable of progressive and critical practice. All I am saying is that the positionality of teachers and researchers needs to be considered in thinking about the pedagogy of any course or knowledge production. Moreover there should be recognition of the particular expertise and vantage points of those who represent historically marginalized communities. These considerations are of course also relevant for employment equity (or affirmative action) and critical pedagogies, topics of great concern to antiracist, anticolonial, and social justice–oriented academics.

The development of critical new interdisciplinary programs, such as the Race, Ethnicity and Indigeneity Program, Human Rights and Equity Studies, CARRP, and the Certificate in Indigenous Thought, contribute to a counter-hegemonic knowledge base, thereby playing a crucial role in antiracism and anticolonial movements in society at large and in creating a space on campus where students, faculty, and staff from marginalized and underrepresented communities can study and work. Apart from challenging the structures and culture of whiteness in universities, the courses in such programs provide opportunities to develop antiracist, anticolonial, and social justice–oriented students who in turn have an impact on arenas outside the university, through their workplaces, friends, family, and community networks. Academics in such programs conduct research, write, publish, and speak in conferences and workshops and participate in community organizations and virtual spaces, bringing their knowledge into activist arenas. Staff members at the administrative, secretarial, and clerical levels model the interpersonal skills and traits that are required to enable such a space to exist.

Summary

This story has a happy ending, as our proposals for new programs passed all the committees, councils, senate, and board requirements. So did our proposal to establish a Department of Equity Studies, which houses these new programs. In the SSS we had a unique interdisciplinary degree in social science developed in the 1970s by faculty members, many of whom are now in DES. Since our department was now going to be called Equity Studies, administrators felt that the social science degree could not be housed there because students would be confused. Instead it would be housed in the Department of Social Science. We spent most of two years negotiating to retain this degree in DES with the argument that equity and social justice were central learning objectives of this degree and therefore rightly belonged in DES. In the end, however, the program was moved to its namesake unit.

Although we were able to consolidate opposition to restructuring and later channeled our energies to create the DES, a small oasis in the midst of the disruption of restructuring, many challenges lie ahead, including making a success of this new unit. We are constantly made aware of neoliberal concerns with performance and enrollments. Gone are the days of pursuing knowledge as an end in itself. Now we are in a period when we have to demonstrate a program's demand, quality, and viability based on standard criteria, otherwise it can be cut back. As of the publishing of this essay, the Race, Ethnicity and Indigeneity Program has been renamed Multicultural and Indigenous Studies, a process that proved to be quite difficult. This was instigated by concerns around insufficient student majors in the degree and administrators' feeling that the old name had not attracted young students from high schools because it seemed they were not interested in the study of race and did not quite understand, nor could pronounce, the term *indigeneity*.

What did restructuring achieve? Exhaustion, burnout, anger, grief, and demoralization. It is only now, after five years, that we are beginning to recover from that process. The amalgamation of the two faculties resulted in a massive faculty representing over 50 percent of the university's students. It did not result in simplification and greater balance of faculties on campus, which had been one of the purported goals of restructuring. Some secretarial staff in Atkinson were redeployed to different units, thus disrupting their working relationships and friendships. The increase in evening courses does not necessarily mean more coherent programming for part-time students who can attend classes only in the evening. This would require a logical planning of course offerings which part-time students need to complete their BA degree. It requires advisory and other support services to be offered to part-time students at accessible hours and places for those who can come to campus only in the evening. Such services require additional resources to be allocated for a coordinator of part-time students in each department and changing the working hours of secretarial staff to keep offices open in the evening. It is not clear whether all this is currently happening.

NOTES

1. Johnson, "Afterword"; Canaan and Shumar, *Structure and Agency in the Neoliberal University*; Newson and Buchbinder, *The University Means Business*; McLaren, *Rage and Hope*.

2. Bourdieu, "The Forms of Capital."

3. Johnson, "Afterword," 292.

4. Brandt, "Protocols and Performances"; Brayboy et al., "Indigenous Epistemologies and the Neoliberal View of Higher Education."

5. Spotton Visano and Taylor, *Room to Grow*.

6. Spotton Visano and Taylor, *Room to Grow*, 11.

7. Spotton Visano and Taylor, *Room to Grow*, 20.

8. Das Gupta, "Teaching Anti-Racist Research in the Academy."

9. Spotton Visano and Taylor, *Room to Grow*.

10. Spotton Visano and Taylor, *Room to Grow*, 145, 140, 12, 144.

11. Undergraduate Program Review, "Undergraduate Program Review, Political Science Program Report."

12. The geography degree in the faculty was terminated on the pretext that there were not enough faculty members to make it viable, although several courses in geography were retained in the SSS to contribute to a social science degree. This meant that new part-time students had no access to a BA degree program in geography.

13. Undergraduate Program Review, "Undergraduate Program Review, Political Science Program Report."

14. Undergraduate Program Review, "Undergraduate Program Review, Political Science Program Report."

TEN

"The Goal of the Revolution Is the Elimination of Anxiety": On the Right to Abundance in a Time of Artificial Scarcity

DAVID LLOYD

The panel for which this essay was initially conceived at the first Critical Ethnic Studies Conference at Riverside was devoted to "social movements and activism." I confess that I was at first uncomfortable with my assignment to this panel: there is something slightly disquieting in the designation of oneself as an activist, the phrase *in my activist life* having all too often something self-regarding about it. More important, for intellectual workers to proclaim themselves *also* activists tends to reinforce the easily assumed division of labor between *scholarship,* which is understood to be disinterested, objective, and professional, and *activism,* which is believed to be tainted by being interested, passionate, and outside the purview of the academy and its evaluations. These are, of course, structural designations, not personal dispositions. They do not have to do with the personal attitude one takes to either scholarship or political engagement but with how the academic-industrial complex segments the world and maintains the systems of value that demarcate the qualities of scholarly work from statements or acts it considers hasty, insufficiently reflective, or strident. Since such a deeply embedded value system, so deeply embedded that it virtually constitutes the political unconscious of the professoriate, has had profound impact on the prospects and careers of all too many scholars in ethnic studies and their allies in other disciplines, we should be wary of reinforcing it.

This division between scholarly disinterest and activism has long structured the academy. It received classic formulation in one of the earliest outlines of the idea of the modern university, Kant's *Conflict of the Faculties*. There Kant defined the role of philosophy, for him a category that embraced all the disciplines that we would now denominate the humanities and social sciences, as the critique of the instrumental disciplines that served the state: theology, law, and medicine. The lower or "minor" discipline judges the higher ones that function as the interested "tools," or *Werkzeuge*, of the state. Its disinterest guaranteed by its lack of instrumental purchase, critical philosophy claims to speak in the name of the universal interest of humankind. The realization of universality, however, turns out to be indefinitely deferred. In the face of an actual transformation of the state, the French Revolution, Kant's response is to fall back on nonparticipatory spectatorship. The "advance towards the better" is revealed not in the social revolution itself but in "the universal and disinterested sympathy" of the philosophical spectator, which recasts revolution "only as an intimation, a historical sign . . . demonstrating the tendency of the human race viewed in its entirety."[1] As Rebecca Comay has nicely put it, "The subject contemplating the scene from the security of a safe place is able to behold itself as a spectatorial collective unified by the *sensus communis* of moral humanity."[2]

Universal humanity thus remains virtual, reduced to the vanishing point of the subject of and in representation. Matthew Arnold's later translation of the Kantian compromise, at a moment in 1865 when the agitation of British workers for the right to political franchise impelled him to reflect back on the French Revolution and its dangers, is at once more brutal and clearer sighted: "*Force till right is ready*; and till right is ready, force, the existing order of things, is justified, is the legitimate ruler."[3]

This little chain of citations offers an abbreviated genealogy of the way the critical, anti-instrumental work of the humanities took on the function of shaping the moral disposition of subjects *for the state* precisely in antagonism to the supposed interest and immediacy of political engagement, "quitting the intellectual sphere and rushing furiously into the political sphere," as Arnold puts it.[4] In the name of an impartial *sensus communis* that grounds the possibility of the universal, the actualization of life in common is perpetually deferred, pending the formation of moral and representative subjects. This brief history also suggests the genealogy of the ego ideal of the scholar, that of the philosophical subject who achieves moral representativeness in standing off from political engagement or "activism." Given that the material condition of possibility of this subjective disposition is, as both Kant and Arnold realized all too well, the protection of the state that in the last instance it serves, its counterpart is an all too ready turn to the invocation of authority and the endorsement of "the existing order of things." Witness the rush by opponents of the American Studies Association's endorsement of the boycott of Israeli academic institutions to invoke the dictates of university presidents, who uniformly pronounced their dedication to the principles of academic freedom in condemnation of this exercise of them.[5] What Fanon ironically dubbed "a unilateral declaration of universality" turns out to be a very shaky foundation from which actually to exercise the critique it supposedly guarantees.[6]

UNDOING THIS SELF-REINFORCING division of labor is one principal task both of critical ethnic studies and of social movements. To interpret the world by thinking critically *is* to change it, insofar as interpreting means refusing the logic of accepting "things as they are." Critique involves not only the establishment of the conditions of possibility of any social phenomenon—its basic definition—but also the perception that because things have *become* what they are, they can and must be made otherwise. Critique of things as they are is historical critique and implies that change is not only possible but inevitable. To name domination is the essential condition of transforming it.

Two projects have been fundamental in the critical work of ethnic studies since W. E. B. Du Bois first questioned how it is to "be a problem"[7]: first, to critique this division of activist and intellectual spheres as an organizing myth of intellectual and political life in modernity by interrogating the economic and political function of the university as a site of the production of knowledge in and for the racial state; second, to deconstruct the distinction between the disinterested or "transparent" subject of knowledge and the pathological or "affectable" object of knowledge that Denise da Silva has shown to be the constitutive racial foundation of academic knowledge.[8] For race-critical practice, the "empirical" can never be invoked as self-evident without the critique of the assumptions that produce its objects, distributing them among the different and aptly named "disciplines" that distinguish the subject of knowledge from the objects on whom it practices. But nor can the critique of the world be detached from its translation into practice, into the practices that it informs and by which it must be constantly transformed, insofar as every practice produces knowledge that is new and therefore not already accommodated by what we thought we knew. To say that these are necessary foundational tasks of a critical ethnic studies is to do no more than return to the initial impetus of ethnic studies, whose roots lie in the insistent demand of antiracist and anticolonial social movements, from civil rights to the antiwar movement and the Third World strikes of the 1960s, not only for access to the university but for the transformation of its structures and ends.

Ironically it has become all the more crucial to critique the academic division of labor—renamed now "professionalism" or "excellence"—precisely at the moment in which the corporatization of the university is breaking down the largely mythical boundaries between pure and applied knowledge. The liberal university of a previous dispensation proudly proclaimed its disinterest and declared its function to be "the development of human beings and society as a whole through the cultivation and enrichment of the human mind and spirit." In a very short time, however, as it has evolved into the "corporate" university, it has forgotten that sense of mission, mystified as it was, and now proclaims a more pragmatic task: "Historic but increasingly archaic divisions between basic and applied research and scholarship often blind both faculty and society at large to the real societal significance of much of university research. By rejecting the false dichotomy between fundamental and applied research, and by creating structures which enable and encourage synergistic interactions among different kinds of research, [it] will secure its status as a university of major societal importance."[9] The corporate university no longer seeks to mask its function as a site of unmediated capitalist reproduction in the language of liberal humanism that was required both by the conditions of the cold war and by the task of producing critical citizens for the democratic state. The former condition determined federal funding of the arts and humanities directly through the National Endowment for the Humanities and the National Endowment for the Arts and indirectly through the funding of university research, student grants, and so forth. The humanities and interpretive social sciences were seen as vital indices of a thriving democratic culture in contradistinction to the Eastern Bloc's totalitarian control of the arts and humanities. The latter condition was inherited from the early function of education as a means to the social integration of a potentially dissident citizenry and was reconfigured and expanded in the course of the struggles for civil rights and affirmative action.[10] With the end of the cold war and the advent of neoliberal regimes, neither condition wields much force, and the educational apparatus is freed to proclaim its directly utilitarian function in the increasingly vocational preparation of students indentured to the labor market by their debt and in the performance of research and development tasks for its corporate sponsors, on whose funding it increasingly relies.

Under such circumstances ethnic studies, like the humanities, can no longer rely for its institutional survival on invoking the function of shaping citizenship for a diverse society (though a corporate version of diversity training has already well learned the lesson of how to serve the business world), nor can it promote its research as a means to creating a more just social order, when neither critical citizenship nor justice seems indispensable to an economic regime increasingly reliant on coercive force to attain its ends. Nor can it rely on the ideal of "academic freedom" that supposedly protects the sacrosanct value of scholarly disinterest. As the recent case of Steven Salaita brutally exemplifies, academic freedom is the first casualty of the bondage of the university to corporate and private donors.[11] By the same token, the drive to corporate efficiencies and monetization of the academy has driven the casualization of academic labor, the erosion of tenure, the steady rise in student fees, and the transformation of universities into PR machines. All these are manifestations of the ongoing drive to appropriate the public good of education that represents about 5.5 percent of the gross domestic product; in their face the philosophical spectator has ever less ground on which to stand and ever less basis for believing itself the representative of common humanity.

This implies that the urgent question of the relation between the production of critical knowledge and those whose interests it serves can no longer be addressed through ethical appeals but regains its direct, political import. A critical ethnic studies can maintain an institutional space only insofar as it affirms its transformative, political role in relation to the communities within and beyond the university whose marginalization, exploitation, and segregation it seeks to redress. It can claim a legitimate intellectual role only insofar as it demands not merely the dispensation of space and resources in the university but a thoroughgoing democratization and transformation of the function and procedures of the university.

Educational institutions indubitably perform a reproductive function for the racial capitalist state. But it is no less true that they remain, for now at least, contested spaces that retain a memory of the struggles out of which they emerged. Schools at all levels, both public and private, constitute a crucial, even strategic sector of what we could call the "second commons." The second commons, a phrase akin to the notion of "second nature" as Georg Lukacs defines it, refers to all those institutions and agencies that were wrested from capital historically by social struggles for the collective means to life that had been expropriated in the process of "accumulation by dispossession" that enclosed the first commons.[12] In place of the immediate means to life that the commons had historically reserved, the social movements that emerged in the course of capitalist development secured such institutional provisions as social welfare, public health, public transportation, power and water—and public educational institutions. This second commons is now the target of the new wave of capitalist accumulation that more or less defines neoliberalism: all these institutions are subject now to an increasingly systematic and violent effort of enclosure that goes by the name of privatization. The financial system seeks to privatize social security and pension funds, releasing these reserves of accumulated capital to the stock market; the private health corporations resist violently any socialization of medical care and exploit attempts to do so in order to capture a larger market of the underinsured; the regents and trustees of public universities collaborate in the increasing privatization of these common resources, raising student fees and integrating campuses with the employment and research goals of private corporations; even public middle and elementary schools are increasingly subject to the inroads of charterization, usually a euphemism for corporate control and profit motivation. As Naomi Klein has documented, cities and towns are increasingly being persuaded to offer up for private control the fundamental resources and services that were hitherto recognized as public goods, from fire departments to water and waste management.[13] Neoliberalism, in other words, everywhere seeks to take hold of and monetize the forms of the second commons that have been the means both to biological life and to life in common. This seizure of public goods is proclaimed to be necessary in the name of the "crisis," of the scarcity of the economic means to fund and maintain these common resources.

Yet paradoxically this time of crisis, in which so many have already suffered immiseration, is in fact a time of abundance. Hunger and homelessness, driven by foreclosure and widespread unemployment, thrive in the midst of plenty, signaling that what we face is an artificial and systemically produced scarcity in and even *through* abundance. Our present scarcity is shadowed by the largest upward redistribution of wealth since the Great Depression. This is, of course, a familiar and fundamental contradiction of capitalism: its cyclical crises are crises of abundance—of overaccumulation—not of scarcity or the failure to produce. As we know, the subprime crisis was itself caused by an *excess* of financial capital, by a glut of unusable investment funds withdrawn from other sectors of the economy. But even in times of crisis, however artificial, there remain abundant resources. Where one hedge fund manager can earn $5 billion and pay only 15 percent in capital gains tax, we know there is no scarcity of means; where the United States can afford to fund Israel $3 billion annually to maintain its settler colonial state, we know there is no shortage of resources; where $1 trillion can be spent on phony wars, while it would take only $25 billion to pay all the tuition and fees of all public universities, we know that the crisis is no less phony than the wars.

Perhaps, then, we need to recognize that precisely what neoliberal capital *fears* is abundance and what it implies. Abundance is the end of capital: it is at once what it must aim to produce in order to dominate and control the commodity market and what designates the limits that it produces out of its own process. Where abundance does not culminate in a crisis of overproduction, it raises the specter that we might demand a redistribution of resources in the place of enclosure and accumulation by dispossession. The alibi of capital is scarcity; its myth is that of a primordial scarcity overcome only by labor regulated and disciplined by the private ownership of the means of production. In a state of generally accessible abundance, on the contrary, could there be exploitation, labor discipline, subjugation? This fear of abundance is deeply inscribed in the history of colonial capital—the instrument that results, according to Rosa Luxemburg, in a process of endless accumulation, crisis by crisis, that can be maintained only by continual incursions into territories that have yet to be subjugated to capital.[14] There the destruction of local economies and ways of life that lays them open to expropriation is always accompanied both by violence and by the artificial production of scarcity.

Abundance is the specter that haunts colonial capitalism as also it haunts the settler. An instance from an early moment in the colonial expansion of the Atlantic world may still stand as an emblem of that anxiety. "Out of the abundance of the heart, the tongue speaks," wrote Edmund Spenser, one of the greatest Elizabethan poets and "a dutiful colonial servant who had acquired a substantial estate in Ireland" as a consequence of the dispossession of the rebellious or resistant native population. The words cited appear in his *View of the State of Ireland*, a text written in 1598 that became notorious for advocating genocide through sword and famine as the only means for overcoming Irish recalcitrance to English civility.[15] The phrase might seem imbued with a poet's appreciation of the fullness of poetic speech or that "spontaneous overflow of powerful feeling" into words of which a later English poet will write.[16] But that is not at all what Spenser the colonialist means. He wants to extirpate, not celebrate this abundance, which is in fact that of the colonial subject who has drunk in the Irish language at the nurse's breast, adjoining the means to life with a life in common in what is, for Spenser, a disturbing and dangerous "infection." He dreads what we might call, after da Silva, the affectable subject's *abundance*. For his fear is of miscegenation and of the engulfment of the settler's children by the native, specifically by the native woman who acts as wet nurse and communicates her tongue to "the childe that sucketh the milke." With the milk the child ingests the language and "the nature and disposition" of the Irish: "For the minde followeth much the temperature of the body: and also the words are the image of the minde, so as they proceeding from the minde, the minde must needs be affected with the words. So that the speach being Irish, the heart must needes bee Irish: for out of the abundance of the heart, the tongue speaketh."[17]

Centuries before postcolonial theory was to identify the ambivalence and hybridity of colonial formations as a cause of anxiety to the colonizer, Spenser fears the contamination of the settler by the language and the culture of the Irish. Specifically, however, what he fears is the specter of an abundance, figured in the breast milk of the native woman, that he is unable to comprehend. It is akin to the abundance of a land that, at the very outset of the text, constitutes the problem that its interlocutors confront, being at once "of so goodly and commodious a soyl" and yet supporting a population obdurately resistant to English conceptions of law and good governance. Accordingly Ireland generates also the fear of an alternative way of life that the English settler can only read as idleness, "theevery," rebellion, and incivility, and yet to which the Irish mysteriously cling. England's perpetual difficulties with Ireland, Spenser fears, may "proceed from the very genius of the soyle."[18]

The dread that Spenser here voices echoes forward through a barrage of settler colonial and colonial capital tracts that provide ample evidence of their fear of a general economy of abundance—and not of some primitive state of necessity or scarcity—which constitutes a challenge to the baleful logic of accumulation by dispossession. Rather than finding a desert and making it bloom, the settler finds a strange abundance and violently reduces it to scarcity, scarcity that is the means to control and exploit. As Luxemburg so clearly saw, "each new colonial expansion is accompanied, as a matter of course, by a relentless battle of capital against the social and economic ties of the natives, who are also forcibly robbed of their means of production and labour power."[19] In the new dispensation of the neoliberal regime, this destruction of "the social and economic ties of the natives" takes the form of the theft of the second commons and of that faint shadow of abundance, freedom from absolute want, that it offered. It is the theft not only of material goods but also of the possibility of imagining a future not determined by the indenture of debt or the terrorism of scarcity and catastrophic illness, unemployment and homelessness; it is the violent denial of the capacity to envisage an alternative to the sheer determining brutality of contemporary capital.

In a letter to Walter Benjamin, Theodor Adorno remarked, "The goal of the revolution is the elimination of anxiety."[20] What Adorno glimpsed was that revolution does not aim principally at rights, political, economic, or even cultural, that represent capitalism's grudgingly allotted compensation for exploitation and dispossession. It aims to pass beyond the regime of mere negative rights to make possible the enjoyment of abundance, of the abundance of the means of life in which lies the potential for the "abundance of the heart" and which would be made feasible by the distribution of the overabundant surplus that capitalism has already produced to the point of provoking its own crisis.

But rather than redistribute, capitalism's response to its cycles of overaccumulation has been to distribute consistently upward to an ever-smaller percentage of the population. Out of potential abundance it creates the semblance of scarcity that it requires to create fear and induce discipline. At the same time, as Luxemburg long ago grasped, in order to continue to accumulate, it must continue to expropriate and dispossess in what is now an increasingly violent frenzy of creative destruction unforeseen even in the *Communist Manifesto*. The wars for the control of oil; the wars to come for water and land; the expansion of the prison system to immobilize the surplus populations that capitalism has produced, like the peasantry evicted in the long decades of enclosure or the subalterns and indigenous people expropriated by colonial settlement; the securitization and militarization of the state: these do not merely take funds from the university and the schools or from health and welfare. They are one with the privatization of education, systematically tied to it as another dimension of the current wave of accumulation by privatization.

This imbrication of privatization and coercion, whose implications have been manifest in the violent suppression of student dissent and of the Occupy movement in the United States and elsewhere, suggests that there is no return to the status quo ante. The liberal university was the institutional and intellectual formation of a particular moment of capitalism, tied to a liberal representative state form by its production of citizen-subjects and contingently compelled to shelter and even foster dissent by the ideological conditions of the cold war. It proved capable of absorbing the first ethnic studies formations into the modes of liberal multiculturalism that corresponded to the "representative" function of the university as a whole. Under the new university regime even the pretence of cultural pluralism has fallen under the insidious shadow of "excellence and diversity," which is the mode of difference's engulfment by the corporate university. Indeed the corporate university has—literally—less and less *use* for the humanities and critical social sciences. Devoted to an ever-increasing instrumentality, linked to a positivism so brutal that it prefers, as Karl Rove once said, to make reality rather than to interpret it, the corporate university—like the emerging neoliberal corporate state—has no use for critique nor for any engagement with alternative possibilities. That is "the real societal significance" of the present formation of the university.[21]

Alternative formations of knowledge like ethnic studies that seek to *enter* the new university—"from the margins to the center"—will succumb to its conditions, be reduced to the empirical study of social problems that transform its subjects back into objects of knowledge or to recreational supplements to applied knowledge. They will be, as the saying goes, incorporated. Angela Davis once spoke—in the era when we were still fighting to defend affirmative action and multiculturalism—of our need to return to the language of *desegregation,* a language prematurely abandoned before even the semblance of racial equity had been achieved. But even that luminous insight may not now be enough. We will need to insist on the language of redistribution and of radical democratization, on the demand not to enter but to break open the enclosures—and that will mean forging again our links with social movements both nationally and internationally.

In the 1980s students on U.S. campuses learned from their involvement in the divestment movement to make the connection between apartheid in South Africa and "apartheid on campus." That imaginative reach from the internationalism of the anti-apartheid struggle back to the "local" issue of desegregating U.S. campuses and transforming the curriculum of the university led to the heady if short-lived successes of the "culture wars" of the 1980s and 1990s. At the same time, it must be confessed, the cultural emphasis of those struggles distracted us from the disastrous economic assault that the Right was conducting under the cover of their attacks on "tenured radicals" or their defense of "Western civilization." The struggle for a culture of critique and possibility is now inseparable from the economic struggle to retrieve real abundance from the illusion of scarcity. Much as we learned in the 1980s from the South African resistance to apartheid, we need now to absorb the lessons of another struggle against settler colonialism and apartheid, that of the Palestinians' defiance of Israel's attempt to dispossess, ethnically cleanse, and culturally destroy them. In particular, as students and academics we need to learn now the full meaning of the Palestinian call for the "right to education" against occupation, closure, and the enforced amnesia that stems from ignorance of the past and destroys the conditions of life in the future. This call, initiated by students and faculty of Birzeit University on the occupied West Bank, insists that Israel's systematic destruction of educational opportunity "not only violates the human rights of individuals, it is an attack on the development of Palestinian society as a whole."[22] It is an assault, as Luxemburg put it, "against the social and economic ties of the natives," and not merely on their employment or vocational opportunities. While the Palestinians' call for us to support their resistance by endorsing the movement for Boycott, Divestment and Sanctions against Israel demands our participation, it also prompts us as intellectuals—as at once scholars and activists—to return to the transformative agenda of a critical ethnic studies. It is a reminder that what we demand is not merely the right to access, the permission to enter, but the right to a life in common predicated on an abundance that will transform the possibilities of thought into the potentials for a revolution that will free us from anxiety.

NOTES

1. Kant, *The Conflict of the Faculties*, 25–29, 43–45, 151–53.
2. Comay, *Mourning Sickness*, 32–33.
3. Arnold, "The Function of Criticism in the Present Time," 265–66.
4. Arnold, "The Function of Criticism in the Present Time," 266.
5. See, for example, this excitable report: Jacobson, "University Statements Rejecting Academic Boycott of Israel."
6. Paraphrased from Fanon, "Racism and Culture," 29.
7. Du Bois, *The Souls of Black Folk* (1989), 3.
8. da Silva, *Toward a Global Idea of Race*, 7–8, 117–18; da Silva, "No Bodies," 224.
9. These statements are taken from the University of Southern California's "Core Documents," the 1993 Mission Statement and the 2004 Strategic Plan, respectively. The transition they exemplify has been no less manifest in public universities like the University of California or the University of Michigan as they have undergone increasingly far-reaching and deliberate processes or corporatization.
10. See Lewontin, "The Cold War and the Transformation of the Academy"; Ohmann, "English and the Cold War."
11. In the summer of 2014, renowned American Indian and Palestinian studies professor Steven Salaita had his appointment to a tenured professorship revoked by the board of trustees of the University of Illinois at Urbana-Champaign. Salaita's employment was terminated in response to his public tweets criticizing the Israeli government's summer assault on Gaza. For his account of the events, see Steven Salaita, *Uncivil Rites: Palestine and the Limits of Academic Freedom* (Chicago: Haymarket Books, 2015).
12. Lukacs, *Theory of the Novel*, 62–64; Harvey, "Accumulation by Dispossession."
13. Klein, *The Shock Doctrine*, 523–34.
14. Luxemburg, *The Accumulation of Capital*, 338–46.
15. Spenser, *A View of the Present State of Ireland*, 71.
16. Wordsworth, preface to *The Lyrical Ballads*, 735.
17. Spenser, *A View of the Present State of Ireland*, 71.
18. Spenser, *A View of the Present State of Ireland*, 11.

19. Luxemburg, *The Accumulation of Capital*, 350.

20. Adorno to Benjamin, March 18, 1936, in *Walter Benjamin and Theodor W. Adorno*, 131.

21. Karl Rove has been identified as the unnamed aide cited in Ron Suskind's "Faith, Certainty and the Presidency of George W. Bush," *New York Times Magazine*, October 17, 2004, accessed February 12, 2015, http://www.nytimes.com/2004/10/17/magazine/17BUSH.html?ex=1255665600&en=890a96189e162076&ei=5090&partner=rssuserland. Wisconsin governor Scott Walker's proposal to eliminate the humanistic language of the "Wisconsin idea" of the university may have backfired, but it expresses no less the neoconservative instrumentalist "idea of the university" that is increasingly the actual operative norm, even as lip service is paid to "truth" and "humanity." See Dan Simmons, "Scott Walker Backtracks from Striking 'Truth,' 'Human Condition' from Wisconsin Idea," *Wisconsin State Journal*, February 5, 2015, accessed February 12, 2015, http://host.madison.com/wsj/scott-walker-backtracks-from-striking-truth-human-condition-from-wisconsin/article_236af72e-acc8–11e4-a807-a74efb453ab4.html.

22. See Birzeit University, Right to Education Campaign; Birzeit University, *Right to Education Bulletin*; U.S. Campaign for the Academic and Cultural Boycott of Israel.

ELEVEN

Subjugated Knowledges: Activism, Scholarship, and Ethnic Studies Ways of Knowing

DAN BERGER

In a 1976 lecture at the Collége de France, Michel Foucault identified the terms of political antagonism. He admonished his listeners to "proceed just as if we had not alarmed [the enemy] at all, in which case it will be no part of our concern to provide a solid and homogenous theoretical terrain for all these dispersed genealogies, nor to descend upon them from on high with some kind of halo of theory that would unite them." Instead, he counseled, the plan of radical critique "will be to expose and specify the issue at stake in this opposition, this struggle, this insurrection of knowledges against the institutions and against effects of the knowledge and power that invests scientific discourse." Later in his talk Foucault argues that "subjugated knowledges" are the forms of knowing that are either co-opted or ignored, interpellated "in a functionalist coherence or formal systemisation" or "naïve knowledges" that are outright "disqualified as inadequate." These forms of knowledge are the popular ways of knowing that emerge from marginalized populations. Without privileging organic intellectual production over and against that of academics, I refer here to the knowledge that emerges within political struggles, knowledge that merges present-day common sense with alternative ways of knowing. Foucault argued that it is in the "re-appearance of this knowledge, of these local popular knowledges, these disqualified knowledges, that criticism performs its work."[1]

A wide variety of critical theorists echoed this theme during the 1970s and since then. I start with Foucault because his formulation of "an insurrection of subjugated knowledges," a celebration of knowledge formed in and useful to popular mobilization, is critical for what I want to argue here. Foucault's provocation can help us reinvigorate the connections between the project of critical ethnic studies and the political movements around which it circulates. I am trying to situate intellectual labor within a historical and social context that makes it inseparable from political work.

This task is critical for ethnic studies scholars. As recent histories have shown, the institutionalization of ethnic studies was born both from social movement demands and elite strategies of co-optation.[2] The result was a privatization of knowledge and a cleavage between academic knowledge and movement knowledge that emerged alongside the retrenchment of state repression through the FBI's counterintelligence program and mass incarceration. The institutionalization of ethnic studies became embroiled in attacks on the "politically correct academy" or the alleged parochialism of "identity politics" as part of the culture wars of the 1980s and 1990s.[3] So while ethnic studies clubs and departments, as well as historically black colleges and universities, have a rich history of campus organizing, their institutionalization is enmeshed in corporate capitalist strategies of containment and assimilation.

Critical scholarship requires us to think through the role of academics as something including but going beyond intellectual labor alone. I want to first sketch some of the tensions between scholarship and activism, and then look at two specific texts to ask how taking on the challenge of subjugating knowledges might shift our work as both scholars and organizers. My examples come from Maoist-influenced movements, but my project is more ambitious than proposing a reconsideration of Maoism.[4] Following Chandan Reddy's recent definition of critical ethnic studies as a project of gaining "access to a different account of political modernity, the politics of knowledge, and the persistent re-emergence of state violence" in and through gendered racial capitalism, I am after a reconsideration of ethnic studies as an epistemology and a political orientation.[5] By revisiting some overlooked but, in my opinion, foundational texts I hope to generate a new archive that can help reinvigorate and reinterpret our practice not just as intellectuals but as participants in social movements at the precise moment when critical ethnic studies has much to contribute to challenging the changing nature of racial capitalism.

That the hidden archive I hope to make visible emerges from sustained encounters with imprisonment is no coincidence, for the prison has been both a critical weapon against radical ethnic studies epistemologies over the past forty years and a critical incubator of them.[6] The prison seeks to contain the mobility not just of people but of ideas as well, which is why struggles over imprisonment, and indeed all social movements, have been struggles over knowledge. Foucault's very call for an insurrection of subjugated knowledges emerged from his own engagement with radical antiprison struggles.[7] Yet his failure to acknowledge his debts to such movements, alongside the broader attack on their physical safety and intellectual legitimacy, obscured the movement origins of his intellectual insights. I lead with Foucault not to reinforce his canonical presence but to destabilize it, or at least to collectivize it by identifying the social movement origins of a diverse range of knowledge production.

A call to understand or make use of subjugated knowledges must proceed through the political formations that give rise to them without merely re-presenting in our language the knowledge formed in and through social movements. I want to peek behind the curtain of academic knowledge to reveal other areas where professionalization has obscured the claims of organic intellectuals and offer a provisional look at the ways critical ethnic studies might recognize the presence and participation of radical social movements. I hope to enlarge the origin stories of ethnic studies, to blur the demarcations that prejudicially separate scholar from activist, and to further collectivize knowledge production.

I want, finally, to move beyond the caricatured dichotomies of anti-intellectual activism versus anti-activist intellectualism to something more dynamic. Indeed while leftist scholars at times bemoan the atheoretical nature of certain political groups, many radicals are inspired by the Marxist dictum that revolutionaries have an obligation to develop new theory.[8] Academic knowledge may be more elegantly formed than movement knowledge but not necessarily more intellectually rigorous. Alternatively our rigor may be no match for the resonance of ideas emanating from radical movements that speak to the demands of the moment. "Another world is possible" is hardly a rigorous notion, yet it captured the world's attention for several years because it named the desire for an alternative to capitalism in ways that little else had done since the collapse of the Eastern Bloc and the nonaligned movement (much in the way that talk of "the 99 percent" Black Lives Matter has done more recently). It opened the door to new ways of thinking about the world, spreading ideas that had been slowly percolating in meetings and classrooms, in zines and journals, at conferences and barricades.

Further, disciplinary and professional requirements place knowledge generated outside the academy as subpar. It may be analyzed, but it is cited far less often. It is not seen as being on the same level as scholarly knowledge. Granted, social movements can flourish best when they remain outside the domestication of academic acceptance. Following the lead of recent anthologies on scholar-activism and discussions of critical ethnic studies as a distinct approach to knowledge and politics, I am interested in pursuing the fine line between identifying with social movements as creators of knowledge and subordinating them to the mandates of the academy.[9] I want to push these provocations further by rooting them in the social movements that can best establish the terms of engagement.

Specifically I want to center activist scholarship, the knowledge produced by activists in social movements, as a form of movement-generated knowledge.[10] If social movements already know some of what academics know, and if they know it earlier or more personally, how might we reconceptualize the relevance of academic knowledge? I want to redirect the scholarly gaze by examining a small but prolific political network of revolutionaries based in Chicago. Since the early 1980s this group has self-published several books, often through a print shop first set up by a revolutionary organization in the 1970s to produce propaganda for different radical groups in the area. Since the start of the twenty-first century this group has been publishing articles online and in an infrequent magazine, the *8th Route Readers Club*, to continue theoretical debates about contemporary class structure, historical analysis, political repression, and the far Right. These discussions are little noticed in the academy, yet they have much to offer thinking about contemporary political possibilities.

While they continue, erratically, to write and publish, for ease of analysis I limit my scope to two self-published, paradigm-setting books, published a decade part, the first one appearing in the early 1980s. These texts develop several ideas that have since become axiomatic within critical ethnic studies about settler colonialism and the shifting political allegiances of race and gender that have marked the neoliberal era. They have done so explicitly through and in relation to a deeper revolutionary tradition. This connection informs every aspect of these texts, from their willful disregard for grammatical norms to the cutting sarcastic wit, lengthy quotes from revolutionary figures such as Amilcar Cabral, Vladimir Lenin, Pancho Villa, and Walter Rodney, and the nontraditional design, including collage-style artwork, of each book.

The books I am referring to are *Settlers: The Mythology of the White Proletariat*, written by J. Sakai and published in 1983, and *Night Vision: Illuminating War and Class on the Neocolonial Terrain*, written by Butch Lee and Red Rover and published in 1993. "Red Rover" is a tongue-in-cheek acknowledgment of a wider research and writing group largely of women but that also included Sakai. (Using the names E. Tani and Kaé Sera, this same group also coauthored a fascinating but challenging book in 1985 called *False Nationalism, False Internationalism: Class Contradictions in the Armed Struggle*. Because of space and analytical clarity, I won't examine that book here.)

Sakai is the child of Japanese immigrants and a former autoworker. Butch Lee is a transfeminist who published the 1980s feminist zine *Bottomfish Blues*. Both were politicized through their involvement with the black freedom struggle, from the civil rights phase through its revolutionary nationalist incarnations that described itself as part of a black liberation movement. These books were written and circulated within a semiclandestine network shaped by revolutionaries close to or part of the Black Liberation Army (BLA), the military offshoot of the Black Panther Party.[11] Sakai and Lee have been key nodes in the circuits of intellectual discourse among imprisoned radicals, especially from the BLA. Their political biographies, like the books they produced, are tied to the fascinating but little known history of revolutionary nationalism based in Chicago from the 1960s to the 1990s. It was a political environment shaped by the racial geography of Chicago, which included a heady mixture of black liberationists, Puerto Rican revolutionary nationalists, Iranian Marxists, Palestinian militants, and white anti-imperialists. As a result the history of these books hints at the hidden history of Chicago's late twentieth-century revolutionaries.[12]

My interest in these books as a way to ground my argument comes from their intellectual significance, their intersections with critical ethnic studies, and their influence on my own political formation. While I hope that I am not simply arguing for the academic legitimacy of texts that have characterized my own intellectual identity, I do think that it is worth charting the ideas that compel us to develop new ideas. I discovered these books as a nineteen-year-old college sophomore and budding antiprison activist. It was a moment in which, to paraphrase Mark Twain, my schooling and my education were separate spheres. More than any class I had taken at that time, these books pushed me to be more thorough and sophisticated—to be, in a phrase, more intellectual—a commitment that led me to graduate school (something they should not be blamed for). They also have advanced my scholarship, priming my interest in studying racialization and constituting vital archives in my study of clandestine organizations of the 1960s era.

Although these books retain a currency in certain revolutionary discourses, especially among some dissident prisoners, few academics seem aware of their work. There appear to be no academic reviews of either book—notwithstanding bell hooks's praise for *Night Vision*—and they are rarely cited in scholarly publications. Yet the arguments they advance have since gained dominance in critical ethnic studies and related fields, such as American studies. This similarity of analysis did not develop within the academy as a result of Sakai's and Lee's writings. But the fact of convergence offers a useful occasion to reflect on the movement-generated intellectual projects that exist beyond the academy and can, at times, be steps ahead of academic knowledge.

Settlers was the first to appear, and its framework shapes their subsequent writings. Sakai writes in the introduction that the book is "a reconnaissance into enemy territory." He argues that ethnic studies programs, the first generation of which were maturing as *Settlers* was being written, were being used cynically to allow "Third World peoples" to study their own history without understanding or challenging the fundamental premise of the dominant society. The conspiratorial language notwithstanding, the premise is the same that would spark the subfield of whiteness studies a decade later: to analyze the mythology (Sakai's word) of whiteness as a political economy and cultural norm. *Settlers* attempts to shatter the "ideological world-view . . . of the oppressor society." Crucially Sakai does so not through an examination of the psyches or cultures of those deemed white but rather through a historically materialist assessment of racial political economy. "The Euro-Amerikan community is not just a conglomeration of stores and residences," he writes toward the end of *Settlers*. "It is a physical structure for settler life, in which the common culture of the Empire garrison still lives on." The book, which took eight years to write and first appeared in leftist circles as a pamphlet, bills itself sensationally as the "true story of the white nation." It analyzes the racialized class structure of American society.[13]

Settlers emphasizes land as a tool in the creation of whiteness and fundamentally connected to the oppression and genocide of black, Native, Latino, and Asian peoples. Sakai argues that whiteness was made not just through national rituals but through the violent appropriation of land. With control of the land, newly defined whites developed exclusive institutions to sustain their control. Sakai reads in various populist and labor revolts proof of the parasitic nature of settler colonialism. By uncovering the colonial dimensions of incidents as diverse as Bacon's Rebellion (1647) and the Flint Sit-Down Strike (1937), Sakai rebukes the standard left celebrations of populist militancy. He argues that white struggles over access to resources have often been parasitic in nature, seeking gains at the expense of "Third World people and nations," both within the United States and internationally. *Settlers* powerfully connects land to racialization in the United States and takes seriously black radicalism as an opposition to settler colonialism specifically. It describes antiblack racism as bound up with settler colonialism and not just akin to it or flowing from it.

Sakai is hardly the first to look at white privilege as a material instead of simply an ideological force. His thinking on the subject follows a long line of independent scholarly engagement on whiteness, going back at least to W. E. B. Du Bois and continuing to animate a range of black critics in and out of the academy. Although *Settlers* received almost no notice from academics, it made a small splash among revolutionaries in the early 1980s and still travels in these circles today.[14] The book is often read as being a dismissal of the possibility that those defined as white could play anything but a reactionary role in social transformation: in that the book echoes Baldwin's contention that "as long as you think you're white there's no hope for you."[15]

It is true that *Settlers* minimizes class and other power differentials among whites. It is far more pessimistic than even the work of other antiracist independent scholars tracking the invention of whiteness at the time, such as Ted Allen. (Allen was for a time part of the Sojourner Truth Organization, members of which ran the publishing company that first printed *Night Vision.*)[16] David Roediger bought *Settlers* at a left bookstore in Chicago in the early 1980s, when it was first published as an oversized pamphlet called *The Mythology of the White Proletariat*. He said recently that he objected to the at times "categorical and transhistorical" dismissal of those defined as white, preferring the formulations of Allen. Yet Roediger was one of the first and remains one of the only people to cite *Settlers* in a scholarly publication, *The Wages of Whiteness*. He said he hoped labor historians would take notice of the book's arguments and also look to the land, although it seems that few, if any, noticed.[17]

A work of labor history, *Settlers* advances our understanding of the material foundation that bonds the creation of whiteness to class betrayal. In later interviews Sakai clarified that this enemy was not whites but the parasitic structure of settler colonialism.[18] Whiteness was the tool through which settlerism established power in the Americas, but whiteness need not always be the dressing in which settler colonialism transpires. Settlerism, then, is the real problem. Settlerism is a way to understand the class structure of the North American racial state, and *Settlers* a uniquely useful text in which to do so. Its framework allows for a cogent theory of racialization and racial struggles in ways few books of its time had done.

Published ten years later, *Night Vision* is a book of political theory and strategy. It centralizes gender as an analytic in ways *Settlers* failed to do. Its gendered framework is one of several factors making *Night Vision* more resonant to contemporary scholarly debates.[19] The book blends social history with political economic analysis using examples drawn from contemporary popular culture to describe the fraught political horizons of the 1990s. The book is a strategic assessment of the shifting political alliances under neoliberalism, which they label *neocolonialism*. Neocolonialism, they argue, requires a fundamental shift in political thinking: "Capitalism is again ripping apart & restructuring the world, and nothing will be the same. Not race, not nation, not gender, and certainly not whatever culture you used to have."[20] They summarize this change as the difference between "old reality" and "new reality." These realities coexist; the old realities of racist police brutality, gay bashing, and Klan violence coexist with the new realities of black political power, gay visibility, and a celebration of multiculturalism. Those who doubt the radical possibilities of cultural studies have never read *Night Vision*. Like good cultural critics, the book analyzes new reality through the postapocalyptic film *Blade Runner*. *Night Vision* does not endorse new reality—"Multiculturalism Won't Save Your Life," they sarcastically title the penultimate chapter—but asks that we adjust our methods accordingly.

They argue that gender increases in saliency under new reality, for reasons both materialist and ideological. The authors quote repeatedly and at length from Maria Mies's classic book of feminist political economy, *Patriarchy and Accumulation on a Global Scale*, arguing that the feminization of poverty and labor make women and children vanguard political subjects of neocolonial reality: "By giving industry a gender—*as they once gave slave agriculture a race*—capitalism can throw a veil over the extreme exploitation and semi-slavery of its women and children workers." Patriarchy also becomes the dividing line between liberatory and parasitic political projects. Their emphasis on antipatriarchal politics leads the authors of *Night Vision* to call nations and nationalism into question more than they did in previous texts. Lee and Red Rover, as with more recent scholarship on black and Native radicalism, are pragmatically agnostic on what doctrinaire Marxists call "the national question." They argue that some people want nations, others want anything but nations—and that both sides have legitimacy.[21]

"New reality" requires a fundamental realignment of political alliances: "The oppressed have to break with parasitism—which means dis-unity with everyone who can't give up parasitism or won't." This assertion extends the discussion of tactics and strategy that concludes *Settlers*. Whereas the earlier book suggested that white Americans were too bought off to participate meaningfully in any lasting movement against empire, *Night Vision* adopts a more sophisticated stance. Here they note that the material foundation of co-optation crosses all lines of race, class, and gender. Years before Wall Street helped elect the first black president of the United States—and in ways that resonate with contemporary critiques of homonationalism—Lee and Red Rover noted that the "white ruling class *wants* Black capitalist government; it promotes, pays for and sponsors Black capitalist government." *Night Vision* ends with a call to assert popular opposition to the racialized and gendered projects of neocolonial capitalism. In language that calls to mind the more recent "delinking" concept proposed by the Latin American coloniality of power theorists, the authors of *Night Vision* title their plea for political unity across identity difference "de-toxing."[22]

For all its stridency, *Night Vision* displays a refreshing political sincerity. In seeking to identify the contours of upheavals to come, it calls for a new political method. Rereading it now asks activist-scholars to expand the rubric of what counts as methodology to include questions of strategy as part and parcel of intellectual labor that extends beyond the academy. Method, in this sense, is not simply about archives and fieldwork but about tactics and goals. The radical elements of the movements pressing for ethnic studies during the 1960s and 1970s had this notion of method in mind when they stormed their college campuses—often with the physical help or political support of members of the community not enrolled at a university. The push for redistribution and not just recognition animates *Night Vision*'s appraisal of new reality as it defines *Settlers*'s critique of the ways that trade unionism became parasitic by demanding greater privileges for white workers rather than greater power for all workers.

Maoism characterizes *Settlers* and *Night Vision*, just as it influenced Foucault's opposition to the prison: Sakai, Lee and their pseudonymous coauthors speak in the idiom of nations, nationalism, and national liberation; they promote armed struggle as the highest form of political engagement; they emphasize the centrality of land as a basis of political power; and they display a biting hostility toward liberalism and social democracy. They are flexible and creative Marxists; they are not wedded to it as holy doctrine but reinterpret it as necessary. They use the concept of imperialism to synthesize the connection between what critical ethnic studies calls racial capitalism and what critical race theorists have dubbed the racial state.[23] Through the framework of imperialism and neocolonialism, they engage the racial and gendered components of the capitalist world system. This approach centers the state in any discussion of local and global politics.

Sakai, Lee, and company are part of a generation of scholarly minded organizers around the world who cut their teeth on 1960s-era upheavals (although for many, including Sakai, politicization came earlier—through the Japanese internment camps, through the communist-inspired sectors of the labor movement).[24] They define settler colonialism as a political framework rooted in dispossession, racialization, and betrayal. They emphasize the material dimensions of racialization and the demands of liberation. They make social movement analysis—historic pitfalls and future potentials—central to analyzing current social and political climate. They fall into sectarianism and essentialism on more than one occasion. But they also have produced a fascinating wealth of knowledge rooted in social movement organizing that is often quite sophisticated.

The critical work of J. Sakai, Butch Lee, and their associates is an example of what is perhaps an article of faith among critical ethnic studies scholars: the ways nonacademic intellectual labor can be intellectually generative on its own terms.[25] Their more recent writings direct our attention to organizing in prison, to contemporary class composition, and to understanding the threat posed by revolutionary movements of the far Right around the world. There are numerous other such theorists outside the academy. The task of activist scholarship, I maintain, is to creatively engage in a task of historical recuperation without reification. Our job is to remember, to make visible, to imagine, and to fight as part of social movements: to read their journals and books, to attend their conferences and meetings, to participate in their organizations and campaigns, to learn from as much as about, to honor the ever-presence of intellectual and physical labor happening outside the academy. Our intellectual labor joins our physical labor in the form of involvement with diverse social movements. As such initiatives gain traction, the dichotomy between academic and organizer, campus and community will wither. Such a development would go a long way toward disarticulating the academy as a privileged location of either activism or intellectualism.

Living under "new reality," as *Night Vision* describes it, clarifies the need to reiterate and sharpen the call—present since ethnic studies first emerged—for greater synthesis between academics and social movements. This relationship has never been easy and cannot be predetermined or prefabricated. Ethnic studies scholarship has always been called to its greatest self in dialogue with political critique informed by the grassroots, and current conditions in and outside the academy provide the generative basis to reexamine how ethnic studies might engage social movement radicals. As when ethnic studies became institutionalized, we live in an era when the academy holds a privileged position in the global political economy. With the academy a key site of production in the neoliberal economy, the threats to insurgent knowledges has grown increasingly severe amid the tightening grip of "professionalization."

At the same time, recent upsurges around the world—mirrored in the 2010–13 prisoner hunger and labor strikes across California, Virginia, Ohio, and elsewhere; reflected in the growing synergy of struggles for land, democracy, and community care and transformative justice that helped create the Occupy and Idle No More movements; illuminated in the growing Black Lives Matter protests against police violence[26]—point to new ways of knowing the world, new ways of understanding love, labor, and life. Such developments take place amid the new racial capitalism of the so-called Obama age, when the first black president of the United States is also the president of drone warfare, deportations, and a marriage-and-militarism "gay rights" program. In this environment of multicultural militarism, critical ethnic studies can provide both the long memory and alternative vision that universities fear and movements need.

Ultimately we need each other. The stakes are too high, and neither nonacademic activists nor nonactivist academics can do it alone. In the mid-1960s James Baldwin told a group of civil rights activists including Student Nonviolent Coordinating Committee's leader Stokely Carmichael that if they, the activists, refuse to accept the lies told about them in society, he, the artist, would refuse to betray them.[27] We might think of the critical scholar as having a similar task—not of loyalty at all costs (which is not what Baldwin promised) but of a direct engagement and ongoing relationship of accountability to the movements from which we draw strength and sustenance, wisdom and encouragement. Accountability as a dynamic process rooted in collective struggle and the passionate exchange of ideas: this is the accountability Toni Morrison spoke of when she said, "The best art is political, and you ought to be able to make it unquestionably political and irrevocably beautiful at the same time."[28]

Baldwin and Morrison are part of a long tradition of critical artists whose work in the world transgresses boundaries of respectability in favor of complex, even counterintuitive notions of accountability to a liberationist ethos.

Such artists have much to teach us about the practice of intellectual work. Just as race can be an empty or reactionary signifier when separated from class, gender, and sexuality,[29] the project of ethnic studies remains barren without social movements to give it meaning. This is a call for the insurrection of subjugated knowledges to blossom.

NOTES

1. Foucault, *Power/Knowledge*, 87, 81–82. See also Choudry and Kapoor, *Learning from the Ground Up*.

2. See Rooks, *White Money / Black Power*; Rojas, *From Black Power to Black Studies*; Biondi, *The Black Revolution on Campus*. Forthcoming work on this subject by Nick Mitchell will contribute a great deal to our understanding of black studies.

3. See, for example, Gates, *Tradition and the Black Atlantic*, 113–63; Brennan, *Wars of Position*.

4. Some of the most insightful writings on Maoism's influence, including an important essay by Robin D. G. Kelley and Betsy Esch, can be found in Ho and Mullen, *Afro-Asia*. See also Prashad, *Everybody Was Kung Fu Fighting*; Frazier, "The Congress of African People."

5. Reddy, *Freedom with Violence*, 19. See also Melamed, *Represent and Destroy*.

6. Of this growing body of literature, see James, ed., *The New Abolitionists*; Rodríguez, *Forced Passages*; Berger, *Captive Nation*.

7. Macey, *The Lives of Michel Foucault*, 257–89; Bourg, *From Revolution to Ethics*, 45–103; Heiner, "Foucault and the Black Panthers"; Hill, *Men, Mobs, and the Law*, 265–314.

8. For example, the Freedom Road Socialist Organization political statement, "Which Way Is Left?" and the rationale that the editors of the Toronto-based journal *Upping the Anti* provide for publishing their journal, which they describe as a consolidation of anticapitalist, anti-imperialist, and anti-oppression politics. See Freedom Road Socialist Organization, "Introducing Our New Strategy Document: 'Which Way Is Left?,'" October 4, 2007, accessed August 10, 2011, http://freedomroad.org/?s=which+way+is+left. Information on *Upping the Anti* can be found at www.uppingtheanti.org.

9. Sudbury, *Activist Scholarship*; Hale, *Engaging Contradictions*; INCITE! Women of Color against Violence, *The Revolution Will Not Be Funded*; Moten and Harney, "The University and the Undercommons"; Hardt and Negri, *Commonwealth*, 117, 127–28; Team Colors Collective, *Uses of a Whirlwind*; Graeber and Shukaitis, *Constituent Imagination*.

10. My thinking on these matters owes much to Bevington and Dixon, "Movement-Relevant Theory"; Dixon, *Another Politics*; and many conversations with Chris Dixon over more than a decade.

11. For more on the BLA, see Berger, *Captive Nation*, 248–50; Muntaqim, "On the BLA"; Shakur, *Assata*; Bukhari, *The War Before*; Umoja, "Repression Breeds Resistance"; Umoja, "The Black Liberation Army and the Radical Legacy of the Black Panther Party"; English, *Savage City*.

12. For an overview of Chicago's radical politics during this time, see Staudenmaier, *Truth and Revolution.*

13. Sakai, *Settlers,* 4, 3, 151.

14. See, for example, Freddy Perlman's review, "The Continuing Appeal of Nationalism," and the response by Kuwasi Balagoon, "The Continuing Appeal of Anti-Imperialism." Perlman was one of the editors of *Fifth Estate,* an anarchist newspaper based in Michigan. Balagoon was a former Black Panther, a defendant in the Panther 21 case, and a political prisoner who died in prison of AIDS-related illness in 1986. See Balagoon, *A Soldier's Story*. For recent engagements with *Settlers,* see J. Moufawad-Paul, "J. Sakai's *Settlers:* A Meta Review," November 2010, http://moufawad-paul.blogspot.com/2010/11/j-sakais-settlers-meta-review.html, accessed August 10, 2011; Sebastian Lamb, "J. Sakai's Settlers and Anti-Racist Working-Class Politics," *New Socialist,* February 6, 2010, accessed August 10, 2011. http://www.newsocialist.org/index.php?option=com_content&view=article&id=92&Itemid=75; Tyler McCreary, review of *Settlers, Upping the Anti* 2 (2005), http://uppingtheanti.org/journal/article/02-settlers-the-mythology-of-the-white-proletariat/, accessed August 10, 2011.

15. Quoted in Roediger, *Towards the Abolition of Whiteness,* 13.

16. See Staudenmaier, *Truth and Revolution*. Some of the group's documents have been archived online: see Sojourner Truth Organization, http://www.sojournertruth.net.

17. David Roediger, email to the author, December 15, 2010. The reference to *Settlers* can be found in *Wages of Whiteness,* 184. *Settlers* is also referenced in Lyons and Berlet, *Right-Wing Populism in America*. Though that book was published by an academic publisher (Guilford), its authors are both independent scholars. Long out of print, *Settlers* was jointly republished by the independent publishers PM Press and Kersplebedeb in 2014. The new edition includes an essay about the reparations given to Japanese Americans for their imprisonment during World War II, as well as an interview conducted with Sakai. It also features a new subtitle, *From Mayflower to Modern,* and a more traditional design than the previous editions.

18. Sakai, "When Race Burns Class."

19. It is also the most traditional of the three in terms of its presentation: it was printed the size of most novels rather than the oversize workbook format of the previous books, and it featured blurbs on the back, unlike the other two. The collage artwork still characterizes the interior design, and the binding is weak, suggesting low production costs.

20. Lee and Red Rover, *Night Vision,* ii.

21. Lee and Red Rover, *Night Vision,* 158, 33. This view is echoed in analyses of social movements by scholars such as Michelle Ann Stephens, Andrea Smith, Nikhil Pal Singh, Robin D. G. Kelley, Donna Murch, and Cynthia Young.

22. Lee and Red Rover, *Night Vision,* 179, 184.

23. In addition to the works cited earlier, see Goldberg, *The Racial State;* Omi and Winant, *Racial Formation in the United States;* HoSang et al., *Racial Formation in the Twenty-First Century.*

24. Author's conversation with J. Sakai, August 29, 2012.

25. Singh's introduction to his edited volume of the collected writings of the black liberationist Jack O'Dell is an excellent example of this intersection in practice (*Climbin' Jacob's Ladder,* 1–69).

26. Of many possible sources on this convergence, see Khatib et al., *We Are Many*; Berger, "Social Movements and Mass Incarceration."

27. Ture and Thelwell, *Ready for Revolution*, 263.

28. Morrison, "Rootedness," 345.

29. Lubiano, "Black Ladies, Welfare Queens, and State Minstrels." This essay concerns the Clarence Thomas–Anita Hill hearings, something that *Night Vision* points to as a pinnacle example of the "new reality."

III. THE BODY AND THE DISPENSATIONS OF RACIAL CAPITAL

TWELVE

Becoming Disabled / Becoming Black: Crippin' Critical Ethnic Studies from the Periphery

NIRMALA EREVELLES

In contemporary social analyses, disability studies has earned provisional inclusion, with claims that alternative theorizations of identity or subjectivity should be rooted in deconstructions or critiques of normative ontologies and epistemologies. I call it provisional because there is no guarantee that disability is always included in the now expanded trinity of race, class, gender, and queer politics. This practice of omission persists even though discourses of disability are intimately imbricated in the construction of the other categories of difference (namely race, class, gender, and queer studies), and yet all the other categories of difference initially appear to repudiate disability, seeking to distance themselves from the "real" physiological "deviance" (not "difference") that hegemonic normative discourses have historically associated with disability. It is in this context that the engagement of social difference from the standpoint of disability could prove to be especially provocative within critical ethnic studies.

The homepage of the Critical Ethnic Studies Association describes the field as laying "the foundation for analyzing how racism, settler colonialism, immigration, imperialism, and slavery interact in the creation and maintenance of systems of domination, dispossession, criminalization, expropriation, exploitation, and violence that are predicated upon hierarchies of racialized, gendered, sexualized, economized, and nationalized social existence in the United States and beyond."[1] Situating itself as undisciplinary by its very nature, critical ethnic studies' main impetus is to engage in decolonizing practices that interrogate and disrupt racial and colonial domination, transnational capitalism, heteropatriarchy, and ongoing settler colonialism. Ironically, though, this radical manifesto of transformative scholarship and praxis makes no obvious mention of ableism or disability, even though disabled subjects abound within all these contexts and disability is often the outcome of most of these oppressive practices.

In this chapter I demonstrate that discourses of disability are an inescapable aspect of the decolonizing practices deployed in critical ethnic studies by employing the analytic practice of crippin.' According to the disability studies scholar Robert McRuer, *crippin'* refers, in part, to critical analytic practices that explore how "cultures of ability/disability are conceived, materialized, spatialized, and populated . . . [within] geographies of uneven development [and] are mapped onto bodies marked by differences of race, class, gender and ability."[2] Locating my analysis in the historical context of the slave trade and the ensuing slave economy in the agrarian southern United States, I demonstrate how disability is imbricated in the violent constructions of race, gender, class, and desire to support colonial exploitation. To foreground this argument I use an essay by the African American literary theorist Hortense Spillers, "Mama's Baby, Papa's Maybe: An American Grammar Book," and discuss the implications of this analysis for critical ethnic studies.

Race, Disability, and the Politics of Enfleshment

In "Mama's Baby, Papa's Maybe: An American Grammar Book," Spillers writes, "Before the 'body' there is the 'flesh,' that zero degree of social conceptualization that does not escape concealment under the brush of discourse, or the reflexes of iconography." Referring specifically to the Middle Passage, where black bodies jammed like animals into the holds of merchant ships were transported as (human) cargo to be sold as slaves in the New World, Spillers describes this terrible journey through the primary narrative of the flesh, with "its seared, divided, ripped-apartness, riveted to the ship's hole, fallen, or 'escaped' overboard."[3]

It is this primary narrative of "wounded" flesh that I turn to in order to conceptualize a historical-materialist theory of disability that also implicates the other categories of difference. I do this with much trepidation, fully aware that I am invoking quite problematically a vision of tattered flesh, of bludgeoned body, of victimized subjectivity—images that fit uncomfortably with any radical aesthetic of disability. But I mean to be provocative, to trouble any easy conceptualization of disability, especially at the intersections of race, class, gender, and sexuality. Spillers's essay painfully unearths the violent history of slavery that gave rise to an American grammar that continues to this day to propagate dehumanizing depictions of black bodies, both male and female. What becomes exceedingly clear in Spillers's analysis is that it is the materiality of racialized violence that becomes the originary space of difference. By *materiality* I mean the actual social and economic conditions that impact (disabled) people's lives and that are concurrently mediated by the politics of race, ethnicity, gender, sexuality, and nation.

I propose that Spillers's essay is as much about the materiality of racialized violence as it is about disability. While there is merit to the argument that disability is the most universal of human conditions,[4] there is an implicit assumption here that the acquisition of a disabled identity always occurs outside historical context. Spillers's argument reminds us otherwise. In the specific historical context of slavery, the attribution of disability to the female captive body, for instance, enabled this body to become a site where the flesh became the prime commodity of exchange in the violent conflation of both profit and pleasure. In this case I situate disability as the condition not of being but of becoming; this becoming is a historical event, and further, it is its material context that is critical in the theorizing of disabled bodies and subjectivities.

There is a danger in associating becoming disabled with a violent and oppressive history because disability is already conceived of as "abject." The "abject," according to Julia Kristeva, is a place of radical exclusion where all meaning collapses and where the "deep well of memory . . . is [both] unapproachable and intimate."[5] Conscious of the danger of invoking an ableist aesthetic, my project is to echo McRuer's provocative question, "What might it mean to welcome the disability to come, to desire it?"[6] McRuer celebrates the transformative potential of disability and queerness to unsettle and radically rewrite abject identities. However, while I also echo McRuer's vision that another world is indeed possible—a world that welcomes and desires disability—I argue that to even reimagine these discursive possibilities necessitates an engagement with the social conditions that constitute disability. Spillers's essay provides the historical context to begin this analysis, even though she never explicitly engages disability. Nevertheless I argue that her essay, in its foregrounding of the brutal violence unleashed against the captive body, not just at the level of the skin but in the very markings of "divided" flesh,[7] has the potential to generate a historical-materialist analysis of disability—an argument that I make later in this essay—that could enable transformative possibilities for all bodies located at the intersections of difference. Put simply, my project angles the analytical frame more purposefully to foreground the transnational historical context that enables becoming disabled.

On one level, my project does not appear very different from either phenomenological or posthumanist disability studies scholars, who also conceptualize disability not as being but as "becoming-in-the-world."[8] According to Margrit Shildrick, "Becoming signifies a process that shifts and flows just as the body itself undergoes changes and modifications . . . as the irregular and contingent transformations and reversals that unsettle subjectivity—and identity—itself. . . . How we come to know ourselves and others in the world is the matter of material engagement, often through the direct contact of flesh and blood encounters that do not simply *affect* us at the surface level but *effect* the very constitution of embodied being."[9]

Where I differ from Shildrick (and other disability studies scholars who use posthumanist theories) becomes apparent in the critical significance I place on the transnational historical contexts in which these social relations and encounters between the self and others occur in the fluid and always incomplete process of becoming-in-the-world. While Shildrick admits that the inequalities produced within the historical context of globalization might disturb or distort the intercorporeal possibilities between diverse bodies, she nevertheless embraces what she calls an "ethics of encounter," which results in an "affective" rather than a transformative response to difference. In fact Shildrick shuns a transformative politics because, following Deleuze, she rejects all hierarchical analyses in favor of the " 'horizontal rhizomatic proliferation of linkages."[10]

The problem with "horizontal rhizomatic proliferation" is that it is rendered inadequate in the historical context of transnational capitalism, where bodies encounter each other often in violent collision such that captivity and mutilation are no longer metaphors but instead inform a brutal materiality that foregrounds the hierarchical binary of master/slave. Here Deleuze and Guattari's "desiring-machines" cannot support the seamless horizontal current of flow between intercorporeal entities,[11] now interrupted by hierarchical social relationships where productive desire that is constitutive of some bodies is enabled through the consumption of the seared, divided, ripped-apart, mutilated flesh of other bodies. It is this violent moment of intercorporeal assemblages that produces disability, and its becoming-in-the-world foregrounds a dialectical tension between the historical and the contemporary, between production and consumption, between desire and need, between continuities and discontinuities, and between the conditions of possibility and the violence of its limits.

I am aware that Deleuze and Guattari frown upon the dialectic, but I am unwilling to dissolve this dialectic in a discursive flourish when confronted by the embodied materiality of this bloodied and broken flesh. To engage materiality at the level of the body in Spillers's essay requires that we recognize the processes by which the body becomes a commodity of exchange in a transnational economic context and how this becoming proliferates a multiplicity of discourses of disability, race, class, gender, and sexuality. By conceptualizing disability as becoming-in-the-world while rejecting at the same time its ahistorical association with lack, I reframe McRuer's question to ask: Within what social conditions might we welcome the disability to come, to desire it? In raising this question I situate "desiring disability" as a historical condition of possibility that does not reproduce economic exploitation on a global scale. I therefore show how race and disability are imbricated in their collective formation of the black disabled body that now becomes a commodity that has economic, social, cultural, and linguistic implications for transnational subjectivities.

Pornotropic Materialities and the Enfleshed Politics of Race and Disability

Spillers's essay focuses on the deliberate and violent process by which the black body is transformed into a commodity—without gender, without genitalia, without subjectivity—a commodity so abject that it exists even outside kinship relations (the most fundamental of social units), such that, in another ironic twist, its very aimlessness constitutes it as "an effective social and economic agent."[12] I underscore both the historical and the economic context that are instrumental in the body's becoming both racialized and disabled. I want to stress that my argument is not that disability is like race or that race is like disability. Rather I am arguing that within the specific transnational conditions of colonialism and neocolonialism, the becoming of black disabled bodies is indeed an intercorporeal phenomenon that foregrounds a violent hierarchical context that contemporary theorists of difference have been reluctant to address or even acknowledge.

Spillers describes this transformation of the enslaved body into a commodity so dehumanized that it is conceived of as mere flesh and proffered for the economic and sexual consumption of the white master as pornotroping. She writes, "(1) The captive body becomes the source of an irresistible, destructive sensuality; (2) at the same time—in stunning contradiction—the captive body reduces to a thing, becoming being for the captor; (3) in this absence from a subject position, the captured sexualities provide a physical and biological expression of 'otherness'; (4) as a category of 'otherness,' the captive body translates into a potential for pornotroping and embodies sheer physical powerlessness that slides into a more general 'powerlessness,' resonating through various centers of human and social meaning."[13]

Because flesh is conceived of as a precursor to the body (an argument that Spillers makes earlier in her essay), "the (white) body—full life—functions as the abstract norm against which (black) flesh—mere life—is measured, and it also serves as an exception due to its unattainability for the black subject."[14] I argue that the practice of pornotroping that results in "the conscription of the victim as lacking both body and full human existence" occurs when the body becomes simultaneously racialized *and* disabled.[15] Here the logic of dehumanization regarded as synonymous with disability in ableist discourses is deployed to justify the abject racialization of enslaved bodies for their economic and sexual consumption by white society.[16] Thus, in the remainder of this chapter, I discuss the process of pornotroping not just as discursive but also as a process that has historical-materialist significance via the deployment of disability.

Spillers's essay begins (and I use this verb very tentatively) in the fifteenth century, in the initial encounters between European adventurers and West Africans, as culled from the 1789 narrative of the Nigerian Olaudau Equiano, or Gustavus Vassa, and the Portuguese Gomes Eannes de Azurara's chronicle of the discovery and conquest of Guinea, 1441–48. In both narratives, written from entirely different perspectives, the initial encounter between the Self and its Other produced the shocked recognition of radical difference. In these initial encounters "white men with horrible looks, red faces, and long hair" came face to face with men and women "black as Ethiops, and so ugly, both in features and in body, as almost to appear (to those who saw them) the images of a lower hemisphere."[17]

The sociocultural and psychic horror expressed by the Self when brought face to face with the *monstrous* Other mimics Julia Kristeva's argument that the abject inspires an irrational fear of engulfment or contamination. At face value it would appear that both parties are guilty of this horror. However, as Spillers is quick to point out, this notion of simultaneous and mutual horror is a solipsism that conceals a more brutal reality: the intention of the One to subjugate the Other on the basis of difference perceived in skin color. To the ship's crew of mostly European men, those bodies, "black as Ethiops, and so ugly, both in features and in body," were nothing more than cargo to be transported to the New World by sea and to be traded for unimaginable profit because of their obvious "physical impairments." It is at this moment of pornotroping that the conceptualization of black subjectivity as impaired subjectivity is not accidental, nor should it be conceived of as merely metaphorical. Rather it is precisely at the historical moment when one class of human beings was transformed into cargo to be transported to the New World that black bodies become disabled and disabled bodies become black. It is also important to note that blackness itself does not stand in for skin color. After all, in his chronicle, de Azurara recognizes that "in the field of captives, some of the observed are 'white enough, fair to look upon, and well-proportioned' [while] Others are less 'white like mulattoes.'"[18] In other words, *black* and *disabled* are not just linguistic tropes used to delineate difference but are instead materialist constructs produced for the appropriation of profit in a historical context where black disabled bodies were subjected to the most brutal violence.

The other factor to recognize in these flesh-and-blood encounters of intercorporeality is that both race and disability are mutually constitutive on account of this form of pornotropic social violence. Here disability is again not just a linguistic trope but the actual bloodied markings on the black body. Spillers cites William Goodell's account of North American slave codes that expose this brutal violation of black flesh: "'The smack of the whip is all day long in the ears of those who are on the plantation, or in the vicinity; and it is used with such dexterity and severity as not only to lacerate the skin, but to tear out small portions of the flesh at almost every stake.' The anatomical specifications of rupture, of altered human tissue, take on the objective description of laboratory prose—eyes beaten out, arms, backs, skulls branded, a left jaw, a right ankle, punctured; teeth missing, as the calculated work of iron, whips, chains, knives, the canine patrol, the bullet." While Spillers describes these markings on the flesh as "the concentration of ethnicity" in a culture "whose state apparatus, including judges, attorneys, 'owners,' 'soul drivers,' 'overseers,' and 'men of God,' apparently colludes with a protocol of 'search and destroy,'" I argue that these same markings on the flesh quite simply also produce impairment. Here impairment is not just biological or natural; it is also produced in a historical, social, and economic context, where the very embodiment of blackness and disability "bears in person the marks of a cultural text whose inside has been turned outside."[19] Here too Rosemarie

Garland-Thomson's depiction of disability as the set of practices that produce disabled and nondisabled bodies via a system of interpreting and disciplining bodily variation takes a brutally violent pornotropic turn.[20]

When the imbrication of blackness and disability produce violent markings on enslaved bodies, the assault on enslaved subjectivities is profound. Take, for example, one historical account cited by Spillers that describes the detailed specifications provided as instruction to the crew of one of the most famous ships associated with the Middle Passage (the *Brookes*) on how to most profitably cram its human cargo on board: "'Let it now be supposed . . . further, that every man slave is to be allowed six feet by one foot four inches for room, every woman five feet ten by one foot four, every boy five feet by one foot two, and every girl four feet six by one foot. . . .' The owner of *The Brookes*, James Jones, had recommended that 'five females be reckoned as four males, and three boys or girls as equal to two grown persons.'"[21] Instructed with much mathematical precision, bodily boundaries collapse and collide, stretch and shrink. The categorical permeability of boundaries has scant regard for the sovereign subject because complex computations of equivalency are not bound by bodily limits. And yet it is difficult to celebrate the fragility, malleability, and instability of these bodily boundaries born out of so much violence as either transgressive or transformative. Rather, more profoundly, the intercorporeal permeability between these ungendered, unnamed, and unremarkable bodies (except for their economic value as cargo) serves only to further erode any form of subjectivity that these bodies could claim for themselves. The historical conditions of a nascent colonialist transnational expansion of capitalism are responsible for the violent reconfiguration of the flesh, such that it becomes almost impossible to claim the sovereign subject, now mutually constituted via race, disability, and gender as a dehumanized commodity. Yet even though the deconstruction of the sovereign subject is cause for celebration, how does one celebrate in the face of so much violated and wounded flesh?

Deterritorializing the Sovereign (Ableist) Subject

What would we make of that tragic cargo of dismembered black bodies described in Spillers's essay? Because their bodies were broken down by the master's whip and their boundaries collapsed by the master's calculations, these bodies become "a collage of segments and significations and propositions," such that they can now be read as the ultimate figures of disorganization that open up possibilities for "profound and complex linkages not only between diverse human beings, but between humans and animals, and human machines instead."[22] As such these black dismembered bodies become *assemblages,* a construct that the philosophers Deleuze and Guattari define as follows: "On a first, horizontal axis, an assemblage comprises two segments, one of content, the other of expression. On the one hand it is a *machinic assemblage* of bodies, of actions, of passion, an intermingling of bodies reacting to one another; on the other hand, it is a *collective assemblage of enunciations,* of acts and statements, of incorporated transformations attributed to bodies. Then on a vertical axis, the assemblage has both *territorial sides,* or reterritorialized sides, which stabilize it, and cutting *edges of deterritorialization,* which carry it away."[23] To read the enslaved dismembered bodies via the concept of the assemblage brings to the fore a disorderly conflation of intermingled bodies, the bodies themselves fragmented by frequent violent lashings (both real and metaphorical) into their molecular components. These assemblages enunciate the violence written on their surfaces via their shifting morphologies—becoming first (human) cargo, then (human) property, and finally the very embodiment of dangerous deviance. In the specific context of colonialism and slavery, such enunciations permitted a further atomization that enabled a more thorough commodification, now becoming not just enslaved labor but also a laundry list of body parts that was distributed by medical institutions for purposes of medical education and medical research, as described in this advertisement from the *Charleston (South Carolina) Mercury* on October 12, 1838: "To planters and others—Wanted, fifty Negroes, any person, having sick Negroes, considered incurable by their respective physicians, and wishing to dispose of them, Dr. S. will pay cash for Negroes affected with scrofula, or king's evil, confirmed hypochondriasm, apoplexy, diseases of the liver, kidneys, spleen, stomach and intestines, bladder and its appendages, diarrhea, dysentery, etc. The highest *cash* price will be paid, on application as above, at No. 110 Church Street, Charleston."[24]

According to Deleuze and Guattari, becoming-other is committed to unravelings, contingencies, fluidities, and contradictions. In the *Mercury* advertisement the constitutive effects of race, disability, and the market coalesce in complex ways to effectively unravel the boundaries between bodies and subjects and destabilize their internal organizations so as to further enable their becoming-other. One of the outcomes of this becoming was that this captive flesh was now reconfigured into its atomized constituents and, in the process, enacted an objectification so complete that the "entire captive community becomes a living laboratory."[25] Moreover, in an ironic contradiction, iterative inscriptions of disability as "abject," "useless eater," and "undue burden" are transformed such that now (black) disabled fragmented bodies become highly valued commodities to be exchanged in the market by their masters for "the highest *cash* price."

Enslaved black disabled bodies were also stripped of all other social markers (e.g., gender) because those invested in transporting those bodies seemed "not [at all] curious about this cargo that bled, packed like so many live sardines among the immovable objects."[26] When enslaved black women were stripped of their gender, they were simultaneously placed outside the narrow confines of white bourgeois femininity, reduced to "bare life" as beasts of burden,[27] and thereby once again subject to violence that reconstituted the intimate contours of their bodies. Spillers describes scenes in which "a female body strung from a tree limb, or bleeding from the breast on any given day of field work because the 'overseer,' standing the length of a whip, has popped her flesh open, adds a lexical and living dimension to the narratives of women in culture and society."[28]

The erasure of gender from black (female) subjectivity enabled the violent inscriptions on black (female) flesh, and as a result the now impaired black (female) body is reconfigured. This brutal violence of history marks another irony. Stripped of gender, the black impaired (female) body (in contrast to her white bourgeois sisters), experiences a form of deterritorialization that enables her to find a line of flight outside the strictures of patriarchal femininity. Exiting the organism that signifies a limiting totality, the enslaved black disabled (female) body, now ungendered, her flesh fissured and organs in disarray, exists in an uneasy tension with another posthumanist analytic: the BwO. In *A Thousand Plateaus* Deleuze and Guattari define the BwO as follows: "The body without organs has replaced the organism and experimentation has replaced all instrumentation, for which it no longer has any use. Flows of intensity [of which pain is one], their fluids, their fibers, their continuums and conjunctions of affects, the wind, fine segmentation, microperceptions, have replaced the world of the subject. Becomings, becomings-animal, becomings-molecular have replaced history, individual or general."[29]

The transgressive possibilities generated via the BwO shift the disabled body outside the restricted strictures of the sovereign subject. In doing so this occlusion avoids confronting the actual violence that breaks bodies up into commodities that are exchanged in the marketplace for profit. By rejecting all moves to analyze social conditions in their totality, posthumanists argue instead for local, fragmented, and partial analyses that fail to foreground the global structures that produce differential effects on different populations. By locating their emancipatory practices within the space of the social imaginary, as opposed to the actual materiality of economic conditions, posthumanists continue to uphold an idealist vision of emancipation that may never be achieved because it exists within the realm of fantasy.

The Materiality of Desire within Racial, Queer, and Crip Politics

On one level the discussion in the previous section could be offered as a tentative response to McRuer's provocative question, "What might it mean to welcome the disability to come, to desire it?"[30] To answer this question I propose a materialist reading of desire as part of my continuing attempt to theorize becoming-as–(disabled) other as a historical event. In his critical reading of Spillers's essay, the Marxist literary theorist Robert Young argues that, when Spillers suggests that the dominant symbolic activity of the ruling episteme regarding race and gender, in particular, is grounded in the economics of slavery, "the logical extension of her argument would put Spillers' project on a firm materialist ground because she articulates the political economy of the symbolic." Young laments that Spillers retracts from engaging this political economy, instead "[deconstructing] the grammar of dominant epistemologies . . . [to end up] in a very surprising and yet familiar space; a reclamation of the [voluntarist] subject."[31]

Echoing Young's critique and expanding it to include theories that engage the discursive conceptualization of disability via desire, I argue that even desire, far from being a "natural" experience, is in fact a historical event. Young defines materialism as "an historical understanding of social relations ensuing from exploitative labor practices, which informs a revolutionary praxis aimed at transformation."[32] Thus returning to Spillers one last time, I join with Young in arguing that to theorize desire as an intimate web of social relations "ensuing from exploitative labor practices" will actually enable us to respond to McRuer's provocative question that promises a world of transformative possibilities for disabled subjects.

Posthumanist theories have shifted the analytical lens away from foregrounding the modes of production, productive forces, and relations of production to focus predominantly on the "regimes of signs, flows of libidinal energy, coding."[33] This is because, according to Deleuze and Guattari, "There is only desire and the social, and nothing else."[34] However, in Spillers's essay, Deleuze and Guattari's argument falters in the face of the historical conditions of slavery. According to Spillers, the actual theft of the body produced a contradictory discourse, wherein the enslaved body became simultaneously "the source of irresistible, destructive sensuality" while "being reduced to a thing, becoming *being for* the captor."[35]

This contradiction was enabled by the determined efforts of the master to intervene in the most intimate social relationships between his slaves—their kinship ties—by transforming even these intimate relationships into an economic asset for profit. With the abolition of the maritime slave trade, the plantation economies in the Americas needed an alternative source of slave labor. As a result, in another ironic twist, previously ungendered (female) enslaved bodies used for production were now perceived as gendered commodities vital to the (re)production of the slave population. Because it was necessary that the children born to the slave mother would not belong to her but to the master who owned her, the master forbade the formation of kinship ties between slaves, often enacting complicated social arrangements to ensure that the slaves were unable to sustain these ties. In this context patrimony in particular was also frowned upon because the father figure (whether he was the slave owner or the male slave) could not or would not claim his children as it would enable the possibility of inheritance (both economic and social) and add an unwanted complication to the economic enterprise of slavery. Thus Spillers explains that the offspring of the enslaved, "being unrelated both to their begetters and to their owners find themselves in the situation of being orphans. . . . I would call this enforced state of breach another instance of vestibular cultural formation where 'kinship' loses meaning, since it can be invaded at any given and arbitrary moment by the property relations."[36]

Clearly property relations played a crucial role in the destruction of kinship ties between enslaved populations. Further, the release from normative (heterosexual, patriarchal, and nuclear) kinships ties did not necessarily signify a release from their oppressive constraints, nor did it enable enslaved bodies to form alternative antipatriarchal, queer relationships unconnected by bloodlines. In a slave economy the very meaning of kinship, both normative and oppositional, was intimately tied to property relations, and enslaved bodies were just that: property. The breakdown of kinship ties occurs in a hierarchical context, where the slave master trades his dehumanized cargo for profit because "slavery creates an economic and social agent whose virtue lies in being outside the kinship system." Located outside the normative kinship system, enslaved bodies nevertheless forged other connections that could loosely be termed *community* in an attempt to survive the brutalities of the slaver. However, Spillers is quick to point out that there is no flattening out of the social relationships here, only a hierarchy that is undeniable. Moreover these relationships are not "natural" but are in fact forged in an intensely political context wherein economic practices take precedence over affective connections between subjects—an observation that causes Spillers to admit that "the feeling of kinship is not inevitable . . . [rather] it describes a relationship that appears 'natural,' but must be 'cultivated' under actual material conditions."[37]

Additionally the justification for the exclusion of enslaved bodies from kinship relations was based on the imbrication of race and disability as inscribed on the enslaved body. This exclusion was justified because of the dominant belief that Africans were of a lower social and intellectual order than their European masters on account of their "natural" inability to forge kinship relationships that allowed "the vertical transfer of a bloodline, of a patronymic, of titles and entitlements, of real estate and the prerogatives of 'cold cash,' from fathers to sons and in the supposedly free exchange of affectional ties between a male and a female of his choice . . . the mythically revered privilege of a free and freed community."[38]

The materialist implications of such exclusions were significant. Africans were transformed into impaired, ungendered, racialized bodies because they were presumed unfit to uphold the economic transactions that kinship relations demand. Concomitantly they were transformed into a commodity precisely because their exclusion from "natural" kinship ties also denied their claims to sovereign subjectivity, to being free to forge relationships that were recognized in a slave society. But it is not just the exclusion from legally recognized kinship ties that impacted enslaved bodies. The imbrication of race and disability also located desire firmly within the social relations of production and consumption such that both male and female slaves were mere commodities in the sexual transactions that ensued in the quest for profit and pleasure.

It is no secret that enslaved women were used for the master's pleasure and for the master's profit. Conceived merely as objects of desire, slave women were utilized not only to meet the master's sexual needs but also in a very concrete way to reproduce the labor force in the slave economy. Drawing from Frederick Douglass's autobiography, Spillers therefore observes that "genetic reproduction becomes, then, not an elaboration of the life-principle in its cultural overlap, but an extension of the boundaries of proliferating properties . . . through the institutional apparatus: war and market."[39]

Within this violent context is it even possible to imagine that the enslaved female or her sexual oppressor could derive pleasure from these intimate couplings? The answer to this question foregrounds the critical importance of articulating a political economy of desire even in the face of posthumanist critiques to the contrary. Posthumanist thought would argue that desire is not constrained by the social because even in the most repressive social organization of slavery held to rigid codes of race, gender, class, and sexuality, erotic desire seemed determined to transgress every boundary. An outlaw erotics flourished, taunting the laws of miscegenation and class antagonisms. Nowhere is this better illustrated than in *Incidents in the Life of a Slave Girl*, an autobiography by Linda Brent (Harriet Jacobs) that Spillers discusses.

Located in a context where rape by the master was a normative experience for black female slaves, Brent describes a fraught relationship between herself and Mrs. Flint, the wife of a doctor who owned Brent. Suspecting that her husband was having sexual relations with his slave, Mrs. Flint, consumed with jealousy, would visit Brent at night, assuming the role of a ghost and attempting to "ride" the victim "in order to exact confession, expiation, and anything else that the immaterial power might want." Here is Brent's account of these visitations: "Sometimes I woke up, and found her bending over me. At other times she whispered in my ear, as though it were her husband who was speaking to me, and listened to hear what I would answer. If she startled me, on such occasion, she would glide stealthily away; and the next morning she would tell me I had been talking in my sleep, and ask who I was talking to. At last, I began to be fearful for my life."[40]

Brent's narrative, clearly a psychodrama, provided yet another discourse of disability that Spillers alludes to but fails to foreground. In Spillers's reading of Brent's narrative she alludes to a discourse of madness associated with each of the three protagonists: the "madness" of the master that "arises in the ecstasy of his unchecked power"; the "madness" of his wife, who, by impersonating the sexual power of her husband, "attempts to inculcate his or her will into the vulnerable, supine body" of his slave; and the attempts by Mrs. Flint to convince Brent that these nightly visitations are the hallucinations of an immoral "mad" woman.[41] Here another becoming is foregrounded, one that is now grounded in the articulation of desire within a violent, abusive, and hierarchical context. Even though these intercorporeal intimacies traverse with impunity the boundaries of race, gender, and sexuality in a complex queering of outlaw desire, the only subject who can enjoy the "freedom to experiment, explore, peek outside of the limits, journey there and back again" is the master, Dr. Flint.[42] Thus Spillers rightly observes that "under these arrangements, the customary lexis of sexuality, including 'reproduction,' 'motherhood,' 'pleasure,' and desire' are thrown into unrelieved crisis."[43]

Additionally Spillers insightfully foregrounds a seemingly improbable alliance that could have been forged between mistress and slave because both were subject to "the same fabric of dread and humiliation." Spillers goes on to explain, "Neither could claim her body and its various productions—for quite different reasons, albeit—as her own, and in the case of the doctor's wife, she appears not to have wanted her body at all, but to desire to enter someone else's, specifically, Linda Brent's, in an apparently classic instance of sexual 'jealousy' and appropriation. In fact, from one point of view, we cannot unravel one female's narrative from the other's, cannot decipher one without tripping over the other."[44]

As Spillers observes, the violent intimate expressions of desire could have been productive in enabling transgressive queer connectivities that had the potential to destabilize the impermeable social boundaries in the slave economy. But I use the verb *could have* because this clearly did not happen in this context. In fact the only possibility for this alliance to flourish would have been if both protagonists were collectively invested in dismantling the social relations of production and consumption that had produced yet another violent instance of the "bare" life.

Finally, this analysis yields yet another discourse of disability that is intimately imbricated with race, gender, and sexuality in a context that foregrounds the continuities between the historical social relations of a slave society and the contemporary social relations supported by neoliberal capitalism. Earlier I discussed the social and economic conditions within which impaired black (female) enslaved bodies were ungendered to enable a more effective appropriation of their (re)productive labor for profit. With the impaired black (female) body becoming ungendered, this becoming also situates becoming queer in a materialist context, such that, as in Brent's autobiographical narrative, the female enslaved body "in an amazing stroke of pansexual potential . . . [can] be invaded/raided by another woman or man."[45] From a materialist perspective, the queering of this enslaved body occurs in a specific historical context wherein femininity loses its sacredness at the precise moment when the flesh becomes the primary commodity of exchange. In fact the very indeterminacy of gender identity occurs at the very moment of captive birth for the only reason that reproductive labor can be appropriated by the master for profit.

While it is true that much of my discussion emerges from a historical period that has substantially been transformed, I argue that the implications of these unsettling practices have transcended several historical periods and continue to have relevance even today. In fact the impetus for Spillers's essay came from the 1965 Moynihan report on the Negro family, which attempted to explain away the continued lack of social and economic progress of African Americans in the United States. Rather than implicating white supremacist capitalist patriarchy, Moynihan laid blame at the door of black female-headed households, implicating the perceived matriarchal culture propagated by (ungendered) black women for emasculating African American men in a culture that is normatively patriarchal. Moynihan wrote, "Ours is a society which presumes male leadership in private and public affairs. . . . A sub-culture, such as that of the Negro American, in which this is not the pattern, is placed at a distinct disadvantage. . . . It is clearly a disadvantage for a minority group to be operating under one principle, while the great majority of the population . . . is operating on another."[46]

To avoid mapping the historical continuities evident in this practice of conceiving black bodies as socially pathological would be a costly mistake. In fact it is in the analysis of these historical continuities that it is possible to foreground the complex ways in which the discourses of race, gender, and sexuality are implicated in African American subjects becoming disabled. The argument continues to play out in contemporary contexts, especially in education, where the "underachievement" of African American males in the lower classes still continues to be blamed on the overachieving matriarchal African American women and the missing patriarchal figures of African American males in the African American female-headed household. Unwilling to read the real material violence against black subjectivities, it seems a little too easy to read disability as embodied otherness (notwithstanding its "inherent" potential for resistance) rather than situate becoming disabled in an economic context "too obviously [committed] to administer to the [master's] own lusts, and make a gratification of their wicked desires profitable as well as pleasurable."[47]

Making (Disabled) Bodies Matter

So then, we are back again to McRuer's question: "What might it mean to welcome the disability to come, to desire it?" In response I have argued that the social meanings of disability, race, gender, and sexuality are constituted within the historical conditions of transnational capitalism. I have also pointed out that it is the economic context (e.g., colonialism) that has blunted the capacity for the *severely disabled desiring machine* to realize its transgressive potential. That the potential for transgression is there is evident in the multiple ways in which the impaired black ungendered enslaved body is nonchalantly tossed across many social boundaries and, as a result, inadvertently (re)writes the social texts that were diligently being monitored by the disciplinary discourses of biopower. Unfortunately, however, in the specific context of slavery these (re)writings came at the cost of the complete erasure of agency of the enslaved body—now transformed into a commodity that was forced to transgress social boundaries purely for the benefit of profit. I define human agency in the context of Marx's famous quote in the *Eighteenth Brumaire of Louis Bonaparte*: "Men make their own history, but they do not make it just as they please; they do not make it under circumstances chosen by themselves, but under circumstances directly found, given and transmitted from the past."[48]

Marx's argument, transforming agency from an autonomous act to a historical event, can also be applied to the concept of desire. Contrary to Deleuze and Guattari's claim that productive desire is autonomous from the social, I join with Rosemary Hennessy to argue that this conceptualization of productive desire conceives of consumption practices as if they occur outside of the exploitative social relations of production, and as a result the BwO now becomes "the undifferentiated subject of self enjoyment."[49] But as I have shown through Spillers's essay, desire is mediated via the social relations of production and consumption, such that the master's ability to consume is dependent on the slave's capacity to produce. Moreover the very articulation of the master's desire is dependent on the appropriation of the ungendered (female) slave body for his pleasure. In contemporary contexts both Hennessy and McRuer draw on the work of John D'Emilio to foreground a materialist analysis of desire in their materialist conceptualizations of queer identity in capitalism. According to Hennessy, D'Emilio posits that the locus of production shifting from the household to the market, and the new demand for women to participate in the workforce and in consumer culture, enabled the "gradual unhinging of sexuality from its pro-creative function as regulated by the family's patriarchal gender system," and this shift enabled the proliferation of "public" queer identities. Hennessy is careful to point out that this does not mean that "class trumps sexual identity" but rather that "the consolidation of new sexual identities that pursues the logic of commodification limits the development of collective agency," or, in other words, the "multitude."[50]

So what does disability have to do with all of this? To answer that question, I take another detour to briefly discuss Young's theorization of race as a commodity fetish and explore its implications for a materialist disability studies. Within the context of literary studies Young is critical of the contemporary trend in cultural theory, where posthumanist scholars eschew metanarratives and humanist scholars extol the experiential, because, he argues, these trends displace a historical understanding of class relations within contemporary transnational capitalism. As a result race theory offers an "idealist notion of race as an expressive causality and an empiricist notion of race as a positivity" and in doing so blocks a materialist understanding of race.[51]

To make the argument for a materialist theory of race, Young turns to Marx's labor theory of value as it manifests in capitalist production. According to Marx, the very basis for participation in labor is to provide for specific needs that are essential for human survival: food, clothing, and shelter. Marx identified this labor as having a use value (i.e., being of use to someone). At the same time, in the context of capitalism, which is predominantly an economy of exchange, labor itself becomes a commodity, which does not merely have a use value but is instead assigned an exchange value in the marketplace—the value of that labor being compensated by a wage. According to Marx's theory of surplus value, labor power—the capacity for work that an employer buys from a worker—produces more value than it is compensated for, thereby producing surplus value in the form of profits that are appropriated by the capitalist. Thus it is productive labor—labor that actually produces surplus value—that has more economic value in capitalist economies. Marx also demonstrates that notions of efficiency and productivity are both historical constructs associated with the modes of production by which the capitalist can extract surplus value from commodity labor power.

It is in this context that Young proposes theorizing race as a commodity fetish, whereby he foregrounds the use value of race as a commodity. Humanist and posthumanist arguments focus on the use value of race outside of economics; in other words, these theories essentially argue that race is useful to deny sameness and mark difference within the social. Young, on the other hand, argues that race has to be understood such that its use value always operates in relation to its exchange value, within the exploitative context of commodity production. Examining race in this context, Young argues that what links racism to capitalism is not just the creation of racial divisions within the working classes; rather "it is the very commodity structure where race is useful precisely because it can be exchanged for less." He continues, "If race signifies 'less than' at the point of (re)production, then it is ideologically (and morally) legitimate for the asymmetrical distribution of resources and thus, this race difference contributes toward increasing surplus value, thereby reinforcing the fundamental logic of capitalism: accumulation."[52]

Then, in an interesting twist to his argument, Young goes on to claim that race is not just a commodity; it is a commodity fetish. In *Capital, Volume 1*, Marx explains:

> The commodity is a mysterious thing, simply because in it the social character of men's labor appears to them as an objective character stamped upon the product of that labor; because the relationship of the

> producers to the sum total of their own labor is presented to them as a social relation, existing not between themselves, but between the products of their labor. . . . There is a definite social relation between men, that assumes in their eyes, the fantastic form of a relation between things. . . . This is what I call the Fetishism which attaches itself to the products of labor, so soon as they are produced as commodities, and which is therefore inseparable from the production of commodities.[53]

Taking up this concept, Young argues that the use value of race fetishizes our conception of the social, and as a result this occludes a critical understanding of the historicity of social relations where race is deployed in the calculus of surplus extraction (its exchange value). Thus by theorizing race as a commodity fetish within the historical context of transnational capitalism, Young is also locating Spillers's conceptualization of pornotroping within a historical materialist context also. Similarly I have argued that becoming disabled is also a historical event whereby disability also has a use value that is deployed simultaneously with race to justify the creation of the enslaved ungendered body. I argue that it is the actual act of impairment that is used to create and at the same time to justify this construction. However, by reading disability as "natural" rather than as a historical event, what is obscured are the social and economic relationships that produce disability as lack. And so, like Young, I too argue that the use value of disability lies in its deployment as a commodity fetish via the historical materialist practice of pornotroping in transnational capitalism.

It could be argued that in reclaiming political economy, I have once again constructed a disembodied disabled subject. In response to that critique, I argue that my project instead seeks to situate embodiment in a historical context in order to foreground the materiality of the flesh. Moreover, in opposition to normative constructions of disability as lack, I answer McRuer's question by simply reframing it: Within what social conditions might we welcome the disability to come, to desire it? I have attempted to answer this question by situating "desiring disability" as a historical condition of possibility that does not reproduce economic exploitation on a global scale. In doing so I offer a critique of posthumanist discourses that see possibility as reinvesting signs with more transgressive meaning. I also echo Young when he argues, "Change will not come by emancipating signs from totalities but by displacing the relations of production. For although the relations of production do not evade, they nevertheless always exceed the fate of the sign."[54]

NOTES

1. Critical Ethnic Studies Association, "About," 2014, accessed October 15, 2015, https://www.criticalethnicstudies.org/content/about.

2. McRuer, *Crip Theory*, 72.

3. Spillers, "Mama's Baby, Papa's Maybe" (1987), 61, 67.

4. Garland-Thomson, "Integrating Disability, Transforming Feminist Theory"; McRuer, *Crip Theory*.

5. Kristeva, *Powers of Horror*, 6.

6. McRuer, *Crip Theory*, 207.

7. Ahmed, "Animated Borders."

8. Paterson and Hughes, "Disability Studies and Phenomenology"; Shildrick, *Dangerous Discourses of Disability, Subjectivity and Sexuality*; Titchkosky, *Reading and Writing Disability Differently*.

9. Shildrick, *Dangerous Discourses of Disability, Subjectivity and Sexuality*, 25.

10. Shildrick, *Dangerous Discourses of Disability, Subjectivity and Sexuality*.

11. Deleuze and Guattari, *Anti-Oedipus*, 5.

12. Spillers, "Mama's Baby, Papa's Maybe" (1987), 74.

13. Spillers, "Mama's Baby, Papa's Maybe" (1987), 67.

14. Weheliye, "Pornotropes," 71.

15. Weheliye, "Pornotropes," 71.

16. Garland-Thomson, "Integrating Disability, Transforming Feminist Theory"; Titchkosky, *Reading and Writing Disability Differently*.

17. Equiano quoted in Spillers, "Mama's Baby, Papa's Maybe" (1987), 67; de Azurara quoted in Spillers, "Mama's Baby, Papa's Maybe" (1987), 70.

18. Quoted in Spillers, "Mama's Baby, Papa's Maybe" (1987), 70.

19. Spillers, "Mama's Baby, Papa's Maybe" (1987), 67.

20. Garland-Thomson, "Integrating Disability, Transforming Feminist Theory."

21. Spillers, "Mama's Baby, Papa's Maybe" (1987), 72.

22. Bogard quoted in Goodley, "Becoming Rhizomatic Parents," 149; Shildrick, *Dangerous Discourses of Disability, Subjectivity and Sexuality*, 157.

23. Deleuze and Guattari, *A Thousand Plateaus*, 88.

24. Goodell quoted in Spillers, "Mama's Baby, Papa's Maybe" (1987), 68.

25. Spillers, "Mama's Baby, Papa's Maybe" (1987), 68.

26. Spillers, "Mama's Baby, Papa's Maybe" (1987), 70.

27. Agamben, *Homo Sacer*.

28. Spillers, "Mama's Baby, Papa's Maybe" (1987), 68.

29. Deleuze and Guattari, *A Thousand Plateaus*, 162.

30. McRuer, *Crip Theory*, 207.

31. Young, *Signs of Race in Poststructuralism*, 119.

32. Young, *Signs of Race in Poststructuralism*, 1.

33. Lecercle, "Deleuze, Guattari and Marxism," 42.

34. Deleuze and Guattari. *Anti-Oedipus*, 29.

35. Spillers, "Mama's Baby, Papa's Maybe" (1987), 67.

36. Spillers, "Mama's Baby, Papa's Maybe" (1987), 74.

37. Spillers, "Mama's Baby, Papa's Maybe" (1987), 75, 76.
38. Spillers, "Mama's Baby, Papa's Maybe" (1987), 74.
39. Spillers, "Mama's Baby, Papa's Maybe" (1987), 75.
40. Spillers, "Mama's Baby, Papa's Maybe" (1987), 76, 77 (quoting Brent).
41. Spillers, "Mama's Baby, Papa's Maybe" (1987).
42. Gibson, "Disability, Connectivity, and Transgressing the Autonomous Body." 95.
43. Spillers, "Mama's Baby, Papa's Maybe" (1987), 76.
44. Spillers, "Mama's Baby, Papa's Maybe" (1987), 77.
45. Spillers, "Mama's Baby, Papa's Maybe" (1987), 77.
46. Quoted in Spillers, "Mama's Baby, Papa's Maybe" (1987), 65.
47. Spillers, "Mama's Baby, Papa's Maybe" (1987), 76.
48. Marx, Engels, and Tucker, 595
49. Hennessy, *Profit and Pleasure*, 71.
50. Hennessy, *Profit and Pleasure*, 103, 106; Hardt and Negri, *Multitude*.
51. Young, *Signs of Race in Poststructuralism*, 4.
52. Young, *Signs of Race in Poststructuralism*, 8, 9.
53. Marx, *Capital, Volume 1*, 320–21.
54. Young, *Signs of Race in Poststructuralism*, 7.

THIRTEEN

Arts and Crafts, Elsewhere and Home, *Mama & Me*: Defying Transnormativity through Bobby Cheung's Creative Modalities of Resignification

BO LUENGSURASWAT

I wanted this because, once I finished the piece, I wanted to be able to say that my relationship with my mother is okay. It's fine. We love each other. And this is the public statement that I want to make to the transgender community.—BOBBY CHEUNG, November 13, 2009

Rather than evoking an imaginary homeland frozen in an idyllic moment outside history, what is remembered through queer diasporic desire and the queer diasporic body is a past time and place riven with contradictions and the violences of multiple uprootings, displacements, and exiles.—GAYATRI GOPINATH, *Impossible Desires: Queer Diasporas and South Asian Public Cultures*

Mama & Me

In the summer of 2009 I attended *Fresh Meat in the Gallery*, the annual visual art exhibition of transgender and gender-variant artists in San Francisco. Organized by Fresh Meat Productions, the nation's first transgender and queer art organization, *Fresh Meat in the Gallery* celebrated its sixth annual exhibition at the San Francisco LGBT Community Center under the theme "Defying Gravities."[1] As I entered the gallery my eyes went directly to Bobby Cheung's work *Mama & Me*, a small, natural-color, beaded curtain arranged in the image of the artist and his mother (figs. 13.1 and 13.2). According to Cheung, an FTM-identified Hong Kong immigrant, this meticulous, labor-intensive work of art represents his effort to rebuild a relationship with his mother.

What does it mean for an Asian immigrant transman to feature himself in an art piece, particularly in the context of a "transgender" and "queer" art exhibition, with his mother? Can a connection be made between the appearance of the work—the sepia color tone and the pixilated visual effect—and the discourses of race, immigration, and globalization? Moreover what are the political implications of craft production techniques in the context of a "white-cube," or the art world? These complex and provocative issues urge me to explore the ways that *Mama & Me,* as an articulation of Asian American transgender masculinity, defies the hegemonic narratives of identity formation central to the discourses of Asian American racialization and transgender identity.

Through my visual analysis of *Mama & Me,* I contend that Cheung engages in the practice of *resignification* as he transforms cultural signifiers of femininity into an articulation of Asian American transgender maleness. Cheung's act of rebuilding a relationship with his mother—more specifically "reestablishing" a connection with womanhood and family—subverts the transnormative logic of "leaving home" or a "female past" as a prerequisite for gender self-determination. In fact the home-elsewhere binary at the core of the teleological coming-out narrative, that which posits "elsewhere"—the new country or corporeal embodiment—as a site of liberation, is irrelevant to subjects whose conditions of existence are implicated in the processes of racialization. If, for Asian American cisgender men, being racialized as Asian American means becoming feminized, then for Asian American transmen, being racialized as Asian American implies a "failed" journey to manhood. In light of this formulation, *Mama & Me* illustrates the impossibility for Asian American transmen to escape the condition of racialization—namely feminization—by conforming to the normative version of transgender masculinity that insists on the possibility of "leaving home" and "leaving one's past behind."

As Cheung's experience of migration from Hong Kong to the United States illustrates, the move from one's home to elsewhere entails less liberation than a confrontation with new conditions of marginalization. Cheung's struggle with cultural difference and declining class status as consequences of immigration astutely undermines the American Dream myth. This reversal of the liberatory narrative of immigrant emancipation that Cheung experiences, I insist, must be understood in relation to queer of color critiques of the teleological coming-out narrative trope through the lens of diaspora studies. As

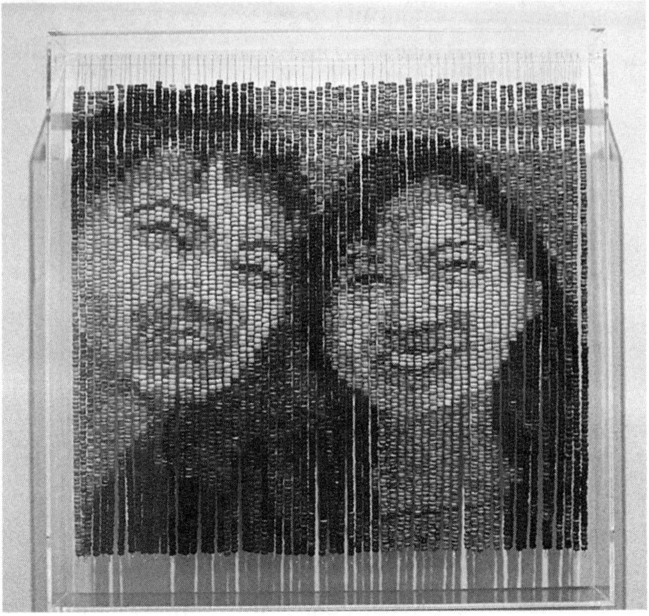

FIGURE 13.1. Bobby Cheung, *Mama & Me,* 2009. Coco beads and metal wires. 14 × 14 inches. *Fresh Meat in the Gallery VI: Defying Gravities,* San Francisco LGBT Community Center, San Francisco, 2009. Photograph courtesy of artist.

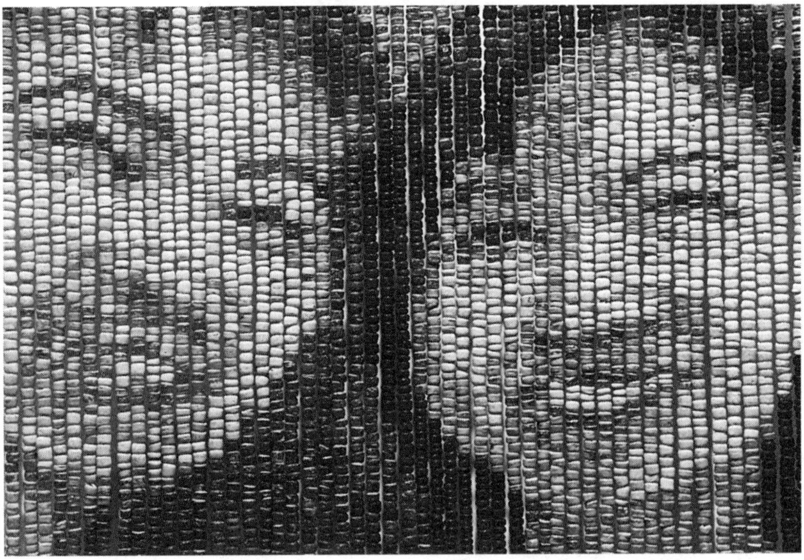

FIGURE 13.2. Bobby Cheung, *Mama & Me,* details. Photograph courtesy of artist.

such it is through critical ruptures and connections among various disciplines of knowledge production that Asian American transmale subjectivity can be adequately conceptualized.

In theorizing Asian American transmasculinity through artistic production, it is crucial to perceive this subject position not as an object of inquiry but as a methodology of decolonization. Cheung's artwork and artistic process underscore that racialization is the process of gendering, thereby transforming the limits of gender construction within Asian American studies as well as reorienting ethnic studies' focus on a single nation-state to transnational critiques of global capital. Critical ethnic studies constitutes a terrain of scholarly activism, where critiques of transnormativity and situated forms of cultural resistance such as Cheung's work translate into world-making methods that are substantively attuned to the effects of racial and economic oppression. Most important, this essay, as a multidisciplinary collaboration between Cheung and me, unsettles the distinctions and hierarchies among knowledge production, artistic practice, and community activism.

Troubling the Home-Elsewhere Binary: Cheung's Journey

Born in Hong Kong and emigrating to San Francisco in 1988, Bobby Cheung is a mixed-media and digital artist and a long-term advocate for the transgender and queer community. As an active member of the Bay Area trans and queer art scene, Cheung had served as a *Fresh Meat in the Gallery* curator and a board member of Fresh Meat Productions for many years. According to Cheung, his feeling of invisibility due to the marginalization of trans people of color in the mainstream LGBT community has been the driving force behind his creative process. However, *Mama & Me* is a path-breaking work in which Cheung not only explored new types of medium and worked sculpturally but also developed a different creative process that did not directly channel anger and frustration into the work of art.

In the description of *Mama & Me* at *Fresh Meat in the Gallery*, Cheung explains his creative process as rather therapeutic, whereby he embarked on a journey to rebuild a relationship with his mother (fig. 13.3):

> My relationship with my mother defies transphobia that typically tears families apart. I created this beaded curtain in honor of our mother-child relationship even after becoming a FTM transsexual. She cuts my hair, and we enjoy exploring different restaurants for dinner. The image of us was transposed from a photo that I took after one of our meals. This

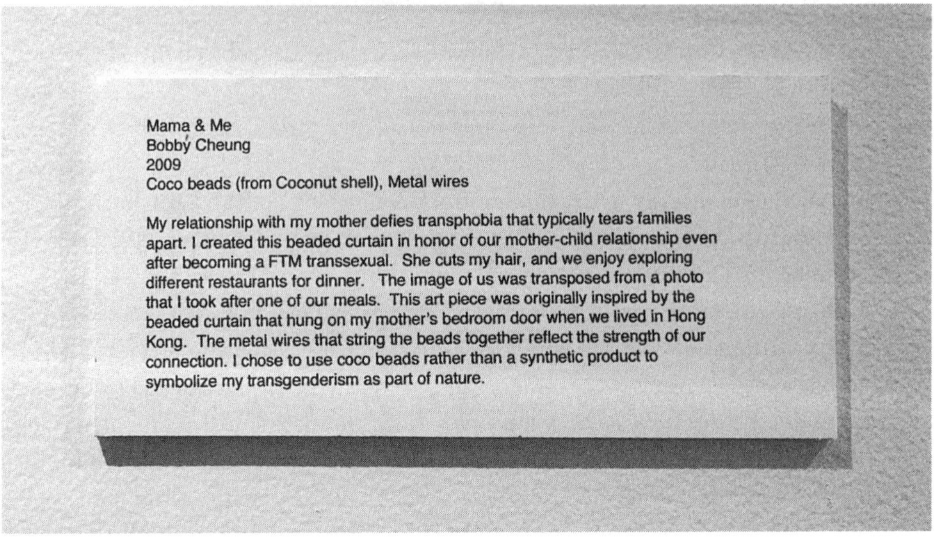

FIGURE 13.3. Bobby Cheung, artwork label, *Mama & Me*. Photograph courtesy of artist.

> art piece was originally inspired by the beaded curtain that hung on my mother's bedroom door when we lived in Hong Kong. The metal wires that string the beads together reflect the strength of our connection. I chose to use coco beads rather than a synthetic product to symbolize my transgenderism as part of nature.

Cheung emphasizes his positive, nurturing relationship with his mother. He references the objects and materials that are associated with the memory of his homeland (the beaded curtain), the strength of his relationship with his mother (metal wires), and the "naturalness" of his transgender and queer self (coco beads). Although Cheung's belief in the naturalness of his gender identity may seem to dangerously align itself with scientific discourses of the biological basis of sexual orientation and gender variance (e.g., the search for a "gay gene"), what he evokes here through the metaphor of nature is the "unexpected" harmony among different aspects of his identity. The fact that Cheung's mother directly participates in his gender presentation by cutting his hair illustrates that family is a possible site for the production of queerness. Evidently Cheung acknowledges that his transgender identity and queerness cannot be understood as separate from family and cultural belonging. Though not directly conveying the feeling of marginalization and invisibility, *Mama & Me* poses a challenge to the hegemonic coming-out narrative that posits the act of leaving home—whether it be family, community, or homeland—as essential for the actualization of one's sexual or gender nonconformity.[2]

The binary of family-home versus freedom-elsewhere is called into question in Cheung's work. By illustrating the possibility of "being oneself at home," Cheung inhabits an in-between space where the embodiment of transgender identity and queerness does not necessarily imply the rejection of family and also challenges the belief that Asian immigrant families are inherently conservative and transphobic. Hence in *Mama & Me* Cheung redefines the notion of home and complicates the understanding of family. For many trans and queer immigrants of color, home—albeit constructed as a site for the repudiation of gender and sexual variance by U.S. immigration measures such as the family reunification program, which grants citizenship strictly through biological inheritance and upholds the supremacy of the heteronormative family structure—is nonetheless a site of struggle because, for the most part, trans and queer immigrants of color rely on their biological family for legal existence and cultural survival.[3] For trans and queer subjects who cannot afford to reject their biological family, or to whom the idea of leaving home is irrelevant, survival by no means implies an individualistic journey toward an enlightened space free from social constraints placed on one's embodiment of identity but rather the complex processes of negotiation and mutual struggle between oneself and one's family and community.

Hong Kong, Hybridity, and the Politics of Migration: Diasporic Queer Belonging

The home-elsewhere binary in the discourse of coming out, which positions home as an oppressive place and elsewhere as an anticipated space of liberation, is complicated by Cheung's relationship to his homeland, Hong Kong, and his experience as a diasporic subject. Interestingly but not surprisingly Cheung describes his move to the United States as "almost like a backward step" due to his encounter with blatant racial discrimination in the United States that he thought never existed in Hong Kong. For Cheung the United States does not stand in for the elsewhere, the American Dream, or that anticipated space of liberation but is rather the site of oppression, as if to reverse the original logic. Thus his experience of migration as a queer diasporic subject reveals the major shortcoming of the developmental narrative of immigrant emancipation—that is, the heteronormatively conceptualized space of the homeland.

Drawing upon Gayatri Gopinath's theorization of diaspora in *Impossible Desires: Queer Diasporas and South Asian Public Cultures,* I contend that Cheung's queer diasporic subjectivity "reorients the traditionally backward-looking glance of diaspora." The "backward-looking glance of diaspora" implies the nostalgic conceptualization of the space of the nation, or one's homeland, as pure, pristine, and authentic—more specifically as ethnically homogeneous, heteronormative, and free from internal contradictions—in order to align diasporic subjects with nationalist ideology. Inasmuch as queer bodies and desires are central to the construction of dominant nationalist and diasporic historiographies, they remain excluded and forgotten.[4] Cheung's work, as an articulation of diasporic queer memory, in turn remembers the space of the homeland as already riven with possibilities of queerness and gender nonconformity. By revealing the inauthentic potential of the nation—that is, the homeland that is already structured as hybrid and queer—*Mama & Me* undermines the belief that the nation is a sanction of purity, an idealized, homogeneous spatiotemporal entity.

Cheung's homeland has been constructed as hybrid since its earliest days, overturning the belief that homogeneity, unity, and rootedness are necessarily the basis of nation-building. Under British occupation from 1841 through 1997, Hong Kong functioned as a capital of exchange between Asia and the West; hence its image was that of a "city of transients," strongly characterized by speed, change, flexibility, and "borderlessness."[5] Although it may seem like Hong Kong (prior to the 1997 handover) was constituted as a nonnation due to the fact that its cultural identity was not bound by either Chinese or British nationalism, I insist that the qualities of fluidity and transience that framed the identity of Hong Kong are precisely a kind of nationalist definition of identity that is completely in line with globalization's emphasis on flexibility.

The notion of home, or the nation, as hybrid, fluid, and heterogeneous per se could have foregrounded Cheung's feeling of alienation when he first arrived in the United States. In 1988, four years after the Sino-British Joint Declaration and one year prior to the Tiananmen Massacre, Cheung's family left Hong Kong in order to avoid the uncertain future after the handover in 1997. For some Hong Kong residents, migration to a different country implied a change in class status, and this shifting class positionality could in turn affect Hong Kong immigrants' perception of home. That Cheung can recall Hong Kong in a nostalgic way as a nonracist paradise could in fact indicate his position of privilege vis-à-vis Hong Kong. In that sense the blatant racial discrimination that Cheung says he experienced when first arriving in the

United States could also be understood in relation to the loss of financial and social entitlements as a condition of his migration.

The diminishment of social status as part of the process of one's immigration to the United States, though neither absolute nor uniformly experienced, subverts the American Dream myth. Truly enough, according to Cheung, his father went from being a white-collar professional in Hong Kong to working menial service jobs in the United States. Formerly an electronics drafter, Cheung's father became a restaurant sous-chef for some time and, later, an aircraft housekeeper. His struggle for employment in the United States and the family's financial strain point to the fact that issues of language barriers, lack of social connections, and cultural difference are indisputably central to the experiences of immigration, such that they cannot be recklessly subsumed into the euphoric discourses of multiculturalism. Thus Cheung's journey from Hong Kong to the United States as a "backward step" importantly underlines the impracticality of positing the West as naturally liberatory and the East as decisively oppressive. The simplistic home-elsewhere binary in the teleological coming-out narrative—the necessity of leaving home for the actualization of one's subjectivity—unwittingly reiterates the American Dream narrative trope and violently endorses the imperialist notion of freedom.

Resignification as Decolonization: Defying Transnormativity and Reconceptualizing Survival

The teleological coming-out narrative can be framed as the temporal colonization of one's being under the guise of liberation. Apparent in the discourse of coming out is the temporal division between *before* and *after*—or the journey from repression to liberation. Coming out is commonly understood as an event in which a trans or queer person begins to acknowledge and embody their gender or sexual nonconformity, and the act is construed as liberatory in contrast to the repressive closet where one had *not yet* become who one *really is*. Since coming out is perceived as a truth-founding instance—the moment when one *begins* to live one's life—the privileging of the post-coming-out self as truthful by all means has material consequences. In the medical discourse, for example, the criteria for hormonal and surgical transition often include proofs of "cross-gender" identification, such as declarations of one's "lifelong" desire to embody the characteristics of the opposite birth sex.[6] Simply put, if becoming recognized as one's chosen gender implies the ontological eradication of one's past, then coming out is the process of dissociating oneself from prior gender socialization and any signifiers of one's assigned sex.

If crossing the gender border equals leaving the past behind—more specifically "becoming a man *equals* dissociating oneself from womanhood"—how can we make sense of the image of Cheung and his mother? Clearly Cheung is not afraid to express his close relationship with his mother, to openly associate himself with the significant female figure in his life, to consider womanhood—motherhood, to be more specific—part of what made him who he is in the present. Not only does Cheung complicate the politics of place and cultural belonging in the discourse of transgender and queer identity, conceptualizing an alternative mode of identity embodiment that does not reference the individualistic, imperialist quest for freedom; he also resignifies what counts as a legitimate expression of transgender maleness. By turning his identification with his mother, womanhood, and femaleness into an articulation of Asian American transmasculinity, he rejects the necessity of renouncing the signifiers associated with one's past in order to validate one's present self.

In lieu of the transnormative recourse to rejection and dissociation, *resignification* is a methodology of survival whereby minoritarian subjects engage in the discursive transformation of the systems of misrecognition into empowering critiques. In essence one could say that resignification is a mode of "disidentification," as José Esteban Muñoz terms it, in the sense that it entails the reconstruction of dominant discursive sites into inhabitable spaces.[7] However, in this context I use the term *resignification* to address the specificity of dealing with hegemonic cultural sources that do not necessarily *pass* as abject or pejorative, yet the circulation of these domains of cultural intelligibility—whether it be within the hetero-, homo-, or transnormative or some women or queer of color systems of signification—contributes to the erasure of certain subjects and positionalities. Amid the conditions of invisibility, resignification is an act of carving out and creating a space within the empire of recognition, laboriously transforming the cultural location within which one's subjectivity is negated and misrecognized into a site of resistance and survival. Against the socially assigned gender of family, domesticity, and crafts, Cheung *reassigns* the meaning to his transition through the performative processes of reuniting with his mother and resituating himself at home.

The Photographic Truth-Effect: Family Reunification and the Performative Processes of Self-Building

Cheung's processes of self-building and reconnection with his family are well illustrated through the medium in which the work *Mama & Me* is made: coco beads. This natural medium notably underscores the performative aspects of signification. First and foremost the sepia tone of the coco beads toys with the idea of the truth-effect, making *Mama & Me* resemble an antique photograph. This photographic effect eloquently renders the happy faces of Cheung and his mother, and their time together, a segment of memory and family history. In light of this reading *Mama & Me* is visual evidence of Cheung's reunification with his mother. Nevertheless, in contrast to the idea of photographic evidence as a mere reflection of reality, a proof of something that already exists, *Mama & Me* functions as an active agent in the process of reality construction, actualizing the relationship between Cheung and his mother. Accordingly this artwork is essentially a significant part of Cheung's long-term effort to rebuild a relationship with his mother after his periodic absences from her life, one of the reasons being his transgender identity and queerness. For Cheung *Mama & Me* is truly a powerful living record of his psychological transformation and self-building.

Cheung's self-building journey—his two-year-long process of creating *Mama & Me*—was by no means straightforward or simply nurturing but was extremely labor intensive and psychologically daunting. He had to accurately match the color of the coco beads with the sepia-filtered photograph, meticulously lace the beads through individual strands of metal wire, and patiently restring the piece countless of times; he also had to deal with the emotional turmoil of looking at the photograph of himself and his mother. He says:

> During the last couple years . . . it was really hard for me to [make] that curtain actually. Sometimes there [were] pieces sitting under a chair for months [because] I wouldn't even touch it. I [couldn't] even do it. . . . Each time I made it I had to look at the photo, the photo of us. That was pretty intense, to do an art piece while I [was] working through all this stuff, processing and [sighing] internally while I was making the piece. Because knowing [that] after it's done . . . I'm going to display this publicly, in front of my friends, in front of my community, talking about my relationship with my mother and that everything's okay. I have to be able to say that, you know, or else I'm lying to the audience.[8]

It is worth noting that Cheung invited his mother to the exhibit, thus officially accomplishing his mission of reuniting with her (fig. 13.4). Particularly remarkable was the fact that the audience of *Fresh Meat in the Gallery* and the San Francisco LGBT Community Center visitors—the mainstream transgender and queer community—were witnesses of Cheung's success in rebuilding a relationship with his family. Through *Mama & Me* Cheung reveals the amount of work, effort, and courage that goes into rebuilding and maintaining

FIGURE 13.4. (From left to right) Bobby Cheung, *Mama & Me*, Cheung's mother. Photograph courtesy of artist.

ties with one's biological family and, most important, highlights the negotiation that trans and queer people of color, particularly those who are immigrants, are dealing with on the daily basis—that is, the pressure to *choose* between one's gender identity and sexuality and one's family and cultural community. By illuminating the inseparability of Cheung's queerness, his familial relations, and his sense of cultural belonging, *Mama & Me* undermines this very notion of choice.

The labor-intensiveness of familial relationship building illustrated through Cheung's artistic process underlines that, for trans and queer immigrants, family reunification entails nothing less than a significant psychological labor and trauma. Since the passage of the Immigration and Nationality Act in 1965, family reunification has been promoted as the main route of immigration to the United States. Currently family reunification, whether through blood relations or marriage to U.S. citizens (or green card holders), accounts for the majority of permanent residency granted each year.[9] According to Chandan Reddy, the family reunification program enables the state to construct immigrant communities of color as conservative and homophobic by way of making the formation of heteronormative biological families a mandatory condition for immigration and survival.[10] In reinforcing compulsory heterosexuality and the supremacy of biological inheritance within immigrant communities of color, the state deliberately produces heteronormative conditions for the reproduction and socialization of racialized immigrant labor in order to fulfill the demands of the transnational economy (the production of surplus populations).[11] Although Cheung's story of having to rebuild a relationship with his biological family does not undermine the stereotype that Asian families are ostensibly patriarchally organized and heteronormative per se, it demonstrates the degree of emotional labor a gender-nonconforming Asian immigrant undergoes in order to reunite with his family and be at home.

Art or Craft? Labor, Globalization, and the Gendering of Creativity

Mama & Me embodies within it the traces of physical and emotional labor, which, whether or not Cheung intends it, directly speaks to the conditions of contemporary Asian migration to the United States. After the Immigration and Nationality Act of 1965 went into effect, we observed the emergence of a substantial Asian American middle class due to transnational capital's demands for managerial, professional, and technical labor. Concurrent with the family reunification program, another aspect of the 1965 immigration reform was the renunciation of all race-based immigration measures in accordance with the U.S. cold war liberal multiculturalist ideal of equality.[12] However, the dismantling of the national origins quota system in U.S. immigration law has in fact paved the way for other immigration restrictions and preferences, predominantly those based on profession and class status. The H-1B work visa in particular authorizes U.S. and multinational corporations and government entities to sponsor overseas college-educated professionals for their residence in the United States.[13] This transformation in immigration law precisely corresponds with shifts in the global economy and the current demands of transnational capital.

From the rise of the info-tech industry in the 1990s to the early 2000s dot-com boom and the continuous evolution of technological empire in the present moment, there has been an uninterrupted influx of professional, managerial, and technical labor from Asian countries, particularly India, Singapore, China, and Hong Kong.[14] The establishment of work visa requirements, which encourages mass migration of professional labor from non-Western countries, and the creation of the family reunification program, which upholds the heteronormative nuclear family ideal as a condition of survival, contribute to the construction of Asian immigrants in the post-1965 era as model minorities.

Unlike Asian immigrants in the era of exclusion, who were seen as "undesirable aliens" due to their lack of capital and "queer" living arrangements (i.e., Chinese bachelors and prostitutes), Asian immigrants in the post-1965 era are commonly regarded as "respectable citizens" because of their perceived upward mobility, economic well-being, and conformity to gender and sexual norms of the American family. Nevertheless, in the midst of global capital development and the rise of the Asian immigrant professional class in the United States, the demands for exploitable, low-wage labor still persist. This bifurcated nature of contemporary Asian migration to the United States illustrates that the U.S. nation-state and economy continue to benefit as much from the affluent labor force as from the low-wage labor force.

In a way *Mama & Me* brings to attention this bifurcated nature of post-1965 Asian immigration. Due to the low ratio between the coco beads and the size of the whole piece, *Mama & Me* appears as a pixilated image, resembling images that are technologically produced. By creating a digital, pixilated image in the most low-tech way possible, Cheung interrogates the idea of Asian immigrants as highly technical workers and calls into question the model minority myth. After all, what are the similarities between software programmers and electronic factory workers in Silicon Valley? Do not both professional technicians and blue-collar workers provide incessant labor for the ever-expanding U.S. info-tech empire? Although college-educated, affluent Asian immigrant professional and technical workers are perceived as desirable subjects of the state, whose image as model minorities has often been deployed to discipline other nonwhite immigrant populations, they nonetheless constitute the new surplus pool of labor for transnational capital. The degree of mobility and agency that Asian immigrant professional workers seem to possess is, in the end, sanctioned through U.S. immigration law. That is, the post-1965 influx of middle-class Asian professionals to the United States by no means indicates the end of racial discrimination but instead implies the effectiveness of the neoliberal regulation of the American citizen body.

What Cheung's work particularly informs us about the contemporary conditions of Asian American racialization is the continued feminization of Asian men well into the era of advanced capitalism. By using a natural medium (coco beads) and a craft production technique (beading) to create a grainy digital image, Cheung merges the "male" domain of information technology with the "female" domain of crafts. Seen from a technological point of view, the irregularly shaped, unevenly sized coco beads and the hands-on method of production undeniably reduce the clarity and sharpness of the image. In the male-dominated field of information technology, where clarity, precision, and exactitude are deemed fundamental to the transmission of ideas and knowledge, the uneven shapes and sizes of natural coco beads and the irregularity of manual spacing can easily be understood as factors contributing to the failure of communication—in other words, the condition of impotency in the world of information technology. In composing a digital image by hand—literally by his corporeal digits—Cheung plays with the notion of potency when masculinity has come to be measured by success in colonizing the visual sphere and penetrating global markets.

Cheung's deployment of a craft production technique effectively resists the subsumption of Asian immigrant labor into the uninterrupted flow of transnational capital and intervenes in the totalizing regime of technological globalization. Through his engagement with the "feminine" domain of crafts, he disrupts the paternalistic logic of the info-tech empire that undermines situated, nonstandardized manual labor in favor of universally standardized technological inventions. Moreover his labor-intensive process of creating *Mama & Me*—a digital image produced in the most low-tech way possible—brings to the fore the most invisible labor force behind the growth of transnational capital: Asian immigrants. As a consequence of the state-sanctioned model minority myth, the *labor* and struggle of Asian immigrants, both professional and working classes, remain largely unacknowledged behind the false façade of upward mobility. In restoring the materiality of labor and struggle that has been rendered invisible under the neoliberal multiculturalist regime of global capital, we must consider crafts and other hands-on, process-oriented creative endeavors as crucial means of bottom-up resistance to capitalist exploitation at this temporal juncture.

In order to contextualize the situated resistance of hands-on creative processes, consider Cheung's work in its context of display: the "white-cube" gallery space. The introduction of craft into the space traditionally created for art is, in and of itself, a profound intervention. Since the founding of the art market and the commercial gallery system, the relegation of handiwork, hand-made utilitarian objects, and decorative arts to the category of crafts has been crucial to the maintenance of the capitalistic structure of the art world. Accordingly the situated processes of craft production are reduced to menial, nonintellectual activities and placed in opposition to "intellectually informed" high art.[15] Nonetheless, as the intensive production process of *Mama & Me* illustrates, crafts are by no means a mindless activity or a monolithic mode of artistic production but the process in which bodily activity comes to influence one's intellectual and emotional life. Within the context of a white-cube gallery, Cheung's work challenges the meaning of art and, furthermore, disrupts the problematically gendered logic underlying the distinction between art and craft, the mind and the body.[16]

Cheung's engagement with crafts—the "feminine" domain of creativity—is as much an act of resistance against the totalizing logic of capitalism as a resignification of the meaning of Asian American masculinity in the era of neoliberal globalization. In the post-1965 immigration reform climate, the rapid development of transnational capital, and the reign of liberal multiculturalism, Asian American male potency cannot be measured in relation to the degree of upward mobility and economic success because the sense of agency that Asian immigrants nowadays experience is merely a consequence of the U.S. nation-state's new strategy of population management. Therefore Cheung's insightful portrayal of the labors of global capital undermines the possibility that Asian Americans and immigrants in the globalization era can simply conform to the norms of respectability and leave their bachelor past—their deviant, queer, and gender-nonconforming history—behind.

The Creative Modalities of Resignification

The work that Asian immigrant professionals and technicians in the post-1965 era do—that is, intellectual and managerial labor—contributes to yet another set of feminized representations of Asian American men as techie, nerd, and computer geek. The fact that Cheung's homeland is one of the technologically advanced countries that provide global supplies of professional and technical labor—the source of Asian geeks and nerds—further emphasizes the impracticality of the immigrant emancipation narrative. The idea of leaving home for freedom elsewhere certainly cannot be applied to post-1965 male-identified Asian immigrants since, for them, coming to the United States implies becoming feminized and regulated as docile subjects of the nation. There is no manhood waiting for them to claim at the end of the journey, whether it be the other side of the world or the gender divide.

By virtue of being female-assigned and racialized as Asian American, Asian American transmen can never successfully escape the processes of feminization. Nevertheless, through the strategy of resignification, *Mama & Me* demonstrates the way Cheung turns this crisis into an opportunity. The impossibility of discursively detaching himself from the gender category in which he was assigned at birth urges Cheung to develop alternative gender expressions and ultimately disidentify with the system that creates and maintains the racially inflected gender distinctions in the first place. In resignifying the markers of femininity—a close relationship with mother and a craft tradition—as expressions of Asian American transgender masculinity, Cheung makes a courageous decision to stay home and struggle at his social location. His willingness to critically engage with his past and challenge the coming-out protocols of transgender identity—the necessity of leaving home in order to attain freedom elsewhere—certainly defies the gravities of the mainstream transgender and queer communities, immigrant communities, and the art world.

In reconceptualizing the meaning of trans identities, experiences, and embodiment through the history of Asian American racialization and the gendering apparatus of immigration, Cheung's creative process exposes the limits of the logic of visibility underlying the discourses of transnormativity and, most important, decolonizes the racially and class-inflected standards of recognition and belonging. As the Euro-American-centric notion of transgender identity is steadily gaining legibility on a global scale, such as in the domains of popular culture, education, health care, and law, it inevitably comes to regulate and discipline gender-nonconforming subjects in the name of inclusion, negating the experiences and desires that cannot be subsumed into the structures of visibility and respectability, turning them instead into surplus. In this sense Cheung's art practice as an Asian American transman reveals the current Western trans discourses' complicity in the exploitative regimes of globalization and the violence of liberal multicultural inclusion, yet optimistically brings forth the alternative forms of trans representation and critique that powerfully connect the seemingly disparate spheres of marginalization. In the face of the hostile conditions of global capital and the colonization of difference in the language of recognition, Cheung's usage of craft and artistic production as a medium through which he reimagines self, temporal relations, and possible lifeworlds underscores the significance of nonlinear modalities of trans of color cultural intervention in expanding the rapidly diminishing horizons of the present.

NOTES

1. Fresh Meat Productions, "Fresh Meat in the Gallery VI."

2. For queer of color critiques of the notion of home, see Gopinath, "Homo-Economics"; Manalansan, *Global Divas.*

3. Reddy, "Asian Diasporas, Neoliberalism, and Family," 110.

4. Gopinath, *Impossible Desires*, 3, 15, 19.

5. Abbas, *Hong Kong*, 4.

6. Harry Benjamin International Gender Dysphoria Association, "The Standards of Care for Gender Identity Disorders, Sixth Version." Although the seventh version of the Standards of Care, published in 2011, no longer considers such proofs of cross-gender

identification as requirements for accessing medical care, the notion of proof nevertheless continues to haunt mainstream conceptualizations of transgender identities.

7. Muñoz, *Disidentifications*, 31.

8. Cheung, telephone interview by author, November 13, 2009.

9. McKay, "Family Reunification."

10. Reddy, "Asian Diasporas, Neoliberalism, and Family," 110.

11. Even after the Defense of Marriage Act was struck down in June 2013, allowing same-sex spouses of U.S. citizens and permanent residents to obtain immigration benefits, the heteronormative familial norms still dominate the discourse of U.S. immigration, particularly through the notion of marriage itself. The legalization of same-sex marriage functions as a means to discipline queer citizens and immigrants into docile subjects of the nation via the formation of the nuclear family structure and the performance of normative gender legibility.

12. Ngai, *Impossible Subjects*, 227–28.

13. U.S. Citizenship and Immigration Services, "H-1B Fiscal Year (FY) 2015 Cap Season."

14. Le, "Asian Immigrants in the Postindustrial Economy."

15. Ioannou, "After the Art/Craft Debate," 26.

16. For more on gender politics and the art world, see Broude and Garrard, "Introduction," 12.

FOURTEEN

Indra Sinha's Melancholic Citizenship: Marking the Violence of Uneven Development in *Animal's People*

ANDREW UZENDOSKI

Globalization has long outsourced risk along with labor. On the night of December 2, 1984, a methyl isocyanate gas leak from a Union Carbide pesticide factory spread through the city of Bhopal, India. The factory's main warning siren failed to respond to the leak for two hours; the city's residents instead awoke to the signs of mass infection and panic. More than eight thousand people would die within days, and the gas leak would affect the health of nearly a quarter of the 900,000 people living in Bhopal at the time of the incident.[1] That the worst industrial disaster in history occurred thousands of miles away from the American headquarters of the culpable corporation is an all too expected expression of uneven geographical development.[2] It was not an accident that this chemical disaster occurred in India. In the service of capital accumulation, the neoliberal state reduces barriers that limit market growth and the movement of capital across national borders, but grounded in the ever-present racial logic of colonialism, neoliberal policies rely on and enable the displacement of risk from the United States to India, from bodies in the West to bodies in the East. With the business *and* racial interests of Union Carbide superseding India's sovereignty—the logic of white supremacy dictating the allocation of risk across a world economic system—the citizens of Bhopal were always already expendable.

Bhopal was the site of the gas leak, but Union Carbide, an American corporation then based in Texas, was the source. Nominally Union Carbide reached a settlement with the Indian government. But as Snehal Shingavi reports, the corporation offered less than $550 for each survivor while abandoning the factory without cleanup: toxic chemicals and contaminated groundwater would be among the disaster's many persistent remainders.[3] Kim Fortun emphasizes that the settlement of the Bhopal case, widely recognized as a failure of historiography in the service of capitalism, "veiled the continuing disaster at the local level, shrouded the need to reassess how we chart progress and shut down productive transactions between past and future."[4] Recourse to health care and human rights was not the only mandate bracketed by such a settlement; modes of recollection were also compromised by a negotiation intent on marking the Bhopal case a settled history.

In his novel *Animal's People* (2007), Indra Sinha confronts this false foreclosure of Bhopal's history through the body of his protagonist. Animal is an emblem of the slow violence of neoliberal globalization.[5] Due to the effects of a chemical disaster in the fictional Khaufpur (the pseudonym for Bhopal), Animal suffers from a severe spinal deformity that from the age of six has required him to crawl rather than walk. Since then he has identified himself as an animal. This epistolary novel, which is structured around Animal's first-person narration recorded on a series of twenty-three tapes, begins with his dissociation from humanity. "I used to be human once," Animal speaks into the recorder. "So I'm told. I don't remember it myself, but people who knew me when I was small say I walked on two feet just like a human being."[6] Walking upright or crawling on his hands and feet: mobility is Animal's initial distinction between human and animal, a difference that is augmented temporally. He *was* a human in a forgotten past. His present inhumanity is marked by a self-identified animal-like deportment and mobility.

At the end of the novel Animal is offered an operation—to be paid for by American benefactors—to walk upright. But after Sinha introduces this intervention of American charity as his novel's potential deus ex machina, Animal declines the operation. He stresses his uniqueness in his refusal: "If I'm an upright human, I would be one of millions, not even a healthy one at that. Stay four-foot, I'm the one and only Animal."[7] He insists on difference, on representing himself as *not* everyone else. But Animal is not a symbol of individualism or cultural relativism. Rather, as an emblem of slow violence, Animal exposes how neoliberalism sustains neocolonial systems of racial exploitation by wearing the cloak of universalism. The citizens of Bhopal were always different in the eyes of Union Carbide—but the displacement of risk onto foreign bodies relies on the formal disavowal of difference. *Animal's People* exposes a structural contradiction that Roderick Ferguson identifies as inherent in liberal capitalism: the nation-state is expected to subscribe to and nominally safeguard "an illusory universality particularized in terms of race, gender, sexuality and class, state . . . but in its production of surplus populations unevenly marked by a racialized nonconformity with gender and sexual norms, capital constantly disrupts that universality."[8] Animal will not serve as a symbol for neoliberalism's ideal citizen, nor will he consent to American charity as the measure of universal incorporation. Instead he remains a citation of slow violence throughout the novel; by the novel's conclusion he even insists on it. If, as Rob Nixon argues, "a neoliberal ideology that erodes national sovereignty and turns answerability into a bewildering transnational maze makes it easier for global corporations like Union Carbide to sustain an evasive geopolitics of deferral," Animal is the emblematic cog that reveals both the foregrounding ideology of global capitalism and sites of endless deferral.[9]

Representing Slow Violence

The predictable result of neoliberal policies, the chemical plant disaster in Bhopal is a manifestation of the racial logic that undergirds such policies. Late in the novel Animal sneaks into the luxury hotel where the American lawyers are staying during the settlement talks between the company and the city. Animal is there to uncover information about the developing settlement. The break-in is surprisingly easy. Representative of the racial logic that governs this space, the visual markers that differentiate him from the American employees—the color of his skin and his filthy clothes—also aid his break-in. At one point during his reconnaissance mission he invisibly slips in and out of a dining room: "My dark bare skin is blended into the jehannum night, my kakadu shorts are dark because filthy. No one sees. People see what they are looking for, no one is looking for me, but what I am looking for is there in abundance, crisp samosas with spicy sauce, bhajias and kebabs of all kinds."[10] He is invisible to both the foreign guests and the hotel workers serving these guests. The scene demonstrates that Animal recognizes the contexts where his body is ultimately rendered imperceptible. A resident of "the kingdom of the poor" dining on Jehannum delicacies, he remains undetected throughout his breach of the hotel security. In this space occupied by representatives of the American company, bodies such as Animal's are never considered. It is all too easy for the hidden Animal to appear nonexistent—and thus expendable within the neoliberal globalized economy—to Western eyes. He contests this presumed expendability throughout the novel, as he works with community activists to represent the true cost of the disaster while disrupting the efforts by the American company to reach an unfair settlement.

The location and operation of Union Carbide's pesticide factory in India displaced risk from American bodies onto Indian bodies. The activist Chamoa Devi, a survivor of the Bhopal disaster, cites the multigenerational effects that still persist even twenty years later: "The women are facing the worst of it. They face the worst illnesses. Their children are born deformed. They get cancer. Girls who are fifteen look like they are six. Women don't have their periods, and then they can't have children."[11] The full extent of this tragedy is till unfolding. Therefore appeals for redress and justice must work against the temporal logic of neoliberalism. Addressing the unique temporal dimensions of this slowly materializing genocide, Nixon defines the term *slow violence* in contrast to *the spectacle.* It is the economics of violence as manifested over a timeline of years rather than days. The documentation of a disaster like Bhopal suffers from the unequal power of spectacular and unspectacular time. Violence as measured and articulated by unspectacular time is harder to observe, quantify, and address.[12]

Sinha exemplifies the gulf between these two temporal yardsticks—spectacular and unspectacular time—with his depiction of the terrorist attacks on the World Trade Center, as observed by Animal in Chunaram's Chai House: "The big thing that happened in Amrika, when I saw it on the tele do you know what I did? I clapped! I thought, fantastic! This plane comes out of nowhere, flies badoom! Into this building. Pow! Blam! Flowers of Flame!" The spectacular is stressed not only by Animal's language—a floral metaphor for the initial explosion, single-syllable exclamations—but also by his reaction: *clapping.* As framed by Sinha, Animal's statement is less a consciously political response and more a visceral reaction to the event. Animal then contextualizes his reaction in cinematic discourse, praising the spectacle as "Fucking Brilliant! Bollywallah special-effects, forget it!"[13] This is not to say that the scene is apolitical; Sinha's critical eye is not focused on naïve consumption. On the contrary, the scene reveals how risk displacement traffics in the reallocation of injury onto non-Western, nonwhite bodies and in the spatial and temporal deferment of recourse.[14] The Bhopal disaster began after nightfall under the concealment of a failed warning system; the World Trade Center tragedy occurred in broad daylight—even when viewed at night in India. The West's response would be so quick, and so seemingly plotted, in large part because of the supplementary relationship between neoliberalism and spectacular time.

In stark contrast, slow violence poses a particular problem for narration, whether expressed in the rhetoric of neoliberalism or social justice: "From the narrative perspective, such invisible, mutagenic theater is slow-paced but open-ended, eluding the tidy closure, the narrative containment, imposed by the visual orthodoxies of victory and defeat." While events characterized by spectacular time are easily mapped onto transition narratives, the histories of unspectacular time betray the ruthless logic of progress that underwrites capitalism. How, then, can an author balance dramatic and ethical needs while narrating a disaster on the temporal scale of Bhopal? Nixon argues that Sinha mediates the dramatic and ethical by "devising a narrator who is at best ambivalent toward the pursuit of justice, yet whose physical form serves as a bodily shorthand for [Bhopal's] transnational plight."[15] As a protagonist Animal narrates particular crimes of neoliberalism; as an emblem he references the economy of violence produced by global capitalism.

The novel is committed to testing the limits of redress and advocacy in our current moment of crisis: How can a public elucidate the various economies of violence that have installed a neocolonial condition in the service of global capitalism? The effects of the gas leak clearly stretched beyond the timeline that was recognized in the settlement. Moreover Animal's invisibility in the hotel dining room is emblematic of how the people of Bhopal were not the random victims of slow violence but the targets of neoliberal policies all along. From this approach we can read slow violence as a form of racial genocide. Indeed slow violence shares with Patrick Wolfe's conception of structural genocide a temporality that reaches beyond the spectacular time of particular violent events while also recognizing how the logic of elimination is employed through various means that evolve along with political and economic developments of (neo)colonial systems.[16] The incorporation of non-Western bodies into the neoliberal economic system serves the logic of elimination, especially when one considers how multinational corporations have surpassed nation-states in sustaining colonial practices of labor exploitation and territorial appropriation.

Mourning Citizenship

Throughout *Animal's People* Sinha delimits the utility citizenship has in guaranteeing human rights in the wake of disasters such as Bhopal. In their account of empire in the twenty-first century, Michael Hardt and Antonio

Negri argue that rather than being a defunct concept, "sovereignty has taken a new form, composed of a series of national and supranational organisms united under a single logic of rule."[17] Multinational corporations regularly undermine the traditional role nation-states have assumed within international law as actors capable of representing their citizens on international stages. As the autonomy of nation-states declines and multinational corporations assert new manifestations of sovereignty, citizenship has lost much of its effectiveness as a marker of political jurisdiction and self-determination. *Animal's People* narrates this deterioration of the nation-state's ability to protect individual citizens. By mourning the failure of citizenship through his emblematic protagonist, Sinha tests the options that remain for communities to represent political and economic interests on an international stage.

Within the context of the nation-state's decline, we must recognize other narratives that "do not look to the state/citizen bind as the ultimate construction of sociality"—those narratives that, according to Dipesh Chakrabarty, "bespeak an antihistorical consciousness, that is, they entail subject positions and configurations of memory that challenge and undermine the subject that speaks in the name of history." *Animal's People* is one such narrative. The preservation of Animal's emblematic body disrupts a potential trajectory, one certainly endorsed by the unnamed American benefactors, for him to become an avatar for what Chakrabarty identifies as a transition narrative. Enabled by historicism's linear investment in a prescribed future, transition narratives traffic in liberal values of development, modernization, and capitalism. Such narratives favor Western subjects while delegitimizing non-Western perspectives; they place the non-Western character on a path toward Western values. The American benefactors targeted the most visually striking (and well-publicized) manifestation of illness in selecting Animal's injury while neglecting the thousands of other health problems that resulted from the chemical disaster. By rejecting surgery Animal will not be a symbol for the settlement between Bhopal and Union Carbide, nor will he silence his community's own history. Chakrabarty laments the totalizing effect the transition narrative imposes over history, within which "other constructions of self and community, while documentable, will never enjoy the privilege of providing the metanarratives or teleologies . . . for our histories."[18] However, when the normalizing promise of the transition narrative (the visual mending of Animal's body) never materializes, the text is able to instead assert a marginal positionality from which to tell Sinha's alternative historiography.

As Gayatri Spivak states, the leading question of so many inquiries into the consciousness of the other—Can the subaltern speak?—is rendered surplus when contextualized within the ideological economies of a world system grounded in the presupposition of the Western subject. All but an axiom for decades, the subaltern *cannot* speak within the context of intellectual appropriation. But then again, that was never really the object of such critical intervention. It is only through the prism of ideology, argues Spivak, that "the banality of leftist intellectuals' lists of self-knowing, politically canny subalterns stands revealed; representing them, the intellectuals represent themselves as transparent."[19] But what if Sinha—the novel's ultimate filter of mediation—engages political action not by trading the authenticity of his victim for an ethical response (one invested in the persistence of the Western subject) but by recognizing how Animal announces the structures of ideology through his quotidian employment of and consistent appeal to allegory?

Constellations of citations to economic violence are embedded in our cultural landscapes. The trick is to articulate their economies. Sinha sidesteps what Spivak identifies as the "transformation of consciousness" by exploiting Animal's body as a monad within larger economies of violence.[20] It is not what Animal says but rather from where he insistently speaks. In the wake of the Bhopal disaster, Animal performs and models a political agency by articulating his positionality within a world system economy bankrolled by white supremacy and a neoliberal agenda. Serving his community, Animal's citizenship is melancholic by his consistent reference to the limited parameters of recourse and activism within the neocolonial reach of corporations such as Union Carbide. Perpetual mourning is as much spatial as it is temporal: it locates the past in a critical historiography of uneven development.

Idelbar Avelar states that the mournful subject acts as a collector of objects that trigger memory of what is lost. As a result, Avelar claims, "his/her mute and melancholy stare upon an object detaches it from all connections, turns it into an emblem of what has been lost, an allegorically charged monad."[21] Telling of Sinha's political project of representation, Animal is both collector and object.[22] He employs Animal to contextualize Bhopal, both by the objects he collects and the placement of his own body against the cityscape, within our operating world system. When histories of violence are silenced by dominant economic and political regimes, Avelar's imperative is to allegorize: "When the most customary is interpreted as a ruin, and the pile of past catastrophes hitherto concealed under that storm called 'progress' at last begins to be unearthed. The most familiar cultural documents become allegorical once they are referred back to the barbarism that lies at their origin."[23] Animal facilitates the avowal of Bhopal's silent past by contextualizing lost objects and places not as discrete points in a silent past but as socially situated texts. Less invested in representing the authentic consciousness of Animal, Sinha's novel seeks to tease out the structural inequalities that ground empire. Ultimately by juxtaposing the Bhopal cityscape (its physical and cultural markers) with Animal (his critical commentary coupled with his own personal exploration and presentation of his physical condition) Sinha articulates his alternative historiography of the Bhopal chemical disaster. This history argues that the disaster was a direct result of neoliberal policies and not an accident.

Leveraging Animal's allegorical body against seemingly apolitical actions, Sinha maps the geographic and temporal cartographies of slow violence. As previously mentioned, when Animal declines the operation, he characterizes his decision as preserving the unique mobility of his body: "Right now I can run and hop and carry kids on my back, I can climb hard trees, I've gone up mountains, roamed in jungles."[24] By characterizing his injury in terms of advanced mobility, Sinha projects the same ability onto his allegorical body. A mobile emblem, Animal's unique body is constantly juxtaposed against a shifting array of objects and landscapes across multiple temporalities. As such he engages a multiplicity of social relations from unexpected entry points. An already allegorized emblem, Animal activates constellations out of otherwise discrete commodities and locations.

Urban mobility not only distinguishes Animal as a unique subject in Khaufpur; it also provides him with a profession. He offers foreigners tours of urban poverty for a fee. When Elli Barber, a recently arrived American doctor intent on administering medical aid to victims of the chemical disaster, wants to visit the neighborhood in Khaufpur referred to as "the kingdom of the poor," she asks Animal to be her guide. During their tour Animal's mobility is defined in contrast to Elli and also in comparison to an accompanying dog. Commenting on Elli's inability to keep pace with his movements, Animal remarks, "The lane's crowded, hard for her to keep me in sight so I lig on slowly, Jara the dog keeps stopping and looking round as if to say, come on Elli, hurry up." Implying how his mobility has informed an emerging class consciousness, Animal then transposes the neighborhood's economic positionality onto the topography of Khaufpur by citing uneven geographical development along a single city street: "At the city end this same road is smarter, there's more money, big shops there are, families with fat children licking ice creams, in our part it's filthy chute with truck exhaust for air."[25] If, as David Harvey asserts, surplus accumulation by dispossession "is a corollary of capitalist stability," then Animal maps such economic imbalances on a local level by constantly wandering throughout various urban landscapes of varying wealth and poverty.[26] Moreover he frequently interrupts the quotidian affairs of the neighborhood. Narrating his tour through "the kingdom of the poor" with Elli, he observes such a series of disruptions: "Low are the doorways we come to now, perfect for a four-foot animal. I know a lot of people here, so I'm in and out, calling greetings to those inside. People come stopping to their thresholds. Some stare. Others beckon us in but I tell them we can't stop."[27] Animal not only exposes hidden economies; he also suspends the daily operations of local economies.

Animal's body fully articulates an extratextual constellation of economic violence when he and Elli walk past the pesticide factory that was the site of the chemical disaster. After mapping economic disparity on a single street in Khaufpur, he narrates their journey past the factory that was built and operated by the American Kampani (Sinha's pseudonym for Union Carbide):

> Across the big road we come to the corner of Kali Parade and take the road that runs past the Kampani's factory. On our left now is the wall, high as a man, covered with writing, some of it's by Zafar and friends, who paint at night when the police are asleep. Zafar's lot never write what they feel which is FUCK YOU WICKED CUNTS I HOPE YOU DIE PAINFULLY FOR THE HORRIBLE THINGS YOU DID TO US AND THE ARROGANT FUCKING CRUELTY YOU'VE DISPLAYED EVER SINCE. They write high-sounding shit like JUSTICE FOR KHAUFPUR and KAMPANI MEET YOUR LIABILITIES but in a few places freer spirits have been at work. HANG PETERESON and DEATH TO AMRIKA. These are the bits the munsipal scrubs out which need repainting more often than any other.[28]

Decontextualized from the horrific gas leak, Animal's body threatens to pathologize the poverty of his community through his physical deformity; dehistoricized from the economies that maintain the condition of poverty that defines "the kingdom of the poor," the factory is but a ruin relegated to history's mistakes. However, when juxtaposed alongside the factory's ruins, Animal appropriates this seemingly settled monument. Supplementing the political commentary produced by local activists, he recovers the pesticide factory as a tragic remainder of economic development facilitated by transnational networks of capital accumulation. His physical condition, no longer readable as a representation of poverty, references the near-permanent and persistent condition of economic violence—as does the factory itself. Tethered to global capitalism, the factory is returned to the here and now as a radical amendment to the Kampani's official historiography.

The graffiti on the pesticide factory walls gives the lie to the framing of the Bhopal chemical disaster as an unprecedented accident, an unforeseeable event easily compartmentalized as a historical aberration. Animal exposes the disaster as the unsurprising result of deliberately outsourcing risk in the service of neoliberal economics of globalization. Perpetuating the idea of the Bhopal disaster as an outlier is central for multinational corporations to sustain what Nixon identifies as the "evasive geopolitics of deferral."[29] In this scene Animal—his body and commentary—emerges as an effective contestation of this geopolitics. Sinha interrupts the settlement's official narrative, a move that employs allegorical intervention to parry integration into neoliberal polices. That Sinha leverages Animal less as a symbol of individuality and more as an emblem of targeted exploitation and deferred redress within neoliberalism's ever-expanding economy of violence provides critical insight into how slow violence may be represented by literary texts. Indeed throughout *Animal's People* Sinha uses allegory to contextualize his protagonist's community within the operating world system.

Prophetic Melancholia

Animal's final choice to decline the aforementioned operation is not motivated by unresolved grief over his disability. Rather it is Animal's identification of his body as emblem of the lives lost from the disaster that spurs this rejection. On the final tape he reveals that his initial desire to tell his story was to "find out what the end should be." He hopes his recorded narrative will inform his response to the medical procedure offered by his American benefactors. However, as he tells his story to the recorder, his spinal injury ceases to be the object of his mourning and instead becomes the emblem from which to mourn the loss of people. "When I started speaking, when I heard dead Aliya's voice calling, it was like she and the others who are no more came back to be with me." The climax of the novel is Animal's choice to remain an emblem of the neoliberal economics of violence that silenced the victims of the chemical disaster: "I can't tell you how I miss them, until I die this wound will never heal. They've been here through every minute of this telling."[30] Walter Benjamin warned us about the fleeting returns of memory; he stressed that "every image of the past that is not recognized by the present as one of its own concerns threatens to disappear irretrievably."[31] Animal captures such lost images, inserting them back into the operating economies of violence. What Nixon sees as the duality of Animal—he provides both an "ambivalent" narration of justice and "bodily shorthand" for neoliberalism—allows Sinha to narrate the melancholic collection of Bhopal's histories.[32]

With each place appropriated as space, Animal provides the necessary conditions for what Benjamin calls a messianic cessation of happening. When the preconditions for voicing a silent past are met, economies of violence can be constellated, allowing allegory to voice Animal's mourning. This temporalized trope, explains Avelar, is specially equipped for "the mnemonic and political task" of recovering the ruins left by the substitutive logic of capitalism—especially when activated by Animal's mastery of urban movement. The silent past remains to be unsettled. But in today's moment of danger, catastrophes rendered in spectacular time are increasingly mourned by the measure of efficiency. Neoliberalism's mandate to forget has become so totalizing that even the succession of subsequent economic crises does not irrevocably expose the contradictions of global capitalism. Therefore, if we are to represent the unspectacular time of slow violence and challenge the limits of historiography, we should engender a productive relationship between allegory and mourning.

Animal's People concludes with a prophecy. The novel's final passage derives its prophetic energy from Animal's melancholic fixation on poverty: "Remember me. All things pass, but the poor remain. We are the people of the Apokalis [Apocalypse]. Tomorrow there will be more of us."[33] Animal actively performs citation. *Remember* Animal, *remember* the poor. But the novel goes further. This brief passage tumbles toward political organization in the midst of an economic and environmental apocalypse presaged by Union Carbide's catastrophic risk deferment. The novel's title is an equation from which to interrogate the limits of political representation, where to allegorize—urban landscapes, economic ruins, commodities, the nation-state, oneself—announces the temporal and structural positionality of the community. The potential for allegory to recognize the prophetic in the tragic hinges on a melancholic response. If mourning the limits of citizenship can be constitutive of community, it is by consolidating a political unit through the marking of its economic positionality within the governing world system. To be sure, the narrative ends with the people of Khaufpur still waiting for justice. But the allegorical economy employed by the text to represent structural violence also remains. That the community's political efficacy is measured by Animal's own access to political agency cannot be discarded. This critical thrust is directed by the title: *Animal's People* recognizes the community as a political unit through Animal's mourning of citizenship and recovery of history.

NOTES

1. Mukherjee, *Postcolonial Environments*, 134.

2. Harvey conceives of a unified theory of uneven development by addressing four conditionalities of the geographic manifestation of global capitalism: the material embedding of capital accumulation processes in the web of socio-ecological life; accumulation and devaluation by disposition; capital accumulation in space and time; and political, social, and "class" struggles at a variety of geographical scales (*Spaces of Global Capitalism*, 75–115).

3. Shingavi, "We Want Real Justice for Bhopal."

4. Fortun, *Advocacy after Bhopal*, 8.

5. Nixon, "Neoliberalism, Slow Violence, and the Environmental Picaresque," 445.

6. Sinha, *Animal's People*, 1.

7. Sinha, *Animal's People*, 366.

8. Ferguson, *Aberrations in Black*, 17.

9. Nixon, "Neoliberalism, Slow Violence, and the Environmental Picaresque," 444.

10. Sinha, *Animal's People*, 270.

11. Shingavi, "We Want Real Justice for Bhopal."

12. Nixon, "Neoliberalism, Slow Violence, and the Environmental Picaresque," 444–45.

13. Sinha, *Animal's People*, 60.

14. Shingavi, "We Want Real Justice for Bhopal."

15. Nixon, "Neoliberalism, Slow Violence, and the Environmental Picaresque," 445, 449.

16. Wolfe, "Settler-Colonialism and the Elimination of the Native," 403.

17. Hardt and Negri, *Empire*, 116.

18. Chakrabarty, *Provincializing Europe*, 37.

19. Spivak, "Can the Subaltern Speak?" (1988), 275.

20. Spivak, "Can the Subaltern Speak?" (1988), 285.

21. Avelar, *The Untimely Present*, 14.

22. Where mourning is marked by Freud as the gradual process of withdrawing the libido from a lost object or ideal, melancholia results from perpetual mourning. This unresolved grief stops the melancholic from replacing the lost object or ideal, allowing ambivalence and psychic conflict to manifest themselves throughout the extended mourning process. In failing to separate the ego from the lost object, the subject incorporates the lost object within the ego. Freud, "Mourning and Melancholia," 243.

23. Avelar, *The Untimely Present*, 8.

24. Sinha, *Animal's People*, 366.

25. Sinha, *Animal's People*, 177.

26. Harvey, *Spaces of Global Capitalism*, 93.

27. Sinha, *Animal's People*, 177.

28. Sinha, *Animal's People*, 177–78.

29. Nixon, "Neoliberalism, Slow Violence, and the Environmental Picaresque," 444.

30. Sinha, *Animal's People*, 365.

31. Benjamin, *Illuminations*, 255.

32. Nixon, "Neoliberalism, Slow Violence, and the Environmental Picaresque," 445.

33. Sinha, *Animal's People*, 366.

FIFTEEN

Cocoa Chandelier's Confessional: Kanaka Maoli Performance and Aloha in Drag

STEPHANIE NOHELANI TEVES

On August 14, 2009, in an old Chinese restaurant converted into a "hip" loft nightclub overlooking N. Hotel and Maunakea Street in Honolulu's Chinatown, the Kanaka Maoli (Native Hawaiian) performance artist Cocoa Chandelier staged what she called "a confessional."[1] The event was a fundraiser for travel to a Miss Entertainer of the Year drag pageant as well as Madonna's forty-ninth birthday. In this ode to the material girl, blondes were granted free entrance as Cocoa Chandelier asked audience members to "confess" their sins. Cocoa Chandelier herself did not confess. She performed a series of numbers from Madonna's body of work, including the songs "Erotica," "Justify My Love," "Cherish," and "Hung Up." Given Cocoa Chandelier's notorious Bollywood performance at the Universal Showqueen Pageant the previous year, it made sense that this evening would be dedicated to Madonna, the ultimate cultural appropriator.

A shoebox asking for donations and confessions circled the room, but the audience greeted her with silence and snickers, which seemed odd considering most local drag show audiences relish the opportunity to shout, read, and applaud the performers. However, this was not a drag show per se, and I was somewhat frightened by the silence. There were many other performers in the crowd, but no one vied for the spotlight. Most people made their comments or confessions from where they were seated on the floor or from the periphery of the space, preferring not to speak at the microphone or be seen and heard by everyone. One prominent drag queen, Kaina Jacobs, walked to the front of the show, donated a handful of money, and walked away without confessing anything.[2] As the evening progressed, most people declined the call to confess, seemingly aware of the cost of their visibility. I wondered, given the intimate space filled with friends and family members, what was the justification for the silent response to Cocoa Chandelier's call to confess?

This chapter draws on recent critiques of the confession and its relationship to the speaking of "truth" that is required of ethnic subjects. As the predominant approach in ethnic studies and Native studies scholarship, the confession fetishizes the narratives of Natives who feel compelled to make our truth known against the historical silencing and belittling effects of colonialism.[3] This approach, however, is increasingly contested by Natives in complicated ways, as evidenced in the audience response at Cocoa Chandelier's confessional. I read the decline to confess as indicative of an unwillingness by Kānaka Maoli to publicly and explicitly confess our truths even among those we are closest to. Through an examination of the confession and its relationship to Hawaiian performance, I aim to tease out the veiled articulations of indigeneity deployed by Cocoa Chandelier in order to analyze how she challenges the ongoing subjection and hypercommodification of Hawaiian indigeneity. As I will show, Kānaka Maoli are encouraged to perform "the aloha spirit" in order to be recognized as Kānaka Maoli. Here I examine the work of Cocoa Chandelier, a well-known Kanaka Maoli performer and drag queen based in Honolulu, whose performance repertoire does not engage in expected displays of aloha or, by extension, Hawaiianness.

Since 2000 the fight for Hawaiian self-determination has set the stage for recurring debates about Native Hawaiian federal recognition, a process that would grant recognition to Kānaka Maoli akin to that for a Native American tribe. These efforts have overshadowed community-based Kanaka Maoli sovereignty efforts by privileging government forms of recognition, which are often presented as the only option left for Kānaka Maoli. Cocoa Chandelier offers us an alternative frame of Hawaiian indigeneity, one that is based in community recognition, not federal recognition. Her performance strategies raise several questions in relation to indigenous subjectivity: How can we recognize one another when we do not perform our indigeneity in prescribed ways? More precisely, how do we perform our aloha or "Hawaiianness" at the same time as we acknowledge that its performance is deeply intertwined with the legacies of colonialism and the tourism industry?

To answer these questions, and to fortify my argument that these performances arise out of a survival instinct that remakes, re-forms, and continually challenges neocolonial efforts to incorporate and assimilate Kānaka Maoli, I turn to the work of the theorists Peggy Phelan and Denise da Silva. Their work, read alongside each other, provides evidence with which to critique the efficacy of the confession, visibility, and politics that are entrenched in questions of recognition. I begin with a theorization of how Hawaiian indigeneity is articulated with aloha, followed by a summary of Phelan and da Silva's arguments and a close reading of Cocoa Chandelier's performance at the 2008 Universal Showqueen Pageant. I argue that Cocoa Chandelier performs aloha in drag, a project that allows Kānaka Maoli to produce new formations of aloha and community recognition that does not rely upon the state and, in turn, sustains Hawaiian indigeneity.

Visibility Is a Trap

Representations of Kānaka Maoli have been circulating globally through multiple discourses since the landing of Captain Cook in the Hawaiian Islands in 1778. Stock imagery of the hula maiden, the surfer boy, the savage queen, and the lazy native, among others, are well known in the American colonial imaginary.[4] Representations in sailor and missionary journals, artistic renderings, photographs, films, nonfictive and fictive literary works, and other formal performances contribute greatly to the perception of Hawai'i and Kānaka Maoli. Aloha in particular has operated as a sign for Hawaiianness. Shortly after statehood Hawai'i was officially named "the Aloha State" in 1959, and ever since aloha has functioned as the state's favorite cultural affect that is harnessed to express and solicit positive feelings.[5] *Aloha* is defined in the Hawaiian dictionary as "love," "affection," "compassion," "mercy"; "to love," "to venerate," "to show kindness"; and as a salutation. Perhaps most significant, according to Mary Kawena Puku'i and George Kanahele, aloha is supposed to be reciprocal.[6] *Aloha,* loosely translated since the mid-nineteenth century as "welcome" or "love," has been harnessed and disarticulated from its Hawaiian cultural context and used to the detriment of the Kanaka Maoli people, which was part of the historical, cultural, and political process that Jonathan Osorio describes as the "dismembering" of the *lāhui,* the nation.[7] Aware of this bastardization, activist iterations of Kanaka Maoli sovereignty have been particularly invested in narrating a version of Kanaka Maoli indigeneity that is confrontational and pushes against the hegemonic imagery of the happy Kānaka Maoli filled with aloha. Still, aloha is something we Kānaka Maoli continue to believe deeply in. My intention is to shift the focus away from disparaging the appropriation of aloha and look instead at the conditions that require Kānaka Maoli to perform aloha and how Kānaka Maoli engage with aloha through performance. Using theories of articulation and performativity, I consider the ways that Kānaka Maoli differentially articulate and perform Hawaiian indigeneity in multiple and competing relations with aloha and for very specific reasons.[8]

According to Stuart Hall, articulation is not just a thing but a process of creating connections, much in the same way that hegemony itself is not domination but rather the process of creating and maintaining consensus among coordinating interests. The so-called unity of a discourse is never final or absolute; it is really the articulation of different and distinct elements, which can be rearticulated in different ways.[9] In other words, a theory of articulation is a way of understanding how ideological elements come together within a discourse; it enables us to think about how an ideology sometimes empowers people, while also locking them as subjects into a spot within a given oppressive discourse, but these meanings are never static. Hawaiian indigeneity and the performance of aloha exemplify that articulation works with certain kinds of performances. Articulation offers us opportunities to think critically about the ways that Kānaka Maoli articulate Hawaiian indigeneity with aloha and gets us out of discourses that posit Kānaka Maoli as simplistically performing aloha as duped by colonialism.

Alongside articulation I rely on theories of performance and, by extension, performativity to critically assess the making and remaking of Hawaiian indigeneity. As Jon McKenzie writes in *Perform or Else,* "The power of discourse to produce what it names is linked with the question of performativity."[10] In performance studies (as well as in queer theory and linguistics) the concept of performativity is frequently used to examine social reality as it is constructed through performances of subjectivity or identity. As Judith Butler explains in *Gender Trouble,* bodily surfaces can be sites where performances become denaturalized to show the performativity of what is considered natural.[11] Understanding that identities are constituted through performance makes possible a critique of how Hawaiian indigeneity is defined vis-à-vis performances of aloha. By assessing how performativity informs what is considered Hawaiian, we are able to look more closely at the structural elements that frame Hawaiianness. We must view Hawaiian performances as part of a system of culture that is actively produced, contested, and articulated in specific contexts, at times to normalize a discourse—like aloha—or to enable a rethinking of how Kanaka Maoli identity is performative. In short, theories of articulation and performativity can work together productively to help us examine cultural performance in new ways.

Bodies of Evidence: Performance Studies and Visibility

Peggy Phelan's book *Unmarked* examines the connections between representational visibility (via performance and visual art) and political power. Phelan documents the complex irony of writing about something that is not "really" there. Her study of performance and representation centers visibility and its futility for advancing political change. In stark opposition to the notion that visibility begets social transformation, Phelan challenges, in the context of performance, the idea that increased visibility or "speaking our truths" promoted cultural understanding.[12] This was a radical perspective within performance studies in the early 1990s, especially in strains of performance studies that were closely affiliated with anthropology, a field that has been criticized for its legacy of institutional mechanisms of classification, surveillance, and training that can inhibit "the other" or keep it locked in a discourse.[13]

Phelan's questioning of visibility and performance resonate with da Silva's *Toward a Global Idea of Race*, in which she critiques the efficacy of inserting the histories of the disenfranchised into dominant discourse. Da Silva challenges the ontohistorical processes that motivated the institutionalization of once marginal knowledges in the name of rewriting history or inserting the history of "others" into dominant discourse. In this configuration non-Western subjects are viewed as containers of knowledge (because of their cultural difference), and Western subjects are normalized as the analysts who adjudicate such "truths." In short, the political subjects addressed in accounts of postmodernity and globalization are constituted by the same tools that codified their marginalized subjectivity.

When applied to Hawaiian performance, Phelan's and da Silva's analyses expose the tensions at the core of cultural performance and resistance. In one sense performance offers the possibility of cultural exchange, but in another, in the context of Hawaiian performance, it remains the norm by which Hawaiianness is evaluated. Anthropologists and cultural historians have shown that there is a rich repertoire of Hawaiian hula performance that Kānaka Maoli used to resist American colonialism, but when read alongside Phelan and da Silva, a deeper critique of colonialism and knowledge production becomes possible. For example, in "Hawaiians on Tour: Hula Circuits through

American Empire," Adria Imada discusses how Kānaka Maoli were called upon to be "ambassadors of aloha," as they were actively recruited to promote Hawai'i's charms on the U.S. mainland throughout the 1930s and 1940s. The hula tours and hula revues in big U.S. cities allowed some Kānaka Maoli to secure a measure of freedom and pleasure, sustain cultural production, and pursue other educational and employment opportunities, while also creating diasporic communities. Indeed Kānaka Maoli exercised agency through these networks under conditions that were increasingly out of their control, but the hula tours also solidified the relationship between Hawai'i and the United States, producing an imagined sense of intimacy between Americans and Hawai'i because of the feminized version of Hawai'i that Kanaka Maoli women performed onstage (i.e., offering "aloha"). This created a fantasy of reciprocal attachment that made it seem unimaginable for Americans to part from "their" colony, Hawai'i. Kanaka Maoli women offering aloha promised intimacy and affection to the United States, making U.S. military and tourist expansion appear "benign."[14] Inadvertently participation in such activities lent credence to the notion that the only value of Kānaka Maoli was their ability to perform aloha and that such performances were "natural," indicative of who we used to and should be.

The latter can be connected to Phelan's arguments when she writes, "It is assumed that disenfranchised communities who see their members within the representational field will feel greater pride in being part of such a community and those who are not in such a community will increase their understanding of the diversity and strength of such communities." Using Imada's study of the hula tours as an example, a realization emerges: Kānaka Maoli became visible in American popular culture, but it was the very visibility of a welcoming Hawaiian culture that justified American colonialism in Hawai'i. With Phelan and da Silva in conversation, it appears that increased "cultural understanding" transmitted via performance does not radically transform the audience into politically conscious actors, nor does it transform power relations. Cultural performance might change the perspective of the audience but not the act of looking. Furthermore, as Phelan explains, visibility politics are symptomatic of capitalism's relentless appetite for new markets and the American way. In short, "you are welcome here as long as you are productive."[15] Alongside Phelan and da Silva, I question the futility of using performance to increase visibility or to facilitate cultural understanding and argue that by performing aloha in drag, the capitalist appetite for the other is momentarily interrupted.

Aloha in Drag

Aloha has emerged as a marker of Hawaiianness, but aloha was just one aspect of precolonial Hawaiian life, and it came from a larger philosophical matrix of Hawaiian ideas and values.[16] Aloha meant "kindness and sharing," especially in the family or *'ohana* setting, where people are welcomed and all is shared with the understanding that people gather to provide mutual helpfulness for collective benefit. This understanding of aloha in relation to 'ohana reiterates the importance of community and the responsibility that comes with membership. The performance strategies of Cocoa Chandelier point to the power of aloha when understood in this way; thus her performance of aloha in drag allows an expansion of Hawaiianness.[17] Drag performance often parodies the very notion of an original—it is a fabrication to begin with. The disruption of normative gender performance has been theorized by a number of scholars, particularly Butler, who is known for positing that drag performance reveals the ways that gender is an imitative structure.[18] Cocoa Chandelier is best known for her work as a drag queen, but rather than deconstruct her performance as purely gender transgression, I am more interested in analyzing how she creates alternative possibilities of Hawaiian indigeneity and aloha by performing it in drag.[19]

At the 2008 Universal Showqueen Pageant, an annual pageant held in Honolulu, Cocoa Chandelier transformed the neocolonial juggernaut known as the Hawai'i Convention Center into a Bollywood "Harem of the Underworld."[20] Situated at the mouth of Waikīkī and adjacent to Ala Moana Center, the Hawai'i Convention Center that opened in 1998 is known for its purported "Hawaiian sense of place." Adorned with Hawaiian plants and promoting *nā mea ho'okipa* (translated as "Hawaiian hospitality"), the convention center is a perfect example of the way Hawaiian indigeneity is actively incorporated into public space throughout Hawai'i in the service of the tourist industry.[21] Draped in Hindu accoutrements, Cocoa Chandelier transformed the space and herself, as she played the role of a bride-to-be who was kidnapped and forced to live in a Harem of the Underworld. Danced to the tune of a world music montage and a remixed Jay Z Bhangra hit, Cocoa Chandelier performed a mishmash of scenes from a Bengali epic. The performance ended with her hanging upside down by her feet from the convention center ceiling, giving herself up to the specter of Orientalism. Refusing to be a Hawaiian subject in this convention center that intends to produce a "Hawaiian sense of place," Cocoa Chandelier's performance of aloha in drag in this fabricated space of aloha is thus all the more provocative.

Read within the ever-visible terrain of Hawaiian performance, Cocoa Chandelier disrupts Hawaiian performance through what Jose Muñoz has termed *disidentification*. Muñoz explains that disidentification is a mode of dealing with dominant ideology that chooses to neither assimilate nor oppose it; instead subjects work on and against dominant ideology. Cocoa Chandelier disidentifies with the dominant ideology of Hawaiianness by employing drag as a method of disguise and disruption. Disidentifying subjects also hold on to what subjects them, and rather than trying to break free of it, they find ways to invest it with new life.[22] As a disidentifying subject, Cocoa Chandelier holds on to Hawaiianness but also invests it with new life by performing aloha in drag. Performers like Cocoa Chandelier, as Sarita See notes, help us "think about identity as a politics of evading rather than securing visibility and legibility." In See's study of Filipino American artists, she ponders the politics of form in art, asking what happens when art offers no explicit or visible markers of ethnic identity? The intent of this question is to think about how the American Empire or imperialist ventures become abstracted and how they are represented in the abstract. As See elaborates, the violence of the American Empire is hidden through particular kinds of performances and resistance might be performed through seemingly apolitical performance genres.[23]

Aloha in drag is the performance of Hawaiian indigeneity by means other than through direct references to Hawaiianness. This is a performance of aloha that is not recognizable to most audiences. Cocoa Chandelier does not perform in ways that physically and culturally mark her as Kanaka Maoli. For example, the practice of self-identifying, common in ethnic beauty pageants, is replicated in the Universal Showqueen Pageant along with a number of other pageant categories. The Kanaka Maoli contestants in particular self-identify by listing all their ethnicities, which is common in Hawai'i; some even comment on the importance of preserving the Hawaiian culture. Cocoa Chandelier is the only contestant who did not state where she was from, what her background is, or her aspirations for the future. Instead, as she walked across the stage, an announcer read a description of Cocoa Chandelier that framed her as a jet-setting artist who associates with famous designers and engages in intellectual conversation in Greek cafés. Later, in the talent competition, she further disembodied Hawaiian indigeneity, while others openly asserted it.

In Cocoa Chandelier's talent portion of the pageant she played the role of the muse, a bride-to-be who is forced to live in the Harem of the Underworld.[24] Throughout this six-minute spectacle, Orientalist signifiers run amuck, performed in drag, by an abstracted Kanaka Maoli body. Cocoa Chandelier's performance begins with a video and narration in which she is adorned with Bindi and surrounded by other Hindu accoutrements and motifs. She introduces herself by telling a story about a muse who was taken on her wedding day and fated to live in the underworld, where she would be forced to sing with other lost brides. Her voice-over explains an attempt to "penetrate the darkness," as Cocoa Chandelier is shown holding and pulling on a rope, trying unsuccessfully to escape from the underworld.

The video sets the stage for the live performance that takes the audience into the underworld, where the brides-to-be perform their songs. The song that begins the piece is "Harem," which was originally recorded by the British world music star Sarah Brightman. At first Cocoa Chandelier dances alone but is soon joined by a young man, whom she kills with her song. The music changes and a group of women and men begin to dance a scene from the 2002 Bollywood film *Devdas*, a film based on a 1917 Hindi novella by Sharat Chandra Chattopadhyay.[25] Then four female backup dancers in red belly dancer outfits approach and the song changes to Kavita Krishnamurthy's "Dola Re Dola," with choreography matching much of the dancing in *Devdas*.[26] Jay Z's song "Beware of the Boys" also begins playing as Cocoa Chandelier dances with another man in a mash-up of hip-hop and Bhangra.[27] Toward the performance's end, Cocoa Chandelier scales a long piece of red fabric that is hanging from the ceiling. Presumably this is the "ray of light" that was sent to save the bride-to-be. When she gets to the top, she spins upside down and slides down slowly. The dancers continue dancing below her. As the music crescendos, Cocoa Chandelier climbs up again, wrapping her feet around the red fabric, only to suddenly flip upside down in an apparently unsuccessful bid to climb out of the dark harem. Hanging by her feet, she sacrifices herself. Hanging from the Hawai'i Convention Center ceiling, Cocoa Chandelier receives a rousing standing ovation. In an interview she describes this story as one in which the woman who attempts to flee her fate, even with the help of a "godlike figure," is doomed to remain a prisoner forever.[28] This performance encapsulates the conundrum of modern Hawaiian indigeneity and subjection.

Cocoa Chandelier performs aloha in a way that aloha cannot be identified: you cannot see the resistance, nor can you *see* the aloha. This is how her performance circumvents neoliberal circuits of exchange: you cannot name it, and subsequently you cannot sell it. Following See's logic, evasive performances like Cocoa Chandelier's participate in abstracting practices; in this specific case Cocoa Chandelier's abstraction of Hawaiianness questions how Kānaka Maoli are supposed to perform. She disrupts the very meaning of

Hawaiianness itself. Through the putting on and taking off of multiple signifiers, the purposeful ambivalences and complexities of Cocoa Chandelier's performance at the Universal Showqueen Pageant offers a space to imagine and engage the agonizing realities of Kanaka Maoli indigeneity. As a disidentifying subject, Cocoa Chandelier rejects Hawaiianness and by extension aloha, but she also reinvests in it.[29]

"Hung Up" at the Feet of Orientalism

The bride-to-be that Cocoa Chandelier portrays lures men to their death with her song, and therefore she must stay in the harem, for she is dangerous. Cocoa Chandelier crafts a performance that references the fear of women's sexuality and the emotive power of sirens' songs. As the story progresses, the bride-to-be cannot escape, for she is continually pulled back into the Harem of the Underworld to perform her song among the other lost brides-to-be. I interpret the bride's punishment as a consequence of her difference, because she is a woman and possesses this ability to confer death through performance. Her difference is her song, her very culture. In the story Cocoa Chandelier explains that a "Sun God, Syria, sends forth a ray of light to penetrate the darkness" in an attempt to save the bride but is ultimately unsuccessful.

The Sun God in the story can be likened to the modern state and its investments in multiculturalism, wherein the state recognizes culture and sanctions life in a God-like fashion. In this story the bride is framed as a victim, such that she is forced to live in the harem. The God-like figure gazes upon her and tries to save her, but it cannot. The bride is offered a chance at freedom, but as she attempts to climb out, she is hailed and interpellated back to the underworld with other lost brides-to-be. The performance of her gender—as the bride—and song is ultimately insufficient, and she cannot climb out of the harem. There she is fated to live out her subjection forever as a gendered and racialized subject. In other words, her racialized and gendered subjectivity pulls her back down; she cannot overcome it through the performance of her song or culture. It is in fact her song, which requires her death.

This performance proves that efforts to overcome subjection through recognizable forms of cultural performance are ultimately futile because the very discourse through which such performances must occur is fundamentally colonial. This exemplifies what da Silva and others have theorized: the very need to recognize cultural difference is proof that the other, or the bride in this story, is inherently inassimilable and cannot be saved. Da Silva contends that it is culture and not race that now doubly disempowers us, and this results in a double bind through discourses of culture rather than through discourses of race. As such the other is always racially encoded, always prisoner of his or her own cultural difference and never self-determining.[30] This is why the bride cannot climb out of the harem. She must always stay there and sing her song. At the performance's end, aware of the problematics of performance and recognition, the bride sacrifices herself. Rather than continue in her attempt to climb out of the harem or be imprisoned there, she chooses death. This act of self-sacrifice is instructive for rethinking Hawaiian indigeneity. Remember, Cocoa Chandelier's performance of the bride's death is a commentary on the bride's inability to overcome her subjection because the performance of her culture is insufficient. In the context of Hawaiian indigeneity Cocoa Chandelier's performance exposes how Hawaiian performance and bodies are deeply inscribed as racialized objects within a representational system, but, as she also shows us, there are ways to enact resistance to that very system.

There is a perception that Kānaka Maoli are performing our interior selves all the time and that this is where the idea of the "aloha spirit' comes from. Historically the aloha spirit has been fabricated as a Hawaiian essence that is shared and transferrable to non-Hawaiians. Aloha's market value counts only when people believe that Kāṇaka Maoli naturally emanate aloha. When Cocoa Chandelier refuses to perform aloha and Hawaiianness in recognizable ways, she shows that both are constructed performances and thus depreciates their worth. She refuses the sharing of Hawaiian culture, that is, the sharing of aloha in obvious modes. What she does do is perform on multiple levels of drag and invoke the trope of the harem to confuse the Western gaze that sees Kānaka Maoli only when they perform aloha. This is why performing aloha in drag is imperative.

At the same time, resisting the performance of culture is not so easy for Native or indigenous peoples when Native aspirations for decolonization and self-determination are predicated on their cultural difference and must be recognized by people in power in order for their claims (such as land claims or entitlement programs) to be acknowledged. In this sense Phelan's critique of the power of performance to advance political change stops short because she completely overlooks the double bind of indigenous peoples who must perform in recognizable ways to be deemed worthy of resources. Scholarship in Native studies has critiqued the desire for recognition or visibility, which promises some form of redress or liberation by the majority.[31] The role of performance is critical in this sense because, as Elizabeth Povinelli explains, Aboriginal groups are forced to perform in certain ways to show themselves worthy, and these performances are sanctioned by the state through a multicultural imaginary that defuses struggles for liberation and ensures the functioning of the modern liberal state. Kēhaulani Kauanui also explains in *Hawaiian Blood* that recognition is tied to a project of selective assimilation where only "authentic" Natives, that is, ones that perform properly before the eyes of the settler state, are recognized. When Natives are not recognized they are regarded as "inauthentic," which in turn facilitates Native dispossession in the service of settler colonialism.[32] Glen Coulthard has similarly referred to recognition as a "death dance" that entraps colonized people into performing nationhood in ways that relies on the state to adjudicate it.[33] The performance of culture thus recuperates colonial power. The reasoning for this, as Phelan notes, is that the spectator dominates and controls the exchange because underrepresented groups are scripted to "sell" or "confess" to someone (a theatrical "audience" or government official) who is in a position to buy or forgive the performer.[34] In sum, while state forms of recognition have a material reality that might be necessary for indigenous groups, aloha in drag foregrounds community recognition, illustrating the alternative paths toward decolonization.

Hiding in Plain Sight

On the verge of this perhaps liberatory performance, Cocoa Chandelier's performance simultaneously exhibits Kanaka Maoli complicity in the racial overdetermination of another subjected group through her appropriation of another other. At the time of this performance in 2008, the so-called War on Terror was in full swing with the ongoing military occupation of Iraq and Afghanistan as well as a military buildup in the Pacific unseen since World War II. Additionally the American media renewed fears of terrorism because of the 2008 Mumbai bombing attacks in India.[35] Cocoa Chandelier's performance of South Asian Orientalism is evidence of the manner in which the War on Terror revived American interest in Middle Eastern, Arab, Muslim, and South Asian cultures that is both an embrace of and a distancing from the brute realities of U.S. war making. Celebrating the other and their culture has always been a tactic of colonialism and nationalism, whereby the inclusion of certain others requires the exclusion of undesirable others, like "terrorists" or "bad Indians," for example.[36]

There is certainly space to critique Cocoa Chandelier for indulging a vague Orientalist notion of a generalized Eastern world. Her use of the Jay Z song is an example of Arab and South Asian rhythms being incorporated, whether through dialogues or sheer appropriation.[37] This repackaging of culture—

via the remix—enters the public sphere and marketplace as commodities to be enjoyed through a multicultural imaginary that celebrates difference without critiquing the political economy upon which it relies. Cocoa Chandelier evades her own commodity status by not performing Hawaiianness, instead choosing to embody a subjectivity that the Western gaze used to produce the Orient itself.[38] Throughout the performance Arab and South Asian cultures are abstracted, which is common in the post-9/11 era, when Arabs, South Asians, Muslims, and anyone perceived to be from a nation with a large Muslim population are wrongly lumped together.[39] For example, the "harems" of the abstracted Arab world are also conflated with indigenous culture when remixed into the *Devdas* Bollywood spectacle that is based on a Bengali novel. Cocoa Chandelier's appropriation of *Devdas* choreography and the story she tells about the harem exhibits this conflation. Historically harems were imagined as an alluring and tantalizingly forbidden world because the Western male gaze could not penetrate it.[40] By embodying this performative realm—the so-called harem—Cocoa Chandelier may well be replicating Orientalism, but she may also be understood to be availing herself strategically of a space that cannot be penetrated by the Western gaze, a space that can be liberating for Natives, especially for Kānaka Maoli, who continue to be hypervisible subjects.

Subjection is something Kānaka Maoli know all too well, as it has been through the embrace and celebration of Hawaiian culture and performance that the material realities of Kanaka Maoli dispossession have been concealed. By articulating Orientalist signifiers with Hawaiian indigeneity, Cocoa Chandelier shows the ways that indigeneity can be articulated with discourses that can also oppress others. Her "liberation" for Kānaka Maoli, then, comes at the expense of another. It makes the appropriation of culture appear both individual and universal, which is at the core of American notions of liberal-democratic freedom, where multiculturalism means appropriating and commodifying ethnic difference to hide ongoing subjection.[41] This performance provides a sense of agency for Cocoa Chandelier to resist recognizable forms of Hawaiian performance, but also evidences how Kānaka Maoli too can participate in the appropriation of other cultures, even if the intention was appreciation. Read within the specific context of Hawaiian performance, however, Cocoa Chandelier temporarily unsettles the grounds upon which Hawaiianness is built because she refuses to perform in prescribed ways. And this is precisely what made this performance so spectacular. Cocoa Chandelier's performances do not represent a desire to be recognized in an easy way. By not performing anything that can be named Hawaiian, she refuses to be a confessing subject fated to live out her subjection forever as a Kanaka Maoli. In this performance of Orientalized femininity she obstructs the disciplinary gaze that seeks to further normalize, contain, and commodify Hawaiian culture.

I am aware that I might be letting Cocoa Chandelier off the hook for her appropriative moves, but I would contend that her numerous performances exemplify what See has called "abstraction as a practice." I view Cocoa Chandelier's usage of the abstract as a tactic, one that See explains is an aesthetic practice, alongside other strategies of indirection, trickery and mimicry.[42] The story that is prerecorded, the Sarah Brightman song, and certainly the *Devdas* choreography are arguably unfamiliar to the general audience. In fact one of the primary moments the audience is heard on the DVD cheering during the performance is when the Jay Z song plays because it is familiar to them. To add to her persona on stage Cocoa Chandelier also carefully crafts her image as a patron of high-fashion designers, and in the Showgirl category of the pageant she enters the stage with her entourage dressed as a court jester. On stilts and holding a long scepter, she wears a black-and-white-checkered skintight bodysuit. Reminiscent of the jester tricksters of *carnivale* and mardi gras, she invokes these notorious scenes of performance play to further set herself apart from the other contestants. She performs what Audra Simpson describes as a mode of triple, even quadruple consciousness that engages in constant play. The play she engages in, as Simpson explains, reveals itself only through refusal.[43] Cocoa Chandelier refuses the hypercommodification of Hawaiian identity and produces a momentary performance event for a specific audience that, as Phelan has noted, finds its greatest strength by "eluding the economy of reproduction" because it "clogs the smooth machinery" of capitalism, as the performance is not easily re-created or marketable to a mass audience.[44]

At the same time, performances of this nature tap into public fantasies, leaving a trace that produces and alters cultural repertoires, making visible not just the live event but "the powerful army of the always already living."[45] These performances thus speak to the presence of a community that can be uplifted by Cocoa Chandelier's performance. What Diana Taylor describes as "the powerful army of the always already living" is, in this case, the army or community of Kānaka Maoli who—whether or not they are recognizable—are always already there through the Kanaka Maoli presence in the convention center space, throughout Hawai'i, through Cocoa Chandelier's very body. In the contained performance event a sense of pride and strength emerges for this particular community, both of Kānaka Maoli as well as the wider LGBTQ community in Hawai'i. Hawaiian indigeneity is articulated with Orientalist discourse tentatively within the performance, which contributes to Cocoa Chandelier's overall power as a performer. The audience recognizes her as a prominent and talented drag queen, which is influenced in part by her ability to not perform "herself," and because of this small community the audience knows who *she really is*. Her "true" identity on stage can be abstracted because the audience is already familiar with her. Her performance of Orientalism is celebrated as an expression of her power as a performer, but as I've shown, this moment of resistance is certainly precarious.

To return to disidentification, Cocoa Chandelier can be seen as a subject that is reworking cultural forms and is neither a "good" nor a "bad" subject operating outside of ideology.[46] Her resistance is never pure. As Hall has discussed, articulation can bring together contradictory elements that are not wholly resistant or liberatory.[47] Drag is also not always transgressive. Whereas drag performance has been theorized as resistance to the normative performance of gender, feminist critics have noted that drag queens often assert male domination, parody femininity, and reconstitute gender norms in oppressive and damaging ways.[48] Taken as a whole, in Cocoa Chandelier's performance Orientalized femininity is reconstituted as Hawaiian indigeneity is hidden and, in a sense, momentarily liberated from itself. It is not one over the other; it is both and in competing relation.

Aloha in drag, then, allows Cocoa Chandelier to perform a version of contemporary Kanaka Maoli life that contends with images of Hawaiian culture that have been bastardized through the spirit of aloha. But aloha is still there. As an affect, aloha is an emotion that is displayed through behavior and can often be felt in physical spaces, moving between individuals and their physical environments. In such instances aloha is omnipresent. As many Kānaka Maoli will tell you, aloha is still something we deeply believe in, even as we pretend to disavow it or publicly critique its commodified nature. We struggle with finding ways to balance this contradiction. We find ways to show it when it does not appear present. Aloha in drag necessitates the contradiction to be held in productive tension when performed or expressed in the appropriate spaces. Cocoa Chandelier's performance at the Universal Showqueen Pageant is one such space, where it appears that Hawaiian indigeneity is not limited or overdetermined by the specter of aloha and all that it carries. Even in the Hawai'i Convention Center space, marred as it is by Hawaiian appropriation at every turn—with rooms named after Hawaiian royalty and Hawaiian imagery adorning its insides—Cocoa Chandelier manages to hide her Hawaiianness while also asserting her Hawaiian indigeneity. In the end this works because the audience recognizes her, knows her, knows her work, has aloha for her—shares in her performance, in its success.

Living (with)in Death

Phelan explains that performance must be experienced live—honoring the idea that a limited number of people in a certain place and time can experience something that leaves no visible trace after the performance. Performance thus disrupts the representation necessary for capitalism by creating something ephemeral, something "there" but not really "there."[49] Phelan explains that once the performance is documented and put into a reproduced form, in this case in a DVD, it is no longer a "performance"; it is an archival video document consisting of a multitude of images of a performance that took place.[50] I wasn't at the Universal Showqueen Pageant; I heard about it from a friend. The fact that I "had to see this," as my friend put it, spoke to the way that word of mouth operates in a small LGBTQ (and Kanaka) community. The spectacular nature of Cocoa Chandelier's performance spread through what people in Hawai'i call the "coconut wireless," the rumor mill. I was told that I had to see it to believe it. This was true. As the audience members left the Hawai'i Convention Center after the performance, word spread: *OMG Cocoa did this Bollywood thing. OMG girl she did that aerial ribbon-dancing thing. OMG she hung herself upside down.* The performance produced an immense feeling of pride; everyone was talking about it. The community somehow felt uplifted by it, connected and affirmed in the fact that this small community was part of this performer who represented the best of the community, something *we* could be proud of. The performance overshadowed the figurative death that is staged at the end. In watching the DVD I was witness to a reenactment of a woman's sacrifice. Her powerful act, in the face of her unbearable existence, could be dealt with only through death, by hanging herself. The song ends. The crowd is heard screaming on the DVD. Cocoa Chandelier chooses to ignore the normal modes of Hawaiian performance and its deep connections to the commodification of aloha, but through her performance she offers the crowd her own embodiment of aloha.

The kind of aloha that Cocoa Chandelier embodies in this performance is in line with a type of performance that Phelan describes as "hardship art" or "ordeal art," which develops an aesthetics of pain and attempts to make a distinction between presence and representation by using the singular body as a substitute for a nonreciprocal experience of pain. Put another way, the audience views pain through one performer as a way to engage their own pain. The performance calls witnesses or the audience to the individual's death. This is what happened during Cocoa Chandelier's performance at the Universal Showqueen Pageant. Phelan explains that in these performances the audience is pushed to see the significance of an individual's death and asks the spectator to "do the impossible": to share the death by rehearsing for it. Phelan likens this experience and performance to ritual, like the ritual that takes place in a Catholic church, where there is a ritualized performative promise to remember and to rehearse for the other's death. The performance evokes a promise to learn and remember what is lost, to recall not only the meaning but the value of what cannot be reproduced or seen (again).[51] Cocoa Chandelier's performance of self-sacrifice forces the audience to experience her—the bride's—figurative death. The death is not just of Cocoa Chandelier; it is of the subjected Kanaka Maoli body, and to that end it is a staging of the death of Hawaiianness, the death of aloha in its most commodified forms.

In the performance the audience witnesses the bride attempting to climb out of the underworld, but the bride transforms into Cocoa Chandelier, a member of the community. Attempting to break out of the underworld, Cocoa Chandelier chooses death. In this death scene the screen flashes and the music comes to an abrupt halt. Cocoa Chandelier's body hangs by her feet, her arms spread in a cross formation, an upside-down crucifixion without the pole, without Jesus (without aloha). As the death occurs we are forced to ponder what is lost and gained in this enactment of death. The multiple attempts to scale the long pieces of fabric hanging from the ceiling exhibit the bride's inability to climb out of the underworld. The bride thus chooses death because she knows that she will never break out of the Harem of the Underworld.

Beneath the costuming Cocoa Chandelier is a Kanaka Maoli performer whom many in the local drag community respect and love. In the end her identity and her Hawaiianness can remain unmarked because of her community recognition. The performance erases Hawaiian indigeneity as it foregrounds it. The aloha that is expressed in her performance cannot be reproduced beyond that very moment. As a viewer of the DVD, I am able to tap into this space where aloha transformed into something available only to those that were present. I am able to share in its emotive power, but it is only a partial experience; the smooth machinery of capitalism remains clogged. As the figurative sacrifice occurs in the performance, it can be read as a staging of the death of commodified forms of Hawaiianness and aloha, but in this sacrifice a new formation of aloha becomes possible.

NOTES

1. The State of Hawai'i distinguishes between the terms *Hawaiian* and *Native Hawaiian*, each of which has a contested legality based on blood quantum. In this work I use the term *Kanaka Maoli* to refer to the native peoples of the Hawaiian archipelago. It is a reference to any person descended from the indigenous people inhabiting the Hawaiian Islands before 1778. *Kanaka Maoli* has recently been taken up by Kānaka Maoli; it translates into "true people" or "real people" in relation to Hawaiian indigeneity. *Kānaka Maoli*, with the macron over the *ā*, is the plural form. Please also note that I use the term *Hawaiian* to refer to categories such as Hawaiian performance and Hawaiian indigeneity.

2. Kaina Jacobs was Universal Showqueen in 2001.

3. Chow, *The Protestant Ethnic and the Spirit of Capitalism*, 114–15.

4. Wood, *Displacing Natives*; O'Brien, *The Pacific Muse*.

5. Hawai'i was named "the Aloha State" in 1959. Haw. Rev. Stat. 5–7.

6. Kanahele, *Kū Kanaka, Stand Tall*; Pukui et al., *Nana I Ke Kumu*.

7. Osorio, *Dismembering Lāhui*.

8. Scholars have used the concept of articulation to add complexity to the category of the Native; see Tengan, *Native Men Remade*; Smith, *Native Americans and the Christian Right*. By the late 1990s a new movement self-identified as Native Pacific cultural studies resignified the category of Native or the indigenous subject in the Pacific in order to convey its deep entrenchment in colonial and postcolonial discourse while also acknowledging its frequent movements and innovations outside of those very discourses. Teresia Teaiwa's work especially contributed to an understanding of Native in terms of diaspora and shifting traditions, an identification with the land and fluid kinship systems that confound colonial, nationalist, and postcolonial representations. See Teaiwa, "Native Thoughts"; Diaz and Kauanui, "Native Pacific Cultural Studies on the Edge."

9. Grossberg, "On Postmodernism and Articulation," 135.

10. McKenzie, *Perform or Else*, 15.

11. Butler, *Gender Trouble*, 146.

12. Phelan, *Unmarked*.

13. Simpson, "On Ethnographic Refusal," 67. For more about the critique of colonial anthropology and its relationship to empire, see Stoler, *Race and the Education of Desire*; Povinelli, *The Cunning of Recognition*.

14. Imada, "Hawaiians on Tour," 112, 113, 112, 114. Imada also notes that through "imperial hospitality" hula dancers and hostesses offered aloha to military officers, notably white men. Through the staging of military lū'au's, the U.S. military scripted Hawaiian hospitality and leisure, embodying a highly mediated form of performance that made visible and available islander bodies, translating Hawai'i into a safe sanctuary for the U.S. military and for Americans ("The Army Learns to Lū'au," 352).

15. Phelan, *Unmarked*, 7, 11.

16. Kanahele, *Kū Kanaka, Stand Tall*, 480; Pukui et al., *Nana I Ke Kumu*, 3.

17. The term *drag* can be used as an adjective or a noun. According to Newton in *Mother Camp*, as a noun *drag* means the act of gender performing another gender. In *Gender Trouble*, Butler focuses on the ways drag performance—in terms of gender—unifies the

category of woman or man through reiteration, in other words, through the constant performance of traits attributed to women or men. Drag exposes the "normal" constitution of gender presentation that is constituted by a set of "disavowed attachments or identifications" (Butler, 160). Drag reveals the ways that gender norms are naturalized, but, as Butler stresses, drag is also contingent.

18. Butler, *Gender Trouble*, 175.

19. Queer studies has been critiqued by Native studies (Smith, "Queer Theory and Native Studies"). Smith advocates using queer theory's subjectless critique to escape ethnographic entrapment, which positions Natives as perpetual objects of study.

20. More information about the pageant DVD can be found at the Universal Showqueen website, http://www.universalshowqueenpageant.com/.

21. For examinations of how Hawaiians are invoked in urban planning, see Marek, "Waikiki Virtual Reality"; Ferguson and Turnbull, *Oh Say Can You See?*; Wood, *Displacing Natives*.

22. Muñoz, *Disidentifications*, 11, 12.

23. See, *The Decolonized Eye*, 128, 138.

24. Not to be confused with Persephone, queen of the Underworld in Greek mythology. Stories told about Persephone reference her abduction into the Underworld and eventual return to regular life on the condition (or curse) that she return to the Underworld during winter. The myth is thought to explain the absence of fertility during winter.

25. *Devdas* (2002) is based on the book by Sharat Chattopadhyay. The film was released in 2002 and was the third Bollywood version to be produced, but the first to be produced in full color. It has been released in English, French, German, Mandarin, Thai, and Punjabi. At the time it was the highest grossing Bollywood film ever.

26. Kavita Krishnamurthy, "Dola re dola," *Devdas Soundtrack*, Fontana Indian, Universal Music India, 2002.

27. Also featured prominently is Panjabi MC, "Beware of the Boys," Sequence Records 2003. It features a remix with Jay Z.

28. Personal communication with Cocoa Chandelier, December 9, 2011. She uses the phrase "God-like figure" to describe the character in the story that is trying to save the bride.

29. Muñoz, *Disidentifications*, 12. Muñoz explains that disidentifying subjects both hold on to the loss of the subject and invest in it a new kind of life.

30. Da Silva, *Toward a Global Idea of Race*, xxxv.

31. See Smith, *Native Americans and the Christian Right* and "Queer Theory and Native Studies"; Simpson, "On Ethnographic Refusal"; Coulthard, "Subjects of Empire."

32. Kauanui, *Hawaiian Blood*, 25.

33. Glen Coulthard, "Indigenous Peoples and the 'Politics of Recognition' in Colonial Contexts," paper presented at the Cultural Studies Now Conference, University of East London, July 22, 2007 quoted in Smith, "Queer Theory and Native Studies," 57.

34. Phelan, *Unmarked*, 163. Phelan notes that in *The History of Sexuality*, Foucault's usage of the confession is akin to how power operates in many forms of performance. She claims that "women and performers" are the ones that are scripted to sell or confess, but I would add that this is applicable to anyone underrepresented who must confess or sell themselves to be included.

35. On November 26, 2008, a Pakistan-based military organization coordinated bombing attacks throughout South Mumbai, India. The attacks lasted two days and killed over a 150 people and wounded over three hundred.

36. Alsultany, "Selling American Diversity and Muslim American Identity through Non-Profit Advertising Post-911," 619. See also Jamal and Naber, *Race and Arab Americans before and after 9/11.*

37. For more on music and appropriation, see Born and Hesmondahalgh, *Western Music and Its Others.*

38. Said, *Orientalism.*

39. See also Puar's chapter "The Turban Is Not a Hat," in *Terrorist Assemblages* for an example of this conflation.

40. See Ahmed, "Western Ethnocentrism and Perceptions of the Harem."

41. For descriptions of how Arab dance is incorporated, see Sellers-Young and Shay, *Belly Dance*; Maira, "Henna and Hip-Hop." Maira explains that the opening up of India's economic market has caused India to be a nation of cheap labor, goods, and emergent markets and trends.

42. See, *The Decolonized Eye,* 128–29.

43. Simpson, "On Ethnographic Refusal," 74.

44. Phelan, *Unmarked,* 148–49.

45. Taylor, *The Archive and the Repertoire,* 143.

46. Muñoz, *Disidentifications,* 12.

47. Hall and Jefferson, *Resistance through Rituals.*

48. Schacht, "Turnabout," 167.

49. Phelan, *Unmarked,* 149, 148.

50. Phelan, *Unmarked,* 146–47.

51. Phelan, *Unmarked,* 152.

IV. MILITARISM, EMPIRE, AND WAR: THE SECURITY STATE AND STATES OF INSECURITY

SIXTEEN

Surrogates and Subcontractors: Flexibility and Obscurity in U.S. Immigrant Detention

DAVID M. HERNÁNDEZ

Merging Instruments of Authority

In the past decade the emerging global dimensions of U.S. "wartime" detentions amplified by the war on terror have cross-fertilized with domestic immigrant detention policy, affecting and being affected by the incarceration of immigrants at ports of entry and within the nation's interior.[1] Both systems achieve increased power and flexibility due to legal exceptionalism and juridical ambiguity, historiographic compartmentalization, muted recognition in contemporary debates about comprehensive immigration reform, and, as discussed in this chapter, the use of surrogate actors and partners in the material execution of noncitizen incarceration. The existence of a parallel, global detention regime dramatically shifts the meaning and scale of immigrant detention and should be considered at once *a part of* the domestic noncitizen detention project but also *apart from* it. Because international detainees are arrested outside the United States and generally on one of the so-called battlefields in the war on terror—the exception being migrants intending to unlawfully enter the United States but who are captured while transmigrating through third-party nations or while at sea—global detainees should not be conflated automatically or uncritically with the majority of immigrant detainees held in the U.S. deportation regime. Nonetheless there are important similarities in terms of their categorical racialization and criminalization, their location vis-à-vis national security frameworks, the conditions of their incarceration, their lack of legal rights and access to due process protections, and, crucially, their invisibility and remoteness from the majority of society as a result of the regime's reliance on surrogate partners in effecting their detentions.

Global detainees, in this way, are a major segment in the unfolding chapter of immigrant detention exacerbated by 9/11 and the war on terror. They are known and unknown at the same time. They stir outrage domestically and internationally and at times shadow and obscure the ongoing domestic counterparts to surrogate detention. Further, each system of antiterror or anti-immigrant suspicion can work as a pretext for the other, enhancing the flexibility of immigrant detention as an enforcement tool. This is to say that, on one hand, the war on terror has allowed the United States to push its borders outward and expand its detention project globally. For example, the international detention structure has included the prisons at Guantánamo Bay Naval Base in Cuba and Abu Ghraib in Iraq under its broad "homeland security" umbrella. Because terrorism is transnational, the argument goes, so should U.S. policies against suspected terrorists. On the other hand, the global war on terror, like past efforts to secure the nation, has doubly underscored the links between homeland security and the control of domestic migration. Whereas the principal concern in the national security context is terrorism and more broadly defined associations with terrorism, the primary result has been an expanded domestic detention regime, impacting noncitizens within the United States from around the world, but in particular the demographically significant and increasingly targeted Latin American immigrant communities throughout the nation.

Boundaries between domestic immigrant detention and the global detention infrastructure are thus blurred. In the popular imagination and strengthened by the federal government, terrorism seems to exist due to the presence of immigrants. As Thomas Faist suggests in his post-9/11 essay "*Extension du domaine de la lutte*: International Migration and Security before and after 11 September 2001" (translation: Extension of the Combat Zone), "The responses to the events on September 11 have reinforced the security-migration nexus, dramatizing a publicly convenient link between international migration and security."[2] Key elements to this "convenient link" are the historical persistence and robust flexibility of detention and deportation laws, policies, and practices. The U.S. detention regime is a critical site of the security-migration nexus, operating at home and abroad to further consolidate state power—formulating and defending U.S. nationalism and sovereignty by constructing and controlling what is foreign *inside* and *outside* the United States.

This chapter briefly contextualizes contemporary securitization efforts, providing examples of cumulative precedents and patterns in immigrant detention that help explain this regime's ongoing obscurity and challenge its exceptionalist foundation. I illuminate the continuities of racial criminalization by exploring the detention regime's historic reliance on surrogate partners domestically and internationally. I also problematize prevailing logics of reform and resistance to detention expansion such as the use of prosecutorial discretion to prioritize so-called criminals and grant relief to low-priority detainees, often referred to as noncriminal or "innocent" noncitizens. Overall I seek to unmask the obscured discursive and institutional formations of immigrant detention in the United States, checking its flexible and coercive technologies used to exercise state power and violence far beyond the control of undocumented migration.

Precedents, Patterns

What legal and political histories paved the way for such "exceptional" detention authority in the war on terror? For over a century immigration law, especially the body of law facilitating the detention process, has been used to address national crises because it is anomalous to and evasive of normative forms of governmental checks and balances and because immigrants are not provided even the limited and deeply flawed constitutional safeguards of criminal law. Because immigration policies are often steeped in frameworks of sovereignty as opposed to constitutional parameters, judicial deference to Congress's extraordinary plenary power over immigration matters has largely been the rule, from the era of Chinese exclusion, through the mid-twentieth-century solidification of anti-Mexican immigration control, to the period prior to and after 9/11.

Even before the consolidation of the federal immigration authority in the late nineteenth century, colonial, federal, and local government entities forcibly removed or restricted the mobility of poor and often nonwhite undesirables. Much like criminal imprisonment, immigrant detention draws from the heritage of slave labor, the control of free black persons, and the recapture of fugitive slaves. In fact the control of nonwhite noncitizen mobility played a critical function in labor management, the industrial development of the U.S. West, and establishment of national sovereignty. For the purported nation of immigrants the exclusion and removal of poor persons from local British colonial communities, federal Indian removal programs, the capture and return of fugitive slaves, and restrictions on free black persons in the United States "foreshadowed," according to Daniel Kanstroom, "the federal deportation system."[3] Although often unrecognized, this "lost century" of immobilization and forced removal is part of the contemporary detention and deportation regime.[4]

Racial anxieties and animosities in particular are paramount in detention history, producing a meandering racial genealogy of detention and deportation that is closely aligned with racial states of emergency.[5] Following the formation of the Bureau of Immigration in the 1890s, we see an unbroken chain of racist immigrant anxieties leading to persistent detention and deportation campaigns against varied groups of immigrants. Whereas anti-Asian angst dominated the late nineteenth- and early twentieth-century fears of immigrants, today anxieties about Latina/o migration play this role, both popularly and in enforcement efforts. Latinas/os, for example, represent 88 percent of all detainees and 93 percent of all removals from the United States.[6] Over the past one hundred years differing security crises occurred in a variety of political contexts, including fears of contagion, the demonization of "foreign" ideologies, international military conflicts, refugee streams, and domestic wars on crime, drugs, and terrorism. Race and racist practices have proven to be malleable and productive across this genealogy, as racist animosities were transposed from one social group to another in immigration enforcement. Racialized immigration enforcement, abetted by surrogate detention partners, discretionary practices of the executive branch, secrecy, and invented legal categories—such as "aliens ineligible to citizenship," "internee," and "enemy combatant"—has thus been a fundamental and flexible tool in the detention process, often uninhibited and thus advanced by the courts, since the inception of the Bureau of Immigration in the late nineteenth century.

Obscurity and Exceptionalism in the Detention Regime

Despite a long, albeit muted, history of immigrant detention in the United States, noncitizen detention and the popular figure of the detainee dramatically entered (or reentered) the U.S. lexicon in the past decade from outside its borders, generating a renewed focus on detention's domestic form. Disturbing photos and unsettling narrative accounts from Abu Ghraib and Guantánamo Bay familiarized the nation and the world with the sensational and deadly consequences of U.S. antiterrorist detention policies. More recently, after the transition from the Bush to the Obama administration, more knowledge has come to light about "black sites" in the war on terror, in which the Bush White House seized extraordinary unchecked powers in labeling "enemy combatants" and effecting the torturous conditions of their incarceration. Despite official protests articulated through the legislative and judicial branches, and because of official acquiescence, such unilateral powers and practices occurred beyond the reach of these ostensibly balancing and regulatory federal branches and with indifference toward supranational bodies of law. The 2006 Military Commissions Act stripping Guantánamo detainees of habeas corpus is but one example of the congressional green light to these practices. The Obama administration, for its part, has "decommissioned" the "remaining sites" for secret rendition of terror suspects.[7] However, it has also retained its authority to render suspects or hold detainees in secrecy.[8] As well, the Obama administration has declined to prosecute interrogators, airline companies, and the principal designers of U.S. torture policies, declaring through the former CIA director that agency officials conducting "past interrogation practices" "should not be investigated, let alone punished."[9] In this manner the Pentagon, CIA, and White House of the past two administrations have constructed and maintained a guise of exceptionalism that cloaks, rationalizes, and absolves the practices of the U.S. war on terror. Under this cover, reports of the U.S. rendition program under Clinton, Bush, and Obama and further details of secret U.S. prisons worldwide indicate a story only partially told, in which the widespread web of detention facilities signals a global detention infrastructure devoid of legal constraints, with limited media coverage, and without an independent evaluation mechanism. That is to say, the U.S. criminalization and incarceration regime for racialized migrants is a global regime, immense and obscured inside the nation but also reliant on global constructions of national security that demonize immigrants.

In its first decade the war on terror has been accompanied by a theory of exceptionalism that distorts perceptions of 9/11 and post-9/11 detentions at home and abroad. For both domestic and global detention spaces and apparatuses, 9/11 as well as the resulting war on terror were certainly astonishing, deeply tragic, and to many unthinkable. The federal government articulated national security as a "state of exception," what Giorgio Agamben calls "a technique of government" facilitating suspensions in existing law—"a suspension of the juridical order itself"—in order to confront national crises.[10] But neither 9/11 nor the extraordinary power to detain noncitizens is without precedent, and whether the state of exception is constructed outside, inside, or incommensurate with the law, it is a recurring tool of power and its accumulation. Terrorism, especially as it has been broadly defined over the past decade—ranging from bombings and political assassinations to lynchings and other racist hate crimes—is not new and has been conducted on U.S. soil by foreign, domestic, and state actors. The genealogy of domestic terrorism in particular is centrally fueled by white supremacist organizations and state apparatuses, and government reactions to terrorism or other national crises bearing these racial contours are similarly fused with popular and racist fears of immigrants producing a long history of violations against noncitizen detainees in the United States.[11] The exceptionalism and sensationalism framing 9/11 and the war on terror, however, endeavor to achieve a status of incomparability, not only justifying any extraordinary governmental response but also contributing to the public suppression of the systematic treatment of noncitizens in the United States prior to 9/11, particularly in the detention process. Detention episodes, largely racialized ones, regularly framed by government authorities as crises in national security, or even by detainee advocates as sensational abuses of power by the government, veil and obscure the precedents, patterns, and century-long consolidation of this institutional authority.

The basic logic entailed in exceptionalist detention rhetoric implies that it is virtually impossible to analyze the historical precursors to the diminished rights of immigrants and detainees. This logic is central to the obscurity of immigrant detention and merges with the spatial execution of the detention authority among diffused actors and remote locations of incarceration. Particularly persons marked by race, religion, or other negatively perceived cultural attributes are further obscured because the national crises usually framing the abuse of noncitizens are regarded popularly and historiographically as having no precedent. Racially targeted enforcement mechanisms, such as those targeting Arabs, Muslims, and South Asians after 9/11, or more recent policies targeting Mexicans, Central Americans, and other Latinas/os in the southern border states over the past decade, make common sense in sensationalist contexts and appear self-evident in a national security framework because, according to John Mueller, "most Americans seem to have developed a false sense of insecurity about terrorism."[12] The much repeated notion since 9/11 that "everything has changed," that we are in a "new era" with "new paradigms of war"—that is, the state of exception—not only masks the history of immigrant detention, but as other scholars have argued, it disappears the larger elephant in the room: the expansion of the U.S. prison industrial complex.[13] Detention episodes, especially those producing evidence of abuse or, as a consequence, popular protest, are thus viewed in history as isolated events—aberrations disconnected from the history of government policies and judicial rulings that enable them.

With the nation's safety professedly at stake, the federal government purportedly responds to distinct security crises utilizing a supposedly temporary strategy of incarcerating noncitizens, thus protecting the nation and homeland from enemies within and, as 9/11 illustrates, from outside its borders. This historical compartmentalization of detention—focused on particular detainee populations, specific historical episodes, or individuated experiences in detention—has further muted its critical importance as an enforcement mechanism that is productive beyond migration control. The obscurity of detention, framed as exceptional in varying political contexts, thus contributes to popular historical amnesia regarding the detention apparatus. While obfuscated by security crises, immigrant detention is also oblique due to its liminal structure in the deportation process, the enormous shadow of the prison system, and its muted location in immigration reform discourse. The regime of detention and deportation thus relies on spatial and discursive obscurity to enhance the flexibility of its power.

In the context of obscurity it is critical to delineate the detention regime's many strands, "third-party actors," and analytical linkages. According to the political scientist Gallya Lahav, "Few attempts have been made to disaggregate the state and to identify the agencies and actors involved in regulating migration."[14] This is critical, in particular for the institution of immigrant detention, in order to grapple with its diffused and stealth intensity as an enforcement initiative domestically, but also its links to expanded border security beyond the United States in a national security and antiterrorism context. The following section thus examines the outsourcing of detention operations and the ongoing use of dispersed, remote, and strategic carceral locations that lead to ambiguities in legal protection, uncertain government accountability, and nebulous limits to the authority of surrogate jailers.

Decentralizing Detention Domestically and Globally

The decentralization, de-federalization, and at times privatization of detention are well-established practices in the configuration of domestic noncitizen detention. In the early twentieth century, for example, privately owned hotels were contracted by the Bureau of Immigration at the U.S.-Mexico border in order to detain immigrants. In El Paso hotels and private residential facilities were widely used through the 1950s when a permanent government-owned and -operated facility was finally constructed in this migrant-heavy region.[15]

This occurred despite documented instances of abuse inflicted upon detainees due to structural inadequacies and mistreatment by surrogate jailers. As late as the 1990s hotel prisons persisted. Christian Parenti writes, "Many of these prisons are nothing more than run-down motels surrounded by barbed wire and infamous for their wretched conditions, overcrowding, and violence."[16] To be sure, federally run facilities are no guarantee of detainee safety, as abuse, medical neglect, and deaths occur in all facilities, public or privatized. The federal government, for example, which often seeks to "stymie outside inquiry," developed a reporting system for in-custody deaths only in the past ten years, and private jailers consistently seek to hide their records behind corporate rights and protections.[17]

Corporate and third-party incarceration is thus a long-standing practice, strengthening and creating elasticity in the detention regime, as well as enriching the private prison industry. The first modern, privately owned and operated prison in the mid-1980s was an immigrant detention facility run by the Corrections Corporation of America in Texas followed by a facility in Colorado run by the Wackenhut Corporation. According to its former CEO, George Zoley, "it was really the INS [Immigration and Naturalization Service] that started privatized corrections in this country."[18] Privatization of detention operations and the use of nonstate actors permits at least three broad goals: the federal government shares the burden of detaining noncitizens while expanding its capacity to do so; it generates profits and revenues, making it attractive to private and other nonfederal institutions; and it deflects accountability for the violent excesses of detention. These three features, much like the legal and rhetorical framing of detention as an exceptional form of alien incarceration, ensure a robust flexibility in detention operations.

First, the use of private and nonfederal detention facilities rapidly expands the total capacity of the federal government to detain noncitizens nationwide and globally. The United States moderates the overall costs and burden of detaining noncitizens in deportation proceedings by contracting out services to local and county prison facilities and also to privately owned properties and jails. Since the late nineteenth century the federal government has utilized private and nonfederal hotels, hospitals, steamships, storage sheds, "tomato warehouses," and other ad hoc facilities to detain immigrants.[19] In 2008, for example, the government used a "cattle exhibit hall" to detain migrant workers raided and detained en masse in Postville, Iowa.[20] Currently the government rents 80 percent of its bed space for detainees from a web of over 250 nonfederal lockups—down from as many as 370 five years ago—in rural counties and small cities nationwide and from private for-profit jails run by the Corrections Corporation of America, Wackenhut Corrections Corporation (now the GEO Group), Cornell Companies, Inc., Management and Training Corporation, and others.[21] This is in comparison to 7.4 percent of contracted bed space for persons incarcerated in the federal and state adult prison and jail population.[22] With detainee bed space tripling in the 1990s, and continuing its rise in the past decade, nearly half of major facilities are privately owned and managed. Private and public efforts to expand this infrastructure, even south of the U.S.-Mexico border, are also under way. The federal government is planning to build a private detention facility in Los Angeles to replace the recently shuttered public Terminal Island federal facility.[23] In 2005 the state of Arizona passed legislation, vetoed by Governor Janet Napolitano, that would have created a foreign private prison commission and constructed a private prison in Mexico to incarcerate Mexican nationals serving time in Arizona.[24] Such a project, if passed, would have bridged the narrowing divide between domestic and international detention. California's governor Arnold Schwarzenegger similarly suggested sending twenty thousand undocumented inmates to Mexico and assisting in building a prison for them.[25] These new proposals and the increased reliance on nonfederal partners and surrogates to rapidly expand detention capacity significantly reconfigure immigration control and enforcement in the Department of Homeland Security—where one of every three dollars flows to private contractors[26]—making permanent the role of private contractors in a sensitive jurisdiction of federal enforcement.

A second result of the de-federalization of detention is the introduction of profit and revenue motives into the rationale behind noncitizen detention. Lahav offers this definition of privatization: "Privatization, loosely defined as the shift of a function from the public to the private sector, involves a dependence on market forces for the pursuit of social goods and may turn local actors or contractors into regulators."[27] In both the domestic and the international sphere of U.S. detention, nonfederal regulators of detention and private military contractors cease to serve merely a social function; now their purview is revenue-driven and catalyzed by financial aims, including the economic motives of war and securitization. As part of what the *New York Times* calls the "'immigrant gold rush' that turned the private prison industry from bust to boom,"[28] immigrant detainees in this scenario are commodities that are accumulated, traded, and transferred for the purposes of creating profits for domestic and foreign jailers and private contractors, as well as political currency for public officials seeking to be considered tough on crime, immigrants, and terrorism, all issues that are linked today.

Private detention thus produces, epiphenomenally, a commerce in immigrant detainees, a microeconomy of public dollars for detention that dramatically informs the way we view immigrants. This includes a variety of for-profit service provision, from food and health care to phone services and transportation. For some poor counties and municipalities in the United States, noncitizen detention serves as a popular development strategy, much like prison construction nationwide. In June 1993, for example, the *Harrisburg Patriot-News* in Pennsylvania carried the headline "Prison Board Shopping for Immigrants to Prevent Layoffs." In this article the county commissioner stated, "We tried like the dickens to get some of the Chinese . . . but it didn't pan out. . . . If no immigrants are secured, some layoffs may be inevitable."[29] Similarly, in response to budget cuts in 2009, the Santa Ana Police Department in California converted two multipurpose rooms at its jail to accommodate additional immigrant detainees and proposed raising its per-bed fee that it charges the federal government. According to Police Chief Paul Walters, "We treat [the jail] like a business. . . . The cuts could have been much deeper if it weren't for the ability to raise money there."[30]

When detention is treated "like a business," the social and legal parameters of immigrant detention as well as its stated administrative functions are rendered meaningless, and the more long-term financial downsides of private prison development give way to political demands for immediate profits. Especially for smaller prison towns, residents have learned that detention centers can result in the opposite of economic development, often producing fewer new jobs than expected and chasing away new businesses as well. As Ruth Wilson Gilmore writes, "Prison development has had the intended, although rarely realized, effect of providing jobs."[31] Moreover, although profit motive or cost savings can be motivating factors for surrogate partners in prison privatization, they are consequent to the public system of immigrant detention, as private and nonfederal monetary benefits still derive from taxpayers' public resources. As related to revenue motives, then, privatization might increase government partnerships in the detention regime, but overall it is a "red-herring,"[32] ancillary to the logic of the carceral structure, and not at its core.

Third, de-federalizing the operations of the detention authority has led to a distant, if not absent, oversight by federal detention authorities. Varying regional, institutional, and political contexts create widespread differences in legal rights (such as access to counsel) and carceral conditions of detention (from health care and religious needs to overcrowding and the use of solitary confinement of so-called administrative detainees). Further, just as the economic pressures mentioned earlier stimulate the incentive to acquire detainees and maintain their long-term detention, they also serve as disincentives to dispense funds to provide structurally and medically safe and humane conditions for detainees. Jody Kent of the ACLU's National Prison Project states, "We have serious concerns about for-profit prison companies because they are notorious for cutting essential costs that need to be provided to maintain a safe and constitutional environment for prisoners."[33] Over one hundred detainees have died in obscurity in nonfederal and federal facilities over the past decade as a result of cost-saving medical neglect, murky government reporting, and lack of investigative inquiries not mandated by policy.[34] Records of such detainee deaths remain buried in agency reports and private companies' annual reports and files.[35] This lack of oversight and evasion of accountability is buttressed by private prison contractors' exemption from the disclosure of records through the Freedom of Information Act. Prison corporations in particular lobby strenuously to block potential legislation, such as the Private Prison Information Act, which would alter this policy.[36] Private partnerships in detention muddy accountability and misdirect advocacy, as the federal government laments privatized abuses endemic to its very system of immigrant criminalization and incarceration and detainee advocates seek piecemeal solutions for individual detainees or particular detention sites. The detention regime overall remains isolated from larger critiques of criminalization and incarceration, often leading lawyers, detainees, and advocates to argue the innocence of detainees, underscoring the criminality of racialized citizens and noncitizens and undermining critiques of the entire system.

The oversight provisions guiding nonfederal immigrant detention further diffuse accountability and criticism of the detention regime's spatial obscurity. When detention operations are decentralized—again, roughly 80 percent of domestic detainees are in nonfederal facilities—enforcement and regulation fall on many others in lieu of federal authorities: state and local law enforcement and prison operators, private security and detention services, and private legal services working on behalf of detainees. In cases where the federal government has been sued for deadly health conditions in contract detention facilities, government lawyers have cagily utilized lack of federal oversight in its own defense, arguing that it is "completely unfair" to hold accountable the government agency "that has no contact with the detainee on a regular basis."[37]

Over the past decade and a half the inspector general of the Department of Homeland Security, human rights groups, and investigative media have issued numerous reports of abuse and poor conditions for immigrant detainees. Although abuses occur in both federal and nonfederal facilities, a key issue affecting contracted and private lockups is that "the treatment of immigration detainees, including living conditions, health care, and access to legal materials is governed by a Department of Homeland Security detention manual, which is neither legally enforceable nor universally applied." One former detainee released from a private facility in San Diego stated, "The standards need some teeth or people with continue to get hurt." As a result detainees and immigrants' rights organizations have petitioned the Department of Homeland Security to issue uniform legal regulations for detention that will "establish clear lines of accountability," which are "especially critical in light of the patchwork system of detention currently employed to house detainees."[38] Enforceable detention standards, it should be noted, are but one step toward improving conditions for detainees. Federal oversight has never been a panacea, as federally run immigrant detention centers, much like federal prisons and other public facilities, are persistently spaces of physical danger, neglect, and abuse. For example, of the over 140 deaths in immigrant detention since 2003, about one fourth occurred in federal service processing centers or Bureau of Prisons lockups.[39] Recurring presidential administrations, however, have refused to enact enforceable detention standards, stating that such protocols and "rule-making would be laborious, time consuming and less flexible."[40]

A critical domestic example of the absence of standards and ad hoc assemblage of detainee facilities is the brief tenure of the T. Don Hutto Residential Center for families in Taylor, Texas. Formerly a state prison, and one of the Bush administration's additions to the domestic detention infrastructure, Hutto has been used as a symbol of reform by both the Bush and the Obama administration—by Bush to signal tough enforcement and the end of the so-called catch-and-release policy for some immigrants, and by Obama as a symbol of post-Bush detention reform, moving toward what the Department of Homeland Security calls a "truly civil detention system."[41] Although dubbed a "residential center" for detained families, Hutto originally was replete with barbed wire, an armed guard tower, at one point prison garb for detainees (or what Immigration and Customs Enforcement calls "medical style-scrubs"[42]), and fully authorized punitive disciplinary actions. The Hutto prison was run for profit as a family detention center by the Corrections Corporation of America and earned $2.8 million per month. Half of its inmates were children. In 2007 it was reported that the children were receiving only one hour of daily academic instruction while incarcerated and that the facility was not licensed by the state for education or other child welfare issues.[43] Also in 2007 administrators at the Hutto facility turned away United Nations human rights expert Jorge Bustamante for his previously scheduled visit.[44] A lawsuit by the ACLU and extensive community-based protest in Texas eventually resulted in a cosmetic makeover of the prison prior to the Obama administration's conversion of Hutto from a family detention center to a women's immigrant prison. Continued allegations of sexual abuse by Corrections Corporation of America guards have been lodged at Hutto both as a family detention facility and, later, as a women's prison. Although Hutto is touted as a symbolic example of Obama's commitment to detention reform, its conversion more accurately reflects the Obama administration's expansion of detention capacity through the continued use of private prison operators despite ongoing abuse.

Surrogates and subcontractors in the detention regime are not limited to domestic incarceration. Detention strategies, impacted by contemporary securitization frameworks targeting terrorism, also exist outside of these global anxieties and are executed as a global arm of domestic migration control. For example, before enemy combatants were imprisoned in what has been a called a "legal black hole," Guantánamo Naval Base was used for the detention of Haitian and Cuban migrants intercepted at sea precisely because the vagaries of sovereignty and the boundaries of constitutional protections of detainees made the offshore facility an uncertain, perhaps ungovernable legal entity. The mass detention of Haitians in particular merged the racial exclusion of black "undesirables" with the discourses of national security and public health—in this case, the fear of HIV—in a legal prologue to the domestic and international detentions in the war on terror. Despite a 1990 Centers for Disease Control advisory eliminating HIV as a rationale for exclusion, the United States quarantined Haitian asylum seekers, creating off its shores what Judge Sterling Johnson Jr. of the federal district court called "the only known refugee camp in the world composed entirely of HIV-positive refugees."[45] This episode, a contemporary parallel to border health policies of the nineteenth and early twentieth centuries, underscores the repetitive logics of racialized noncitizen detention and reaffirms the importance of cognizance of detention history. The Haitian HIV detentions also demonstrate the recurrence of what Nayan Shah calls "contagious divides"—that is, fears of contagion and their use as rationales for control of racialized immigrant undesirables, especially the use of off-shore, global detention sites.[46] Moreover Haitian detentions at Guantánamo helped to construct the legal groundwork and material infrastructure for confining enemy combatants in the war on terror.

As with Guantánamo, U.S. military bases overseas are often used for the detention of interdicted migrants destined for the United States. For example, from April to December 1999 the U.S. Coast Guard intercepted seven Chinese boats destined for the United States and detained almost one thousand migrants at Tinian and Midway islands in the Pacific as well as in detention centers in Guatemala.[47] Other detention sites for interdicted migrants have included U.S. bases in Panama, Ecuador, and Guam and a hospital ship anchored in Kingston, Jamaica.[48] In the late 1990s the United States established the Regional Conference on Migration, or Puebla Process, to create hemispheric partners in drug and immigration control, permitting the U.S. Coast Guard access to the territorial waters of twenty-five nations. Under the guise of drug interdiction, U.S. Immigration and Customs Enforcement (ICE) has worked directly with the Ecuadoran National Police to combat human smuggling, leading to complaints of detainee abuse by U.S. sailors, the destruction of Ecuadoran sea vessels, and the eventual ouster of ICE from Ecuador.[49]

These global detention efforts reflect a diffusion of immigration enforcement, a policy that usually focuses, myopically, on border enforcement—attempting to seal the border from undocumented immigration. Except in this case the border and its enforcement jurisdiction are pushed outward into international waters. As seen in the Caribbean border zone—where apprehension at sea as opposed to the shores of southern Florida significantly alters would-be migrants' legal rights—the government seeks to maintain its detention infrastructure away from the United States. Such transnational border enforcement, even when conducted with binational cooperation, should not be confused with a transnational immigration control policy that might take social networks and global economies into consideration and utilize international development to bolster the economies of immigrant sending nations. This is explicitly border enforcement, exported globally.

The largest and most well-known target of U.S. border enforcement is the undocumented migration coming from and through Mexico. As a result the United States spends billions of dollars fortifying and militarizing the two thousand–mile U.S.-Mexico border. In addition in the late 1990s the United States launched an international anti–human smuggling operation called "Operation Global Reach," which established over forty international offices in cooperation with "source-country" governments.[50] In the first four years of Operation Global Reach immigration officials claim to have apprehended seventy-four thousand migrants passing through Central American nations. Mexico, for its part, launched its Plan Sur (Southern Plan) in 2001 to control migration across its borders with Belize and Guatemala. Mexico's National Migration Institute detained annually over 100,000 Central Americans and other migrants from twenty-five nations on their way to the United States in the late 1990s.[51] In 2006 Mexico apprehended over 170,000 migrants.[52] Large numbers of such persons are incarcerated in detention centers funded by the United States in Guatemala and Honduras. Such efforts are consistent with Mexico's partnership in U.S. immigration control during the twentieth century. According to Kelly Lytle Hernández, "Mexican officials actively participated in the imagination and implementation of policing unsanctioned migration along the U.S.-Mexico border."[53] Third-party surrogates abroad, capturing and detaining would-be immigrants, make U.S. security a global effort.

Detaining migrants internationally at surrogate facilities, often with little oversight or accountability by U.S. officials, mirrors detention privatization domestically, increasing stealthily U.S. detention capacity and providing dramatic financial savings. It is far less expensive than detaining and deporting undocumented migrants from the United States. "The cost savings are enormous," stated one U.S. immigration representative in Honduras.[54] In 2000, for example, the United States paid only $173,000 to detain and deport six hundred smuggled migrants from Honduras at an estimated savings of $5 million.[55] Similarly U.S.-funded detention centers in Guatemala housing would-be migrants captured in Mexico are paid a fraction of the cost for daily bed space compared to centers and jails in the United States.[56] Effectively pushing the U.S. southern border and detention infrastructure into Central America, the southern migration of U.S. border policies into Latin America, much like the global relocation of the detention infrastructure in the war on terror, has resulted in an increase in criminalization of and human rights violations against immigrants as well as an increase in the militarization of Latin American borders.

Internationally the dispersion of detention operations in the war on terror has also created a sense of havoc, wherein apprehension, interrogation, and punishment are unstandardized and the absence of accountability and training fosters abuse and deflects responsibility. The U.S. wars in the Middle East, for example, have been called the most privatized war efforts on record, relying on 180,000 private contractors—more than deployed military personnel.[57] Civilian contractors are an intimate part of the detention regime, performing military and intelligence interrogations, security tasks, and medical support, and contractor ranks have been filled with former military personnel, such as when "former military psychologists working under contract for the [Central Intelligence] agency helped design the hard interrogation procedures."[58] Further, it is not insignificant that many of the civilian interrogators (not bound by military law) and military jailers at Abu Ghraib were trained in U.S. jails and immigrant detention centers. As Michelle Brown has pointed out, the biographies of the reservists in the Abu Ghraib scandal reveal a combination of experience working in U.S. prisons in addition to a total lack of corrections training or cultural knowledge of Iraq.[59] Detention, diffused globally and relying on private contractors, thus provides capacity and flexibility. It permits the deflection of government criticism of the systemic procedures of jailers and accountability of leadership, whereby culpability instead supposedly lies with a "few bad eggs" or simply the "nightshift" at Abu Ghraib. That is, as detention at home and abroad is couched in exceptionality, so are detainee abuses. Curbing carceral state violence is stymied by these constructions and other articulations of state secrets and corporate privacy, making accountability for detainee abuse the exception. Although distinct from the domestic detention of immigrants, the U.S. global detention infrastructure linked to the war on terror produces similar results: increased prison capacities and authority, profiteering and growth by private and governmental agencies, and deniability and obfuscation of detainee abuse.

From Bad to Worse: Obama's Reforms and Record-Breaking Detention Regime

Three days after the inauguration of Barack Obama in January 2009, Dana Priest reported on the front page of the *Washington Post,* "With the stroke of his pen, he effectively declared an end to the 'war on terror' . . . signaling to the world that the reach of the U.S. government in battling its enemies will not be limitless."[60] Priest was referring to the intended closure of Guantánamo Bay Naval Base as a detention site. "The house of cards is finally falling down," said Vincent Warren of the Center for Constitutional Rights, which helped to defend Guantánamo detainees.[61] The public accounting of the abuses that took place during the previous administration's war on terror, however, would never happen. In the same year the Obama administration began instituting a series of administrative reforms to the domestic detention infrastructure. Director of ICE John Morton stated, "We're trying to move away from [a] 'one size fits all'" model for detaining immigrants toward a "truly civil detention system."[62] Other reforms at ICE and the Department of Homeland Security included replacing workplace immigration raids with audits of employers' immigrant employment records, the shuttering of the Hutto family detention center (and converting it to a women's detainee facility), a retooling of the fugitive operations program targeting persons with existing deportation orders, and instituting comprehensive reviews of deportation orders to prioritize so-called violent criminal offenders.

The Obama administration drew from the long-term practices of surrogate and diffused detention enforcement in two ways: first, it distributed immense discretionary powers from the cabinet level to field officers for the detention and deportation of noncitizens or for granting relief; second, it broadly expanded the use of local partners in immigration enforcement. For example, the Department of Homeland Security under Obama deferred deportations for young immigrants who arrived without authorization as children, recognized same-sex partnerships as potential rationales for fighting deportation, and reformed the use of immigrant detainers in local jails, permitting release from jail or prison instead of uniformly initiating further detention and deportation proceedings. In other words, detention reform, with support from advocates, carefully singled out "sympathetic" detainee populations, articulating their "innocence" or exceptional vulnerabilities or merits in relation to the costliness of their detention. The execution of such discretionary relief, however, reflected old practices of uniform criminalization and zero tolerance. For example, a report from the American Immigration Lawyers Association and the American Immigration Council concluded, "The overwhelming conclusion is that most ICE offices have not changed their practices since the issuance of these new directives." "This is a classic example of leadership saying one thing and the rank and file doing another," said Gregory Chen of the AILA.[63]

In addition the diffusion of discretionary relief in the execution of detention and deportation from the president downward was accompanied by dramatic expansions in Bush-era enforcement initiatives leading to record-breaking detention and deportation statistics in each of Obama's years in office. In particular a trio of programs—the Criminal Alien Program, 287(g) Memoranda of Understanding, and Secure Communities—utilizes partnerships with local jails, police, and sheriffs' departments and has resulted in the detention and removal of over 400,000 noncitizens annually.[64] Although ICE chief Morton pledged to prioritize "serious criminal offenders," ICE has been criticized for establishing enforcement quotas in internal documents that pressure ICE officers to pursue the low-hanging fruit in a "surge" in enforcement efforts. ICE's labor union spokesperson, Chris Cane, stated, "For ICE leadership, it's not about keeping the community safe. It's about chasing this 400,000 number." These numerical goals increase the need for detention space not only because of the volume of deportation cases but because deporting criminal aliens takes on average forty-five days, instead of eleven for so-called noncriminals, which creates a shortage of detention beds and the need for expanding capacity.[65]

Criminals-first priorities guided by discretionary powers have been largely condemned as smokescreens, as majorities of detainees and deportees have included persons unconvicted or unindicted for crimes and many others who are deported for minor, nonviolent offenses. These policies placed criminality and innocence in stark relief, with the government claiming removal of the worst of the worst and advocates articulating the voices of innocent victims of the deportation regime. In other words, the prevailing solutions of the Obama reforms reinforce serious limitations for detainee advocates who often rely on the continued articulations of innocence—and thus the criminality of others—in the ongoing context of obscured detention practices. For instance, the Mexican columnist Carlos Puig lamented the return of "thousands of convicted murders, sex offenders and drug dealers being sent back to their countries or origin,"[66] reinforcing the commonly held belief, based largely on stated U.S. enforcement priorities, that deportees are indeed dangerous. Puig leaves unchallenged the basic claims and legitimacy of U.S. enforcement policy, more or less telling the United States, *You keep them.* Trolling local jails for deportable migrants and deputizing local law enforcement signal the devolution of detention operations. Immigrant criminality and the legitimacy of immigration enforcement practices are reinforced, moving immigrants into a far more flexible and unrestrained system of punishment and incarceration.

Summary

Third-party surrogate jailers have been institutionalized by the United States, compartmentalizing detention in remote and obscure entities, dodging accountability, and making collective resistance more difficult. As Angela Davis suggests, "the prison industrial complex is much more than the sum of all jails and prisons in this country. It is a set of symbiotic relationships among correctional communities, transnational corporations, media conglomerates, guards' unions, and legislative and court agendas."[67] To understand the labyrinthine U.S. immigrant detention regime, one must look at the use of surrogate partners involved in this federal authority, whether they extend national borders outward or intensify detention and deportation in the interior of the country. Further, the export of U.S. immigration policies and legal structures to our North American neighbors, allies, former colonial territories, and current military outposts requires a broader, more global purview to understand historically the global reach of U.S. imperial power and the contemporary detention authority. It's important to reiterate that immigrant detainees and enemy combatants captured in the U.S. global war on terror are two different populations with vastly different desires and designs vis-à-vis the United States. Less different, however, are the spatial and legal patterns in their incarceration, enforcement priorities and racist criminalization, and the context of national security that envelops both sets of detainees. Detention at home and abroad in a global security context is invigorated by the regime's flexibility and obscurity. The diffused and surrogate system of detention produces a pliable, biased, productive, and deeply advantageous state power over immigrants and foreigners. In short, security of the nation comes at the expense of the security of migrants and foreigners abroad. For both groups of detainees the diffused and remote systems of detention compromise physical safety and legal recourse. The intensified migration-security nexus makes aliens' and outsiders' presumed criminality more visible, while the structurally obscure system of incarceration disappears the detainee from public view.

Any confrontation, resolution, or abolition of detention at home or abroad will have to contend with the mutually constitutive migration-security nexus and its principal characteristic, obscurity. That is, existing efforts at accountability in this remote system of incarceration are structured in the very obscurity of the overall system and reflect the diffused spatiality of the detention regime. In seeking the innocence or targeted relief of particularly sympathetic detainees, the larger castigatory system remains immune to the piecemeal relief of existing detainee advocacy. A chief concern, then, is not only the international application or adoption of U.S. detention practices but the transposition and implementation of racial fears often at the foundation of U.S. immigration policies. Detention, when founded in racial xenophobia and executed with little opposition because of the legal vulnerabilities of noncitizens, will serve to cement racialized constructions of criminality, enemy behavior, or terrorist activity in the global arena. Additionally surrogate detention, as witnessed in the war on terror, does not just flow from the nation outward. Because the war on terror distorts the meaning of national security, it also has a dramatic effect on the constitution of domestic detention practices, bringing global imperatives and legal strategies home. As Jeanne Theoharis writes in her article "Guantánamo at Home," "Guantánamo is a particular way of seeing the Constitution, of constructing the landscape as a murky terrain of lurking enemies where courts become part of the bulwark against such dangers, where rights have limits and where international standards must be weighed against national security."[68] Migrants and foreigners in detention are bound to a legal system with vast extralegal methods and accepted practices that are amplified in the securitization context. Contradictory in every way, immigrant detention is morally bankrupt yet profitable, is meant to securitize the nation through the insecurity of others, and is bound by inflexible rules and consolidated authorities, yet immigrant detention is robust in its flexibility and obscurity as an enforcement mechanism.

NOTES

1. Parenti notes a parallel form of "legal cross-fertilization" along the U.S.-Mexico border in the early 1990s, when Border Patrol agents were "empowered" to perform the duties of Drug Enforcement and Customs agents, and "a de facto form" of merging enforcements when the Border Patrol works jointly with local police. Parenti writes, "Thus, when a joint INS-police patrol makes contact with a 'subject,' the police officers and Border Patrol agents can simply pass the person back and forth, from the enforcer of state criminal codes to the enforcer of federal immigration and contraband laws" (*Lockdown America*, 145).

2. Faist, "*Extension du domaine de la lutte*," 7–8.

3. Kanstroom, *Deportation Nation*, 22.

4. Neuman, *Strangers to the Constitution*, 19.

5. Hernández, "Undue Process."

6. Simanski and Sapp, "Immigration Enforcement Actions," 3–5.

7. Karen De Young, "CIA Has Quit Operating Secret Jails, Chief Says," *Washington Post*, April 10, 2009.

8. A Somali detainee, for example, was incarcerated aboard a U.S. Navy ship for two months as recently as 2011. See Ken Dilanian, "Terrorism Suspect Secretly Held for Two Months," *Los Angeles Times*, July 6, 2011.

9. De Young, "CIA Has Quit Operating Secret Jails, Chief Says."

10. Agamben, *State of Exception*, 2–4.

11. Hernández, "Undue Process."

12. Mueller, *Overblown*, 3.

13. For a critical discussion of how the spectacle of torture at Abu Ghraib obscures "the naturalized landscape" and "unspectacular" punishment of persons in U.S. prisons, see Rodríguez, "(Non)Scenes of Captivity."

14. Lahav, "The Rise of Nonstate Actors in Migration Regulation in the United States and Europe," 216, 217.

15. T. F. Schmucker, letter to the Commissioner-General of Immigration, "Recommending certain alterations of the detention station at El Paso," National Archives I, "Subject Correspondence 1906–1932," Box 45, Entry 9, Folder 51646/1-C, part 1; Swing, *Annual Report of the Immigration and Naturalization Service*, 35–36.

16. Parenti, *Lockdown America,* 141.

17. Nina Bernstein, "Officials Hid Truth of Immigrant Deaths in Jail," *New York Times,* January 9, 2010, accessed May 16, 2010, http://www.nytimes.com/2010/01/10/us/10detain.html?ref=incustodydeaths&_r=0.

18. Alisa Solomon, "Detainees Equal Dollars," *Village Voice,* August 14–20, 2002, 46.

19. Lee, *At America's Gates,* 124; Hernández, "The Crimes and Consequences of Illegal Immigration," 441.

20. Spencer S. Hsu, "Immigration Raid Jars a Small Town," *Washington Post,* May, 18, 2008, accessed August 9, 2011, http://www.washingtonpost.com/wp-dyn/content/article/2008/05/17/AR2008051702474.html.

21. Spencer S. Hsu and Sylvia Moreno, "Border Policy's Success Strains Resources," *Washington Post,* February 2, 2007; Kirk Semple, "Plan to Upgrade New Jersey Jail into Model for Immigrant Detention Centers," *New York Times,* January 27, 2011, accessed August 9, 2011, http://www.nytimes.com/2011/01/28/nyregion/28detain.html?pagewanted=all; Welch, *Detained,* 90.

22. Stephanie Chen, "Larger Inmate Population Is Boon to Private Prisons, *Wall Street Journal,* November 19, 2008, accessed July 25, 2010, http://online.wsj.com/article/SB122705334657739263.html?mod=todays_us_page_one.

23. Anna Gorman, "Immigration Detention Center Considered," *Los Angeles Times,* February 3, 2009.

24. Howard Fischer, "Napolitano Vetoes Include Mexico Prison for Mexicans," *Arizona Daily Star* (Tucson), May 3, 2005, accessed January 4, 2015, http://www.freerepublic.com/focus/f-news/1395788/posts.

25. Kevin Yamamura, "Schwarzenegger: Send Illegal Immigrant Inmates to Mexico," *Sacramento Bee,* January 25, 2010, accessed July 21, 2010, http://www.sacbee.com/static/weblogs/capitolalertlatest/2010/01/schwarzenegger-143.html.

26. Tom Barry, "Privatizing Homeland Security," Border Lines, October 28, 2009, accessed January 4, 2015, http://borderlinesblog.blogspot.com/2009/10/privatizing-homeland-security.html.

27. Lahav, "The Rise of Nonstate Actors in Migration Regulation in the United States and Europe," 228–29.

28. Nina Bernstein, "City of Immigrants Fills Jail Cells with Its Own," *New York Times,* December 27, 2008.

29. Maruskin, "Voices from Around the Country Call for INS Detention Reform," 32. The Chinese to which the *Patriot-News* article refers are the captured migrants who were smuggled aboard the ill-fated *Golden Venture* that ran aground at New York Harbor in 1993.

30. Anna Gorman, "Cities and Counties Rely on U.S. Immigrant Detention Fees," *Los Angeles Times,* March 17, 2009. In the Bay Area, in the absence of a dedicated immigrant detention facility, Santa Clara County began housing detainees in 2003. Its chief of corrections, Edward Flores, states, "It was a strategy to help us financially. . . . We have become very reliant on this revenue."

31. Gilmore, *Golden Gulag,* 106.

32. I thank Dylan Rodríguez for clarifying this critical point.

33. Chen, "Larger Inmate Population Is Boon to Private Prisons."

34. Nina Bernstein, "Few Details on Immigrants Who Died in Custody," *New York Times*, May 5, 2008, accessed January 2, 2013, http://www.nytimes.com/2008/05/05/nyregion/05detain.html?fta=y.

35. Andrew Becker, "Rebranding at ICE Meant to Soften Immigration Enforcement Agency's Image," *Washington Post*, June 17, 2010.

36. Christopher Petrella, "Private Prisons Currently Exempt from Freedom of Information Act," Nation of Change, September 25, 2012, accessed January 12, 2015, http://www.nationofchange.org/private-prisons-currently-exempt-freedom-information-act-1348581256.

37. Nina Bernstein, "Lawsuits Renew Questions on Immigrant Detention," *New York Times*, March 3, 2010.

38. "Immigration Detainees Petition Homeland Security to Issue Enforceable, Comprehensive Immigration Detention Standards," National Immigration Project of the National Lawyers Guild, press release, January 25, 2007.

39. U.S. Immigration and Customs Enforcement, "List of Deaths in ICE Custody."

40. Nina Bernstein, "U.S. Rejects a Call for Enforceable Immigration Detention Rules," *New York Times*, July 29, 2009.

41. Nina Bernstein, "U.S. to Overhaul Detention Policy for Immigrants," *New York Times*, August 6, 2009.

42. U.S. Immigration and Customs Enforcement, "Fact Sheet: The ICE T. Don Hutto."

43. Michael Martinez, "U.S. Sued over Detention of Immigrants," *Chicano Tribune*, April 9, 2007, accessed November 5, 2014, http://articles.chicagotribune.com/2007–04–09/news/0704080408_1_immigrants-border-crackdowns-catch-and-release.

44. Anabelle Garay, Associated Press, "U.N. Representative Visit to Immigration Center Rejected," May 3, 2007, accessed May 4, 2007, http://www.chron.com/disp/strory.mpl/ap/tx/4773525.html.

45. Farmer, *Pathologies of Power*, 66.

46. Shah, *Contagious Divides*.

47. Schneider et al., "Human Cargo."

48. Mitchell, "The Costs of State Power," 88. See also Wilch, "Delegation Brings Hope," 6.

49. Hiemstra, "The U.S. and Ecuador," 20, 21–22.

50. Flynn, "¿Dónde Está La Frontera?" See also Tom Barry, "Pushing Our Borders Out," IRC Americas Program Policy Brief, Hispanic Vista, February 17, 2005, accessed January 12, 2015, http://www.hispanicvista.com/hvc/Opinion/Guest_Columns/022805barry.htm.

51. Mohar and Alcaraz, "U.S. Border Controls," 146.

52. James C. McKinley, "Despite Crackdown, Migrants Stream into South Mexico," *New York Times*, January 28, 2007.

53. Hernández, "The Crimes and Consequences of Illegal Immigration," 442.

54. Flynn, "¿Dónde Está La Frontera?"

55. Frances Robles, "Illegal Immigrants Languish in Guatemala," *Miami Herald*, December 26, 2001.

56. Flynn, "¿Dónde Está La Frontera?"

57. James Risen, "Use of Iraq Contractors Costs Billions, Report Says," *New York Times*, August 11, 2008, accessed January 2, 2013, http://www.nytimes.com/2008/08/12/washington/12contractors.html.

58. Scott Shane, "C.I.A. to Close Secret Prisons, Scenes of Harsh Interrogations," *New York Times*, April 10, 2009.

59. Brown, "'Setting the Conditions' for Abu Ghraib," 983.

60. Dana Priest, "Bush's 'War' on Terror Comes to a Sudden End," *Washington Post*, January 23, 2009.

61. William Glaberson, "Rulings of Improper Detentions as the Bush Era Closes," *New York Times*, January 19, 2009.

62. Bernstein, "U.S. to Overhaul Detention Policy for Immigrants."

63. Julia Preston, "Obama Policy on Deporting Used Unevenly," *New York Times*, November 13, 2011.

64. U.S. Immigration and Customs Enforcement. "FY 2012: ICE Announces Year-end Removal Numbers."

65. Spencer S. Hsu and Andrew Becker, "ICE Officials Set Quotas to Deport More Illegal Immigrants," *Washington Post*, March 27, 2010.

66. Carlos Puig, "Crime and Banishment," *New York Times*, June 26, 2013, accessed July 10, 2013, http://latitude.blogs.nytimes.com/2013/06/26/crime-and-banishment/.

67. Davis, *Are Prisons Obsolete?*, 107.

68. Jeanne Theoharis, "Guantánamo at Home," *Nation*, April 20, 2009, 16–21.

SEVENTEEN

Of "Mates" and Men: The Comparative Racial Politics of Filipino Naval Enlistment, circa 1941–1943

JASON LUNA GAVILAN

On November 3, 1943, Mrs. D. M. Salgado, the wife of a navy enlistee, sent a letter of concern to Frank Knox, secretary of the U.S. Navy. In this letter Salgado spoke on behalf of a "collective body" of enlistees who were protesting against their placement and treatment as the "Chief Officer's Steward" and "Chief Officer's Cook." Her first complaint was that Filipinos and African Americans were the only enlistees assigned to those largely segregated positions. Her second grievance was the lack of respect given to these marginalized stewards by those ranked below them, as well as by the ones ranked above them. Her third complaint was that these officer's chief stewards lacked decent uniforms, unlike ranked chiefs from other branches of the U.S. Navy. And Salgado's fourth grievance was that the naval officers were overworking these enlisted stewards, especially during the busy holiday celebrations.[1]

What were the structural conditions, particularly during World War II, that permitted the marginalization and exploitation of Filipinos, African Americans, and other ethnoracial minorities as enlisted stewards in the U.S. Navy? Why did Salgado, and likely other navy wives and civilians, write letters of protest to navy officials regarding the placement and treatment of their enlisted counterparts—rather than the enlistees themselves—during this time of war? How did the wartime response(s) of navy officials, or lack thereof, confirm such racial hierarchies in the U.S. Navy while spurring further challenges to the racial order by civilians and enlistees during World War II? In this essay I closely examine these questions by drawing upon a wide array of military and civilian correspondence, largely between 1941 and 1943. Such correspondence includes letters and telegrams between navy officials, along with letters between civilians and officials, especially regarding the comparative racial policies and politics of Filipino enlistment.

I address these questions and correspondence under the scope of comparative race and ethnicity, making three main arguments. First, Filipinos were one segment in a complex web of military segregation and service desires among white naval officers, particularly during World War II. Whereas some naval officers preferred Filipino enlistees serving such needs, others preferred African Americans, Mexican Americans, Chamorros, or Chinese Americans as cooks, messmen, and stewards. Factors determining such preferences often were contingent upon regional dominance or dominant conceptualizations of at least one of these minority groups on these U.S. bases. While local bases and transnational military bureaus had conflicting racial and ethnic preferences for their mess attendants, the continual policies and politics of enlistment among people of color in the U.S. Navy, coupled with the increasing U.S. wartime interventions abroad, facilitated the escalating recruitment of people of color as marginalized cooks, stewards, and messmen by navy officials during World War II.

Second, I argue that civilian responses by D. M. Salgado and others to the exclusive placement and discriminatory treatment of Filipinos and other ethnoracial minorities in the U.S. Navy suggest the relatively increasing power of women in the heterofamily in catalyzing social change within the U.S. nation-state. Their letters of protest on behalf of racialized enlistees in the U.S. Navy demonstrate their increasing political power during the wartime period. Simultaneously these acts of protest demonstrated the limited agency of ethnoracial enlistees in vocalizing or collectively organizing their own grievances against the policies and practices of inclusive minority enlistment during World War II.

Third, the strategic responses (or lack thereof) by naval officials to civilians' grievances were part and parcel of what I call the politics of enlistment. In the specific context of U.S.-Philippine relations, the politics of Filipino enlistment, as practiced in naval officials' inclusive enlistment and exclusive marginalization of Filipinos as cooks, stewards, and messmen, shaped the contours and tensions of what I call the "U.S.-Philippine nation" during the wartime period, particularly on the ground level. For these officials the U.S.-Philippine nation was defined just as much by the inclusion of Philippine commonwealth subjects as allied forces of the U.S. Empire as it was by the ethnoracial separation and subjugation of these subjects as cooks, messmen, and stewards in the U.S. domestic militarized space. In other words, the conditions for their inclusion were also conditions for their exclusion within the U.S. nation-state. This specific tension between inclusion and exclusion facilitated the politics of Filipino enlistment and the enlistment of other foreign nationals, colonial subjects, and racial minorities. One naval official in particular, W. E. Moore, was an exceptionally important figure who implemented racial policies of enlistment during (and following) World War II. I examine his correspondence to officials and civilians regarding the marginal enlistment of foreign nationals, colonial subjects, and racial minorities in the U.S. Navy during this time. My primary focus is on Filipino enlistment set in the larger context of U.S. military segregation.

The Politics of U.S. Navy Minority Enlistment: 1941–1943

Between 1941 and 1943 more and more enlistees were being deployed in the infantry and armed forces.[2] This left vacancies in the mess branch.[3] To fill this vacancy U.S. naval officials turned primarily to African Americans and secondarily to Filipinos, Chamorros, and other minorities. In other words, U.S. officials preferred African Americans over Filipinos and other ethnic minorities as enlisted stewards during the early stages of U.S. involvement in World War II. For instance, in order to address the increasing demand for mess attendants, the director of enlisted personnel, H. A. Badt, made the recommendation to recruit a "limited quota" of Filipino mess attendants into Class v6 of the U.S. Naval Reserve.[4] Badt immediately followed by stating his actual preference for "sufficient Negroes" over Filipinos if African Americans were able to fulfill his "limited quota." His third and last request in his memorandum emphasized the following: "If such enlistments are authorized it is recommended that these mess attendants pass through 3 weeks detention in Cavite and then be transferred to ships of the Asiatic Fleet for training. It will be necessary to find out what facilities obtain in the Sixteenth Naval District for such detention."[5] It is unclear whether Badt is referring to Filipinos or African Americans, or simply a conflated group of nonwhite messmen. American recruits, likely including African Americans, were shipped to detention centers in the Philippines and elsewhere in the Asia-Pacific Theater. These new recruits stayed in detention centers (primarily living in barracks) while undergoing extensive physical and mental training before they became officially enlisted in the U.S. Navy. The general purpose of boot camp training centers was to make newly recruited enlistees as physically and mentally capable as possible for military service. This included intense daily regimens that tested their disciplinary capabilities, mental fortitude, and physical endurance.

While detention centers served primarily as living facilities for the new recruits, *detention* seems to be used especially in reference to newly recruited people of color, as evidenced in Badt's statement. By placing these new recruits in detention, officials aimed to confine—if not isolate—them from the civilian population before they became the enlistees that U.S. officials sought. Detention would effectively discipline, make loyal, and confirm the obedience of recruited messmen in accordance with the national standards of their official (white) superiors. The systematic isolation of these new recruits of color in training centers before their official integration in the U.S. Navy arguably parallels the process of immigration detention in places like Angel Island in San Francisco and Ellis Island in New York City. Whereas military training at the detention center prioritized minority integration through immediate behavioral and physical modification, the immigration detention center privileged minority exclusion through extensive interrogations, health inspections, and legal classifications of incoming immigrants, resulting in admission or deportation. Despite the distinctive natures of the two types of detention centers, the common intent and outcome of including citizen and noncitizen minorities under conditions of subjugation (if not subservience) made them central to the politics of inclusion, effecting a simultaneous integration and segregation within the United States.[6]

Nonetheless the U.S. Navy's preference for African American over Filipino enlistees was evident in different geographical and temporal contexts where demands for mess enlistees were increasing. For instance, a September, 24, 1941 memorandum to the chief of the Bureau of Navigation from Commandant A. C. Read of the U.S. Naval Air Station in Pensacola, Florida, announced several related matters. First, Commandant Read requested training preparations for seventy newly enlisted mess attendants on a four-week basis. Second, he requested more mess attendants to work in the mess branch of the Pensacola Naval Station. His third request adhered more to the racial politics of enlistment prevalent in this period: "The Bureau is requested, when filling existing vacancies in the mess attendant complement of this station, to send Negroes, rather than Filipinos, especially in the cooks and stewards ratings."[7] While it may have been cheaper for U.S. naval officials to hire regionally available African American citizens within the United States rather than Filipino foreign nationals from the Philippine archipelago, the bottom line was that naval officials were formally restricted from enlisting Filipinos during the Philippine Commonwealth period (though they were still enlisted informally through individual official requests). Based on that formal restriction, African Americans were more readily and legally available during this early stage of the war—and Filipinos apparently were not.[8]

Despite the fact that Filipinos in the Philippines were not yet allowed to be officially recruited into the U.S. Navy, those who were previously enlisted legally during the Philippine-American colonial period (1901–34) were continually reenlisted and transferred within the circuits, or registers, of the U.S. naval stations and ships on both coasts of the continental United States. In some cases messmen of other ethnicities were included in such policies of transfer. In a 1941 telegram to the Bureau of Naval Personnel (previously the Bureau of Navigation) the Immigration and Naturalization Service requested confirmation that the present policy of transferring messmen was to "transfer Chinese and Filipino MATS [mess attendants] [in] San Francisco and other MATS [in] Norfolk."[9]

The significance of transferring existing and former personnel, especially personnel of color, is that it permitted the continuing racial and ethnic inclusion of minorities in the U.S. military—on the condition that the military would not have to recruit more racial and ethnic minorities in the process. This allowed officials to continue reenlisting Filipinos, especially those in the United States, during the Philippine Commonwealth period. This policy would also give officials the privilege of transferring personnel who, for any reason, did not perform in accordance with the standards of these (white) officials. Thus the transfer policy of Filipino and Chinese personnel likely added one more layer of racial and ethnic exclusion in the U.S. military—in addition to the placement and marginalization of enlisted minorities as cooks, messmen, and stewards.

The U.S. Navy's racial and or ethnic preference among mess attendant recruits was also contingent upon the local base's position in relation to the multiethnic civilian space immediately surrounding it. For instance, in early 1942 an officer from the Naval Air Station in Corpus Christi, Texas, sent a brief telegram to the Bureau of Naval Personnel requesting more information on the "races which can be enlisted [in the] messman branch." This naval official (whose name is not mentioned) specifies his "desire [for] enlist[ed] white officers[,] stewards[,] and cooks[,] and men of Mexican extraction for messmen if applicable." Given the historically high population of whites and Mexicans in Corpus Christi, it is likely that the officers on this base had a conceptual preference for and positive relationship with white officers and white and Mexican messmen.

The Bureau of Naval Personnel responded with a telegram on May 21 stating that the "enlistment [of] men of Mexican extraction . . . [was] not approved" and that the current instructions for recruitment permitted "enlistment of negro . . . , filipino and chinese extraction only as messmen."[10] What is significant about this telegram is that it illustrates the politics of blackness, whiteness, and citizenship within these enlisted service jobs of the U.S. Navy Stewards Branch. The Navy Bureau was not willing to enlist Mexicans, who were considered racially white before and during this period. Instead Mexicans were more likely accepted for service jobs in the defense industry and as soldiers on the front line.

The telegram also illustrates that local bases and transnational military bureaus had conflicting racial and ethnic preferences for their mess attendants. The translocal Naval Air Station in Corpus Christi desired Mexican enlistees from the civilian spaces immediately surrounding the base. However, the transnational-based Naval Bureau preferred the enlistment of Filipinos and Chinese to all militarized stations across the globe. Given the structural superiority of the Bureau of Naval Personnel in matters of mess enlistment, it is more than likely that this and other naval stations enlisted more Filipinos and Chinese as mess attendants, regardless of the civilian racial and ethnic demographic immediately surrounding the local militarized zone. More particularly, Filipinos continued to be restricted to work only as messmen, alongside African American and Chinese men.

While African Americans, Filipinos, and Chinese have historically (and unevenly) been normativized to work in positions of subservience, there appear to be no direct reasons or logic as to why the Naval Bureau preferred particular racial or ethnic minorities over others as enlisted messmen in specific temporal and geographic contexts. Even one of the officials stationed at Corpus Christi asked the following question to the Bureau of Naval Personnel in 1942: "Is there any reason why we can't enlist U.S. citizen Mess Attendants?"[11] It seems there was no clear and logical response to this inquiry, but in response to the ambiguity and partially regional nature of racial recruitments, there began to be increasing pressure to develop more national standards for recruitment and enlistment of messmen personnel. In 1941, for example, the African American community exerted pressure on the Roosevelt administration to develop national standards of racial inclusion in the U.S. military and defense industry. Shortly after the March on Washington that year, Roosevelt agreed to implement Executive Order 8802, enforcing equal racial opportunity in the defense industry on the condition that the March on Washington drop its demand that the military be desegregated. Despite this compromise, debates surrounding the standards of military segregation, and the racialization of the Stewards Branch in particular, are still evident in correspondence between civilians and military officials during the 1940s. These standards, as confirmed by the Bureau of Naval Personnel, would be determined in reaction to civilian responses, many by women, to the working conditions and racial criteria of the messmen.

Women, Civilians, and the Shifting Politics of Naval Minority Enlistment

The role of women in U.S. domestic and public spaces was changing during the World War II period, particularly as American male soldiers were away fighting, leaving mass employment vacancies in the industrial and defense sectors. The wartime increase in women's employment also occurred in response to political and public pressure to promote and enforce gender equality in the workplace, especially after President Franklin Delano Roosevelt's global proclamation of the United States as the "arsenal of democracy." Pressure by First Lady Eleanor Roosevelt and other political figures enhanced women's integration in the military and industrial workplace. Subsequently more women worked in factories that were supplying weapons and machinery to the U.S. Armed Forces or as enlisted nurses, photographers, and in some cases spies in the U.S. Army.[12] More than 350,000 women worked in medical and administrative fields of the auxiliary military as well.[13] Many also enrolled as college students in educational institutions.[14] While white women in particular were placed in higher paying and learning positions within these industries, more women of color—African American women in particular—were often hired in domestic work positions in civilian households.[15] Some of these women also emphasized their presence in the military sphere, specifically when it came to matters regarding the placement and treatment of their enlisted steward counterparts. Several of these women were wives or relatives of these enlisted men. Navy wife D. M. Salgado was one example, as mentioned at the outset.[16]

Military strategies toward addressing public complaints about the placement and treatment of enlisted cooks, stewards, and messmen—whether by women, political officials, or other concerned citizens—were being discussed as early as 1941.

In a January 24, 1941, memo to the Bureau of Navigation the commander in chief of the U.S. Fleet expresses considerable concern about press statements on the working and living conditions in the mess branch. Rather than trying to solve the problem itself (i.e., race and class discrimination), the commander suggests ways to avoid press complaints about treatment of the messmen.[17]

Similar concerns about public inquiries were evident two years later in a letter prepared on October 11, 1943, by Assistant Chief of Bureau Rear Admiral L. E. Denfield in response to a letter from U.S. Senator Arthur H. Vandenburg. Denfield emphasizes the voluntary nature of "all personnel entering the Stewards Branch of the Navy" rather than the actual placement of these personnel by the officers themselves. Hence "no one is forced into the Stewards Branch or transferred to that branch without his consent." He also points out how "important to the welfare and fighting efficiency of the Navy" these men of the Stewards Branch really are and adds, "It is regrettable that there are some who do not realize the importance of the part they are playing in the war effort."[18]

While Denfield and other officers were quick to respond to the concerns of more privileged and powerful figures such as the senator, they appear less willing to address the concerns of women such as Salgado. Direct responses by navy officials to Salgado's complaint are not evident in the written historical record. Perhaps (white) navy officials simply did not feel it was necessary to address or redress complaints by a likely civilian of color who was directly affiliated with one of the cooks, stewards, or messmen of color. Or perhaps the officials' response to Salgado's complaint is simply yet to be found.

Nevertheless it is likely that Salgado's complaint preceded inquiries by other civilians (including Senator Vandenburg) challenging officials who denied or justified the racial subjugation of ethnic minorities, foreign nationals, and colonial subjects in the U.S. Navy.

From "Cooks" to "Steward's Mates": Reinforcing the Politics of Minority Enlistment

External pressure from civilians' material concerns for the welfare of the mess attendants and internal dialogues such as navy officials' perceptions of the "lack of efficiency" among African American mess attendants prompted the Bureau of Naval Personnel to ponder the mess conditions and to offer suggestions on ensuring stability and mess attendant efficiency on base. These suggestions were also intended to ameliorate civilians' concerns for the enlistees. In a January 20, 1943, memorandum to the director of mess training, a military official in the Bureau of Naval Personnel, W. E. Moore, attributed the problem to several factors, largely regarding the issue of race. The Bureau's immediate concern was the circulation of newspaper publications read by African American mess attendants, particularly the *Chicago Defender* and "several other Negro publications." In the memorandum Officer Moore claims that the *Chicago Defender* specifically publicized civilian issues of black employment that generated unrest among African American mess attendants dissatisfied with their labor conditions on base.[19] Moore attributes their unrest to their reading of such materials containing "inflammatory matter." He further states that if not for the availability of these "Negro publications," such situations of unrest and instability "would not otherwise have occurred."[20]

It is not clear in the written historical records the extent to which these ethnic news reports exposed the maltreatment of African American enlistees, or the degree to which U.S. naval officers were successful in censoring these news reports in the militarized space. However, it is clear that naval officials were anxious about the increased enlistment and visibility of African Americans as cooks, messmen, and stewards and about the potential unrest due to newspapers as politically powerful as the *Chicago Defender* in and beyond the African American community. Officers' anxieties arguably spurred not only efforts to place African Americans in other enlisted positions but also their replacement as cooks, messmen, and stewards by Filipinos and other minorities.

In addition one cannot underestimate the influence that Moore had on navy policy in matters of minority enlistment. Not only did he reinforce the racialist terms of minority enlistment during World War II, but his policies also beget more racism in the postwar U.S. military. While his historical relevance is largely undermined in many previous studies on minority enlistment, his empirical relevance in this study is certainly not. In fact one can even argue that his pattern of hiring and limiting the enlistment of racial and ethnic minorities as stewards was the hallmark of racial policies of segregation in the military. The racialist logic that facilitated white supremacist notions of U.S. Empire also guided Moore's policies of enlistment and segregation of African Americans and other ethnoracial minorities in the U.S. Navy.

Racial legacies and essentialist traces of nineteenth-century social Darwinism permeated and reinforced the racialist logic of Moore's leadership, who wrote his January 30, 1943, letter on (primarily) African American mess attendant enlistment. Along with the circulation of African American publications in militarized spaces, Moore suggested the mess attendants' "low intelligence" was a source of their conflicts with officers and their "lack of efficiency" in work performance. He concluded, "If it were possible to raise the average intelligence of Negro recruit mess attendants above those that were brought in a year ago, and [are] now being brought in, the mess attendant problem aboard ship would be made easier."[21]

In his attempt to look at "all interrelated factors" on this issue, Moore also held some naval officers accountable for their conflicts with the messmen:

> A small percentage of officers have a poor attitude toward, and lack of consideration for, members of the messmen branch, be they Filipinos or Negroes. By and large, these officers are equally inconsiderate of other enlisted men outside the messman branch. In other words, most officers who can handle enlisted men can handle messmen well, and vice versa. It is true that a very limited number of officers, due to previous environment prior to entering the service, have had no experience whatever with servants of any sort, and do not treat them fairly. These few officers are found among newly graduated regulars as well as among newly commissioned reserves.[22]

This excerpt illuminates several interesting points. First, officers who had more experience being served by stewards of color were more "friendly" in their racialist attitudes toward these stewards than the newer officers, who tended to display "a poor attitude" toward African American and Filipino enlistees. Second, Moore, a massively influential policymaker of minority enlistment, had dichotomous racial perceptions that transpired in the way he approached the problematic encounters between white officers and stewards of color. In other words, Moore was not looking at the environment informing and shaping the lives of African American and Filipino mess attendants as much as he was pondering the reasons for the lack of efficiency and intelligence among the white naval officers. This evident dichotomy between racialist essentialism toward enlisted mess attendants and the sense of historical understanding toward his fellow officers shaped the politics of enlistment among mess attendants and also determined the actual proposals, practices, and policies of enlistment among racial and ethnic minorities during the wartime period. On the one hand, according to Moore, the messmen of color, rather than the broader structures of racial hierarchy and prejudice, were the primary problem that needed correction. On the other hand, Moore considered the "few" problematic officers to be inexperienced individuals who just needed some extra teaching and guidance to be as "benevolent" toward the stewards as the veteran officers were—primarily in order to stabilize and preserve the existing racial order in the U.S. Navy. More specifically Moore's recommendations include the extended education and institutional training of the captain assisting the president of the Mess Branch, as well as the officers whom the messmen served. Moore writes, "It is believed that the required reading and explanation of the Navy Training Course for Messman Branch at the Naval Academy and at the Indoctrination Schools would reduce the number of officers who are totally unfamiliar with the servant problem in general."[23] In other words, with additional education and training white officers would be taught proper behavior in the racial order of the U.S. military.

Another suggestion that Moore proposed, which actually came to fruition later in the war, was changing the name of the ratings, which at the time was "cooks" or "messmen." The purpose of the name change was to improve the working relationships between officers and messmen on base and to secure the structural stability of the domestic confines of the navy space. In his memorandum Moore first suggests changing the name to "Officers' Mates," but he immediately discounts this recommendation because he believes it does not "appropriately" define the mess attendants' working relationship with their superior officers and does not address "the question of miscegenation" between officers and mates.[24]

Why Moore used the term *miscegenation* is not entirely clear. In the context of his correspondence he likely did not believe that the name *officers' mates* defined clearly enough the racial, gendered, and class-based boundaries between the officers and their servants within the militarized and domestic space of the mess rooms and officers' headquarters. Subsequently he writes, "If any change of the rating is eventually made, the terms 'Stewards' Mates' or 'Stewards' Assistants' are suggested." In order to support this change he patronizingly recalls his own experience and observations about the pride and collective sense of responsibility felt by the people assigned to such positions, as well as the domestic and additional work required from it.[25]

Thus Moore's documented naval correspondence is historically vital because it expresses the need to stabilize and secure discursively an already existent racial and ethnic hierarchy in the U.S. Navy. Taking up Moore's suggestions, officials within and beyond the navy eventually approved the name changes for messmen. On February 15, 1943, the chief of naval personnel submitted the name changes to Secretary of the Navy Frank Knox for approval. Subsequently the Messman's Branch became the Stewards' Branch; the officer's chief steward became chief steward; the officer's chief cook became chief cook; the officer's steward, first class became steward's mate, first class. The name changes also applied to the second and third classes of the enlisted ranks in the U.S. Navy, and so on. Collectively known as the 1943 Naval Appropriation Act, these policies created changes mostly in terminology, not in the actual pay or "rating insignia, duties, and qualifications"—which would remain unchanged.[26]

The name changes reflected a desire for a boost in image and morale. Naval officials believed "that assignment to this rating branch would be more desirable and would attract a better class of personnel."[27] Naval officials thought that the name changes would enhance the image of the mess branch for those working within the branch, those recruited into the branch, and concerned civilians. Eleven days later, on February 26, 1943, the secretary of the navy transmitted an updated version of the approved memorandum to the Planning and Control Division of the Bureau of Naval Personnel. While this version confirmed the official name changes from the previous memorandum, it also emphasized the conditions in which the name changes did *not* apply. As previously stated, such conditions included enlistees' previous terms of duty in their service records, health records, and pay accounts—up until the official date of the change itself (February 26, 1943). After that date all official references to enlistees would be made according to their newly named rank.[28]

Another condition of the name changes was temporal-based. Naval officials considered the transition to the common usage of the new terminology to be "indefinite." Because of this they allowed (and in turn practiced) the interchangeability of the old and new names. The purpose of this interchangeability, according to naval officials, was for "establishing identity of men in the Steward's branch."[29] Therefore, while naval officials rhetorically formalized the name changes on behalf of the enlistees and concerned civilians, these same naval officials *informally*—if not contradictorily—permitted use of the old names along with the new in the discursive space (e.g., service records, officers' correspondence) and the material space (e.g., naval ships and stations).

While on paper the purpose of this interchangeability was to establish "the identity of men in the steward's branch," one can argue that such interchangeability was more for the naval officials *themselves* to determine the stewards' identity and enforce their own identity as "superiors." Simultaneously and subsequently the continued use of old ranks and classifications reinforced the class- and race-based boundaries between the subjects of the Stewards' Branch and the officers. These hierarchical boundaries, as evident from previously cited historical records, were determined and continued to racialize, feminize, and spatially segregate the people of color enlisted as "stewards" rather than "mess attendants."

Summary

Between 1941 and 1943 the U.S. nation-state's inclusionary and exclusionary politics of Filipino enlistment served to reinforce the United States as an empire in the general sense and to reconfigure its hegemony in the Philippines in particular. Throughout the twentieth century the U.S. nation-state considered the Philippines a strategic military site for expanding and policing socioeconomic interests overseas. Additionally the U.S. Navy consistently saw wartime recruitment of Filipinos and other racial, foreign, and colonial subjects as integral to the U.S. imperial project, despite their evident anxieties that these minorities would integrate into the U.S. nation-state. While their policies of inclusion shaped the enlistment and relative privileging of various ethnoracial minorities within and beyond the navy, their politics of enlistment facilitated the marginalization of minorities within the Stewards Branch to work as cooks and messmen and in other segregated military units.

Although the uneven segregation and mistreatment of racial and ethnic minorities in the U.S. military is clear, 1944 and 1945 were watershed years in inclusive enlistment of ethnic minorities in general, particularly Filipinos. Filipino and African American enlistment grew dramatically. Moreover in 1944 and 1945 the United States and the Philippines shared disdain for the daily atrocities committed by Japanese occupying forces in the Philippines and applauded the increasing fervor among surviving Filipinos in their local provinces for the return of General MacArthur's allied forces to aid in the evacuation of Japanese forces from the archipelago. In this context the U.S. Navy resumed official enlistment of Filipino and other minoritized stewards in 1944. Simultaneously the Selective Service Act of 1944 made these minority enlistees eligible for GI Bill benefits.[30]

Despite congressional passage of the GI Bill and grassroots emergence of the Double Victory movement in the racial desegregation of the defense industry, minority enlistees were still largely placed and marginalized as cooks, messmen, or stewards in the U.S. Navy during these watershed years of minority enlistment, and civilian women continued to protest the nature of minority exploitation and segregation in the U.S. Navy. In 1944 and 1945 several women wrote to military officials about the enlistees' lack of paid uniform allowances, the continued placement of minorities as stewards, the replacement of Filipino stewards with African Americans, and the private enlistment of stewards for individual navy officers rather than for the U.S. Navy.[31] Officials continued to acknowledge and ameliorate the women's concerns. Thus the politics of enlistment simultaneously signified continued de facto discrimination in an era of de jure equality, much as it would on the postwar home front. Not until 1948 did Truman's Executive Order 9981 formally enforce black-white racial integration in the U.S. military, and not until 1973 did the order apply officially to Filipinos, when Admiral Elmo Zumwalt promised the horizontal and upward mobility of Filipinos into a relatively wider array of naval ranks—not merely as mates but as seamen.[32]

NOTES

Without the following people and groups, the publication of this essay might not have been possible: the Critical Ethnic Studies Editorial Collective for accepting my essay for further revision and completion; Scott Kurashige, Damon Salesa, Sarita See, Rudolf Mrázek, and Nadine Naber for your support and guidance of my research on this essay since its initial conception; Matthew Andrews, Joi Barrios, Jan Christian Bernabe, Sony Corañez Bolton, Bradley Cardozo, Deirdre de la Cruz, Vicente Diaz, Maria Paz Gutierrez Esguerra, Marco Garrido, Aprilfaye Manalang, Ricky Punzalan, Cynthia Marasigan, Victor Román Mendoza, Dean Ijutsi Saranillio, Charley Sullivan, Ginang Deling Weller, and the Philippine Study Group and the Philippine Study Group Student Association; the Students of Color of Rackham for accepting my paper on this topic for your 2007 conference, along with Mark Villegas, Josephine Sirineo, and other conference participants, panelists, and attendees who commented on my presentation; Vernadette Gonzalez, Brandi McDougall, Mari Yoshihara, Robert Perkinson, and Dylan Rodríguez for your inquiries and input in previous meetings and conferences; the Filipino American National Historical Society for your insightful critiques and reflections on earlier configurations of this essay; cohort and founding members of the Asian/Pacific Islander American Caucus at the University of Michigan for your unwavering support—Brian Chung, Cathryn Fabian, Monica Kim, Isabella Quintana, Mark A. Villacorta, among many more folks; Jesse Carr, Christina Finley, Jessica Gan, Sharon Heijin Lee, Isabel Millan, Kiri Sailiata, Lani Teves, Lee Ann Wang, Kathy Zasur, and the Critical Ethnic Studies Writing Workshop for providing comprehensive critiques of an outlined version of this essay; David Hernández from the Critical Ethnic Studies Editorial Collective for your support, guidance, and concise editorship; Francis A. Gealogo, Marichi C. Guevara, and the Institute of Philippine Culture at Ateneo de Manila University for allowing me to continue this work during the postdoctoral stage of my academic career; and last but not least, many thanks to you, the reader, for taking the time to read and possibly comment on this essay. All errors and omissions are my own.

1. Mrs. D. M. Salgado, letter to Frank Knox, Secretary of the Navy, and Bureau of Naval Personnel, November 3, 1943, pp. 1–2, Record Group 24, Stack Area 470, Box 901, Row 53, Compartment 5, Shelf 2, National Archives and Records Administration (hereafter NARA), College Park, Maryland.

2. My temporal focus on the early to middle World War II period of Filipino enlistment is not meant to erase the period of American colonization in the Philippines prior to the war. In fact between 1901 and 1934 Filipino enlistment was instrumental in

assisting the U.S. war, annexation, and colonization of the Philippines. Rather, in the context of Asian American historical scholarship particularly, it is meant to decenter our understanding of Asian immigration as a post-1965 phenomenon, limited to migrating bodies on the U.S. mainland. Moreover, from a historiographical standpoint, I counter Jesse Quinsaat's claim in "An Exercise on How to Join the Navy . . . and Still Not See the World" (*Counterpoint: Perspectives on Asian America*, Emma Gee et al., Los Angeles: Asian American Studies Center, 1976) that Filipinos were not recruited as enlisted messmen during World War II until the watershed year of 1944, when the U.S. Navy recruited massive numbers of enlistees as messmen (Filipino and African American) from the Philippines. On the contrary, Filipinos were sought after as messmen prior to 1944 through existing enlistees, reenlisted or transferred naval personnel, and eventually from the islands, and also were mentioned in pre-1944 naval correspondence.

3. For example, in a 1941 memorandum Captain H. A. Badt, director of enlisted personnel, reported to the assistant chief of the Bureau of Navigation that, given the high demand and low recruitment of messmen, there was a need to fill messmen vacancies. H.A. Badt, Director of Enlisted Personnel, memorandum to USN Captain to Assistant Chief of Bureau of Navigation, "Subject: Recruitment of Filipinos . . . as Mess Attendants," 1941, p. 1, Record Group 24, Stack Area 470, Box 901, Row 53, Compartment 5, Shelf 2, NARA.

4. Enlistees who are classified by the U.S. Naval Reserve as Class V6 specialize in "general service." This includes specialties in generally any field in the naval service (mess stewardship included). This categorization is inclusive to any naval enlistment rank, whether third class, second class, first class, or chief petty officer.

5. Badt memorandum, 1.

6. Since the American Revolutionary War the promise of citizenship historically compelled African Americans to enlist in the U.S. military in times of war. In turn U.S. officials have displayed more trust in minority populations who fight in U.S. wars, especially on the front lines, as stewards, or in other less privileged positions. In various celebratory public narratives, African Americans have been portrayed fighting side by side with white Americans on behalf of the ideals of freedom, justice, and liberty. However, the promise and portrayal of citizenship were met with the daily realities and varying degrees of segregation in the civilian U.S. nation-state as well as in the military. For African Americans military loyalty also included subservient labor with peers, such as Filipino noncitizens.

7. A. C. Read Commandant, U.S. Naval Air Station, Pensacola, Florida, memorandum to Chief of Bureau of Navigation, "Subject: Mess Attendant Training," September 24, 1941, p. 1, Record Group 24, Stack Area 470, Box 901, Row 53, Compartment 5, Shelf 2, NARA.

8. One might also make the case that U.S. officials in Pensacola preferred African American messmen because of a historically affirmative relationship between officers and messmen on that base, as well as the likely large local population of civilian African Americans. This point of inquiry can be an additional topic for further research.

9. Immigration and Naturalization Services, telegram to Bureau of Naval Personnel, 1941, p. 1, Record Group 24, Stack Area 470, Box 901, Row 53, Compartment 5, Shelf 2, NARA.

10. Webb C. Haynes, Bureau of Naval Personnel, Washington, DC, telegram to Naval Air Station Corpus Christi, "Enlistment of Men of Mexican Extraction not approved . . . Current Recruiting Instructions Permit Men of Negro Filipino and Chinese Extraction only as Messmen," May 21, 1942, p. 1, Record Group 24, Stack Area 470; Box 901, Row 53, Compartment 5, Shelf 2, NARA.

11. NAS Corpus Christi, Texas, telegram to Bureau of Naval Personnel, ". . . Is there any reason why we can't enlist Mexican US citizens [as] mess attendants?," May 13, 1942, p. 1, Record Group 24, Stack Area 470, Box 901, Row 53, Compartment 5, Shelf 2, NARA.

12. Weatherford, *American Women and World War II.*

13. Chambers, *Oxford Guide to American Military History*, 808.

14. Norton et al., *A People and a Nation*, 751.

15. Brown and Stentiford, *The Jim Crow Encyclopedia*, 245.

16. Salgado letter, 1–2.

17. Commander in Chief, U.S. Fleet, USS *New Mexico* Flagship, Washington, DC, memorandum to FLEET [?], "Mess Attendants, Examination of Living and Messing Conditions," January 24, 1941, pp. 1–2, Record Group 24, Stack Area 470, Box 901, Row 53, Compartment 5, Shelf 2, NARA.

18. Commander in Chief memorandum, 1–2.

19. Moore did not elaborate in this written correspondence on which specific issues of the *Chicago Defender* he was referring to. I hope to further investigate the *Chicago Defender* and other "ethnic press" during this period to better assess their impact on the policies and politics of naval enlistment, especially the enlistment of African Americans and other ethnic minorities.

20. W. E. Moore, Bureau of Naval Personnel, Washington, DC, memorandum to Director of Training, "Comments Letter Re Mess Attendants," January 30, 1943, pp. 1–2, Record Group 24, Stack Area 470, Box 901, Row 53, Compartment 5, Shelf 2, NARA.

21. Moore memorandum, 1.

22. Moore memorandum, 1.

23. Moore memorandum, 2.

24. Moore memorandum, 2.

25. Moore memorandum, 2.

26. Chief of Naval Personnel, Washington, DC, memorandum to Frank Knox, Secretary of the Navy, February 15, 1943, pp. 1–2, Record Group 24, Stack Area 470, Box 901, Row 53, Compartment 5, Shelf 2, NARA.

27. Chief of Naval Personnel memorandum, 1–2.

28. Frank Knox, Secretary of the Navy, Washington, DC, memorandum to Planning and Control Division of the Bureau of Naval Personnel, February 26, 1943, pp. 1–2, Record Group 24, Stack Area 470, Box 901, Row 53, Compartment 5, Shelf 2, NARA.

29. Knox memorandum, 2; such interchangeability was also noted in Chief of Naval Personnel, Washington, DC, memorandum to BurPers Planning, February 1943, pp. 2, Record Group 24, Stack Area 470, Box 901, Row 53, Compartment 5, Shelf 2, NARA.

30. The GI Bill was a main source of what Lipsitz called "the possessive investment in whiteness" because the bill was constrained by domestic racism and how the money was distributed. Ira Katznelson also makes this argument in *When Affirmative Action Was White: An Untold History of Racial Inequality in Twentieth-Century America* (New

York: W.W. Norton, 2005). Nevertheless the impact of the GI Bill, coupled with the 1940 Nationality Act that promised citizenship after three years of military service, on informing and shaping the wartime enlistment of U.S. racial and ethnic minorities and foreign nationals in general cannot be overstated. The GI Bill promised benefits for veterans that included subsidized navy housing and residence on bases, retirement pensions, college grants, public college tuition fee waivers for familial descendents under the age of twenty-four, postwar civilian employment services and training, mortgage loan guarantees for home purchases, and cash payments for the honorably discharged and unemployed personnel. For many enlisted racial and ethnic groups and foreign nationals, including Chamorro, African American, Japanese American, Chinese American, Mexican American, Puerto Rican, Native American, and Filipino enlistees, the GI Bill provided material means for U.S. citizenship and upward financial mobility. Moreover, while the 1946 Rescission Act barred allied Philippine national soldiers from obtaining similar benefits, for others enlisted into the main branches of the U.S. military as foreign nationals, the promises of the GI Bill were more likely to be realized.

31. Mrs. Paul Gurley and Mildred I. Yemmans, for example, questioned—if not criticized—the continuing placement, marginalization, and exploitation of ethnoracial minorities as cooks or stewards during 1944 and 1945. Parallel to and distinct from their responses to Salgado and Vandenburg, military officials reacted to Gurley's and Yemmans's complaints by reassuring them of the U.S. Navy's positive—if not dignified—placement and treatment of enlistees of color as chief cooks and stewards. However, officials also emphasized the structural integrity of those placed in this branch of duty by proclaiming that "*it was not intended that cooks and stewards would exert military authority* or assume the responsibility of petty officers, and, therefore, they have not been classified as such [italics mine]." Additionally "all grades of cooks and stewards receive the same uniform allowances as chief petty officers, in view of similarity in type and hence cost of uniform." One official's final response to Gurley's concerns in particular was highlighted in the following statement: "It is the considered opinion of this Bureau [of Naval Personnel] that the best interests of the service are served by the present policy, and you may be advised that no change is contemplated. The Bureau, however, appreciates the thought which prompted your inquiry." Mrs. Paul Gurley, Chula Vista, California, letter to Naval Bureau of Naval Personnel, January 1944, p. 1; W. F. Calkins, Lt. Cmdr., USN, Washington, DC, letter to Mrs. Paul Gurley, February 14, 1944, pp. 1–2; Mildred I. Yemmans, Newark, New Jersey, letter to Office of Dependency Benefits, February 7, 1945, p. 1; Captain W. B. McHugh, Plans and Operations Division, USN, Washington, DC, letter to Mildred I. Yemmans, February 21, 1945, p. 1, all in Record Group 24, Stack Area 470, Box 901, Row 53, Compartment 5, Shelf 2, NARA.

32. Though U.S. officials officially banned Filipino naval enlistment from the Philippines in 1992, officials would continue to enforce their militaristic presence in the Philippines and (re)enlist Filipino Americans in and beyond the U.S. Navy for many years to come. While the inclusion and upward mobility of Filipino Americans (in the United States) and other ethnoracial minorities have since become more and more visible in public and academic spheres, certain historical questions remain that should not be forgotten: To what extent is the U.S. military actually desegregated—based not just on race but on class, gender, indigeneity, geography, sexuality, and other intersect-

ing markers of difference? How might the inclusion and privileging of one ethnoracial group imply the exclusion and exploitation of another? To what degree does the institutional and informal prevalence of U.S. militarism, and its role in reinforcing the United States as an empire, rely upon the very celebration and marginalization of its integrated racialized subjects, whether ranked V6 in general service, stewards' mates, or even seamen? While answers to these questions remain to be researched, this essay provides a window into how such inquiries were being addressed (or not) during, and since, a time of global war.

EIGHTEEN

The Thickening Borderlands: Bastard Mestiz@s, "Illegal" Possibilities, and Globalizing Migrant Life

GILBERTO ROSAS

Thickening Borderlands

Borders thicken. Their reach expands beyond international boundaries. Military-like police or police-like military inspect; they divide; they scrutinize.[1] They erase distinctions between strangers and enemies,[2] between the criminal and the law-abiding, between immigrant and disenfranchised citizens in regimes of immigration enforcement. Anxieties about *the* territorial border translate into anxieties about those bearing "figurative borders."[3]

"The border" cuts through the nearby glass door of this restaurant in a small community on the outskirts of Chicago momentarily severing our communion. She erupts, amid the loud din of young families at this restaurant. Gone is the sparkling eye contact of this stocky, olive-skinned woman, modestly dressed in a white, flowered dress. Her confident gaze, cradled in deep folds of warm flesh, and warm smile of this mother of five give way as she begins to relate her experience of the ever thickening, painful effects of undocumented border crossing. Her head tilts farther downward as she recounts her arrest for driving without a license. Her voice is now a whisper. But she, this person I call Maria, speaks, definitely and defiantly: "I had always done it. I had driven [without a driver's license] taking my husband to work, my kids to school, and going to work. And, yes, I'd been stopped before. But I would show them my National ID card. The officers usually let me off with a warning and I'm careful driver. But this time the officer was a woman. She was different." She continues to study the floor. "I was arrested." She repeats, "I was arrested. I'm a careful driver. And they took me to the police station. It was like two in the morning and I had just gotten out of work. I was exhausted. I was by myself." She describes her processing:

> The officer asked me my legal status and I was quiet. I told them I wouldn't answer their questions. The officer said to me people brought to the station are "illegal" and they are sent to immigration. And, if you're illegal, ICE [Immigration and Customs Enforcement] would come in early in the morning to pick up the people. And I began to think to myself, is this true? And then they began to take my fingerprints. And I immediately began to think of my family, of my children. The woman police officer said, "Look call your family and with luck they can get you a lawyer and he can get you out of custody before Immigration comes." And then a couple of hours passed and Immigration showed up. And the official told me to sign some paper, and I said I wouldn't sign anything, because I didn't understand what the paper said and he [the ICE officer] got angry. And I still refused and then he got me and put on handcuffs and they took me to the immigration center. And then Immigration took my fingerprints, and that other stuff. And they asked me if I had children and I said yes, I have five. And then they asked if I had crossed the border illegally. Well of course, I did. They knew. They knew I had passed illegally. They already knew. They had taken my fingerprints years ago.

Maria had not crossed the U.S.-Mexico border since the 1990s. Instead its late neoliberal permutation now reached her here, thousands of miles away. The mammoth and seemingly ever intensifying policing regime once largely arrayed against undocumented migrations and drug smugglers in the U.S.-Mexico border region now grasps at undocumented life in the interior of the United States. They are exemplified by the notorious immigration laws of Arizona and Georgia and the far more pervasive, if less recognized, federal enforcement initiatives such as 287(g), Criminal Alien Programs, and Secure Communities. They are illustrated by Sheriff Joe Arpaio's "concentration camps," his spectacles of incarceration and humiliation that crystallize how the dynamics of international boundaries are now thickening, their reach longer, their edges sharper.[4] Indeed vast new regimes of deportation, incarceration, and criminalization extend the border into the interior of nation-states amid the ruins of neoliberal globalization across much of the globe.

The arrest rendered María "subject to deportation." The authorities could drop by her home or work and sever her from her family, deporting her. Her potent memories of crossing the U.S.-Mexico border, its steel walls, its surveillance towers, its armed personnel, the swirling rumors of vigilantism and "killing deserts," haunt her, a culturally specific manifestation of racial terror (Gilroy 1993).

But "the border" cuts southward too. Listen to Nancy, the bespectacled director of an immigrant shelter in Oaxaca City, deep in southern Mexico. Her organization is one of many that began long ago as sites to steel Mexican migrants as they headed north to the United States or to deal with the remains of those who died in the United States. But things have changed. New migrations from Central America, the drug war in Mexico and the war on terror in the United States, and the security arrangements between the United States and Mexico cut deeply.

"Mexico," remarks Nancy, "is like the wall of the United States. There are so many obstacles for [Central American] migrants going through Mexico. It is like a wall that is put up to exclude the migrants." The U.S.-Mexico—or best the U.S.-Latin America—border now reaches southward and deep into Mexico.

Forms of old rifle through the new. Contemporary forms of market dispossession, new regimes of racial subjugation as criminalization and criminalization as racial subjugation, the fraying seams between the military and law enforcement, once reserved for the international boundary between the United States and Mexico, now cut through both countries. But, the *borderlands* thicken as well. As Alejandro Lugo has noted, "There is a difference between those who write about borderlands and border crossings metaphorically, psychologically, sexually, and intellectually, and those who write about the border as imposed and sanctioned by nation-state policy makers and by government officials."[5]

Nancy's organization in this respect sustains life in the borderlands. It provides respite. It offers temporary shelter, meals, and clothing to undocumented migrants. But it also offers solidarity. Nancy explains: "We understand the migrant experience." She has friends and allies who have experienced daily life as undocumented migrants in the United States. Experiences of criminalized life circulate through the organization and inform its aid to migrants from Central America that violate Mexico's southern international boundary.

And listen. Listen to a dreamer celebrate her defiance of the United States and the borderlands begin to crystallize: "I went up there, and I did it. Undocumented, Unafraid, Unashamed. I stood strong, and let them know who I was. I crossed the border. I'm undocumented. . . . I am undocumented, exercising my first amendment rights, asking the world to be fair! This is my home, this is my country, this is OUR LAND. Yours and mine." Inhabitants of the borderlands hold close the raw memories of fights in the making of borders.[6] They foreground the new horizons of post- or antiborder possibilities. That is to say, be it the international boundary between United States and Mexico or that between Israel and Palestine or the borders being made between Baghdad's Green Zone and the rest of Iraq, the *borderlands* assert that such arrangements are fraught, incomplete, subject to contestation.

Borders, that is, incite dreams. The suggestion that the borderlands are thickening captures how the cordoning of old commons, the vigilance by the petty sovereigns of new racisms,[7] and the violent spectacle of the drug war in Mexico's north signify both renewed vulnerabilities and renewed possibilities. They render the intellectual tradition of the U.S.-Mexico border region increasingly paradigmatic, challenging "illegality" and its hermeneutics currently dominating the social sciences. Such currents urgently recast *mestizaje*, Latin America's generally and Mexico's specific iteration of dominant racial ideologies and processes of asymmetrical cultural and racial fusion and their resultant hybridities. Borders, checkpoints, undocumented migrations are becoming increasingly significant across the globe, as are the oppositional subjectivities that they engender.

Although the promise of earlier migration was the social and economic incorporation of immigrants in the receiving countries under the alternative paradigms of multiculturalism or cultural assimilation, vile ethnic and religious divisions have become the rule.[8] The new frontiers of immigration, these sovereign dictates over life and death or the permanent wars of the margins, the failed promises of economic integration now turned into dark dystopias, do not prohibit transnational migration. Rather they contain it. The concentration of security forces and their necessary incompleteness cause undocumented migrants to risk life and limb to cross international boundaries, effectively subjugating, criminalizing, and forging an irreconcilable difference on them, in the subject par excellence of neoliberalism "in the struggle and the work through which he or she confronts death."[9]

The discoveries of decapitated corpses in Mexico's north tell of new dominations of Other life in Mexico. The gruesome, violent exhibitions are another dimension of thickening borders, another illustration of "the governmentality of immigration in dark times" in the U.S.-Mexico borderlands.[10] Thickened borders signal how how mortality is the lethal edge of contemporary anti-immigrant racism.[11] It enables a state-mediated racisms or a "fatal coupling[s] of power and difference."[12] That is, the exposure of undocumented life to death effectively racializes migrants. *Humans—not bodies*—become objectified in the context of the new frontiers of the neoliberal Americas. They become dismember-able, detain-able, deport-able, incarcer-able in this latest amplification of the decidedly unexceptional "high intensity policing and low intensity warfare."[13] Thickening borderlands effectively capture the complicity of governing rationalities in these practices, how for migrants it has become a necessary strategy of economic survival for migrants and remittance-hungry nation-states alike and how civilian migrants must suffer the consequences.

The vulnerability of the undocumented illustrates how thickening borders, or an amplification and perceived failure of security practices, inculcate virulent "anti-immigrant racism."[14] The recent history of intensified migration, particularly undocumented border crossings, from Mexico into the United States is quite telling in this respect. Consider that with the advent of the North American Free Trade Agreement, which lowered barriers for transnational commerce among Canada, Mexico, and the United States, the U.S. government intensified militaristic strategies of social control at the border largely on populations of civilian migrants. In the El Paso area Operation Blockade, later renamed Hold the Line to be more politically palpable, commenced on the eve of NAFTA.[15] Four hundred Border Patrol agents and their vehicles were positioned along a twenty-mile stretch of the border, and helicopters went up in a show of force. Shortly thereafter the Immigration and Naturalization Service modeled southern California's Operation Gatekeeper, south Texas's Operation Lower Rio Grande, and southern Arizona's Operation Safeguard on the success of this first campaign.[16]

The *Border Patrol Strategic Action Plan 1994 and Beyond* is instructive in this respect. Experts from the Department of Defense and chief patrol agents authored a strategic roadmap for the implementation of low intensity warfare as the government of unauthorized border crossers. It advanced a strategy of border and migration controls called "prevention through deterrence." It holds that with the militarized campaigns of the Border Patrol "violence will increase as effects of strategy are felt." The document further describes the strategy: "The Border Patrol will achieve the goals of its strategy by bringing a decisive number of enforcement resources to bear in each major entry corridor. . . . The prediction is that with traditional entry and smuggling routes disrupted, illegal traffic will be deterred, or forced over more hostile terrain, less suited for crossing and more suited for enforcement."[17] The fatal coupling of power and anti-immigrant difference dramatizes the thickening powers of new frontiers in the neoliberal age. Several thousands of undocumented migrants have died of exposure avoiding the Border Patrol and, one can speculate, vigilantes. Hundreds more unidentified humans fill the coroners' offices in communities in the southwestern United States. And likely hundreds more unidentified remains remain buried and undiscovered in the desert, alongside the abandoned water bottles, torn shirts, boxers and panties, and footprints in the steep sandy hills and hundred-plus-degree heat of "the killing deserts."[18]

But again, undocumented migrants traveling from or through Mexico have overwhelmingly succeeded in crossing the securitized border. This is evident demographically and, more important, in terms of the nightmares of insecurity about undocumented migration currently reverberating across the United States.[19] Thus undocumented migrants evade the Border Patrol but are contained in the economic and racial order of the United States, while inciting ethnonationalist nightmares of insecurity among an aggrieved public, particularly following 9/11, and dramatically diffusing the effects of the U.S.-Mexico border deep in the interior of Mexico.[20] Such nightmares dehumanize *civilian immigrants*, casting them as an invading force and, increasingly, as an "enemy within."

This phenomenon is captured in the influential Center for Immigration Studies publication "Coming to America: The Weaponization of Immigration":

> America, historically secure and prosperous, with vast oceans as moats and peaceful trading partners buffering its unguarded frontiers, is the spiritual and material envy of the world. Yet the changing dynamics of war and warfare, from symmetrical to asymmetrical, confront it with the ugly reality that a nation uncertain in the defense of its borders, from even the casual trespass of those fleeing hunger to seek work, is, in turn, at the mercy of those who trespass it. The war on terror affirms that threats to liberty abound. America's borders are the tripwires of this war. Their violations sound an alarm heard in debates over immigration, terrorism, and national security. Over these debates looms the memory of laws and borders easily and violently broken on September 11, 2001. The story of 9/11 reveals this breaking began well before American Airlines Flight 11 struck the North Tower of the World Trade Center at 8:46 on that fate-filled Tuesday morning. If American intelligence is correct, that breaking continues and with it the sieve-like

migration of terror across United States borders, especially those of the Southwest.[21]

Calls for antiterrorist strategies transpose the deep histories of international divisions onto bodies crystallized in the pernicious laws, ordinances, and practices, such as the checkpoints on the highways across the southwestern United States.

As do certain anti–Central American currents coursing through Mexico. They experience "the wall" of Mexico amid the turmoil of the drug war. Fighting between the new regional cartels has spiraled into a battle for profits by territorial expansion. Tens of thousands of people in Mexico have been killed, disappeared, decapitated, and dismembered in the past four years, more than the toll of U.S. adventurism in Afghanistan over the same period. Fifty thousand Mexican federal troops and thousands more private security contractors, many of them from U.S. security firms employed by Mexico, are now deployed. The conjunction of spiraling poverty rates and U.S. addictions thickens borders southward.

Certainly military repression in Mexico is not new. During the dirty war, from the 1960s through the 1980s, the Mexican Army was given carte blanche to put down student demonstrations and guerrilla groups, and it carried out disappearances and illegal detentions, torture, and killings on such a scale that the United States noted "an emerging security problem." When President Felipe Calderón describes the current campaign as a "war," the word holds multiple political meanings. He and his ministers constantly spoke in these martial terms, and he compared the fight against the cartels to Mexico's celebrated defeat of an invading French expeditionary force on May 5, 1862.[22] But this war now is routine. Necropolitical government has become how neoliberal crisis is managed.

Imagined enemies that span borders, such as migrants from Central America, become its grotesque casualties. The stories of mass kidnappings and demands for ransom and the recent discovery of mass graves with nameless bodies only confirm it. Central American women traveling through Mexico are particularly vulnerable. Listen to Nancy, the director of the migrant shelter in Oaxaca City, hundreds of miles away from the U.S.-Mexico border: "We were not hearing four years ago about the kidnapping of two hundred migrants, the mass making of seventy, the killing of seventy-two here, one hundred twenty in Tamaulipas, and those are the ones we know about. Because there's a lot more."

Nancy notes:

> Central American migrants come and they say a man stripped my clothes off he took everything and afterwards he told me take your pants and get out of here, no? And so begins migrant fear of certain people that look like delinquents, right? And they walk through the jungle, and there they find delinquents who will rob them, or trap them in the jungle. Sometimes they have to go around the migration *garritas* [checkpoints] and they know that around there they surround there there's going to be someone that's going to rob them, right? And not just the delinquents but also maybe in stores in places where a soda costs five and to migrants they sell it for twenty and they say if you don't pay me then I'll call Migration. Everyone knows, but no one talks about it. Everyone knows that those who talk with those accents or who wear *traje (indigenous clothing)*—everyone knows they're not from here. Everyone knows that there are lots of migrants. Everyone knows that the officials take advantage of them.

But, silence rules. The blood of migrants courses through this latest thickening border.

The Thickening Borderlands of Mestizaje

Listen to Nancy and others who assist migrants from Central America in Oaxaca: "We provide them food, clothing, and temporary shelter." Her willingness to work with Central American immigrants crossing the wall of Mexico emerges from her knowledge of the racist practices against Mexican immigrants in the United States. Meanwhile scholars like Alejandra Aquino-Moreschi have charted indigenous mobilization in the immigrant rights marches of 2006 in the United States.[23] She holds that experiences as a subordinated population in Mexico spark the moral indignation against anti-immigrant legislation and infuse an unprecedented collective and transnational mobilization. The thickening of the borderlands, that is, captures how the sovereign dictates over life and death produce subjects whose "ideological and material agency move in counter-purpose to 'fatal couplings of power and difference,'" what Ruth Wilson Gilmore terms racism.[24]

As the materiality of borders cut deeper north and south and deepen divisions across other parts of the globe, new identities resignify the old. The thickening of the borderlands captures how migrants and their allies transform mestizaje, or the processes and ideologies of racial and cultural mixing in the Americas as a result of contact with Spanish colonialism. It must be emphasized that mestizos, as Marisol de la Cadena notes, "are not simple, empirical hybrids, a plain result of biological or cultural 'mixture' of two (formerly discreet) entities."[25] Rather, as Ana Alonso writes, mestizos inscribe "a notion that has been a product of long-term, unequal dialogues in social fields of domination, exploitation, and subjectification."[26]

In Mexico the so-called cult of the mestizo emerged from the ashes of this country's revolution as a remarkably successful attempt to exorcise its violent legacy. A cadre of intellectuals, ranging from Manuel Gamio—trained at Columbia University and a disciple of the famed anthropologist and public intellectual Franz Boas—to the Hispanophile scholar of letters José Vasconcelos, himself a child of the border, imposed a new politics of subjugating life: a state-organized aesthetic of mestizaje. Bolstered by the new science of anthropology, mestizaje situated the beginnings of Mexican history firmly in the indigenous past.

The natives of Mexico were presumed to be a dead or dying culture. They were romanticized as Mexico's vital origins, but living ones were seen as backward after centuries of colonialism and oppression. Indians, then, had to be redeemed by the postrevolutionary science of racial fusion between the Spanish and the indigenous peoples, marshaled by the Mexican state. This new mythic revolutionary history considered racial mixture to be positive and became the cornerstone of a new state-driven cultural and aesthetic project that was explicitly anti-imperialist and anticolonial and that permeated state institutions such as schools and the mass media.[27]

Mestizaje, south of the border, thus provides an enduring map of social relations in Mexico as well as throughout much of Latin America. Its all too often racist sensibilities circulate in government statistics and in public schools. It flows among the blondes of the elite barrio of Santa Fe in Mexico City who, sheathed in black, tell themselves that there is no racism in Mexico.

Such problematic currents reverberate in Mexico's diaspora in the United States. It can be heard among those who celebrate the Sambo-like characters of la India Maria or the Memín Pinguín and who express bewilderment at the outrage toward the latter and other parallel images in the United States. Such latent racisms similarly emerge among elderly grandmothers in Mexico's north and the U.S. Southwest who insist that their grandchildren remain covered in the sun so as not to grow "too dark." Mestizaje dissolves black and brown into white in a national space thick with the dialectics of racial formation and in synchronization with always reconstructing—and always contested—borders.

Indigenismo is a related cultural current inextricably tied to mestizaje and further thickens the border. As a derivative of mestizaje, it celebrates an abstracted dehistoricized Indian identity. The ever-present specter of revolutionary violence haunts this official management of the indigenous. Indeed despite the profound disagreements that plunged Mexico into a half century of political chaos, in the immediate context of the Revolution liberals and conservatives shared a common concern about the Indian problem.[28] In this respect Manuel Gamio, probably indigenismo's architect, held positivist vision of Mexico's "national race." A key player in the eugenics movement, he recognized his commitment to "bettering" Mexico's indigenous peoples and to preparing them for "racial fusion . . . cultural generalization and linguistic unification."[29] In *Forjando Patria* (Forging a Nation) he ruminated on the "central, troubling issue of how to forge one nation out of the two races inhabiting the country—one of Indian descent, the other of European descent."[30] Moreover Gamio held that the return of émigrés from the United States would effectively whiten Indians. Contemporary interpretations of indigenismo underscore how it "repeatedly celebrates the Indians' spectacular contributions in realms historical, artistic, cultural, and scientific . . . all the while meticulously plotting out their absorption into a future nation" built on a whitening trajectory of racial and cultural fusion.[31]

These problematic roots lead many thinkers to caution against a problematic indigenous essentialism, if not racism, in the mobilization and analysis of mestizaje north of the border, or in the United States. Chicano studies, in this respect, a U.S.-based, decidedly post- or antidisciplinary field, resignifies the now hegemonic racial and cultural meanings of mestizaje. It privileges the indigenismo currents of mestizaje discourse, which are central to the decolonizing currents that oscillate from it. Yet a paradigm of Chicanos/as as Indians "run[s] the risk of representing the [mestizo] body as the realm of 'the real,'" superimposing a physical essence on ethnicity.[32] Relatedly, as Nicole Guidotti-Hernández has put it, "in privileging an 'Indian essence,' mestizaje be it north or south of the border fetishizes a residual, abstract, dehistoricized Indian identity."[33]

Moreover, mestizaje in neoliberal Mexico increasingly no longer signifies ideologies of racial mixture. Instead the term approaches the racial project of whiteness in the United States. An effect of the asymmetrical integrations of the U.S. and Mexican economies, to be mestizo in Mexico is to be nonindigenous, to be nonblack, and to definitely *not* be the bleached elite of Mexico.[34] It is the taken for granted; the unremarkable.

Yet, as the border thickens, the roots and routes of transnational migrants,[35] particularly migrant experiences of competing racial projects in Mexico and the United States, interrupt certain processes of normalization. They informs new horizons of complex comminglings of Central Americans in Mexico and movements like the Dreamers in the United States. Such movements openly refuse their marginal status as "illegal aliens" or "undocumented" border crossers or their progeny do. That is, migrations and (un)documentation, identity and power birth a new mestizaje, echoing Anzaldúa's *Borderlands* from years ago.

In this respect certain theorists, such as Paul Gilroy, have argued that diaspora and the hybridities it provokes offer "a ready alternative to the stern discipline of primordial kinship and rooted belonging." Diaspora does not constitute "successive stages in a genealogical account of kin relations, equivalent to single branches on a family tree. One does not beget the other in a comforting sequence of ethnic teleology."[36] Diaspora, or in this case the ever thickening borderlands with respect to undocumented migrations, becomes an antidote to what Gilroy calls "camp-thinking."[37]

The thickening borderlands, similarly, thus disrupt oppositional, exclusive, and essentialist modes of thought about people and culture that rest on assumptions of purity and absolute cultural identities. Liberal modern exclusions of mestizaje and accompanying painful projects of incorporation of Latin American mestizaje must be held in critical abeyance to the emergent, alternative orientations and frequencies of a way of possible alternative ways of life that seek to become, incited by those living in exclusion in both Mexico and the United States. One can speculate that such migrant identities have a global relevance. As more and more people or their friends and their families live in the restless in-betweenness of undocumented immigration, the thickening borderlands become a global condition.

The New Reach of Borders

To dwell on such dark governmentalities or the condition of "illegality" or even the thickening border risks erasing the insistence by theorists of the U.S.-Mexico borderlands that borders birth vibrant alternatives. Borders kindle new dreams. A critical appreciation of Maria's experience or Nancy's analysis would insist on not only recognizing the disabling nature of contemporary order making as border making; it would likewise insist on recovering the formation of oppositional consciousness that border making and accompanying regimes of illegality birth. These oppositional dynamics are frequently neglected in the social sciences. Néstor Rodríguez long ago reminded scholars that defying international boundaries could be taken as acts of autonomy, as acts of an autonomous working class engaged in projects of existence.[38] I would add that defying international boundaries can spark tremendous decolonial imaginaries, to echo Emma Perez.[39] Undocumented migrant life, stripped bare of protections, its kin, collaborators, and allies, birth new possibilities. That is, migrant subjectivities in Mexico, or those from Mexico or Central America in the United States, bring new energies, new frequencies, new orientations, ranging from quotidian techniques of survival to mass political mobilization. In the act of defying borders the repressed histories of colonization, conquest, enslavement, and domination nourish effective forms of resistance under contemporary global conditions: they are key to the imagination of decoloniality—and accompanying reversals of ideology—in its most utopian sense.[40] The mass graves of dismembered bodies of Central American migrants caught in the vicious crossfires of the drug wars in Mexico or undocumented life caught in the dynamics of racial terror in the United States generate new theories of the flesh and bring new flesh to theory.[41]

Such oppositional consciousness is irrevocably tied to what I have elsewhere termed the necessary incompleteness of borders, their radical defiance by undocumented border crossers, and the subsequent "nightmares of insecurity" that they generate.[42] Anxieties about incomplete borders, about walls between countries that are never finished, about bodies burrowing under borders hail aggrieved subjectivities in both Mexico and the United States. The demonization of migrants from Central America in Mexico and of Mexicans in the United States feeds dystopic narratives of contamination and national deterioration and spiraling calls for greater immigration controls. But the challenges and rebellions that such powers engender invite critical analysis and reflection.

The concept of the thickening borderlands scandalizes debates on immigration and race. They and our concepts are too often limited by the nation-state and its multiple horizons. Borders, in the words of Gloria Anzaldúa, are "una herida abierta [an open wound] where the Third World grates against the First and bleeds." Before a scab can form "it hemorrhages again, the lifeblood of two worlds merging to form a third country—a border culture."[43] Anzaldúa's iconic and original bloody metaphor seems ever more appropriate as the border cuts deeper into both the United States and Mexico. This year at least two dozen states have considered laws modeled on Arizona's heinous SB 1070; officials from fourteen states have pledged to try to repeal birthright citizenship in their states; and others are working to curtail public services to undocumented immigrants.

Conceptually the thickening of the borderlands captures how borders now cut deep, sometimes deep enough to decapitate in Mexico or to sever parents from children, as with Maria in Chicago and millions of others across the United States. Wars on crime, drugs, and terror merge. In regimes anchored in permanent warfare, traffickers and undocumented migrants are depicted as insurgents and terrorists. The discovery of mass graves, of caches of guns in Mexico, and the lower intensity draconian anti-immigrant policing initiatives and legal measures in the United States illuminate the logics of war-like policing and policing-like warfare as contemporary government. They thicken the border.

And, they thicken the borderlands.[44] To emphasize such dark arts in the governmentality of migration risks neglecting the renewed "methodologies of the oppressed"; the living dreams of Dreamers who openly claim their undocumented status, the daily workings of NGOs and their constituencies in Mexico and the United States in support of their undocumented status, the marchers of 2006, and countless other examples across the globe speak to how defying international boundaries and their internal reaffirmations reignite longings, hail subjugated knowledges of the making of borders, and consequently decolonial imaginaries, which dominant trends in the humanities and social sciences would neglect. Dreamers organize; sovereignty bends. The president of the United States recently put in a program called "deferred action," designed to give some relief to immigrant youth. Nancy's organizations and countless other, less formal solidarities survive.

The new borderlands likewise births alternative racial recognitions. A gradual reworking of mestizaje is born. The drug war in Mexico and the war against undocumented migration in the United States illuminate a perpetual thickening of the U.S.-Mexico border in the ruins of NAFTA and disturbing reverberations across the globe. But migrants and their allies do not experience social death.[45] They suffer gross marginalization. They suffer politically organized, premature near-death experiences as they cross international boundaries and the daily in the informal wars against immigrant—and those imagined as immigrant—Others fueled by anti-immigrant racisms, be they in Mexico, in the United States, or elsewhere in the globe, where to be imagined as a foreigner casts one as a source of insecurity and toward an ever greater proximity to death. In the process some, if not many, become politicized in living these thickening borders of exclusion, or the actual or gradual strangling of life as "the undocumented," as "illegal aliens," or even beheadings. This phenomenon demands a certain diasporic sensibility that divorces mestizaje from its increasingly problematic roots in Mexico and other parts of the Americas.

It is emergent. The tremendous new horizons, solidarities, and methodologies of the oppressed are evident in Mexico, in the United States, and in other parts of the globe. They demand the globalization of scholarship from the U.S.-Mexico border region.

NOTES

Research undertaken in Mexico for this essay was made possible by University of Illinois Research Board and by the generous support of CIESAS PACIFICO-Sur, specifically that of Drs. Alejandra Aquino-Moreschi and Manuel Rios Rama.

1. Lugo, "Theorizing Border Inspections"; Rosaldo, *Culture and Truth.*

2. Balibar, *Strangers as Enemies.*

3. Chang, "A Meditation on Borders," 247.

4. For more information, see Mahwish Khan, "Arpaio Boasts about His "Concentration Camp," Calls Out Puente Arizona for Challenging Him," America's Voice, June 6, 2012, accessed July 7, 2012, http://americasvoice.org/blog/arpaio-boasts-about-his-concentration-camp-calls-out-puente-arizona-for-challenging-him/.

5. Lugo, "Theorizing Border Inspections," 356. See also Lugo, *Fragmented Lives, Assembled Parts.*

6. Foucault, *Society Must Be Defended,* 8.

7. Chappell, "Rehearsals of the Sovereign."

8. Appadurai, *Fear of Small Numbers.*

9. Mbembe, "Necropolitics," 14.

10. Fassin, "Policing Borders, Producing Boundaries."

11. Mbembe, "Necropolitics."

12. Gilmore, "Fatal Couplings of Power and Difference."

13. Rosas, "The Thickening Borderlands," 337.

14. Rana and Rosas, "Managing Crisis," 229.

15. Agent Silvestre Reyes had implemented similar polices in McAllen, Texas, prior to becoming chief of the Border Patrol in El Paso and, later, a state senator and implementing Operation Hold-the-Line in El Paso. Peter Brownell writes, "These operations did not draw Washington's attention until October and November 1993; just before implementation of NAFTA, Operation Blockade caught presidential attention and became the basis for a border-wide strategy." Peter Brownell, "Border Militarization and the Reproduction of Mexican Migrant Labor," *Social Justice* 28.2 (2001): 278.

16. As Nicholas De Genova contends, "U.S. immigration law has generated the juridical categories of differentiation among various migrations, defined the parameters of 'legality,' and continually revised the possibilities for 'legal' migration in ways that have been disproportionately restrictive for Mexicans in particular." Nicholas De Genova, *Working the Boundaries: Race, Space, and "Illegality" in Mexican Chicago* (Durham: Duke University Press, 2005), 8.

17. U.S. Border Patrol, *Border Patrol Strategic Plan,* 5–8.

18. Rosas, *Barrio Libre.*

19. Although border enforcement funding has more than doubled between 2001 and 2006, the Mexican-born population in the United States, both legal and illegal, has continued to grow at an average rate of 500,000 per year over the past decade. Between 2000 and 2005 America's undocumented population increased by 24 percent, from 8.4 million to 11.1 million. At the end of the 1990s and continuing into this decade, the pace of unauthorized new arrivals began to accelerate, averaging 850,000 per year. Indeed increased enforcement at certain sections of the border has rerouted illegal crossers to less fortified areas, but the U.S. Border Patrol has had no more success apprehending illegal entrants in 2005 than it did in 1996. Statistical information can be found at Faye Hipsman and Doris Meissner, "Immigration in the United States: New Economic, Social, Political Landscapes with Legislative Reform on the Horizon," Migration Information Source, April 16, 2013, accessed September 22, 2013, http://www.migrationpolicy.org/article/immigration-united-states-new-economic-social-political-landscapes-legislative-reform.

20. See Rosas, *Barrio Libre.*

21. Cato, "Coming to America," 311.

22. Gregory, "The Everywhere War."

23. Aquino-Moreschi, "De la indignación moral a las protestas colectivas."

24. Gilmore, "Fatal Couplings of Power and Difference," 16.

25. Cited in Alonso, "Conforming Disconformity," 460.

26. Alonso, "Conforming Disconformity," 460.

27. Alonso, "Conforming Disconformity," 463.

28. Guidotti-Hernández, *Unspeakable Violence.*

29. Buffington, *Criminal and Citizen in Modern Mexico*, 152–54.

30. Gamio, *Forjando Patria*, 206.

31. Saldaña-Portillo, *The Revolutionary Imagination in the Americas and the Age of Development*, 206.

32. Perez-Torres, *Movements in Chicano Poetry*, xv.

33. Guidotti-Hernández, *Unspeakable Violence*, 6

34. Korinta Maldonado, Totonac "usos y custombres": Racial Sensibilities and Uneven Entitlements in Neoliberal Mexico. PhD diss., University of Texas, Department of Anthropology, 2012.

35. Clifford, *Routes.*

36. Gilroy, *Between Camps*, 123, 128.

37. Wade, "Hybridity Theory and Kinship Thinking," 84.

38. Rodríguez, "The Battle for the Border."

39. Perez, *The Decolonial Imaginary.*

40. Sandoval, *Methodology of the Oppressed.*

41. Moraga, *Loving in the War Years.*

42. Rosas, *Barrio Libre.*

43. Anzaldúa, *La Frontera/Borderlands*, 25.

44. Thickening borders speaks to how violent technologies of criminalization are the modus operandi and chart their migration from the margins of nation-states and the globe to the centers. Low-intensity conflict, once reserved for the so-called Third

Worlds, has moved from the margins to the core. Conflicts now proliferate across the constantly thickening U.S.-Mexico border. Border inspections, a concept theorized by Lugo, and not just "border crossing" but their radical defiance, have a way of life (Lugo, "Theorizing Border Inspections").

45. Compare Cacho, *Social Death*; see Zavella, *I'm Neither Here nor There.*

NINETEEN

Up in the Air and on the Skin: Drone Warfare and the Queer Calculus of Pain

RONAK K. KAPADIA

This essay examines the critical and social potential of the contemporary aesthetic works of Wafaa Bilal, an Iraqi artist based in New York City. I argue that close attention to the nonvisual sensory elements of his performance projects offers a way to glean evidence of the histories, geographies, and sentiments of those disappeared by U.S. military operations in the Middle East and South Asia. I propose the concept of a "queer calculus" as an alternative mode of understanding the proliferation of drone warfare and the dominant militarized vision of U.S. imperialism that lies at its core. Queer calculus is a theoretical strategy that generates an account of both persistent systems and structures undergirding U.S. global counterinsurgency warfare and alternative logics, affects, and affiliations produced by racialized subjects in response. Through close readings of Bilal's visual and performance works the essay identifies ethical practices and perceptual regimes that access the untold histories absented by the abstractions of the long war.[1] This work contributes to the intellectual and political project of critical ethnic studies by questioning the abstractions and rationalities of U.S. imperial discourse and the statistical modes through which the collateral damage of counterinsurgency warfare is calculated. In the process my reading exposes another calculus, a queer calculus of bodies in pain and of bodies that imagine alternatives to that pain. By employing the critical tools of ethnic studies, queer studies, and visual studies, this chapter gestures at alternative ways of understanding drone weaponry and the effects of this violent practice on the gendered, racialized, and sexualized bodies that are its targets. An account of Bilal's queer calculus of pain thus responds to the call by critical ethnic studies scholars to identify new epistemological frameworks and vocabularies from which to understand these enduring forms of gendered racial violence and also signals an entirely different mode of inhabiting the world collectively and in relation to others in times of war.

Body Counts and the Price of Life and Death

When, in August 1990, President Saddam Hussein of Iraq invaded neighboring Kuwait just two years after the end of the Iran-Iraq War, Wafaa Bilal was forced to flee.[2] The Iraqi-born painter and visual artist was part of the secular student movement that refused to enlist in Saddam's army, which was newly tasked with suppressing the Shia-led popular uprisings that raged against his iron rule. Bilal fled to Kuwait before escaping to an American-sponsored refugee camp in Saudi Arabia, where he lived for nearly two years. He was eventually granted political asylum in the United States around September 11, 1992. In the context of contemporary U.S. wars in Iraq, Afghanistan, Pakistan, Yemen, and beyond, Bilal's story of exile and displacement serves as a potent reminder that the U.S. military presence in Iraq long predates our more recent preoccupations with the post-9/11 period. If we include the U.S. involvement in the Iran-Iraq War and the thirteen years of near-total economic sanctions that starved millions of Iraqis between the two ground occupations, the United States has had a fatal hand in the country for at least three decades. When asked in a May 1996 interview if the deaths of nearly half a million Iraqi children caused by economic sanctions and United Nations–mandated trade embargoes had been justified, U.S. Secretary of State Madeleine Albright famously replied, "We think the price is worth it."[3]

The present-tense violence of U.S. militarism and aerial bombardment in Iraq can help explain Albright's calculus of what counts as a "livable and grievable life."[4] In the performance works of Bilal sensory knowledge of the discourses of the U.S. racial security state and the Arab diasporic experimental art practices responds to the violent effects of the long war. The crucial force of Bilal's artwork hinges primarily on the pain he inflicts on his own body—especially his skin, that organ of touch and feeling that connects the body to the social world and provides a key platform for his artistic interventions. In these aesthetic works embodiment and the senses attempt to account for the subjective experiences and lived vulnerabilities of populations that are both produced and obscured by U.S. racial regimes of security.[5]

If we want to understand modern security politics and practices, particularly the modes of intelligence gathering and killing technologies perfected in the domestic and international contexts of the long war, we need an alternate approach to the maps of strategic thinkers and security analysts. When read alongside the escalating use of drone technologies in U.S. military operations, Bilal's performance projects allow for a more complicated understanding of the ethical and affective relations that can emerge between Americans and Iraqis under the conditions of U.S. security and warfare. This understanding is framed by the interplay between what's "up in the air"—namely the discourses shaping the use of aerial surveillance and twenty-first-century military technologies—and what's "on the skin" as a way of capturing the painful intimacies of seemingly discrete peoples, histories, and geographies. These modes reveal two distinct but intersecting cartographic representations of landscape and the human terrain, with very different implications and blueprints for the future.[6] Bilal is one artist who uses his own body to map the uneven contours of human vulnerability in times of war, uncovering the intimate and affective politics of U.S. imperial violence, those animated traces and "disqualified secrets" discarded by official accounts of the war, as well as the alternative models of affiliation these politics engender.[7]

A recent performance by Bilal entitled *. . . and Counting* highlights this approach by examining the ongoing U.S.-led massacre of Iraqi civilians, including the artist's own brother, who was killed by a drone missile strike in the family's hometown of Kufa, Iraq, in 2004. In this March 2010 piece staged in New York City, the artist transforms his body into a canvas by tattooing the names of Iraqi cities on his back and then, during a twenty-four-hour live performance, tattooing 105,000 dots onto this borderless map as audience members stand as witnesses while a select few solemnly recite the names of Iraqis and Americans killed in the U.S. occupation since 2003. Five thousand dots are marked first in red ink to represent dead American soldiers. The remaining 100,000 dots, meant to memorialize the "official" Iraqi death toll from the war, are in ultraviolet ink, invisible unless viewed under a black light. As this cursory description suggests, Bilal's piece asks its audience whose death "counts" in times of war, erecting what Neferti Tadiar calls "living memories, living histories, as openings into other futures."[8] But the piece also elicits timely questions about the Central Intelligence Agency's proliferating use of missile-armed unmanned aerial vehicles, or drones, in targeted assassinations across

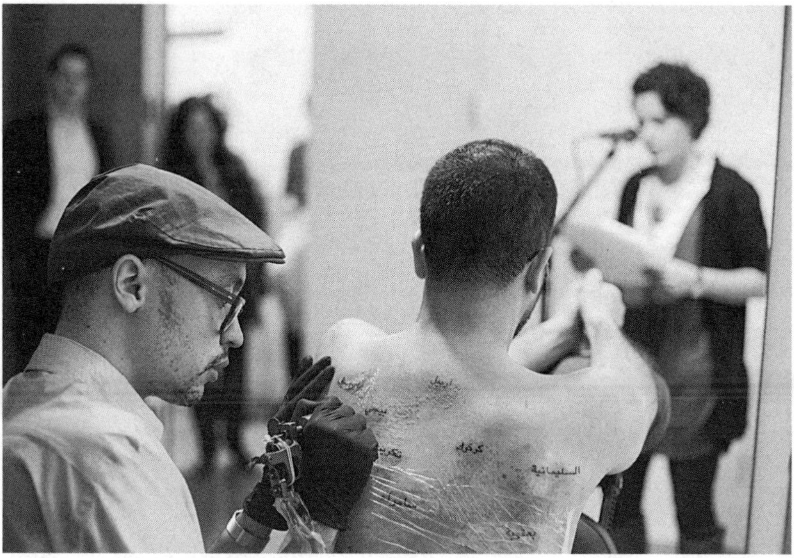

FIGURE 19.1. Wafaa Bilal, detail from *. . . and Counting,* performance, 2010. Photo by Brad Farwell. Courtesy of Driscoll Babcock Galleries.

Iraq and the Af-Pak borderlands.[9] Bilal's own sensate body in pain, with ink pressed into bare skin, depicts my focus on how we might glean evidence of the histories, geographies, and sentiments of those disappeared by U.S. global warfare in tactile and corporeal forms.

How to Shoot an Iraqi and Collateral Damages

Bilal first gained international recognition for his 2007 performance *Domestic Tension,* in which he confined himself to a gallery space in Chicago for a month, inviting the public to visit a website where they could "shoot" him by remotely firing a paintball gun at his body. Originally known by the more straightforward, if provocative, title *Shoot an Iraqi,* this interactive performance piece had more than sixty-five thousand online users fire at the artist by month's end, transforming this virtual experience about collective unfeeling toward militarized warfare into a very tactile experience, most of all for its subject. Bilal's self-imposed spatial confinement conjures the dilemma that contemporary Iraqis face every day, living in domestic confinement due to the miseries of foreign occupation and sectarian conflict.[10]

Recognized for his controversial video installations, Bilal made national headlines again in November 2010 by announcing that he would have a tiny

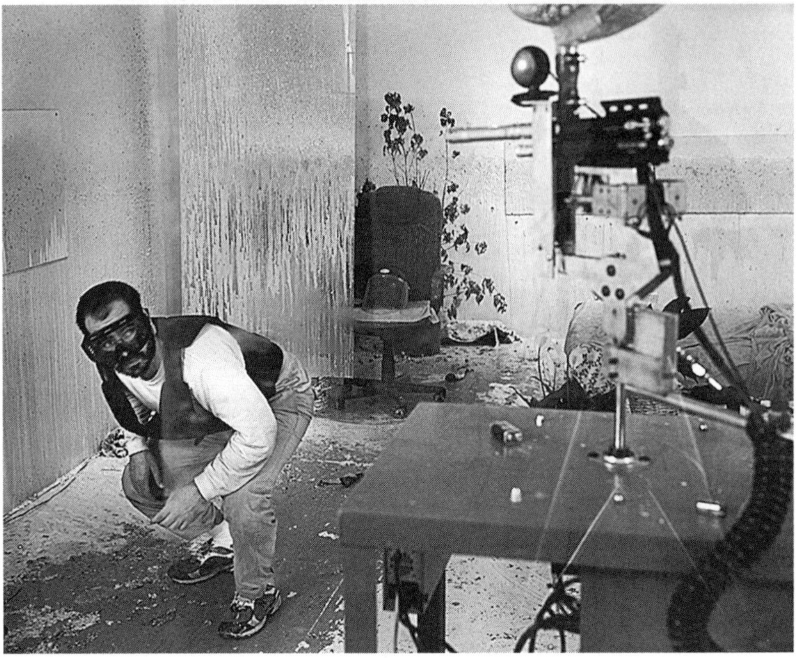

FIGURE 19.2. Wafaa Bilal, detail from *Domestic Tension*, performance, 2007. Copyright Wafaa Bilal. Courtesy of Driscoll Babcock Galleries.

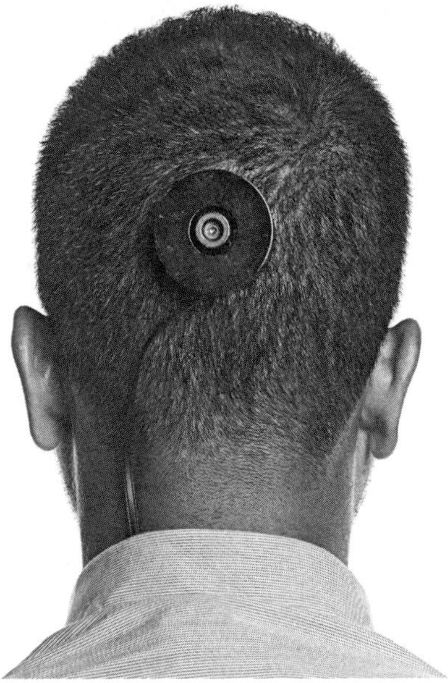

FIGURE 19.3. Wafaa Bilal, detail from *3rdi*, year-long performance, 2010–11. Copyright Wafaa Bilal. Courtesy of Driscoll Babcock Galleries and Mathaf: Arab Museum of Modern Art.

fist-size camera surgically installed into the back of his head for a year. The embedded camera captured a photograph every minute of the artist's daily life and then transmitted that visual record to a website; the inaugural images are displayed at the Arab Museum of Modern Art in Doha, Qatar, as part of its new permanent collection. *3rdi* sutures the technological apparatus of photography onto the artist's own body; the arbitrary images captured by Bilal's cyborg creation, with more than 500,000 pictures taken by the end of 2011, compose a visual record that awaits interpretation and reception.[11] With its backward glance, the piece asks us to confront the tyranny of the visual register and its renewed salience in the context of elevated surveillance and security panics in the contemporary period, as well as the critical histories of pain, humiliation, and subordination in performance art.

Bilal's larger ensemble of work exemplifies the complex ways in which diasporic expressive culture can provide diagnoses of and alternatives to the geopolitical and epistemological maps produced by the U.S. global security state. In particular his works ask us to consider how the visual field is constitutive of both the logic and the materiality of war. This is true not only in the case of pilotless drones over the conflict zones of Iraq and Af-Pak, where cameras are quite literally appended onto missiles and bombs, but also in what he names "the comfort zone," those more mundane settings far from killing fields in which war enlists and acts upon our senses. Thus an encounter with Bilal's artwork elicits a transformation in our affective relationship to dominant visual and discursive frames of war.

My focus on the aerial perspective as central to U.S. global security regimes joins a range of critical ethnic and postcolonial feminist scholars in a collective effort to challenge the systematic embrace of the visual in cultural and intellectual responses to U.S. global warfare and surveillance. This concern stems from the argument that visual and conceptual frames have contributed to the manufacture and obliteration of populations as objects of knowledge and targets of war. The links between vision and epistemology have been well theorized and rehearsed.[12] From these studies we learn that perspectival vision is in fact constitutive of the logic of surveillance and the materiality of war. As the eye became the privileged organ of knowledge and authority, the power to *see* became equated with the power to *know* and to *dominate*. Throughout the twentieth century we see this enduring alliance between vision and war. As military fields increasingly became reconfigured as fields of visual perception, preparations for war increasingly became indistinguishable from the preparations needed to make a film. Rey Chow, for instance, writes, "War would mean the production of maximal visibility and illumination for the purpose of maximal destruction."[13] We might conceive of the long war, then, as Anne McClintock observes, not only as a struggle over "oil, water, and the resources of globalization but [also quite centrally a struggle over the] control of the global image and data worlds."[14]

Given the dense interconnectivity among vision, knowledge, and warfare, what system of knowing and writing might adequately address both the violence the imperial state tries to render invisible and the "invisible obscene," as McClintock puts it, of civilian populations exposed endlessly to this violence?[15] We benefit from turning away from the visual and discursive frames of war and toward analyses that feature lesser studied senses, including touch and sound. These extravisual sensory relations have become newly vital to U.S. security governance, both as actual military weapons (the use of music in torture) and as resources for diasporic public cultures.[16] However, rather than dispense with the visual altogether, we benefit from attending more closely to the ambiguities and particularities of the visual experience produced by diasporic and racialized subjects responding to these conditions as they reveal alternative clues for knowing and mapping the world. I trace this line of thinking back through the performances of Bilal, arguing that diasporic visual and performance art provides a particularly privileged terrain from which to interrogate the expansion of the U.S. global security state (its logics, frames, desires, and tactics), and it further offers a perspective from which we might develop alternatives to imagine and inhabit.

What the aesthetic works of Bilal make possible is an alternative sensorial understanding of the long war. . . . *and Counting* is offered as a way of archiving both personal and collective traumas. Bilal is a blacklisted political refugee from Saddam-era Iraq mourning the loss of his brother, who was killed by a drone for simply being in the way—the "collateral damage" that belies the imprecision of the war machine as it misses its target.[17] Bilal's use of tattooing and body art here is particularly instructive for reasons worth elaborating. First, we must contend with the map of Iraq tattooed onto Bilal's body. Although maps regularly function as instruments of centralized surveillance, as tactics of information retrieval and war making, the cartography that Bilal quite literally prints on his back resonates instead with what the literary historian Jonathan Flatley calls an "affective map," that is, a map that "not only gives us a view of a terrain shared with others in the present but also traces the paths, resting places, dead ends and detours we might share with those who came before us."[18]

Flatley's work allows for a reconsideration of Bilal's individual art practices as part of a larger epistemological project engaged in a politics of knowledge,

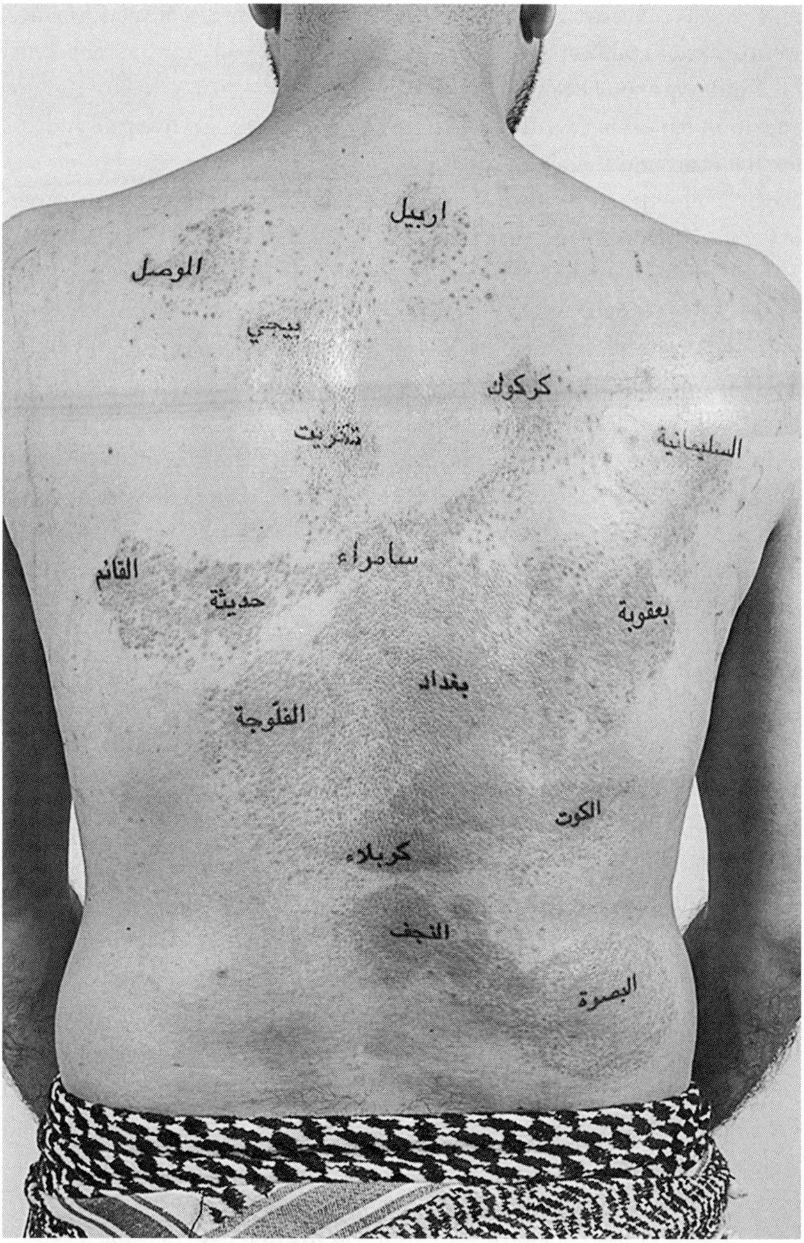

FIGURE 19.4. Wafaa Bilal, detail from *... and Counting*, performance, 2010. Photo by Brad Farwell, with illustration by Kyle McDonald. Courtesy of Driscoll Babcock Galleries.

one that has collective and social effects.[19] When viewing Bilal's performance, we are asked to think about individual and collective pain, sorrow, mourning, loss, and hope concurrently. To think of Bilal's pain—that is, to give it shape and meaning—is necessarily to attempt an account of collective pain and loss for Iraqis around the globe, a diaspora whose connective tissue is felt and forged in bloodshed, death, and related miseries produced by the state of permanent war. Bilal's performances of pain (and the mourning that emanates from his pieces) are hence not solely metaphors but also "evidence of the historicity of [his and our] subjectivity."[20]

Yet it is important to note that the source of this affective connection is the artist's own skin—that sensory organ of touch and feeling that sutures the body to the social world. Thus while this performance is surely a visual experience for his audience, it is only through the tactile—where we are asked to confront Bilal's body in pain—that this affective relation to past histories is drawn. It is touch, not vision, that provides this affective relationality and makes possible new ways of conceptualizing the self and others. This impulse to "touch the past" by charting the "dead ends and detours" shared with those who came before him thus becomes crucial in specifying Bilal's sensorial interventions, as it suggests another way of archiving the long war.[21]

Queer Calculus of Pain and Deadly Inscriptions

While arguing for an alternative archival relation to U.S. security wars, I want to briefly elaborate on the concept of a queer calculus as an interpretative framework salient to this discussion. *Calculus* in mathematics refers to a particular method or system of reasoning. Central to my concern here are questions of expertise, mastery, and evidence—concepts finely calibrated to serve the super-panoptic ambitions of the United States in the long war. How does the U.S. global security archipelago "see"? How does it know what it knows about its citizens, subjects, economies, and geographies? I am interested in the forms of modern security expertise and the knowledge practices through which security threats are visualized, rationalized, and managed (thus highlighting the aerial perspective, or paying close attention to what is up in the air).

While the politics of global knowledge production have long been central to postcolonial criticism, the topic remains noticeably underinvestigated in critical ethnic and queer studies. My project responds by analyzing the complex array of knowledge workers who together produce a wide and divergent set of claims about the state of contemporary global racial regimes of security and the evidence of its archives. Unlike security planners and military intellectuals, however, cultural producers like Bilal do not claim any relationship to expert knowledge. Their work instead highlights the random, provisional, indiscriminate, and altogether uncoordinated ways in which material resistance to imperial violence erupts. Indeed it is this mode of queerness that we might elaborate in our work by employing reading practices that denaturalize or queer—that is, make strange—processes like security and warfare that rely upon the presumption of their naturalness, thus unmooring sexuality as the fixed referent for queer studies.[22]

The other, less circulated sense of *calculus* is biological in origin. This notion of calculus underscores the role of affects, sensations, and embodiment. In medicine, calculus (or calcification) describes the concretion of minerals formed within the body, in places like the kidney and gall bladder. This process is often painful, as these stones prove to be difficult to displace or dissolve. Their destructive power accrues as they grow in number, wreaking havoc on different organs, first one by one and then on the system as a whole. This organic sense of calculus also conjures the idea of residue, a palimpsestic view of time that carries with it the sedimentation of older histories, encounters, and legacies of violence. This interpretation opens up a particularly generative way of describing the long war as a violent, corporeal process working on racialized populations and bodies. It allows me to accentuate not only the sensorial and somatic life of empire but also the sedimentation of different forms of violence over time. An account of the queer calculus of the long war thus takes up the conjoined biological and discursive meanings of the phrase to capture how affects, fantasies, sentiments, and the senses have figured in and mattered to the shaping of U.S. imperial statecraft and its resistance from the late cold war through and beyond the Global War on Terror.

Bilal's queer calculus of pain thus demands a more complex relation to the ensemble of the senses. We achieve better conceptual clarity on the operations of killing and violence perfected in the theaters of the long war by isolating touch and other modes of affective transmission that circumvent the visual field, that might even contradict the scopic altogether. The critical import of turning to the tactile realm stems from the hope that knowing through touch might elicit an alternative, sometimes contradictory conceptualization of social relations than that offered by visually based epistemologies. Sensations can reveal an account of feeling otherwise inaccessible to the regime of the visible and might make possible other ways of organizing collective social life beyond the logic of security. The idea here is not simply to discard the visual register but to elaborate a fuller epistemology that understands touch in relation to sight and other sensorial processes.

With this perspective in mind, we must question further what this borderless map on Bilal's back really represents. How does death sort livable from grievable lives? What is the "unspoken calculus of the value of a life and a death on this planet"?[23] With Bilal's work we are forced to contend with the failure of numbers to represent the disappeared and the relations of force that produce such disappearances.[24] Of course we can never know how many people have died in the name of security and freedom in the terror wars we currently wage. There is no evidence of that in the material archive of war. This fact suggests the failure of enumeration and quantitative reasoning to understand state violence fully and the populations most vulnerable to its destructive force.

What is called for instead is what Herman Gray and Macarena Gómez-Barris term "a sociology of the trace." This method offers "a way to attenuate the distance between empirically social worlds and those things that are not easily found through methodologies that attempt to empirically account for social reality." In contrast to the sociological imperative toward "generalizability, systematicity and a normative notion of rigor," Gray and Gómez-Barris suggest an alternative methodological approach that "points toward inscriptions, traces, the audible, the inaudible, cacophonies, incoherences, assemblages, translations, appearances, and hauntings as methodological necessities rather than those things that do not quite fit into overtly social categories."[25] Their emphasis on "archives of traces and inscriptions" speaks to the larger political dimension of my approach in this essay. By connecting Bilal's abstract performance works to histories and theories of aerial bombardment, this project attempts to decenter the primacy of the visual, given its centrality in U.S. global security logics, attending instead to extravisual sensory relations as a way of "attenuating the distance" between the views from "above" and "below" in the context of aerial warfare.

In other words, Bilal's work reveals that positivist framings of loss, including numbers, cannot always contain what these dominant representations seek to make visible or readable. While this dominant frame of war jettisons the "de-legitimated alternative versions of reality," it is busily generating what Judith Butler calls "a rubbish heap whose animated debris provides the potential resources for resisting." Given that the archive of U.S. global security continues to violently unfold (even as it refuses to see itself *as* an archive), a queer impulse to follow the specters that haunt the "animated and de-ratified traces" of killing provides a trenchant methodological antidote to archival-based studies of U.S. racial formation, state secrecy, and imperial warfare.[26] This approach thus demonstrates how conventional representations of the death toll fail to capture what Gayatri Gopinath has described as the "inner amalgamation of memory, imagination and pain," thereby suggesting the failure of vision and the impossibility of transparent access to the effects of the long war in its operations of killing and violence.[27]

If a queer account of this work rejects the politics of enumeration, in its place we are left simply to confront Bilal's back under black light. His back is transformed by the tattoo performance into a craggy terrain that looks like the remnants of a surface scarred by cluster bombs and missile strikes. There are no numbers present. Instead the assemblage of tattoos conjures the heat of burn marks, the glow of a starry night, the faint impression of a galaxy or cosmos from outer space, or satellite imagery, which is all too pervasive in this era of global positioning systems. Yet we should recall that this view from above is permanently imprinted on his skin.

Finally, while there is no official tradition of body art in Iraq, Bilal's use of tattooing powerfully captures the missing history of the disappeared. In an interview the artist recounts how, while living in a refugee camp as a young person in Saudi Arabia after escaping Iraq in 1991, he was granted asylum in the United States on the condition that the U.S. delegation interrogate his brother first, also in the camp.[28] One of the American translators who befriended Bilal informed him that Americans would not take three kinds of people: criminals, communists, and people with tattoos. Bilal's brother had a tattoo, and the reason that he got it was related to the war. During the Iran-Iraq War of the 1980s many young people lost family members on the front lines, and their bodies came back unidentifiable. Young Iraqis started getting tattoos of their names and cities, sometimes on one or two of their body parts, so that if they were killed and their bodies were mutilated beyond recognition, their families would still be able to identify them. If the Americans saw the tattoo on his brother's arm—this inscription of a future death—they would not grant Bilal asylum. That night Bilal's brother decided to burn the tattoo off his arm using a hot spoon.[29]

Here we see a paradoxical queer calculus at work: in order to gain access to refuge in the United States one needs to efface this other, unseen record of the bodily effects of U.S. proxy war in the Middle East, as evidenced by U.S. participation in and financing of the Iran-Iraq War. Bilal's story captures the nexus of the body in pain and the violence of the regulatory security state as it reveals the evidence of the somatic and sensorial life of empire. In short, the burned-off tattoo provides "material evidence of power's whereabouts."[30] What lies outside the visual archive are these sense memories and feelings that conjure affective attachments full of individual, familial, and collective histories and that escape or elide official archives of war.

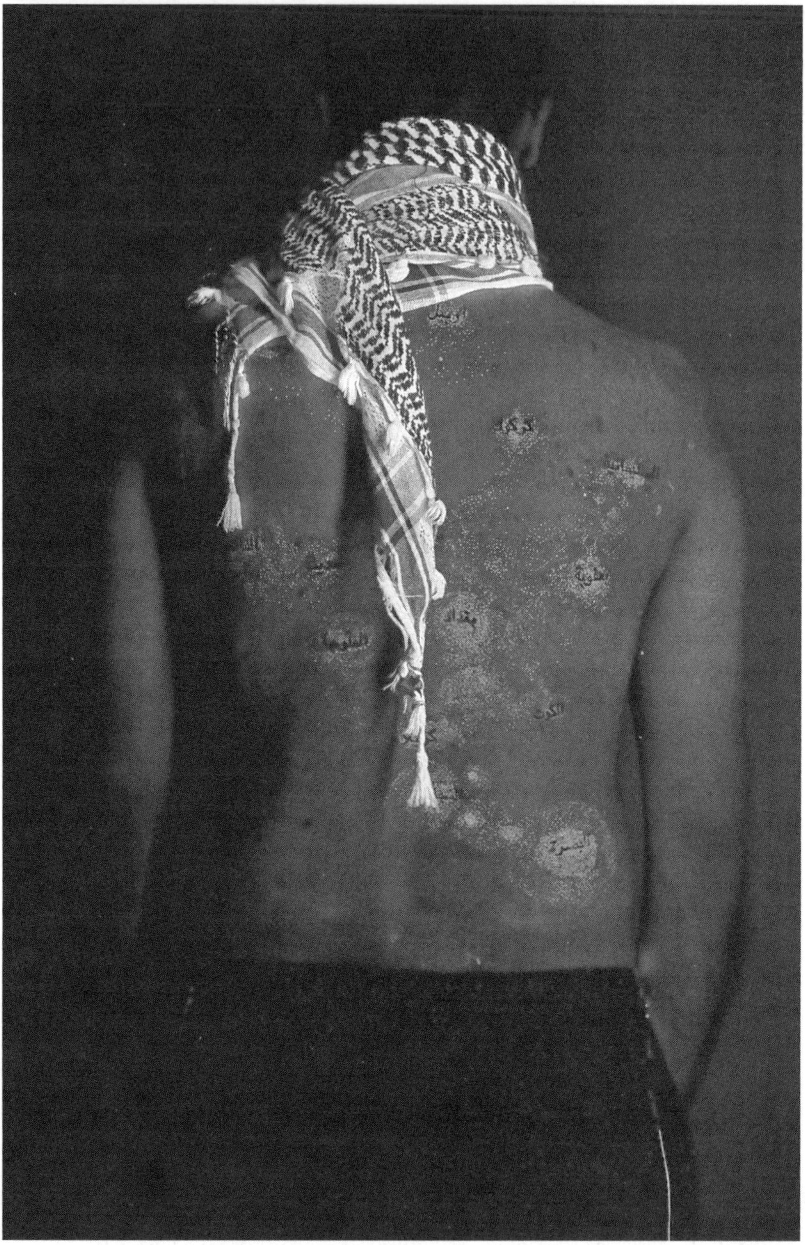

FIGURE 19.5. Wafaa Bilal, detail from . . . *and Counting,* performance, 2010. Photo by Brad Farwell. Courtesy of Driscoll Babcock Galleries.

Critically analyzing Bilal's work thus better captures the sensorial logics of imperial governance and its manifold resistance. In the midst of enduring bloodshed in Afghanistan and Iraq, population displacements and drone attacks in Pakistan and Yemen, the drumbeat of war against Iran, the normalization of intensified disciplinary tactics against racialized immigrant and nonimmigrant people of color in the United States, and the complex unfolding of imaginative geographies of liberation across the Middle East and North Africa today, a queer relation to these war archives advances critical genealogies of the long war and its affective afterlives. Our political imaginations have been impoverished by the prevailing logics of state security in discourses of terrorism, militarism, and war. Analyzing diasporic archives, and specifically experimental performance works, as epistemological projects engaged in a politics of knowledge offers a moment of refreshment—an opportunity to think antiracist, anti-imperialist queer politics anew. An analysis of long war diasporic culture lets us move beyond the calculus of counterinsurgency to propose urgently needed alternatives to security, militarism, and war. A queer calculus of the long war thus provides blueprints for sensuous affiliations as expansive as the Pentagon's long war, without the violence of its vision.

NOTES

1. My use of the term *the long war* refers to the Pentagon's counterinsurgent defense strategy in Iraq, Afghanistan, Pakistan, the Horn of Africa, and beyond. Imagined as a permanent cold war against Al Qaeda with small "hot wars" along the way, the long war provides a geopolitical frame through which the United States has come to know itself and its enemy Others in the Global South.

2. Bilal and Lydersen, *Shoot an Iraqi*, 67.

3. Madeleine Albright, interview by Leslie Stahl, "Punishing Saddam," *60 Minutes*, aired May 12, 1996.

4. See Butler, *Frames of War*.

5. In a forthcoming manuscript I analyze the ways innovative state practices of coding, aggregating, managing, and dividing populations under contemporary forms of securitization have produced new populations, with differing degrees of precarity in relation to the state and its various apparatuses, while scrambling older ones. This project seeks to contribute to studies of U.S. racial formation by thinking through the complex intersections of foreign and domestic policy, citizenship and governance in the context of longer genealogies of colonial violence, decolonization, migration, and present-day forms of less spectacular racial dehumanizations.

6. I allude here to the Human Terrain System (HTS), run by the U.S. Army Training and Doctrine Command. HTS was billed as an effort to counteract the security and intelligence communities' perceived inadequate cultural and historical knowledge and

cultural-interpretive capacities in the Middle East and South Asia. In a forthcoming work I offer a more detailed analysis of what constitutes the human terrain, both for the U.S. warfare state and for the interconnected movements that are working to oppose its particular strand of violence. This includes analyzing the relation among these art interventions, their global circuits, and the broader political coalitions necessary to forge global political challenges to U.S.-led imperial wars and violent neoliberalisms.

7. Gordon, "The Prisoner's Curse," 19. Gordon's critical extension of Foucault's theorization of "subjugated knowledges" provides a formative resource for my project.

8. Tadiar, "The War to Be Human," 92.

9. The political theorist Kiren Aziz Chaudhry's essay on U.S. militarism along the Af-Pak border, "Dis(re)membering \Pä-ki-ˈstän\," provides an important source for my understanding of the changing geopolitical dimensions of the region. In a forthcoming work I elaborate on the politics of the "Af-Pak" designation, both the geopolitical implications for the region and for area studies projects more generally. This joins a larger collective argument that examines how Pakistan has increasingly become disentangled from "South Asia" and newly sutured to the "Middle East," given its renewed importance as a failed state and reluctant collaborator in the U.S. Global War on Terror over the past decade.

10. In his analysis of global Muslim racial formations, "More than Nothing," Rana describes *Domestic Tension*, following Butler, as an "aesthetic of grievability."

11. *3rdi*'s first images were captured in Doha on December 14, 2010. The images are often quite mundane, sometimes cryptic, but always antimonumental. The artwork is part of the museum's first exhibit, entitled *Told/Untold/Retold*, featuring twenty-three contemporary artists from the Arab world. In a mirrored room forty-two monitors display images from Bilal's online archive. The images are uploaded every minute with the GPS location. The speed of the changing pictures is altered according to the museum visitor's movements. Bilal created a series of platforms: viewers in the museum, viewers online, those willingly or unwillingly captured on camera. The piece provides an important commentary in the context of debates on privacy amid proliferating personal data on the internet. See the images at http://www.3rdi.me/.

12. On the links between vision and warfare, see Kaplan, "Dead Reckoning" and "Mobility and War." See also Ngo, "Sense and Subjectivity."

13. Chow, *The Age of the World Target*, 30–31.

14. McClintock, "Paranoid Empire," 91.

15. McClintock, "Paranoid Empire," 103.

16. See Goodman, *Sonic Warfare*.

17. On collateral damage, see Yoneyama, *Hiroshima Traces*; Feldman, "The Structuring Enemy and Archival War."

18. Flatley, *Affective Mapping*, 1. On the early cold war production of spatial knowledge as a weapon of war, see Farish, *The Contours of America's Cold War*; Dalby, "The Pentagon's New Imperial Cartography."

19. My thinking on the alternative epistemological projects of Asian American cultural forms is most directly indebted to Chuh, *Imagine Otherwise*; Kim, *Ends of Empire*.

20. Flatley, *Affective Mapping*, 3.

21. Here I evoke Dinshaw's evocative metaphoric of touch, which suggests that historical inquiry can be motivated by an affective relation between past and present rather than mere causalities alone. See Dinshaw, *Getting Medieval.*

22. This framework builds on and is informed by the writings of women of color and queer of color intellectuals who have complicated conventional genealogies of queer studies by radically altering the proper objects of the field, critiquing multiple social antagonisms, including race, gender, class, nationality, and religion, in addition to sexuality. These works further interrogate the differential social processes that produce and sustain normative constructions of the nation-state, citizenship, migration, imperialism, and empire. My formulation of a queer calculus draws on and extends this genealogy of queer of color criticism and transnational queer studies through a more direct engagement with the national security apparatus and discourses of counterterrorism and counterinsurgency.

23. Engelhardt, *The American Way of War*, 29.

24. The Body Count provides an entry into thinking about ethical systems of life, death, violence, and war. A major source that I draw upon is the Iraq Body Count (IBC) database, http://www.iraqbodycount.org/. It records violent civilian deaths resulting from the 2003 military invasion of Iraq. A public database of deaths caused by U.S.-led coalition forces and paramilitary or criminal acts by others, IBC has been working to process and analyze the Iraq War Logs released by WikiLeaks on October 22, 2010, which contain over 54,910 records compiled by the U.S. military and noting "109,032 violent deaths between January 2004 and December 2009." See IBC's initial analysis of the document drop: "Iraq War Logs: What the Numbers Reveal," October 23, 2010, accessed September 15, 2015, http://www.iraqbodycount.org/analysis/numbers/warlogs/. See also "Iraq War Logs," https://www.thebureauinvestigates.com/category/projects/iraq-war-logs/, which is run by the Bureau of Investigative Journalism, a U.K.-based organization created on April 26, 2010, to "analyze the secret U.S. military war logs released to us by the whistleblowing internet site WikiLeaks."

25. Gómez-Barris and Gray, *Toward a Sociology of the Trace*, 5, 4.

26. Butler, *Frames of War*, xiii.

27. Gopinath, "Archive, Affect and the Everyday."

28. Kamat, "Interview with Iraqi Artist Wafaa Bilal."

29. Bilal and Lydersen, *Shoot An Iraqi*, 140.

30. Gómez-Barris and Gray, *Toward a Sociology of the Trace*, 6.

TWENTY

Empire's Verticality: The Af-Pak Frontier, Visual Culture, and Racialization from Above

KEITH P. FELDMAN

From the original watch-tower, through the anchored balloon to the reconnaissance aircraft and remote-sensing satellites, one and the same function has been indefinitely repeated: the eye's function being the function of a weapon.—PAUL VIRILIO, *War and Cinema: Logistics of Perception*

Maman, look, a Negro; I'm scared!—FRANTZ FANON, *Black Skin, White Masks*

First of all, we often call the problem AfPak, as in Afghanistan Pakistan. This is not just an effort to save eight syllables. It is an attempt to indicate and imprint in our DNA the fact that there is one theater of war, straddling an ill-defined border.—RICHARD HOLBROOKE, U.S. special envoy for Afghanistan and Pakistan, March 2008

Geronimo E-KIA.—U.S. NAVY SEAL COMMUNIQUÉ from Abbottabad, Pakistan, to White House Situation Room to confirm the death of Osama bin Laden, May 1, 2011

How might a critical ethnic studies frame the relationship between the borders of the United States as nation-state and the United States as "homeland"? How do these borders become defined, and where are they extended? How do they draw on and innovate processes of racialization, and what forms do such processes take? These types of questions remain pressing, especially given the advancement, in the name of "homeland security," of a cartography of open-ended counterinsurgency in West and Central Asia, a cartography whose remains, as the "Geronimo" codename for the mission to kill Osama bin Laden attests, are the residues of a late nineteenth-century settler colonial violence resuscitated in a contemporary project of extraterritorial jurisdiction. The mission initiated by Bill Clinton in the late 1990s and intensified under the war on terror to apprehend bin Laden as the racialized nonstate actor par excellence has culminated in a targeted killing on the homeland's globalized frontier, a zone that the prominent U.S. diplomat Richard Holbrooke called the "ill-defined" border between Pakistan, a supposed U.S. ally in the war on terror, and Afghanistan, where U.S. empire has been haltingly advancing a mix of counterinsurgency and nation-building. Recall George W. Bush's pronouncement at the dawn of the Afghanistan invasion in 2001: "We're steady, clear-eyed, and patient, but pretty soon we'll have to start displaying scalps."[1] Almost ten years later there is Geronimo, enemy, killed in action.

How should we come to see this late-modern resuscitation of frontier violence, a move whose own reiterative logic is strewn across a history of U.S. imperial warfare's double-voiced linkage of secure national borders and their persistent eclipse?[2] With the ideological contours and practices of state violence organizing the U.S. war on terror at a historical inflection point, conspicuously not on display in bin Laden's assassination are images of a mutilated body extricated from the ambiguous Af-Pak frontier, that key site for the performance of Holbrooke's singular "theater of war." There are no "spider holes" or grainy cell-phone images of death by hanging, à la Saddam Hussein after the U.S. invasion of Iraq. Instead, in the immediate aftermath of bin Laden's killing, we are invited to view the widely circulated photograph of a crowded White House Situation Room, with Barack Obama surrounded by a dozen prominent figures in his administration. They gaze at an off-camera screen whose video content was supplied by feeds from both the Central Intelligence Agency's RQ-170 Sentinel unmanned aerial vehicle hovering several miles above the Abbottabad, Pakistan, compound where bin Laden was located and killed, and the cameras mounted on the helmets of the Navy SEAL Team 6 operatives penetrating the compound's fortifications (figure 20.1). In an image variously described in the blogosphere as "mesmerizing" and "captivating," the target of imperial retribution remains just outside the visual field, even as its presence haunts our reading. We are drawn to witness the witnessing of bin Laden's assassination, its spectral performance registered in the attempt to represent the imperial state's right to extraterritorial killing.

In this way the Situation Room photograph frames sovereign power through the absent presence of the homeland security state's constitutive frontier

FIGURE 20.1. Pete Souza, *Situation Room*, May 1, 2011.

violence, one whose geography abruptly extended from the "ill-defined" space of the Durand Line to a zone deep in one of Pakistan's urban regions. While this highly mediated scene captures something new about the recent present—an innovation elaborated below—the photograph likewise allows us to see how the production of ambiguous national borders and their modes of racialization are hardly novel. Such forced ambiguity punctuates histories of U.S. imperial sovereignty, whose settler contours and anti-Black animus routinely exceed the fiction of a stably bounded nation-state. Indeed they were drawn with typical blur in the late nineteenth-century U.S. policy to apprehend inside Mexico Geronimo himself, the Chiricahua Apache, through what one historian calls particularly "elastic approaches to issues of extraterritorial jurisdiction."[3] The longue durée of the modern colonial world system itself evidences how nation-state borders as a stable geographic homology promised by the Treaty of Westphalia have refused to remain still. Instead they have been constituted by persistent reproduction, constellation, and contestation, an instability indexed by the infusion of the Euro-American juridical order with the "externalized" violence of the colony and the "internalized" circumscription of political life under transatlantic slavery and indigenous genocide.[4] Cultural analyses premised on this insight are obliged to track carefully histories of what Ann Laura Stoler calls imperial sovereignty's "shifting categories and moving parts whose designated borders at any one time were not necessarily the force fields in which they operated."[5]

The contemporary U.S. homeland security state has elaborated and capitalized on this instability through practices of "ubiquitous bordering" at a variety of local, regional, and transnational scales that persistently rub against the Westphalian system.[6] In doing so it propagates zones of differentiated inclusion and exclusion that constitute the geographic warp and weft of globalized warfare. Amy Kaplan suggests that the ideological function of the term *homeland security* is itself meant to legitimize these practices by suturing the intranational contraction of proper spaces and subjects of the political with the transnational expansion of U.S. imperial sovereignty.[7] For Allen Feldman the borders of the homeland function no longer solely as barriers between nationally defined zones but operate instead as "a flexible spatial pathogenesis that shifts around the globe and can move from the exteriority of the transnational frontier into the core of the securocratic state."[8] "In this heteronymous organization of territorial rights and claims," argues Achille Mbembe, "it makes little sense to insist on distinctions between 'internal' and 'external' political realms, separated by clearly demarcated boundaries."[9]

This transmutation and persistent eclipse of national borders by the contemporary U.S. homeland security state has at least two key effects. Felicitously captured in the phrase "Papers, please," the ubiquity of borders generates forms of verification meant to stabilize, make legible, and manage the ineluctable plurality of a population. In doing so this ubiquity incites the truth-telling desired by the nation-state of increasingly inscrutable—and increasingly surveilled—subjects of power in sites both beyond and beneath the horizon of the national. At the same time, the extension of bordering processes outside the geography of the nation-state creates flexible biopolitical zones capable of traversing and encompassing the globe, where certain subjects—whose apogee in this case is represented by the sovereign figures in the Situation Room photograph, the operators of the unmanned aerial system, the members of Navy SEAL Team 6, and, if the photograph retains its structure of address, those viewers interpellated into its frame—are invited to inhabit categories of life and wield power over the lives of others, while others are banished from sociality to the point of death.

I submit that this latter figure, of life-in-death, constitutes the kernel of the raciality of the war on terror, whose inclusion as figure emerges precisely through its social exclusion. While its genealogy emerges out of a history of settler colonial violence that reanimates indigenous genocide, manifest destiny, and other expressions of U.S. imperial sovereignty, it is saturated by what Jared Sexton calls the "structure of gratuitous violence in which a body is rendered as flesh to be accumulated and exchanged"—in other words, the afterlife of slavery.[10] Junaid Rana calls this the "fungibility of comparative racialization," which can move swiftly between the criminal, the illegal alien, the security threat, and the terrorist.[11] The reproduction of biopolitical frontiers reenacts older imperial patterns that also remain connected to modalities of antiblackness that legitimize the production of targets understood through rubrics of threat, fear, and terror. Theorizing and intervening in the production, specificity, and motility of the figure of life-in-death thus animate the task of a critical ethnic studies, inviting an account of the relational constitution and effects of national and imperial race-making as domestic borders of the U.S. nation-state are transmuted by conceptions of the globalized homeland.

Building on recent scholarship in critical human geography, critical race theory, and visual culture studies, this chapter charts how the fungibility of comparative racialization operates through a "dynamic sociospatial process" that traverses local, national, and imperial geographies.[12] This traffic across geographic scales has developed a vector of verticality, what I call racialization from above, which supplements the well-documented contours of racialization on the ground. Racialization from above accomplishes what racialization on the ground has been ill-equipped to achieve: it contorts the temporality of warfare through notions of preemption and endurance; it recalibrates Orientalist imagined geography through far more porous concepts of proximity that challenge received notions of state territoriality and national borders; and it fixates on the mystique of "precision targeting" in highly ambiguous structures of race and space.[13] In this way racialization from above arrays visual technologies along a vertical vector in order to supplement imperial sovereignty's practices of ubiquitous bordering on the ground. In charting this verticality as it arose in the decade between the formal emergence of the homeland security state and the killing Osama bin Laden, this chapter attempts to apprehend how contemporary "logistics of perception" utilize the sight of imperial visioning to inform the raciality of the war on terror.[14]

Two Vectors of Racialization

While the paradigmatic figure for framing processes of racialization may remain the color line theorized by Du Bois at an earlier moment of imperial terror's link with antiblackness, the mid-twentieth-century break with white supremacy and the absorption of a nominal antiracism by the neoliberal state has given way to forms of race making that exceed Du Bois's mapping.[15] That the raciality of the war on terror—its capacity to produce a fungible constellation of figures exposed to the everyday violence of life-in-death—no longer adheres to white supremacist rubrics of the color line is among the so-called postracial era's signal achievements. The moment the effects of racism are no longer addressed by the state as structurally unequal distributions of human value and valuelessness and instead seen as operating solely through the market logic of individual preference and choice is simultaneously the moment when the raciality of the war on terror becomes inscribed in the homeland security state's governing legal, military, and policing apparatus and infuses its visual logics.

In this contemporary regime, racialization's spatial vectors illuminate the state's ambiguous borders in order to expose categories of embodied difference to an interpretive grid of threat. One vector of this process has been reproduced in horizontally defined sociospatial relationships, what I call *racialization on the ground*. Through processes of inclusion, seclusion, exclusion, and extermination, the dialectic that racializes space and spatializes race generates what David Theo Goldberg calls "territorializations and regionalizations . . . of life's possibilities."[16] This geography links frontier expansion to an imperial defense of internalized space, tidily activating a genealogy of U.S. racialization on the ground. Histories of settler colonial violence, for instance, narrate a persistent telos that expands the boundaries of civilization westward; the imperial construction of U.S. national borders routinely draws on the legacy of the War of 1848; walls, barriers, fences, and other assorted passage points dramatize a form of territorial sovereignty increasingly on the wane; and regimes of confinement transfer bodies from the space of the slave plantation through cartographies of Jim Crow and the urban ghetto to the largest and most racially stratified prison system in human history.[17]

Under contemporary regimes of homeland security, racialization on the ground has been supplemented by a differentially embodied vertical vector of racialization, what I call racialization from above. As it heads skyward this "politics of verticality" leaves beneath it the border crossing, the fence, the passport check, the guard tower, the high ground, and the hilltop.[18] A prominent technology of *racialization from above* has been condensed in the assemblage of aerial surveillance, policing, and state-sanctioned killing known as the unmanned aerial system (UAS). By fusing visuality, preemption, and a disregard for territorial sovereignty, unmanned aerial systems have become among the most popular technologies of the homeland security state. In the past hundred years more than forty countries have developed UAS capacities, but the past decade has seen massive growth in these machines of death dealing, with widespread expansion predicted for years to come. Under the auspices of security they have been deployed across police, surveillance, and military theaters, not to mention the increasingly privatized domains of commercial commodification. However, assuming that unmanned aerial systems leave behind either the human or territory obfuscates the centrality of visual perception so important to racialization from above. As Derek Gregory has explicated, over 180 people are involved in any single U.S. drone operation, including pilots, sensor operators, mission controllers, senior commanders, intelligence officers, military lawyers, data analysts, image technicians, and military personnel in theater.[19] Many of these people train their gaze on a collage of video screens whose content is generated by infrared and daylight color TV cameras, satellite mappings, and laser rangefinders. This "human element," the military emphasizes, "is at the core of the overall system."[20]

As with all racial geographies, the spatial is complemented by the temporal. Boundaries between civilization and barbarism, whiteness and nonwhiteness, human and inhuman, are buttressed by asynchronous and even extratemporal temporalities whose past-tense grammar limns the elsewhere of racialized difference. Racial naturalism and racial historicism are most notable here, differentiating populations based upon framing past-tense relations to present political, cultural, and ontological norms.[21] While U.S. empire's liberal ideologies all hinge on such notions of history's waiting room and its dynamics of racialized exclusion and inclusion, under the homeland security state the waiting room has become especially infiltrated by threat and risk. To address this, racialization from above weaves permanently temporary observation into permanently temporary warfare, with "endurance" its organizing chronos.[22] This future anterior grammar of preemption provides the temporal frame for the raciality of the war on terror, whose substantial differentiation from earlier forms of colonial warfare—when accumulation by dispossession was accomplished through extraterritorial conquest and settlement from without—brings to bear geographic ambiguities made sensible only through preventing what "will have been."[23] The war on terror's speculative regimes seize upon and attempt to make seeable the imminent, probable, or possible. While questions of territorial sovereignty remain figured in the predictable rhythm of oscillating troop deployments and withdrawals, they remain irresolvable when the horizon of war making is always already marked by an open-ended and indefinite futurity for some, and a permanent withholding of futurity for others.

Visualizing the "Human Element"

In 2010 the U.S. Army published *Eyes of the Army,* a document premised on the idea that "the global security environment is more ambiguous and unpredictable than in the past. . . . Future operations [of UAS] will likely span the spectrum of conflict from peacekeeping operations to counterinsurgency to major combat."[24] This premise underwrote the exponential growth of UAS in the first decade of the war on terror. Prior to 2001 the U.S. Department of Defense inventoried approximately fifty drones; in October 2009 Defense counted more than 6,800 in its arsenal, with appropriations for procurement, research, testing, and evaluation above $20 billion. About 6,200 of these were "small systems" (handheld, carried in backpacks, launched by catapult, etc.), while almost five hundred, including the popular Predator and Reaper systems, required significant training, maintenance, and technology to operate. By July 2013 inventory had grown to nearly eleven thousand.[25] This growth happened with such alacrity that training time for operators was greatly reduced, ground space for storage and maintenance dwindled, and the Federal Aviation Administration's regulation on access to the national airspace impeded where training missions could be run. Since airspace above missions in Afghanistan and Iraq was less regulated, trainings were increasingly completed "in theater."[26]

Drone deployments yoke together varied geographic sites, each with their own rubrics of proximity. Since they traverse space at speeds slower than other aerial materiel, drones are launched by operators from facilities proximate to their target. Once they are airborne, control is ceded to operators based in the United States, who are then responsible for directing navigation, targeting, and killing technologies. Video feeds and communication technologies link these operators to Central Command's Combined Air and Space Operations Center in Qatar and Langley Air Force Base in Virginia.[27] At least twelve army installations in the United States carry out UAS missions, with a coordinating center at Fort Rucker, Alabama; these squadrons logged their millionth hour piloting drones above Iraq and Afghanistan in December 2010. U.S. Air Force systems are more substantial, with squadrons managed at Holloman Air Force Base in New Mexico and Creech Air Force Base in southern Nevada, the latter designated a "center for excellence" to coordinate "concepts," training, tactics, and "procedural solutions" across all branches of the military. Tonopah Test Range Airport in Nevada services the RQ-170 Sentinels. Air National Guard squadrons fly Predators and Reapers out of Texas, North Dakota, California, and Arizona. Fort Huachaca in Arizona supports reconnaissance along the U.S.-Mexico border and, increasingly, in the Mexican interior. In 2010 the

Department of Homeland Security (DHS) announced it had deployed UAS to patrol the entire southwestern border and received FAA clearance to run UAS surveillance along the U.S. border with Canada. This activity supplements enforcement measures on the ground, such as the buildup of law enforcement officers, the erection of fences and walls, and the implementation of various means of surveillance at border crossings.

The DHS program was initiated in 2004 using the popular Hunter and Hermes drone systems. The Hunter was produced jointly by the U.S. firm Northrop Grumman and Israel Aircraft Industries, one of the primary UAS producers in Israel. Elbit Systems, the largest private security company in Israel, builds the Hermes, among the most popular UAS packages for Britain's Ministry of Defense. (Elbit also provided a suite of surveillance technologies for the U.S.-Mexico border developed in conjunction with the Israeli wall snaking through the West Bank.) Battle-tested in the assaults on Lebanon in 2006 and Gaza in 2009, Hermes routinely run surveillance over the Palestinian Occupied Territories. Since 2001 this dense transfer of technologies of militarized perception between the U.S. homeland security state and the Israeli occupation regime has been routed through state, military, and cultural production, even as it builds on a larger genealogy linking the Israeli state to the raciality of U.S. imperial formation.[28] The motility of the U.S. war on terror's geography brings the Israeli "security threat," the "illegal," and the "terrorist" into its capacious ambit.

At the time of bin Laden's killing, the most discussed and debated, and least transparent, UAS program was run by the U.S. Central Intelligence Agency. Initially developed for reconnaissance, in 2002 the Bush administration authorized the weaponized use of Predators, first pursuing "high-level targets" in Sana'a, Yemen. CIA Operators are based in Langley, Virginia, among other places, and until May 2011 were launching and recovering aircraft out of the Shamsi Air Field in the southwestern Pakistan province of Balochistan. In the wake of the bin Laden assassination, under pressure from the Pakistani regime, these localized outposts were moved to the Afghan side of the Durand Line, though missions were still conducted in Pakistan's Federally Administered Tribal Areas of North and South Waziristan. This frontier zone is a key imagined geography for the neologism *Af-Pak*, revealing precisely the homeland security state's investment in enacting and legitimizing violence on sovereignty's ambiguous borders. Leaving aside the pressing questions raised by the deceptively "simple" enumeration of drone attacks and their deadly effects—questions that press on the grids of intelligibility through which we account for imperial violence—nevertheless the New

America Foundation counted 192 deadly strikes from the time Obama was inaugurated in January 2009 until bin Laden's assassination at the beginning of May 2011, more than quadrupling the prior administration's forty-four.

These geographies of warfare contort any simple distinction between domestic home front and foreign battlefield, reproducing highly ambiguous concepts of sovereignty within the territorial borders of the United States. The spatiotemporal distinctions between civilian and combatant within the United States are increasingly blurred. "Even if they are sitting in Langley," writes the legal scholar Gary Solis, "the CIA pilots are civilians violating the requirement of distinction, a core concept of armed conflict."[29] The maintenance and regulation of the U.S. national airspace has become increasingly contested, described by the legal scholar Joseph Vacek as nothing less than "an aeronautical Wild West."[30] At the end of 2010 the FAA counted approximately fifty U.S. companies, universities, and government agencies engaged in designing and producing more than 150 types of UAS, while certifying individual applications for use of national airspace through a Certificate of Waiver or Authorization to public entities like local and state law enforcement, the federal security apparatus, and research institutions. At the time of bin Laden's killing, there were 273 active Certificates of Waiver or Authorization. A multiagency task force links the FAA to NASA, DHS, and Defense to streamline and integrate a policy to expand accessibility to the U.S. national airspace. Not surprisingly this task force sees UAS as the most likely kind of aerial operations to increase in the coming decade, particularly by local and state law enforcement, with the police departments of Houston and Miami already integrating UAS into their arsenal and a broad swath of North Dakota's airspace was granted FAA approval for extensive UAS testing, making the frontier state what some have begun calling the "Silicon Valley" of drones.

Understanding the array of UAS technologies across increasingly militarized spaces reveals the centrality of vision lodged in the raciality of the war on terror, with the "way of seeing" proffered by the UAS framing how U.S. border zones are construed. Following Nicholas Mirzoeff, we can link the rule of the eye to imperial culture, with sight functioning as the paramount modern sense through which techniques of dominance have been understood: "As sovereign, visuality envisages a top-down view of the world in which only it can see what is to be done. As governance, visuality trains and commodifies vision to acculturate to the prevailing mode of production."[31] Commentators since at least Paul Virilio have connected vertical technologies of visuality to cultures of war, though few have gauged these technologies' racializing force. In the case of UAS specifically, Gregory has argued that the "scopic regime" produced by drones "renders 'our' space familiar even in 'their' space—which remains obdurately Other."[32]

Intensified as part of the raciality of the war on terror is its peculiarly Muslim target. Since the time of the Spanish Inquisition, as Rana reminds us, processes of Muslim racialization have invested the visual with a heightened truth regime meant to extract the otherwise inscrutable core identity of its racial object through sustained visual scrutiny. The kernel of truth embodied in the "Islamist" or "radical fundamentalist" or "Jihadi" has required intensified forms of seeing that collapse sartorial, physiognomic, and behavioral signifiers into a racial threat. "Profiling the racialized Muslim," writes Rana, "means imagining levels of terror potential intertwined as fields of visible identity."[33] The identification of such a threat draws on the broader visual register of racialization, whose dialectic was captured in Frantz Fanon's signal phrase describing race making's colonial interpellation: "Look, a Negro; I'm scared!" This practice of hailing, according to Fanon, deploys sight as the primary racial technology to lock a subject in place and force its ontology into a terrifying relation to white supremacy.

The consolidation of the visual's regime of truth as a sign of verification under modernity thus resuscitates the fantasy of precision structuring the visual logic of Muslim racialization. The fungible figures of threat that give the raciality of the war on terror its coherence are exposed to the open-ended duration of targeted observation and perpetual video feeds—creating a video archive that routinely exceeds the capacity of the military to process. These fantasies of logistical precision become all the more valued in sites like Af-Pak, whose long history of ambiguous sovereignty is mirrored in the drones being deployed with little recourse to any stably defined borders of the U.S. homeland security state. Even as Al Qaeda's deterritorialized organizational structure propped up the legitimacy narrative necessary for an extraterritorial logic of counterinsurgency, the genealogy of North and South Waziristan's unruly relation to imperial sovereignty provides a useful object for imperial violence. The very grounded contingencies of the region—its inhuman mountainous topography and harsh weather conditions—have been easily and quite literally overcome by the eye of the unmanned aerial vehicles.

Returning to the Grounds of "Indian Country"

Designating the operation to apprehend bin Laden "Geronimo" reveals how certain parts of the globe are envisioned at the frontier of the U.S. homeland. The Apache warrior utilized porous borders between Arizona and Mexico to evade capture, even as the increasingly complex technologies of policing and surveillance devised by those sovereign powers and legitimized by their pursuit of Geronimo were extended into wider social fields, and upon whose incarceration hinged the temporal close of the Indian Wars.[34] The colonial residues sedimented in the Durand Line between Afghanistan and Pakistan, drawn in the late 1890s to demarcate the border of British rule in the region, and where bin Laden was presumed to reside, generate a resonant geopolitical ambiguity whose own porosity underwrites the legitimizing logic to expand the geographical zone of U.S. imperial violence.[35] That the bin Laden operation was completed outside the Waziristan provinces and instead within a midsize city whose jurisdiction falls under the Pakistani state suggests that the bounds of this kind of violence have likewise remained porous. And that this city is called Abbottabad, named after its founder, British major James Abbott, in 1853, circles us back to another genealogy of imperial intervention, administration, and regulation.

Even as practices of racialization from above have cast shadows across the Durand Line, to remediate the condition of bin Laden's own shadowy existence, the Geronimo operation involved bringing back to earth the necessity for veracity and verifiability of life-in-death. On the one hand, racialization from above was accomplished through a constellation of "pattern of life" data that could construct a spectral version of bin Laden's identity, whose corporeality evaded capture, with his presence in the Abbottabad compound never visually verified. Imaging data from the Sentinel drone flying several miles overhead and operated out of Langley and Shamsi Airfield suggested there was a resident whose physical size and stature was comparable to bin Laden's. Yet given his own capacity to wield control over the circulation of his visibility, such partial imaging was not permitted to enter the war on terror's visual archive. Something more grounded was required. The Obama administration ruled out a missile strike because the intensity of destruction would not only destroy what was presumed to be a "treasure trove" of intelligence about the inner workings of Al Qaeda, but the body of bin Laden itself would become unrecognizable as such, replaced by yet another screened image from the air. Deploying Navy SEAL Team 6 would place the "human element" in close contact with its target, capture the image of bin Laden on camera, and buttress the truth claims embedded in the war on terror's visual archive.

A strategy of unmediated proximity was required, whose "rush to the intimate" could adequately respond to 9/11's wound of punctured domesticity.[36] Members of Navy SEAL Team 6 wore night-vision contact lenses, "cat vision," as well as video cameras that purportedly relayed images to the White House

Situation Room. Unlike much of the war on terror's visual archive, the video feeds whose collage was screened in the Situation Room have to date remained publicly unseen. The postmortem images of bin Laden himself have received nominal, if highly restricted, circulation. After a brief public disagreement inside the Obama administration, the CIA made available a portfolio of photographs to select members of Congress, who then released statements verifying the existence of the photographs, that they were of bin Laden, and also, importantly, that such visual verification was unnecessary. The ability of sovereign power to point to the existence of a visual archive, and hence its truth, without making it visible reproduces the flickering dance of light and shadow that remains an effect of racialization from above.

Standing in for a "scalp on display" is the photograph of the Situation Room, taken by the official White House photographer, Pete Souza, and initially published on the White House's Flickr photostream, itself lauded as an innovation in executive transparency. We come to see the death of bin Laden through its absent presence, that just outside the frame he will have been executed. We are asked to identify with the sovereign power of observation, each gaze focused on a singular point just outside the frame. The out-of-frame flat-screen monitor collaged with visual data contrasts with the blank laptop computers positioned in front of Robert Gates and Hillary Clinton. Necks crane from the rear of the room for an unobstructed view. While Joe Biden reclines slightly and watches with the calm demeanor of experience, Obama leans forward with a stare whose intensity is rarely captured in photos. Lips are tightly pursed, save Clinton's. She has covered her mouth with her hand in a look of astonishment, dismay, concern. Yet when asked later, Clinton says she has "absolutely no idea" what was on screen during that particular moment; she was "somewhat sheepishly concerned that it was my preventing one of my early spring allergic coughs. So it may have no great meaning whatsoever."[37] The photograph thus calibrates our identification with the sovereign for whom the execution provides legitimacy, whose variegated affective response is meant, like Clinton's remark, to be rendered meaningless, and whose violence remains obfuscated by a fiction of embodied disembodiment.

While this chapter has meant to detain precisely such a fiction, what remains is training ourselves to see otherwise. One possible entry point is through the specter of lynching photography in the raciality of the war on terror, with its deft concatenation of antiblackness and colonial violence. The prolific archive of torture images produced at Abu Ghraib activated this genealogical and resolutely relational way of seeing, revealing the mutilated body's double performance for both the U.S. military personnel and the viewers of the photographs themselves. In those photos the embodied objects and tactics of imperial violence are placed in full view, while the observing subject remains abstracted outside the frame.[38] Rather than consign these images to the externalized logics of aberration or exception, a critical ethnic studies intervention reminds us that such hypervisualized scenes of captivity have as their condition of possibility the "nonscenes" of torture that structure the everyday lives of people held captive in the U.S. carceral regime.[39]

Another pedagogy is achieved through the remarkable visual art of Ken Gonzales-Day. A cultural historian, Gonzales-Day assembled a large collection of photographs and postcards from scenes of lynching that became crucial evidence for his landmark research on racial technologies of violence in the western United States. In *Lynching in the West,* he comprehensively documents how the 350 instances of lynching in California between 1850 and 1935, particularly of Native, Mexican, and Chinese men, were inextricably linked to the expanding borders of U.S. sovereign power. Inspired by the work of Ida B. Wells-Barnett and the NAACP to document black lynchings, Gonzales-Day reconstructs the embodied nuance of human particularity otherwise lost in glosses of imperial culture. Their virtual erasure from national histories of racial violence in the borderlands, he argues, was enabled in part by a tacit refusal to track the workings of comparative racialization as it labored to both consolidate and persistently exceed the contours of the national. Gonzales-Day reproduced and displayed many of these images in museum installations, only now with the tortured bodies withdrawn from view, literally expunging their presence from the frame. The result, entitled *Erased Lynching,* foregrounds the site and scene of lynching where, in the installation space, the viewer is himself folded into the scene. Gonzales-Day calls the project "a conceptual gesture intended to direct the viewer's attention, not upon the lifeless body of the lynch victim, but upon the mechanisms of lynching themselves."[40] (See figure 20.2.)

The stakes animating my analysis of the Situation Room photograph are to develop a perspective that can see the contemporaneity of erasure otherwise, to account for the ways that mechanisms of life-in-death produced by the homeland security state have become articulated to visual technologies of racialization from above. How might we contextualize, document, and disrupt this articulation, a move performed so evocatively by Gonzales-Day vis-à-vis racialization on the ground? By the time you read this, the locations where unmanned aerial systems yoke visuality and life-in-death will have been contorted still further. Since I began writing on drones in spring 2011, racialization from above has expanded and envisioned the borders of the U.S.

FIGURE 20.2. Ken Gonzales-Day, *der Wild West Show*, 2006. 3.8 × 6 inches, Lightjet mounted to cardstock. Courtesy of Ken Gonzales-Day.

homeland in Yemen, Libya, and Somalia; the day after Obama's reelection in November 2012 included a strike in Yemen.[41] Even as state and parastate agents of security and surveillance remain enthralled by those concepts of endurance, proximity, and precision that give form to racialization from above, *Erased Lynching* brings us back to the firmament on which such violence is appended and apprehended. Doing so demands an accounting of the bodies that appear and disappear before our eyes at blistering speed. Perhaps in such an accounting we might grasp a momentary antidote to an archive whose tempo is complicit with the future anterior of preemptive war.

NOTES

An earlier version was originally published in *Comparative American Studies* 9.4 (December 2011): 325–41. The publisher has granted permission for its reprint.

1. Quoted in Singh, "The Afterlife of Fascism," 71.
2. Silliman, "The 'Old West' in the Middle East."
3. Margolies, "Geronimo, Bin Laden, and U.S. Foreign Policy."
4. See Mbembe, "Necropolitics"; Mignolo, *Local Histories / Global Designs*; Sexton, "People-of-Color-Blindness."
5. Stoler, "On Degrees of Imperial Sovereignty," 138.

6. Graham, *Cities Under Siege*, 132.

7. Kaplan, "Homeland Insecurities," 87.

8. Feldman, "Securocratic Wars of Public Safety," 336.

9. Mbembe, "Necropolitics," 31–32.

10. Sexton, "People-of-Color-Blindness," 38.

11. Rana, *Terrifying Muslims*, 50–57.

12. Pulido, "Rethinking Environmental Racism," 13. On critical human geography, see Elden, *Terror and Territory*; Graham, *Cities Under Siege*; Gregory, *The Colonial Present*; Weizman, *Hollow Land*. On critical race theory, see Goldberg, *The Threat of Race*; Lipsitz, *How Racism Takes Place*. On visual culture studies, see Chow, *The Age of the World Target*; Kaplan, "'A Rare and Chilling View.'"

13. Kaplan, "Precision Targets."

14. Virilio, *War and Cinema*.

15. Kramer, *The Blood of Government*; Melamed, *Represent and Destroy*; Winant, *The World Is a Ghetto*.

16. Goldberg, *The Threat of Race*, 30.

17. Drinnon, *Facing West*; Slotkin, *Regeneration through Violence*; Sadowski-Smith, *Border Fictions*; Streeby, *American Sensations*; Brown, *Walled States, Waning Sovereignty*; Alexander, *The New Jim Crow*; Gilmore, *Golden Gulag*; Wacquant, "From Slavery to Mass Incarceration."

18. Weizman, *Hollow Land*.

19. Gregory, "From a View to a Kill."

20. UAS Center for Excellence, *Eyes of the Army*, 9.

21. Goldberg, *The Racial State*.

22. Weizman, *Hollow Land*.

23. Goldberg, *The Threat of Race*; Harvey, *The New Imperialism*; Pease, *The New American Exceptionalism*.

24. UAS Center for Excellence, *Eyes of the Army*, 19.

25. U.S. Department of Defense, *Unmanned Systems Integrated Roadmap, FY2013–2038* (14-S-0553), 5.

26. U.S. Government Accountability Office, *Unmanned Aircraft Systems*.

27. Gregory, "From a View to a Kill."

28. Feldman, *A Shadow over Palestine*; McAlister, *Epic Encounters*; Graham, *Cities Under Siege*; Gregory, *The Colonial Present*.

29. Gary Solis, "America's Unlawful Combatants," *Washington Post*, March 12, 2010.

30. Vacek, "Big Brother Will Soon Be Watching," 675.

31. Mirzoeff, "War Is Culture," 1741.

32. Gregory, "From a View to a Kill," 201.

33. Rana, *Terrifying Muslims*, 54.

34. Sadowski-Smith, *Border Fictions*; Margolies, "Geronimo, Bin Laden, and U.S. Foreign Policy."

35. Gregory, "The Everywhere War."

36. Gregory, "Rush to the Intimate"; Kaplan, "Homeland Insecurities."

37. Barry Moody, "Clinton: Allergy, Not Anguish in My bin Laden Photo," Reuters News Service, May 5, 2011.

38. Butler, *Frames of War*; Puar, *Terrorist Assemblages*; Razack, *Casting Out.*

39. Rodríguez, "(Non)Scenes of Captivity."

40. Gonzales-Day, *Erased Lynching.*

41. Indeed since this chapter was originally published in December 2011, both the scope of drone warfare and the scholarship on it have grown exponentially. Rather than a full-scale updating of the original essay (which I am currently conducting for a larger project), I point to the following book-length studies: Adey, Whitehead, and Williams, eds., *From Above*; Chamayou, *A Theory of the Drone*; Neocleous, *War Power, Police Power.*

V. FUGITIVE SOCIALITIES AND ALTERNATIVE FUTURES

TWENTY-ONE

Decolonization, "Race," and Remaindered Life under Empire

NEFERTI X. M. TADIAR

To speak of empire today is to speak about a global dispensation of power predicated on, and furthering, the aims of capitalist accumulation in an era when the familiar components and dynamics of the international order of sovereign states, by means of which such accumulation took place, seem to have been dramatically, perhaps irrevocably, reorganized. To understand empire's workings is hence to grasp an order of common ideals, sensibilities, and practices that no longer entail simply the protocols of proper belonging defined by the nation-state or protocols of full citizenship that defined the rights of peoples in the age of national sovereignty. Certainly race, gender, and sexuality, as identitarian codes for understanding and regulating human differences cut against the measure of Man, have long served to organize the social divisions of economic production and political power within and across nation-states—perhaps exemplarily so during the age of decolonization (the true and obverse content of the age of freedom)—and continue to do so in the present. Yet over the past several decades these codes have operated beyond a normative cultural logic of social identities (where they act as means of specification, disciplining, and representation of individuals, groups, and nations as integral units of modern sovereignty). These codes now also operate within numerous calculative procedures of attribution, where they act as variables for partitioning and bundling organic and inorganic masses, matters, and potentials in new modes of value production and life extraction, which have resulted in both a proliferation of social differences (in shifting scales) and a staggeringly profound breach in the fates of human beings.

Beyond the protocols and ideals of political community established by a still expanding Euro-American humanism and rule of democratic sovereignty, which defined an older world order, today's imperial order entails protocols for the enhancement and furtherance of life of an already recognized humanity,[1] whose guaranteed rights to such life of the already human can be extended, but only to deserving candidates: those becoming-human, who aspire to the protocols of living that obtain under a transnational free market economy and expanding liberal-democratic rule of law, and those periodically expelled from humanity who petition for asylum from the ravages of that existence beyond the pale of empire. Seeing in the latter the making of a new humanitarian order, Mahmood Mamdani argues, "If the rights of the citizen are pointedly political, the rights of the human pertain to sheer survival; they are summed up in one word: protection. The new language refers to its subjects not as bearers of rights—and thus active agents in their emancipation—but as passive beneficiaries of an external 'responsibility to protect.' Rather than rights-bearing citizens, beneficiaries of the humanitarian order are akin to recipients of charity."[2]

I describe these features of the present to call attention to the shifting imperial mandates that racial and sex and gender regimes—as conjoined systems of producing, managing, and understanding (perceiving and naturalizing) social divisions of labor, discrepancies of privilege, resources, and life chances and qualities—have been crucial for fulfilling. But how? What is the role, for example, of racial logics in the work of empire? If struggles of decolonization in the past were always critiques and struggles against racism, insofar as colonialism was itself the invention of racism as we know it, how, in this present moment, are we to critically understand the role of racial logics in the contemporary work and history of empire? How, in other words, can this critical work be the work of decolonization today?

"Race" and Empire Studies

Since the more blatantly brutal policing wars launched by the United States in the past twenty years, a growing body of work in empire studies has sought to take account of earlier moments of U.S. imperialism, which decades of academic scholarship had actively forgotten.[3] Analyzing the ideological representations and machineries of social practice of U.S. colonial government, public administration, medicine and public health, state and civic projects, and popular culture in the Philippines, Puerto Rico, Cuba, Hawaii, Guam, and Samoa in the late nineteenth and early twentieth century, this work has been invaluable for foregrounding transnational processes of racism and racial (and gendered) formation across metropole and periphery, as well as for enabling an alternative genealogy of dominant U.S. institutions and apparatuses that are key sites and instruments of racializing processes.

For example, Warwick Anderson's work argues that the shift in Filipino resistance to U.S. imperial occupation at the turn of the twentieth century, from practices of diplomatic negotiations to guerrilla warfare, shaped the logics and practices of the new American public health after 1910. Colonial health officers in the Philippines were among the first advocates of this new public health, which entailed a shift from a focus on sanitation to a focus on the private activities of individuals and the control of public spaces and social life in accordance with what he calls the "white American racial grid of intelligibility" of tropical pathology. This regime of "racial hygiene," as he calls it, served as "a mode of population management and identity formation," disciplining natives' corporeal and social practices to contain their predispositions to be bearers of disease and contamination, shaping the way Filipinos thought about their own bodies and their societies, but also in turn symbolically and directly influencing the new public health in the United States through the Pacific crossings of ideas and personnel. Reflecting further on these crossings, Anderson urges us to think seriously "about the extent to which urban health services in America that targeted immigrants and minorities were legacies of empire," and to consider, more broadly, "the imperial dimensions of national embodiment in the United States."[4] His own study traces the genealogy of the later international development regime, particularly in the arena of public health services, as well as the more contemporary global regime of biomedical citizenship to these early U.S. colonial projects of hygiene and bodily reform in the Philippines.

Similarly Paul Kramer's work provides, on the one hand, "a history of the racial politics of empire, of the ways in which hierarchies of difference were generated and mobilized in order to legitimate and to organize invasion, conquest, and colonial administration," and, on the other hand, "a history of the imperial politics of race, of the way that empire-building interacted with, and transformed, the process of racial formation." Looking at public statements, debates, state policies, private journals, and media representations of U.S. and Filipino politicians, military and civil government authorities, and soldiers during and after the Filipino-American war in 1899 until World War II, Kramer argues that the mutual imbrication of Filipino and American nation-building during those four decades led not only to racialized differences between the two populations but to a proliferation of new forms of racialized difference in both places, differences through which political capacity and agency were calibrated, delimited, and excepted in the process of negotiating the meaning and scope of national sovereignty. As he puts it, "It was not simply that difference made empire possible: empire remade difference in the process."[5]

The importance of this scholarship for foregrounding transnational processes of race making and racism across metropole and periphery and for enabling an alternative genealogy of dominant U.S. institutions and apparatuses that are key sites and instruments of racializing processes cannot be underestimated. At the same time, in a moment of late imperial capitalism when, as I described earlier, the principles for establishing humanity as the new globopolitical subject is concordant with new modes of extracting value through the discrepant subsumption and surplusing of life—that is, in this arguably different moment of empire, in which globopolitical citizenship depends less on any particular normative national culture (not even imperial U.S. culture) than on valorizable life (a calculus of social values)—the rapidly burgeoning histories of imperial race making and, most important, a widely shared analytical focus on *race as difference* from a putative unmarked identitarian norm (of whiteness) raise questions about the political consequences of this knowledge. In the strong focus on dominant logics and institutions of producing, regulating, stratifying, measuring, and specifying individuals and populations, through the racial differentiation of identities—indeed in the disciplinary focus on race as difference—such works risk shoring up the very "grid of intelligibility" of disciplinary and regulatory power that U.S. Empire studies purports to critique.

I would venture further that the attention to processes of race making as the primary object of study transnationalizes, without radically altering, the social analytic of a liberal democratic politics. Indeed Kramer sees colonial race making as "intimately tied up in a broader politics of recognition," which he argues provided the ideological basis for brokering both empowerment and disenfranchisement for colonial subjects negotiating the treacherous road to political independence.[6] On the one hand, this social analytic elides racisms and processes of racialization embedded in the successful assimilation to and inhabiting of the norm, such as nationality (and not just differences or exclusion from the norm). On the other hand, such an analytic overwrites historical imperial racial processes in the terms of what Jodi Melamed calls "racial liberalism," a fantasy of official antiracism sutured to postwar U.S. nationalism that she argues facilitated the containment of radical anticolonial and antiracist movements and fueled the further expansion of U.S. global hegemony after World War II.[7] Melamed observes that racial liberalism employs a paradigm of race as culture, which in its neoliberal revision increasingly displaces racial reference altogether, addressing racial inequalities as a matter of culture and casting more conventionally legible racisms, such as those associated with slavery and colonialism, as (ultimately) disappearing. I read the social analytic of histories of imperial race making as bearing the imprints of racial liberalism insofar as it understands race primarily through the rubric of political representation, that is, as a problem of lack or failure (or unevenness) of political recognition and rights on the juridical field stipulated on the liberal ideals of universal freedom and equality.[8] It is from precisely the point of view of these ideals that race making and racial formation are understood to be projects (and problems) of difference.

Such an analytic thus serves to obscure other forms of racism not primarily predicated on juridical subjects, including the racist violence of dominant forms of humanization embedded in everyday practical structures and protocols of living historically instituted through colonialism and now reorganized as the very basis for a new global political economy of life. Elsewhere I write about the racist violence of this global political economy of life in terms of a distinction that is crucial to the operation of new processes of value production, characteristic of the global financial economy, that is, a distinction between *life worth living*, life with the capacity to yield value as living labor, and *life worth expending*, life with the capacity to yield value as disposable existence.[9] It is this contemporary mode of racism, whose productivity is manifested in global industries of war, security, bioeconomics, and humanitarian protection and is also at work in the conversion of the promised lifetimes of large swathes of national populations into monetized assets (securitized liquid reserves) by their own states in their respective bids to play the global financial market,[10] that I fear is occluded (and, more, aided) by the shoring up of a grid of intelligibility of race as social difference.

If race as social difference is given both as object of analysis and analytical principle (with gender as an additional, value-adding variable), it loses its critical force as a theoretical question and political intervention. For example, in U.S. Empire studies of U.S.-Philippines colonial relations, natives, in this case Filipinos, come to be seen as having agency in and through this already given racialized identity of their nationality, despite its relatively recent emergence in struggle under late Spanish rule and its continuing inchoateness decades later and arguably up until the present. What the U.S. colonizers themselves sought to accomplish—the conversion of a radical political claim ("Filipino") that instigated and emerged out of revolutionary struggle against Spanish colonialism into a disciplinary project of assimilation and tutelage under the imperial aegis of the United States ("Filipinization")—is itself taken for granted as an established fact by contemporary scholarship.[11]

Historicizing the construction and self-making of "Filipino" as processes of racialization, even as part of a broader process of race making, would seem only to affirm race as *properties* of total social formations, however contingent, flexible, and constructed those properties are contended to be. Such an analytic confirms the established *fact* of existence of the social subjects whose racialization (the mechanism of inscribing those value-laden meanings and qualities constituting race as difference) it meticulously critiques. In this dominant coding of sociality, academic knowledge furthers rather than radically alters the practices of an imperial project.

It would seem that, even in critical work on empire, there is more decolonizing to be done.

Imperial Reproduction as Race Making

To my thinking decolonization demands that we reconsider the reflexive ways we understand and code sociality, as well as the ways we think about historical continuity and change in genealogies of empire, both of which imply a particular notion of reproduction. If imperialism is the generalization or extended reproduction of the social relations of capital constituted through subjective norms of gender, race, and sexuality, it is undoubtedly an inheritance of particular institutions and codifications of human life and being. One of the most important of these institutions is the law. Angela Mitropolous asserts that what distinguishes the United States from the British was the United States's use of common law to expand and push through frontier spaces. "Common law, with its reliance on case law, unfolds through a subtle play between precedence and approximation. . . . It navigates power through repetition and variation." Mitropolous argues further that "it is the heteronormative household that determined, through precedent and approximation in common law's unfolding, the extent to which property, contract and credit were recognized, considered as heritable and therefore guaranteed across time." As the basic architectural unit of a Jeffersonian domestic economy, the heteronormative household figured centrally in U.S. imperialism by modeling "the space through which the legal form of value was defined and imposed."[12]

Through this conception of U.S. domestic space working within the imagination of colonial legislative law, inhabitants of the nonsovereign Philippine Islands (Las Filipinas) who were formerly subjects of Spain were deemed unsuitable for U.S. citizenship. Instead of being fully incorporated into the domestic space of the U.S. nation, upon their colonization by the United States Filipinos were given the imperially recognized status of nationals, members of a "dependency—an unincorporated territory belonging to the United States and under it's complete sovereignty—a part of the United States in an international sense," as the dean of the College of Law of the University of the Philippines, George Malcolm, defined the Philippines in the *Michigan Law Review* in 1916.[13] Filomeno V. Aguilar Jr. argues that such a status—invented with the country's "first organic act," the Philippine Bill of 1902—was founded on the immediate political precedent set by legislation for Puerto Rico and by the application of the U.S. Chinese Exclusion Law to the Philippines in 1902.[14] It is notable that through the colonial application of this U.S. legal act, which was among the many immigrant acts racializing the U.S. nation against the figure of Asia, in the making of Philippine nationality, *Filipino* would be officially racialized as *not* Chinese, despite the fact that the core of the emerging national elite, including the intellectual stratum that formed the propaganda movement against Spain in the late nineteenth century, consisted of *mestizo* Chinese-Filipinos.[15] Furthermore it is particularly important to underscore the fact that against the politically inclusive citizenship provision of the revolutionary Philippine government's Malolos Constitution of 1899, the invention of Filipino nationality legislated under U.S. colonialism was most directly shaped by the nonextension of the 1868 Fourteenth Amendment of the U.S. Constitution to the new colonial acquisition.[16] Insofar as the Fourteenth Amendment was framed to give citizenship to African American former slaves (excluding Native Americans), we could understand this nonextension as racializing Filipino nationality against the defining cases of both. (Indeed we could say Filipino is racialized as *not* black and *like* Indian.)[17]

I would hence argue that this national status of Filipino bore the legal memory of the earlier precedents set by the landmark cases *Cherokee Nation v. Georgia* (1831) and *Scott v. Sandford* (1857), in which the U.S. Supreme Court judged both "Indians" and the "descendants of Africans" as neither citizens nor aliens, on the basis of their disqualification from the right to own property. Insofar as indigenous people and slaves or the descendants of slaves constituted "two ways of not owning the self," the Lockean condition of citizenship as self-ownership, they were not legally representable; that is, they did not have recourse to the law in asserting or seeking protection of their rights.[18] Although both indigenous people and slaves and their descendants would subsequently achieve citizenship, these and other cases ideologically affirmed the values of white property-owning subjects, upholding "possessive individualism" (the individual as sole proprietor of his or her skills) as the criterion of citizenship and legal representation. These legal decisions and acts set precedents for deeming what is outside of the national rule of law as also outside of the bounds of civil and human status, which continues to be reflected in the attitudes today toward "illegals" (as forms of nonpersonhood). Similarly the "Filipino nationality" recognized and presupposed by the U.S. imperial government in preparing the Philippines for eventual independence would require these conditions of legal subjectivity and the heteronormative household as the proper form of the self-managed territorialized domestic economy.

Part of my argument, then, is that there are complex relations of mutual *inter-* and *intra*constitution between "minority" populations and colonial "nationalities" as they are forged as subsidiary, *normative* forms of citizenship under empire. Following the logic of precedent and approximation, it is no accident that the experimental U.S. colonial mass educational system tasked with making citizen-subjects out of Philippine natives found its test cases at the Hampton Institute for the schooling of Native Americans and the Booker T. Washington's Tuskegee Institute for African Americans. In 1900 the first director of the colonial education bureau, Fred Atkinson, wrote Washington to seek his advice on establishing education in the Philippines along industrial lines.[19] Atkinson's visits to Tuskegee and the Hampton Institute provided him with models of an industrial education that placed considerable emphasis on agricultural instruction, an emphasis that would facilitate the further integration of the national economy based on the export of raw materials within a broader international economy.[20]

It is precisely through the heteronormative household installed by means of the political, economic, social institutions of independent nationhood as norm (the imperial program of "humanization" of colonial peoples through the protocols of citizen-man, the precursor of the proper subject of globopolitical life) that the U.S. technocratic production of Filipino subjects as particular forms of social relation to work, nature, and value, indeed as particular dispositions toward oneself and others, bears the gender, race, and sexuality imprints of the putatively unmarked culture of freedom of U.S. liberal democracy. Put more broadly, it is through accession to, and not merely exception or exclusion from, a putative universal norm of modern free subjects that social groups are gendered and raced.

The installation of dominant U.S. gendered roles through the heteronormative household can be glimpsed in the home economics programs of this mass educational system, which sutured a reformed private domestic life to a Jeffersonian domestic national economy and to an emerging international economic order. Jefferson's ideal of an independent yeomanry informed the colonial Philippine rural education emphasis on training in farming and housekeeping, the growing of home gardens, and so on. The gendered roles that such a household ideal were to foster are manifest in the differences between the Barrio Boy's Creed and Barrio Girl's Creed and their respective areas of training as stipulated in the educational readers widely disseminated in the schools. While boys were to be trained in productive labor ("to kill weeds, increase crops, double the output of flock by keeping more chickens and careful breeding; growing larger crops; keeping a home garden to increase, vary and improve the diet; increasing the value of the land with fruit trees, fence vines, shrubs and flowers"), girls were trained for naturalized, free, domestic, "caring" labor ("to love chickens and pigs and goats and puppies as well as dolls and dresses . . . to take care of some domestic animals as well as my brother, who does not love them as much as I; homemaking; to give away flowers and cook vegetables which I myself raised").[21] Such a division of labor clearly entails the subjective imperatives and object relations constitutive of the proper social relations of heteronormative households.

To see the interplaying constitution of subsidiary forms of citizenship under empire is to think beyond the discrete genealogies of particular racialized social groups and to think beyond the homologies that buttress the perspective of imperial comparatism. To employ these discrete genealogies (even in arguments of mutual constitution) is to reproduce the effects of the juridical fictions of imperialism (and to think and imagine from within the rule of law that is its buttress). It is indeed to see that George W. Bush's preposterous statement that the U.S. colonial occupation of the Philippines at the turn of the twentieth century could serve as a model for the contemporary occupation of Iraq was a genealogical claim that needs to be made for empire to continue. More than a hundred years after the Philippine-American War (1900–1913), which left between a tenth and a sixth of the native population dead and a legacy of military techniques of counterinsurgency and torture as well as police procedures of surveillance and domestic security that persist in the contemporary context, this earlier imperial project of capitalist expansion is deemed a success, serving as an instructive precedent for democratizing regime change today. Cited as precedent, this episode does in fact become part and parcel of the autobiographical narrative of imperial democracy. It confirms the geopolitical order whose installation over the next four decades until World War II (and with it the solidification of "the American Century") it helped to inaugurate. Empire studies risks a similar confirmation of this geopolitical order when its location of historical precedents for today's imperial actions traces the very same narrative lines of continuity through which the imperial subject maintains its privileged representational being. It risks, in other words, being a discursive means of imperial reproduction.

In contrast that earlier moment of imperial expansion might serve as a historical passageway connecting contemporary scenes of warehoused disposable populations within the United States and scenes of populations surplused through an ongoing global antiterrorist war waged not only by U.S. forces but also by subsidiary or franchise state military forces everywhere. It foregrounds the submerged side of a general process of *racialization through freedom* that traverses the given racial orders of both metropole and colony, which are so central to the material and symbolic organization of imperial democracy.

In fact John Blanco argues that for many of the white rank and file in the U.S. Army fighting in the Philippines, "the new episode of imperial conquest [was] the concluding chapter to the unfinished racial conquest of whites over blacks and native Americans." We see evidence of what Blanco calls "the counterhistory of white redemption [that] draws from the popular memories of the Confederacy's war against the emancipation of slavery, as well as the self-identified Anglo-Saxon wars against the indigenous populations on the westward frontier," not only in the racialized representation of Filipinos as African Americans and Native Americans in public arenas of debate and visual culture but also in the fact that the height of U.S. atrocities in the genocidal campaigns in the Philippines in the early 1900s coincided with the escalation of lynchings of black men in the United States during the same moment.[22] Blanco shows that U.S. public officials attempted to frame the violence of war in domestic metaphors and discourses of civil society. This domestication of violence in paternalistic metaphors of discipline, hygiene, and education attested to by countless political cartoons of the period was also in effect the suppression and internalization of the violence of a translocal, imperial war through civil institutions like the Bureau of Health, the Bureau of the Interior, and the Bureau of Public Security.[23]

The domestication of racist violence (what Blanco calls "race as the sign of war, the state of war as constitutive of race relations") through civil structures and institutions in the postcolony can be viewed as playing out the geopolitical race narrative that Melamed argues is at the core of racial liberalism, that is, the integration of minoritized populations within U.S. democratic society and advancement toward equality defined through a liberal framework of legal rights and inclusive nationalism.[24] We see the way a shared logic of imperial reproduction is at work in the construction of racialized socialities here and abroad, indeed of ethnicities as particular, minority subjects within universal projects of enfranchisement, empowerment, and even liberation.

Social Reproduction as Life Making

So far I have argued that it is crucial to see such intricate connections between racialized subpopulations as the invisible latticework or circuit board of a shared logic or order of imperial reproduction, that is, the production of the social relations of the global free world. These connections do not imply a simple continuity of being of these discrete social identities but rather a continuum of processes of social making that cut across and confound the very racialized collectivities they importantly help to constitute.

However, if we only track this imperial reproduction of racialized socialities and maintain the grid of intelligibility through which such socialities are produced, we miss another level of social reproduction, this time on the side of quotidian social struggle, which is neither tethered to nor constrained by continuity, succession, lineage, or consistency of sociality as subject. This level of social reproduction, sometimes understood through the category of reproductive labor, consists of those generative associations and acts, social capacities and aspirations, agencies of imagination and practice, that can also act in fugitive, dispersive, and insurgent fashion. As the designation of this array of life-making, life-renewing capacities and practices, reproductive labor is wrongly conflated with the conception of reproduction as the production and conservation of dominant social relations, and indeed as the production and maintenance of a stable sameness. For life making, perhaps especially under conditions of foreclosure, negation, and dispossession, may very well and often does consist of practices that can corrode rather than preserve the putative sociality of one's naturalized belonging, in part by involvement in and mediations of other socialities.

We might consider, for example, the role of native wives in the southern Philippines, Aceh, Borneo, and elsewhere across the arc of the Indian Ocean to East Africa, in the anchoring and shaping of that transnational skein of networks composing the Muslim diaspora of the Hadhrami—Arabs from Hadhramaut, Yemen—which Engseng Ho shows constituted itself over centuries as a potential rival empire to European and U.S. empires. Counting Osama bin Laden as its most prominent recent figure, this specter of diasporic sociality now draws out some of the most virulent forms of racialization of Muslims in Europe and North America in the contemporary context of resurgent U.S. imperialism. As Ho describes it, the Hadhrami diaspora

> brought together not just peoples from the homeland, but peoples in destinations throughout the Indian Ocean as well. Here, Hadramis played a major role in the expansion of Islam. . . . In their marriages with local women, Hadramis and their offspring become Swahilis, Gujaratis, Malabaris, Malays, Javanese, Filipinos. They became natives everywhere. At the same time, the men and their offspring continued to move throughout this oceanic space, for reasons of trade, study, pilgrimage, and politics. Throughout this space, a Hadrami could travel and be put up by relatives, who might be Arab uncles married to foreign local aunts. Many men had wives in each port. In the arc of coasts around the Indian Ocean, then, a skein of networks arose in which people socialized with distant foreigners as kinsmen and as Muslims.[25]

Native wives served as anchors, port homes, seemingly fixed milieus of accommodation in the geography of this diaspora's movements, yet they do not figure prominently in this or any other account of emergence of a counterempire. They were nevertheless vital to the social reproduction of the local and transnational peoples for whom they were enabling means of life. Like the local, "native" wives of the Hadhrami, Filipina domestic workers and caregivers in Europe, Asia, America, and the Middle East (including Israel/Palestine, where Filipina women as well as transwomen work on both sides of an ongoing racialized war) mediate and shape socialities that ultimately may not claim them as one of their own or as bearing the proper lineage and agency of cultural transmission of their host or patron communities.

If we stick to given continuist narratives we may miss what passes between and among given social identities in ways indiscernible, too indeterminate, or too destabilizing—perhaps too infrasubjective and infrasocial—to be thought through the macroprocess called "identification" or even subjectification, as the other side of racialization. We miss forces that are transient and fleeting despite the pivotal role they might play in the renewal as well as the mutation of the social geography of global empire, which we might equally understand as the racial and gendered relations of production of capitalism. The imperial reproduction of these relations might subsume the life-making practices of social reproduction of its subjects, yet the very foreclosure of other forms of life entailed by such imperial reproduction, not to mention the harshness of living exploited, devalued life under capitalism, sets the conditions for the uneasy alignments and discordance as well as outright antagonisms between the reproduction of imperial relations and the social reproduction of individual and collective lives.

We cannot therefore think about the continuity or reproduction of capitalist production without also considering the necessary violence of preventing workers from running away, that is, from flight from their function within capitalist relations. It is in this context that we can recognize the salience of what Marx understood as processes of "original accumulation," those processes of annihilation of the means of subsistence, which secures workers from running away: "Individual consumption provides, on the one hand, the means for the workers' maintenance and reproduction; on the other hand, by the constant annihilation of the means of subsistence, it provides for their continued re-appearance on the labour-market."[26] Destruction of the means of subsistence might be understood in terms of the assault on the social reproductive capacities of particular populations and groups. The destruction of welfare services serves as only one contemporary example of such assault. Permanent war, land appropriation through agribusiness, speculative settlement, and real estate development continue to be some of the more spectacular forms of dispossession, but there are also quotidian forms of exclusion from material and cultural resources, or forms of enclosure of the so-called general intellect that serve as emergent nonsubjective modes of racist dispossession. Meanwhile the gendered reproductive capacities of individual disenfranchised women as well as men from those very disposable populations whose own social reproductive capacities remain under assault are harnessed to the social reproduction of advanced industrial households and families. In this latter context migrant Third World domestic workers' desires are often outlawed, their naturalized families and kin splintered transnationally, even as they form new, informal networks, nonnormative families to assist in their own reproduction. Thus, on the one hand, racial, gendered norms are deployed to reproduce the class subjects of globopolitical humanity. On the other hand, these social forces of reproductive labor are continuously prohibited or impeded from becoming subjects at all.

Within this uneven and contradictory arena of social reproduction it is therefore important to attend to practices of dissolution that might issue out of the excess and leftovers of life making on the part of those serving as the means of reproduction of others. We might attend, for example, to the practice and discourse of Filipina wives of Japanese men running away from their homes and roles as reproducers of the Japanese family. As Lieba Faier shows in her ethnography of Filipina wives in rural Japan, the acts and stories of Filipinas running away (stories told and circulated by Filipinas themselves) serve to create potential and actual spaces of extradomestic life and in this way contribute to conditions of instability and insecurity for the very Japanese family that they were expected to stabilize and restore.[27] Running away was at once an alternative strategy for survival, allowing some Filipinas to continue supporting their families in the Philippines while leveraging better conditions of life for themselves in Japan, and a tempting but also terrifying life option that was dangerous, promising, and unsettling. Running away is not only an act of freedom on the part of the enslaved but also a risk-taking, adventurous, and ordinary practice, part of the historical repertoire of everyday life making on the part of native wives, the gendered mediators and means of interethnic, international social reproduction and exchange.

Running away is one example of social practices of making viable life for those who serve as the means of reproduction of others that both supports and corrodes privileged forms of sociality. It highlights a realm of actions and processes that exists beneath the threshold of intelligibility of imperial race making and its racial liberal critique, actions and processes that I designate and understand as forms of *remaindered life*. Remaindered life is an analytical category for thinking about life-sustaining forms and practices of personhood and sociality that, despite being pushed into permanent outmodedness and illegibility by the discursive and practical mandates of imperial reproduction, persist in creative, transformed ways as practices of living—important soft technologies or means of social reproduction—particularly among more disenfranchised social groups. It is, in my own thinking, also a political imperative to attend to and continue the work of decolonization.

Remaindered Life: Vital Platforms of Social Reproduction

Anna Tsing writes about the defining tracks and grounds, channels and landscape elements enabling global flows as relations of production that are hidden by a dominant model of circulation that many scholars adopt to frame their analyses of globalization. Rather than following money as the *ur*-object of flow, she urges attention to the social conditions of that flow, the means and infrastructure of place making that circulation requires.[28] Tsing's perspectival shift is useful here to think about the way that contemporary immigrant domestic workers and caregivers, as much as the native wives of the Hadhrami diaspora, serve similarly as the enabling channels of not just a geographic movement of privileged forces of agency (money and its sociosubjective correlatives, i.e., sovereign subjects) but also a chronohistorical movement of privileged forms of sociality (discrete communities persisting through time). To the extent that these workers and wives serve as feminized means for the transgenerational survival, renewal, continuity, and futurity of social subjects made legible within the political frame of empire (whether as legitimate or illegitimate nations or diasporic peoples), it is important to understand the forms of life and practices of life making that shape their role as vital *media* of other lives. As conduits of other people's wills and aspirations, accommodating and conforming to the bodily, emotional, psychical, and metaphysical requirements of individuals and communities, to which they are attached as vital component yet alienable parts, they act in a very practical but also otherworldly sense forms of human media (technologies of reproduction) rather than fully fledged sovereign (self-determining, self-owning) individual subjects.[29]

To understand the life-making capacities of such human media beyond their role in the reproduction of legible subjects under empire (i.e., beyond the conservation of the sameness of social being of the latter) means to consider the plural ontologies enabling and guiding their performances of this mediatic role. It means considering the permeability, extendability, divisibility, and mutability of selves, the porousness of social belonging (family, household, kin, community), and the transmissibility of potency and life across persons as well as across divisions of the living and the dead that this mediatic role entails, salient features of lifeworlds in which histories and practices of spirit-mediumship and debt-bonds continue to bear contemporary significance.

Fenella Cannell insightfully describes social processes of interaction in the contemporary context of lowland Christianized Philippines in such terms, foregrounding an array of habits and gestures in the context of everyday life that evidence the extant workings of practices that appear to have their origins in precolonial and early colonial times. Cannell observes in contemporary practices of spirit-mediumship, marriage, funerals, and transvestite beauty contests the workings in particular of the social logic and model of power characteristic of precolonial and early colonial Philippine societies, "which functioned dynamically on the basis of infinite gradations of debt-bondage." She notes the way everyday social encounters operate as dynamic engagements with and negotiations of a specifically Southeast Asian notion of power (an energy animating all organic and inorganic matter) that entail possibilities of either depletion or augmentation among persons who act both as mediating bearer-agents of power and as "their own mediatory objects" in such negotiations; the way wives might construct themselves as "the reluctant objects of other wills and other desires," "a kind of forced gift of [themselves]" that in turn (as a kind of return gift) obligates others, compelling others' obligations for the gendered value of their submission; the way spirit-mediums serve as conduits of a patronage that functions ambivalently as both benevolent and predatory forms of "help," while at the same time becoming themselves, through the gift of healing, a kind of patron to those they help; and finally, in their mastery of a genre of transformative performance in which all members of the community have a shared interest, the way transgender *bakla* beauty contestants and singers "become the temporary bodily 'lodging places for potency' . . . [epitomizing] recapturings of power, not literally through possession, but through a wrapping of the body in symbols of protective status, and a transformation of the person by proximity to the power it imitates, which are in many ways akin to it."[30]

In all these specific contexts human actors engage in forms of mediation in which their own bodies and selves are offered up as mediatory apparatuses (as object and site) for the transaction and transmission of quantities and qualities of power and value across realms of social interaction (both visible and invisible) that are to some extent congruent but also importantly imperfectly aligned with the social field of exchange under capitalist democracy.

I too have written on the different ways that Filipino women in particular participate in their own export and exchange, as a *medium of exchange*, the way they and their families speak of their bodily lives as collateral for loans they take to gain overseas placement, while they themselves offer that very bodily life as the ante they risk in the cosmic gamble of overseas adventure that they embark upon.[31] Rather than simply an ideological effect of capitalism, these practices of self-lending draw on the same seemingly anachronistic "political economy" and ontology, which the extant practice of spirit-mediumship, in its instantiation of fungible, extendable, divisible, alienable, transformable, and combinable selves continues to be based on as well as renovates.

The kinesthetic, aesthetic (sensorial and perceptual), affective, and cognitive entailments of using and inhabiting bodily selves as media suggest precisely what I call remaindered life, which I view as the unabsorbed residue of an epistemic translation and real subsumption of "non-human" forms of life by capitalist production and exchange. Women (and men) who become helpers of other communities, as well as their own, whether as domestic workers, nurses, caregivers, or foreign or native wives, draw on and revitalize older vocabularies and repertoires of action wherein the lines between submission and volition, bondage and sentimental attachment, obligation and gift, servitude and care are constantly negotiated in transactions of personal and social well-being and potency. As the means of generation and renewal of the life of communities, and the means of transmission of the properties and values that ensure affective, identificatory, and genealogical continuity across spatial and temporal distances, such helpers (vital yet auxiliary agents of reproduction of legible social subjects) perform functions and services that issue from older social mediatic capacities, which I have elsewhere shown were designated for regression and outright eradication by the imperial project of instituting the practical subjective ideal of the self-possessed citizen-man through the apparatuses of colonial governmentality.[32]

The exercise of such regressive mediatic capacities—adaptable and mimetic bodily, kinesthetic, and sensorial tendencies seen as inimical to the development of the proper capacities of autonomous, free subjects[33]—can be gleaned in the high-fidelity analog performances of Filipino jazz musicians coursing throughout East and Southeast Asia throughout the twentieth century, historically mediating the transmission of U.S. black and Latin American musical sensibilities and modernities across Asian worlds and beyond (such that the languorous tropical structure of postcolonial feeling conveyed in Wong Kar-Wai's trilogy of films of the late twentieth century becomes indelibly marked by and traceable to Filipino Latin jazz musicians in the nightclubs of Shanghai and Hong Kong in the 1950s and 1960s). Indeed in these musicians' technically exact bodily rendition of voices, sounds, styles, looks, and other qualities of the performing arts that they did not themselves author (their "slavish" or "mechanical" mimetic bodily capacities of reproduction of the performances of others) as much as in the intimate caring bodily mediatic performances of domestic workers, nurses, caregivers, and wives, we glimpse some persons' real, practical function as what I call "vital platforms of social reproducibility."[34] Such examples should make us attend to that level of social reproduction occluded by proper genealogies of national and transnational, ethnoracial belonging and to glimpse other orders of being and action through which discontinuous itineraries (of flight, of fate playing, of magical transformation, or of redemption) are pursued.

TO BE ABLE TO see and trace the meandering itineraries of these human mediatic performances of immaterial social production across discrepant sociogeographical landscapes (East, Southeast, and West Asia as well as Europe and the Americas) and across discontinuous histories (ethnoracial, national, regional) and also within the dispersed transpersonal space-times of intimate, affective, kinesthetic interaction and communication in everyday life is to see examples of reproductive labor producing a surplus (of life, of labor) no longer as accumulative or eliminable excess (value or waste) as entailed by the global capitalist economy, but rather as a nonidentical permutation and proliferation of plural qualities, conditions, and effects.

I want to emphasize the importance of attending to these remaindered forms of life making as potentially radical, corrosive, transformative supplements to our critiques of dominant processes of racial inscription. Beneath the level of given social identities, whose genealogies we participate in making and revising so they become the proper protagonists of our critique, remaindered forms of life point to subaltern human pathways of transmission and influence through which life-making affective properties and sensibilities are invisibly passed across distinct communities.

What, then, might it mean to reconsider race as a theoretical question and political intervention rather than a category of social exemption or exclusion or a descriptive category of difference (as a sign of marginalized social being)? It seems to me that it means attending to these subaltern pathways of social and self-formation that remain beneath the threshold of visibility of raced subjects (both dominant and subordinate), the proper borders of their own self-presencing. It means to ask how race operates within and results from practices of reproducing social life, generating lines of affiliation, stratification, and descent; determining and allocating proper distributions of value, right, power, and futurity; producing and maintaining relations of exploitation, expropriation, and violence at levels and through means beyond the ideological field within which race operates as a discriminatory, representational sign of social being. It means letting go of our uninterrogated attachment to the ideal of abstract, free subjects that undergirds the grid of intelligibility of racial liberalism and its critique of empire, with its premise and promise of a state of freedom already achieved, a humanity already realized. It means opening up the histories of capitalism, racism, and empire to the plurality and heterogeneity of extant and shifting social logics and practices of naturalized obligation and bondage—the conditions and inventions, the untold creative agencies and impeded potentials, as well as pain, of *nonfree life*—operating as both productive forces of capitalism and imperialism and as subaltern forces of other life making.

To decolonize thus means to ask: How do we mobilize other social analytics to bring into operation remaindered forms of social intelligence, imagination, and sensibility that might not only dispute what is given in empire and the very frames within which such things (like "race as difference") are given, but also, in doing so, set the stage (create the platforms) for radical departure from the given conditions of life under empire now?

NOTES

1. This is a world order that renewed itself through the crises of the two world wars (particularly, according to Hannah Arendt, the crisis of fascism and totalitarianism that precipitated World War II) but up until the present moment continued to be politically and philosophically organized around the 1789 Declaration of the Rights of Man and of the Citizen. See Arendt, *The Origins of Totalitarianism*; Agamben, *Homo Sacer*.

2. Mahmood Mamdani, "The New Humanitarian Order," "The New Humanitarian Order," *Nation*, September 29, 2008.

3. The literature is vast. Besides more traditional military-political histories of the United States (Karnow, *In Our Image*; Johnson, *Sorrows of Empire*), a whole new body of work on U.S. Empire that focuses on the cultural dimensions with particular focus on race and gender has emerged. See, for example, Kaplan and Pease, *Cultures of U.S. Imperialism*; Kaplan, *The Anarchy of Empire in the Making of U.S. Culture*; Rowe, *Literary Culture and U.S. Imperialism*; Stoler, *Haunted by Empire*; Wexler, *Tender Violence*; Kramer, *The Blood of Government*; Greenberg, *Manifest Manhood and the Antebellum American Empire*; Anderson, *Colonial Pathologies*; Briggs, *Reproducing Empire*; McCoy and Scarano, *Colonial Crucible*. Though there is some overlap, I do not include under empire studies the growing body of critical work in Filipino American studies and Native studies that has also undertaken historical studies of U.S. imperialism insofar as conversation and exchange between these fields (i.e., between empire studies and critical race and ethnic studies) are rare or discordant, issuing from quite discrepant methods and premises.

4. Warwick Anderson, "Race, Empire, and Transnational History," in *Colonial Crucible*, ed. McCoy and Scarano, 283, 287.

5. Kramer, *The Blood of Government*, 2–3, 7.

6. Kramer, *The Blood of Government*, 3.

7. Melamed, "The Spirit of Neoliberalism."

8. Whatever the claims about the material effects of this conceptualization of race in terms of a politics of recognition (e.g., lack of recognition as enabling and contributing

to substantive racial inequality, viewed as a matter of distribution), they are set in terms of an understanding of representation that is predicated on a liberal democratic separation between the political and the economic. See Spivak, "Can the Subaltern Speak?"; Brown, *States of Injury*.

9. Tadiar, "Life-Times in Fate-Playing."

10. Tadiar, "Life-Times of Disposability within Global Neoliberalism."

11. As a category of national identity, "Filipino" is certainly also central to the social analytic of postcolonial Philippine nationalist historiography, but it is not predominantly deployed as a racial category. While contemporary empire studies might historicize the "invention" of the Filipino (following nationalist scholarship), much of this new work deploys Filipino as a category of racialized national identity, which functions simultaneously as the object of study and an organizing principle of the analysis. That is to say, "Filipino" continues to stand in as a particular totality, in contradistinction with but also in relations with, other ethnoracial identities, such as American, African American, and Native American, preconstituted subjects who are racialized by these colonial, historical representations (but presumably not by the representational apparatus of the scholarship on empire).

12. Mitropolous, *Contract and Contagion*, 101, 102, 103. See also Joanne Barker, "The Specters of Recognition," Joanne Barker, "The Corporation and the Tribe," M. A. Jaimes Guerrero, "Civil Rights versus Sovereignty: Native American Women in Life and Land Struggles," in *Sovereignty Matters*, ed. Joanne Barker.

13. Quoted in Aguilar, "Between the Letter and the Spirit of the Law," 438. The notion of "foreign in a domestic sense" has become a key concept for thinking about the cultural ramifications for Filipino and Filipino American communities. See Sarita See, *The Decolonized Eye*; Isaac, *American Tropics*.

14. Aguilar, "Between the Letter and the Spirit of the Law," 438.

15. Lowe, *Immigrant Acts*. The recommendation of the extension of this law was made by Brigadier General Elwell S. Otis, head of the military government set up in 1898 after the U.S. takeover, and was supported by anti-Chinese sentiments among the collaborating Filipino elite. The complex, contradictory history of *indios* (natives) and the Chinese within the archipelago shows that the processes of racialized differentiation began earlier, with the colonial Spanish state, but it is with the invention of Philippine citizenship that "Filipino" is transformed into a racialized legal status. See Hau, "'Who Will Save Us from the Law?'"; Chu, *Chinese and Chinese Mestizos of Manila*.

16. Aguilar, "Between the Letter and the Spirit of the Law."

17 How Filipinos become racialized as *not* Indian, that is, as *not* savages (the split between *indio* and savage), is another story that also traverses Spanish and U.S. colonialism.

18 Wald, "Terms of Assimilation," 65.

19 May, *Social Engineering in the Philippines*.

20 Constantino, *The Philippines* and "The Miseducation of the Filipino."

21 Camilo Osias, *Barrio Life and Barrio Education*, 37–38.

22 Blanco, "Race as Praxis in the Philippines at the Turn of the Twentieth Century," 382; Schirmer, "U.S. Racism and Intervention in the Third World, Past and Present," *Friends of the Filipino People Bulletin*, 1994.

23 Ignacio et al., *The Forbidden Book.*

24 Blanco, "Race as Praxis in the Philippines at the Turn of the Twentieth Century," 382.

25 Ho, "Empire through Diasporic Eyes," 215–16.

26 Marx, *Capital,* vol. 1: 719.

27 Faier, *Intimate Economies.*

28 Tsing, "The Global Situation."

29 I write about migrant domestic workers as *replicants* and as domestic technologies in *Fantasy-Production.*

30 Cannell, *Power and Intimacy in the Christian Philippines,* 10, 231, 46, 95, 223.

31 Tadiar, *Fantasy-Production,* chapter 3; Tadiar, *Things Fall Away,* chs. 2, 3.

32 Tadiar, "Remaindered Life of Citizen-Man."

33 See also Ness's perceptive observations in *Body, Movement, and Culture* about the social value of permissive surfaces, fluid kinesthetics, and intensified multiplicity of temporal action in the habitual modes of urban conduct in Cebu.

34 Tadiar, "Remaindered Life of Citizen-Man." These capacities and the life-making practices they enable are not cultural in any (anthropological) sense of inhering in a given people, however historicized that construction might be. They are cultural perhaps only in the sense of what is bracketed as the particular raced domain or burden of subjects of affectability, which da Silva argues in *Toward a Global Idea of Race* serve as the constitutive other of transparent self-determining subjects of universal reason.

TWENTY-TWO

Critical Ethnic Studies, Identity Politics, and the Right-Left Convergence

ROBERT STAM AND ELLA SHOHAT

Critical ethnic studies and identity politics must be seen against the backdrop of what we call the "seismic shift" constituted by the decolonization of world culture. Central twentieth-century events—World War II, the Jewish Holocaust, Third Worldist anticolonialism, the civil rights struggle, and minority liberation movements—all simultaneously delegitimized the West as the axiomatic center of reference and affirmed the rights of non-European peoples emerging from the yoke of colonialism and racism. In the wake of centuries of struggles, decolonization achieved climactic expression with Indian independence in 1947, the Chinese Revolution in 1949, Algerian independence in 1962, up through the independence of Mozambique and Angola in the mid-1970s. Thus if Nazism, fascism, and the Holocaust revealed in all their horror the internal sickness of Europe as a site of racism and totalitarianism, Third World liberation struggles revealed the external revolt against Western domination, in tandem with minority struggles within the metropole, thus provoking a crisis in the taken-for-granted narrative of European-led Progress. The seismic shift refers to the intellectual and discursive fallout of these events, seen as catalytic for a broad decolonization of knowledge and academic culture.

What often gets lost in the culture war polemics is the actual scholarly work—what might be awkwardly called "the decolonizing corpus"—generated by the postwar seismic shift. The broader corpus includes work practiced under diverse names and rubrics and performed by hundreds of scholars in many countries. At this point the corpus includes such diverse currents of thought as Third Worldism, the modernity and coloniality project, anti-imperialist media studies, critical race theory, critical whiteness studies, Latin American subaltern studies, (multi)cultural studies, transnational feminism, minor and feminist Francophone studies, Latino studies, Asian studies, visual culture, social movement analysis, cross-racial and cross-national literary history, race-conscious queer theory, critical science theory, radical pedagogy, reflexive and experimental anthropology, postmodern urbanism and geography, counter-Enlightenment philosophy, border theory, alter-globalization theory, and postcolonial studies, to name just a few of the many adversarial currents and formations. Although our rubrics are schematic, and although there are tensions between and even within the diverse modes of critique, what all these heterogeneous fields have in common is a critical engagement with the historical legacies of colonial and racial oppression.

In the 1980s and 1990s terms such as *multiculturalism* and *identity politics* came to crystallize these trends. Just as the American Right had opposed Third Worldism and civil rights in the 1960s, it opposed multiculturalism and identity politics in the 1980s. What provoked the Right's howls of execration in this period was not the indisputable fact of the dappled variety of the world's cultures—what we call multiculturality—but rather the larger decolonizing and critical race projects. Predictably conservatives in many countries were not enthusiastic about the seismic shift manifested in these decolonizing projects. In the United States, in a faux populist attack stage-managed by elite circles in the Republican Party, the Right ridiculed these projects as a new, politically correct version of the communist menace. Right-wing polemicists mocked what they saw as oversensitive do-gooders stifling free speech in the name of touchy-feely sympathy for minorities. Recycling cold war rhetoric, conservative figures such as Allan Bloom, William Bennett, Dinesh D'Souza, and Lynne Cheney, in tandem with liberals such as the historian Arthur M. Schlesinger Jr., denounced any identity-based critique of inequality as un-American and divisive. Thus on May 4, 1991, George H. W. Bush publicly denounced the "political extremists . . . setting citizens against one another on the basis of their class or race."[1] In a sense the

Right was retrofitting its old "class warfare" rhetoric—that is, the notion that to call attention to class inequality was to wage class warfare—to issues of race and gender. To speak of racial inequality, by analogy, was to wage "race warfare," just as speaking of gender inequality was to wage "gender warfare."

The virulence of these attacks manifested a fear not only of greater racial, economic, and political equality but also of nonexceptionalist and non-Eurocentric narrativizations of history. Thus Schlesinger ridiculed "underdog," "compensatory," and "there's-always-a-black-man-at-the-bottom-of-it" approaches to historiography, whose sole function was to provide "social and psychological therapy" and "raise the self-esteem of children from minority groups."[2] But if minorities have indeed been traumatized by their experience in dominant educational institutions, therapy is clearly preferable to trauma. Why should only the dominant Euro-American group have its narcissism massaged by official histories, while others suffer the body blows of stereotype and marginalization? The most frequently reiterated charge was that of "separatism," as evidenced in the constant recourse to metaphors of "balkanization," "Lebanonization," and "tribalism." For Charles Krauthammer, multicultural identity politics "poses a threat that no outside agent in this post-Soviet world can match—the setting of one ethnic group against another, the fracturing not just of American society but of the American idea."[3] The most extreme accusation was to speak of ethnic cleansing as a logical end product of multiculturalism, as when P. J. O'Rourke defined multiculturalism as "that which is practiced today in the former Yugoslavia."[4] The Right thus gave the impression that the Serbs, the Bosnians, and the Croatians, fresh from reading Cornel West and bell hooks, were rushing into fratricidal slaughter brandishing the banner of "identity politics."

Schlesinger was the most vocal proponent of the "disuniting" perspective and, not by coincidence, a vociferous opponent of the "rainbow curriculum" designed for New York schools. Formulations such as Schlesinger's that portray a "common culture" threatened by ethnic difference come close to blaming the victim by implying that cultural difference itself causes social strife, when in fact it has always been the inequitable distribution of power that generates divisiveness and tension. The critics were generally unable to cite any actual writers or activists calling for separatism, for the simple reason that the "separatists" did not exist; they were imaginary creatures, ideological ogres invented to frighten the uninformed. In fact many of the multiculturalists were shaped directly or indirectly by the struggle *against* segregation. Yet the separatist charge has been repeated so often that it has become part of the received wisdom, even, as we shall see, for many on the Left.

The Right also portrayed left identity politics, in an oxymoronic characterization, as at once puritanical and hedonistic. One of the Right's public relations coups was to associate the Left with negative personal attributes such as self-righteousness as a diversion from what was really an argument about social change and political power. Thus the label of "political correctness" was affixed only to those who were calling for more egalitarian relations between races, genders, ethnicities, and sexualities. In a new twist on cold war imagery, the multicultural Left was portrayed as lugubrious, dour, and drab, in short, as neo-Stalinist. In a historical inversion of letters, the CP (Communist Party) became PC (political correctness).[5] At the same time, paradoxically, the Right depicted the cultural Left as the heirs of the permissive 1960s. An incoherent portrait, based on the melding of the negative portrayals of two very different historical lefts (the Stalinist Communist Party Left of the 1930s to the 1950s and the more ludic "New Left" of the 1960s and 1970s), presented the same people as at once uptight puritans and self-indulgent do-your-own-thingers.

In any case the PC rubric generated its own ontology, ultimately taking on a life of its own and spreading, due to the reach of U.S. media, to other regions such as Europe and Latin America. The various decolonizing projects unleashed fierce polemics not because they were separatist but because they called for a decisive transformation in the ways history would be written, literature taught, art curated, films programmed, cultural resources distributed, and political representation shaped. What was left unsaid by the Right was the assumed desirability of the status quo ante. At least by implication the Right was calling for a return to the pre-1960s default position of white male heteronormative hegemony, a time when there were virtually no students of color and relatively few women on campuses, when history texts were blandly noncommittal about slavery and segregation, and when Native Americans, African Americans, Latinos, and other minorities, along with women, gays, lesbians, and transsexuals, had very little voice. What was for the Right an object of nostalgia was for minorities a searing memory of trauma.

If the Right was hostile to identity politics, liberals and some on the Left were critical as well. Some feminists, such as Susan Moller Okin, called multiculturalism "bad for women."[6] Some liberals lamented the assault on the Western canon. Some Marxists, meanwhile, saw identity politics as dividing the Left through a cultural detour that distracted from "real" struggles over class and power. In his 1995 book, *The Twilight of Common Dreams,* Todd Gitlin blamed the decline of the American Left on "identity politics" as expressed by "groups overly concerned with protecting and purifying what they imagine to be their identities."[7] The Left, in Gitlin's view, abandoned the real struggle in favor of a narcissistic quest for a chimerical identity. Neglected in his account are the diverse causes of left decline: the right-wing attack on the '60s legacy, the murderous repression of the Black Panthers, the conservative agitprop of well-funded think tanks, a rigged two-party system, winner-take-all politics and laissez-faire economics, a constitution favoring conservative rural states, the corporate corruption of Congress, the wedge-issue tactics of the Republican Party, and the ideological vacillations of an ever more corporate-dominated Democratic Party. An analysis that scapegoats multicultural identity politics for left decline offers a flattened version of a complex historical narrative, forgetting the global and local factors that have undermined the Left generally as an overarching progressive project: globally the end of actually existing socialism, the *embourgeoisement* of Third World liberation movements, and the weakening of unions and the workers' movement.

The scapegoating analysis forgets that (1) the Left has historically often been fragmented for reasons having little to do with identity politics—one need only recall the Left's self-cannibalizing due to the Stalinist, Trotskyist, Marxist, Leninist, Anarchist, Socialist, Spartakist schisms that plagued the Left during much of the twentieth century; (2) the Old Left versus New Left debate had more to do with ideological vision, generational tensions, and political tactics than with identity politics; (3) the Marxist Left has declined in much of the world due to the collapse of actually existing socialism, often in situations where identity politics played little role; (4) anxieties around race, class, gender, and sexuality were present in U.S. left politics long before the advent of identity politics (evident, for example, in black intellectuals' disenchantment with the CP in the 1930s); (5) participation in race-inflected left politics in no way precludes participation in other forms of left politics; and (6) the major exceptions to left decline in the world—Latin America and now the Arab Spring—have often embraced cultural identity and social movements as an integral part of coalitionary politics. If it is true that the multicultural Left has been more effective in defending the right to difference than in guaranteeing political-economic equality, that does not mean that the Left has not achieved political-economic equality *because* of the multicultural achievements.

We find a recent illustration of the partial convergence of Left and Right on these issues in two February 2011 denunciations of multiculturalism, one by the conservative British prime minister David Cameron, the other by the "radical leftist" Slavoj Žižek. The former asserted in a speech that multiculturalism had failed, that tolerance had led to Islamic radicalism, and that what was needed was a "robust liberalism" and a return to Western values and pride in British identity. For Cameron (and other conservative leaders such as Nicolas Sarkozy and Angela Merkel), multiculturalism—and not discrimination—creates separate communities; thus he blames the proponents of a solution to a problem for the problem itself. Žižek, meanwhile, in an interview on *Al Jazeera* (February 1, 2011) about the democratic movement in Egypt, also denounced the putative multiculturalists who believe that "Egypt has a separate culture and does not need democracy." While Cameron sees liberalism as the answer to radicalism, Žižek has long argued that multiculturalism is not the opposite of neoliberalism but its ideal form. Both Cameron and Žižek were speaking up for Western Enlightenment values, although Cameron was channeling Adam Smith and John Locke, while Žižek was channeling Hegel and Marx.[8]

What is surprising, then, is not the Right's hostility to identity politics but rather that of some on the Left. After mapping the general direction of the left arguments, we address specific interventions by Walter Benn Michaels and Žižek. Some left critics expressed apprehension about what they saw as the supervalorization of culture over political economy. This critique was less about the *multi-* than about the *culture*, seen as an inconsequential distraction from the economy as the determinative instance shaping all other spheres. Yet while political economy is absolutely essential to any substantive left critique, it is also important to articulate culture and economy together, to conceive of them as existing in and through each other. Here many people have questioned forms of Marxism that exalt class struggle while belittling struggles revolving around other modalities of social inequality. Feminist theory, postcolonial theory, subaltern studies, queer theory, coloniality and modernity theory, critical whiteness studies, and indigeneity theory all offer conceptual instruments relevant to multiple, historically sedimented forms of inequality. Rather than replace class struggle, these projects complicate it, seeing multiaxial forms of oppression as engendering similarly multiaxial forms of resistance and struggle, shaping new social actors, new vocabularies, and new strategies.

Quite apart from identity politics, divisions based on race, class, and gender have shaped American history from the very beginning. Propertied, slave-holding white men have classically used race to hide class by "conferring" the cultural capital of whiteness on nonpropertied whites. The color line also subtly marked even left organizations, from the Communist Party to labor unions, which privileged whites over working-class people of color despite ideologies of equality. Blaming identity politics for left division is thus a form of sideways scapegoating. Gitlin's derisive reference to "groups overly concerned with protecting and purifying what they imagine to be their identities" is an especially low blow.[9] It betokens a privileged, pseudo-objective standpoint that deems itself in a position to judge which identities are authentic and which imaginary, as if Gitlin knows the "real" identities of people of color better than people of color themselves do. Social identities are neither a luxury nor imaginary; they are historically shaped and have consequences for who gets jobs, who owns homes, who gets racially profiled, and so forth. Rather than an investment in a phantasmatic affiliation, identities have to do with a differential relation to power as lived in the world, with discrepant experiences of the judicial system, the medical system, the economy, and everyday social interchange. Social identities are not fixed essences; they emerge from a fluid set of diverse experiences within overlapping circles of belonging. It is these overlapping circles of identity and identification that make possible transcommunal coalitions based on historically shaped affinities. Anxieties about identity are asymmetrical. While the disempowered seek to affirm a precariously established right, the traditionally empowered feel relativized by having to compete with previously unheard voices. What is missed in the dividing-the-Left argument is that each "division" can also be an "addition" within a coalitionary space. Disaggregation and rearticulation can go hand in hand.

The debates over identity have featured a complex range of positions, ranging from essentialism to social constructivism. If the Right's attack on identity politics was framed in nationalist terms, the Left's critique was framed either in political or in philosophical poststructuralist or skeptical postmodernist terms. For many scholars the goal was therefore to avoid both essentialist and antiessentialist traps, whence "strategic essentialism."[10] That identities are socially constructed does not mean that they do not exist and have real-life consequences. In this vein the postpositivist "realist" approach advanced by such scholars as Linda Martin Alcoff, Satya P. Mohanty, and Chandra Mohanty offers an alternative conceptualization to the postmodern skeptical view of identities as merely fictional constructs. For advocates of this approach identities are markers of history, social location, and positionality, lenses through which to view the world. Rather than ethnocharacterological essences, identities are chronotopic positionings within social space and historical time, the place from which one speaks and experiences the world. The class-based argument against identity politics ignores the difference that race makes and the ways that the refusal of cross-racial coalitions have hurt the Left itself. One axis of analysis (class) is applauded, while others (race, gender, sexuality) are derided. Opposition to the "special" claims of racial minorities, as George Lipsitz has suggested, often masks the hidden identity politics of the dominant group's possessive investment in white Europeanness.[11] Although a certain kind of salami-slicing identity politics can turn identity into a form of cultural capital in a competitive fight for status, the denunciation of identity politics itself can also subtly normativize white supremacy.

The various left critiques of multicultural identity politics share certain motifs but also touch on distinct notes. Here we address just two examples beginning with Walter Benn Michaels's *The Trouble with Diversity.* His argument, in its simplest form, is that "we love race and identity because we don't love class." Most of the book consists of formulaic permutations of the same basic structural grammar of mutually exclusive paradigms, in the manner of "We love to talk about A (race, diversity) because we refuse to talk about B (class, economics, capitalism)." In a zero-sum approach each and every invocation of race implies a denial of class. Within a grammar familiar with only two conjunctions—*either/or*—we are exhorted to choose between "a vision of our society as divided into races" or as divided "into economic classes." Sentence after sentence is premised on a rhetoric of stark dichotomy—"We would much rather get rid of racism than get rid of poverty"—or of invidious comparison: "We like the idea of cultural equality better than we like the idea of economic equality."[12]

While we applaud Michaels's critique of the erasure of class, especially in the United States, we lament the fact that he merely replaces one erasure (of class) with other erasures (of race, culture, identity). Although his vaguely socialist politics differ sharply from those of D'Souza, he shares with D'Souza the fantasy that racism was basically outlawed and eliminated in the 1960s. Deploying a tacitly white liberal "we," Michaels writes, "We like programs such as Affirmative Action because they tell us that racism is the problem we need to solve and that solving it requires us to give up our prejudices."[13] The formulation is unfortunate, however, since (1) affirmative action today is under constant attack, including by the Supreme Court; (2) even its supporters are not defending it very vigorously (President Barack Obama seems to prefer a William Julius Wilson–style class-over-race approach); and (3) affirmative action was about concrete legal and practical issues such as hiring minorities and correcting past injustice, not about a mushy and unrealizable "giving up prejudices."

Michaels's sunny portrait of an America "in love with diversity," moreover, ignores many ominous clouds. Although university brochures prominently feature the word *diversity* and proudly display photographs of chromatically diverse students and faculty, that is hardly the same as achieving substantive social equality. There seems to be a race-informed difference of perception here. While Michaels describes campuses as "in love with diversity," many black, Latino, and Middle Eastern students find American campuses, including supposedly diversity-friendly campuses such as UC Berkeley, "hostile environments." A 2004 survey at the University of Virginia, for example, found that 40 percent of the black students had been the target of a direct racial slur, while 91 percent had either experienced or witnessed an act of racial discrimination or intolerance.[14] Meanwhile black students are vanishing from U.S. campuses as the race and class divides worsen under the onslaught of predatory capitalism, high-priced educational institutions, and the assault on affirmative action.

As evidence of the American "love of diversity," Michaels cites the absence of "pro-hate rallies."[15] But this sets a terribly low bar. The KKK and the white militias do not call their demonstrations "hate rallies," but that is what they are. Even Hitler, after all, did not call the Nuremberg rallies "hate rallies," but one suspects that Jews and Bolsheviks, gays and gypsies got the drift. Building on a long tradition of paranoid, nativist political speech, venomous celebrities such as Ann Coulter and Glenn Beck stage the mediatic equivalents of hate rallies, with TV audiences larger than those of any Nuremberg spectacle. The galling experience of watching TV shows such as *Lou Dobbs Tonight* and *The O' Reilly Factor* or of listening to the hate radio of Michael Savage or Rush Limbaugh reveals at the very least a deep ambivalence about "diversity." And while the election of Obama offered evidence of another America that does indeed love diversity, right-wing voices that do not love diversity have become even more strident since his election. Rather than demonstrate that Americans have become "postracial," the irrational hostility to Obama has shown that one of the major parties, representing around half of the populace, are comfortable with voter repression and racist appeals.

Race as an analytical category is crucial because racism structures social advantage. Every economic crisis that afflicts whites—for example, the subprime lending crisis—impacts racialized communities even more dramatically. When white America sneezes, black America gets influenza. The Great Depression, as a bitter black joke has it, was a time when white Americans got to live the way blacks had always been living. The wealth divide, meanwhile, is even larger than the income divide: "For every dollar owned by the average white family in the U.S., the average family of color has less than one dime."[16]

For blacks, as Mel King puts it, "white men of means" often coincide with "mean white men."[17] Yet race and class must be seen as interarticulated, since they are so completely "imbricated in the consciousness of working-class Americans," as David Roediger puts it, "that we do not 'get' class if we do not 'get' race." Indeed the refusal to engage the complexities of race can result in the "retreat from class" just as surely as can "a reductive obsession with race as an ahistorical essentialist category."[18] A certain Left wants to move "beyond race," but in fact a retreat from race, as Roediger points out, will not solve the problem of the denial of class and will ultimately "get us closer to addressing neither."[19] Although Michaels thinks "we" are overly "eager" to centralize race, in fact race and class (and gender and sexuality) are at the burning core of American politics. Underscoring the symbiotic interconnection of race and class, Marx saw chattel slavery as the pedestal on which wage slavery was based. W. E. B. Du Bois spoke of "the wages of whiteness," arguing, "It must be remembered that the white group of laborers, while they received a low wage, were compensated in part by a sort of public and psychological wage. They were given public deference and titles of courtesy because they were white. They were admitted freely with all classes of white people to public functions, public parks, and the best schools."[20] Later Martin Luther King Jr. asked, "What does it profit a man to be able to eat at an integrated lunch counter if he doesn't earn enough money to buy a hamburger and a cup of coffee?"[21] Henry Louis Taylor Jr. noted that "the black job ceiling has been the floor of white opportunity."[22] Black Marxism told us that race and class were interarticulated, while black feminism reminded us that race, class, and gender all intersect.

Throughout most of the twentieth century the black liberation movement has been engaged in a complex debate about the strengths and weaknesses of Marxism in terms of explaining and remedying black oppression. Critical race theory, for example, points to the political limitations of both liberalism and Marxism. While liberalism reduces racism to attitudinal bigotry, Marxism reduces racism to an epiphenomenon of class. Although Marxism has provided a powerful theory of the dialectic of social oppression, the historical forces that produced Marxism as a theory, as Charles Mills points out, "have now thrown up other perspectives, other visions, illuminating aspects of the structured darknesses of society that Marx failed to see."[23] Although Michaels claims to shift our attention from individual prejudice to the social system, he sets up a false dichotomy between individual and society when he asserts that even when "we" as individuals "are racist, the society to which we are committed is not."[24] Bypassing all the critical race scholarship on institutional, systemic, and even epistemic racism, this claim of societal innocence is ultimately rooted in a U.S. American exceptionalist discourse.

An emerging left consensus assumes that (1) race is not a biological reality—human beings share 99.9 percent identical DNA, and all humanity shares a common ancestor in Africa; (2) the issue is not race but racism and racialization; and (3) race as a social construct and racism as a social practice shape the contemporary world by skewing the distribution of power and resources. Rather than move from race to discrimination, it is in some ways more useful to move in the opposite direction, from the discrimination revealed by statistics (e.g., the disproportionate incarceration of black people) to the categories that explain the discrimination, whether having to do with race, color, national origin, religion, accent, or some other visible or audible difference. The very concept of race, moreover, has been historically transfigured. Nowadays Du Bois's color line has been retraced and blurred. Some prominent American blacks, such as Colin Powell and Condoleezza Rice, can be deracialized to join the white side. Islamophobia and the War on Terror, meanwhile, have racialized a religion (Islam) embracing people of many colors, rendering its followers subject to suspicion and profiling.[25] Today the color line involves not only what is visible—color—but also less visible social demarcations involving religion, clothing, body language, speech, etiquette, cultural capital, and Europeanness. Yet *race* and *racism* still serve to designate the persistence of strong inequalities linked to race, despite the lack of scientific substance to the notion of race itself.

Michaels mocks the politics that "consists of disapproving of bad things that happened a long time ago." Here he forgets that such radically reconstructive historiography is aimed at countering a dominant historiography that ignores those "bad things" or even paints them as "good things" and that those "bad things" still shape and help explain the present. Michaels echoes the conservative caricature of identity politics as invested in preserving "the differences between blacks and whites and Native Americans and Jews and whoever."[26] But the issue is not preserving difference for difference's sake, a notion redolent of salvage anthropology rescuing "tribes on the verge of extinction," but rather recognizing discrepancies in historical experience. Like French intellectuals such as Alain Finkielkraut, Michaels belittles accounts of the victimization of racialized communities as a form of narrative envy in relation to Jews, an accusation already mounted against Edward Said's articulation of a Palestinian counternarrative in the late 1980s.[27] Citing Leslie Marmon Silko's mention of the sixty million Native Americans eliminated by Europeans, Michaels responds, "They aren't just engaging in a kind of victimization one-upsmanship. They aren't trying to replace the Jews; they're trying to join them."[28] In this account of competition over ethical and narratological capital, it is as if Native Americans, who have been lamenting (and fighting) genocide since 1492, were trying to hitchhike on the prestige of the Holocaust.

The ethnocentric limits of Michaels's dichotomization of class-versus-race and culture-versus-economy become manifest in his analysis of Latin American activism. "There's a big difference," he writes, "between dealing with indigenous peoples who want to protect their culture and socialists who want to nationalize their industry.... When Evo Morales talks about 'nationalizing industry,' he is speaking as a socialist; when he talks about fulfilling the dreams 'of our ancestors,' he is speaking as an Indian."[29] In his embrace of the socialist Morales as against the Indian Morales, Michaels overlooks not only Morales's self-characterization as both socialist and Indian (specifically Aymara) but also the mutual imbrication of culture and political economy in present-day Bolivia. By lauding Morales *only* as a socialist, Michaels ignores the public perception of Morales as *indio*, as well as the cultural politics that got him elected. The victory of Morales and Movement for Socialism, confirmed again in the elections of December 2008, forms a historic landmark for a country shaped by the oligarchy's racism toward the Quechua and Aymara majority. The new constitution recognizes the "multinational" character of the nation. For much of Bolivia's history, as Morales himself has frequently pointed out, Indians were not allowed to share the sidewalks with *criollos*. Morales's enemies, for their part, are defined not only as capitalists but also as Bolivian "whites." Thus it was in great part by "speaking as Indians" that the indigenous movement managed to coalesce into a powerful force able to challenge transnational corporations and the Bolivian oligarchy.

Any analysis like Michaels's that is based on the stigmatization of an abstract identity per se is likely to create a number of theoretical problems. First, the stigmatization of identity is usually asymmetrical; it rejects certain identities but not usually the identity of the analyst, which is empowered and assumed but remains unnamed. Second, the very abstraction of the term makes it easy to practice guilt by association between the various identitarians. Michaels, for example, compares the Aymara in Bolivia to Samuel Huntington, on the basis that both Huntington and the Aymara want to preserve identities. Such a formulation completely overlooks the question of power, rather like equating Hitler and his Jewish victims since both wanted to preserve their (respectively Aryan and Jewish) identities. Michaels amalgamates the situations of a well-connected geopolitical strategist speaking a dominant language with an Aymara people victimized by a five-century siege. Renewing the linguistic spirit of the Conquest, he calls the disappearance of languages such as Aymara a "victimless crime."[30] As anyone knows who has lived without a language available for communication, language is a form of power; to lose one's language is to be disempowered. It is passing strange to hear someone whose identity and livelihood derive from mastery of a hegemonic language be so cavalier about language, but that is perhaps why Michaels can be so cavalier; he knows *his* language is not about to disappear.

There is increasing recognition on the Left that the social movements in Latin America, from Zapatismo to the indigenous movements in Bolivia, Peru, and Ecuador, are now at the cutting edge of social change. In the wake of indigenous activism and the UN declaration of indigenous rights, Ecuador and Bolivia have begun to inscribe indigenous rights and even the "right of Nature not to be harmed" into their constitutions, and Bolivia now has a Ministry of Decolonization. The era of neoliberalism and the weakened nation-state has brought more and more direct confrontations pitting transnational corporations against indigenous groups defending their rights, in a new "contact zone" where land, biodiversity, and intellectual copyright are all at stake. While classical Marxism is anticapitalist yet ultimately productivist, the Andean movements are often more radically anticapitalist in their assertion that mother earth should not be commodified. This culturally instilled refusal of commodification was one force-idea that helped energize the Bolivian movement and enabled it to prevent the corporated privatization of water. Activists speak of communal forms of politics and of what Arturo Escobar calls "the political activation of relational ontologies." In Escobar's account, the activists call for substantive rather than formal democracy, "biocentric" sustainable development, and interculturality in polyethnic societies. The goal is to move beyond capitalism, liberalism, statism, monoculturalism, productivism, Puritanism, and the ideology of "growth."[31]

For many indigenous people and societies, *culture* implies a norm of egalitarian economic arrangements, ecological balance, and consensus governance. Thus indigenous culture and economic globalization confront each other in the form of very real battles fought in the name of biodiversity, communal intellectual property rights, and the noncommodification of nature.[32] Culture and economics, in sum, are deeply enmeshed in the Andes, with some ancestral traditions of communal property and collective decision making combined with a rejection of instrumental and productivist attitudes toward nature. Indigenous resistance thus passes through culture.

The Bolivian Left won victories against the transnational corporations by mobilizing the cultural memory of the *ayllus*, the chronotopic space-time of indigenous sovereignty. They won by *not choosing* between socialism and culture and instead constructing a socialist culture and a culturally inflected socialism.

We conclude with a few remarks about another figure, the theorist Žižek, who has raised his voice against multicultural identity politics. Like Michaels, Žižek deploys a class-over-race prism. The distorting power of this prism becomes manifest in his casual dismissal elsewhere of black demands for reparations. Gleaning his information not from reparations advocates but from the media—in this case from a press report on an August 17, 2002, Rally for Slave Reparations—Žižek sarcastically asks "if the working class should get compensation for the surplus value appropriated by capitalists over the course of history." He misses the "nuances" that the white working class was not violently kidnapped from another continent and that working-class labor, unlike slave labor, is in principle voluntary and paid! For Marx a metaphoric "wage slavery" was built on the pedestal of literal chattel slavery. Žižek then moves to a reductio ad absurdum comparison meant to discredit the whole reparations project, wondering if we should not "demand from God himself a payment for botching up the job of creation."[33] His tone and argument are reminiscent of the conservatives who lament the "culture of complaint" in the United States or the "cult of repentance" in France.

Behind Žižek's derisive attitude lies a failure of the historical imagination, an inability even to imagine why oppressed communities might feel the urgency and justice of reparations. While the "true task" is indeed "not to get compensation from those responsible, but to deprive them of the position which makes them responsible," it strikes us that massive transfers of wealth from exploiters to their victims might actually help restructure power relations and thus deprive "those responsible . . . of the position which makes them responsible." Here "the best"—the goal of overturning global capitalism—has become the enemy of "the good." Critics of identity politics like Žižek get hung up on one horn of the Enlightenment antinomy of the universal and the particular, by choosing to opt only for the universal rather than seeing the mutual imbrication of the two categories. For Žižek true politics is predicated on "universality, in its eminently political dimension," as opposed to "identifying the specific problems of each group and subgroup, not only homosexuals but African American lesbians, African American lesbian mothers, African American single unemployed lesbian mothers, and so on."[34] But what makes certain struggles particular and others universal? Referring to political movements in the former Yugoslavia, Žižek applauds their appeal to specific demands that at the same time invoked a notion of universality. Yet other activist "specificities," which happen to be those of people of color, get immediately beaten down with the police truncheon of the universal. An isomorphism operates between the hierarchy of real-world social domination and the hierarchy of the universal/particular asserted in Žižek's writing. Unemployed black lesbian single mothers, one of the most abused segments of any population, also happen to be the most abused in Žižek's prose. Their travails simply do not register within his view of political or emotional economy—they are the butt of his joke.

In this sense Žižek incarnates what Adrienne Rich called "white solipsism," that is, the "tunnel vision which simply does not see nonwhite experience or existence as precious or significant."[35] His blindness resembles that of the Republican U.S. senators who applauded future Supreme Court justice Samuel Alito's claim that his Italian-immigrant background had a positive impact on his role as an appellate judge but who quickly condemned as racist Justice Sonia Sotomayor's parallel claim that being Latina would make her a better judge. One expects the mockery of socially induced human pain from the social Darwinist Right but not from a leftist such as Žižek. Indeed the situation of unemployed black lesbian single mothers can be seen as condensing a series of socioeconomic disadvantages: those of African Americans, those of women, those of the unemployed, of lesbians, and of single mothers lacking the financial security provided by an employed (male) partner. Subjects dwelling on multiple margins, as victims of multiple prejudices—of sexism, racism, and homophobia—one would think, might possess the epistemological advantage of being aware of the oppressive aspects of many borders. Multiple subalternizations in terms of class (as being unemployed), race (as blacks), sexuality (as lesbians), and marital status (as single), one might think, would grant this social category more, rather than less, claim on the universal, once the universal is conceived not as an abstract Neoplatonic ideal but as a mottled profusion of intersecting particularities. For Žižek the idea that unemployed black lesbian single mothers might make intellectual claims or political demands with a universal dimension is simply ridiculous on its face. Union activists, meanwhile, are something else entirely. But why assume that such women are not activists in unions or critics of global capitalism? Thus Žižek reproduces not only the classic Marxist class-over-race paradigm but also the class-over-gender-and-sexuality paradigm, along with the hierarchies of white over black, heterosexual males over lesbian females, and the West over the non-West.

Žižek echoes the right-wing charge that identity politics calls for "separate" identities, but he adds a leftist touch. "The postmodern identity politics of particular (ethnic, sexual, and so forth) lifestyles," he writes, "fits perfectly the depoliticized notion of society," one "in which every particular group is accounted for and has its specific status (of victimhood) acknowledged through affirmative action or other measures."[36] As arbiter of political legitimacy, Žižek depoliticizes movements based on gender and ethnicity by calling them mere "lifestyles" and then blames the movements themselves for depoliticization. He dismisses feminism, multiculturalism, and affirmative action as mere diversions from real politics into the dead end of identity, yet all these projects could be seen as an integral part of a progressive left coalitionary politics. Perhaps lurking behind this dismissal are the vestiges of a base or superstructure model, combined with reminiscences of a gendered tropology that favors real, hard politics over soft cultural matters, where a post-Marxist cultural politics does not enter the picture. Nor does Žižek see that gender and sexuality also have an economic dimension in terms of glass ceilings, unequal pay, and tax code discrimination against gay couples. Extrapolating the same dismissive logic to working-class activism, one might just as easily condemn workers for practicing the "politics of the particular" by complaining about their pensions and their health benefits.

Žižek productively defines the political struggle proper as "the struggle for one's voice to be heard and recognized as a legitimate partner." When those who are excluded protest against the ruling elite, he points out, "the true stakes [are] not only their explicit demands but their very right to be heard and recognized as an equal participant in the debate."[37] His formulations echo myriad similar formulations from advocates of the various projects that he so breezily dismisses. His insight that universal claims can be inferentially embedded within concrete local demands, furthermore, can easily be extended to all those groups concerned with social and cultural justice and equity. Alert to the overtones of the universal in some protests, he becomes deaf to the universal in the cries of "unemployed black lesbian single mothers," relegated to an amusing particularity. Some identities remain locked up in the solitary cells of their specificity, while others open up toward the bright skies of the universal. Indirectly relaying the venerable Hegelian binarism of historical and nonhistorical peoples, of European universal and non-European local, Žižek's universalizing formulation is paradoxically nonuniversal, in that it refuses to extend its circle of reference.

Žižek frankly privileges class over all other axes of social domination: "I disagree with the postmodern mantra: gender, ethnic struggle, whatever, and then class. Class is not just one of the series." (The adolescent shrug of "whatever" here downgrades gender and ethnic struggle.) In a move reminiscent of Louis Althusser's "the economy in the last instance," Žižek accords the economy a "prototranscendental status."[38] And while political economy is absolutely essential, that does not mean that we can simply "return" to exclusively class-based analyses. An understanding of capitalism, moreover, must pass through colonialism, empire, slavery, and race. In an intersectional perspective, all of the axes of stratification work in concert and mutually inflect one another. It is not clear why Angela Davis's work on class, race, gender, and sexuality, within an overall Marxist and feminist grid, should be any less universal than Žižek's own work. One could easily argue precisely the opposite: that her multiply intersectional prisms engender a more inclusive universal, one rich in conflictual particularities, a universal in the Shakespearean concrete universal sense rather than an abstract Racinian universal, cleansed of the vulgar materialities of existence.[39]

We have a fairly good idea why the Right hates identity politics; it is too black, too foreign, too Muslim, too activist. But it is not so clear why some on the Left also dislike identity politics. Usually they dismiss it as essentialist, binarist, Manichaean, and if they are French (right or left), they call it *identitaire, commmunitairiste,* and Anglo-Saxon. In France, François Durpaire points out, "critics of black or Arab activism say that they are not opposed to blacks or Arabs but only to 'black communitarianism' and 'Arab communitarianism.'"[40] In other words, the actual people discriminated against on the basis of their visible or audible difference disappear into the mists of stigmatized abstractions. While it is easy to mock a caricatural identity politics—the Right does it all the time—millions of people, such as blacks and Latinos in American cities, immigrant *racailles* in the banlieues of France, favela *marginais* in Brazil, are daily profiled, brutalized, and even killed for what is projected as their identity. The Right forbids us to speak of race because to speak of race is to be racist; a certain Left, meanwhile, warns us not to speak of identity politics because it is essentialist and philosophically unsophisticated, thus disarming us in the struggle against identity-based oppressions.

NOTES

1. Bush, "Remarks at the University of Michigan Commencement Ceremony in Ann Arbor."

2. Schlesinger, *The Disuniting of America,* 35.

3. See Charles Krauthammer, "An Insidious Rejuvenation of the Old Left," *Los Angeles Times*, December 24, 1990.

4. O'Rourke quoted in the Brazilian newsmagazine *Isto É*, February 1, 1995, 61.

5. This portrayal served as a decoy to distract attention from the deep substratal strains of moralistic puritanism within the Right itself, evidenced in its obsession with controlling women's bodies and adults' sexual preferences. It was the Right, after all, that narrativized HIV/AIDS as divine vengeance against homosexuals, that objected to the orifice-stuffing performance art of Karen Finley, and that censured the homoerotic photographs of Robert Mapplethorpe and the films of Marlon Riggs. Subsequent to the 1990s and the sexualized prosecutions of Bill Clinton, the hypocrisy of the Right became more than evident, as most of the figures who berated Clinton were subsequently caught in their own sexual shenanigans.

6. Okin, *Is Multiculturalism Bad for Women?*

7. Gitlin, *The Twilight of Common Dreams.*

8. On *Al Jazeera* Žižek as usual mixed valid political critiques (of U.S. and Israeli policies in the Middle East) with a rant against an imaginary bogeyman: multiculturalists as anti-universalists rejecting freedom and democracy in the bane of culturalist separatism. We have no idea where he finds multiculturalists who claim that "Egypt does not need freedom because it has a separate culture." There are of course people who say such things; we call them "colonialists," "racists," "Orientalists," and "Samuel Huntington." (Žižek actually associates the phrase *clash of civilizations* with the multiculturalists, exactly those who have most combated his ideas.) Žižek patronizingly told the *Al Jazeera* audience what they already know: that "Egypt deserves democracy just like everyone else." One would think that the relevance of multiculturalism to Egypt would be to point to that country's fantastic multiculturality, to argue for an interfaith Egypt featuring equality between Muslims and Copts, for example, and to teach Egyptian history in Western schools. Žižek also spoke of his discovery in a Qatar museum of a "wonderful plate" inscribed with a phrase from an Iranian philosopher to the effect that "only the foolish man invokes Fate as an excuse," for Žižek evidence that "even" the Islamic world can be enlightened. We are reminded of the ironic response of a Tunisian friend (Moncef Cheikhrouhou) to a European interlocutor's "reassuring" assertion that she believed "Arabs are human beings": "Merci!"

9. Gitlin, *The Twilight of Common Dreams*, 33.

10. Spivak, *In Other Worlds.*

11. Lipsitz, *The Possessive Investment in Whiteness*, vii.

12. Michaels, *The Trouble with Diversity*, 7, 3, 12, 17.

13. Michaels, *The Trouble with Diversity*, 89.

14. Cited in Wise, *Speaking Treason Fluently*, 71.

15. Michaels, *The Trouble with Diversity*, 72.

16. Lui et al., *The Color of Wealth*, 1.

17. Quoted in Lui et al., *The Color of Wealth*, 268.

18. Roediger, *Towards the Abolition of Whiteness*, ix.

19. Roediger, "The Retreat from Race and Class."

20. Du Bois, *Black Reconstruction in America*, 700–701.

21. King, "All Labor Has Dignity."

22. Taylor quoted in Mills, *Blackness Visible*, 135.

23. Mills, *Blackness Visible*, 39.

24. Michaels, *The Trouble with Diversity*, 82.

25. The problem of "racing Islam" has been addressed by critics such as Rabab Abdulhadi, Evelyn Alsutany, Moustafa Bayoumi, and Nadine Naber.

26. Michaels, *The Trouble with Diversity*, 74.

27. See debate with Edward Said, 1986.

28. Michaels, *The Trouble with Diversity*, 60.

29. Michaels, *The Trouble with Diversity*, 143.

30. Michaels, *The Trouble with Diversity*, 65.

31. Escobar, "Latin America at a Crossroads."

32. During the course of history, culture and economics have gone hand in hand in the United States as well, for example, in the case of conflicts between the U.S. government and Native Americans. The ethos of private property and the imposition of individual allotments on Indian tribes, through the Dawes Act, meant nothing less than the social death of indigenous culture as a living mode of praxis.

33. Žižek and Daly, *Conversations with Žižek*, 134.

34. Žižek and Daly, *Conversations with Žižek*, 134, 22.

35. Rich, *On Lies, Secrets and Silence*, 306.

36. Žižek, "A Leftist Plea for 'Eurocentrism,'" 1006.

37. Žižek, "A Leftist Plea for 'Eurocentrism,'" 989.

38. Žižek and Daly, *Conversations with Žižek*, 147.

39. We refer here to Auerbach's famous comparison of Racine and Shakespeare in *Mimesis*.

40. See Durpaire, *France Blanche, Colere Noire*.

TWENTY-THREE

Césaire's Gift and the Decolonial Turn

NELSON MALDONADO-TORRES

A civilization that proves incapable of solving the problems that it creates is a decadent civilization. A civilization that chooses to close its eyes to its most crucial problems is a stricken civilization. A civilization that uses its principles for trickery and deceit is a dying civilization.—AIMÉ CÉSAIRE, *Discourse on Colonialism*

Aimé Césaire's indictment of European civilization occurred at a point when Europe's crisis reached its climax. It was only a decade after the end of World War II, when the impact of the first decolonization struggles on European discourse and on the minds of other colonized peoples throughout the world had already become obvious. From that point on Europe gradually became more marginal than ever in its not so recent history. Today Europe is politically, economically, and intellectually important, but not as important as before the war and certainly not "defensible" in Césaire's terms—even though post–cold war admirers from Eastern Europe, Russia, and the former Soviet republics sometimes ignore or forget the lesson.[1] Relative admiration of Europe in the post–cold war era, however, does not hide a present crisis in European identity. This new crisis can be understood, using Boaventura de Sousa Santos's terms, as a standing in between the new imperial Prospero and the old Caliban.[2] For Sousa Santos this setting best describes the position of Portugal in relation to European countries such as France and Great

Britain on the one hand, and the colonial world on the other. But the term could be extended to refer to the way many other Europeans feel today. As the United States has asserted its independence from Europe more openly than ever since World War II, Europeans begin to experience some degrees of subalternity, a feeling that often breeds or increases xenophobia. The responses to such a position have been predictable.

One response to the crisis of Europe today consists in reminding the United States of the Western origins of its roots and the need for partnership with Europe.[3] This response is part of an imperial dialectic between Eurocentrism and a form of Americanism that is also facing a moment of crisis with distinct internal and external "menaces."[4] It fights the provincial imperialism of U.S. Americanism with another form of provincialism grounded in the European experience. A second response calls attention to the need to define a European common foreign policy based on the political viability of the European Union.[5] Also part of the imperial dialectics of recognition, this response, asserted in a particularly eloquent form by the philosophers Jürgen Habermas and Jacques Derrida involves recasting and reaffirming the value of European cultural and intellectual roots. It is almost as problematic as the first, not because it searches for common ground among members of the European Union but because it gestures toward the formerly colonized non-European world only very vaguely and thus fails to address the challenges that Europe still has to overcome in relation to its imperial and colonial legacy.

The third response is more promising. It consists in the idea of de-investing from U.S. interests.[6] This response goes together with the realization of a certain commonality between Europe and its former colonies. It is the emergence of a certain European postcolonialism—not of Europeans who support decolonization but of the perception of Europe itself as a colony. To be sure, this idea is not by any means widespread or without risks. For although the identification with the colonies opens unsuspected possibilities of mutual respect and collaboration, it can easily follow the path of a Eurocentric appropriation of the legacy and work of intellectuals from the periphery—that is, a recentering of Europe and a new marginalization of the colonized and their perspectives. There is also the risk of erasing the significant differences between Europe's subaltern status today and the legacies of its own forms of racial colonialism in the former European colonies. The effective evasion of these risks necessitates constant vigilance together with a process of self-decolonization. This would imply the need for Europeans to give more priority to seeing themselves through the eyes of the colonized and to seriously reflecting on the various historical, social, political, and ethical implications of such observation. This, in place of the continued validation of their identity, their roots, and their geopolitical relevance. Europeans, like the formerly colonized, cannot take any idea for granted in the production of their refashioned identity and political projects. They need to critically revise their history and their ideas in light of questions and concerns that appear prominently not only in the marginalized spaces within Europe but also in the colonial context.

In a historical moment when Europeans and others look to the South for responses to the crisis of the age, it is important to clarify and elaborate on the contributions of intellectuals from the colonial world. If, as Immanuel Wallerstein has pointed out, we live in a *kairos* moment, when choice is both necessary and important,[7] then we need to investigate more the intellectual resources that might shed light on our current predicament and that may provide guidelines for the future. It is therefore necessary to expand on insights and projects that have remained marginal and have been silenced because their premises or proposals question the very bases of the European civilization project as well as our modern identities. Translation and transgression of different projects on critical theorizing are also necessary if we want to widen and refine the alternatives that we have as we attempt to collectively respond to the future. Exercises in what I have called elsewhere transgresstopic critique and post-continental theorizing are today as important as ever.[8] This essay is an exercise in such a kind of criticism and theory making. It joins other efforts in subverting the tables of what is considered legitimate theorizing, and in augmenting the space for reflection about our collective present and future, by engaging in the epistemic practice of what the Caribbean Philosophical Association refers to as *shifting the geography of reason*.[9] The first section of this essay seeks to elucidate the significance of decolonization as a project and to elaborate a genealogy of what I refer to as "the decolonial turn." The decolonial turn (different from the linguistic or the pragmatic turns) refers to the recognition and propagation of decolonization as an ethical, political, and epistemic project, which arguably had its highest moment yet in the twentieth century. This project reflects changes in historical consciousness, agency, and knowledge, and it also involves a method or series of methods that facilitate the task of decolonization at the material and epistemic levels.

The second part focuses on method. I identify basic principles of decolonial methodology as they appear in Césaire's *Discourse on Colonialism*, which provides one of the most penetrating analyses of both the crisis of Europe in and after World War II and the beginnings of twentieth-century decolonization movements around the world. Césaire's *Discourse* seeks to show Europeans certain truths about themselves as well as provide an intellectual framework for conceiving of and advancing decolonization. In this sense *Discourse on Colonialism* can be read as a discourse on decolonial methodology: it facilitates the decolonization of both the European and the colonized. The *Discourse* appears to relate to the project of decolonization in a way similar to how other discourses on method stand in relation to the project of European civilization. I am thinking quite clearly of Descartes. I take the relationship between Césaire's *Discourse on Colonialism* and Descartes's *Discourse on Method* further by suggesting that the former can actually be read as a response to the latter. In this sense Césaire joins figures like Husserl and Heidegger, among others, who reflected deeply on the connection between the nature and crisis of Europe and Cartesian premises. It is widely known that while Husserl wished to radicalize Descartes and to strengthen the European rationalist vein and the French cosmopolitan impetus, Heidegger, a German nationalist who at one point served as a functionary of the Nazi administration, enlisted Descartes as one of the pivotal thinkers on the path that led to and continued the forgetting of the question of Being. Heidegger also celebrated German language and customs and questioned the philosophical relevance of Romance languages. Appropriation or rejection of the Cartesian legacy stood behind philosophical formulations of cosmopolitanism and nationalism. Césaire, as well as his one-time student Frantz Fanon, had a different view, a different project, as well as a different geopolitical point of departure: not a Germany in crisis with varied reactions to French liberal cosmopolitanism and the Cartesian legacy in Europe, but the colonial world, and more specifically the French Caribbean colonies. Césaire's *Discourse* is the response of a black colonial subject to the Cartesian project. He mobilizes those aspects of his identity and geopolitical orientation toward a critical reflection on the basis of the European civilization project. It is such a critical theory that I wish to locate historically and then to explicate with the hope of providing more tools for the understanding of decolonization as an unfinished project. The critical theory in question helps to better understand the concept of critique in Critical Ethnic Studies and can inform processes of theoretical and methodological innovation and change in multiple other fields.

From the *Idea* to the *Project* of Decolonization in the Twentieth Century

Decolonization not only refers to the critique of and effort to dismantle neocolonial relations that continue and renew dependency and vertical relations of power between northern and southern countries in different ways.

It also refers to the radical transformation of the modern/colonial matrix of power that continues to define modern identities as well as the relations of power and epistemic forms that go along with them. We owe the concept of the modern/colonial to Walter Mignolo, who is indebted to Aníbal Quijano's theorizations of modernity and the coloniality of power.[10] There are subtle but important differences in their accounts of the relationship between modernity and coloniality that are necessary to have in mind when the term is used. While for Mignolo coloniality is modernity's constitutive darker side, for Quijano modernity is an ambiguous formation that includes coloniality as a founding moment but that also gives expression to legitimate human demands for individual freedom. Thus Quijano has been hesitant, if not resistant, to the idea of joining together modernity and coloniality in a single expression. Mignolo does not necessarily oppose the idea that modernity contains positive elements that cannot be reduced to coloniality, but he sees in the very concept of the modern an idea that inevitably makes reference to the colonization of time.[11] Thus while it may be true that there are aspects of modernity that escape the logic of coloniality, such recognition does not do away with the inherent colonial aspect of the term. This leads Mignolo to talk about alternatives *to* modernity rather than simply alternative modernities. For his part Quijano would insist that ideas such as individual freedom and the socialization of power must be conceived as universal human achievements or imperatives that are not to be diffused by appeals to the geopolitics of knowledge or "diversality."[12] It is an open question whether Mignolo's concepts of diversality and the geopolitics of knowledge as well as his critique of abstract universals can or cannot accommodate the universalistic grain of Quijano's claims, or whether Quijano's appeal to universality collapses into the problematic dimensions of abstract universals and an appeal to diversality would be more consistent with a decolonial epistemology. To be sure, a systematic and more complete elucidation of these issues requires more ample space.[13]

My use of modernity/coloniality here refers mainly to the idea that it is necessary always to historicize and theorize modernity with the concept of coloniality in mind. This leaves open the question about the exact extent of modernity's achievements or failures. Seen in this light, decolonization refers to the task of building an alternative world to modernity, without simply falling back into many of the ideas and practices that are now regarded, even if problematically, as premodern. Decolonization also makes reference to the construction of a new horizon of meaning that includes new conceptions about the human being and material relations that do not conform to the dictatorship of capital and that are not limited by the empire of law in the modern/colonial nation-state form. Decolonization, in short, is the comprehensive process that seeks to dismantle the "coloniality of power." It is best understood, as Chela Sandoval and Catherine Walsh, among others, have suggested in different contexts, as "decoloniality."[14] Here "decoloniality" means the dismantling of relations of power and conceptions of knowledge that foment the reproduction of racial, gender, and geopolitical hierarchies that came into being or found new and more powerful forms of expression in the modern/colonial world.

Césaire's *Discourse on Colonialism* is central to the project of decoloniality. It is a critical reflection on the European civilization project that gives expression to the *disenchantment* with European modernity that was increasingly felt in many places after the First and particularly the Second World War.[15] The *Discourse* is an indictment of Europe and a rejection of its racist and imperial ways. His critique is not without precedents. Césaire questions Eurocentrism and the racism of the modern episteme as or more strongly than Descartes questioned the criteria of rationality sustained by the Church throughout the Middle Ages and early modernity up until the seventeenth century. Césaire also takes discourses on colonialism to a new level. Critiques of coloniality are as old as coloniality itself. They first appeared in the cries of despair of subjects who either lost their lives or observed the expansion of the modern/colonial system in early modernity. From despair and cries the skepticism of the modern/colonial project turned into the idea of decolonization, which presupposed the possibility of achieving some kind of independence. The idea of decolonization was nurtured during the first moment of decolonization toward the end of the eighteenth until the first half of the nineteenth century. The first wave of decolonization was critical of imperialism but not so much of racism, and thus of the coloniality of power. It was also still for the most part enchanted with Europe or with ideas of progress that had emanated from Europe. What I call the project of decolonization emerges when the critique of racism intensifies, the absolute goodness of the nation-state form is put into question, the disenchantment with Europe becomes strong, and the question of postcolonial agency acquires global relevance.[16] This occurs at the point when the end of the most devastating war in the twentieth century coincides with the start, and in some cases with the expansion, of liberation struggles in European colonies throughout the Caribbean, Asia, and Africa.

The project of decolonization represents a third pathway among the intellectual and ideological options that became more prominent after World War II.[17] The first two political and ideological pathways were defined by the new geopolitical powers that took a protagonist role during the war. On the one hand, there was the United States, which had already become an international force after the expansion of its territory beyond the original thirteen colonies, the war with Mexico, and the Hispanic-American war. The United States would come to assist as well as to displace northern Europe as a fundamental geopolitical axis of world-systemic forces. With this displacement Americanism is introduced into the world as a triumphalist and assimilationist ideology. Americanism had already entered the scene at the end of the nineteenth century and the start of the twentieth with the likes of Theodore Roosevelt. It worked then as an ideology that dictated the terms of the assimilation of European immigrants, particularly Catholic and non-Christian, some of whom were regarded as people of dark skin.[18] Americanism took new shapes with McCarthyism and today finds new forms of expression in reactions to foreign threats that include the war on terror and the hysteria about Mexican immigration, as manifested in writings such as those of Samuel P. Huntington.[19] To be sure, Americanism has never entirely reconciled itself with other subjects, such as indigenous peoples and blacks in the United States who in some way represent constitutively subaltern or racial components of the U.S. nation.

The second historical door or pathway that opened after the fall of Europe in World War II was that of communism. Communism represented for many a viable option for a different future from those offered by fascism, European liberalism, or U.S. Americanism. The cold war put Soviet communism and Americanism at the center, with some other, related projects as satellites. Europe itself became physically and ideologically divided between these two spheres of influence, while former European colonies attempted to negotiate or steal spaces of freedom to forge alternative projects or at least political formations that allow them to enjoy some autonomy. Some of these projects were defined by neocolonial elites in the former colonies and others by ultraconservative anti-Western sectors. But there also emerged a sophisticated anticolonial discourse that raised itself beyond *ressentimment* while also offering new grammars to do critique and new ideas to forge a post-Eurocentric future that also overcomes the limits of modernity/coloniality. This is what I am referring to as the third historical pathway that opens up in the twentieth century. Césaire's *Discourse on Colonialism* is one of the key texts that put forward this type of discourse. We also find many figures and texts that might be located in two or more projects simultaneously.

In sum, if, as Wallerstein argues, the distinctive ideologies of modernity after the French Revolution were conservatism, liberalism, and Marxism, World War II would bring into visibility particular expressions of these ideologies, now forged primarily outside of the European continent.[20] European liberalism's sphere of influence subsides and U.S. American liberalism dominates. Unlike European liberalism—particularly French liberalism—U.S. American liberalism tends to reconcile itself more easily with religion, in particular with Christian Protestantism, which tends to be taken as the norm for understanding religiosity in the United States. Marxism gives way primarily to Soviet communism, which was deeply antireligious and held aspirations of empire building. Conservatism in this context became primarily the view of those who wanted to hold onto a picture of the world as dominated by Europe or by a European nation, as was the case of intellectuals such as Heidegger, who adopted strong forms of Germanocentrism after his complicity with fascism.[21] In more general terms Eurocentrism itself became the new conservatism since it continued to affirm European centrality in a world that no longer had faith in Europe and that was gradually moving beyond the European Age. Indeed Eurocentrism represents today an option similar to that taken by those who defended a Christian-centered view of the world after Copernicus had defied Christian cosmology, after Columbus had broken with classical and Christian geography,[22] and after Descartes offered a new epistemology. At least this is how it appears after reading Césaire's *Discourse on Colonialism* and Fanon's *The Wretched of the Earth*. The same can be said, if we follow Sylvia Wynter, of much of what often passes as "minority" literature.[23] But from the perspective introduced by these texts conservatism can hardly be said to appear only in Eurocentric ventures. Conservatism also transpires in U.S. American liberalism, which tends to valorize the world through religious themes (such as Manifest Destiny), the perversity of which has already been more than historically tested. As problematic as European liberalism may be, U.S. American liberalism undoes some of its victories. The same occurred with Soviet communism. But all of them appear to be in some measure conservative when compared with the project of decolonization. In short, while liberalism, Marxism, and decolonization projects left conservatism to some extent by the wayside during the cold war, conservatism gradually came back strongly not only as a separate or distinct ideology but also in the form of the Eurocentrism of liberals and Marxists who resist decolonization. Conservative republicanisms and a liberal form of conservatism have become the strongest ideologies after the cold war.

The fall of Europe in and after World War II makes possible the opening of a new historical horizon, that of decoloniality, which, as Fanon put it, is the path of the *condemned of the earth*. If modern philosophy began in the Caribbean, as Enrique Dussel suggests, it is possible to say that transmodern decolonial philosophy also finds a strong anchor in the Caribbean.[24] Césaire's *Discourse* and Fanon's *Wretched of the Earth* and *Black Skin, White Masks* are the primary representatives. The pathway of decoloniality that I wish to highlight is opened in a definitive form by the combination of the internal and the external devastation of Europe, that is, not only by the racist and genocidal force of Nazism within but also by the hopeful force of decolonization in many of the colonial territories. Contrary to the decolonization struggles in Latin America throughout the nineteenth century, which remained fascinated with Europe or northern countries (primarily France and the United States; Haiti is an exception to what appears as a rule here), the second wave of decolonization took place at a point when Europe was "indefensible," as Césaire puts it in the *Discourse*.[25] Thus the newly (dependent) nations, as well as the territories that had already achieved their formal independence in the late eighteenth and nineteenth century, suddenly found themselves in a context where Eurocentrism raised more suspicion than enchantment. The new door that opens up after World War II is that of the disenchantment with Eurocentrism and a renewed affirmation of decoloniality as a project. This is also where the decolonial turn emerges as a widely shared epistemic perspective among many Third World thinkers. One can trace it, for instance, from Césaire and Fanon in the Caribbean, Europe, and North Africa, to Dussel's *Philosophy of Liberation* (1985) in Latin America, to Linda Tuhiwai Smith in her *Decolonizing Methodologies* (1999) in New Zealand, and to Chela Sandoval's *Methodology of the Oppressed* (2000) in the United States, among other locales.[26] The list of precursors is also ample, including W. E. B. Du Bois and the Pan-African movement, intellectuals of the Haitian Revolution, Guaman Poma de Ayala and other indigenous intellectuals in the Americas and elsewhere for more than five hundred years now, and others in Africa, Asia, and the Americas.

The disenchantment not simply with "tradition" largely defined or with religion, as Max Weber would accentuate in regard to what he perceived as the progressive historical development of Europe, but with Eurocentrism or the "myth of modernity" itself, became a central component of the second wave of decolonization.[27] The fall of Europe was a symptom of a larger crisis of the world-system as a whole, which made visible the ways in which colonial structures still defined geopolitical relations, even in places that had achieved independence. From here the suspicion or disenchantment with Eurocentrism began to propagate rapidly in different spaces in the second half of the twentieth century, including Europe and the United States themselves.[28]

Discourse on Colonialism, the "Crisis" of Europe, and the Third Path of Decolonization

What I call the third way, that of decolonization, transmodernity, and pluriversality,[29] is not parallel or equivalent to the other two pathways that opened up after World War II. Americanism and communism are more recent historical projects and are less ambitious than the project of decolonization. Americanism has its founding moment in 1776, and communism is grounded on modern ideologies that were born out of the European Enlightenment. The project of decolonization, on the other hand, has been articulated in different ways since the very beginning of the European expansion in the Americas.[30] Americanism and communism are also more limited than the project of decolonization because they are circumscribed by modernity. That is, they are expressions of modernity's ideologies: conservatism, liberalism, and Marxism. The project of decolonization represents a "spatial rupture" with modernity.[31] This does not mean that the project of decolonization is necessarily antiliberal or anti-Marxist, or that it could dispense with elements from them. It means, first, that the bases for the project of decolonization not only precede the European Enlightenment, but that they are developed outside of the metropolitan centers of European empires or inside of those centers but predominantly by subjects who are considered to be outsiders, and, second, that it subsumes modern ideas in the effort to produce alternatives to Western modernity, which Dussel refers to as transmodern.[32] The project of decolonization also implies that Europe has been called from the very beginning of the modern/colonial project to abandon its imperialist posture and to adopt a different historical project. That is to say, the project of decolonization is not only different from that of European modernity; it also confronts modernity with a series of ethical, political, and intellectual imperatives. Decolonization has the character of denunciation and demand. Its viability, however, does not rest on their recognition. These different dimensions of the project of decolonization appear in *Discourse on Colonialism*.

As I suggested previously, Césaire's *Discourse on Colonialism* and Fanon's *The Wretched of the Earth* are the texts that perhaps more clearly and strongly articulate the third path that opened up after the war. They were written with full awareness of the new world dynamics that began to unfold after World War II. Both aim to understand the world that began to emerge from the perspective of groups that suffered constant and consistent exclusion throughout modernity. They refer to these groups as the *wretched* or *condemned*. Césaire's *Discourse* focuses on the understanding of the crisis of

Europe and the possibilities that began to open after its fall. Fanon's *Wretched of the Earth* focuses more on the struggles and possibilities of colonized peoples as they began to claim independence from Europe.

My main thesis here is that *Discourse on Colonialism* should be read as a response from the colonized world, and particularly from the perspective of the African diaspora, to the European modern civilization project, which finds one of its strongest roots in the philosophy of Descartes. Césaire takes a variety of postures that go from internal critique and "subversive complicity" to the introduction of new critical perspectives beyond the European interpretive and epistemological framework.[33] He deploys a complex rhetorical arsenal in his diagnosis and indictment of European Man.[34]

With his reflections on the crisis of Europe, Césaire joins a wide and diverse group of thinkers who diagnose Europe and who aim to articulate responses to it. Many of these European theorists took Descartes's philosophy as a point of reference. I have referred to Husserl and Heidegger already, but one can add Sartre, Freud, and Lacan as well, among many others. They interpreted the crisis of Europe as the result of a departure from Cartesianism, or else as the contrary, that is, as the expression of the inability to break away from Descartes. They thus attempted to provide a new view of the subject, of knowledge, and a new methodology, philosophical perspective, or science, beyond the Cartesian or Newtonian sciences. Of the different European voices trying to provide a new orientation for thought it was undoubtedly Sartre who took most seriously questions and ideas that emerged in the colonial world. But even Sartre failed to note the extent of radicality in the proposals of such figures. From here we see the need to attend to Césaire and others as philosophers or theorists in their own right, which includes analyzing the extent to which intellectuals from the periphery, and not only those from Europe, were critically and originally engaging the Cartesian legacy and other foundations of modern Western thought.

Césaire writes at a moment of heightened disenchantment with Europe. He offers the first sustained diagnosis and critique of Europe at a point when the crisis of Europe looked more like Europe's very end. And this becomes for him and others a new point of departure for critique. While in the nineteenth century it was believed that critique found its starting point in the critical assessment of religion—indeed for Marx, with the possibility of religion's very end—Césaire's text makes the point that critique in the second half of the twentieth century can only begin with the critique of Europe. It also seems to follow from his text that, just as Europe had to pass through the disenchantment with religion in order to access modernity, the world (including

Europe) has to pass through the disenchantment with Europe in order to aspire to what Dussel calls transmodernity.[35] This remains a goal fifty years after Césaire wrote his *Discourse*. But this should cause no surprise. Just as many religions have the capacity to survive even after their main tenets have been undermined, Eurocentrism will keep its priests and mausoleums for some time. The realization of its bankruptcy will be gradual and not by any means immediate. And at the end of it all Césaire's *Discourse* will still be waiting for us.

Discourse on Colonialism and the Crisis of Europe

Césaire opens the *Discourse on Colonialism* by describing Europe as a "decadent civilization." In this statement he has in mind not only the proliferation of fascism in Europe but also the more general issue that European civilization has been unable to solve the problems that it creates. The main problems are proletarianism and colonialism. The problem of the proletariat is very present in Europe and is thus taken seriously by many. But colonialism hardly emerges as a problem in the same way. If anything, it is colonized peoples that appear as problems. In this Césaire exercises one of the central features of the decolonial attitude: the problem is located in the structures, not the people.[36] This move is characteristic of a critical attitude in general. What makes it decolonial is that the "people" in question are not even considered to be "people" under the racial and colonial lenses.[37] That is, they are racialized subjects who inhabit the world of superfluous visibility.[38] In regard to these "subjects" the shift of perspective that leads to critique requires a more radical turn. Here the European tradition of critical theory usually finds its limits.

A clear expression of the "decolonial attitude" is Césaire's resistance to subordinating the question of the proletariat to the colonial problem. The colonial problem raises for him specific questions and requires an exploration of its own, which includes reference to capitalism but which is not reducible to economics, class struggle, or exploitation. Instead he points to the specificity of colonial and racial domination. However, he does not proceed to show the connections between world capitalism and race or colonialism; he focuses on the connections between fascism and the colonial experience. He uses drastic but legitimate means to bring to European consciousness the harsh gravity of the colonial problem. This is a decolonial strategy. Once the "master" recognizes as a principle the gravity of something that has affected him, the colonized uses those principles or those "evidences" in order to bring the master to the awareness of gravities that he did not even want to see. This is not always a mere strategy. In some cases, as in Césaire's, the colonized has more complex and convincing articulations of those principles than does the master himself. Gaining the master's recognition about some evil serves the practical goals of gaining degrees of freedom and also serves the theoretical task of educating those in position of master about ethics and reason. Here the practical and the theoretical are entangled without being entirely reducible to each other.

Discourse on Colonialism is written in poetic prose, but the style is very different from Césaire's poems, which follow the surrealist trend of the time. Surrealism employs unconscious forces and prerational elements in order to debunk the attempt to reduce the psyche and our experience of the world in rationalist formulas. As Robin Kelley points out, surrealism is "an extension of [Césaire's] search for a new black subjectivity."[39] Césaire makes very illuminating comments in this regard: "Well then, if I apply the surrealist approach to my particular situation, I can summon up these unconscious forces. This, for me, was a call to Africa. I said to myself: it's true that superficially we are French, we bear the marks of French customs; we have been branded by Cartesian philosophy, by French rhetoric; but if we break with all that, if we plumb the depths, then what we will find is fundamentally black."[40] Césaire infuses his poems with *négritude. Discourse on Colonialism,* written only a few years after the end of World War II, uses different rhetorical devices. His narrative takes more sober, argumentative, and rational tones. Moreover Césaire focuses on Europe, not black subjectivity. By no means does this represent an inconsistency or betrayal to his surrealist intuitions. Surrealism allows Césaire, among other things, to undermine the bases of Cartesianism. In this Césaire to a degree approaches Heidegger and others who found in poetry important ingredients to overcome the limits of Cartesianism. But while Heidegger searched for European roots in Greece and Germany, Césaire was trying to establish an intimate connection with Africa. Césaire, however, was not tied to African roots. While négritude took him away from Europe, his Marxist commitments and his view of the structural conditions of colonization led him far from relying solely on cultural politics. It would be a mistake, though, to reduce his political commitments to Marxism. It is not only the problem of the proletariat that he addressed, but also the colonial and racial problem. And he does not think that one can be reduced to the other. As I pointed out earlier, Césaire does not spell out the relationship between these two. This work had been done by figures such as the Trinidadean sociologist Oliver Cox in the 1940s and would continue by Cedric Robinson and the Peruvian sociologist Aníbal Quijano, among others.[41] Quijano's theorization of capitalist exploitation and racial domination, along with their impact on spheres of power in society such as control of sex, knowledge, labor, and authority, provides a particularly rich framework for the understanding of modernity and capitalism. Césaire does not articulate these ideas, but he and others make their articulation possible. This reveals important levels of continuity and collaboration in the larger and collective project of decolonization.

While Césaire's poetic and surrealist vein puts him closer to Heidegger than to Husserl's project, the *Discourse on Colonialism* is definitely closer to Husserl. In his *Cartesian Meditations,* Husserl attempts to provide a response to the crisis of modernity through the transformation of Cartesian thought.[42] *Discourse on Colonialism* can be seen as an effort in the same direction, but it decisively breaks from Cartesianism as well. While Descartes and Husserl attempt to establish or reformulate the basis of the European historical project through the centrality of the subject and the epistemic value of "clarity" and "distinction" (or phenomenological intuition in Husserl's case), Césaire aims to introduce a new type of critical reason, which rests on the "clarity" that colonized subjects have of the perversity of the European civilization project. Let's consider this carefully.

There are clear parallels between Césaire's *Discourse on Colonialism* and Descartes's *Discourse on Method*. Both are brief texts divided into six sections. It is almost as if Césaire was emulating Descartes, responding to him, or trying to write a new *Discourse* for a new historical project. The brevity of both texts is explained by their focus on the most basic aspects of the scientific attitude; that is, they aim to provide new perspectives on basic philosophical principles. Both focus on impediments to the search for truth. But they highlight different forms of deception. Descartes focuses on the deception of the senses, tradition, and assumed certainties, while Césaire focuses on the deception of those who, after apparently following Descartes's method, believe they are not being deceived but deceive themselves nonetheless in regard to the most fundamental elements: themselves and their relations with others. Otherwise put, in *Discourse on Colonialism* Césaire aims to elucidate the dark side of the "deception" and "self-deception" that Descartes attempts to exorcize in his *Discourse on Method*. He also provides ideas about correcting these evils and falsehoods through decolonization. Thus Césaire's *Discourse,* like Descartes's, is a discourse on method. It is a discourse on decolonial methodology, on how to achieve and maintain a decolonial consciousness and a decolonial attitude.

Discourse on Colonialism is premised on the *fact* that "Europe is unable to justify itself either before the bar of 'reason' or before the bar of 'conscience'; and that, increasingly, it takes refuge in a *hypocrisy* which is all the more odious because it is *less and less likely to deceive*."[43] It is clear here that for Césaire Europe took the role in modernity of a failed evil demon of sorts who could no longer, after the war, deceive others about the grandiosity of its civilization or about the alleged obviousness of the racial, sexual, religious, and geopolitical categories that were so instrumental for its hegemony. This bar of reason, on the other hand, is not a privileged epistemic subject but an intersubjective community: the whole world. The devastation of World War II and the Holocaust showed the world very clearly the bankruptcy of Europe. Césaire comments that the U.S. opinion of Europe was not necessarily wrong but that it clearly reflected its own interests for supremacy. That is, the critique by the United States served its own interests in hegemony. Césaire knew, as did so many others in the U.S. Southwest and Latin America, and some in Europe, that the United States posed a menace to Europe and the world. He also knew that Europeans might be tempted to respond to the situation by holding onto their roots with more determination. From Husserl and Heidegger at the beginning of the twentieth century, to Habermas and Derrida, among others, more recently, we find the repeated gesture of searching for European roots as a response to its "crisis."[44] Some Europeans continue to believe that the door of Eurocentrism is still open, or is a lived possibility. To be fair to these efforts, it must be said that Eurocentric epistemologies still dictate to a great extent recognized ways of thinking and critique.[45] But conscious adherence to Eurocentric projects is quite different from opposing Eurocentrism while nonetheless collapsing into it. Césaire's judgment of the former is unforgiving. He considers them to be hypocrites who lie to themselves and who aim to hide what has appeared with "clarity" and "distinctness" to everyone: Europe's perversity.

Césaire accuses Europeans of attempting to hide from themselves by different means knowledge about the reality and character of European civilization. That is, Europe has not only deceived the world but also itself. Césaire's *Discourse* aims to elucidate the nature of the deception and self-deception in question:

> Yes, it would be worthwhile to study clinically, in detail, the steps taken by Hitler and Hitlerism and to reveal to the very distinguished, very humanistic, very Christian bourgeois of the twentieth century that without his being aware of it, he has a Hitler inside him, that Hitler *inhabits* him, that Hitler is his *demon,* that if he rails against it he is being inconsistent and that, at bottom, what he cannot forgive Hitler for is not *crime* in itself, *the crime against man,* it is not *the humiliation of man*

as such, it is the crime against the white man, the humiliation of the white man, and the fact that he applied to Europe colonialist procedures which until then had been reserved exclusively for the Arabs of Algeria, the coolies of India, and the blacks of Africa.[46]

Like Descartes, Césaire knows that deception leads humans away from the "truth" and the achievement of "true science,"[47] but he adds to this that the European form of self-deception is also homicidal. While Europe, through the Eurocentrism endemic to European modernity, took the role of deceiving others, and thus of becoming an evil demon of sorts, Europe itself, Césaire notes, has its own demon, or agent of deception. This is Hitler himself. And Hitler showed himself an effective agent of European thought and action long before fascism existed. Hitler was already present in Europe's mind since the time of colonization and systematic racism in modernity. Like many of Hitler's victims, colonized and racialized subjects have suffered extermination, genocide, enslavement, and violence for centuries. Hitler is, in short, the name that Césaire uses to refer in retrospect to the European evil demon that has deceived Europe and led it to create and sustain the *color line,*[48] which is a fundamental source of its own identity and historical agency. Hitler precedes fascism but also survives it. European humanists and the Christian bourgeoisie itself, according to Césaire, continue to be duped by Hitler. Their critiques of the historical Hitler rely on their unshakable commitment to Hitler, the internal demon of European consciousness. Thus their critique is "inconsistent" as it presupposes a commitment to that which they allegedly criticize. For instance, critiques of "the crime and humiliation of man" are critiques of the use of colonial violence toward the typical colonizers, the Europeans. That is why Hitler's crime has been unforgivable. That is also why he keeps been denounced, but only partially, as Hitler the demon continues to define the terms of such critique, and thus of its outcome. Following this very logic it could be said not only that fascism was preceded by colonialism, but also that elements of it continue to shape "civilized" life through the coloniality of power and the continued production of what Du Bois referred to as the color line. In that sense, European Man in many ways continues to be deceived about himself and those realities.

The emergence and spread of fascism in Europe along with its tragic consequences made it impossible for the European to hide some truths about his civilization. Yet European Man has for the most part remained blind to the reality of the colonized, and has thus failed to know more about himself. The "slave," however, has known about the perversity and the inconsistency of the "master" for centuries. Césaire points out that the slaves know that their masters "lie" (to themselves and the slaves) and that, inasmuch as they hide from themselves a truth about themselves, they are "weak." This is particularly true after the collapse of Europe in World War II. The slaves and the colonized people appear in the *Discourse on Colonialism* as a necessary epistemic source for Europe to achieve "clear" and "distinct" ideas about its identity and the character of its historical project. Their failure to take the colonized seriously as a subject of knowledge means at the same time a betrayal of the Cartesianism to which they are allegedly committed. Lies, more than clarity and distinctness, are central aspects of the European project.

To be sure, the knowledge that enslaved and colonized subjects have, while clear and distinct, is not necessarily achieved by a rigorous Cartesian method. Descartes's method rests on hyperbolic doubt. He imagines an evil demon who plays with the epistemological powers and the sensorial capabilities and who "deceive[s]" people about their most fundamental convictions. The *condemned* do not need to imagine an evil demon in order to know the truth about European Man. The violence of the master is enough for that. Or else, as I indicated previously, Europe itself is an evil demon of sorts, as in Césaire's text. Now its evil character shows not only in deceit but also in the propagation of violence and death as well as in the naturalization of the institutions, ideas, and practices that perpetuate social death and colonial violence.[49] Instead of a process of methodic doubt, the *condemned* go through a process of methodical suffering based on their alleged lack of humanity. But the slaves know themselves to be human. They also know that the master can legitimate his conceptions and the violence that he perpetrates only through a process of methodical and brutal self-imposed blindness, facilitated by the dominant symbolic structure and forms of knowledge, including the often lauded Western sciences and "liberal arts," which Césaire take as an object of critique in the *Discourse*. The crux of the matter is that the modern masters hide from themselves knowledge about the humanity of those whom they consider nonhuman. According to Césaire, the forgetfulness of the humanity of the racialized and the colonized, rather than the forgetfulness of Being, as Heidegger would have it, is the true crime and inconsistency of Europe. This is bad faith in its most destructive expression.[50]

While Descartes's *Discourse on Method* gave form and shape to the European rationalist project and fomented a certain form of self-critique (process of doubt), *Discourse on Colonialism* makes explicit the failure of the European commitment with the Cartesian project while also pointing to intrinsic problems with the Cartesian approach itself. Even though Descartes attempted to articulate a solid ground for reason, and thus to combat lies and deceit, he adopted a method that concealed the epistemological relevance of the relation between master and slave, colonizer and colonized. Descartes's method is based on an internal dialogue whereby the subject can arrive at the truth about itself and about the true nature of reason. Cartesian individualism and Descartes's monological process of doubt leave dialogue by the wayside and place obstacles before the flourishing of intersubjective reason. There is a different route, which consists in conceiving reason as dialogical and intersubjective from the beginning. From that perspective, slavery and colonization, rather than the tricks of an "evil genius," represent the highest betrayals of reason. The perspective of the slave is more conducive to this kind of reflection than that of the master. That is why we see in the periphery or the Third World continued affirmation of ethics and politics as first philosophy. Césaire's *Discourse* itself is a manual to teach us the right kind of skepticism, whose negative function (doubt) is grounded on the ethical mode of reception of otherness and whose positive goal is none other than love, understood as a force of social activism and a social formation premised on the primacy of ethical human contact.[51] This ground and this goal are basic ideas that appear in the third way of decolonization. They are also the most fundamental elements of the decolonial turn.[52] His dismissal or ignorance about this type of reflection led Descartes not so much to conceal Being as to make invisible racialized and colonized subjects as well as to severely hinder the power of decolonial loving, giving, and receiving.

Decolonial giving or the *decolonial gift* refers in this case to the reason of the enslaved or the condemned. Césaire finds in the general character of this form of reason a fundamental contribution to responses to the European crisis. The very existence of the slave may be interpreted as a claim or exigency, or as a radical questioning of the decision to maintain slavery.[53] The blindness or lack of hospitality toward the free gift of the slave is not accidental. It is inherent in the colonial situation and in racial slavery. The notion of *damnation,* which both Césaire and Fanon use to refer to the colonized, makes reference to a situation wherein "gifts" are not received but taken before they are even offered.[54] Dispossession and possession take precedence over the logic of the gift. I base this insight on the etymology of *damné* (condemned), which makes reference to the French *donner* (to give).[55] *Damné* refers to someone who cannot give because her or his offerings have been taken from her or him. Both Césaire and Fanon understand colonization as a *despojo* (dispossession) of the resources that subjects and people count to offer to others. The offering (*la ofrenda*) enacts (does not represent) the humanity of such subjects. This moment of humanization cannot be spelled out with reference to the Hegelian conception of the struggle for recognition. The gift, not struggle, is the means of obtaining recognition—particularly by one slave from another, not from the master. But even the master searches for recognition in this way. Lordship itself can be understood as a peculiar form of the logics of giving, a skewed form in which giving and receiving turn into selective giving and possession. Césaire favorably cites Malinowski on this point, who describes the nature of the European gift:

> Every conception according to which Europe is a cornucopia or a place where everything is freely given is mistaken. One does not need to be a specialist in anthropology in order to know that the "European gift" is always highly selective. We never offer and we [never will offer] to the indigenous peoples who live under our control the following elements of our culture:
>
> (1) The instruments of physical force: firearms. . . .
> (2) Our instruments of political power. . . .
> (3) We will never share with the indigenous peoples the essential part of our riches and our economic advantage. . . .
>
> At no moment will we offer full political equality, or complete social equality, or even full religious equality. Indeed, when we consider all the points that we just listed it is easy to observe that it is not a matter of "giving" [*donner*] but rather of "taking" [*prendre*].[56]

Europe pretends to give generously to the colonized, but that which it gives is inessential. The irony of the colonizing endeavor is that the European *imperial gift* presents itself as donation, but, as Malinowski points out, it is very selective, and it establishes a logic of possession. Thus colonization can be seen as a perversion of the paradox of the gift. Giving is paradoxical because the subject or its interests cannot fully account for its condition of possibility. Its paradoxical character is most evinced at the point where a subject gives her or his own life for a subject who is not even considered to be a subject and from whom one cannot therefore expect anything on return.[57] Colonialism fundamentally distorts this paradox. The paradox of giving turns into the perverse paradox of possession whereby the European takes away the possibilities of giving from the colonized, while paradoxically also expecting gratitude. The imperial gift takes away from the colonized the very possibilities of giving: that which the colonized could give has been taken away from them. This is precisely the condition of damnation. The colonizer-colonized relation fundamentally distorts and makes impossible reciprocal relations of generosity between colonizer and colonized. The colonized are banned from affirming their humanity through donation, while the colonizers lie to themselves by thinking that they give to the colonized when what they do is steal from them, including stealing the very possibility of giving. In colonialism what takes the place of reciprocity and generosity is permanent debt, which allows colonization to take the form of recurrent dependence. Thus colonialism, which begins in conquest, gradually turns into a process that demands permanent gratitude and permanent dependence. In this process both colonizer and colonized fail to affirm their humanity in a way that is consonant with the paradox of the gift, which is necessary for reciprocal recognition to take place.

For Césaire the slave perceives with clarity and distinction that the master enacts a logic of possession when he wants to make colonization appear as if it were an expression of generosity, the "white man's burden." And since generosity is basic to the affirmation of humanity, this insight is relevant for knowledge about Europe and its crisis. Colonialism alters the coordinates of relations that allow subjects to affirm themselves as humans. In this sense it could be said that colonialism has metaphysical implications, which require philosophical anthropology to spell them out. Fanon made clear, for instance, how black subjects were led to affirm their humanity by adopting white masks.[58] This is another way in which the paradox of giving, with its constructive and life generating elements, turn into the production of deception and death—starting with the demonization and then elimination of blackness. But colonialism dehumanizes both the colonizer and the colonized.

Césaire's and Fanon's analyses introduce peculiar visions of subjectivity and sociality that defy Cartesian tenets, but they nonetheless remain committed to universalism. This combination serves as the basis to new *decolonial sciences*.[59] Césaire proposes what I would refer to as decolonial sciences as an alternative and antidote of sorts to the European sciences. The relationship between European humanity and its sciences, as Husserl formulated them, makes clear that the decolonial sciences must be included in the preparation of any diagnosis of and cure for the crisis of European Man. At least it appears that way with clarity and distinctness from the perspective of the slave and the colonized. It is from this perspective that Césaire contributes to the discourse on the crisis of the European sciences. Concerning European scientists Césaire proclaims that "their highly problematical subjective good faith is entirely irrelevant to the objective social implications of the evil work they perform as watchdogs of colonialism."[60] He offers several illuminating examples in which he makes reference to Descartes's *Discourse on Method*:

From the Rev. Tempels, missionary and Belgian, his "Bantu philosophy," as slimy and fetid as one could wish, but discovered very opportunately, as Hinduism was discovered by others, in order to counteract the "communistic materialism" which, it seems, threatens to turn the Negroes into "moral vagabonds."

From the historians or novelists of civilization (it's the same thing)—not from this one or that one, but from all of them, or almost all—their false objectivity, their chauvinism, their sly racism, their depraved passion for refusing to acknowledge any merit in the non-white races, specially the black-skinned races, their obsession with monopolizing all glory for their own race.

From the psychologists, sociologists, *et al.*, their views on "primitivism," their rigged investigations, their self-serving generalizations, their tendentious speculations, their insistence on the marginal, "separate" character of the non-whites, and—although each of these gentlemen, in order to impugn on higher authority the weakness of primitive thought, claims that his own is based on the firmest rationalism—their barbaric repudiation, for the sake of the cause, of Descartes's statement, the charter of universalism, that "reason . . . is found whole and entire in each man," and that "where individuals of the same species are concerned, there may be degrees in respect of their accidental qualities, but not in respect of their forms, or natures."[61]

Due to their racism the European sciences go as far as betraying part of their fundamental elements, such as Cartesian universalism. We have already seen that Césaire's surrealism, as well as some aspects of *Discourse on Colonialism*, part ways with Cartesian premises. Césaire, however, continues to hold onto a universalist vision. To be sure, by no means must one be led to believe that universalism is *only* a Cartesian legacy or that it belongs only to a European tradition of thought. Césaire's own formulation of universalism is nonetheless very original as it is founded on dialogue and the imperative of decolonization rather than on a monological and monotopical Cartesian vision. It is from this perspective that the gift of the colonized appears so important for him. The colonized have been stripped of the means of giving (not only the means of production), but they nonetheless count with the resources to offer something to the masters or colonizers, that is, an epistemic perspective that would help them to understand themselves better and address their crisis in a way that leads to the formation of a more humane world. Certainly the colonizer is most resistant to the gift of the colonized. To recognize such a gift as a gift would entail accepting certain finitude and limitation as well as the full humanity of the colonized. These ideas and actions erode the very ground of colonialism and racial superiority.

Césaire reveals the complicity of the European sciences with the racist perspective that sustains the colonizing mission. He deplores them for that. Such racism and its conciliation with epistemology is a characteristic feature of the "barbarity" that for Césaire distinguishes the colonizer. Failure to observe the epistemological implications of the colonizer-colonized relation as well as the continuous affirmation of imperial politics and attitudes led Europe to a state of "savagery." Césaire remarks, "First we must study how colonization works to *decivilize* the colonizer, to *brutalize* him in the true sense of the word, to degrade him, to awaken him to buried instincts, to covetousness, violence, race hatred, and moral relativism."[62] It is notable that "racial hatred" directly precedes "moral relativism" on Césaire's list. Husserl believed that relativism and skepticism were decisive markers of the crisis of European Man and indicated a fundamental departure from its Cartesian roots. For Césaire racial hatred seems to be as fundamental as relativism, if not more so, in understanding the crisis of Europe. He invites reflection about the relationship between the two terms and leads us to ask ourselves whether it is not so much that relativism leads to racial hatred as it is that, at least in the European case, racial hatred undergirds the preference for relativism at a certain point in Europe's history—just as in another period racial hatred undergirded the preference for monotopical and monological universalism. Or one could perhaps say that extreme doubt and relativism have always been a central part of the European civilization project inasmuch as that project has been premised on the permanent skepticism concerning the full humanity of non-European and racialized subjects, particularly indigenous people, blacks, people of Asian descent and non-Europeans in general, including those considered to have various degrees of mixture. The distorting effects of such skepticism do not appear clearly and cannot be properly understood until the epistemological and ethical dimensions of the colonizer-colonized relationship have come to light. To do this is precisely the task of *Discourse on Colonialism*. It seeks to correct the historical project that is grounded on Descartes's *Discourse on Method*. In this sense it also offers itself as an obligatory reference point to the articulation of any decolonial and post-Eurocentric point of view.[63]

Summary

Discourse on Colonialism is the contribution of a colonized and racialized black subject to European discourses about the crisis of Europe and its Cartesian legacy. It is a direct response to Descartes's *Discourse on Method.* Césaire confesses, "We have been branded by Cartesian philosophy, by French rhetoric," but beyond such brands one finds the ideas and experiences that survived colonial violence and others that emerged in response to such violence.[64] They are the sources for a "clear" and "distinct" understanding of problems that the European refuses to confront. They are also at the base of new ideas and proposals for human conviviality. Césaire highlights the promise of universalism under the rubric of decolonization, as well as its problematic expression in the European project. He leads us to ask ourselves what would have happened if Descartes had been attentive to the reason of the slave. What kind of method would he have proposed to address the perversity of colonization and the relation of the emerging sciences with it? What does it mean for the European humanity of the twentieth and twenty-first century that the "slaves" have spoken and continue to speak, or that their perspective has been at least partly articulated and voiced?

Discourse on Colonialism offers itself as a mirror to or a view of Europe from a position that is not entirely European and that Europe continues to subalternize. The *Discourse* articulates the point of view of the slave using discursive forms that are characteristic of European reason, but it also points to its limits, its silences, and its racism. For a very long time Europe has evaded this look, and for this very reason Europe has not been able to gain a full understanding of its own condition. Perhaps now, over fifty years after Césaire published his *Discourse,* at a moment when responses to Europe's declining geopolitical significance and financial crises only seem to awaken old forms of traditionalism, Eurocentrism, and racism, the look from the colonized and the very view of the colonized as an agent and thinker who has something to offer that cannot be simply "included" in existing frameworks is needed but also resisted most. The fascination with European roots is still strong, however. A serious engagement with Césaire thus remains a challenge. His discourse, like the decolonial gift, has the form of the classic *pharmakon* which is both medicine and poison.[65] It is an offering that promises to initiate a process that leads to the decolonization of Europeanness, and along with it to the decolonization of the sciences and humanities that still define the contour of what is considered legitimate knowledge globally. It is also at the very basis of a post-Eurocentric and postcontinental discourse.[66] *Discourse on Colonialism* is perhaps as important for twenty-first century humanity as *Discourse on Method* was in the seventeenth century for European civilization. While modern Europe found its basis in Descartes's *Discourse*, global transmodernity has to come into terms with Césaire. *Discourse on Colonialism* aims to take us beyond modernity/coloniality to transmodernity. This is the task that it poses for twenty-first-century humanity.

NOTES

This essay is an expanded version of "Césaire y la crisis del hombre europeo," later published in English (in a slightly revised form) as "Césaire's Gift and the Decolonial Turn." Thanks to George Ciccariello-Maher for assistance in the translation and to the *Radical Philosophy Review* for permitting use of the English version that appeared in the journal. Thanks are also due to Carolyn Ureña for careful and thoughtful editorial suggestions; the current version incorporates a number of those and a few other changes. This essay is a genealogical and phenomenological reflection inspired by and in dialogue with Césaire's *Discourse on Colonialism*, of which it is in part a philosophical analysis; Lewis Gordon's existential phenomenology, especially *Fanon and the Crisis of European Man*; Sylvia Wynter's theorizing; and the work of the Modernity/Coloniality network. Previous versions were presented at the meeting of the African Studies Association (2004) and the second annual meeting of the Caribbean Philosophical Association (2005). The argument was gradually enriched in conversations with students and colleagues at the Center for Global Studies and the Humanities at Duke University, the Department of Ethnic Studies at the University of California, Berkeley, the Doctoral Program in Latin American Intercultural Studies at the Universidad Andina Simón Bolivar in Ecuador, and elsewhere.

1. I thank the participants of the workshop Transcultural Humanities at the University of Bremen, June 17–19, 2006, for discussion of related ideas, particularly Sabine Broeck, one of the organizers, and Madina Tlostanova. Broeck explicitly brought out the Césairean theme of the indefensibility of Europe, and Tlostanova provided ample reflections on the crisis of Russia's intellectual and political environment in relation to the enchantment with Europe.

2. Santos, "Between Prospero and Caliban."

3. For example, Hutton, *A Declaration of Interdependence.*

4. Maldonado-Torres, "Decolonization and the New Identitarian Logics after September 11."

5. Habermas and Derrida, "February 15, or What Binds Europeans Together."

6. Richard Senett talked about this in a meeting of the Academy of Latinity (New York University, October 7, 2004).

7. Wallerstein, *Utopistics.*

8. Maldonado-Torres, "Post-imperial Reflections on Crisis, Knowledge, and Utopia."

9. Gordon, *Fanon and the Crisis of European Man*; Gordon, "Shifting the Geography of Reason in an Age of Disciplinary Decadence"; Gordon and Gordon, *Not Only the Master's Tools.*

10. Mignolo, "José de Acosta's *Historia natural y moral de las Indias*"; Quijano, "Modernity, Identity, and Utopia in Latin America"; Quijano, "Coloniality of Power, Eurocentrism, and Latin America."

11. Mignolo, "José de Acosta's *Historia natural y moral de las Indias*."

12. Mignolo, *Local Histories / Global Designs*; Mignolo, "The Geopolitics of Knowledge and the Colonial Difference"; Mignolo, "Os esplendores e as misérias da 'ciência.'"

13. For articulations of different aspects of this tension, see Maldonado-Torres, "Post-imperial Reflections on Crisis, Knowledge, and Utopia." These and related issues have emerged and been discussed in the Modernity/Coloniality Research Group, a network of scholars working primarily, but not only, in the United States and Latin America on the redefinition and intersections between critical theory and decolonization, world-system analysis and ethnic studies, liberation thought and subaltern knowledges. They include Manuela Boatca (Rumania, Germany), Santiago Castro-Gómez (Colombia), Enrique Dussel (Mexico), Arturo Escobar (Colombia, United States), Angela Figueiredo (Brazil), Oscar Guardiola (Colombia, England), Ramón Grosfoguel (Puerto Rico, United States), Edizón León (Ecuador), Madina Tlostanova (Russia), Nelson Maldonado-Torres (Puerto Rico, United States), Walter Mignolo (Argentina, United States), Anibal Quijano (Peru), José David Saldívar (United States), and Catherine Walsh (United States, Ecuador).

14. Sandoval, *Methodology of the Oppressed*; Walsh, "'Other' Knowledges, 'Other' Critiques."

15. I take the notion of disenchantment from Wynter, "On Disenchanting Discourse."

16. For different theorizations on the project of decolonization, Grosfoguel et al., "Latin@s and the 'Euro-American' Menace"; Mignolo, *Local Histories / Global Designs*; Mignolo, "The Zapatistas' Theoretical Revolution"; Walsh, "'Other' Knowledges, 'Other' Critiques."

17. Maldonado-Torres, "Enrique Dussel's Liberation Thought in the Decolonial Turn."

18. I owe Shimberlee Jirón-King references about this point.

19. Huntington, *Who Are We?*

20. For a discussion of the modern Western ideologies in the late eighteenth and through the nineteenth centuries, see Wallerstein, *Unthinking Social Science.*

21. Maldonado-Torres, "The Topology of Being and the Geopolitics of Knowledge."

22. Wynter, "Columbus and the Poetics of the Propter Nos"; Wynter, "1492."

23. Wynter, "On Disenchanting Discourse."

24 For an elucidation of the concept of transmodernity, see the following by Dussel: "Modernity, Eurocentrism, and Trans-Modernity"; *Posmodernidad y transmodernidad*; "World System and 'Trans'-Modernity."

25. Césaire, *Discourse on Colonialism*, 9. On Haiti, see Fischer, *Modernity Disavowed.*

26. Even though Fanon has been much more influential than Césaire, the influence of Césaire cannot be overestimated. Chela Sandoval told me in conversation, for instance, that the first decolonial book that she read was Césaire's *Discourse on Colonialism.*

27. For an elaboration of the "myth of modernity" see Dussel, *The Invention of the Americas.*

28. In the United States there were theories of "internal colonialism" and decolonial proposals by women of color. See, among others, Allen, *Black Awakening in Capitalist America*; Barrera, *Race and Class in the Southwest*; Blauner, *Racial Oppression in America*; García, *Chicana Feminist Thought*; Moraga and Anzaldúa, *This Bridge Called My Back*.

29. Dussel, "World System and 'Trans'-Modernity"; Mignolo, *Local Histories / Global Designs*.

30. Adorno, *Cronista y principe*; Dussel, *The Invention of the Americas*; Mignolo, *The Darker Side of the Renaissance*.

31. Mignolo, "Globalization and the Geopolitics of Knowledge."

32. Mignolo, *Local Histories / Global Designs*; Dussel, *Etica de la liberación en la edad de la globalización y de la exclusión*; Dussel, "World System and 'Trans'-Modernity."

33. Grosfoguel, "The Divorce of Nationalist Discourses from the Puerto Rican People."

34. By "European Man" I refer to an ideal of European humanity, which is closely tied to its difference with colonized subhumanity. It also denotes a strong masculinist bias in favor of conceptions of self and civilization that fit ideals of manliness. I distinguish European Man from Europeans in that while the former refers to an idea, the latter refers to European people as such, whose self-conception has been informed by the ideal but who can identify or not identify with it in different respects.

35. Dussel, "Modernity, Eurocentrism, and Trans-Modernity"; Dussel, "World System and 'Trans'-Modernity."

36. Maldonado-Torres, "Decolonization and the New Identitarian Logics after September 11."

37. Maldonado-Torres, *Against War*.

38. Gordon, "Context"; Gordon, "Existential Dynamics of Theorizing Black Invisibility."

39. Kelley, "Poetry and the Political Imagination."

40. Césaire, *Discourse on Colonialism*, 68.

41. See the following by Quijano: "Colonialidad y modernidad/racionalidad"; "'Raza, etnia, y nación'"; "Colonialidad del poder y clasificación social"; "Coloniality of Power, Eurocentrism, and Latin America."

42. Husserl, *Cartesian Meditations*.

43. Césaire, *Discourse on Colonialism*, 9, italics mine.

44. Habermas and Derrida, "February 15, or What Binds Europeans Together."

45. Quijano, "Coloniality of Power, Eurocentrism, and Latin America."

46. Césaire, *Discourse on Colonialism*, 14.

47. Descartes, *Discourse on Method*, 21.

48. See Du Bois, *The Souls of Black Folk*.

49. For an elucidation of social death, see Patterson, *Slavery and Social Death*. For the links between death and colonialism, see Maldonado-Torres, *Against War*.

50. Sartre introduced the philosophical concept of bad faith with the intent to build a critical theory out of the implications of the Cartesian cogito, as interpreted and reformulated by Husserl in his phenomenology (see Sartre, *Being and Nothingness*). He used it to examine anti-Semitism (Sartre, *Réflexions sur la question juive*). Fanon makes reference to Sartre's analysis in his account of the "lived experience of the black" in

Black Skin, White Masks. Building on Sartre and Fanon, Gordon uses the concept to examine antiblack racism (*Bad Faith and Antiblack Racism*). On Sartre's own indebtedness to Third World intellectuals, see Ciccariello Maher, "Beyond the Debate on Humanism."

51. It is no accident that Césaire's *Discourse* was the first and one of the most powerful texts on decolonization that the Chicana theorist Chela Sandoval, who offers an account of love as a decolonial force in her *Methodology of the Oppressed*, encountered (conversation April 22, 2005). Sandoval's *Methodology of the Oppressed* is directly inspired by the writings of Third World women of color in the United States and by theorists such as Fanon, who, as I have mentioned, studied Césaire carefully and who insisted on the primacy of the self-other relation. Sandoval's *Methodology* is a self-conscious effort to elevate some of the insights on the decolonization of self, society, and knowledge to the level of method, just as Césaire himself began to do in the *Discourse*. The *Discourse*, written in the early years of the wave of decolonization in the twentieth century, focuses on the fundamentals of decolonization as perceived by many in the periphery upon Europe's demise. It stands today, as before, as a propaedeutics to decolonial methodology as it also continues to inspire new approaches. Césaire's and Sandoval's reflections on method and the sciences, along with those of Fanon, Wynter, Gordon, and others, form part of the rich and complex genealogy of the decolonial turn.

52. Maldonado-Torres, "Decolonization and the New Identitarian Logics after September 11."

53. Gordon, *Fanon and the Crisis of European Man*.

54. Fanon highlights the relevance of the concept of damnation in *The Wretched of the Earth* (*Les damnés de la terre*). Césaire also uses the term. He writes that the culture of the colonized is "condemned to remain marginal in relation to European culture" ("Culture et colonisation," 119).

55. Benveniste, "Gift and Exchange in the Indo-European Vocabulary."

56. Césaire, "Culture et colonisation," 115, translation mine.

57. Maldonado-Torres, "The Cry of the Self as a Call from the Other."

58. Fanon, *Black Skin, White Masks*.

59. Césaire notes, "Je trouve que Malinowski a eu le mérite, par sa théorie du don sélectif, de fournir une contribution très intéressante à la science, une contribution positive à ce que j'appelle l'anticolonialisme" ("Débat [extraits]," 132). The most systematic continuations of this project appear in the work of Wynter ("The Ceremony Must Be Found"; "Unsettling the Coloniality of Being/Power/Truth/Freedom") and Gordon (*Fanon and the Crisis of European Man*; "Shifting the Geography of Reason in an Age of Disciplinary Decadence"). See also Gordon and Gordon, *Not Only the Master's Tools*.

60. Césaire, *Discourse on Colonialism*, 34.

61. Césaire, *Discourse on Colonialism*, 34.

62. Césaire, *Discourse on Colonialism*, 13.

63. This project continues today in the work of the Modernity/Coloniality Research Group, the Caribbean Philosophical Association, Latin@ philosophers and critical thinkers, and in the work of Latin American liberation philosophers, among others. Figures who belong to these groups met in 2005 in the conference Mapping the

Decolonial Turn: Post/Trans-Continental Interventions in Theory, Philosophy, and Critique at the University of California, Berkeley, April 21–23, 2005, to discuss their commonalities and differences. They included Linda Alcoff, Enrique Dussel, Lewis R. Gordon, Paget Henry, José David Saldívar, Chela Sandova, and Sylvia Wynter. I edited two special issues of a journal with various works that were originally presented in this conference and some others; see *Transmodernity: Journal of Peripheral Cultural Production of the Luso-Hispanic World* 1.2 (2011) and 1.3 (2012).

64. Césaire, "Culture et colonisation," 68.

65. Maldonado-Torres, "Reconciliation as a Contested Future."

66. Dussel, "The 'World-System'"; Maldonado-Torres, *Against War*.

TWENTY-FOUR

Checkered Choices, Political Assertions: The Unarticulated Racial Identity of La Asociación Nacional México-Americana

LAURA PULIDO

The current century has witnessed a vibrant conversation surrounding Latina/o racial identity. This discussion has been triggered by scholarship that troubles the assumption that Mexican Americans have always identified as a nonwhite population. Martha Menchaca, looking back to the nineteenth century, has shown how the Treaty of Guadalupe Hidalgo's (1848) requirement that conquered Mexicans be eligible for U.S. citizenship conflicted with the 1790 Naturalization Act, which set whiteness as a precondition for naturalization and citizenship. From their incorporation, then, Mexicans' citizenship rights were violated and their racial status was rendered ambiguous. This in turn put pressure on Mexicans, especially Mexican Indians, to claim whiteness and denounce markers of nonwhiteness in a defensive posture against a broader society that was hostile to their incorporation. Neil Foley, looking at the League of United Latin American Citizens (LULAC) in the 1930s, demonstrated that activists in Texas resisted state-led efforts to categorize Mexicans as nonwhite. And Ian Haney-Lopez, focusing on the Los Angeles Chicana/o movement of the 1960s and 1970s, argued that previous to *el movimiento*, Mexican Americans did not embrace wholly a nonwhite identity. Since then numerous historians and legal scholars have explored the question of Mexican racial subjectivity.[1] Collectively this work suggests that Mexican Americans have not hesitated to claim whiteness as a strategy to overcome racial discrimination and that discussions of their racial subjectivity are far more complex that often presumed. This is particularly the case in Texas, which has been the site of the majority of studies.

Latina/o racial subjectivity is also a pressing contemporary issue because of the U.S. census. For several decades now a significant portion of the Latina/o population has chosen Some Other Race (SOR) rather than claim an officially sanctioned racial category. Indeed, 97 percent of all persons checking the SOR box are Latinas/os. Given that Latinas/os are now the largest racial or ethnic group in the United States, the nation is grappling with the fact that up to 40 percent of that population does not racially "conform."[2] Accordingly, social scientists have sought to understand what variables are associated with particular racial identities. Key variables include age, gender, nativity, number of years in the United States, as well as education and income. While the overall results of this literature do suggest some relationship between racial identity and level of integration in U.S. society, they are hardly conclusive and point to a vast complexity in racial choices and strategies.[3]

One of the features that characterizes both literatures is the desire to ascertain a "true" Latina/o racial identity. For example, Thomas Guglielmo and Brian Behnken, both of whom provide compelling evidence of Mexican Americans' commitment to whiteness as an antidiscrimination strategy, suggest that this desire for whiteness was not limited to middle-class Latinas/os and elites but extended to the working class.[4] Indeed in an otherwise excellent book, Behnken acknowledges that working-class Mexican Americans may have had alternative racial subjectivities, but he overlooks them because LULAC, a large and established organization, best represents the trajectory of mid-twentieth-century Mexican American racial subjectivity.[5] What interests me is our desire to develop a singular racial narrative regarding Latina/o racial identity. Why is this so important? What gets left off the table? What are the implications for building an antiracist movement? One of the consequences of the historical literature is that it compels us to see Mexican racial identity as a choice. For some Chicana/o studies scholars this is an uncomfortable literature, as it becomes painfully obvious that some ethnic Mexicans embraced white supremacy in order to alleviate their own oppression. While there has not been sufficient research across space and time to draw definitive conclusions about the larger *Mexicana/o* population outside of Texas, there is no doubt that Latinas/os, as one of the most racially subordinated groups today, have a checkered history when it comes to their relationship with whiteness and nonwhiteness.

As a critical ethnic studies scholar I am particularly interested in the political responses and interpretations of such findings. I welcome this scholarship as it provides a more accurate picture of Latina/o racial subjectivity both past and present. As any U.S. Latina/o knows, our families and communities are filled with a diversity of racial and political identities. Too often it is assumed and hoped that Latinas/os, as racially subordinated people, should get their act together, identify as nonwhite, and join the antiracist struggle. But one reason there has been uneven movement in this direction is because a significant number of Latinas/os insist on whiteness as their racial identity. And as Chicana/o studies scholars we have been slow to accept that fact.

Eduardo Bonilla-Silva has tried to capture some of this complexity by suggesting that U.S. Latinas/os are shifting to a triracial structure similar to Latin America's.[6] The top of the hierarchy consists of those considered white. Second are the "honorary" whites, and at the bottom is the "lumpen black," which comprises those who cannot pass as white, immigrants, and the working class. Part of the power of Bonilla-Silva's analysis is that he does not claim that any single racial identity is more authentic than others. And the evidence *is* compelling that Latinas/os are becoming increasingly fragmented along economic, political, immigration, and racial lines.[7]

In this essay I argue that we need to accept that a segment of the Latina/o population is invested in claiming whiteness. Equally important, however, is the fact that others are invested in claiming nonwhiteness. While these positions may be associated with such variables as income and education, they are first and foremost *political decisions* that are informed by one's experiences and environment. Reading recent quantitative analyses of Latina/o racial identity, it is easy to forget that political agency is involved. Often researchers position Latinas/os as gravitating toward whiteness because it represents the best strategy to counter discrimination. Alternatively Latina/o racial identity is seen as a function of specific variables or racial markers. In her study of naturalized Mexican immigrants who voted along conservative lines, Carleen Basler argues that conservative voting was an active and conscious way of declaring one's whiteness and distancing oneself from recent immigrants, dark-skinned Latinas/os, and African Americans.[8] Her work illuminates the agency involved in articulating a racial identity, as well as how white supremacy informs such responses.

I explore these issues by examining one particular case of Mexican American racial identity: the Asociación Nacional México-Americana (ANMA), a radical political organization in the southwestern United States in the 1940s and 1950s that was connected to the Communist Party and the International Union of Mine, Mill and Smelter Workers (aka Mine Mill). Though it did not articulate an overt racial identity, a close reading of the archives indicates an implicit but strong and consistent nonwhite racial subjectivity. Some may dismiss ANMA because of its relatively small size or the fact that it lasted only five years, but that is missing the point. Disregarding ANMA because it is not necessarily "representative" not only reproduces the idea that there is a single or true Mexicana/o racial identity or political voice, but it also overlooks the power that collective action can yield. ANMA created power among its individual membership as well as within the larger community and across the larger political landscape. Although small and fleeting, ANMA represents an important segment of the Mexican American population who consciously and actively articulated a nonwhite identity in solidarity with other people of color. Instead of seeing ANMA as an outlier that can be dismissed, we should see it as part of a much richer tapestry of Mexican American racial politics, one that is especially important to acknowledge prior to el movimiento. ANMA asserted a nonwhite racial identity by never claiming whiteness, by allying with other minoritized groups, and through the development of an antiracist, materialist analysis.

The Roots of the Asociación Nacional México-Americana

ANMA was initially the political arm of Mine Mill, which had roots in the militant Western Federation of Miners.[9] The Federation was notable for its Wobbly influence, which contributed to a strong class identity that facilitated the formation of worker organizations across racial lines. In the U.S. Southwest, Mine Mill was composed largely of ethnic Mexicans with strong Mexican American leadership. ANMA was created because of the need for a permanent, national organization to defend Mexican Americans' rights. It emerged in 1949 in Albuquerque, and its founding convention was in Phoenix.[10] The influence of mining culture can be seen in figure 24.1, in which both a smelter and the earth from which the metals and minerals are drawn are depicted in the background.[11]

Although ANMA was linked to Mine Mill, the Communist Party quickly saw its strategic importance, as it sought to partner with Mexican Americans during this period.[12] Consequently the Communist Party and ANMA were

FIGURE 24.1. Program cover of ANMA's second National Convention, 1952. Source: Program of Segunda Convención Nacional, July 1952. El Paso Public Library, Nathalie Gross Collection, 1948–75, Archive 819, Mexican American Box 1, Folder Mexican American—Civil Rights—ANMA. Courtesy of the Nathalie Gross Collection.

close, as were ANMA and Mine Mill and various other labor organizations.[13] ANMA's national office relocated from Albuquerque to Los Angeles in 1951. In addition each state had its own central office and numerous local offices; for instance, in Colorado there were locals in Denver, Boulder, Pueblo, Walsenburg, Trinidad, and Greeley.[14] Many of the locals were formed in response to police abuse, a key concern of ANMA.[15] It is difficult to say how large ANMA was. According to one source, it claimed four thousand members, but Mario Garcia found a source claiming fifty thousand.[16] It would seem that the smaller figure is more likely.

As a political organization ANMA described itself as "a national association for the protection of civil, economic, and political rights, and for improving the education, culture, and progress of the Mexican people in the United States."[17] ANMA did this in a variety of ways, including through its newspaper, *Progreso*, which reported the various activities of the state chapters and locals and was also an educational tool to promote its political ideology. Its slogan, "In the field and in the city, in the factory and the home ANMA educates, benefits, and protects,"[18] attests to the organization's efforts to reach all spheres of Mexican American life.

While there were some issues that all chapters engaged in, such as opposition to the Korean War, the deportation of immigrants, and the McCarren Walter Act, ANMA also pursued very specific causes. In one case ANMA defended Mexican culture by successfully boycotting the Colgate Palmolive Petty Company, which sponsored the Judy Canova radio show; ANMA opposed its stereotypic depictions of Mexicans.[19] Locals focused on geographically specific concerns. As an active promoter of the Spanish language, the Chicago chapter ran the Lazaro Cardenas School, which taught English, Spanish, and art classes.[20] In Los Angeles members established the Los Angeles Trade Union Committee of ANMA, which spearheaded an organizing drive to improve Mexicans' standard of living and to protect their economic rights.[21] In New Mexico there was tremendous support for the mining strike in Bayard, depicted in the film *Salt of the Earth*.[22] It appears that all locals regularly held dances and celebrated Cinco de Mayo and other cultural events that honored Mexican culture.

Despite the intensity of its activities, ANMA folded in 1954. The primary reason for its demise was the intense red-baiting of the cold war era. Mine Mill was expelled from the Congress of Industrial Organizations because of its leftist tendencies, which had a significant affect on ANMA. The union had provided various forms of support to ANMA, including giving a New Mexican local funds to attend an ANMA convention in Los Angeles and providing lodging to ANMA delegates participating in a convention in New Mexico. But perhaps more important, as Shana Bernstein has documented, was the intense pressure on less radical organizations to break ties with explicitly left groups in order to save themselves. This can be seen most vividly in such legislation as the Internal Security Act of 1950 that sent a chill through all progressive organizations. [23] It is important to point out that ANMA did not quietly acquiesce to political attacks. When the *El Paso Herald Post* of Texas described a forthcoming ANMA convention as "red submarines in the Rio Grande," ANMA responded with a scathing critique emphasizing the dominant society's unwillingness to recognize and act upon the hardship and discrimination that Mexican Americans faced—and thus the need for ANMA.[24]

The Racial Subjectivity of the Asociación Nacional México-Americana

Examining the historical record indicates little explicit mention of ANMA's racial subjectivity or that of its membership. This should not be terribly surprising for several reasons. First, as has been noted by other scholars, Mexican Americans, particularly during midcentury, frequently collapsed race, ethnicity, and language in their discussions of difference. This practice was especially pronounced in New Mexico, where there has been a long tradition of eschewing "racial difference" in favor of "cultural" and "ethnic conflict."[25] Nevertheless the archive reveals a robust discourse on racial subjectivity in which ANMA clearly positioned itself as nonwhite. This can be discerned in three ways. First, ANMA and its members never claimed to be white. This may sound insignificant, but it is not when compared to the dominant antidiscrimination strategies of contemporaneous Mexican Americans. Second, ANMA regularly identified with and aligned itself with other people of color. Again this may not sound significant by today's standards, but we know that this was not a widely popular choice among Mexican Americans at the time. Third, ANMA advocated a clearly antiracist approach to solving social problems.

During the 1940s and 1950s many Mexican American political organizations sought to challenge discrimination and Mexicans' subordinated status. A common strategy, especially in Texas, was to insist that Mexicans were Caucasian and therefore should not be discriminated against. Not surprisingly, this generated numerous assertions of whiteness on the part of Mexican Americans. Indeed at one point activists tried to pass a Texas law that declared Latinas/os to be Caucasian. (It never passed.)[26] However, nowhere in the historical record could I find evidence of ANMA claiming whiteness, let alone pursuing a whiteness strategy. The organization never used the terms *white, Anglo,* or *Caucasian* to refer to itself collectively or to individual members. Instead it consistently referred to itself and its members as Mexican Americans or Mexicanas/os, both of which were imbued with a nonwhite racial meaning. There is no doubt that ANMA was aware of other Latina/o civil rights organizations and their strategies. Although it was closest to labor and antiracist left organizations, ANMA tried to maintain civil and respectful relations with more mainstream Latina/o groups.[27] Accordingly its silence on whiteness should be read as salient.

While many contemporary scholars have been critical of the whiteness strategy, Maria Josefina Saldaña-Portillo offers an alternative interpretation by reminding us that racial subjectivity is not simply a matter of choice.

Drawing on the work of Haney-Lopez, she points to the degree to which the law establishes available racial categories. While I appreciate Saldaña-Portillo's intervention, I argue that ANMA did in fact *choose* to identify as nonwhite.[28] It was cognizant of the strategies of the LULAC and the GI Forum, another civil rights organization and consciously chose an alternative path precisely because it disagreed with the political implications of such racial subjectivities.

ANMA's racial subjectivity is also evident in how and the degree to which it identified with other minoritized groups. In its publications, speeches, and events it is apparent that ANMA consistently sought to align itself with "other minorities." It insisted that a coalition could more vigorously attack the white power structure rather than each group individually. For example, one publication points out, "Mexican Americans represented only one of several minorities, who in some cases were worse off than Mexicans. The struggle and gains of one minority aid those of the rest. We should unite with Blacks who suffer from similar conditions as our own, and in this way reinforce both groups."[29] Certainly ANMA was not alone in partnering with other people of color; however, its strategy was distinctive. For example, in *Mendez v. Westminster* the American Jewish Congress, the National Association for the Advancement of Colored People, and the Japanese American Citizens League all supported Mexican Americans' struggle against school segregation. However, interracial support was slow to develop, emerging only in the appeals process. In other cases such interracial alliances were hindered by questions of racial subjectivity—namely Mexican American resistance to seeing themselves as a racial minority.[30]

In contrast ANMA articulated a more organic and comprehensive culture of solidarity. Publications routinely asserted the need to ally with "Negros," as well as Jews and sympathetic whites.[31] Besides encouraging general solidarity, ANMA also offered specific support to African Americans. Virginia Ruiz, ANMA's executive secretary, "pledg[ed] . . . joint action of the ANMA with the Negro people against another legal lynching such as the Martinsville Seven, the Lt. Gilbert Case and the Trenton Six."[32]

Interracial solidarity can also be seen in ANMA's events. Semana de Historia y Cultural Mexicana was held in Belvedere in 1950, and both Jewish and Black groups were invited to perform.[33] Similarly ANMA observed Negro History Month and on another occasion hosted a lecture titled "Negro History."[34] Importantly, there appears to be some reciprocity with communities of color. In the program for its second national convention, for instance, there is a prominent message of support from the Los Angeles Negro Labor Council.

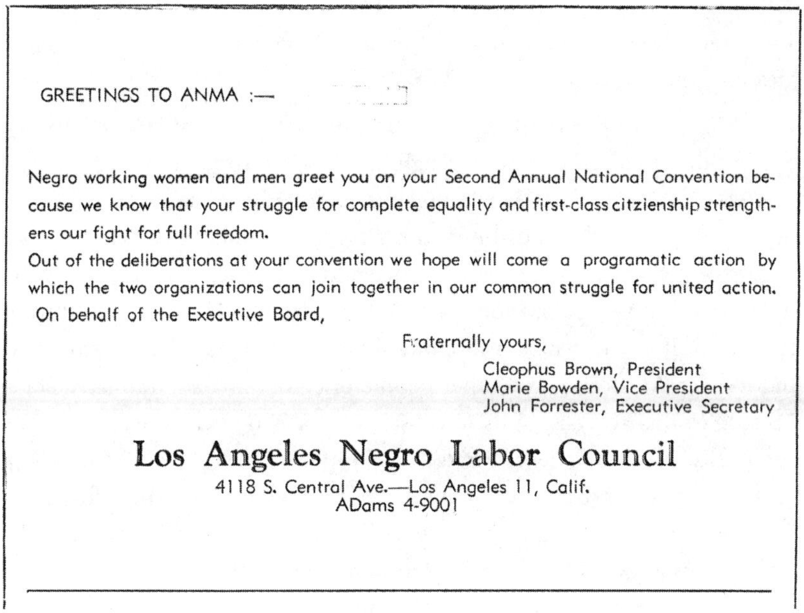
GREETINGS TO ANMA :—

Negro working women and men greet you on your Second Annual National Convention because we know that your struggle for complete equality and first-class citzienship strengthens our fight for full freedom.

Out of the deliberations at your convention we hope will come a programatic action by which the two organizations can join together in our common struggle for united action.

On behalf of the Executive Board,

Fraternally yours,

Cleophus Brown, President
Marie Bowden, Vice President
John Forrester, Executive Secretary

Los Angeles Negro Labor Council

4118 S. Central Ave.—Los Angeles 11, Calif.
ADams 4-9001

FIGURE 24.2. Message of solidarity from the Los Angeles Negro Labor Council to ANMA, 1952. Source: Program of Segunda Convención Nacional, July 1952. El Paso Public Library, Nathalie Gross Collection, 1948–75, Archive 819, Mexican American Box 1, Folder Mexican American—Civil Rights—ANMA. Courtesy of the Nathalie Gross Collection.

These values and practices stand in stark contrast to Behnken's research on Latina/o and African American solidarity in Texas, or rather the lack thereof. He provides dramatic evidence of antiblack racism on the part of Felix Tijerina, a LULAC leader who would not serve African Americans in his restaurant and actively opposed Black civil rights protests.[35] In comparison ANMA took the question of solidarity to a whole different level—with important implications for its racial subjectivity. Solidarity was not merely strategic; it was a central part of ANMA's political identity. As numerous writers have pointed out, participating in antiblack racism is one of the steps through which non-white immigrants assert whiteness. This is painfully evident in Behnken's account of Tijerina, who was so terrified of his proximity to blackness that he consciously participated in white supremacy. ANMA did not fear blackness because it saw itself in a similar racial position and was committed to joining forces to end white supremacy. Such an understanding was predicated on its larger political ideology.

The Conception of Racism in the Asociación Nacional México-Americana

This brings us to the third manifestation of ANMA's racial subjectivity: its conception of racism and how to fight it. Coming from a Marxist perspective, ANMA insisted that "Mexicans were exploited as cheap labor, but they were also oppressed as a distinct ethnic racial community."[36] While ANMA understood that anti-Mexican racism could not be challenged solely via class struggle, the organization insisted there was a link between racism and capitalism. It saw racism as a tool that was used to divide the working class and to keep Mexicans (and other people of color) in a subordinated state. Because of this analysis, in its discussions of racism—which frequented its publications—writers never berated Anglos per se, but they were critical of a white, racist power structure. For instance, in a meeting of the local chapter of Downey, California, members "discussed three instances of 'White Supremacy' involving several Mexican American families." Ultimately the members were able to "provide relief" for those families.[37] The very acknowledgment of the concept of white supremacy is a powerful marker of ANMA's racial consciousness. How could ANMA ever claim whiteness knowing its role in an oppressive racial structure?

Conversely ANMA did not attribute Mexicans' inferior social position to "cultural misunderstandings" or to Mexican Americans' alleged shortcomings. Instead Mexicans' subordinated status was seen as a function of racism, which in turn was a function of capitalism. The existence of this worldview contributed to a fuller understanding of what racism was and how it worked: racism was not an unknowable, unpredictable, irrational force; it was a knowable thing that needed to be systematically challenged.

This understanding of racism is evident in how ANMA conceptualized larger social problems—beginning with how Mexicans saw themselves. Among oppressed peoples there are always those who seek acceptance by attempting to make themselves more acceptable to the dominant group. ANMA would have none of that: "Discrimination has forced some of us to deny our heritage. The word 'Mexicano,' which refers to the country and culture of our ancestors has been given a bad connotation. As a result, there are some of us who have sought refuge in labels like, 'Spanish-American, Latin-American, Spanish Californian, Spanish-speaking' etc. Discrimination has made us do this."[38] Here we see a direct challenge to those who would adopt a more accommodating or conservative politics. ANMA understood *why* people might do so, but would still not accept it. In another instance ANMA discussed housing segregation at length in *Progreso*. The author, writing in a mocking tone, suggests that the most "advanced" Mexican Americans (who often pass as "Spanish" or "Nice Mexicans") articulate highly problematic understandings of the causes of segregation: "La raza is responsible; if everyone behaved well we would not all lose-out because of one person's behavior. . . . No one takes me to be a Mexican. I can live wherever I want. But I do care about the others. . . . It is not certain that segregation actually exists; if you are decent, you have nothing to fear."[39] The author offers a series of "common-sense" understandings of Mexican racial inferiority that were (and still are) in circulation. These explanations are largely linked to blaming the victim and the merits of passing. ANMA demonstrates a fairly sophisticated understanding of how racism operates and the degree to which it had been internalized by Mexican Americans. The solution, according to ANMA, was certainly not to pass nor to claim whiteness but to embrace their *Mexicanidad*, including its nonwhite elements, specifically indigeneity. This solution required ANMA to challenge fellow Mexicans who were too accommodating and to unite with like-minded people.

Summary

Even though ANMA did not explicitly articulate a racial identity, its larger discourse and practice were in fact based on a nonwhite racial subjectivity that was manifest in at least three ways. First, the fact that ANMA never claimed whiteness is quite significant, as this claim was common at the time. Second, the consistency and depth with which ANMA sought to ally with other nonwhite groups suggests a deep commitment to solidarity with other people of color. This position makes it difficult to believe that ANMA would have pursued a strategy that advanced Mexican American rights while further subordinating others. Third, ANMA conceptualized social problems in clearly antiracist terms. Its particular conception of racism was firmly linked to a larger materialist analysis that saw racism as a function of capitalism.

The contemporary politics of Latina/o racial subjectivity has enormous implications for the evolving U.S. racial formation, in particular, antiracist strategies. Hence it needs to be taken very seriously by ethnic studies scholars. The first wave of scholarship has dispelled the idea that Latinas/os, especially Mexicans, are an unambiguously nonwhite population. But perhaps in our quest to trouble the inherited wisdom of Chicana/o studies—that ethnic Mexicans are unambiguously nonwhite—we have lost sight of the fact that racial identity can in some places and sometimes be a choice—a political choice. And just as some ethnic Mexicans insisted on whiteness as an antidiscrimination strategy, some also insisted on being a person of color.

The fact that researchers have uncovered such differing racial subjectivities should not be a surprise. The Latina/o community continues to reflect such splits today. It is our task to understand these dynamics as completely as possible in order to develop the most effective strategies to achieve social justice.

NOTES

1. Menchaca, "Chicano Indianism"; Foley, "Partly Colored or Other White"; Haney-Lopez, *Racism on Trial*; Gomez, *Manifest Destinies*; Guglielmo, "Fighting for Caucasian Rights"; Saldaña-Portillo, "'How Many Mexicans [Is] a Horse Worth?'"; Wilson, "Brown over 'Other White'"; Gross, *What Blood Won't Tell*; Behnken, *Fighting Their Own Battles*; Blanton, "George I. Sanchez, Ideology and Whiteness in the Making of the Mexican American Civil Rights Movement."

2. See Rodriguez, *Changing Race*, for a detailed discussion of the Census Bureau's efforts to address this problem. Since 1980 the state-sanctioned racial choices include American Indian, Asian/Pacific Islander, black, white, and SOR. In 2000 the category "multiracial" was added. However, the Census Bureau has proposed making "Hispanic" a racial category in the 2020 census.

3. Part of this ambiguity is due to the fact that researchers employ a variety of methodological approaches and data sources. For a sampling of this literature, see Tafoya, *Shades of Belonging*; Michael and Timberlake, "Are Latinos Becoming White?"; Logan, "How Race Counts for Hispanic Americans"; Golash-Boza and Darrity, "Latino Racial Choices"; Dowling, *Mexican Americans and the Question of Race*; Pulido and Pastor, "Where in the World Is Juan?"

4. Guglielmo, "Fighting for Caucasian Rights"; Behnken, *Fighting Their Own Battles.*

5. While it is true that LULAC was a large established organization, it is also true that it has an excellent set of records—an important point to appreciate. I am grateful to David Hernandez for this insight.

6. Bonilla-Silva, "From Bi-racial to Tri-racial."

7. See, for example, Vallejo, *Barrios to Burbs*; Ochoa, *Becoming Neighbors in a Mexican American Community.*

8. Basler, "White Dreams and Red Votes."

9. The fullest treatment of ANMA is Garcia, "Mexican American Radicals and the Cold War." On Mine Mill, see Garcia, "Border Proletariats."

10. On the founding of ANMA, see Garcia, "Mexican American Radicals and the Cold War," 200–204; "Una Breve Historia," Convención Nacional Fundadera de ANMA, program, El Paso Public Library, Nathalie Gross Collection, 1948–75, Archive 819, Mexican American Box 1, Folder Mexican American—Civil Rights—ANMA (hereafter Nathalie Gross Collection).

11. Equally important is the heteropatriarchal nature of the family, which is beyond the scope of this chapter.

12. FBI report 100–5176, Denver, May 3, 1951, 11–12; FBI report 100–31499, San Francisco, August 20, 1951, 12–13. All FBI reports obtained under the Freedom of Information Act.

13. The FBI generated over 1,500 pages on ANMA through its informants. The number of informants ranged from twenty-seven in Los Angeles to four in Arizona and focused on ideological and membership overlap between ANMA and the Communist Party. According to Garcia, the FBI investigated ANMA in order to prove a link with the Communist Party and thus declare ANMA subversive. For example, it was reported that ANMA's president, Alfredo Montoya, was seen acting as secretary at CP meetings (FBI Report 100–30990, Los Angeles, July 5, 1951, 5). However, Garcia questions the significance of these observations, pointing out that shared politics does not necessitate collusion. While Garcia is correct, I am more apt to believe that there was in fact significant overlap between the two organizations based on their similar organizational culture, their objectives, the allies each group associated with, and the tendency toward solidarity among the Left during the cold war. As an example, the FBI submitted the ANMA document, "Resolution on the Mexican People" as evidence that the Communist Party controlled the San Francisco chapter. While there is no evidence of actual control, it does suggest overlap. FBI report 100–31499; Garcia, "Mexican American Radicals and the Cold War," 222–26.

14. FBI Report 100–5176, May 3, 1951, Denver, 1.

15. Urrutia, "An Offspring of Discontent"; FBI report 100–3464, Phoenix, May 17, 1951, 5–6; FBI report 100–30990, Los Angeles, July 5, 1951, 7.

16. Garcia, "Mexican American Radicals and the Cold War," 202.

17. "Constitucion de la Asociación Nacional Méxicana-Americana," Nathalie Gross Collection, translation mine.

18. *Progreso* 4.9 (1952): 2, Nathalie Gross Collection, Folder Mexican American—Civil Rights—ANMA—*Progreso*.

19. "Sigue en Pie," *Progreso*, April, 1952, 4, Nathalie Gross Collection; FBI Report 100–5176, January 5, 1952, Denver, 19–20.

20. FBI report 100–22449, Chicago, July 2, 1951, 5.

21. *Eastside Sun*, August 7, 1952, Chicano Resource Center, Los Angeles County Public Library.

22. FBI report 100–4596, El Paso, November 24, 1951, 2.

23. Bernstein, *Bridges of Reform*, especially chapter 4. On efforts to resist, see Healey and Isserman, *California Red*.

24. Letter to Mr. Pooley, editor, *El Paso Herald Post*, from ANMA, no date, Nathalie Gross Collection.

25. See Gomez, *Manifest Destinies*, 79.

26. Guglielmo, "Fighting for Caucasian Rights."

27. Garcia, "Mexican American Radicals and the Cold War," 221–22.

28. Saldaña-Portillo, "'How Many Mexicans [Is] a Horse Worth?'"

29. Alfonso Sena, "Discurso Principal Conferencia Estatal de Colorado," Nathalie Gross Collection; see also Garcia, "Mexican-American Radicals and the Cold War," 208.

30. On *Mendez v. Westminster* more generally, see Strum, *Mendez v. Westminster*. On the complexities of interracial alliances, see Robinson and Robinson, "The Limits of

Interracial Coalitions"; Blanton, "George I. Sanchez, Ideology and Whiteness in the Making of the Mexican American Civil Rights Movement."

31. Asian Americans make only rare appearances in ANMA's discourse. This is consistent with subsequent Chicana/o political organizing. See Pulido, *Black, Brown, Yellow and Left,* chapter 5.

32. FBI Report 100–31499, San Francisco, August 20, 1951, 11.

33. "ANMA Inicia Su Gran Campaña Pro-Cultura," *Progreso* 2.4 (1950): 1, Nathalie Gross Collection.

34. Garcia, "Mexican American Radicals and the Cold War," 222; FBI Report, 100–30990, Los Angeles, July 5, 1951, 14.

35. Behnken, "Elusive Unity"; Behnken, *Fighting Their Own Battles,* chpt. 2 While it is undoubtedly true that Tijerina was an outlier, it is also true that he was repeatedly elected to LULAC office.

36. Garcia, "Mexican American Radicals and the Cold War," 205.

37. FBI Report, 100–30990, July 5, 1951, 19.

38. Alfonso Sena, "Discurso Principal Conferencia Estatal de Colorado," translation mine.

39. "Segregan a los Mexicanos Aqui: Venden Propiedades con Restricciones Raciales," *Progreso* 2.4 (1950): 5, Nathalie Gross Collection.

TWENTY-FIVE

Racializing Biopolitics and Bare Life

ALEXANDER G. WEHELIYE

Michel Foucault's notion of biopolitics and Giorgio Agamben's idea of bare life have enjoyed great critical currency within different formations of critical ethnic studies (Arab American studies, Asian American studies, Black studies, Latino/a studies, Native American studies, postcolonial studies, etc.). Though several critical ethnic studies scholars have highlighted their limits, Foucault's and Agamben's ideas are frequently invoked in mainstream discourses without scrutinizing the historical, philosophical, or political foundations upon which they are constructed, which bespeaks a broader tendency in which theoretical formulations by white European thinkers are granted a conceptual carte blanche, while those uttered from the purview of minority discourse that speak to the same questions are almost exclusively relegated to the jurisdiction of ethnographic locality. I show how Foucault and Agamben, by placing racial difference in a field prior to and at a distance from conceptual contemplation, inscribe race as a "real object" or a "primitive notion."[1] In doing so I want to underscore just how comprehensively the coloniality of Man suffuses the disciplinary and conceptual formations of knowledge we labor under, and how far we have yet to go in decolonizing these structures.[2] This is especially unfortunate, and perhaps a result of the fact that most of the recent innovative impulses in critical theory have been formulated in the context of minority discourse (critical ethnic studies, postcolonial theory, queer theory, etc.).

The challenges posed to the smooth operations of Western Man since the 1960s by continental thought and minority discourse, though historically, conceptually, institutionally, and politically relational, tend to still be segregated because minority discourses seemingly cannot inhabit the space of proper theoretical reflection. This applies especially to the critical conversations about bare life and biopolitics, given that they revolve around racism, genocide, legal exclusion, torture, and humanity, topics that have been debated and theorized in black and ethnic studies for some time. The concepts of Foucault and Agamben are deemed transposable to a variety of spatiotemporal contexts because the authors do not speak from an explicitly racialized viewpoint (in contradistinction to nonwhite scholars who have written about racial slavery, colonialism, indigenous genocide, etc.), which lends their ideas more credibility and, once again, displaces minority discourse. If I didn't know any better, I would suppose that scholars not working in minority discourse seem thrilled that they no longer have to consult the scholarship of nonwhite thinkers now that European master subjects have deigned to weigh in on these topics.

Bare life and biopolitics discourse in particular is plagued by a strong anti-identity politics strain in the Anglo-American academy in its positioning of bare life and biopolitics as uncontaminated by and prior to reductive or essentialist political identities such as race and gender. Supposing that analyses of race and racism are inherently essentialist whereas those concerning bare life and biopolitics are not—because they do not suitably resemble real-world identities—allows bare life and biopolitics to appear unaffected by identitarian locality and thus as proper objects of knowledge. This occurs because the ideas of white European theorists are not regarded as affectable by a "critical consciousness" that would to open them "up toward historical reality, toward society, toward human needs and interests, to point up those concrete instances drawn from everyday reality that lie outside or just beyond the interpretive area."[3] Traveling theories, particularly those supposedly transparent and universal soldiers in Man's philosophical army, should be exposed to and reconstructed not only according to the factors Edward Said mentions but also in concordance with a critical consciousness that probes the conceptual constraints of these theories, especially as it pertains to the analytics of race, and exhumes their historico-geographical affectability.[4]

Since bare life and biopolitics discourse largely occludes race as a critical category of analysis (and not race as such), as do many other current articulations of critical theory, it cannot provide the methodological instruments for diagnosing the tight bonds between humanity and racializing assemblages in the modern era. The volatile rapport between race and the human is defined above all by two constellations: first, there exists no portion of the modern human that is not subject to racialization, which determines the hierarchical ordering of the *Homo sapiens* species into humans, not-quite-humans, and nonhumans; second, as a result humanity has held a very different status for the traditions of the racially oppressed. Man will be abolished "like a face drawn in sand at the edge of the sea" only if we disarticulate the modern human (Man) from its twin: racializing assemblages.[5] My principal question, phrased plainly, is this: What different modalities of the human come to light if we do not take the liberal humanist figure of Man as the master subject but focus on how humanity has been imagined and lived by those subjects excluded from this domain? Some scholars associated with black and ethnic studies have begun to undertake the project of thinking humanity from perspectives beyond the liberal humanist subject, Man. [6] There humanity emerges as an object of knowledge, which offers the means of conceptualizing how the human materializes in the worlds of those subjects habitually not thought to define or belong to this field. The greatest contribution to critical thinking by black studies—and critical ethnic studies more generally—is the transformation of the human into a heuristic model and not an ontological fait accompli, which seems particularly important in our current historical moment.

Though the human as a secular entity of scientific and humanistic inquiry has functioned as a central topos of modernity since the Renaissance, questions of humanity have gained importance in the academy and beyond in the wake of recent technological developments, especially the advent of biotechnology and the proliferation of informational media. These discussions, which in critical discourses in the humanities and social sciences have relied heavily on the concepts of the cyborg and the posthuman, largely do not take into account race as a constitutive category in thinking about the parameters of humanity. Reading thinkers such as Jacques Derrida, Michel Foucault, or Louis Althusser today, one cannot help but notice the manifesto-like character of their writings, historicizing the Western conception of Man (Foucault) providing a more scientific, nonhumanist version of Marxism (Althusser), or attempting to think at the limits of humanism while being aware that this just reinscribes the centrality of Man (Derrida). Going back further, the axial project of linguistic, anthropological, and literary structuralism that emerged in the aftermath of World War II was to displace a holistic notion of the human through various structural features that constitute, frame, and interpellate Man. We can also locate these tendencies in the German philosophical traditions that inspired a number of poststructuralist projects, or, for that matter, in the works of Sigmund Freud, Karl Marx, and Ferdinand de Saussure. These thinkers, however, are hardly regarded as posthumanist philosophers; instead they are classified as antihumanist.

Here we would do well to retrieve the deracination of poststructuralism once annexed by the U.S. academy in the 1970s and rechristened "theory." As Robert Young, among others, has shown, the Algerian war in particular, and decolonization in general, provided the impetus for a generation of French intellectuals (Derrida, Pierre Bourdieu, Hélène Cixous, Jean-François Lyotard, for example, who would later be associated with poststructuralism), to dismantle Western thought and subjectivity.[7] The near simultaneous eruptions of ethnic studies and poststructuralism in the American university system has been noted by critics such as Hortense Spillers, yet these important convergences hardly register on the radar of mainstream debates.[8] That is to say, the challenges posed to the smooth operations of Western Man since the 1960s by continental thought and minority discourse, though historically, conceptually, institutionally, and politically relational, tend to be segregated because minority discourses seemingly cannot inhabit the space of proper theoretical reflection.

We also find this in current studies of posthumanism associated with theories of technological virtuality, as well as in the embryonic field of animal studies. In these modes of inquiry, Man interfaces with a plethora of informational technologies or, in the case of animal studies, sheds its superiority complex vis-à-vis nonhuman animals and enters into the space and time of the posthuman. Moreover many invocations of posthumanism, whether in antihumanist poststructuralist theorizing or in current considerations of technology and animality, reinscribe the humanist subject (Man) as the personification of the human by insisting that this is the category to be overcome, rarely considering cultural and political formations outside the world of Man that might offer alternative versions of humanity.[9] Posthumanism and animal studies isomorphically yoke humanity to the limited possessive individualism of Man because these discourses also presume that we have now entered a stage in human development when all subjects have been granted equal access to Western humanity and that this is indeed what we all want to overcome. It is remarkable, for instance, how the (not so) dreaded comparison between human and animal slavery is brandished in the field of animal studies and how black liberation struggles serve as both positive and negative foil for making a case for the sentience and therefore emancipation of nonhuman beings.[10] This sleight of hand comes easy to those critics attempting to achieve animal rights and is frequently articulated comparatively vis-à-vis black subjects' enslavement in the Americas—"the moral and intellectual jujitsu that yielded the catachresis, person-as-property."[11] In supposing that all human subjects occupy the space of humanity equally, post- and antihumanist discourses cannot conceptualize how "the transubstantiation of the captive into the volitional subject, chattel into proprietor, and the circumscribed body of blackness into the disembodied and abstract universal seems improbable, if not impossible."[12] Much post-1960s critical theorizing either assumes that black subjects have been fully assimilated into the human qua Man, or it continues to relegate the thought of nonwhite subjects to the ground of ethnographic specificity.

Consequently the figuration of humanity found in black cultures forms an amalgamation of technologies—the application of knowledge—that have generally not been construed as central to or even as part of this category. These assemblages remain muffled in mainstream critical thinking, which either consigns minority intellectuals or thought to the language of radical particularity or, conversely, places them on the Olympus of the deracinated master subject, which, of course, they cannot comfortably occupy.

Take, for instance, Judith Butler's passing reference to Wynter's oeuvre: "[Fanon's] project has been extended by contemporary scholars, including the literary critic Sylvia Wynter, to pertain to women of color and to call into question the racist frameworks within which the category of the human has been articulated."[13] While Fanon might not have been a champion of feminism as we have come to understand it—though one could contest this, seeing how easy it has become to brush aside in a single sentence Fanon's work on the basis of his androcentrism while this does not occur nearly as frequently in the case of Hegel or Foucault—it is not quite clear how his theorization of interior colonies would not pertain to women of color, unless Butler were writing under the presumption that writers of color could produce thought only for and about their particular identities. Viewing Wynter's colossal project, with which Butler does not engage in any sustained way, of both critiquing the current Western instantiation of the human as coterminous with the white liberal subject and of crafting a new humanism, should not be reduced to observing the historicity of this concept with the aim of showing how women of color and other groups are excluded from its purview. Or to put it in Butlerian terms: Wynter is interested in human trouble rather than "merely" woman of color trouble, even while she deploys the liminal perspective of women of color to imagine humanity otherwise.[14] In response to Butler and Western feminism more generally, Wynter has stated on several occasions that her object of knowledge is not gender but genre—genres of the human: "Our struggle as Black women has to do with the destruction of the genre; with the displacement of the genre of the human of 'Man.'"[15] For Wynter, destroying only Western bourgeois conceptions of gender leaves intact the genre of the human to which it is attached and thus cannot serve as a harbinger of true emancipation, which requires abolishing Man once and for all. It seems as if we have yet to countermand the "unrecognized contradiction" that, as Gayatri Spivak so fittingly diagnosed in1988, "valorizes the concrete experience of the oppressed, while being so uncritical about [how] the historical role of the intellectual is maintained by a verbal slippage."[16] Rather than contending with Wynter's thinking as an intellectual project in the same manner as she does with Foucault, Hegel, or Luce Irigaray, Butler privileges her concrete experience as a woman of color.

In addition to rejecting gender as a category independent of other axes of subjugation, Wynter states that in her writings "'race' is really a code-word for 'genre.' Our issue is not the issue of 'race.' Our issue is the issue of the genre of 'Man.' It is this issue of the 'genre' of 'Man' that causes all the '-*isms*.' . . . Now when I speak at a feminist gathering and I come up with 'genre' and say 'gender' is a function of 'genre,' they don't want to hear that."[17] Thus Wynter does not privilege race over gender as much as she insists that the master's tools (a universal notion of gender) cannot dismantle the master's house (Man), in Audre Lorde's formulation. Rather Wynter's is a feminism typified by a critique of race and coloniality that focuses on the liberation of humans from all *-isms* versus only one specific form of subjection such as sexism, and it does not contradict the majority of women of color feminisms, which have not taken gender as an isolatable—or even primary—category of analysis but have instead highlighted the complex relationality between different forms of oppression.[18] Mainstream feminism in contrast sees itself "as an autonomized particularity, rather than as a particularity constitutive of a new non–middle class mode of universality." For Wynter, a feminism that does not aspire to create a different code for what it means to be human merely sketches a different map of Man's territorializing assemblages; however, in order to abolish these assemblages feminism's insurrection must sabotage "its own prescribed role in the empirical articulation of its representations in effect by coming out of the closet, moving out of our assigned categories."[19] Spillers makes a similar point when she maintains, "We are less interested in joining the ranks of gendered femaleness than gaining the insurgent ground as female social subject."[20] In this context "gendered femaleness" denotes gender as a purely natural and sovereign modality of difference, while the revolt of a "female social subject" articulates gender as an integral component in the abolition of the human as Man. As phrased by one of the defining texts in the recent history of black feminism: "If Black women were free, it would mean that everyone else would have to be free since our freedom would necessitate the destruction of all the systems of oppression."[21] Moving away from discourses of inclusion and recognition, the Combahee River Collective dwells on the specific positions of black women within Western modernity to launch global critiques, expansive theories, poetic tactics, and relational political projects that spurn the ethnographic encampment of Man's racializing assemblages.[22] Neither Wynter nor Spillers asks us to choose between race and gender; instead their thinking demands vigilance about how different forms of domination create both the conditions of possibility and the "semiosis of procedure" necessary to hierarchically distinguish full humans from not-quite-humans and nonhumans.[23] Spillers's and Wynter's ideas have been essential to formulating my arguments because they represent systems of thought—both individually and taken together—that tackle notions of the human as it interfaces with gender, coloniality, slavery racialization, and political violence without mapping these questions onto a mutually exclusive struggle between either the free-flowing terra nullius of the universally applicable or the terra cognitus of the ethnographically detained.

In contrast to Agamben's disavowal of race, racism plays a crucial role in Foucault's genealogy of biopolitics, the power of the European state to "make live and let die," which begins to shatter the hitherto unitary body politic of European nations at the end of the eighteenth century and comes to fully engulf these societies that must be defended throughout the nineteenth century.[24] This is the moment in which politics takes hold of the biological and the biological health of the national population defines the exercise of state power; according to Foucault, it produces a "racism that society will direct against itself, against its own elements, and its own products. This is the internal *racism of permanent purification*, and it will become one of the basic dimensions of social normalization." Careful to establish that racism preexists this moment, even though both its quality and primary function shift, Foucault shows that racism "had already been in existence for a very long time. But I think it functioned *elsewhere*." Racism, which up to this point had led a peaceful conceptual and historical life in an unspecified terra incognita, thus journeys from the uncharted periphery into the heart of the modern European nation-state. Yet despite locating the naissance of modern racism in "colonization or, in other words, with colonizing genocide," for Foucault racism only becomes relevant once it penetrates the borders of Fortress Europe.[25] Because Foucault does not describe this *allieurs* or even mention it again in the text, it materializes as a primitive topography, operating as a constitutive outside for his theory of biopolitics throughout these lectures. In logic primitive terms or notions, also referred to as axioms or postulates, name instantly understandable terms that are used without elucidating their signification. The meanings of all other concepts in a logical system are determined by these primitive terms and by previously established expressions. Over the course of his argument about the genesis of biopolitics in the lectures, Foucault will continue to distinguish European state racism and biopolitics from those primeval forms of racism that continue to linger in the aforementioned philosophical, geographical, and political quicksand of an unspecified elsewhere; at least this is what we are asked to infer as a consequence of Foucault's taciturnity about the reach and afterlife of those other modalities of racialization.

In several of the 1975–76 lectures Foucault also employs the term *colonization* figuratively.[26] The slippage between colonialism as a historical phenomenon and colonization as a synonym for hegemonic appropriation or annexation underscores the primitiveness of this concept in Foucault's system of thought, in much the same way as the idea of ethnic racism, which I will discuss shortly. That is, despite the fact that the histories of colonialism and racism secure his definition of biopolitics, for Foucault the meaning of colonization and ethnic racism are immediately understandable, and as such they are exploited without the peripheral benefits of explication. More generally Foucault positions biopolitics against rather simplified definitions of, on the one hand, an "ordinary racism . . . that takes the traditional form of mutual contempt or hatred between races" and, on the other, racism as an "ideological operation that allows States, or a class, to displace the hostility that is directed toward them . . . onto a mythical adversary." In its place modern European racism provides a deeper domain because it supplies the conditions of possibility for biopolitics, and although Foucault sees modern racism as originating in colonialism, he ultimately uses the Third Reich to illustrate the full reach of biopower when he writes, "Of course, no state could have more disciplinary power than the Nazi regime. Nor was there any other State in which the biological was so tightly, so insistently, regulated."[27] We should remain vigilant about not acquiescing to these monumentalizing protocols (and Agamben's) because, more often than not, they achieve their aggrandizing effect by not taking into account the historical relationality and conceptual contiguity between Nazi racism and the other forms of biopolitics I discussed earlier, those perfected in colonialism, indigenous genocide, racialized indentured servitude, and racial slavery, for instance. They also foreclose discussions of those racializing assemblages that Foucault and Agamben consign to a theoretico-geographical no-Man's-land. Given Foucault's principal point about the overall pervasiveness of biopolitics in Europe, why must its most severe incarnation bear the heavy burden of paradigmatic exemplariness, just as it does in Agamben? Why not simply examine the biopolitics of Nazi racism qua Nazi racism? Why must this form of racism necessarily figure as the apex in the telos of modern racializing assemblages?

Even when considering modes of biopolitical racialization in the socialist state, Foucault's interpretation hinges on setting it apart from a narrow definition of racism: "Quite naturally, we find that racism—*not a truly ethnic racism* but racism of the evolutionist kind, biological racism—is fully operational in the way socialist States (of the Soviet Union type) deal with the mentally ill, criminals, political adversaries, and so on."[28] Initially the caesura Foucault places between "ethnic" and "biological" racism seems to productively counteract some of his foregoing remarks about this question; at a closer look, however, the distinction exposes the shortcomings of his approach to race and racism. Because he fails to probe the decidedly undemonic ground of his argument, he uncritically embraces an ontological differentiation between ethnic and biopolitical racism, leaving the door open for the naturalization of racial categories and the existence of a biological sphere that is not always already subject to ethnic racism. However, all modern racism is biological, first, because it maintains the believed natural—often evolutionary—inferiority of the targeted subjects and, second, because racialization is instituted, as elucidated by Wynter, in the realm of human biochemistry as the sociogenic selection of one specific group in the name of embodying all humanity. So rather than deselecting phenotypically nonwhite or Jewish subjects, socialist biopower racializes sets of humans (criminals, dissidents, etc.) that are not distinctive in Man's racial epidermal schema but are nevertheless classified as deviating from full (socialist) humans according to an established pecking order that is deemed beyond the authority of human culture or politics.[29] Put bluntly, there exists no significant difference between ethnic and biological racism in the way Foucault imagines, since both rely on the same tools of the trade: racializing assemblages. Nevertheless it appears as if Foucault can authenticate the uniqueness and novelty of European biopolitical racism only by conjuring the antithetical spirits of racisms always already situated in a primitive elsewhere.

Foucault concedes that the idea of race has no stable anchor in the biological; rather it names "a certain historico-political divide" in which "two races exist whenever one writes the history of two groups which do not, at least to begin with, have the same language or, in many cases, the same religion." If divergences in language and religion between different humans serve as the markers for racial difference within the confines of Europe, this passage cannot explain how the operations of race differ constitutively from those of nationalism, to name one obvious example. Foucault, then, moves quite swiftly to explain that races "exist when there are two groups which, although they coexist, have *not become mixed* because of the differences, dissymmetries, and barriers created by privileges, customs and rights, the distribution of wealth, or the way in which power is exercised."[30] Here he supplies so broad a definition of racism that it could be applied to any number of categories that have been brandished to create caesuras among different humans: economic and social class, nationality, or gender, for instance. We are confronted with these resulting questions: How does this definition of race diverge from ethnic racism? Are the racialized classes in ethnic racism not segregated as a result of the distribution of wealth or the deployment of power? Moreover Foucault does not explain how these groups come to exist as different, how we are to understand the distinction between coexistence and mixing, or what their particular mixing might entail. Thus he positions hybridity as a panacea for racial difference without querying the foundation upon which the very idea of racial differences among humans is built.

Ultimately, despite stressing the importance of racism to the machinations of biopolitics, Foucault restrains its full conceptual reverberations because he relies on a commonsensical notion of racism as his primitive straw man and because he remains confined to a version of nineteenth-century Europe oddly unscathed by colonialism and ethnic racism. Of course colonial configurations in the late eighteenth and early nineteenth century would at least partially derive from the intramural tensions within and between European nations, given that these tensions were exported to the colonial elsewhere around the globe. As a result colonization unavoidably reflects the racializing assemblages interior to Europe, while techniques that discipline humanity into full humans, not-quite-humans, and nonhumans developed in the colonies inflect those at home, and which Foucault, following Hannah Arendt, terms the "boomerang effect" of colonialism.[31] The fundamental problem, then, is not that Foucault largely omits colonialism and the non-Western world from the province of his discussion of racism but, to be more precise, that he and some of his followers assume there to be substantial inconsistency between a "confrontation of two alien races" and the "bifurcation within Europe's social fabric," which demarcates the inadequate and limiting theoretical parameters of his conception of racism.[32] Though Foucault does not deploy the term *alien races*, his insistence on the spatiotemporal disjuncture between the race from here and the race that came from another place as well as the reemergence of the race from the past within it cannot but echo colonialist tropes and recapitulation theory: "The other race is basically not the race that came from *elsewhere* . . . but . . . it is a race that is permanently, ceaselessly infiltrating the social body. . . . What we see . . . as a binary rift within society is not a clash between two distinct races. It is the splitting of a single race into a superrace and a subrace. To put it a different way, it is the reappearance, within a single race, of the past of that race."[33] Within this context, alien races—Ann Stoler's very unfortunate rephrasing of Foucault's ethnic racism, to be sure—dodge the brush of discourse, dwelling in a speculative state of organic truth. This line of reasoning rests on the assumptions that such a thing as alien races exist, that the confrontation between them (ethnic racism) need not be explained, and that Europe—remember it is immaterial whether this signifies France or Europe as whole—was internally cohesive, because racism dwelled elsewhere prior to the ascent of biopolitics in the late eighteenth and early nineteenth century. Hence in Foucault's schema race and racism, insofar as they have yet to achieve proper biopolitical credentials, take on the shape of an inevitable clash between unacquainted civilizations.

There lies a vast gulf between an argument that explores the particular techniques of racialization that appeared in Europe over the course of the eighteenth and nineteenth centuries and one that attests to some form of cultural, social, or ontological anteriority of alien races. Put simply, Foucault never interrogates the bare existence of racial difference and those hierarchies fabricated on this primordial notion and, as a result, reinscribes racial difference as natural. Because ethnic racism is based on established variances among different ethnicities it evidently demands no further elaboration in Foucault's genealogical deduction of modern racializing assemblages, and thus emerges as a fixed category rather than as the biopolitical apparatus it actually is. Conversely the fission that appears within Europe's autochthonous population in this period assumes the fragmentation of a formerly cohesive body politic: the proliferation of biopower produces the hierarchal differentiation of internal groups as races, whereas the caesuras between European and alien races exist outside the vicissitudes of biopolitics. In Foucault's model race and ethnicity remain always already beyond the administrative, ideological, and conceptual precincts of Europe; they function *as and in* an unnamed elsewhere.[34] Thus the elision and active disavowal of racism, colonization, and ethnic racism in these lectures are not mere glitches in Foucault's thought but serious conceptual limitations.

Agamben has even less to say about racism, colonialism, and the world beyond Fortress Europe. In his system of thought bare life accomplishes a conceptual feat that race as an analytical category seemingly cannot: it founds a biological sphere above and beyond the reach of racial hierarchies. For Agamben the Muselmann, who represents the most extreme incarnation of bare life, heralds "an absolute biological substance that cannot be assigned to a particular bearer or subject, or divided by another caesura."[35] Nevertheless in order for the Muselmann to function as the most radical paradigm of bare life, Agamben must insist on the indivisibility of this state so that it does not resemble traditional racial identities. The barring of subjects that belong to *Homo sapiens* from the jurisdiction of humanity depends upon the workings of racialization (differentiation) and racism (hierarchization and exclusion); in fact the two are often indistinguishable. *Bare life* is but an alternative term for *racism*, though a designation that attempts to conjure a sphere more fundamental to the human than race.

In this vein I argue that black studies and other formations of critical ethnic studies provide crucial viewpoints, often overlooked or actively neglected in current scholarly debates about bare life in Agamben's work and beyond. And, as with Foucault, in both cases theories of racism or race appear almost exclusively in conjunction with the extremity of Nazism: "The link between politics and life instituted by [Nazism] is not (as is maintained by a common and completely inadequate interpretation of racism) a merely instrumental relationship, as if race were a simple natural given that had merely to be safeguarded."[36] In a vein similar to Foucault's brushing aside of ethnic racism, Agamben perfunctorily dismisses the instrumental definition of racism without explicating its historical or conceptual provenances. As untenable as an instrumental form of racism might be, does this disqualify all other analyses of race and racism, and, if so, on what grounds? If Agamben and Foucault are to be believed, all interpretations of race, ethnicity, and racism that are not immediately tied to Nazism or concerned with caesuras among European populations are crude, simplistic, prehistorical, and undeserving of sustained critical attention, which, as a consequence, naturalizes traditional racial or ethnic delimiters. In other words, while Foucault and Agamben render biopolitical racism an object of knowledge, that is, an object constituted by particular modes of knowledge production, racism that is based on ethnic difference, because it is camouflaged by a reading at sight, acts as a real object against which their proper objects of knowledge—biopolitics and bare life—are gauged. This is why we cannot cede speaking of race in terms of biology or ontology to either the proponents of bare life and biopolitics discourse or those who would conflate race with nature, now frequently done in the language of genetics rather than phenotype. Viewed in this light, the transcendence of race Agamben ascribes to the Muselmann rests on the philosophical unseeing of racializing assemblages. *Pace* Agamben, the Muselmann not only names the conditions of possibility for violent exclusions but also serves as the foundation for policing the borders between bare life, life, and death. As a result the pure organic essence born of the biopolitics of racism is a form of racial classification and most definitely not its supersession. There can be no absolute biological substance because in the history of modernity this field always already appears in the form of racializing assemblages.

Assemblages (*agencement* in French, which translates literally to "arrangement"), in accordance with Gilles Deleuze and Félix Guattari's thinking, constitute continuously shifting relational totalities comprising spasmodic networks between different entities (content) and their articulation within "acts and statements" (expression). [37] However, content does not antecede expression, or vice versa, as much as these two forces and their constituent components must enter into mutually co-constitutive machinic becomings that coalesce at certain points while seceding at others. That is, the differing elements articulated in an assemblage become components only in their relational connectivity with other factors. For Deleuze and Guattari assemblages pivot on both a vertical and a horizontal axis. The horizontal line, consisting of content and expression, features "*machinic assemblages* of bodies, actions and passions, passions, an intermingling of bodies reacting to one another" as well as "*collective assemblages of enunciation,* of acts and statements, of incorporeal transformations of bodies," while the vertical dimension is marked by "*territorial sides,* or reterritorialized sides, which stabilize it, and *cutting edges of deterritorialization,* which carry it away."[38] Assemblages are inherently productive, entering into polyvalent becomings to produce and give expression to previously nonexistent realities, thoughts, bodies, affects, spaces, actions, ideas, and so on. However, the fecundity of these becomings, what Deleuze and Guattari term "machinic," ought not be cognized as unavoidably positive or liberating, particularly when set off against putatively rigid structures such as race and colonialism, since assemblages transport potential territorializations as often as lines of flight: "The identity of any assemblage at any level of scale is always the product of a process (territorialization and, in some cases, coding) and it is always precarious, since other processes (deterritorialization and decoding) can destabilize it."[39] In addition to highlighting the double-pronged milieu of assemblages, Manuel De Landa's concise account also shows how these circumvent the structure versus agency problematic, because assemblages do not assume change to inhere in full, self-present, and coherent subjects.

We should remain cautious, as Barbara Christian, Stuart Hall, and Spivak urge us to do, about the complete disavowal of subjectivity in theoretical discourse because in the context of the Anglo-American academy more often than not an insistence on transcending limited notions of the subject or identity leads to the neglect of race as a critical category, as we have seen in scholars such as Butler, Foucault, and Agamben.[40] In this context Spivak's remarks concerning Deleuze and Guattari's refusal "to consider the relations between desire, power and subjectivity" remain acutely relevant because it "renders them incapable of articulating a theory of interests" while "their indifference to ideology (a theory of which is necessary for an understanding of interests) is striking but consistent." In addition "Foucault's commitment to 'genealogical' speculation . . . has created an unfortunate resistance . . . to 'mere' ideological critique."[41] The resistance to ideology as a metaterritorializing category on the part of Foucault and Deleuze and Guattari is understandable within the context of post-1960s French thought, given the then au courant disenchantment with Marxism and grand narratives. Nevertheless notions such as power, ideology, gender, coloniality, identity, and race jinglingly dawdle in the margins of Deleuze and Guattari's putatively asubjective and disinterested universes, since otherwise, as Hall remarks, "there is no reason why anything is or isn't potentially articulatable with anything. The critique of reductionism has apparently resulted in the notion of society as a totally open discursive field."[42] It should be noted that Hall and Spivak, two of the most significant contemporary Anglo-American theorists of cultural studies and deconstruction, are not simply rejecting poststructuralist tenets for their arbitrariness or relativism but asking about the stakes of evacuating seemingly retrograde concepts such as identity, especially within the context of "societies structured in dominance."[43]

Hall's elaboration of the Marxian notion of articulation, which Marx referred to as *soziale Gliederung*, represents "the necessity of thinking unity and difference; difference in complex unity, without this becoming a hostage to the privileging of difference as such."[44] Hall's outline of articulation here emphasizes relational connectivity in much the same way as Deleuze and Guattari's notion of assemblages while still retaining some of the political traction called for by Spivak and Hall. Hall is also careful to acknowledge the existence of "tendential combinations," which are "not prescribed in the fully determinist sense" but are nevertheless the "'preferred' combinations, sedimented and solidified by real historical development over time."[45] Preferred articulations insert historically sedimented power imbalances and ideological interests, which are crucial to understanding mobile structures of dominance such as race or gender into the modus operandi of assemblages. Accordingly a robust fusion of articulation and assemblage accents the productive ingredients of social formations while not silencing questions of power, reinstituting an innocent version of the subject, or neglecting the deterritorializing capabilities of power, ideology, and so on. Articulated assemblages such as racialization materialize as sets of complex relations of articulations that constitute an open articulating principle—territorializing and deterritorializing, interested and asubjective—structured in political, economic, social, racial, and heteropatriarchal dominance.

With regard to the category of race, racializing assemblages ascribe "incorporeal transformations . . . to bodies," etching abstract forces of power onto the human body and flesh in order to create the appearance of a naturally expressive relationship between phenotype and sociopolitical status: the hieroglyphics of the flesh.[46] As a result the legal and extralegal fictions of skin color and other visual markers obscure and therefore facilitate the continued existence and intergenerational transmission of the hieroglyphics of the flesh. Spillers adds to and recasts the concept of bare life by forcefully showing that, in the context of racial slavery, it gives birth to a cluster of classifying assemblages that stands at the center of modernity. Racializing assemblages articulate and create relational intensities between the human body and flesh, producing racial categories, which are subsequently coded as natural substances, whether pure or impure, rather than as the territorializing articulations of these assemblages. The flesh, although not synonymous with racialization in toto, represents one such racializing assemblage within the world of Man.

Though these viscous assemblages may not be equivalent to physicochemical indices such as skin pigmentation, Spillers's idea of the hieroglyphics of the flesh nevertheless touches this register through what Wynter terms the sociogenic institution of punishment-reward systems, or "the *relativity* of our modes of being human, and of the invented practices/institutions by means of which our culture-specific conceptions of being human (e.g., theory) are inscribed, turned into *flesh*."[47] Spillers's theorization of the flesh highlights one significant instance of this biocultural stigmatic apparatus in which ideas are literally and figuratively deformed into racialized assemblages of human flesh that invest human phenomenology with an aura of extrahuman physiology. The hieroglyphics of the flesh still dwell among us in the fissures of our current governing configuration of the human as Man.[48] Racializing assemblages, which, although born partially of political violence, cannot be reduced to it. Put differently, instances of systemic political violence moored in the law and beyond not only herald the naissance of bare life and its racialized progeny but also produce a surplus, a line of flight in Deleuze and Guattari's and George Jackson's parlance, that evades capture, that refuses rest, that testifies to the impossibility of its own existence. Taking the workings of flesh seriously frees and sets in motion the deviances that lay dormant in the concept of bare life and that repudiate by their very existence the equation of domination and violence with the complete absence of subjectivity, life, enjoyment, hunger, and so on.

I am by no means contending that critical minority discourse scholars should not engage the thought of Agamben and Foucault or other European thinkers, nor am I emphasizing and bemoaning the exclusion of race as a conceptual category from these conceptual apparatuses. Instead I am asking scholars in critical ethnic studies not to replicate the shortcomings of biopolitics and bare life discourse, while also considering the racial and gender politics of knowledge production that continue to construct certain forms of theorizing as more universal than others in a neocolonial model. Though the critique of colonial reason still so prominent in the writings of white European theorists is significant, we would also do well to highlight—through extensive exegeses, for instance—the varied traditions of critical thought that lie beyond the European canon to counteract the methodical disremembering of the extensive intellectual contributions critical ethnic studies has made to modern knowledge formations.

NOTES

1. See Tarski, *Introduction to Logic and to the Methodology of Deductive Sciences*, 110.

2. On the coloniality of being and knowledge in modernity, see Lugones, "Heterosexualism and the Colonial/Modern Gender System"; Chen, *Asia as Method*; Quijano, "Coloniality and Modernity/Rationality"; Wynter, "Unsettling the Coloniality of Being/Power/Truth/Freedom."

3. Said, "Traveling Theory," 241.

4. Within post-Enlightenment European thought da Silva distinguishes between the transparent white master subject of Man and his various affectable non-European others. Global raciality, then, "produces both (a) the affectable (subaltern) subjects that can be excluded from juridical universality without unleashing an ethical crisis

and (b) the self-determined things who should enjoy the entitlements afforded and protected by the principle of universality said to govern modern social configurations" (*Toward a Global Idea of Race*, 35).

5. Foucault, *The Order of Things*, 387.

6. Besides the thinkers discussed here, see Ong, *Neoliberalism as Exception*; Mignolo, "Citizenship, Knowledge, and the Limits of Humanity"; Gilroy, *Postcolonial Melancholia*; Tadiar, "In the Face of Whiteness as Value"; Radhakrishnan, *History, the Human, and the World Between*; Esmeir, *Juridical Humanity*.

7. See Ahluwalia, *Out of Africa*.

8. Spillers, "The Crisis of the Negro Intellectual." See also Chandler, "Originary Displacement." I have addressed some of these questions on the discussion of identity and the subject as critical categories; see Weheliye, *Phonographies*, 46–72.

9. For an elaboration of the nexus between posthumanism and black culture, see Weheliye, "Feenin."

10. This is a reference to Spiegel's *The Dreaded Comparison*.

11. Spillers, "Introduction," 20.

12. Hartman, *Scenes of Subjection*, 123.

13. Butler, *Undoing Gender*, 13.

14. On black women's liminal vantage point in Wynter's work, see McKittrick, *Demonic Grounds*, 133–36.

15. Thomas, "*Proud Flesh* Inter/Views: Sylvia Wynter."

16. Spivak, "Can the Subaltern Speak?" (1988), 275. Of course Spivak, in what has now become a locus classicus of postcolonial critical theorizing, is referencing the limitations of Foucault's and Deleuze's work vis-à-vis subaltern subjectivity.

17. Thomas, "*Proud Flesh* Inter/Views: Sylvia Wynter."

18. See Opitz et al., *Showing Our Colors*; Moraga and Anzaldúa, *This Bridge Called My Back*; Smith, *Home Girls*; Boyce Davies and Savory, *Out of the Kumbla*.

19. Wynter, *Beyond Liberal and Marxist*, 14, 16.

20. Spillers, "Mama's Baby, Papa's Maybe," 229.

21. Combahee River Collective, "A Black Feminist Statement," 215.

22. Simpson, "On Ethnographic Refusal."

23. Spillers, "Introduction," 21.

24. Foucault states, "This will allow power to treat that population as a mixture of races, or to be more accurate, to treat the species, to subdivide the species it controls, into the subspecies known, precisely, as races. That is the first function of racism: to fragment, to create caesuras within the biological continuum" (*Society Must Be Defended*, 255).

25. Foucault, *Society Must Be Defended*, 60, 254, 257.

26. Foucault, *Society Must Be Defended*, 11, 33, 38–39, 58, 215.

27. Foucault, *Society Must Be Defended*, 258, 259.

28. Foucault, *Society Must Be Defended*, 261–62. Race and colonialism do not figure prominently in the remainder of Foucault's oeuvre, neither in the works published during his lifetime nor in the eight volumes of posthumously issued lectures that were given at the Collège de France from 1973 to 1984.

29. I would distinguish the socialist racism Foucault invokes here from the racializing assemblages that I have been discussing only on the grounds that the former does not

necessitate the optic cum biological grounding of difference among human groups that is the defining property of ethnic racism.

30. Foucault, *Society Must Be Defended,* 77.

31. Foucault writes of the "boomerang effect" that "colonial practice can have on the juridico-political structures of the West. . . . While colonization, with its techniques and its political and juridical weapons, obviously transported European models to other continents, it also had a considerable boomerang effect on the mechanisms of power in the West, and on the apparatuses, institutions, and techniques of power. A whole series of colonial models was brought back to the West, and the result was that the West could practice something resembling colonization, or an internal colonialism, on itself" (*Society Must Be Defended,* 103). He takes this idea from Arendt without citing its source (*The Origins of Totalitarianism,* 155, 206, 223).

32. The quoted phrases are taken from Stoler's summary of Foucault's lectures on racism: *Race and the Education of Desire,* 66, 60.

33. Foucault, *Society Must Be Defended,* 61.

34. For an analogous critique of Foucault's erasure of racialized, gendered, and colonial violence in his argument about the changing nature of modern punishment and incarceration in *Discipline and Punish,* see James, *Resisting State Violence,* 24–43.

35. Agamben, *Remnants of Auschwitz,* 85.

36. Agamben, *Homo Sacer,* 147–48.

37. See Deleuze and Guattari, *A Thousand Plateaus,* 87–88. See also Puar, *Terrorist Assemblages,* 211–16.

38. Deleuze and Guattari, *A Thousand Plateaus,* 88.

39. De Landa, *A New Philosophy of Society,* 28.

40. Christian, "The Race for Theory"; Hall, "Who Needs 'Identity'?"; Spivak, "Can the Subaltern Speak?"

41. Spivak, "Can the Subaltern Speak?" (1988), 273.

42. Hall, "On Postmodernism and Articulation," 146. Hall is referring to Ernesto Laclau and Chantal Mouffe's 1985 text, *Hegemony and Socialist Strategy: Towards a Radical Democratic Politics.*

43. Hall, "Race, Articulation, and Societies Structured in Dominance."

44. Hall, "Signification, Representation, Ideology," 93. See also Althusser and Balibar, *Reading Capital.*

45. Hall, "On Postmodernism and Articulation," 330.

46. Deleuze and Guattari, *A Thousand Plateaus,* 98.

47. Wynter, "'Genital Mutilation' or 'Symbolic Birth,?'" 513. For Spillers's theorization of the flesh, see *Black, White, and in Color.*

48. This confers an altogether different signification on the biblical adage "And the Word was made flesh, and dwelt among us" (John 1:14).

BIBLIOGRAPHY

Abbas, Ackbar. *Hong Kong: Culture and the Politics of Disappearance*. Minneapolis: University of Minnesota Press, 1997.

Adorno, Rolena. *Cronista y principe: La obra de don Felipe de Guamán Poma de Ayala*. Lima: Pontificia Universidad Católica del Perú, 1989.

Adorno, Theodor W., and Walter Benjamin. *Walter Benjamin and Theodor W. Adorno: The Complete Correspondence, 1928–1940*. Ed. Henri Lonitz. Trans. Nicholas Walker. Cambridge: Harvard University Press, 1999.

Agamben, Giorgio. *Homo Sacer: Sovereign Power and Bare Life*. Stanford: Stanford University Press, 1998.

———. *Remnants of Auschwitz: The Witness and the Archive*. Trans. Daniel Heller-Roazen. New York: Zone Books, 1999.

———. *State of Exception*. Chicago: University of Chicago Press, 2005.

Agathangelou, Anna, Morgan Bassichis, and Tamara Spira. "Intimate Investments: Homonormativity, Global Lockdown, and Seductions of Empire." *Radical History Review* 100 (2008): 120–43.

Aguilar, Filomeno V., Jr. "Between the Letter and the Spirit of the Law: Ethnic Chinese and Philippine Citizenship by Jus Soli, 1899–1947." *Southeast Asian Studies* 49.3 (2011): 431–63.

Ahluwalia, Pal. *Out of Africa: Post-Structuralism's Colonial Roots*. New York: Routledge, 2010.

Ahmed, Leila. "Western Ethnocentrism and Perceptions of the Harem." *Feminist Studies* 8.3 (1982): 521–34.

Ahmed, Sara. "Animated Borders: Skin, Color, and Tanning." In *Vital Signs: Feminist Reconfigurations of the Bio/logical Body*, ed. Margrit Shildrick and Janet Price, 45–65. Edinburgh: Edinburgh University Press, 1998.

———. *The Cultural Politics of Emotion*. Edinburgh: Edinburgh University Press, 2004.

———. *The Promise of Happiness*. Durham: Duke University Press, 2010.

———. *Queer Phenomenology: Orientations, Objects, Others*. Durham: Duke University Press, 2006.
Alexander, Michelle. *The New Jim Crow: Mass Incarceration in the Age of Colorblindness*. New York: New Press, 2010.
Alfred, Taiaiake. "Sovereignty." In *Sovereignty Matters: Locations of Contestation and Possibility in Indigenous Struggles for Self-Determination*, ed. Joanne Barker, 33–50. Lincoln: University of Nebraska Press, 2005.
Allen, Robert. *Black Awakening in Capitalist America*. Garden City, NY: Doubleday, 1969.
Alonso, Ana. "Conforming Disconformity: 'Mestizaje,' Hybridity, and the Aesthetics of Mexican Nationalism." *Cultural Anthropology* 19.4 (2004): 459–90.
Alsultany, Evelyn. *Arabs and Muslims in the U.S. Media Post-9/11*. New York: New York University Press, 2012.
———. "Selling American Diversity and Muslim American Identity through Non-Profit Advertising Post-911." *American Quarterly* 59.3 (2007): 593–622.
Althusser, Louis, and Étienne Balibar. *Reading Capital*. Trans. Ben Brewster. London: Verso, 1970.
Anderson, Warwick. *Colonial Pathologies: American Tropical Medicine, Race, and Hygiene in the Philippines*. Durham: Duke University Press, 2006.
Anzaldúa, Gloria. *La Frontera/Borderlands: The New Mestiza*. 2nd edition. San Francisco: Aunt Lute Books, 1999.
Appadurai, Arjun. *Fear of Small Numbers: An Essay on the Geography of Anger*. Durham: Duke University Press, 2006.
Aquino-Moreschi, Alejandra. "De la indignación moral a las protestas colectivas: La participación de los migrantes zapotecos en las marchas de migrantes de 2006." *Norteamérica* 5.1 (2010): 63–90.
Arendt, Hannah. *The Origins of Totalitarianism*. Orlando, FL: Harcourt, Brace, Jovanovich, 1968.
———. *The Origins of Totalitarianism*. 1951. New York: Houghton Mifflin Harcourt, 1994.
Arnold, Matthew. "The Function of Criticism in the Present Time." In *Lectures and Essays in Criticism*, ed. R. H. Super, 258–85. Ann Arbor: University of Michigan Press, 1962.
Auerbach, Erich. *Mimesis: The Representation of Reality in Western Literature*. Princeton: Princeton University Press, 2003.
Avelar, Idelber. *The Untimely Present: Postdictatorial Latin American Fiction and the Task of Mourning*. Durham: Duke University Press, 1999.
Baier, Dirk, et al. *Kinder und Jugendliche in Deutschland: Gewalterfahrungen, Integration, Medienkonsum. Zweiter Bericht zum gemeinsamen Forschungsprojekt des Bundesministeriums des Inneren und des KFN*. Hanover: Criminological Research Institute Niedersachen, 2010.
Balagoon, Kuwasi. *A Soldier's Story*. Montreal: Solidarity, 2002.
_______. "The Continuing Appeal of Anti-Imperialism." Prison News Service #49 (1985) http://theanarchistlibrary.org/library/kuwasi-balagoon-the-continuing-appeal-of-anti-imperialism

Balibar, Étienne. *Strangers as Enemies: Further Reflections on the Aporias of Transnational Citizenship*. McMaster University, Hamilton, Ontario, Canada. MCRI Globalization and Autonomy, 2006.

Bambach, Charles. *Heidegger's Roots: Nietzsche, National Socialism, and the Greeks*. Ithaca: Cornell University Press, 2003.

Barrera, Mario. *Race and Class in the Southwest: A Theory of Racial Inequality*. Notre Dame, IN: University of Notre Dame Press, 1979.

Barskanmaz, Cengiz. "Rasse—Unwort des Antidiskriminierungsrechts?" *Kritische Justiz* 4 (2011): 382–89.

Basler, Carleen. "White Dreams and Red Votes: Mexican Americans and the Lure of Inclusion in the Republican Party." *Ethnic and Racial Studies* 31.1 (2008): 123–66.

Bassichis, Morgan, and Dean Spade. "Queer Politics and Antiblackness." In *Queer Necropolitics*, ed. Jin Haritaworn, Adi Kuntsman, and Silvia Posocco, 191–210. London: Routledge, 2014.

Bayoumi, Moustafa. *This Muslim American Life: Dispatches from the War on Terror.* New York: New York University Press, 2015.

Behnken, Brian. "Elusive Unity: African Americans, Mexican Americans, and Civil Rights in Houston." In *Seeking Inalienable Rights: Texans and Their Quest for Justice*, ed. Debra Reid, 123–75. College Station: Texas A&M Press, 2009.

———. *Fighting Their Own Battles: Mexican Americans, African Americans and the Struggle for Civil Rights in Texas.* Chapel Hill: University of North Carolina Press, 2011.

Bell, Derrick. "Racial Realism." In *Critical Race Theory: The Key Writings That Formed the Movement*, ed. Kimberle Crenshaw, Neil Gotanda, Gary Peller, and Kendall Thomas, 302–12. New York: New Press, 1996.

Benjamin, Walter. *Illuminations: Essays and Reflections*. Ed. Hannah Arendt. Trans. Harry Zohn. New York: Schocken Books, 2007.

Ben-Moshe, Liat. "Resistance to Incarceration: The Intersections of Prison Abolition, Anti-Psychiatry and Deinstitutionalization" Paper presented at the PsychOut Conference, University of Toronto, May 7–8, 2010.

Benveniste, Émile. "Gift and Exchange in the Indo-European Vocabulary." In *The Logic of the Gift: Toward an Ethic of Generosity*, ed. Alan D. Schrift, 33–42. New York: Routledge, 1997.

Ben-Zohar, Michael. *Ben-Gurion: A Biography*. New York: Delacorte Press, 1978.

Berger, Dan. *Captive Nation: Black Prison Organizing in the Civil Rights Era*. Chapel Hill: University of North Carolina Press, 2014.

———. "Social Movements and Mass Incarceration: What Is to Be Done?" *Souls* 15.1 (2013): 3–18.

Berlant, Lauren. "On the Case." *Critical Inquiry* 33.4 (2007): 663–72.

Berlin, Ira. *The Making of African America: The Four Great Migrations*. New York: Penguin, 2010.

Berman, Tressa Lynn. *Circle of Goods: Women, Work, and Welfare in a Reservation Community*. Albany: State University of New York Press, 2003.

Bernstein, Shana. *Bridges of Reform: Interracial Civil Rights Activism in Twentieth Century Los Angeles*. New York: Oxford University Press, 2011.

Bevington, Douglas, and Chris Dixon. "Movement-Relevant Theory: Rethinking Social Movement Scholarship and Activism." *Social Movement Studies* 4.3 (2005): 185–208.

Bhabha, Homi K. *The Location of Culture.* New York: Routledge, 1990.

Bilal, Wafaa, and Kari Lydersen. *Shoot an Iraqi: Art, Life and Resistance under the Gun.* San Francisco: City Lights, 2008.

Biondi, Martha. *The Black Revolution on Campus.* Berkeley: University of California Press, 2012.

Birzeit University. *Right to Education Bulletin* 1, July 31, 2004. Accessed February 12, 2015. http://www.miftah.org/Display.cfm?DocId=4407&CategoryId=8.

———. Right to Education Campaign. Accessed February 12, 2015. http://right2edu.birzeit.edu/.

Blanco, John D. "Race as Praxis in the Philippines at the Turn of the Twentieth Century." *Southeast Asian Studies* 49.3 (2011): 356–94.

Blanton, Carlos. "George I. Sánchez, Ideology and Whiteness in the Making of the Mexican American Civil Rights Movement, 1930–1960." *Journal of Southern History* 72.3 (2006): 569–604.

Blauner, Robert. *Racial Oppression in America.* New York: Harper and Row, 1972.

Bonczar, Thomas. "Prevalence of Imprisonment in the U.S. Population, 1974–2001." Bureau of Justice Statistics Special Report, August 2003. Accessed June 19, 2015. http://www.bjs.gov/content/pub/pdf/piusp01.pdf.

Bonilla-Silva, Eduardo. "From Bi-racial to Tri-racial: Towards a New System of Racial Stratification in the USA." *Ethnic and Racial Studies* 27.6 (2004): 931–50.

Born, Georgina, and David Hesmondahalgh, eds. *Western Music and Its Others: Difference, Representation, and Appropriation in Music.* Berkeley: University of California Press, 2000.

Bourdieu, Pierre. "The Forms of Capital." In *The Sociology of Economic Life,* ed. M. Granovetter and R. Swedberg, 96–111. 2nd edition. Boulder, CO: Westview Press, 2001.

Bourg, Julian. *From Revolution to Ethics: May 1968 and Contemporary French Thought.* Montreal: McGill-Queen's University Press, 2007.

Boyce Davies, Carole, and Elaine Savory, eds. *Out of the Kumbla: Caribbean Women and Literature.* Trenton, NJ: Africa World Press, 1990.

Brandt, Carol B. "Protocols and Performances: Scientific Discourses in the Molecular Biology Laboratory." In *Structure and Agency in the Neoliberal University,* ed. Joyce E. Canaan and Wesley Shumar, 153–71. New York: Routledge, 2008.

Braun, Bruce. *The Intemperate Rainforest: Nature, Culture, and Power on Canada's West Coast.* Minneapolis: University of Minnesota Press, 2002.

Brayboy, Bryan McKinley Jones, Angelina E. Castagno, and Emma Maughan. "Indigenous Epistemologies and the Neoliberal View of Higher Education." In *Structure and Agency in the Neoliberal University,* ed. Joyce E. Canaan and Wesley Shumar, 172–92. New York: Routledge, 2008.

Breggin, Peter. "Campaigns against Racist Federal Programs by the Center for the Study of Psychiatry and Psychology." *Journal of African American Studies* 1.3 (1995): 3–22.

Breitman, George, ed. *Malcolm X Speaks: Selected Speeches and Statements*. New York: Grove Press, 1994.

Brennan, Timothy. *Wars of Position: The Cultural Politics of Left and Right*. New York: Columbia University Press, 2006.

Briggs, Laura. *Reproducing Empire: Race, Sex, Science, and U.S. Imperialism in Puerto Rico*. Berkeley: University of California Press, 2002.

Broude, Norma, and Mary D. Garrard. "Introduction: Feminism and Art in the Twentieth Century." In *The Power of Feminist Art: The American Movement of the 1970s. History and Impact*, ed. Norma Broude and Mary D. Garrard, 10–29. New York: Harry Abrams, 1994.

Brown, Michelle. "'Setting the Conditions' for Abu Ghraib: The Prison Nation Abroad." *American Quarterly* 57.3 (2005): 973–97.

Brown, Nikki L. M., and Barry M. Stentiford, eds. *The Jim Crow Encyclopedia*. Westport, CT: Greenwood Press, 2008.

Brown, Wendy. *States of Injury: Power and Freedom in Late Modernity*. Princeton: Princeton University Press, 1995.

———. *Walled States, Waning Sovereignty*. New York: Zone Press, 2010.

———. "Wounded Attachments." *Political Theory* 21.3 (1993): 390–410.

Bryant, Karl, and Salvador Vidal-Ortiz. "Introduction to Retheorizing Homophobias." *Sexualities* 11.4 (2008): 387–96.

Buckley, R. Philip. *Husserl, Heidegger and the Crisis of Philosophical Responsibility*. Dordrecht: Kluwer Academic, 1992.

Buffington, Robert M. *Criminal and Citizen in Modern Mexico*. Lincoln: University of Nebraska Press, 2000.

Bukhari, Safiya. *The War Before: The True Life Story of Becoming a Black Panther, Keeping the Faith in Prison and Fighting for Those Left Behind*. New York: Free Press, 2010.

Bush, George H. W. "Remarks at the University of Michigan Commencement Ceremony in Ann Arbor." American Presidency Project, May 4, 1991. Accessed June 22, 2015. http://www.presidency.ucsb.edu/ws/?pid=19546.

Butler, Judith. "Critically Queer." In *Performance Studies*, ed. Erin Striff. New York: Palgrave Macmillan, 2003.

———. "Endangered/Endangering: Schematic Racism and White Paranoia." In *Reading Rodney King / Reading Urban Uprising*, ed. Robert Gooding-Williams, 15–22. New York: Routledge, 1993.

———. *Frames of War: When Is Life Grievable?* London: Verso, 2009.

———. *Gender Trouble*. New York: Routledge, 1990.

———. *Undoing Gender*. New York: Routledge, 2004.

Butler, Octavia. *Mind of My Mind*. New York: Warner, 1977.

Byrd, Jodi. *The Transit of Empire: Indigenous Critiques of Colonialism*. Minneapolis: University of Minnesota Press, 2011.

Cacho, Lisa. *Social Death: Racialized Rightlessness and the Criminalization of the Unprotected*. New York: New York University Press, 2012.

Canaan, Joyce E., and Wesley Shumar, eds. *Structure and Agency in the Neoliberal University*. New York: Routledge, 2008.

Canclini, Néstor García. *Hybrid Cultures*. Minneapolis: University of Minnesota Press, 1990.
Candido, Luciana. "O Haiti é Aqui, no Complexo do Alemão." *Partido Socialista dos Trabalhadores Unificado*, June 29, 2007. Accessed February 20, 2012. http://www.pstu.org.br/nacional_materia.asp?id=6995&ida=40.
Cannell, Fennella. *Power and Intimacy in the Christian Philippines*. Cambridge: Cambridge University Press, 1999.
Carbado, Devon, and Cheryl Harris. "The New Racial Preferences." *California Law Review* 96.5 (2008): 1139–214.
Carby, Hazel. "It Jus Be's Dat Way Sometime: The Sexual Politics of Women's Blues." *Radical America* 20.4 (1986): 9–22.
Carson, E. Ann, and W. J. Sabol. "Prisoners in 2011." U.S. Department of Justice, Bulletin December 2012. http://www.bjs.gov/content/pub/pdf/p11.pdf.
Castells, Manuel. "The University System: Engine of Development in the New World Economy." In *Revitalizing Higher Education*, ed. Jamil Salmi and Adriaan M. Vespoor, 14–40. Oxford: Pergamon Press, 1994.
Castells, Manuel, and Peter Hall. *Technopoles of the World: Making of Twenty-First-Century Industrial Complexes*. New York: Routledge, 1994.
Cato. "Coming to America: The Weaponization of Immigration." *Washburn Law Journal* 46 (2007): 309–33. Accessed November 12, 2010. http://contentdm.washburnlaw.edu/cdm/ref/collection/wlj/id/5590.
Césaire, Aimé. "Culture et colonisation." In *"Lire" . . . le* Discours sur le colonialisme *d'Aimé Césaire*, by Georges Ngal, 107–21. Paris: Présence Africaine, 1994.
———. "Débat (extraits)." In *"Lire" . . . le* Discours sur le colonialisme *d'Aimé Césaire*, by Georges Ngal, 122–34. Paris: Présence Africaine, 1994.
———. *Discourse on Colonialism*. Trans. Joan Pinkham. New York: Monthly Review Press, 1972.
Chakrabarty, Dipesh. "Belatedness as Possibility: Subaltern Histories, Once More." In *The Indian Postcolonial: A Critical Reader*, ed. Elleke Boehmer and Rosinka Chaudhuri, 163–76. London: Routledge, 2011.
———. *Provincializing Europe: Postcolonial Thought and Historical Difference*. Princeton: Princeton University Press, 2007.
Chambers, John Whiteclay, ed. *Oxford Guide to American Military History*. Oxford: Oxford University Press, 2000.
Chan, Wendy, Dorothy Chunn, and Robert Menzies. *Women, Madness and the Law: A Feminist Reader*. London: Glass House, 2005.
Chandler, Nahum D. "Originary Displacement." *boundary 2* 27.3 (2000): 249–86.
Chang, Robert S. "A Meditation on Borders." In *Immigrants Out! The New Nativism and the Anti-Immigrant Impulse in the United States*, ed. Juan F Perea, 244–53. New York: New York University Press, 1997.
Chappell, Ben. "Rehearsals of the Sovereign: States of Exception and Threat Governmentality." *Cultural Dynamics* 18.3 (2006): 313–34.
Chatterjee, Piya, and Sunaina Maira, eds. *The Imperial University: Academic Repression and Scholarly Dissent*. Minneapolis: University of Minnesota Press, 2014.

Chaudhry, Kiren Aziz. "Dis(re)membering \Pä-ki-ˈstän\." *Informed Comment*, April 30, 2010. http://www.juancole.com/2010/04/chaudhry-disremembering-pa-ki-%CB%88stan.html.

Chavez, Leo R. *The Latino Threat Narrative: Constructing Immigrants, Citizens, and the Nation*. Stanford: Stanford University Press, 2008.

Chen, Jeremy. "The Spy Who Shanghaied Me." *Hardboiled: The Asian American Newsmagazine!* 9.2 (2005): 3.

Chen, Kuan-Hsing. *Asia as Method: Toward Deimperialization*. Durham: Duke University Press, 2010.

Choudry, Aziz, and Dip Kapoor, eds. *Learning from the Ground Up: Global Perspectives on Social Movements and Knowledge Production*. New York: Palgrave Macmillan, 2010.

Chow, Rey. *The Age of the World Target: Self-Referentiality in War, Theory, and Comparative Work*. Durham: Duke University Press, 2006.

———. *The Protestant Ethnic and the Spirit of Capitalism*. New York: Columbia University Press, 2002.

Christian, Barbara. "The Race for Theory." *Cultural Critique* 6 (1987): 51–63.

Christie, Nils. *Crime Control as Industry: Towards Gulags, Western Style*. 3rd edition. New York: Routledge, 2000.

Chu, Richard. *Chinese and Chinese Mestizos of Manila: Family, Identity, and Culture, 1860s–1930s*. Leiden: Brill, 2010.

Chuh, Kandice. *Imagine Otherwise: On Asian Americanist Critique*. Durham: Duke University Press, 2003.

Churchill, Ward, and Jim Vander Wall. *Agents of Repression: The FBI's Secret Wars against the Black Panther Party and the American Indian Movement*. Boston: South End Press, 2001.

Ciccariello Maher, George. "Beyond the Debate on Humanism: Césaire, Fanon, and the Limits of the European Gaze." *Radical Philosophy Review* 9.2 (2006): 139–65.

Clark, Elizabeth B. "'The Sacred Rights of the Weak': Pain, Sympathy, and the Culture of Individual Rights in Antebellum America." *Journal of American History* 82.2 (1995): 463–93.

Clifford, James. *Routes: Travel and Translation in the Late Twentieth Century*. Cambridge: Harvard University Press, 1997.

Cohen, Cathy. "Death and Rebirth of a Movement: Queering Critical Ethnic Studies." *Social Justice* 37.4 (2010–11): 126–32.

———. "Punks, Bulldaggers and Welfare Queens: The Radical Potential of Queer Politics?" *GLQ: A Journal of Lesbian and Gay Studies* 3.4 (1997): 437–65.

Comay, Rebecca. *Mourning Sickness: Hegel and the French Revolution*. Stanford: Stanford University Press, 2011.

Combahee River Collective. "A Black Feminist Statement." In *This Bridge Called My Back: Writings by Radical Women of Color*, ed. Cherríe Moraga and Gloria Anzaldúa, 210–18. 2nd edition. New York: Kitchen Table, Women of Color Press, 1983.

Conrad, Ryan, ed. *Against Equality: Prisons Will Not Protect You*. Lewiston, ME: Against Equality Publishing Collective, 2012.

Constantino, Renato. "The Miseducation of the Filipino." In *Sinaglahi: An Anthology of Philippine Literature*, ed. M. L. Santaromana, 210–19. Quezon City: Writers Union of the Philippines, 1975.
———. *The Philippines: A Past Revisited*. Vol. 1. Manila: Renato Constantino, 1975.
Coulthard, Glen. Keynote speech at Critical Ethnic Studies and the Future of Genocide, University of Riverside, Riverside, California, March 10–12, 2011.
———. "Subjects of Empire: Indigenous Peoples and the 'Politics of Recognition' in Canada." *Contemporary Political Theory* 6.4 (2007): 437–60.
Crandell, Gina. *Nature Pictorialized: "The View" in Landscape History*. Baltimore: Johns Hopkins University Press, 1993.
Crispus Attucks Brigade. "The Mission of the Crispus Attucks Brigade." Accessed September 20, 2012. http://tedhayes.us/uscab/.
Critical Ethnic Studies Association. "Mission and Vision." Accessed June 3, 2015. https://www.criticalethnicstudies.org/content/mission-vision.
Critical Resistance Oakland. *Annual Report*. 2011. Accessed January 1, 2015. http://crwp.live.radicaldesigns.org/wp-content/uploads/2012/03/CR-Annual-Report-2011-final.pdf.
Dalby, Simon. "The Pentagon's New Imperial Cartography: Tabloid Realism and the War on Terror." In *Violent Geographies: Fear, Terror and Political Violence*, ed. Derek Gregory and Allan Pred, 295–308. New York: Routledge, 2007.
Das Gupta, Tania. "Teaching Anti-Racist Research in the Academy." *Teaching Sociology* 31.4 (2003): 456–68.
da Silva, Denise Ferreira. "No Bodies: Law, Raciality and Violence." *Griffith Law Review* 18.2 (2009): 212–36.
———. *Toward a Global Idea of Race*. Minneapolis: University of Minnesota Press, 2007.
Davis, Angela. *Are Prisons Obsolete?* New York: Seven Stories Press, 2003.
Davis, Angela, and Dylan Rodriguez. "The Challenge of Prison Abolition: A Conversation." *Social Justice* 27.3 (2000): 212–18.
Decolonize Queer. "From Gay Pride to White Pride? Why It Is Racist to March on the East End." Decolonizing Sexualities Network, March 15, 2011. Accessed May 17, 2013. http://www.decolonizingsexualities.org/decolonize-queer/.
De Landa, Manuel. *A New Philosophy of Society: Assemblage Theory and Social Complexity*. New York: Continuum International, 2006.
De Leon, Arnoldo. *They Called Them Greasers: Anglo Attitudes towards Mexicans in Texas*. Austin: University of Texas Press, 1983.
Deleuze, Gilles, and Félix Guattari. *Anti-Oedipus: Capitalism and Schizophrenia*. Trans. Brian Massumi. Minneapolis: University of Minnesota Press, 1983.
———. *A Thousand Plateaus: Capitalism and Schizophrenia*. Minneapolis: University of Minnesota Press, 1987.
Denetdale, Jennifer. "Securing Navajo National Boundaries: War, Patriotism, Tradition, and the Diné Marriage Act of 2005." *Wicazo Sa Review* 24.2 (2009): 131–48.
Descartes, René. *Discourse on Method and Meditations on First Philosophy*. Ed. David Weissman. New Haven: Yale University Press, 1996.

Diaz, Vicente M., and J. Kēhaulani Kauanui. "Native Pacific Cultural Studies on the Edge." *Contemporary Pacific* 13.2 (2001): 315–42.
Dinshaw, Carolyn. *Getting Medieval: Sexualities and Communities, Pre- and Post-Modern.* Durham: Duke University Press, 1999.
Dissidentenfunk. "Massregelvollzug/Forensische Psychiatrie." January 13, 2005. Accessed January 1, 2014. http://www.dissidentenfunk.de/archiv/s0501/index.html.
Dixon, Chris. *Another Politics: Talking across Today's Transformative Movements.* Berkeley: University of California Press, 2014.
Doherty, Caroll. "Attitudes towards Immigration: In Black and White." Pew Research Center, April 25, 2006. http://www.pewresearch.org/2006/04/25/attitudes-toward-immigration-in-black-and-white/.
Dowling, Julie. *Mexican Americans and the Question of Race.* Austin: University of Texas Press, 2014.
Drinnon, Richard. *Facing West: The Metaphysics of Indian-Hating and Empire-Building.* Minneapolis: University of Minnesota Press, 1980.
Driskill, Qwo-Li. "Doubleweaving Two-Spirit Critiques: Building Alliances between Native and Queer Studies." *GLQ: A Journal of Lesbian and Gay Studies* 16.1–2 (2010): 69–92.
Du Bois, W. E. B. *Black Reconstruction in America, 1860–1880.* 1935; New York: Free Press, 1995.
———. *The Souls of Black Folk.* New York: New American Library, 1969.
———. *The Souls of Black Folk.* Harmondsworth, UK: Penguin, 1989.
Duggan, Lisa. *The Twilight of Equality: Neoliberalism, Cultural Politics and the Attack on Democracy.* Boston: Beacon Press, 2004.
Durpaire, François. *France Blanche, Colere Noire.* Paris: Odile Jacob, 2006.
Dussel, Enrique. "The Caribbean Origin of Modern Philosophy: The Right to the Expansion of Christendom. Ginés de Sepúlveda and Bartolomé de las Casas." Paper presented at the second annual Meeting of the Caribbean Philosophical Association, San Juan, Puerto Rico, 2005.
———. *Etica de la liberación en la edad de la globalización y de la exclusión.* Madrid: Editorial Trotta, 1998.
———. *The Invention of the Americas: Eclipse of "the Other" and the Myth of Modernity.* Trans. Michael D. Barber. New York: Continuum, 1995.
———. "Modernity, Eurocentrism, and Trans-Modernity: In Dialogue with Charles Taylor." In *The Underside of Modernity: Apel, Ricoeur, Rorty, Taylor, and the Philosophy of Liberation,* ed. and trans. Eduardo Mendieta, 129–59. Atlantic Highlands, NJ: Humanities Press, 1996.
———. *Philosophy of Liberation.* Trans. Aquilina Martinez and Christine Morkovsky. Maryknoll, NY: Orbis Books, 1985.
———. *Posmodernidad y transmodernidad: Diálogos con la filosofía de Gianni Vattimo.* Puebla, Mexico: Universidad Iberoamericana, Golfo Centro; Instituto Tecnológico y de Estudios Superiores de Occidente; Universidad Iberoamericana, Plantel Laguna, 1999.
———. "World System and 'Trans'-Modernity." *Nepantla: Views from South* 3.2 (2002): 221–44.

———. "The 'World-System': Europe as 'Center' and its 'Periphery' beyond Eurocentrism." In *Beyond Philosophy: Ethics, History, Marxism, and Liberation Theology*, ed. and trans. Eduardo Mendieta, 53–84. Lanham, MD: Rowman and Littlefield, 2003.

Elden, Stuart. *Terror and Territory: The Spatial Extent of Sovereignty*. Minneapolis: University of Minnesota Press, 2009.

Elia, Nada. 2012. "The Brain of the Monster." In *The Case for Sanctions on Israel*, ed. Audrea Lim, 51–60. New York: Verso Books.

El-Tayeb, Fatima. "Begrenzte Horizonte: Queer Identity in der Festung Europa." In *Spricht die Subalterne deutsch? Migration und postkoloniale Kritik*, ed. Hito Steyerl and Encarnación Gutiérrez Rodriguez, 129–45. Münster: Unrast, 2003.

———. *European Others: Queering Ethnicity in Postnational Europe*. Minneapolis: University of Minnesota Press, 2011.

Engelhardt, Tom. *The American Way of War: How Bush's Wars Became Obama's*. Chicago: Haymarket, 2010.

English, T. J. *Savage City: Race, Murder, and a Generation on the Edge*. New York: William Morrow, 2011.

Escobar, Arturo. "Latin America at a Crossroads: Between Alternative Modernizations, Postliberalism, and Postdevelopment." Lecture at the Center for Latin American and Caribbean Studies, New York University, October 29, 2009.

Esmeir, Samera. *Juridical Humanity: A Colonial History*. Stanford: Stanford University Press, 2012.

Espiritu, Yen Le. *Asian American Panethnicity: Bridging Institutions and Identities*. Philadelphia: Temple University Press, 1992.

Faier, Lieba. *Intimate Economies: Filipina Women and the Remaking of Rural Japan*. Berkeley: University of California Press, 2009.

Faist, Thomas. "*Extension du domaine de la lutte*: International Migration and Security before and after 11 September 2001." *International Migration Review* 36.1 (2002): 7–14.

Fanon, Frantz. *Black Skin, White Masks*. 1952. Trans. Charles Lam Markmann. New York: Grove Press, 1968.

———. "Racism and Culture." In *Toward the African Revolution: Political Essays*. Trans. Haakon Chevalier, 29–44. New York: Grove Press, 1988.

———. *The Wretched of the Earth*. Trans. Constance Farrington. New York: Grove Press, 1991.

Farish, Matthew. *The Contours of America's Cold War*. Minneapolis: University of Minnesota Press, 2010.

Farley, Najah. "Alabama Immigration Law and a Modern-Day Civil Rights Movement." *Harvard Law and Policy Review*, November 16, 2011.

Farmer, Paul. *Pathologies of Power: Health, Human Rights and the New War on the Poor*. Berkeley: University of California Press, 2003.

Fassin, Didier. "Policing Borders, Producing Boundaries: The Governmentality of Immigration in Dark Times." *Annual Review of Anthropology* 40 (2011): 213–26.

Favela em Foco. "Assassinato na Favela do Jacarezinho." April 5, 2013. Accessed May 1, 2013. http://favelaemfoco.wordpress.com/2013/04/05/assassinato-na-favela-do-jacarezinho/.

Feldman, Allen. "Securocratic Wars of Public Safety." *Interventions: International Journal of Postcolonial Studies* 6.3 (2004): 330–50.
———. "The Structuring Enemy and Archival War." PMLA 124.5 (2009): 1704–13.
Ferguson, Kathy, and Phyllis Turnbull. *Oh Say Can You See? The Semiotics of the Military in Hawai'i*. Minneapolis: University of Minnesota Press, 1999.
Ferguson, Roderick. *Aberrations in Black: Toward a Queer of Color Critique*. Minneapolis: University of Minnesota Press, 2003.
———. *The Reorder of Things: The University and Its Pedagogies of Minority Difference*. Minneapolis: University of Minnesota Press, 2012.
Fischer, Sibylle. *Modernity Disavowed: Haiti and the Cultures of Slavery in the Age of Revolution*. Durham: Duke University Press, 2004.
Flatley, Jonathan. *Affective Mapping: Melancholia and the Politics of Modernism*. Cambridge: Harvard University Press, 2008.
Flynn, Michael. "¿Dónde Está La Frontera?" *Bulletin of the Atomic Scientists*, July/August 2002, 25–35.
Foley, Neil. "Partly Colored or Other White: Mexican Americans and Their Problems with Color Line." In *Beyond Black and White: Race, Ethnicity, and Gender in the U.S. South and Southwest*, ed. Stephanie Cole and Alison Parker, 123–44. College Station: Texas A&M Press, 2004.
Fortun, Kim. *Advocacy after Bhopal: Environmentalism, Disaster, New Global Orders*. Chicago: University of Chicago Press, 2001.
Foucault, Michel. "About the Concept of the 'Dangerous Individual' in Nineteenth-Century Legal Psychiatry." *International Journal of Law and Psychiatry* 1 (1978): 1–18.
———. *The Birth of Biopolitics: Lectures at the Collège de France 1978–1979*. 1978. London: Palgrave, 2004.
———. *Discipline and Punish: The Birth of the Prison*. New York: Vintage Books, 1995.
———. *The History of Sexuality*. New York: Vintage, 1990.
———. *The Order of Things: An Archaeology of the Human Sciences*. Trans. Alan Sheridan. New York: Vintage, 1970.
———. *Power/Knowledge: Selected Interviews and Other Writings, 1972–1977*. New York: Pantheon, 1980.
———. *Society Must Be Defended: Lectures at the Collège De France, 1975–76*. New York: Picador USA, 2003.
———. "The Subject and Power." In *Michel Foucault: Beyond Structuralism and Hermeneutics*, ed. Hubert L Dreyfus and Paul Rabinow, 208–28. Chicago: University of Chicago Press, 1982.
Frazier, Robeson Taj. "The Congress of African People: Baraka, Brother Mao, and the Year of '74." SOULS: *A Critical Journal of Black Politics, Culture, and Society* 8.3 (2006): 142–59.
Fresh Meat Productions. "Fresh Meat in the Gallery VI: Defying Gravities." Accessed December 27, 2014. http://freshmeatproductions.org/fresh-meat-in-the-gallery-vi-defying-gravities/.
Freud, Sigmund. "Mourning and Melancholia." In *The Standard Edition of the Complete Psychological Works of Sigmund Freud*, ed. James Strachey, 243–58. London: Hogarth Press, 1957.

Friedman, Debra, and Doug McAdam. "Collective Identity and Activism: Networks, Choices, and the Life of a Social Movement." In *Frontiers in Social Movement Theory*, ed. Aldon D. Morris and Carol McClurg Mueller, 156–73. New Haven: Yale University Press, 1992.

Gamio, Manuel. *Forjando Patria (Pro Nacionalismo)*. Mexico City: Librería de Porrúa Hermanos, 1916.

———. "Observations on Mexican Immigration into the United States." *Pacific Affairs* 2.8 (1929): 463–69.

García, Alma M., ed. *Chicana Feminist Thought: The Basic Historical Writings*. New York: Routledge, 1997.

Garcia, Mario. "Border Proletariats: Mexican Americans and the International Union of Mine, Mill and Smelter Workers." In *Mexican Americans: Leadership, Ideology, and Identity, 1930–1960*, 175–98. New Haven: Yale University Press, 1989.

———. "Mexican American Radicals and the Cold War." In *Mexican Americans: Leadership, Ideology, and Identity, 1930–1960*, 199–227. New Haven: Yale University Press, 1989.

Garland-Thomson, Rosemary. "Integrating Disability, Transforming Feminist Theory." *NWSA Journal* 14.3 (2002): 1–32.

Gates, Henry Louis. *Tradition and the Black Atlantic: Critical Theory in the African Diaspora*. New York: Basic Books, 2010.

Gee, Emma et al. *Counterpoint: Perspectives on Asian America*. Los Angeles: Asian American Studies Center, 1976.

Gibson, Barbara E. "Disability, Connectivity, and Transgressing the Autonomous Body." *Journal of Medical Humanities* 27.3 (2006): 187–96.

Gilmore, Ruth Wilson. "Fatal Couplings of Power and Difference: Notes on Racism and Geography." *Professional Geographer* 54.1 (2002): 15–24.

———. "Globalisation and US Prison Growth: From Military Keynesianism to Post-Keynesian Militarism," *Race & Class* 40.2–3 (1999): 171–88.

———. *Golden Gulag: Prisons, Surplus, Crisis, and Opposition in Globalizing California*. Berkeley: University of California Press, 2007.

Gilroy, Paul. *Between Camps: Nations, Cultures, and the Allure of Race*. London: Allen Lane, Penguin Press, 2000.

———. *The Black Atlantic: Modernity and Double Consciousness*. Cambridge: Harvard University Press, 1993.

———. "British Cultural Studies and the Pitfalls of Identity." In *Cultural Studies and Communications*, ed. J. Curran, D. Morley, and V. Walkerdine, 34. London: Arnold, 1996.

———. *Postcolonial Melancholia*. New York: Columbia University Press, 2005.

Gitlin, Todd. *The Twilight of Common Dreams: Why America Is Wracked by Culture Wars*. New York: Holt, 1995.

Golash-Boza, Tanya, and William Darrity. "Latino Racial Choices: The Effects of Skin Colour and Discrimination on Latinos' and Latinas' Racial Self-Identifications." *Ethnic and Racial Studies* 31.5 (2007): 899–934.

Goldberg, David Theo. *The Racial State*. Malden, MA: Blackwell, 2002.

———. *The Threat of Race: Reflections on Racial Neoliberalism.* Malden, MA: Wiley-Blackwell, 2008.

Gomez, Laura. *Manifest Destinies: The Making of the Mexican American Race.* New York: New York University Press, 2007.

Gómez-Barris, Macarena, and Herman Gray, eds. *Toward a Sociology of the Trace.* Minneapolis: University of Minnesota Press, 2010.

Gonzales-Day, Ken. *Erased Lynching.* Accessed January 25, 2016. http://www.kengonzalesday.com/projects/erasedlynching/index.htm.

———. *Lynching in the West, 1850–1935.* Durham: Duke University Press, 2006.

Goodley, Dan. "Becoming Rhizomatic Parents: Deleuze, Guattari, and Disabled Babies." *Disability and Society* 22.2 (2007): 207–31.

Goodman, Steve. *Sonic Warfare: Sound, Affect, and the Ecology of Fear.* Cambridge: MIT Press, 2009.

Gopinath, Gayatri. "Archive, Affect and the Everyday: Queer Diasporic Re-Visions." In *Political Emotions,* ed. Ann Cvetkovich et al., 165–92. New York: Routledge, 2010.

———. "Homo-Economics: Queer Sexualities in a Transnational Frame." In *Burning Down the House: Recycling Domesticity,* ed. Rosemary Marangoly George, 102–24. Boulder, CO: Westview Press, 1998.

———. *Impossible Desires: Queer Diasporas and South Asian Public Cultures.* Durham: Duke University Press, 2005.

Gordon, Avery F. "Methodologies of Imprisonment." *PMLA* 123.3 (2008): 651–58.

———. "The Prisoner's Curse." In *Toward a Sociology of the Trace,* ed. Macarena Gómez-Barris and Herman Gray, 17–56. Minneapolis: University of Minnesota Press, 2010.

Gordon, Lewis R. *Bad Faith and Antiblack Racism.* Atlantic Highlands, NJ: Humanities Press, 1995.

———. "Context: Ruminations on Violence and Anonymity." In *Her Majesty's Other Children: Sketches of Racism from a Neocolonial Age,* 13–23. Lanham, MD: Rowman and Littlefield, 1997.

———. "Existential Dynamics of Theorizing Black Invisibility." In *Existence in Black: An Anthology of Black Existential Philosophy,* ed. Lewis R. Gordon, 68–80. New York: Routledge, 1997.

———. *Fanon and the Crisis of European Man: An Essay on Philosophy and the Human Sciences.* New York: Routledge, 1995.

———. "Shifting the Geography of Reason in an Age of Disciplinary Decadence." Paper presented at Mapping the Decolonial Turn: Post/Trans-Continental Interventions in Philosophy, Theory, and Critique, at University of California, Berkeley, April 21, 2005.

Gordon, Lewis R., and Jane Anna Gordon, eds. *Not Only the Master's Tools: Theoretical Explorations in African American Studies.* Boulder, CO: Paradigm Press, 2005.

Gorman, Rachel. "Mad Nation? Thinking through Race, Class, and Mad Identity Politics." in *Mad Matters: A Critical Reader in Canadian Mad Studies,* ed. Brenda LeFrançois, Robert Menzies, and Geoffrey Reaume, 269–80. Toronto: Canadian Scholars Press, 2013.

Graeber, David, and Steven Shukaitis, eds. *Constituent Imagination.* Oakland, CA: AK Press 2007.

Graham, Stephen. *Cities Under Siege: The New Military Urbanism.* London: Verso, 2010.
Greenberg, Amy. *Manifest Manhood and the Antebellum American Empire.* Cambridge: Cambridge University Press 2005.
Gregory, Derek. *The Colonial Present: Afghanistan, Palestine, and Iraq.* Malden, MA: Blackwell, 2004.
———. "The Everywhere War." *Geographical Journal* 177.3 (2011): 238–50.
———. "From a View to a Kill: Drones and Late Modern War." *Theory, Culture & Society* 28.7–8 (2011): 188–215.
———. "Rush to the Intimate: Counterinsurgency and the Cultural Turn." *Radical Philosophy* 150 (2008): 8–23.
Grosfoguel, Ramón. "The Divorce of Nationalist Discourses from the Puerto Rican People: A Sociohistorical Perspective." In *Puerto Rican Jam: Rethinking Colonialism and Nationalism,* ed. Frances Negrón-Muntaner and Ramón Grosfoguel, 57–76. Minneapolis: University of Minnesota Press, 1997.
Grosfoguel, Ramón, Nelson Maldonado-Torres, and José David Saldívar. "Latin@s and the 'Euro-American' Menace: The Decolonization of the US Empire in the 21st Century." In *Latin@s in the World-System,* ed. Ramón Grosfoguel, Nelson Maldonado-Torres, and José David Saldívar, 3–27. Boulder, CO: Paradigm Press, 2005.
Gross, Ariela. *What Blood Won't Tell: A History of Race on Trial in America.* Cambridge: Harvard University Press, 2008.
Grossberg, Lawrence. "On Postmodernism and Articulation: An Interview with Stuart Hall." In *Stuart Hall: Critical Dialogues in Cultural Studies,* ed. David Morhey and Kuan-Hsing Chen, 131–50. New York: Routledge, 1996.
Guglielmo, Thomas. "Fighting for Caucasian Rights: Mexicans, Mexican Americans, and the Transnational Struggle for Civil Rights in World War II Texas." *Journal of American History* 92.4 (2006): 1212–37.
Guidotti-Hernández, Nicole M. *Unspeakable Violence: Remapping U.S. and Mexican National Imaginaries.* Durham: Duke University Press, 2011.
Gutierrez, David. *Walls and Mirrors: Mexican Americans, Mexican Immigrants, and the Politics of Ethnicity.* Berkeley: University of California Press, 1995.
Haakenson, Thomas. "Queers in Space: The Queer Art of Michael Elmgreen and Ingar Dragset." Paper presented at the Queer Futurities Symposium, Finland Institute, Berlin, May 18–19, 2009.
Habermas, Jürgen, and Jacques Derrida. "February 15, or What Binds Europeans Together: A Plea for a Common Foreign Policy, Beginning in the Core of Europe." *Constellations* 10.3 (2003): 291–97.
Hale, Charles R., ed., *Engaging Contradictions: Theory, Politics, and Methods of Activist Scholarship.* Berkeley: University of California Press, 2008.
Hall, Stuart. "New Ethnicities." In *"Race," Culture and Difference,* ed. James Donald and Ali Rattansi, 252–59. London: Sage, 1992.
———. "On Postmodernism and Articulation: An Interview with Stuart Hall." In *Stuart Hall: Critical Dialogues in Cultural Studies,* ed. David Morley and Kuan-Hsing Chen, 131–50. New York: Routledge, 1986.
———. "Race, Articulation, and Societies Structured in Dominance." In *Sociological Theories: Race and Colonialism,* 303–45. Paris: UNESCO, 1980.

———. "Signification, Representation, Ideology: Althusser and the Post-Structuralist Debates." *Critical Studies in Media Communication* 2.2 (1985): 91–114.

———. "Who Needs 'Identity'?" In *Questions of Cultural Identity*, ed. Paul Du Gay and Stuart Hall, 1–17. London: Sage, 1996.

Hall, Stuart, and Tony Jefferson. *Resistance through Rituals: Youth Subcultures in Post-War Britain*. London: HarperCollins Academic, 1991.

Halmi, Alice. "Kontinuitäten der Zwangspsychiatrie." Master's thesis, Freie Universität Berlin, 2008.

Hamzeh, Mona. *Refugees in Our Own Land: Chronicles from a Palestinian Refugee Camp in Bethlehem*. London: Pluto Press, 2001.

Haney-Lopez, Ian. *Racism on Trial: The Chicano Fight for Justice*. Cambridge: Harvard University Press, 2003.

Hanhardt, Christina B. "Butterflies, Whistles, and Fists: Gay Safe Streets Patrols and the New Gay Ghetto, 1976–1981." *Radical History Review* 100 (2008): 61–85.

Hardt, Michael, and Antonio Negri. *Commonwealth*. Cambridge: Harvard University Press, 2010.

———. *Empire*. Cambridge: Harvard University Press, 2000.

———. *Multitude: War and Democracy in the Age of Empire*. New York: Penguin Books, 2004.

Haritaworn, Jin. "Colorful Bodies in the *Multikulti* Metropolis: Vitality, Victimology and Transgressive Citizenship in Berlin." in *Trans-Migrations: Bodies, Borders, and the (Geo)politics of Gender Trans-ing*, ed. T. Cotton, 11–31. New York: Routledge, 2011.

———. "Kiss-Ins, Demos, Drag: Sexuelle Spektakel von Kiez und Nation." In *Verqueerte Verhälnisse. Intersektionale, ökonomiekritische und strategische Interventionen*, ed. AG Queer Studies, 41–65. Hamburg: Männerschwarm, 2009.

———. *Queer Lovers and Hateful Others: Regenerating Violent Times and Places*. London: Pluto Press, 2015.

Haritaworn, Jin, Adi Kuntsman, and Silvia Posocco. Introduction to *Queer Necropolitics*, ed. Jin Haritaworn, Adi Kuntsman, and Silvia Posocco, 1–27. London: Routledge, 2014.

———. "Introduction: Murderous Inclusions." *International Feminist Journal of Politics* 15.4 (2013): 445–52.

Haritaworn, Jin, Adi Kuntsman, and Silvia Posocco, eds. *Queer Necropolitics*. London: Routledge, 2014.

Haritaworn, Jin, and Jennifer Petzen. "Invented Traditions, New Intimate Publics: Tracing the German 'Muslim Homophobia Discourse.'" In *Islam in Its International Context: Comparative Perspectives*, ed. Stephen Hutchings et al., 48–64. Cambridge, UK: Cambridge Scholars Press, 2011.

Haritaworn, Jin, and C. Riley Snorton, "Trans Necropolitics." In *Transgender Studies Reader*, vol. 2, ed. A. Aizura and S. Stryker, 66–76. New York: Routledge, 2013.

Haritaworn, Jin, and Alex Weheliye. "Ethnic Studies in Deutschland? Über die Grenzen und Potenziale der universitären Institutionalisierung von minorisierten Wissensformen." In *Geschlossene Gesellschaft*, ed. Noa Ha and Kien Ngi Ha. Berlin: Heinrich-Böll-Stiftung, forthcoming.

Harry Benjamin International Gender Dysphoria Association. "The Standards of Care for Gender Identity Disorders, Sixth Version." *International Journal of Transgenderism* 5.1 (2001).

Hartman, Sadiyya. *Lose Your Mother: A Journey along the Atlantic Slave Route*. London: Farrar, Straus and Giroux, 2008.

———. *Scenes of Subjection: Terror, Slavery and Self-Making in Nineteenth Century America*. New York: Oxford University Press, 1997.

Harvey, David. "Accumulation by Dispossession." In *The New Imperialism*, 137–82. Oxford: Oxford University Press, 2003.

———. *The New Imperialism*. Oxford: Oxford University Press, 2005.

———. *Spaces of Global Capitalism: Towards a Theory of Uneven Geographical Development*. New York: Verso, 2006.

Hau, Caroline S. "'Who Will Save Us from the Law?' The Criminal State and the Illegal Alien in Post-1986 Philippines." In *Figures of Criminality in Indonesia, the Philippines, and Colonial Vietnam*, ed. Vicente L. Rafael, 128–51. Ithaca: Southeast Asian Studies Program, Cornell University, 1999.

Haug, Sonja. *Jugendliche Migranten—Muslimische Jugendliche: Gewalttätigkeit und geschlechterspezifische Einstellungsmuster.* Berlin: Federal Ministry for Family, Seniors, Women and Youth, 2010.

Healey, Dorothy Ray, and Maurice Isserman. *California Red: A Life in the Communist Party*. Urbana: University of Illinois Press, 1993.

Heidegger, Martin. "'Only a God Can Save Us': *Der Spiegel*'s Interview with Martin Heidegger (1966)." In *The Heidegger Controversy: A Critical Reader*, ed. Richard Wolin, 91–116. Cambridge: MIT Press, 1993.

Heiner, Brady Thomas. "Foucault and the Black Panthers." *City* 11.3 (2007): 313–56.

Heisig, Kirsten. *Das Ende der Geduld: Konsequent gegen jugendliche Gewalttäter.* Munich: Herder, 2010.

Hennessy, Rosemarie. *Profit and Pleasure: Sexual Identities in Late Capitalism*. New York: Routledge, 2000.

Hernández, David M. "Undue Process: Racial Genealogies of Immigrant Detention." In *Constructing Boundaries / Crossing Borders: Race, Ethnicity and Immigration*, ed. Caroline B. Brettell, 59–86. Lanham, MD: Lexington Books, 2007.

Hernández, Kelly Lytle. "The Crimes and Consequences of Illegal Immigration: A Cross-Border Examination of Operation Wetback, 1943–1954." *Western Historical Quarterly* 37 (Winter 2006): 420–44.

Hiemstra, Nancy. "The U.S. and Ecuador: Is Intervention on the Table?" *NACLA Report on the Americas* 45.4 (2013): 20–24.

Hill, Rebecca N. *Men, Mobs, and the Law: Antilynching and Labor Defense in U.S. Radical History*. Durham: Duke University Press, 2008.

Ho, Engseng. "Empire through Diasporic Eyes: A View from the Other Boat," *Comparative Studies in Society and History*, Vol. 46, No. 2 (Apr., 2004): 210–246

Ho, Fred, and Bill V. Mullen, eds. *Afro-Asia: Revolutionary Political and Cultural Connections between African Americans and Asian Americans*. Durham: Duke University Press, 2008.

Hobsbawm, Eric. "Introduction: Inventing Traditions." In *The Invention of Tradition*, ed. Eric Hobsbawm and Terence Ranger, 1–14. Cambridge: Cambridge University Press, 1983.

Holland, Sharon Patricia. *Raising the Dead: Readings of Death and (Black) Subjectivity*. Durham: Duke University Press, 2000.

Hong, Grace. "Past Legacies, Future Projects: Asian Migration and the University." *Diaspora* 10.1 (2001): 117–27.

hooks, bell. *Killing Rage: Ending Racism*. London: Penguin, 1996.

Horsman, Reginald. *Race and Manifest Destiny: Origins of American Racial Anglo-Saxonism*. Cambridge: Harvard University Press, 1981.

HoSang, Daniel Martinez, Oneka LaBennett, and Laura Pulido, eds. *Racial Formation in the Twenty-First Century*. Berkeley: University of California Press, 2012.

Huck, Wolfgang. "Intensivtäter aus jugendpsychiatrischer Sicht." In *Jugendliche Intensivtäter: Interdisziplinare Perspektiven*, ed. Annette Boeger, 141–71. Wiesbaden: VS, 2011.

Human Rights Watch/Americas. *Police Brutality in Urban Brazil*. New York: Human Rights Watch, 1997.

Huntington, Samuel P. *Who Are We? The Challenges to America's National Identity*. New York: Simon and Schuster, 2004.

Husserl, Edmund. *Cartesian Meditations: An Introduction to Phenomenology*. Trans. Dorion Cairns. Dordrecht: Kluwer Academic, 1960.

Hutson, Christiane. "Unverschämt—Wir im Spannungsfeld von Rassismus, Hetero-/Sexismus und Ableism." Paper presented at Hamburg University, May 13, 2009.

Hutton, Will. *A Declaration of Interdependence: Why America Should Join the World*. New York: Norton, 2003.

Ignacio, Abe, Enrique de la Cruz, Jorge Emmanuel, and Helen Toribio. *The Forbidden Book: The Philippine-American War in Political Cartoons*. San Francisco: T'Boli, 2004.

Imada, Adria. "The Army Learns to Lūʻau: Imperial Hospitality and Military Photography in Hawaiʻi." *Contemporary Pacific* 20.2 (2008): 328–61.

———. "Hawaiians on Tour: Hula Circuits through the American Empire." *American Quarterly* 56.1 (2004): 111–49.

INCITE! Women of Color against Violence. "Critical Lessons from the New Jersey 7." *New Left Turn*, September 2008. Accessed August 1, 2014. http://www.incite-national.org/sites/default/files/incite_files/resource_docs/9908_toolkitrev-nj7.pdf.

———. *The Revolution Will Not Be Funded: Beyond the Nonprofit Industrial Complex*. Boston: South End Press, 2007.

Ioannou, Noris. "After the Art/Craft Debate: Critical Writing into the 1990s." *Artlink* 12.2 (1992): 26–28.

Isaac, Allan Punzalan. *American Tropics: Articulating Filipino America*. Minneapolis: University of Minnesota Press, 2006.

Iton, Richard. *In Search of the Black Fantastic: Politics and Popular Culture in the Post–Civil Rights Era*. New York: Oxford University Press, 2008.

Jabotinsky, Vladimir. 1923. "The Iron Wall: We and the Arabs." 1923. Trans. Lenni Brenner. Reds—Die Roten. Accessed January 3, 2015. http://www.marxists.de/middleast/ironwall/ironwall.htm.

Jacobson, William A. "University Statements Rejecting Academic Boycott of Israel." Legal Insurrection, December 22, 2013. Accessed March 5, 2015. http://legalinsurrection.com/2013/12/indiana-wash-u-st-louis-gwu-northwestern-cornell-reject-academic-boycott-of-israel/.

Jacoby, Karl. *Crimes against Nature: Squatters, Poachers, Thieves, and the Hidden History of American Conservation*. Berkeley: University of California Press, 2003.

Jamal, Amaney A., and Nadine Christine Naber. *Race and Arab Americans before and after 9/11: From Invisible Citizens to Visible Subjects*. Arab American Writing. Syracuse, NY: Syracuse University Press, 2008.

James, Joy, ed. *The New Abolitionists: (Neo)Slave Narratives and Contemporary Prison Writings*. Albany: State University of New York Press, 2005.

———. *Resisting State Violence: Radicalism, Gender, and Race in U.S. Culture*. Minneapolis: University of Minnesota Press, 1996.

———. *Warfare in the American Homeland: Policing and Prison in a Penal Democracy*. Durham: Duke University Press, 2007.

Johnson, Chalmers. *Sorrows of Empire: Militarism, Secrecy, and the End of the Republic*. New York: Metropolitan Books, 2004.

Johnson, Richard. "Afterword: University Challenge. Neoliberal Abstractions and Being More Concrete in Canaan." In *Structure and Agency in the Neoliberal University*, ed. Joyce E. Canaan and Wesley Shumar, 278–97. New York: Routledge, 2008.

"Jornal Hoje 25 11 2010 Vila Cruzeiro Penha Invasão de Favela no Rio de Janeiro." YouTube, November 25, 2010. Accessed February 20, 2010. http://www.youtube.com/watch?v=MedHp8vFh_0.

Jung, Moon-Kie. "Constituting the U.S. Empire-State and White Supremacy: The Early Years." In *State of White Supremacy: Racism, Governance, and the United States*, ed. Moon-Kie Jung, João H. Costa Vargas, and Eduardo Bonilla-Silva, 1–23. Stanford: Stanford University Press, 2011.

Kamat, Anjali. "Interview with Iraqi Artist Wafaa Bilal." *Arab Studies Journal* 18.1 (2010): 316–29.

Kanaaneh, Rhoda, and Isis Nuseir, eds. *Displaced at Home: Ethnicity and Gender among Palestinians in Israel*. New York: State University of New York Press, 2010.

Kanahele, George. *Kū Kanaka, Stand Tall: A Search for Hawaiian Values*. Kolowalu Book. Honolulu: University of Hawaii Press, Waiaha Foundation, 1986.

Kanani, Nadia. "Race and Madness: Locating the Experiences of Racialized People with Psychiatric Histories in Canada and the United States." *Critical Disability Discourse / Discours Critiques dans le Champ du Handicap* 3 (2011): 1–14.

Kanazi, Remi. "This Poem Will Not End Apartheid." Yahoo. Accessed December 30, 2014. http://video.search.yahoo.com/search/video?p=remi+kanazi++this+poem+will+not+end+apartheid&fr=my-myy&toggle=1&cop=&ei=UTF-8.

Kanstroom, Daniel. *Deportation Nation: Outsiders in American History*. Cambridge: Harvard University Press, 2007.

Kant, Immanuel. *The Conflict of the Faculties*. Trans. Mary J. Gregor. Lincoln: University of Nebraska Press, 1979.
Kaplan, Amy. *The Anarchy of Empire in the Making of U.S. Culture*. Cambridge: Harvard University Press 2002.
———. "Homeland Insecurities: Reflections on Language and Space." *Radical History Review* 85 (2003): 82–93.
Kaplan, Amy, and Donald Pease, *Cultures of U.S. Imperialism*. Durham: Duke University Press, 1994.
Kaplan, Caren. "Dead Reckoning: Aerial Perception and the Social Construction of Targets." *Vectors* 2.2 (2007). Accessed January 25, 2016. http://www.vectorsjournal.org/index.php?page=7&projectId=11.
———. "Mobility and War: The Cosmic View of US 'Air Power.'" *Environment and Planning* A.38 (2006): 395–407.
———. "Precision Targets: GPS and the Militarization of U.S. Consumer Identity." *American Quarterly* 58.3 (2006): 693–714.
———. "'A Rare and Chilling View': Aerial Photography as Biopower in the Visual Culture of 9/11." *Reconstruction: Studies in Contemporary Culture* 11.2 (2011).
Kapur, Ratna. *Erotic Justice: Law and the New Politics of Postcolonialism*. London: Glasshouse Press, 2005.
Karnow, Stanley. *In Our Image: America's Empire in the Philippines*. New York: Ballantine Books, 1990.
Kauanui, J. Kēhaulani. *Hawaiian Blood: Colonialism and the Politics of Sovereignty and Indigeneity*. Durham: Duke University Press, 2008.
Kauanui, J. Kehaulani, Robin D. G. Kelley, Bill V. Mullen, Nikhil Pal Singh, and Neferti Tadiar. "Educators Can't Stay Silent about Israeli Apartheid." *Electronic Intifada*, February 13, 2012. Accessed December 30, 2014. http://electronicintifada.net/content/educators-cant-stay-silent-about-israeli-apartheid/10928.
Kelley, Robin. *Freedom Dreams: The Black Radical Imagination*. Boston: Beacon Press, 2002.
Kelley, Robin D. G. "Poetry and the Political Imagination: Aimé Césaire, Negritude, and the Applications of Surrealism." *Lip Magazine*, July 9, 2001.
Kent, Mary Mederios. "More U.S. Scientists and Engineers Are Foreign-Born." Population Reference Bureau, January 2011. Accessed December 12, 2013. http://www.prb.org/Publications/Articles/2011/usforeignbornstem.aspx.
Khalass!!! We're vex! *We Are Here—We Have Always Been Here! Wir sind da—wir waren schon immer da!* Unpublished manifesto. Berlin, 2013.
Khalidi, Walid. *All That Remains: The Palestinian Villages Occupied and Depopulated by Israel in 1948*. Washington, DC: Institute for Palestine Studies Press, 2006.
———. *Before Their Diaspora: A Photographic History of the Palestinians, 1867–1948*. Washington DC: Institute for Palestine Studies Press, 2010.
Khatib, Kate, Margaret Killjoy, and Mike McGuire, eds. *We Are Many: Critical Reflections on Movement Strategy from Occupation to Liberation*. Oakland, CA: AK Press, 2012.
Kim, Claire. *Bitter Fruit: The Politics of Black-Korean Conflict in New York City*. New Haven: Yale University Press, 2003.

Kim, Jodi. *Ends of Empire: Asian American Critique and the Cold War.* Minneapolis: University of Minnesota Press, 2012.
King, Martin Luther, Jr. "All Labor Has Dignity." 1968. In *"All Labor Has Dignity,"* ed. Michael Honey, 167–78. Boston: Beacon Press, 2011.
Klein, Naomi. *The Shock Doctrine: The Rise of Disaster Capitalism.* New York: Picador, 2007.
Kramer, Paul A. *The Blood of Government: Race, Empire, the United States, and the Philippines.* Durham: University of North Carolina, 2006.
Kristeva, Julia. *Powers of Horror: An Essay on Abjection.* New York: Columbia University Press, 1982.
Kuntsman, Adi. *Figurations of Violence and Belonging: Queerness, Migranthood and Nationalism in Cyberspace and Beyond.* Oxford: Peter Lang, 2009.
Lahav, Gallya. "The Rise of Nonstate Actors in Migration Regulation in the United States and Europe: Changing the Gatekeeper or Bringing Back the State?" In *Immigration Research for a New Century: Multidisciplinary Perspectives,* ed. Nancy Foner, Rubén Rumbaut, and Steven J. Gold, 215–41. New York: Russell Sage Foundation, 2000.
Le, C. N. "Asian Immigrants in the Postindustrial Economy." Asian-Nation: Asian American History, Demographics, and Issues. 2015. Accessed June 19, 2015. http://www.asian-nation.org/postindustrial.shtml.
Lecercle, Jean-Jacques. "Deleuze, Guattari and Marxism." *Historical Materialism* 133.3 (2005): 35–55.
Lee, Butch, and Red Rover. *Night Vision: Illuminating War and Class on the Neocolonial Terrain.* New York: Vagabond Press, 1993.
Lee, Erika. *At America's Gates: Chinese Immigration During the Exclusion Era, 1882–1943.* Chapel Hill: University of North Carolina Press, 2003.
Lee, Sharon. "The De-Minoritization of Asian Americans: A Historical Examination of the Representations of Asian Americans in Affirmative Action Admissions Policies at the University of California." Asian American Law Journal 129 (2008): 129–52.
Lee, Wen Ho, with Helen Zia. *My Country versus Me: The First-hand Account by the Los Alamos Scientist Who Was Falsely Accused of Being a Spy Author.* New York: Hyperion, 2001.
Lees, Loretta. "Gentrification and Social Mixing: Towards an Inclusive Urban Renaissance?" *Urban Studies* 45.12 (2008): 2449–70.
Lenoir, Gerald. Lecture delivered at Northwestern University, Evanston, Illinois, April 17, 2008.
Lewontin, Richard. "The Cold War and the Transformation of the Academy." In *The Cold War and the University: Toward an Intellectual History of the Postwar Years,* ed. André Schiffrin et al., 1–34. New York: New Press, 1997.
Lipsitz, George. *How Racism Takes Place.* Philadelphia: Temple University Press, 2011.
———. *The Possessive Investment in Whiteness: How White People Benefit from Identity Politics.* Philadelphia: Temple University Press, 1998.
Logan, John. "How Race Counts for Hispanic Americans." Lewis Mumford Center for Comparative Urban and Regional Research, State University New York,

Albany, July 14, 2003. Accessed June 19, 2015. http://mumford.albany.edu/census/BlackLatinoReport/BlackLatino01.htm.
Lorde, Audre. *Sister Outsider*. 1984. New York: Ten Speed Press, 2007.
Love, Heather. "Compulsory Happiness and Queer Existence." *New Formations* 63.1 (2007): 63–52.
Lowe, Lisa. *Immigrant Acts: On Asian American Cultural Politics*. Durham: Duke University Press, 1996.
LSVD. "Feier zum Tag des Gedenkens an die Opfer des Nationalsozialismus." 2009. Accessed August 15, 2009. http://www.berlin.lsvd.de/cms.
———. "Schluss mit Diskriminierung und Gewalt: Migranten müssen Verhältnis zu Homophobie klären." Press release. July 18, 2003.
Lubiano, Wahneema. "Black Ladies, Welfare Queens, and State Minstrels: Ideological War by Narrative Means." In *Race-ing Power, En-gender-ing Justice*, ed. Toni Morrison, 323–63. New York: Pantheon, 1992.
Lugo, Alejandro. *Fragmented Lives, Assembled Parts: Culture, Capitalism, and Conquest at the US-Mexico Border*. Austin: University of Texas Press, 2008.
———. "Theorizing Border Inspections." *Cultural Dynamics* 12.3 (2000): 353–73.
Lugones, Maria. "Heterosexualism and the Colonial/Modern Gender System." *Hypatia* 22.1 (2007): 186–219.
Lui, Meizhu, Bárbara J. Robles, Betsy Leondar-Wright, Rose M. Brewer, and Rebecca Adamson. *The Color of Wealth: The Story behind the U.S. Racial Wealth Divide*. New York: New Press, 2006.
Lukacs, Georg. *Theory of the Novel*. Trans. Anna Bostock. Cambridge: MIT Press, 1971.
Luxemburg, Rosa. *The Accumulation of Capital*. Trans. Agnes Schwarzschild. London: Routledge, 2003.
Lyons, Matthew N., and Chip Berlet. *Right-Wing Populism in America: Too Close for Comfort*. New York: Guilford, 2000.
Lyons, Scott Richard. *X-Marks: Native Signatures of Assent*. Minneapolis: University of Minnesota Press, 2010.
Macey, David. *The Lives of Michel Foucault: A Biography*. New York: Pantheon, 1993.
Maira, Sunaina. "Henna and Hip-Hop: The Politics of Cultural Production and the Work of Cultural Studies." *Journal of Asian American Studies* 3.3 (2000): 329–69.
Maldonado, Korinta. 2012. "Totonac 'usos y custombres': Racial Sensibilities and Uneven Entitlements in Neoliberal Mexico." PhD dissertation, University of Texas, 2012.
Maldonado-Torres, Nelson. *Against War: Views from the Underside of Modernity*. Durham: Duke University Press, 2008.
———. "Césaire's Gift and the Decolonial Turn." *Radical Philosophy Review* 9.2 (2006): 111–38.
———. "Césaire y la crisis del hombre europeo." In *Discurso sobre el colonialismo*, ed. Aimé Césaire, 173–96. Madrid: Ediciones Akal, 2006.
———. "The Cry of the Self as a Call from the Other: The Paradoxical Loving Subjectivity of Frantz Fanon." *Listening: Journal of Religion and Culture* 36.1 (2001):46–60.
———. "Decolonization and the New Identitarian Logics after September 11: Eurocentrism and Americanism against the Barbarian Threats." *Radical Philosophy Review* 8.1 (2005): 35–67.

———. "Enrique Dussel's Liberation Thought in the Decolonial Turn." *Transmodernity: Journal of Peripheral Cultural Production of the Luso-Hispanic World.* 1.1 (2011): 1–30.
———. "Post-imperial Reflections on Crisis, Knowledge, and Utopia: Transgresstopic Critical Hermeneutics and the 'Death of European Man.'" *Review: A Journal of the Fernand Braudel Center for the Study of Economies, Historical Systems, and Civilizations* 25.3 (2002): 277–315.
———. "Reconciliation as a Contested Future: Decolonization as Project or Beyond the Paradigm of War." In *Reconciliation: Nations and Churches in Latin America*, ed. Iain S. Maclean, 221–41. Aldershot, UK: Ashgate, 2006.
———. "Thinking through the Decolonial Turn: Post-Continental Interventions in Theory, Philosophy, and Critique—An Introduction." *Transmodernity: Journal of Peripheral Cultural Production of the Luso-Hispanic World* 1, no. 2 (2011): 1–15.
———. "The Topology of Being and the Geopolitics of Knowledge: Modernity, Empire, Coloniality." *City* 8.1 (2004): 29–56.
Manalansan, Martin F., IV. *Global Divas: Filipino Gay Men in the Diaspora.* Durham: Duke University Press, 2003.
Maneo. "Zum Tod von Kirsten Heisig." Press release. 2010. Accessed January 25, 2016. http://www.maneo.de/presse/archiv/year/2010/article/zum-tod-von-kirsten-heisig.html.
Marek, Serge. "Waikiki Virtual Reality: Space, Place and Representation in the Waikiki Master Plan." Masters thesis. University of Hawai'i, 1997.
Margolies, Daniel S. "Geronimo, Bin Laden, and US Foreign Policy." *History News Network*, May 5, 2011. Accessed January 20, 2015. http://hnn.us/articles/139017.html.
Márquez, John D. *Black-Brown Solidarity: Racial Politics in the New Gulf South.* Austin: University of Texas Press, 2013.
———. "The Browning of Black Politics: Foundational Blackness and New Latino Subjectivities." *Subjectivity* 4.1 (2011): 47–67.
———. "Latino/as as the 'Living Dead': Raciality, Expendability, and Border Militarization." *Latino Studies* 4.10 (2012): 473–98.
Maruskin, Joan M. "Voices from Around the Country Call for INS Detention Reform." *Migration World Magazine* 23.4 (1995): 32.
Marx, Karl. *Capital.* Vol. 1. New York: Vintage Books, 1977.
———. *Capital. Volume 1.* In *The Marx-Engel's Reader*, ed. R. C. Tucker, 294–438. New York: Norton, 1972.
———. *The Eighteenth Brumaire of Louis Bonaparte.* In *The Marx-Engel's Reader*, ed. R. C. Tucker, 594–617. New York: Norton, 1972.
May, Glenn. *Social Engineering in the Philippines: The Aims, Execution, and Impact of American Colonial Policy, 1900–1913.* Westport, CT: Praeger, 1980.
Mbembe, Achille. "Necropolitics." *Public Culture* 15.1 (2003): 11–40.
McAlister, Melani. *Epic Encounters: Culture, Media, and US Interests in the Middle East, 1945–2000.* Berkeley: University of California Press, 2001.
McClintock, Anne. "Paranoid Empire: Specters from Guantánamo and Abu Ghraib." In *States of Emergency: The Object of American Studies*, ed. Russ Castronovo and Susan Gillman, 88–115. Chapel Hill: University of North Carolina Press, 2009.

McCoy, Alfred W., and Francis A. Scarano, eds. *Colonial Crucible: Empire in the Making of the Modern American State*. Madison: University of Wisconsin Press, 2009.
McKay, Ramah. "Family Reunification." Migration Policy Institute. May 1, 2003. Accessed December 27, 2014. http://www.migrationpolicy.org/article/family-reunification.
McKenzie, Jon. *Perform or Else: From Discipline to Performance*. London: Routledge, 2001.
McKittrick, Katherine. *Demonic Grounds: Black Women and the Cartographies of Struggle*. Minneapolis: University of Minnesota Press, 2006.
McLaren, Peter, ed. *Rage and Hope: Interviews with Peter McLaren on War, Imperialism and Critical Pedagogy*. New York: Peter Lang, 2006.
McNeil, Genna Rae. "Joanne Is You and Joanne Is Me: A Consideration of African American Women and the 'Free Joan Little' Movement, 1974–75." In *Sisters in Struggle: African American Women in the Civil Rights–Black Power Movement*, ed. Bettye Collier-Thomas and V. P. Franklin, 259–79. New York: New York University Press, 2001.
McRuer, Robert. *Crip Theory: Cultural Signs of Queerness and Disability*. New York: New York University Press, 2006.
Melamed, Jodi. "Reading Tehran in Lolita: Making Racialized and Gendered Difference Work for Neoliberal Multiculturalism." In *Strange Affinities: The Gender and Sexual Politics of Comparative Racialization*, ed. Grace Hong and Roderick Ferguson, 76–109. Durham: Duke University Press, 2011.
———. *Represent and Destroy: Rationalizing Violence in the New Racial Capitalism*. Minneapolis: University of Minnesota Press, 2011.
———. "The Spirit of Neoliberalism: From Racial Liberalism to Neoliberal Multiculturalism." *Social Text* 24.4 (2006): 1–24.
Melter, Claus, and Paul Mecheril, eds. *Rassismustheorie und -forschung in Deutschland: Kontur eines wissenschaftlichen Feldes*. Schwalbach: Wochenschau Verlag, 2009.
Menchaca, Martha. "Chicano Indianism: A Historical Account of Racial Repression in the United States." *American Ethnologist* 20.3 (1993): 583–603.
Michael, Joseph, and Jeffrey Timberlake. "Are Latinos Becoming White? Determinants of Racial Self-identification in the US." In *Racism in Post-Race America: New Theories, New Directions*, ed. Charles Gallagher, 107–22. Chapel Hill, NC: Social Forces, 2008.
Michaels, Walter Benn. *The Trouble with Diversity*. New York: Holt, 2006.
Mies, Maria. *Patriarchy and Accumulation on a Global Scale*. London: Zed Books, 1986.
Mignolo, Walter D. "Citizenship, Knowledge, and the Limits of Humanity." *American Literary History* 18.2 (2006): 312–31.
———. *The Darker Side of the Renaissance: Literacy, Territoriality, and Colonization*. 2nd ed. Ann Arbor: University of Michigan Press, 2003.
———. "The Geopolitics of Knowledge and the Colonial Difference." *South Atlantic Quarterly* 101.1 (2002): 57–96.
———. "Globalization and the Geopolitics of Knowledge: The Role of the Humanities in the Corporate University." *Nepantla: Views from South* 4.1 (2003): 97–119.
———. "José de Acosta's *Historia natural y moral de las Indias*: Occidentalism, the Modern/Colonial World, and the Colonial Difference." In *Natural and Moral History of the Indies*, by José de Acosta, 451–18. Durham: Duke University Press, 2002.

———. *Local Histories / Global Designs: Coloniality, Subaltern Knowledges, and Border Thinking*. Princeton: Princeton University Press, 2000.
———. "Os esplendores e as misérias da 'ciência': Colonialidade, geopolítica do conhecimento e pluri-versalidade epistémica." In *Conhecimento Prudente para uma Vida Decente: Um Discurso sobre as Ciências' revistado*, ed. Boaventura de Sousa Santos, 667–709. Edições Afrontamento, 2003.
———. "The Zapatistas' Theoretical Revolution: Its Historical, Ethical, and Political Consequences." *Review* 25.3 (2002): 245–75.
Mills, Charles W. *Blackness Visible: Essays on Philosophy and Race.* Ithaca: Cornell University Press, 1998.
———. "Liberalism and the Racial State." In *State of White Supremacy: Racism, Governance, and the United States*, ed. Moon-Kie Jung, João H. Costa Vargas, and Eduardo Bonilla-Silva, 27–46. Stanford: Stanford University Press, 2011.
Mirzoeff, Nicholas. "War Is Culture: Global Counterinsurgency, Visuality, and the Petraeus Doctrine." *PMLA* 124.5 (2009): 1737–46.
Mitchell, Christopher. "The Costs of State Power: U.S. Border Control in South Florida." In *The Wall around the West: State Borders and Immigration Controls in North American and Europe*, ed. Peter Andreas and Timothy Snyder, 81–97. Lanham, MD: Rowman and Littlefield, 2000.
Mitropolous, Angela. *Contract and Contagion: From Biopolitics to Oikonomia*. Brooklyn, NY: Minor Compositions, 2012.
Mohar, Gustavo, and María-Elena Alcaraz. "U.S. Border Controls: A Mexican Perspective." In *The Wall around the West: State Borders and Immigration Controls in North American and Europe*, ed. Peter Andreas and Timothy Snyder, 139–50. Lanham, MD: Rowman and Littlefield, 2000.
Montejano, David. *Anglos and Mexicans in the Making of Texas, 1836–1986*. Austin: University of Texas Press, 1987.
Moraga, Cherríe. *Loving in the War Years: Lo Que Nunca Pasó por Sus Labios*. Cambridge, MA: South End Press, 2000.
Moraga, Cherríe, and Gloria Anzaldúa, eds. *This Bridge Called My Back: Writings by Radical Women of Color*. 2nd ed. New York: Kitchen Table, Women of Color Press, 1983.
Morgensen, Scott Lauria. "Settler Homonationalism: Theorizing Settler Colonialism within Queer Modernities." *GLQ: A Journal of Lesbian and Gay Studies* 16.1–2 (2010): 105–31.
Morrison, Toni. "Rootedness: The Ancestor as Foundation." In *Black Women Writers*, ed. Mary Evans, 339–45. New York: Anchor Press, 1984.
Moten, Fred "The Case of Blackness." *Criticism* 50 (2008): 177–218.
———. *In the Break: The Aesthetics of the Black Radical Tradition*. Minneapolis: Minnesota University Press, 2003.
———. "The New International of Insurgent Feeling." Palestinian Campaign for the Academic and Cultural Boycott of Israel. November 7, 2009. Accessed December 30, 2014. http://www.pacbi.org/etemplate.php?id=1130.
Moten, Fred, and Stefano Harney. "The University and the Undercommons: Seven Theses." *Social Text* 79 (2004): 101–15.

Moynihan, Daniel P. *The Negro Family: The Case for National Action*. Washington, DC: Office of Policy Planning and Research, U.S. Department of Labor, 1965.

Mueller, John. *Overblown: How Politicians and the Terrorism Industry Inflate National Security Threats, and Why We Believe Them*. New York: Free Press, 2006.

Mukherjee, Upamanyu Pablo. *Postcolonial Environments: Nature, Culture and the Contemporary Indian Novel in English*. New York: Palgrave Macmillan, 2010.

Muñoz, José Esteban. *Disidentifications: Queers of Color and the Performance of Politics*. Minneapolis: University of Minnesota Press, 1999.

Muntaqim, Jalil. "On the BLA." In *Imprisoned Intellectuals: America's Political Prisoners Write on Life, Liberation and Rebellion*, ed. Joy James, 107–13. Lanham, MD: Rowman and Littlefield, 2003.

Naber, Nadine, and Amaney Jamal, eds. *Race and Arab Americans before and after 9/11: From Invisible Citizens to Visible Subjects*. Syracuse, NY: Syracuse University Press, 2007.

Nair, Yasmin. "Why I Won't Come Out on National Coming Out Day." October 9, 2008. Accessed June 1, 2013. http://www.yasminnair.net/content/why-i-won%E2%80%99t-come-out-national-coming-out-day-9-october-2008.

Nesper, Larry. *The Walleye War: The Struggle for Ojibwe Spearfishing and Treaty Rights*. Lincoln: University of Nebraska Press, 2002.

Ness, Sally Ann. *Body, Movement, and Culture: Kinesthetic and Visual Symbolism in a Philippine Community*. Philadelphia: University of Pennsylvania Press, 1992.

Neuman, Gerald L. *Strangers to the Constitution: Immigrants, Borders, and Fundamental Law*. Princeton: Princeton University Press, 1996.

Neumann, Roderick P. *Imposing Wilderness: Struggles over Livelihood and Nature Preservation in Africa*. Berkeley: University of California Press, 2002.

Newson, Janice, and Howard Buchbinder. *The University Means Business*. Toronto: Garamond Press, 1988.

Ngai, Mae M. *Impossible Subjects: Illegal Aliens and the Making of Modern America*. Princeton: Princeton University Press, 2004.

Ngo, Fiona. "Sense and Subjectivity." *Camera Obscura* 26.1 (2011): 95–129.

Nixon, Rob. "Neoliberalism, Slow Violence, and the Environmental Picaresque." *Modern Fiction Studies* 55.3 (2009): 443–67.

Norton, Mary Beth, et al. *A People and a Nation: A History of the United States*. Boston: Houghton Mifflin, 1990.

O'Brien, Michael. *Exxon and the Crandon Mine Controversy*. Middleton, WI: Badger Books, 2008.

O'Brien, Patty. *The Pacific Muse: Exotic Femininity and the Colonial Pacific*. Seattle: University of Washington Press, 2006.

Ochoa, Gilda. *Becoming Neighbors in a Mexican American Community: Power, Conflict and Solidarity*. Austin: University of Texas Press, 2004.

Ohder, Claudius, and Lorenz Huck. *Intensivtäter in Berlin: Hintergründe und Folgen vielfacher strafrechtlicher Auffälligkeit. Teil 1: Eine Auswertung von Akten der Abteilung 47 der Berliner Staatsanwaltschaft*. Berlin: Berliner Forum Gewaltprävention, 2006.

Ohmann, Richard. "English and the Cold War." In *The Cold War and the University: Toward an Intellectual History of the Postwar Years*, ed. André Schiffrin, 73–106. New York: New Press, 1997.

Ohnuma, Keiko. "'Aloha Spirit' and the Cultural Politics of Sentiment as National Belonging." *Contemporary Pacific* 20.2 (2008): 365–94.

Okin, Susan Moller. *Is Multiculturalism Bad for Women?* Ed. Joshua Cohen, Matthre Howard, and Martha S. Nussbaum. Princeton: Princeton University Press, 1999.

Oliveira, Ney dos Santos. "O Caso do Estado e as Questões Raciais, Origem e Características Sócio-Econômicas de uma Favela em Niterói, Estado do Rio de Janeiro." In *Espaço Urbano e Afrodescendência: Estudos da Espacialidade Negra Urbana para o Debate das Politicas Públicas*, ed. Henrique Cunha Jr. and Maria Estela Rocha Ramos, 137–54. Fortaleza: UFC Edições.

Omatsu, Glenn. "The 'Four Prisons' and the Movements of Liberation." In *The State of Asian America: Activism and Resistance in the 1990s*, ed. Karin Aguilar San-Juan, 19–69. Boston: South End Press, 1994.

Omi, Michael, and Howard Winant. *Racial Formation in the United States*. New York: Routledge, 2014.

Ong, Aihwa. *Neoliberalism as Exception: Mutations in Citizenship and Sovereignty*. Durham: Duke University Press, 2006.

Opitz, May, Katharina Oguntoye, and Dagmar Schultz, eds. *Showing Our Colors: Afro-German Women Speak Out*. 1986. Amherst: University of Massachusetts Press, 1992.

Osias, Camilo. *Barrio Life and Barrio Education*. Chicago: World Book Company, 1921.

Osorio, Jonathan. *Dismembering Lāhui: A History of the Hawaiian Nation to 1887*. Honolulu: University of Hawai'i Press, 2002.

Paixão, Marcelo, Irene Rossetto, Fabiana Montovanele, and Luiz M. Carvano. *Relatório Anual das Desigualdades Raciais no Brasil: 2009–2010*. Rio de Janeiro: Editora Garamond, 2010.

Parenti, Christian. *Lockdown America: Police and Prisons in the Age of Crisis*. London: Verso, 1999.

Paterson, Kevin, and Hughes, Bill. "Disability Studies and Phenomenology: The Carnal Politics of Everyday Life." *Disability & Society* 14.5 (1999): 597–610.

Patterson, Orlando. *Slavery and Social Death: A Comparative Study*. Cambridge: Harvard University Press, 1982.

Pease, Donald E. *The New American Exceptionalism*. Minneapolis: University of Minnesota Press, 2009.

Pellow, David. "Activist-Scholar Alliances for Social Change." In *Transforming the Ivory Tower: Challenging Racism, Sexism, and Homophobia in the Academy*, ed. Brett Stockdill and Mary Yu Danico, 106–19. Honolulu: University of Hawai'i Press, 2012.

Pellow, David, and Lisa Park. *The Silicon Valley of Dreams: Environmental Injustice, Immigrant Workers, and the High-Tech Global Economy*. New York: New York University Press, 2002.

Perez, Emma. *The Decolonial Imaginary: Writing Chicanas into History*. Bloomington: Indiana University Press, 1999.

Perez-Torres, Rafael. *Movements in Chicano Poetry: Against Myths, against Margins*. Cambridge: Cambridge University Press, 1995.

Perlman, Freddy. "The Continuing Appeal of Nationalism." Fifth Estate 1984. http://theanarchistlibrary.org/library/fredy-perlman-the-continuing-appeal-of-nationalism.

Petzen, Jennifer. "Gender Politics in the New Europe: 'Civilizing' Muslim Sexualities." PhD dissertation, University of Washington, 2008.

Phelan, Peggy. *Unmarked*. New York: Routledge, 1993.

Piterberg, Gabriel. "Erasures." *New Left Review* 10 (July–August 2001): 31–46.

Povinelli, Elizabeth A. *The Cunning of Recognition: Indigenous Alterities and the Making of Australian Multiculturalism*. Durham: Duke University Press, 2002.

Prashad, Vijay. *Everybody Was Kung Fu Fighting: Afro-Asian Connections and the Myth of Cultural Purity*. Boston: Beacon, 2001.

———. *The Karma of Brown Folk*. Minneapolis: University of Minnesota Press, 2001.

President's Executive Office. "University of California Briefing Binder." May 2010. Accessed December 12, 2013. http://www.ucop.edu/impac/_files/regents-briefing-materials.pdf.

Puar, Jasbir. "The Cost of Getting Better: Suicide, Sensation, Switchpoints." Paper presented at Racialization, Neoliberalism and Queering Public Spheres, University of California at San Diego, April 22–23, 2011.

———. *Terrorist Assemblages: Homonationalism in Queer Times*. Durham: Duke University Press, 2007.

Pukui, Mary Kawena, E. W. Haertig, and Catherine Lee. *Nana I Ke Kumu (Look to the Source) Vol 1*. Honolulu: Hui Hanai, 1983.

Pulido, Laura. *Black, Brown, Yellow and Left: Radical Activism in Los Angeles*. Berkeley: University of California Press, 2006.

———. "Rethinking Environmental Racism: White Privilege and Urban Development in Southern California." *Annals of the Association of American Geographers* 90.1 (2000): 12–40.

Pulido, Laura, and Manuel Pastor. "Where in the World Is Juan—and What Color Is He? The Geography of Latina/o Racial Identity in Southern California." *American Quarterly* 65.2 (2013): 309–41.

Quant, Ted. "Slavery in the Fields: Amite, Louisiana." The People's Tribune. March 2008. Accessed January 13, 2012. http://www.peoplestribune.org/PT.2008.03/PT.2008.03.10.html.

Quijano, Aníbal. "Colonialidad del poder y clasificación social." *Journal of World-Systems Research* 11 (2000): 342–86.

———. "Colonialidad y modernidad/racionalidad." *Perú indígena* 29 (1991): 11–20.

———. "Coloniality and Modernity/Rationality." *Cultural Studies* 21.2–3 (2007): 168–78.

———. "Coloniality of Power, Eurocentrism, and Latin America." *Nepantla: Views from South* 1.3 (2000): 533–80.

———. "Modernity, Identity, and Utopia in Latin America." In *The Postmodernism Debate in Latin America*, ed. John Beverly, Michael Arona and José Oviedo, 201–16. Durham: Duke University Press, 1995.

———. "'Raza, etnia, y nación': Cuestiones abiertas." In *José Carlos Mariátegui y Europa: La otra cara del descubrimiento*, ed. Roland Forgues, 167–87. Lima, Peru: Amauta, 1992.

Radhakrishnan, Rajagopalan. *History, the Human, and the World Between*. Durham: Duke University Press, 2008.

Rana, Junaid Akram. "More than Nothing: The Persistence of Islamophobia in Post-Racial Racism." *Global Dialogue* 12.2 (2010). http://www.worlddialogue.org/print.php?id=482.
———. "The Story of Islamophobia." *Souls* 9.2 (2007): 148–61.
———. *Terrifying Muslims: Race and Labor in the South Asian Diaspora*. Durham: Duke University Press, 2011.
Rana, Junaid, and Gilberto Rosas. "Managing Crisis: Post-9/11 Policing and Empire." *Cultural Dynamics* 18.3 (2006): 219–34.
Razack, Sherene. *Casting Out: The Eviction of Muslims from Western Law and Politics*. Toronto: University of Toronto Press, 2008.
———. "When Place Becomes Race." In *Space, Race and Law: Unmapping a White Settler Society*, ed. Sherene Razack, 1–20. Toronto: Between the Lines, 2002.
Reddy, Chandan. "Asian Diasporas, Neoliberalism, and Family: Reviewing the Case for Homosexual Asylum in the Context of Family Rights." *Social Text* 23.3–4 (2005): 101–19.
———. *Freedom with Violence: Race, Sexuality, and the U.S. State*. Durham: Duke University Press, 2011.
Reina. "SRLP Announces Non-support of the Gender Employment Non-Discrimination Act." Sylvia Rivera Law Project. April 6, 2009. Accessed January 5, 2010. http://srlp.org/genda.
Rich, Adrienne. *On Lies, Secrets and Silence*. New York: Norton, 1979.
Rifkin, Mark. *When Did Indians Become Straight? Kinship, the History of Sexuality, and Native Sovereignty*. New York: Oxford University Press, 2011.
Roberts, Dorothy. "Crime, Race, and Reproduction." *Tulane Law Review* 67 (1993): 1945–77.
Robinson, Cedric. *Black Marxism: The Making of the Black Radical Tradition*. Chapel Hill: University of North Carolina Press, 1983.
Robinson, Toni, and Greg Robinson. "The Limits of Interracial Coalitions: Mendez v. Westminster Reexamined." In *Racial Transformations: Latinos and Asians Remaking the United States*, ed. Nicholas de Genova, 93–119. Durham: Duke University Press, 2006.
Rodriguez, Clara. *Changing Race: Latinos, the Census, and the History of Ethnicity in the United States*. New York: New York University Press, 2000.
Rodríguez, Dylan. "The Black Presidential Non-Slave: Genocide and the Present Tense of Racial Slavery." *Political Power and Social Theory* 22 (2011): 17–50.
———. *Forced Passages: Imprisoned Radical Intellectuals and the U.S. Prison Regime*. Minneapolis: University of Minnesota Press, 2006.
———. "Forced Passages." In *Warfare in the Homeland: Policing and Prison in a Penal Democracy*, ed. Joy James, 35–57. Durham: Duke University Press, 2007.
———. "Inaugurating Multiculturalist White Supremacy." *Colorlines*, November 10, 2008. Accessed December 30, 2012. http://colorlines.com/articles/dreadful-genius-obama-moment.
———. "(Non)Scenes of Captivity: The Common Sense of Death and Punishment." *Radical History Review* 96 (2006): 9–32.

———. *Suspended Apocalypse: White Supremacy, Genocide, and the Filipino Condition.* Minneapolis: University of Minnesota Press, 2010.
Rodríguez, Néstor. "The Battle for the Border: Notes on Autonomous Migration, Transnational Communities, and the State." *Social Justice* 23.3 (1996): 21–37.
Roediger, David. "The Retreat from Race and Class." *Monthly Review* 58.3 (2006): 40–51.
———. *Towards the Abolition of Whiteness.* London: Verso, 1994.
———. *The Wages of Whiteness.* London: Verso, 1999.
Rojas, Fabio. *From Black Power to Black Studies: How a Radical Social Movement Became an Academic Discipline.* Baltimore: Johns Hopkins University Press, 2007.
Rooks, Noliwe M. *White Money / Black Power: The Surprising History of African American Studies and the Crisis of Race in Higher Education.* Boston: Beacon Press, 2006.
Rosaldo, Renato. *Culture and Truth: The Remaking of Social Analysis.* Boston: Beacon Press, 1989.
Rosas, Gilberto. *Barrio Libre: Criminalizing States and Delinquent Refusals of the New Frontier.* Durham: Duke University Press, 2012.
———. "The Managed Violences of the Borderlands: Treacherous Geographies, Policeability, and the Politics of Race." *Latino Studies* 4.4 (2006): 401–18.
Rose, Nikolas. *Governing the Soul: The Shaping of Private Life.* London: Routledge, 1989.
———. "Screen and Intervene: Governing Risky Brains." *History of the Human Sciences* 23.1 (2010): 79–105.
Roth, Marcus, and Inge Seiffge-Krenke. "Frühe Delinquenz und familiäre Belastungen in der Kindheit." In *Jugendliche Intensivtäter: Interdisziplinare Perspektiven,* ed. Annette Boeger, 255–76. Wiesbaden: VS, 2011.
Rowe, John Carlos. *Literary Culture and U.S. Imperialism: From the Revolution to World War II.* Oxford: Oxford University Press 2000.
Sadowski-Smith, Claudia. *Border Fictions: Globalization, Empire, and Writing at the Boundaries of the United States.* Charlottesville: University of Virginia Press, 2008.
Said, Edward. *Culture and Imperialism.* New York: Vintage Press, 1993.
———. *Orientalism.* New York: Random House, 1978.
———. *Representations of the Intellectual.* New York: Vintage Press, 1994.
———. "Traveling Theory." In *The World, the Text, and the Critic,* 226–47. Cambridge: Harvard University Press, 1983.
Sakai, J. *Settlers: The Mythology of the White Proletariat.* Chicago: Morningstar Press, 1989.
———. "When Race Burns Class: An Interview with J. Sakai." Revolutionary Anti-Imperialist Movement (Denver), May 1, 2007. Accessed February 2, 2016. http://raimd.wordpress.com/2007/05/01/when-race-burns-class-interview-with-j-sakai/.
Saldaña-Portillo, María Josefina. "'How Many Mexicans [Is] a Horse Worth?' The League of United Latin American Citizens, Desegregation Cases, and Chicano Historiography." *South Atlantic Quarterly* 107.4 (2008): 809–31.
———. *The Revolutionary Imagination in the Americas and the Age of Development.* Durham: Duke University Press, 2003.
Salles, Marcelo. "A Chacina do Complexo do Alemão." *A Nova Democracia* 6.36 (2007). Accessed February 20, 2012. http://www.anovademocracia.com.br/no-36/256-a-chacina-do-complexo-do-alemao.

Sanchez, Rosaura. "Ethnicity, Ideology and Academia." *Cultural Studies* 4.3 (1990): 294–302.
Sandoval, Chela. *Methodology of the Oppressed*. Minneapolis: University of Minnesota Press, 2000.
Santos, Boaventura de Sousa. "Between Prospero and Caliban: Colonialism, Postcolonialism, and Inter-identity." *Luso-Brazilian Review* 39 (2002): 9–43.
———. *Toward a New Common Sense: Law, Science and Politics in the Paradigmatic Transition*. London: Routledge, 1995.
———. "The World-Social Forum: Toward a Counter-Hegemonic Globalization." July 2003. Accessed 2003. http://www.ces.fe.uc.pt/bss/documentos/wsf.pdf.
Sarrazin, Thilo. *Deutschland schafft sich ab: Wie wir unser Land aufs Spiel setzen*. Munich: DVA, 2010.
Sartre, Jean Paul. *Being and Nothingness: A Phenomenological Essay on Ontology*. Trans. Hazel E. Barnes. New York: Washington Square Press, Pocket Books, 1966.
———. *Réflexions sur la question juive*. 1944. Paris: Gallimard, 1954.
Schacht, Stephen. "Turnabout: Gay Drag Queens and the Masculine Embodiment of the Feminine." In *Revealing Male Bodies*, ed. Nancy Tuana, Willian Cowling, Maurice Harrington, Greg Johnson, and Terrance MacMullan, 155–77. Bloomington: Indiana University Press, 2002.
Schlesinger, Arthur M., Jr. *The Disuniting of America: Reflections on a Multicultural Society*. Knoxville, TN: Whittle Direct Books, 1991.
Schneider, Diana, Robert Steiner, and Joan Romaine. "Human Cargo: Health Conditions of Chinese Migrants Interdicted Offshore by U.S. Authorities." *Journal of Community Health* 28.1 (2003): 19–39.
See, Sarita Echavez. *The Decolonized Eye: Filipino American Art and Performance*. Minneapolis: University of Minnesota Press, 2009.
Segar, Maggie. 2011. "Palestinian Queer Activists Challenge the Pinkwashing of the Israeli Occupation." Mondoweiss, February 16, 2011. Accessed December 30, 2014. http://mondoweiss.net/2011/02/palestinian-queer-activists-challenge-the-pinkwashing-of-the-israeli-occupation.
Sellers-Young, Barbara, and Anthony Shay, eds. *Belly Dance: Orientalism, Transnationalism, and Harem Fantasy*. Costa Mesa, CA: Mazda, 2005.
Sexton, Jared A. *Amalgamation Schemes: Antiblackness and the Critique of Multiracialism*. Minneapolis: University of Minnesota Press, 2008.
———. "People-of-Color-Blindness: Notes on the Afterlife of Slavery." *Social Text* 28.2 (2010): 31–56.
———. "The Social Life of Social Death: On Afro-Pessimism and Black Optimism." *InTensions* 5 (2011): 1–47.
———. "The Vel of Slavery: Tracking the Figure of the Unsovereign." *Critical Sociology* (December 19, 2014).
Shah, Nyan. *Contagious Divides: Epidemics and Race in San Francisco's Chinatown*. Berkeley: University of California Press, 2001.
Shakur, Assata. *Assata: An Autobiography*. London: Zed Books, 1987.
Shavit, Ari. "Cry the Beloved Two-State Solution." Righteous Jews. August 2003. Accessed December 30, 2014. http://www.righteousjews.org/article4.html.

Shildrick, Margrit. *Dangerous Discourses of Disability, Subjectivity and Sexuality*. New York: Palgrave Macmillan, 2009.
Shingavi, Snehal. "We Want Real Justice for Bhopal." Counterpunch, July 5, 2004. Accessed November 23, 2011. http://www.counterpunch.org/2004/07/03/quot-we-want-real-justice-for-bhopal-quot/.
Shooman, Yasemin. "Der Topos 'Deutschenfeindlichkeit' in rechtspopulistischen Diskursen." In *Rechtspopulismus in Berlin: Rassismus als Bindeglied zwischen der Mitte der Gesellschaft und Neonazismus?*, ed. Bündnis "Rechtspopulismus stoppen," 45–47. Berlin: Bündnis "Rechtspopulismus stoppen," 2011.
Silliman, Stephen W. "The 'Old West' in the Middle East: US Military Metaphors in Real and Imagined Indian Country." *American Anthropologist* 110.2 (2008): 237–47.
Simanski, John, and Lesley M. Sapp. "Immigration Enforcement Actions: 2011." In *Annual Report: Office of Immigration Statistics*, 1–7. U.S. Department of Homeland Security, September 2012.
Simon, Bernd. "Einstellungen zur Homosexualität." *Zeitschrift für Entwicklungspsychologie und Pädagogische Psychologie* 40.2 (2008): 87–99.
———. "Einstellung zur Homosexualität." *Arbeitsblätter News*, February 2, 2009. Accessed August 1, 2014. http://arbeitsblaetter.stangl-taller.at/news/104/einstellung-zur-homosexualitaet.
Simpson, Audra. "On Ethnographic Refusal: Indigeneity, 'Voice' and Colonial Citizenship." *Junctures: The Journal for Thematic Dialogue* 9 (2007): 67–80.
Simpson, Jacqueline. "Segregated by Subject: Racial Differences in the Factors Influencing Academic Major between European Americans, Asian Americans, and African, Hispanic, and Native Americans." *Journal of Higher Education* 72 (2001): 63–100.
Singh, Ilina, and Nikolas Rose. "Biomarkers in Psychiatry." *Nature* 460.7252 (2009): 202–7.
Singh, Nikhil. "The Afterlife of Fascism." *South Atlantic Quarterly* 105.1 (2006): 71–93.
———. *Climbin' Jacob's Ladder: The Black Freedom Movement Writings of Jack O'Dell*. Berkeley: University of California Press, 2010.
Sinha, Indra. *Animal's People*. New York: Simon and Schuster, 2007.
Skeggs, Beverley. "The Value of Relationships: Affective Scenes and Emotional Performances." *Feminist Legal Studies* 18.1 (2010): 29–51.
Slater, David. *Geopolitics and the Post-Colonial: Rethinking North-South Relations*. London: Blackwell, 2004.
Slotkin, Richard. *Regeneration through Violence: The Mythology of the American Frontier, 1600–1800*. Middletown, CT: Wesleyan University Press, 1973.
Smith, Andrea. "Against the Law: Indigenous Feminism and the Nation-State." *Affinities: A Journal of Radical Theory, Culture, and Action* 5.1 (2011): 56–69.
———. "Indigeneity, Settler Colonialism, White Supremacy." *Global Dialogue* 12.2 (2010): 66–90.
———. *Native Americans and the Christian Right: The Gendered Politics of Unlikely Alliances*. Durham: Duke University Press, 2008.
———. "Queer Theory and Native Studies: The Heteronormativity of Settler Colonialism." In *Queer Indigenous Studies: Critical Interventions in Theory, Politics, and*

Literature, ed. Qwo-Li Driskill, Chris Finley, Brian Joseph Gilley and Scott Lauria Morgensen, 43–65. Tucson: University of Arizona Press, 2011.

———. "Unmasking the State: Racial/Gender Terror and Hate Crimes." *Australian Feminist Law Review* 26 (2007): 47–57.

Smith, Barbara, ed. *Home Girls: A Black Feminist Anthology*. New York: Kitchen Table, Women of Color Press, 1983.

Smith, Linda Tuhiwai. *Decolonizing Methodologies: Research and Indigenous Peoples*. New York: Zed Books, 1999.

Snorton, Riley, and Jin Haritaworn. "Trans Necropolitics." In *Transgender Studies Reader Vol. II*, ed. Aren Aizura and Susan Stryker, 66–76. New York: Routledge, 2013.

Solomon, Robert C. "Sympathy and Vengeance: The Role of the Emotions in Justice." In *Emotions: Essays on Emotion Theory*, ed. Stephanie H. M. Van Goozen, Nanne E. Van de Poll, and Joseph A. Sergeant, 291–321. Hillsdale, NJ: Lawrence Erlbaum, 1994.

Spade, Dean. "Fighting to Win." In *That's Revolting! Queer Strategies for Resisting Assimilation*, ed. Mattilda Bernstein, 49–57. Brooklyn, NY: Soft Skull Press, 2004.

———. *Normal Life: Administrative Violence, Critical Trans Politics and the Limits of the Law*. Cambridge, MA: South End Press, 2011.

Spade, Dean, and Craig Willse. "Confronting the Limits of Gay Hate Crimes Activism: A Radical Critique." UCLA *Chicano-Latino Review* 21 (2000): 38–52.

Spenser, Edmund. *A View of the Present State of Ireland*. Ed. Andrew Hadfield and Willy Maley. Oxford: Blackwell, 1997.

Spiegel, Marjorie. *The Dreaded Comparison: Human and Animal Slavery*. New York: Mirror Books, 1996.

Spillers, Hortense J. *Black, White, and in Color: Essays on American Literature and Culture*. Chicago: University of Chicago Press, 2003.

———. "The Crisis of the Negro Intellectual: A Post-Date."

———. "Introduction: Peter's Pans. Eating in the Diaspora"

———. "Mama's Baby, Papa's Maybe: An American Grammar Book." *Diacritics: A Review of Contemporary Criticism* 17.2 (1987): 65–81.

———. "Mama's Baby, Papa's Maybe: An American Grammar Book." In *Black, White, and in Color: Essays on American Literature and Culture*, 203–29. Chicago: University of Chicago Press, 2003.

Spivak, Gayatri. "Can the Subaltern Speak?" In *Marxism and the Interpretation of Culture*, ed. Cary Nelson and Lawrence Grossberg, 271–316. Urbana: University of Illinois Press, 1988.

———. "Can the Subaltern Speak?" In *Colonial Discourse and Post-Colonial Theory: A Reader*, ed. Patrick Williams and Laura Chrisman, 66–111. Hertfordshire, UK: Harvester Wheatsheaf Press, 1994.

———. *In Other Worlds: Essays in Cultural Politics*. London: Taylor and Francis, 1987.

Spotton Visano, Brenda, and Kristin Taylor. *Room to Grow: Celebrating Atkinson's Living Legacy*. Toronto: York University Press, 2009.

Stanley, Eric A., and Nat Smith, eds. *Captive Genders: Trans Embodiment and the Prison Industrial Complex*. Oakland, CA: AK Press, 2011.

Staudenmaier, Michael. *Truth and Revolution: A History of the Sojourner Truth Organization, 1969–1986*. Oakland, CA: AK Press, 2012.
Stober, Dan. "Lee Case Discourages Asian American Scientists." Model Minority, 2000. Accessed April 15, 2014. http://www.modelminority.com/joomla/index.php?option=com_content&view=article&id=125:lee-case-discourages-asian-american-scientists-&catid=34:academia&Itemid=56.
Stoler, Ann Laura, ed. *Haunted by Empire: Geographies of Intimacy in North American History*. Durham: Duke University Press, 2006.
———. "On Degrees of Imperial Sovereignty." *Public Culture* 18.1 (2006): 125–46.
———. *Race and the Education of Desire: Foucault's History of Sexuality and the Colonial Order of Things*. Durham: Duke University Press, 1995.
Streeby, Shelley. *American Sensations: Class, Empire, and the Production of Popular Culture*. Berkeley: University of California Press, 2002.
Strum, Philippa. *Mendez v. Westminster: School Desegregation and Mexican American Rights*. Lawrence: University Press of Kansas, 2010.
Sudbury, Julia, ed. *Activist Scholarship: Antiracism, Feminism, and Social Change*. Boulder, CO: Paradigm, 2009.
———. "Celling Black Bodies: Black Women in the Global Prison Industrial Complex." *Feminist Review* 80 (2005): 162–79.
Support CeCe McDonald. "Background." Accessed August 1, 2014. http://supportcece.wordpress.com/about-2/background/.
SUSPECT. "Where Now? From Pride Scandal to Transnational Movement." Bully Bloggers, July 26, 2010. Accessed March 1, 2015. http://bullybloggers.wordpress.com/2010/06/26/where-now-from-pride-scandal-to-transnational-movement/.
Sweet Honey in the Rock. *Sweet Honey in the Rock*. Compact disk. Flying Fish, 1976.
Swing, Joseph M. *Annual Report of the Immigration and Naturalization Service*. Washington, DC: Government Printing Office, 1955.
Tadiar, Neferti Xina M. *Fantasy-Production: Sexual Economies and Other Philippine Consequences in the New World Order*. Quezon City: Ateneo de Manila University Press, 2004.
———. "In the Face of Whiteness as Value: Fall-Outs of Metropolitan Humanness." *Qui Parle* 13.2 (2003): 143–82.
———. "Life-Times in Fate-Playing." *South Atlantic Quarterly* 111.4 (2012): 783–802.
———. "Life-Times of Disposability within Global Neoliberalism." *Social Text* 31.2 (2013): 19–47.
———. "Remaindered Life of Citizen-Man, Medium of Democracy." *Southeast Asian Studies* 49.3 (2011): 464–95.
———. *Things Fall Away: Philippine Historical Experience and the Makings of Globalization*. Durham: Duke University Press.
———. "The War to Be Human / Becoming Human in a Time of War." In *The Color of Violence: The Incite! Anthology*, ed. Incite! Women of Color against Violence, 90–93. Cambridge, MA: South End Press, 2006.
Tafoya, Sonia. *Shades of Belonging*. Washington, DC: Pew Hispanic Center, 2004.
Takagi, Dana. *The Retreat from Race: Asian-American Admissions and Racial Politics*. New Brunswick, NJ: Rutgers University Press, 1992.

Tam, Louise. "Governing through Competency: Race, Pathologization, and the Limits of Mental Health Outreach." Master's thesis. University of Toronto, 2012.

Tarski, Alfred. *Introduction to Logic and to the Methodology of the Deductive Sciences*. 4th edition. Ed. Jan Tarski. New York: Oxford University Press, 1936.

Taylor, Diana. *The Archive and the Repertoire: Performing Cultural Memory in the Americas*. Durham: Duke University Press, 2003.

Teaiwa, Teresia. "Native Thoughts: A Pacific Studies Take on Cultural Studies and Diaspora." In *Indigenous Diasporas and Dislocations*, ed. Graham Harvey and Charles Johnson, 15–36. Burlington, VT: Ashgate, 2005.

Team Colors Collective, ed. *Uses of a Whirlwind*. Oakland, CA: AK Press, 2010.

Tengan, Ty Kawika. *Native Men Remade: Gender and Nation in Contemporary Hawai'i*. Durham: Duke University Press, 2008.

"Texas Juvenile Probation Commission." Accessed February 27, 2012. http://www.tjjd.texas.gov/publications/reports/RPTOTH201202.pdf.

Thomas, Greg. "*Proud Flesh* Inter/Views: Sylvia Wynter." *ProudFlesh: New Afrikan Journal of Culture, Politics, and Consciousness* 4 (2006).

Titchkosky, Tanya. *Reading and Writing Disability Differently: The Textured Life of e\ Embodiment*. Toronto: University of Toronto Press, 2007.

TOPOS. "Sozialstruktur und Mietentwicklung im Erhaltungsgebiet Luisenstadt (SO 36)." 2008. Accessed April 1, 2010. http://www.berlin.de/imperia/md/content/bafriedrichshain-kreuzberg/abtstadtpg/amtstapl-verm_baa/stapl/stadterneuerung/luise_endbericht.pdf?start&ts=1264082523&file=luise_endbericht.pdf.

Toprak, Ahmet. "Machtausübung." *Siegessäule*, November 2011. Accessed October 25, 2012. http://www.siegessaeule.de/uploads-img-printausgaben-sis_11–09.pdf.

Toprak, Ahmet, and Katja Nowacki. *Gewaltphänomene bei männlichen, muslimischen Jugendlichen mit Migrationshintergrund und Präventionsstrategien*. Berlin: Bundesministeriums für Familie, Senioren, Frauen und Jugend, 2010.

Torres, Arlene, and Norman E. Whitten Jr. "General Introduction: To Forge the Future in the Fires of the Past. An Interpretive Essay on Racism, Domination, Resistance, and Liberation." In *Blackness in Latin America and the Caribbean*, ed. Arlene Torres and Norman E. Whitten Jr. Vol. 1 of *Social Dynamics and Cultural Transformations: Central America and Northern and Western South America*, 3–33. Bloomington: Indian University Press, 1998.

Treuer, Anton. *Ojibwe in Minnesota*. St. Paul, MN: Minnesota Historical Society Press, 2010.

Tsing, Anna. "The Global Situation." *Cultural Anthropology* 15.3 (2000): 327–60.

Ture, Kwame, with Michael Thelwell. *Ready for Revolution*. New York: Scribner's, 2003.

Umoja, Akinyele Omowale. "The Black Liberation Army and the Radical Legacy of the Black Panther Party." In *Black Power in the Belly of the Beast*, ed. Judson Jeffries, 224–51. Urbana: University of Illinois Press, 2006.

———. "Repression Breeds Resistance: The Black Liberation Army and the Radical Legacy of the Black Panther Party." In *Liberation, Imagination, and the Black Panther Party*, ed. Kathleen Cleaver and George Katsiaficas, 3–19. New York: Routledge, 2001.

Undergraduate Program Review. "Undergraduate Program Review, Political Science Program Report." Atkinson Faculty of Liberal and Professional Studies, York University, Toronto, 2008.
UAS Center for Excellence. *Eyes of the Army: U.S. Army Unmanned Aircraft Systems Roadmap, 2010–2035*. Fort Rucker, AL: U.S. Army UAS Center for Excellence, 2010.
U.S. Border Patrol. *Border Patrol Strategic Plan: 1994 and Beyond, National Strategy*. Washington, DC: U.S. Border Patrol, July 1994.
U.S. Campaign for the Academic and Cultural Boycott of Israel. Accessed March 5, 2015. http://www.usacbi.org/.
U.S. Citizenship and Immigration Services. "H-1B Fiscal Year (FY) 2015 Cap Season." March 31, 2014. Accessed December 27, 2014. http://www.uscis.gov/h-1b_count.
U.S. Government Accountability Office. *Unmanned Aircraft Systems: Comprehensive Planning and a Results Oriented Training Strategy Are Needed to Support Growing Inventories*. Accessed January 25, 2016. March 26, 2010. http://www.gao.gov/products/GAO-10-331.
U.S. Immigration and Customs Enforcement. "Fact Sheet: The ICE T. Don Hutto Family Residential Facility." Department of Homeland Security. February 2007.
———. "List of Deaths in ICE Custody: October 2003–December 2, 2013." Department of Homeland Security. Accessed January 12, 2015. http://www.ice.gov/doclib/foia/reports/detaineedeaths2003-present.pdf.
———. News release. "FY 2012: ICE Announces Year-end Removal Numbers, Highlights Focus on Key Priorities and Issues New Detainer Guidance to Further Focus Resources." Department of Homeland Security. December 20, 2012. Accessed December 31, 2012, http://www.ice.gov/news/releases/1212/121221washingtondc2.htm.
University of Southern California. "Core Documents: The 1993 Mission Statement and the 2004 Strategic Plan." Accessed March 5, 2015. http://strategic.usc.edu/.
Urrutia, Liliana. "An Offspring of Discontent: The Asociación Nacional México-Americana, 1949–1954." *Aztlan* 15.1 (1984): 179–81.
Vacek, Joseph J. "Big Brother Will Soon Be Watching—Or Will He? Constitutional, Regulatory, and Operational Issues Surrounding the Use of Unmanned Aerial Vehicles in Law Enforcement." *North Dakota Law Review* 85 (2010): 673–92.
Valdez, Rene, and Czarina Thelen. *I Come from a Teardrop*. Austin, TX: Red Salmon Press, 2010.
Vallejo, Jody. *Barrios to Burbs: The Making of the Mexican-American Middle Class*. Palo Alto, CA: Stanford University Press, 2012.
Vargas, João H. Costa. "Apartheid Brasileiro: Raça e Segregação Residencial no Rio de Janeiro." *Revista de Antropologia* 48.1 (2005): 75–131.
———. "The Inner City and the Favela." *Race & Class* 44 (2003): 19–40.
———. *Never Meant to Survive: Genocide and Utopias in Black Diaspora Communities*. Lanham, MD: Rowman and Littlefield, 2010.
Vargas, João Costa, and Joy James. "Refusing Blackness-as-Victimization: Trayvon Martin and the Black Cyborgs." In *Pursuing Trayvon Martin: Historical Contexts and Contemporary Manifestations of Racial Dynamics*, ed. George Yancy and Janine Jones, 193–204. Plymouth, UK: Lexington, 2012.

Vasconcelos, José. *The Cosmic Race / La raza cósmica*. 1979. Trans. Didier T. Jaén. Baltimore: Johns Hopkins University Press, 1997.

Vergès, Françoise. *Monsters and Revolutionaries: Colonial Family Romance and Métissage*. Durham: Duke University Press, 1999.

Vila, Pablo. *Crossing Borders, Reinforcing Borders: Social Categories, Metaphors, and Narrative Identities on the U.S.-Mexico Frontier*. Austin: University of Texas Press, 2000.

Virilio, Paul. *War and Cinema: The Logistics of Perception*. Trans. Patrick Camiller. London: Verso, 1989.

Voronka, Jijian. "Rooting Out the Weeds: Resisting White Settler and Psychiatric Supremacy through a Critique of 'The Review of the Roots of Youth Violence.'" Paper presented at PsychOut Conference, University of Toronto, May 7–8, 2010. Accessed August 1, 2014. http://individual.utoronto.ca/psychout/papers/voronka.html.

Wacquant, Loïc. "From Slavery to Mass Incarceration: Rethinking the 'Race Question' in the US." *New Left Review* 13 (2002): 41–60.

Wade, Peter. "Hybridity Theory and Kinship Thinking." *Cultural Studies* 19.5 (2005): 602–21.

Wald, Priscilla. "Terms of Assimilation: Legislating Subjectivity in the Emerging Nation." In *Cultures of U.S. Imperialism*, ed. Amy Kaplan and Donald Pease, 59–84. Durham: Duke University Press, 1993.

Wallerstein, Immanuel. *Unthinking Social Science: The Limits of Nineteenth-Century Paradigms*. Cambridge, UK: Polity Press, 1991.

———. *Utopistics: Or, Historical Choices of the Twenty-First Century*. New York: New Press, 1998.

Walsh, "Interculturality and the Coloniality of Power: An Other Thinking and Positioning from the Colonial Difference." In *Coloniality, Transmodernity, and Border Thinking*, ed. Ramon Grosfoguel, José David Saldívar, and Nelson Maldonado-Torres, in press.

Walsh, Catherine. "'Other' Knowledges, 'Other' Critiques: Reflections on the Politics and Practices of Philosophy and Decoloniality in the 'Other' America." *Transmodernity* 1.3 (2012): 11–27.

Wang, L. Ling-chi. "Model Minority, High-Tech Coolies, and Foreign Spies: Wen Ho Lee and Asian Americans in Science and Technology." *Amerasia Journal* 33.1 (2007): 49–62.

Weatherford, Doris. *American Women and World War II*. New York: Facts on File, 1990.

Weheliye, Alexander G. "Feenin: Posthuman Voices in Contemporary Black Popular Music." *Social Text* 20.2 (2002): 21–47.

———. *Phonographies: Grooves in Sonic Afro-Modernity*. Durham: Duke University Press, 2005.

———. "Pornotropes." *Journal of Visual Culture* 7.1 (2008): 65–81.

Weizman, Eyal. *Hollow Land: Israel's Architecture of Occupation*. London: Verso, 2007.

Welch, Michael. *Detained: Immigration Laws and the Expanding I.N.S. Jail Complex*. Philadelphia: Temple University Press, 2002.

Wexler, Laura. *Tender Violence: Domestic Visions in an Age of U.S. Imperialism*. Durham: Duke University Press 2000.

Whaley, Rick, and Walter Bresette. *Walleye Warriors: An Effective Alliance against Racism and for the Earth*. Philadelphia: New Society, 1994.

White, Ben. *Palestinians in Israel: Segregation, Discrimination, and Democracy*. London: Pluto Press, 2011.
Wilch, Matt. "Delegation Brings Hope to Stranded Refugees from Burma." *Detention Watch Network News* (Spring 2001): 6.
Wilderson, Frank. "The Prison Slave as Hegemony's (Silent) Scandal." In *Warfare in the American Homeland: Policing and Prison in a Penal Democracy*, ed. Joy James, 23–34. Durham: Duke University Press, 2007.
———. *Red, White and Black: Cinema and the Structure of U.S. Antagonisms*. Durham: Duke University Press, 2010.
———. "The Vengeance of Vertigo: Aphasia and Abjection in the Political Trials of Black Insurgents." *InTensions* 5 (2011): 1–41.
Wilson, Steven. "Brown over 'Other White': Mexican Americans' Legal Arguments and Litigation Strategy in School Desegregation Lawsuits." *Law and History Review* 21.1 (2003): 145–94.
Wilson, William Julius. *The Declining Significance of Race: Blacks and Changing American Institutions*. Chicago: University of Chicago Press, 1978.
Winant, Howard. *The World Is a Ghetto: Race and Democracy Since World War II*. New York: Basic Books, 2001.
Wise, Tim. *Speaking Treason Fluently: Anti-racist Reflections from an Angry White Male*. Berkeley: Soft Skull Press, 2008.
Wolfe, Patrick. "Settler-Colonialism and the Elimination of the Native." *Journal of Genocide Research* 8.4 (2006): 387–409.
Wood, Houston. *Displacing Natives: The Rhetorical Production of Hawai'i*. Pacific Formations. Lanham, MD: Rowman and Littlefield, 1999.
Wordsworth, William. Preface to *The Lyrical Ballads*. In *Poetical Works*. Ed. Thomas Hutchinson. Revised by Ernest de Selincourt. Oxford: Oxford University Press, 1969.
Wynter, Sylvia. *Beyond Liberal and Marxist Leninist Feminisms: Towards an Autonomous Frame of Reference*. San Francisco: Institute for Research on Women and Gender, 1982.
———. "The Ceremony Must Be Found: After Humanism." *Boundary 2* 12.3 (1984): 19–65.
———. "Columbus and the Poetics of the Propter Nos." *Annals of Scholarship* 8.2 (1991): 251–86.
———. "'Genital Mutilation' or 'Symbolic Birth'? Female Circumcision, Lost Origins, and the Aculturalism of Feminist/Western Thought." *Case Western Reserve Law Review* 47 (1997): 501–52.
———. "1492: A New World View." In *Race, Discourse, and the Origin of the Americas: A New World View*, ed. Vera Lawrence Hyatt and Rex Nettleford. Washington, DC: Smithsonian Institution Press, 1995.
———. "On Disenchanting Discourse: 'Minority' Literary Criticism and Beyond." In *The Nature and Context of Minority Discourse*, 207–44. New York: Oxford University Press, 1990.
———. "Unsettling the Coloniality of Being/Power/Truth/Freedom: Towards the Human, After Man, Its Overrepresentation—An Argument." *New Centennial Review* 3.3 (2003): 257–337.

Yıldız, Yasemin. "Turkish Girls, Allah's Daughters, and the Contemporary German Subject: Itinerary of a Figure." *German Life and Letters* 62.4 (2009): 465–81.
Yılmaz-Günay, Koray, ed. *Karriere eines konstruierten Gegensatzes: Zehn Jahre "Muslime versus Schwule."* Sexualpolitiken seit dem 11. September 2001. Berlin: Self Publishing, 2013.
Yoneyama, Lisa. *Hiroshima Traces: Times, Space, and the Dialectics of Memory*. Berkeley: University of California Press, 1999.
Young, Iris Marion. *Justice and the Politics of Difference*. Princeton: Princeton University Press, 1990.
Young, Robert M. *Signs of Race in Poststructuralism: Toward a Transformative Theory of Race*. Lanham, MD: University Press of America, 2009.
Zavella, Patricia. *I'm Neither Here nor There: Mexicans' Quotidian Struggles with Migration and Poverty*. Durham: Duke University Press, 2011.
Zia, Helen."Oh, Say, Can You See?" In *Asian Americans on War and Peace*, ed. Russell Leong and Don Nakanishi, 1–10. Los Angeles: UCLA Asian American Studies Center Press, 2005.
Žižek, Slavoj. "A Leftist Plea for 'Eurocentrism.'" *Critical Inquiry* 24.4 (1998): 988–1009.
Žižek, Slavoj, and Glyn Daly. *Conversations with Žižek*. Malden, MA: Polity Press, 2003.
Zuberi, Tukufu, and Eduardo Bonilla-Silva, eds. *White Logic, White Methods: Racism and Methodology*. Lanham, MD: Rowman and Littlefield, 2008.

CONTRIBUTORS

DAN BERGER is the author of *Captive Nation: Black Prison Organizing in the Civil Rights Era* (2014), among other titles. He is an assistant professor of comparative ethnic studies at the University of Washington Bothell and a founding member of Decarcerate PA.

LONG T. BUI is a visiting assistant professor at Wesleyan University in the Department of American Studies. In his work, Bui explores the political economy of race, gender, and sexuality to discuss issues of globalization, militarism, and empire.

GLEN COULTHARD (Yellowknives Dene) is an assistant professor in the First Nations studies program and the Department of Political Science at the University of British Columbia.

TANIA DAS GUPTA is a professor in the Department of Equity Studies, York University. Her publications, teaching, and research interests are in the following areas: South Asian diaspora, race and racism, antiracism, immigration and refugee issues, state policies, women, work, and families, and community activism. Her publications include *Real Nurses and Others: Racism in Nursing* (2009) and *Racism and Paid Work* (1995).

NADA ELIA is a Palestinian Diaspora activist and a founding member of the U.S. Campaign for the Academic and Cultural Boycott of Israel. She resides in Seattle, where she also coordinates the grassroots activist umbrella organization NorthWestBDS. She has taught at Brown University, Tufts University, the University of Massachusetts, Purdue University, Western Washington University, and Antioch University–Seattle. Elia is currently completing "Who You Callin' 'Demographic Threat?' Notes from the Global Intifada," a gendered analysis of the racism at the core of Israel's settler colonialism.

NIRMALA EREVELLES is a professor of social and cultural studies in education at the University of Alabama. Her teaching and research interests lie in the areas of disability studies, critical race theory, transnational feminism, sociology of education, and postcolonial studies. She has published articles in the *American Educational Research Journal, Educational Theory, Studies in Education and Philosophy, Disability & Society,* and *Disability Studies Quarterly,* among others. Her book, *Disability and Difference in Global Contexts: Towards a Transformative Body Politic,* was published in 2012.

KEITH P. FELDMAN is an assistant professor of comparative ethnic studies at the University of California, Berkeley. He is the author of *A Shadow over Palestine: The Imperial Life of Race in America* (2015).

JASON LUNA GAVILAN is a recent postdoctoral scholar via Ateneo de Manila University in Quezon City, Philippines. Historical and literary approaches to Filipino/American studies, Asian American studies, U.S. empire history, critical ethnic studies, and disability issues inform and shape his continuing research, writing, and teaching interests. Gavilan is currently working on three projects: an essay-length article about disavowed Filipino workers in the U.S. military during the early cold war period; a book-length manuscript titled "The Politics of Enlistment: Empire and the 'U.S.-Philippine Nation'"; and a meditative and interdisciplinary project that examines intersectionalities shaping transnational politics, labor, and capital in disability services.

JIN HARITAWORN is an assistant professor of environmental studies at York University. They have authored numerous articles (in journals such as GLQ, *Society & Space,* and *Sexualities*), four coedited collections (including *Queer Necropolitics,* 2014), and two monographs (including *The Biopolitics of Mixing,* 2012, and *Queer Lovers and Hateful Others: Regenerating Violent Times and Places,* 2015).

DAVID M. HERNÁNDEZ is an assistant professor of Latina/o studies at Mount Holyoke College. His research focuses on immigration enforcement, in particular the U.S. detention regime. He is completing a book manuscript on this institution, titled "Undue Process: Immigrant Detention and Lesser Citizenship." His article "Pursuant to Deportation: Latinos and Immigrant Detention" was reprinted in *Governing Immigration through Crime: A Reader* (2013).

RONAK K. KAPADIA is an assistant professor of gender and women's studies and affiliated faculty in Asian American studies at the University of Illinois at Chicago. He is completing his first book, "Shadow Atlas: Race, Security, and the Sensorial Life of Empire," a study of contemporary visual and performance art practices and their critical intersections with the logics and tactics of U.S. counterinsurgency warfare. With Simone Browne and Katherine McKittrick he is coeditor of the forthcoming special issue of *Surveillance & Society* on race and surveillance.

JODI KIM is an associate professor of ethnic studies at the University of California, Riverside.

DAVID LLOYD, Distinguished Professor of English at the University of California, Riverside, works primarily on Irish culture and on postcolonial and cultural theory. His most recent books are *Irish Times: Temporalities of Irish Modernity* (2008) and *Irish Culture and Colonial Modernity: The Transformation of Oral Space* (2011).

BO LUENGSURASWAT is an interdisciplinary artist, scholar, and activist. He earned an MA in Asian American studies from the University of California, Los Angeles, and a BA in visual studies from the California College of the Arts. His areas of research include critical ethnic studies, feminist studies, queer/trans studies, disability studies, popular culture, and comics studies.

NELSON MALDONADO-TORRES is an associate professor and chair of the Department of Latino and Hispanic Caribbean Studies, a member of the core faculty of the Comparative Literature Program at Rutgers University, a research fellow in the Department of Political Sciences at the University of South Africa, a member of the international board of the Frantz Fanon Foundation in Paris, France, and an honorary member of the Fundación Fausto Reinaga in Bolivia. His publications include *Against War: Views from the Underside of Modernity* (Duke University Press, 2008) and the coedited book *Latin@s in the World-System* (2005), and he is a coeditor of a book series on critical Caribbean studies (with Rutgers University Press) and global critical Caribbean thought.

JOHN D. MÁRQUEZ is an associate professor of African American studies and Latina/o studies at Northwestern University. He is the author of *Black-Brown Solidarity: Racial Politics in the New Gulf South* (2013) and is a coeditor of the journal *Critical Ethnic Studies.*

LAURA PULIDO is a professor of American studies and ethnicity at the University of Southern California, where she teaches classes on race, Chicana/o studies, Los Angeles, and environmental justice. Her books include *Black, Brown, Yellow and Left: Radical Activism in Los Angeles* (2006), and, with Laura Barraclough and Wendy Chang, *A People's Guide to Los Angeles* (2012).

SHANA L. REDMOND is an associate professor of American studies and ethnicity at the University of Southern California and the author of *Anthem: Social Movements and the Sound of Solidarity in the African Diaspora* (2014). She is the recipient of numerous awards and fellowships, including the inaugural Ella Baker Visiting Associate Professor fellowship at the University of California, Santa Barbara.

DYLAN RODRÍGUEZ is a professor of ethnic studies at the University of California, Riverside.

GILBERTO ROSAS is an associate professor in the Department of Anthropology and the Department of Latin@ Studies at the University of Illinois at Urbana Champaign. He was a fellow at the Center for the Study of Race, Politics, and Culture at the University of Chicago, where he was also visiting faculty in the Department of Anthropology, and held the Mellon at Northwestern in Latin@ studies. His award-winning book, published in 2012 by Duke University Press, is titled *Barrio Libre: Criminalizing States and Delinquent Refusals of the New Frontier.*

LINDSEY SCHNEIDER is a Ph.D. candidate in ethnic studies at the University of California, Riverside, and a descendant of the Pembina Band of Turtle Mountain Chippewa and of Scandinavian settlers. Her dissertation, "Dammed by the State: Indian Fishing and the Geographies of Settler Colonialism," interrogates the connections between nature, race, and property and explores Indian food production in the Columbia River Basin as a generative praxis that contests the genocidal logics of settler colonialism. She received her MA in ethnic studies from the University of California, Riverside, and her BA from Willamette University.

SARITA ECHAVEZ SEE is an associate professor of media and cultural studies at the University of California, Riverside.

ELLA SHOHAT is professor of cultural studies at the Culture & Representation track. Her books include *Taboo Memories, Diasporic Voices* (Duke University Press, 2006); *Israeli Cinema: East/West and the Politics of Representation* (1989; updated edition, 2010); *Talking Visions: Multicultural Feminism in a Transnational Age* (1998); *Dangerous Liaisons: Gender, Nation and Postcolonial Perspectives* (coedited, 1997); *Between the Middle East and the Americas: The Cultural Politics of Diaspora* (coedited, 2013, Honorable Mention in the nonfiction category of the 2014 Arab American Book Award, The Arab American Museum); and with Robert Stam, *Unthinking Eurocentrism* (winner of the Katherine Kovacs Singer Best Book Award, 1994, 2nd ed., 2014); *Multiculturalism, Postcoloniality and Transnational Media* (2003); *Flagging Patriotism: Crises of Narcissism and Anti-Americanism* (2007); and *Race in Translation: Culture Wars Around the Postcolonial Atlantic* (2012). Her writing has been translated into over ten languages. She is a recipient of such fellowships as Rockefeller and the Society for the Humanities at Cornell University and was awarded a Fulbright research / lectureship at the University of São Paulo, Brazil.

ROBERT STAM is a University Professor at New York University. He has authored, coauthored, and edited seventeen books on film and cultural theory, national cinema (French and Brazilian), comparative race, and postcolonial studies. His books include *Francois Truffaut and Friends: Modernism, Sexuality, and Adaptation* (2006); *Literature through Film* (2005); *Film Theory: An Introduction* (2000); *Tropical Multiculturalism* (Duke University Press, 1997); *New Vocabularies in Film Semiotics* (1992); *Subversive Pleasures: Bakhtin, Cultural Criticism and Film* (1989); *Reflexivity in Film and Literature: From Don Quixote to Jean-Luc Godard* (1995); and *Brazilian Cinema* (1982). He is coauthor, with Ella Shohat, of *Race in Translation: Culture Wars Around the Postcolonial Atlantic* (2012); *Flagging Patriotism* (2006); *Multiculturalism, Postcoloniality, and Transnational Media* (2003); and *Unthinking Eurocentrism: Multiculturalism and the Media* (1994). He has taught in France, Tunisia, Brazil, and Abu Dhabi. His work has been translated into French, Spanish, German, Portuguese, Italian, Greek, Farsi, Korean, Japanese, Chinese, Hebrew, Estonian, Turkish, Serbo-Croatian, and Arabic. A twentieth anniversary edition of *Unthinking Eurocentrism* was published in 2014. His most recent book is *Keywords in Subversive Film/Media Aesthetics* (2015)..

NEFERTI X. M. TADIAR is author of *Things Fall Away: Philippine Historical Experience and the Makings of Globalization* (Duke University Press, 2009) and *Fantasy-Production: Sexual Economies and Other Philippine Consequences for the New World Order* (2004). She is professor of women's, gender, and sexuality studies at Barnard College, Columbia University and coeditor of the journal *Social Text*. Her current book project is titled "Remaindered Life."

STEPHANIE NOHELANI TEVES is a Kanaka Maoli feminist scholar. She is currently an assistant professor of ethnic studies and women's and gender studies at the University of Oregon and is a member of Hinemoana of Turtle Island, a Pacific Islander feminist group of activists, poets, storytellers, and scholars located in California and Oregon.

ANDREW UZENDOSKI received his Ph.D. in English at the University of Texas at Austin in 2015. His research focuses on Indigenous and Latin@ speculative fiction, applying critical attention to how Indigenous and Latin@ speculative texts theorize the reform of international legal norms and human rights law. He has published work in *American Indian Quarterly* and *Western American Literature*, and has essays forthcoming in *Extrapolation*, *Aztlán*, and *The Chican@ & Latin@ Speculative Discourses Anthology*.

JOÃO H. COSTA VARGAS works at the University of Texas, Austin.

ALEXANDER G. WEHELIYE is a professor of African American studies at Northwestern University. He is the author of *Phonographies: Grooves in Sonic Afro-Modernity* (Duke University Press, 2005), which was awarded the Modern Language Association's William Sanders Scarborough Prize for Outstanding Scholarly Study of Black American Literature or Culture, and *Habeas Viscus: Racializing Assemblages, Biopolitics, and Black Feminist Theories of the Human* (Duke University Press, 2014).

INDEX